Christianity

Christianity

—— A Brief Survey ——

Michael D. Robinson

CASCADE *Books* · Eugene, Oregon

CHRISTIANITY
A Brief Survey

Cascade Books
An Imprint of Wipf and Stock Publishers
199 W. 8th Ave., Suite 3
Eugene, OR 97401

www.wipfandstock.com

PAPERBACK ISBN: 978-1-5326-1832-1
HARDCOVER ISBN: 978-1-4982-4380-3
EBOOK ISBN: 978-1-4982-4379-7

Cataloguing-in-Publication data:

Names: Robinson, Michael D. (Michael Dale, 1958), author.

Title: Christianity : a brief survey / by Michael D. Robinson.

Description: Eugene, OR: Cascade Books, 2022. | Includes bibliographical references and index.

Identifiers: ISBN 978-1-5326-1832-1 (paperback) | ISBN 978-1-4982-4380-3 (hardcover) | ISBN 978-1-4982-4379-7 (ebook)

Subjects: LCSH: Christianity. | Theology, Doctrinal. | Christian ethics. | Worship—History. | Christianity and other religions. | Bible—Criticism, interpretation, etc. | Bible—Hermeneutics.

Classification: BR121.3 R635 2022 (print). | BR121.3 (ebook).

To Eric and Ariel,

God's Immeasurable Gifts
to Me and Your Mother

Contents

Introduction | ix

Part One: Christian Foundations

1 Sacred Text and Sacred History | 1

2 Sacred Person and Sacred Community | 32

Part Two: Christian Theology

3 Revelation, God, Creation, and Providence | 63

4 Humanity and Sin | 92

5 Christ and Salvation | 119

6 The Church | 156

7 Last Things | 195

Part Three: Christian Ethics

8 Foundations of Christian Ethics | 237

9 Christian Ethics in the Classical, Medieval, and Reformation Eras | 276

10 Christian Ethics in the Modern and Contemporary Eras | 303

Part Four: Christian Worship

11 Christian Worship: Biblical Foundations and Early Centuries | 341

12 Christian Worship: From the Middle Ages to the Contemporary Era | 365

Part Five: Christian Issues

13 Christian Issues: Christianity, the Problem of Evil, and Other Religions | 393

14 Christian Issues: Christianity and Science | 425

15 Christianity Issues: Christianity and Women in Ministry | 459

Epilogue | 495

Appendix | 497

Bibliography | 501

Index | 517

Introduction

WHAT IS CHRISTIANITY? THE question is deceptive in its simplicity, for many answers can be and have been offered. One response to this query is to tell of Christianity's development through history. Indeed, in a previous work titled *Christianity: A Brief History*, I offer just such a description. In this book, *Christianity: A Brief Survey*, I develop a more thematic approach, seeking to describe Christianity topically. With this objective in mind, then, what is Christianity? For the purpose of this survey, I tender the following beginning definition—a definition that admittedly is inadequate in many ways, but one that will serve as a starting point for our conversation: *Christianity is a religious way of life centered on the person, life, teaching, death, and resurrection of Jesus the Christ.*

Of course, this definition is not without ambiguity. For starters, one might wonder, what is a religious way of life? Religion itself is complicated. Numerous definitions have been proposed, each highlighting some distinct essential characteristic of religion. Often such definitions fall short, not so much because they fail to identify an important element of religion, but because they often miss other vital aspects. Perhaps it is safest simply to state that religion is multifaceted. William Austin, in his seminal article on religion, suggests that rather than try to name some essential attribute of religion, one should think in terms of family resemblances—that is, characteristics often shared by religions. While some religions do not manifest all of these characteristics, all religions harbor some of them. According to Austin, some representative religion-making characteristics are these.

1. Belief in supernatural beings or powers

2. Recognition of sacred versus profane objects or places

3. Ritual acts

4. A moral code

5. Religious feelings, experiences, or both (including awe, mystery, guilt, adoration)

6. Forms of human communication with the supernatural

7. A distinctive view of reality, including an understanding of human beings

8. Formation of a social group or community[1]

To Austin's list we might add two more traits. First are ordering narratives (sometimes referred to as mythologies). These are stories (fictional or historical) that help the religious individual or community comprehend reality and learn how to behave appropriately in that reality. Second is an existential commitment or a resolve. More than merely recommending a set of beliefs to coldly affirm, or rituals to endure, or moral norms to formally sanction, many religions call for earnest commitment to such beliefs, practices, and norms. This commitment helps separate the living out of religion from a mere academic study of religion and contributes to religion being "a way of life." Most religions manifest most if not all of these characteristics. And all religions seem to realize some of them.

As a religious way of life, then, Christianity is multidimensional. It too possesses its own (often diverse) beliefs about humanity and reality as a whole, including beliefs about supernatural beings and ultimate reality. It recommends sets of moral norms, ritual acts, and means of communing with God. It recognizes the occurrence and validity of various religious experiences throughout history and today. And usually Christianity calls for earnest commitment to the ideas and ideals expressed in its traditions, forming communities around these principles. Part of the intent of this book is to expose readers to the multiplicity of beliefs, values, practices, narratives, and experiences that make up Christianity in its various forms. Christianity is a religious way of life, or perhaps more accurately: it is several religious ways of life.

With these broad ideas in mind, we may outline the content of this book as follows. In the first two chapters, we examine four core foundations of the Christian way of life. These are a sacred text (commonly called the Bible), a sacred story or history (especially describing the story of the ancient Jewish people), a sacred person (namely, Jesus of Nazareth), and a sacred community (especially the earliest followers of Jesus). With these foundations established, we turn—in chapters 3 through 7—to describe the central teachings (beliefs, theology) of the Christian faith. Discussed in these chapters are the doctrines of divine revelation, God, creation, providence, humanity, sin, Christ, salvation, the church, and last things. In chapters 8, 9, and 10, we discuss central elements of Christian ethics, especially exploring the broad contours of biblical ethics as well as numerous models of Christian ethics proposed across the ages. In chapters 11 and 12, we examine many of the central worship practices of Christians through the centuries—identifying how Christians both celebrate and attempt to perpetuate their relationship with God. Finally, in chapters 13 through 15, we wrestle with several intellectual issues faced by the Christian faith, specifically problems posed by the existence of evil, religious diversity, social exclusivism (specifically the role of women in ministry), and the relationship of faith and science.

1. Austin, "Religion," 141–42.

As is the case with any introductory work, this book cannot fully investigate the intricacies of the Christian way of life. The same could be said of whole libraries dedicated to such exploration. Still, hopefully this composition provides a helpful introduction to many of the themes and practices of the Christian faith and will spur readers on toward fuller investigations. On a technical note, dates given throughout this text are assumed to occur in the Common Era unless otherwise noted with the designation BCE (which stands for Before the Common Era).

A final note of gratitude is needed for all those who, in one way or another, aided me in putting together this book. Thanks first to the trustees, faculty, President Randy O'Rear, and other administrators of the University of Mary Hardin-Baylor for supporting me in my efforts to research and to produce this work—including a summer research grant in 2013 and a semester sabbatical in fall 2018. Appreciation also goes to several readers who examined preliminary chapters of the book, offered helpful commentary, and suggested revisions along the way. Especially, thanks to Adam Winn, Steve Oldham, Carol Holcomb, and Dan Stiver for their helpful advice. Ever and always, thanks to my best friend and wife, Carol Robinson, whose patience made this process possible.

Part One: **Christian Foundations**

1

Sacred Text and Sacred History

CHRISTIANITY IS ANCHORED IN four important foundations: a sacred text, a sacred history, a sacred person, and a sacred community. In the next two chapters, we explore these four groundworks. At the core of Christianity is the conviction that God has been active in human history, interacting and communicating with human beings. From this divine-human exchange a sacred history or "ordering narrative" has unfolded; this history began in the story of the Hebrew people (also called Israelites and Jews), continued in the person and work of Jesus of Nazareth, and took further shape in the community that grew up around Jesus. In turn, Christians believe that much of this sacred chronicle has been described in the pages of Christian Scriptures, often called the Bible. The Bible is both a written account of and a product of this divine-human interface; therefore, the Bible is both a source for knowledge of God and a catalyst for ongoing divine-human encounters.

For Christians, the apex of sacred history is in the person, life, and deeds of Jesus. In turn, Jesus' life emerged and was interpreted within the complex cultural context of first-century Palestinian Judaism, which itself was grounded in the ancient sacred story of the Israelites. Further, even within that first-century context, the significance of Jesus—who he was and what he accomplished—was not immediately evident. It certainly was not obvious to his contemporaries, at least not according to the biblical accounts. Some of Jesus' contemporaries saw him as a blasphemer and his teachings as an aberration of the Hebrew sacred tradition, while others (his followers) saw him as the fulfillment of Jewish religious insights and hopes. Thus, to understand Jesus (and the community that formed around him) requires a basic knowledge of the Jewish tradition out of which Jesus (and Christianity) came, as well as an awareness of the earliest Christian accounts and interpretations of Jesus' identity and accomplishments.

In this chapter, in the section entitled Sacred History, we explore the core narratives and religious teachings of the Hebrew tradition from which Jesus and Christianity emerged. In many ways, the story of the Israelites is only a portion of the sacred history of Christianity. That history continues in the life and work of Jesus, as well as in the activities of his earliest followers. Still for the sake of convenience, we will refer to the Hebrew story as "the sacred history" and will discuss the story of Jesus and of the community that grew up around him using different headings. Specifically, in Chapter 2, in the section called Sacred Person, we discuss the basic interpretations of Jesus and his significance as assessed by the earliest Christians. In turn, in chapter 2, in the section called Sacred Community, we examine the emergence of the earliest societies that rose up around Jesus, discussing the nature and mission of those groups. Before exploring these topics, however, it will be helpful to say a word about the Bible, for it is largely from that literature that we learn of the sacred history of Israel, of the person and work of Jesus, and of the faith-movement that sprang-forth from Jesus. We will discuss this literature under the title *sacred text*, to which we now turn.

Sacred Text

The Bible is less a single book than it is a library of books. It contains multiple independent writings composed by numerous authors over a more-than-thousand-year span. Typically, these books are separated into two major groupings: the Old Testament and the New Testament. The Old Testament contains sacred Jewish writings prior to Jesus. The New Testament contains sacred Christian Scriptures that arose within the first hundred years of Jesus' death. The label "Old Testament" is largely a Christian expression. The term "testament" is from a Latin translation of the Greek word *diathēkē*, which is perhaps better translated "covenant." The central idea behind the division of the Christian Bible into the Old and New Testaments is that the Old Testament deals with matters of God's first covenant (agreement, contract) with the people of Israel, whereas the New Testament deals with God's new covenant with believers in Jesus Christ (see Exod 19–20; Luke 22:20; 1 Cor 11:23–26; Heb 9:11–15, 10:14–25). Since the Bible is from the ancient world, it is written in the languages of that world. The Old Testament is written primarily in ancient Hebrew; the New Testament is written in first-century Greek.

In recent years, many have contended that using the label "Old Testament" is inappropriate or in bad taste. A preference is to call these materials "the Hebrew Bible." This certainly is understandable since these writings were produced by the ancient Jewish people and remain today the primary scripture of Judaism. Further, these scriptures are (for the most part) written in the ancient Hebrew language. In this work, I will use the terms "Old Testament" and "Hebrew Bible" synonymously, attempting to honor these writings both as the sacred text of the Jewish tradition and as the foundational scriptures of the Christian tradition.

Canon and Content

While most Christians agree about which writings constitute the New Testament, there is some disagreement about which books should be included in the Old Testament.

There are three major divisions of Christians—Roman Catholics, Eastern Orthodox, and Protestants.[1] (We will discuss these groups in more detail later in the book, as well as a few outside these three). The Protestant Old Testament canon (official list of books) differs from the Roman Catholic list, which in turn differs somewhat from the Eastern Orthodox canon. Furthermore, there is disagreement over the ordering of the Old Testament books. Here are the books and book arrangements of the Old Testament found in Judaism and in the three major branches of Christianity.

Hebrew Canon	Protestant Canon	Roman Catholic Canon	Orthodox Canon
Torah (Law)	**Pentateuch**	**Pentateuch**	**Pentateuch**
Genesis	Genesis	Genesis	Genesis
Exodus	Exodus	Exodus	Exodus
Leviticus	Leviticus	Leviticus	Leviticus
Numbers	Numbers	Numbers	Numbers
Deuteronomy	Deuteronomy	Deuteronomy	Deuteronomy
Nevi'im (Prophets)	**Historical Books**	**Historical Books**	**Historical Books**
Former Prophets	Joshua	Joshua	Joshua
Joshua	Judges	Judges	Judges
Judges	Ruth	Ruth	Ruth
Samuel	1 & 2 Samuel	1 & 2 Samuel	1 & 2 Kingdoms (1 & 2 Samuel)
Kings	1 & 2 Kings	1 & 2 Kings	3 & 4 Kingdoms (1 & 2 Kings)
	1 &2 Chronicles	1 & 2 Chronicles	1 & 2 Chronicles
Latter Prophets	Ezra	Ezra	1 Ezra (2 Esdras)
Isaiah	Nehemiah	Nehemiah	2 Ezra (Ezra/2 Esdras)
Jeremiah	Esther	Tobit	Nehemiah
Ezekiel		Judith	Tobit
(The Twelve)	**Writings**	Esther (& additions)	Judith
Hosea	Job	1 & 2 Maccabees	Esther (& additions)
Joel	Psalms		1, 2, 3 Maccabees
Amos	Proverbs	**Writings**	
Obadiah	Ecclesiastes	Job	**Writings**

1. We might include Non-Caledonian Christians as a fourth major division of Christians. For a discussion of this Christian heritage, see Robinson, *Christianity: A Brief History*, chapter 8.

Hebrew Canon	Protestant Canon	Roman Catholic Canon	Orthodox Canon
Jonah	Song of Solomon	Psalms	Psalms
Micah		Proverbs	Job
Nahum	**Prophets**	Ecclesiastes	Proverbs
Habakkuk	Isaiah	Song of Solomon	Ecclesiastes
Zephaniah	Jeremiah	Wisdom of Solomon	Song of Solomon
Haggai	Lamentations	Sirach/Ecclesiasticus	Wisdom of Solomon
Zechariah	Ezekiel		Sirach/Ecclesiasticus
Malachi	Daniel	**Prophets**	
	Hosea	Isaiah	**Prophets**
Ketuvim (Writings)	Joel	Jeremiah	Isaiah
Psalms	Amos	Lamentations	Jeremiah
Proverbs	Obadiah	Baruch	Baruch
Job	Jonah	Ezekiel	Lamentations
(Five Scrolls)	Micah	Daniel (& additions)	Letter of Jeremiah
Song of Songs	Nahum	Hosea	Ezekiel
Ruth	Habakkuk	Joel	Daniel (& additions)
Lamentations	Zephaniah	Amos	Hosea
Ecclesiastes	Haggai	Obadiah	Joel
Esther	Zechariah	Jonah	Amos
Daniel	Malachi	Micah	Obadiah
Ezra-Nehemiah		Nahum	Jonah
Chronicles	**The Apocrypha**	Habakkuk	Micah
	1 & 2 Esdras	Zephaniah	Nahum
	Tobit	Haggai	Habakkuk
	Judith	Zechariah	Zephaniah
	Additions to Esther	Malachi	Haggai
	Wisdom of Solomon		Zechariah
	Ecclesiasticus/Sirach	*Appendix*	Malachi
	Baruch	Prayer of Manasseh	
	Letter of Jeremiah	1 Esdras	*Appendix*
		Appendix	
		Prayer of Manasseh	
		1 Esdras	

Hebrew Canon	Protestant Canon	Roman Catholic Canon	Orthodox Canon
	Additions to Daniel:	2 Esdras	Prayer of Manasseh
	Prayer of Azariah and Song of Three		4 Maccabees
	Susanna		
	Daniel, Bel & the Snake		
	Prayer of Manasseh		
	1 & 2 Maccabees		

A quick glance at these canons shows that there is much overlap between them. Indeed, all of the books listed in the Hebrew canon are also contained in all of the Christian listings. A minor difference is that some of the books of the Hebrew canon are divided into two books in the Christian canons—namely, Samuel, Kings, and Chronicles. An important difference between the Hebrew and Christian canons is the partitioning used. The Hebrew canon divides the books into three sections: Torah, Prophets, and Writings; often the Hebrew Bible is called the Tanak, which is an acronym for the *Torah* (Law or Instruction), the *Nevi'im* (Prophets), and the *Ketuvim* (Writings). The Christian canons divide the books into four sections: the Pentateuch (meaning "five books"), the Histories, the Writings, and the Prophets. Perhaps the greatest difference between the Hebrew and Christian canons comes with the books listed under the title of Apocrypha in the Protestant canon. The Hebrew canon does not contain these works; but the apocryphal books have been incorporated into different sections of the Roman Catholic and Eastern Orthodox canons; and at least two additional works appear in the Eastern Orthodox Canon— namely, 3 and 4 Maccabees. Protestants have tended to reject the books of the Apocrypha as authoritative scripture, seeing them at best as helpful for devotional life but not for formal doctrine. Roman Catholics and Eastern Orthodox typically consider these books to be authoritative even for doctrine, thus including them in various sections of their Old Testament listings.

The New Testament canon is agreed upon by all three major branches of Christianity. The list is as follows:

Gospels & Acts	Pauline Epistles	General Epistles & Revelation
Matthew	Romans	Hebrews
Mark	1 & 2 Corinthians	James
Luke	Galatians	1 & 2 Peter

Gospels & Acts	Pauline Epistles	General Epistles & Revelation
John	Ephesians	1, 2, 3 John
Acts	Philippians	Jude
	Colossians	Revelation
	1 & 2 Thessalonians	
	1 & 2 Timothy	
	Titus	
	Philemon	

Multiple genres are found in the biblical literature. In the Old Testament, there are legal and religious codes (especially in Exodus through Deuteronomy), hymns for personal and corporate worship (Psalms), an extended love poem (Song of Solomon or Song of Songs), a protracted lament (Lamentations), collections of poetic and prosaic oracles and sermons (especially throughout the Prophets), aphoristic wisdom sayings (Proverbs), religious-philosophical treatises (Job, Ecclesiastes, portions of Proverbs), short stories (Ruth, Esther, Jonah), and foreboding apocalyptic writings (Daniel). There are also historical narratives. Indeed, there is a grand narrative running through the core of the Old Testament that serves as a framework for understanding the Hebrew tradition as a whole. This narrative is expressed especially in portions of the Pentateuch, in Joshua through 2 Kings, and in 1 and 2 Chronicles, Ezra, and Nehemiah. We will discuss this grand historical narrative along with some key theological themes in the next major section of this chapter.

The New Testament also contains assorted genres of literature. Nearly half of it is made up of four separate theological-historical narratives about the life and significance of Jesus. These narratives are called Gospels and include Matthew, Mark, Luke and John. The first three are often called Synoptic Gospels since they have a similar narrative structure and share some written content (sometimes word for word). The Gospel of John offers a more independent account of the life and person of Jesus. All four Gospels spend considerable space describing the last week of Jesus' life, including his death and resurrection. Another important New Testament theological–historical narrative details the activities of the earliest Christians from the time shortly after Jesus' resurrection through much of the missionary activities of the apostle Paul. This narrative is called the Acts of the Apostles (often shorted to Acts) and was composed by the author of Luke.

With the exception of the book of Revelation, the rest of the New Testament is composed of letters (also called epistles) by various leaders of the early church. Many of these letters were written by the apostle Paul; others were written either by Paul or by persons sympathetic to Paul's theology. These letters are listed as Pauline Epistles in the table above. Another set of letters has come from authors other than Paul; these are often called the General Epistles. As the names in the table indicate, many of these general letters are attributed to well-known early Christian leaders such as the apostle Peter, or James and Jude (brothers of Jesus), but not all scholars agree with these ascriptions of authorship. The book of Revelation stands alone in the New Testament as an apocalyptic text, filled with mysterious symbolism, including images of God's final victory over sin and evil. Later in this chapter, we will explore some of the chief theological themes of the New Testament, including especially the basic narratives and interpretations of the life and person of Jesus.

Literary Development

The literature of the Bible developed over a long and complex history. This especially is true of the *narratives* found in the Old Testament.

Old Testament Literary Development

The precise evolution of the Old Testament narratives is controversial, but scholars generally agree about the broad sweep of their development. First, there were oral traditions. Early in the history of Israel, various stories arose that were passed down from generation to generation, passed down by word of mouth within families, and clans, and whole tribes. Among the more notable oral traditions were those dealing with the patriarchs of Israel and with God's deliverance of the Hebrews from slavery in Egypt. The next step in the development of the Old Testament narrative was the production of various written sources, which were eventually combined into a grand story. Over time many of the oral traditions were written down and integrated into narrative units. Scholars believe that there was a long history (beginning around 1,000 BCE and running through 400 BCE) of writing and rewriting, of adding, deleting, combining and recombining various literary materials.[2] Evidence for this adding, deleting, and reordering is found throughout the Old Testament narrative.[3]

---

2. Sometimes this perspective is referred to as the Documentary Hypothesis of Old Testament literary development.

3. Here is one example: A comparison of 1 and 2 Chronicles with 1 and 2 Samuel and 1 & 2 Kings shows that much of the material in Chronicles is (word for word) identical to materials in Samuel and Kings. Indeed, over half of the writings are essentially the same. But there are also several important differences in Chronicles. Significantly, unlike the accounts in Samuel, no mention is given in Chronicles of King David's conflict with King Saul or of David's affair with Bathsheba. Most scholars believe that these omissions were made by the writers and editors of Chronicles in an effort to avoid making David look bad, because they had a pro-David, pro-Judah agenda. They were trying to make important religious and political points, and like us all, they were selective in the materials they put in their texts. Whatever their reasons, it is clear that the writers of Chronicles left some materials out (and put some materials in) precisely because they were trying to make a point that they felt was important. The same appears to be the case for much of the Old Testament.

By closely examining the literature, scholars have identified four major periods of literary activity involved in constructing the Old Testament narrative. First was the *Yahwist Tradition* or J. This was a *written* tradition that appears to have accumulated and combined many oral traditions from the Southern Kingdom of Judah. It was likely composed between 1,000 to 950 BCE, probably around the time of King Solomon. Some of the chief characteristics of this tradition are the use of the name YHWH (*Yahweh*) for God and the telling of elaborate stories. Typically, these narratives are vivid and earthy, often describing God anthropomorphically (with human characteristics). The second major period of literary activity was the *Elohist Tradition* or E. This *written* tradition combined oral traditions from the Northern Kingdom of Israel, anywhere from 850 to 750 BCE. Some of its characteristics are the use of the word *elohim* for God (which was a general Hebrew word for "God" or "gods") and a tendency to make God more remote (than in the J tradition). Instead of directly communicating with people (as often is the case in the J source), the E tradition depicts God as revealed indirectly, through dreams (e.g., Gen 20:3), divine messengers or angels (e.g., Gen 21:17; Exod 3:2), and prophets. There is greater mystery associated with God in the E tradition. Most Old Testament scholars believe that somewhere around 750 BCE, the J and E sources were edited into a whole.

The third major period of literary activity involved the *Deuteronomic Tradition*, which likely emerged between 621 to 580 BCE. This tradition was closely tied to the reign of King Josiah of the Kingdom of Judah. Josiah lived from 640 to 609 BCE. During his reign, a "book of the law" was discovered, (see 2 Kgs 22:8) and was consulted as a source for political and religious reform in Judah. Many scholars believe that this "book of the law" was an early version of the book of Deuteronomy. The Deuteronomistic tradition likely produced considerable portions of the book of Deuteronomy as well as the books of the Former Prophets (often called the Deuteronomistic History)—that is, the books of Joshua, Judges, 1 and 2 Samuel, and 1 and 2 Kings. Further, several books of the Latter Prophets share many themes found in this tradition, including the books of Isaiah, Hosea, Amos, Micah, Zephaniah, and (especially) Jeremiah. Among the key characteristics of this tradition are emphases on the need for a central place of worship, for proper worship practices, and for Israel to be faithful to its covenant with God.

A final period of literary activity centered on the *Priestly Tradition*, which is thought to have arisen between 550 to 440 BCE, during and just after the Babylonian exile of the people of Judah. (We will say more about the history of Israel and Judah below.) The priestly tradition grew out of the concerns of the religious priests of Judah, who hoped for a return to religious and ritualistic purity. Some of the key characteristics of this literature are portrayals of God as even more distant (than depicted by either J or E) and stress on ritual purity and right religious practice—including especially sacrifices and holiness requirements. While the priestly group drew from ancient traditions, especially those about worship in the Jerusalem temple, it is believed that the *final shape* of the legal and ritual codes in Exodus, Leviticus, and Numbers were formed by this priestly group. The members of the priestly school are often seen as the last great editors of the Old Testament narrative and broader tradition, shaping especially the Torah and the Prophets into their current form, and piecing the Old Testament oral and written traditions into a more unified system. The books of 1 and 2 Chronicles, Ezra, and Nehemiah typically are especially associated with the Priestly tradition.

A final step in the development of the Old Testament was *canonization*. The word *canon* comes from a Greek word meaning "measuring rod." Thus, a religious canon is a list of writings considered to be authoritative—a standard by which religious truth is judged. As we have seen, the narratives of the Old Testament developed over a long period. The same can be said of other literary works found in the Old Testament, such as the Latter Prophets and the Writings. These writings would have been possessed by different people in diverse places throughout ancient Jewish territories. But eventually these separate pieces of literature began to be pieced together, recognized as units, and ultimately seen as one large singularity. Two major ancient Jewish canons eventually emerged: a *Hebrew canon* and a *Greek canon*. The Hebrew canon is essentially the one described above in our table of the various canons of the Old Testament. No one knows for sure exactly how or when the various books in the Hebrew canon were deemed authoritative. This recognition was gradual, and some books were more readily accepted than others. The books of the Torah were affirmed as authoritative first (by c. 400 BCE), followed by the Prophets (by c. 200 BCE), and finally the Writings (some, such as the book of Daniel, perhaps as late as 100 BCE). The criteria for choosing writings for the canon are not clear. At least two tests seem to have been employed: (1) the usage test (most books or writings were selected because they had been and continued to be useful to the religious community) and (2) the age test (some texts were rejected because they were written after the time of Ezra).

Another important ancient canon of the Old Testament was the *Greek* or *Alexandrian canon*. In 332 BCE, Persian rule over Israel was ended by the forces of Alexander the Great. And for the next several centuries, the Jews were ruled by various Hellenistic dynasties. The result was that many Jews were dispersed throughout the Mediterranean and learned Greek as their primary language. Because of this, various Hebrew Scriptures were translated into Greek so that people could understand their own scriptures. Eventually a canon of these texts was established among Jews living in Alexandria, Egypt, perhaps between 200 to 150 BCE. This canon, more or less, became the standard of Greek-speaking Jews throughout the Mediterranean, including Palestine (at least by the later part of the first century). It is not certain when or by whom these Hebrew scriptures were translated into Greek. But tradition held that seventy Jewish scholars did this and established the Greek canon. For this reason, the ancient Greek version of the Old Testament became known as the *Septuagint* (Greek for "seventy") or the LXX (Roman numeral for the number 70). The

Greek canon had fifteen more books than the Hebrew canon. These are those books listed above in the Protestant canon as the Apocrypha. While many first-century Greek-speaking Jews knew that the LXX differed from the Hebrew canon, they accepted the authority of the LXX anyway. This shows the fluidity of the early Jewish perspective on its religious traditions and texts.

The Septuagint was the primary Scripture of the earliest Christians—that is of Christians of the first century CE. Often when an Old Testament passage is quoted in the New Testament, it is in the wording of the Septuagint. (It is interesting to note, however, that no Apocryphal book is directly quoted in the New Testament, although there are some allusions to these books in the New Testament.) In turn, as the first Christians began to die off, and the church moved into the second and third centuries, church leaders accepted not only the twenty-four or thirty-five books of the Hebrew canon but also the fifteen additional works of the Greek canon (known to Protestants as the Apocrypha). The oldest Latin translation of the Christian Bible, dating back before the fourth century, was a translation of the Greek Septuagint plus the Greek New Testament. Thus, it contained the additional books of the Septuagint. In turn, the authoritative Latin Vulgate, translated by Jerome (354–420 CE) in the fourth century, also contained these books of the Septuagint known to Protestants as the Apocrypha (even though Jerome translated the other Old Testament books from Hebrew rather than from the Septuagint). In short, early and medieval Christianity accepted more books as authoritative than are in the Hebrew Canon.

The Protestant Reformation[4] (1590–1680s) changed this. Protestantism emphasized going back to the original biblical languages. As a result, many in the movement thought that the Hebrew canon was superior to the Greek canon. Martin Luther did not regard the additional texts of the Septuagint as scripture. But even he kept them in his German translation of the Bible, for he felt that they were useful to Christians. Calvinists, on the other hand, excluded these apocryphal works from the Bible, contending that they were not Scripture and thus not helpful. Anglicans, following Luther, kept many of the apocryphal books in their Bibles, but claimed that such works could not be used to establish doctrine. Roman Catholics (during the Counter-Reformation) responded to the Protestant scriptural challenge by officially declaring many of these additional works to be part of the Bible. The Eastern Orthodox Church also formally included these books in the Bible and added others as well. Often this additional set of Roman Catholic and Eastern Orthodox Scriptures is referred to as the Deuterocanonical (second canon) books. As we have seen, this set is also called the apocryphal (hidden) books.

---

4. For a discussion of the Reformation era, see Robinson, *Christianity: A Brief History*, chapter 7.

New Testament Literary Development

The New Testament also shows signs of evolution, although not as complex or temporally extended as the development of the Old Testament. The New Testament was produced by the early Christian community and was grounded in that community's experience of Jesus of Nazareth. From the standpoint of the academic historian, Jesus was a Jewish peasant and itinerant religious teacher in Roman-occupied Palestine during the early part of the first century CE. It is fairly clear historically that Jesus' teachings and activities somehow got him into trouble with both the Jewish religious and political authorities as well as with the local Roman government, resulting in his execution by crucifixion sometime between 30 and 33 CE. Further, soon after his death several of his followers began claiming that Jesus had been raised from the dead by the God of Israel, and that God had vindicated his teachings and life.

Many claims and stories about Jesus emerged in the ensuing decades, as his original disciples shared their experiences of and insights about him. Soon converts were added and a larger community of believers began to materialize; a growing tradition unfolded, initially passed down orally. The first Christians[5] were primarily Aramaic-speaking Jews in and around Judea and Galilee (Jesus' home region); the first major Christian community appears to have been centered in Jerusalem, led by Peter and James (a relative of Jesus).[6] By the 40s CE a second important Jewish Christian center arose in Syrian Antioch. And soon efforts were being made to draw Gentiles (non-Jews) into the Christian community. The apostle Paul played an especially important role in these missionary efforts to Gentiles. Paul initially was a persecutor of Christians but was converted (apparently in the mid-30s) when he experienced a profound revelation of the resurrected Jesus. Soon he and others were spreading the gospel (good news) of Jesus to Gentiles throughout Asia Minor (present-day Turkey), Greece, and Rome. As time passed, the number of Gentile Christians and congregations out-grew the number of Jewish Christians. More and more, Christian thought came to be expressed through the Greek language (rather than in Aramaic, the language Jesus likely spoke). All the books of the New Testament are written in Greek. The earliest surviving writings of Christianity are letters of Paul. His undisputed letters are 1 Thessalonians, Galatians, 1 and 2 Corinthians, Romans, Philemon, and Philippians. Most of these were written throughout the 50s CE. Scholars debate Paul's authorship of the other so-called Pauline

---

5. It is somewhat anachronistic to refer to these early followers of Jesus as Christians since according to the book of Acts (11:26), they did not take on that name until later, in Antioch. Indeed, it appears that early on the first followers of Jesus did not clearly distinguish themselves from adherents of Judaism proper, nor did many of their early Jewish adversaries.

6. Contemporary Christians disagree about the relationship between James and Jesus. The canonical biblical text seems to straightforwardly say James was Jesus' brother, a view that most Protestant groups accept. But Catholic tradition finds such a view problematic due to affirmations about the virginity of Mary.

letters (namely, 2 Thessalonians, Colossians, Ephesians, 1 and 2 Timothy, and Titus), so the dating of these letters is more controversial.

The book of Mark likely was the first Gospel written, composed in the late 60s CE or later. The Gospels of Matthew and Luke appear to have been written somewhere between the late 70s to the late 80s CE Both Matthew and Luke used existing written sources to construct their accounts. One of those sources was the Gospel of Mark itself. In many places, Matthew's and Luke's accounts follow Mark's exact wording or alter Mark's phrasing ever so slightly to stress some theological nuance. In addition to Mark's Gospel, Matthew and Luke apparently shared another written source (often referred to as Q for *Quelle*, the German word for "source"). Q included many of the sayings or teachings of Jesus and perhaps some narrative material. Finally, Matthew and Luke appear to have used sources unique to their respective Gospels: the one unique to Luke is often called L, and the one unique to Matthew is called M. It is uncertain when these earlier written sources were composed or precisely what their content was. The literary development of John's Gospel is disputed. It too shows signs of dependence upon earlier written sources and may have undergone a series of revisions over a decade or more. Its final form likely took shape between the late 80s to late 90s CE. The authorship of the four Gospels is uncertain. The four names now associated with these Gospels are not in the earliest manuscripts and likely were ascribed to these books later in Christian tradition.

While there is considerable overlap among the Gospels, especially among the first three (together called the Synoptic Gospels, as noted), there are also important distinctions. Each writer stresses different aspects of Jesus' life and significance. Mark's Gospel emphasizes the role of Jesus as a suffering messiah. While acknowledging Jesus as the Messiah (14:61–62) and as a worker of wonders and healings, Mark also stresses the need to rightly understand Jesus' messiahship as involving suffer and give his life as a ransom for others (8:27–33; 10:45). The Gospel of Matthew emphasizes the role of Jesus in fulfilling Old Testament prophecy and law (torah), and Jesus' role as the teacher of genuine righteousness (5:17–20). The Gospel of Luke stresses Jesus role as the merciful Savior for all people (2:10–11; 23:34) and the role of Jesus as the giver of God's empowering Spirit to the church (Luke 24:49; Acts 1:8; 2:1–4). The Gospel of John emphasizes Jesus' identity as the Word of God and Son of God that became incarnate (in-fleshed) as a human being. For John, Jesus uniquely reveals God's will and nature. The dating and authorship of the various General Epistles is also uncertain. Most scholars see these works as produced late in the first century or even early in the second century CE. The letters of 1, 2, and 3 John as well as the book of Revelation are typically seen as tied to the community of believers that produced the Gospel of John.

Gradually, the late ancient church came to recognize an official New Testament scriptural canon. Diverse works were acclaimed to be authoritative by different churches in the first and second centuries. But as various conflicts arose among Christians, lists of authorized (and unauthorized) texts began to emerge. Over several centuries, a gradual consensus arose regarding which books were most sacred and were to be recognized as authoritative. The process was gradual and at times controversial; and no truly official consensus was derived for many centuries. Nevertheless, it is fair to say that by the fourth century (and perhaps earlier than that) a general consensus existed among Christians regarding the core works of the New Testament. In 367 CE, bishop Athanasius of Alexandria endorsed a list of books identical to the modern New Testament canon, and other writers soon followed. In turn, in synods (official meetings of church bishops) at Hippo (393) and Carthage (397) Athanasius's collection was confirmed as final and authoritative (at least by those synods).

Sacred History

The Bible forms one of the foundations of the Christian faith. A second base of Christianity is the sacred story of the Jewish people that is described especially in the Hebrew biblical tradition (or what Christians often call the Old Testament). To this second pillar of Christianity we now turn.

Out of the conviction that God has been active in human history, the writers of the Hebrew Bible constructed a grand narrative describing central events in the divine-human dialogue and offering theological assessments along the way. Major portions of the Old Testament chronicle this sacred history, especially Genesis through Numbers, Joshua through Kings, and Chronicles, and Ezra and Nehemiah. Some of this history is also pieced together from inferences drawn from other literature in the Old Testament, including materials in the Deuterocanonical (Apocryphal) writings. In this section, titled Sacred History, we describe the grand narrative of God's interactions with humans—especially with the Jewish people—up to the appearance of Jesus. We also briefly note other themes found in other books of the Hebrew canon, especially as they interface with themes of this sacred narrative.

The Hebrew Biblical Narrative

According to the sacred narrative of the Old Testament, in the beginning God created the heavens and the earth, formed the basic features of the world, and filled it with numerous creatures. Among these creatures were humans, created in the divine image. Soon after their creation, humans sinned against God. This sin was fueled by desire, mistrust, and deception, resulting in disobedience of God's command. Soon enmity with God, with one another, and with the created order befell humans; and violence became a pattern of human interaction. Through it all, divine judgment and grace intermixed as the Lord (a title often given to the Hebrew God) sought both to judge the evil of humanity but also to save humanity from its own unrighteousness. As time passed, violence filled the earth so that, in judgment, God destroyed most life on the planet through a flood; but God preserved a small remnant on an ark through a man named Noah.

Despite the new start with Noah and his family, sin continued to plague humanity. But God did not abandon humankind or the world. In a key moment in sacred history, God called forth a man named Abraham (initially known as Abram) to go to a land that God would show him, and God promised to bless Abraham and his descendants, and through them to bless all nations. Abraham obeyed God, and the Lord counted his faith (faithfulness) as righteousness (see Gen 15:6). Once Abraham arrived in the land, God promised that one day Abraham's offspring would possess it. A core element of the Lord's promise to Abraham was many descendants, but through most of his life Abraham had no children. Eventually, a son named Isaac was born to Abraham and his wife Sarah. In turn, Isaac and his wife Rebekah had two sons: one was named Jacob (eventually called Israel); Jacob and his four wives had twelve sons. From these boys the twelve tribes of Israel emerged. One of these twelve sons—Joseph—was sold into slavery by his brothers and ended up in Egypt. There, Joseph prospered, eventually becoming a leading official in the pharaoh's government. Years later a famine forced Joseph's family (including his father and brothers) to seek aid in Egypt. Upon arriving, Joseph's brothers discovered (much to their consternation) that their lives were now in the hands of the sibling they had sold into slavery. But much to their relief, Joseph forgave their treachery; that is, Joseph saw God's providential hand involved in all that had transpired so that God's people—the descendants of Abraham—might survive (see Gen 37–50).

The descendants of Abraham (often called Hebrews or Israelites) prospered and increased in Egypt for many centuries, until a pharaoh arose who did not recognize or honor Joseph, and who saw the people of Israel as a threat to his regime. Soon, the new pharaoh pressed the Israelites into forced labor building various public-works. In these dire circumstances, however, God raised up a leader named Moses to challenge the pharaoh to release the Israelites from political oppression so that they might worship God. To Moses was revealed the personal name of God—Yahweh (see Exod 3). Pharaoh refused to free the Israelites. So, God exacted great plagues upon the Egyptians until the pharaoh released the people. The last plague was the death of the firstborn of every household throughout Egypt, except in the houses of those who (per God's instructions) participated in a ritual called Passover: in this ceremony a lamb was killed and roasted, and its blood was painted on the doorposts of each Hebrew domicile as a signal for God's destroyer to "pass over" that home. After their release by the pharaoh, the Hebrews went to Mount Sinai (also called Horeb) and there entered a covenant or agreement with God wherein the Lord promised to be their God and they promised to be Yahweh's people. Numerous stipulations eventually were included as part of the agreement, but at its core were the Ten Commandments. Essentially, these commands stated:

1. Worship Yahweh alone.

2. Make no images of Yahweh or other deities.

3. Honor Yahweh.

4. Keep the Sabbath.

5. Honor parents.

6. Do not murder.

7. Do not commit adultery.

8. Do not steal.

9. Do not bear false witness.

10. Do not covet.

The story of Abraham and his descendants is described in the book of Genesis, as are the narratives about primordial events before Abraham. The stipulations of the covenant between God and Israel are found in the books of Exodus, Leviticus, and Deuteronomy. Included in these regulations are sacrifices that provide the Israelites a way to express gratitude to God, as well as to attain ritual cleanliness and forgiveness for breaching covenant expectations. After receiving the covenant from God, the people of Israel wandered in the wilderness for forty years, eventually entering the land promised to Abraham—the land of Canaan.

The sacred history of Israel continues in the books of Joshua, Judges, 1 and 2 Samuel, and 1 and 2 Kings. These accounts, sometimes called the Deuteronomistic History, describe the Israelite conquest of the promised land (in the book of Joshua), the lingering temptations and threats that the Canaanite occupants presented to the Israelites (in the book of Judges), and the emergence of a united kingdom under Kings David and Solomon (in the books of Samuel and 1 Kings). In the books of 1 and 2 Kings, the Deuteronomistic History tells about the split of the united kingdom into two realms (the kingdom of Israel in the north and the kingdom of Judah in the south) after the reign of King Solomon, about the fall of the Northern Kingdom to the Assyrians in 722 BCE, and about the fall of the Southern Kingdom to the Babylonians in 587/586 BCE. Throughout these narratives, principles affirmed in the book of Deuteronomy resound. One important theme is the promise of blessing to those who are faithful to God's covenant and the warning to those who are unfaithful to God's covenant of falling under a curse. Also significant are calls to love Yahweh with all of one's being (Deut 6:4; 2 Kgs 23:24–25) and to worship God at a central shrine. The latter of these ideals came to fruition through King David's establishment of Jerusalem as his capital and through King Solomon's building the temple of the Lord in that city. A particularly important theme in the Deuteronomistic History (the books of Joshua through Kings) is that God promises David that his dynasty will be everlasting (2 Sam 7:3–17). Another

significant theme or principle is that obeying God is better than merely following rituals or performing sacrifices (1 Sam 15:17–23).

The sacred story of Israel does not end with the fall of Jerusalem to the Babylonians. In 539 BCE, a Persian ruler named Cyrus the Great conquered the Babylonians and soon (in 538) allowed some Jews[7] to return to their homeland in Judah
(called Yehud by the Persians). These events, as well as others that followed, are
described in the books of Ezra and Nehemiah. Among the first to return to Judah
was a man named Sheshbazzar, who was the son of Jehoiachin, the former king of
Judah (see Ezra 1). With Sheshbazzar were several former exiles hoping to restore
Jerusalem to its glory, including to rebuild the temple of the Lord. Unfortunately,
these pilgrims faced considerable economic hardships and political opposition, and
only were able to lay the foundations of the temple. In 520 BCE, however, another
group of exiles, led by a nephew of Sheshbazzar named Zerubbabel and by a priest
named Joshua, was permitted to rebuild the temple. There were even whispers that
Zerubbabel or Joshua might restore the Davidic dynasty (Hag 2:23; Zech 6:9–15).
But no such restoration occurred, and the names Zerubbabel and Joshua disappeared from history. During the decades that followed, something of a spiritual and
"national" morass befell the residents of Judah. Hopes of a restored independent
Jewish kingdom ruled by a Davidic king dissipated quickly as the realities of Persian
authority set in. While Persians kings were religiously tolerant, allowing diverse
peoples to honor their spiritual heritages, these kings were not open to political insurrection or indigenous autonomy. And they seem to have sought some uniformity
within each religious community that they sanctioned.[8]

Perhaps for these reasons, a new strategy for survival under foreign rule emerged
in Judah in the mid-fifth century BCE. Rather than advocating for political autonomy
or voicing hopes for a concrete political messiah, two key Jewish leaders, Ezra and
Nehemiah, proposed strict adherence to the Torah—the law of Moses—as a way to preserve the heritage of Israel and Judah. Historians quarrel over when these two leaders
arrived in Judah.[9] Regardless of the exact dates, Ezra and Nehemiah did much to shape
the future of the Jewish faith. In a pivotal moment in the biblical narrative, Ezra reads
the law of Moses to the people of Jerusalem, and many of them repent and dedicate
themselves to earnest adherence to the covenant. Many Jewish men agree to sever ties

7. At this point in the biblical narrative, the people of Judah are called Jews—meaning, people
from Judah.

8. This is suggested in the narrative about Ezra, wherein the Persian king authorizes Ezra to teach
and impose certain religious practices upon all persons who understand themselves to be followers of
the Jewish God in the province (satrap) "Beyond the River" (7:21, 25).

9. A straightforward reading of the books of Ezra and Nehemiah suggests that Ezra arrived first, in
the seventh year of Artaxerxes I (reigned 465–424 BCE): thus, Ezra arrived in 458 BCE. Nehemiah arrived in Artaxerxes I's twentieth year—thus in 445 BCE. Some scholars, however, propose (for various
reasons) that Ezra arrived in the seventh year of Artaxerxes II (reigned 404–358 BCE), so in 397 BCE.
Most agree that Nehemiah arrived in 445 BCE, served twelve years, and then returned for a second
term, perhaps around 430 BCE

with non-Jews, including divorcing their foreign wives. Only in this way (some seem to have thought) could the people of Abraham preserve their heritage, remain faithful to Yahweh, and again receive the blessing lost due to unfaithfulness. Depending on how one reads the timeline, Nehemiah concurrently or later imposed similar sanctions during his tenure (see Ezra 9:1–5; Neh 8–10; 13:23–27).

The books of 1 and 2 Chronicles reinforce many of the ideas expressed in Ezra and Nehemiah. These histories retell the story of Israel up to the fall of Judah, often duplicating word for word passages from Samuel and Kings, but also shaping the narrative to stress the importance of the Torah, Israel's priesthood, and the role of King David in supporting Judah's ritual practices. The function of Israel's high priests also is emphasized, and at times is depicted as usurping the authority of Judah's kings (2 Chr 19:8–11; 26:16–21). And the roles and linage of priests and Levites are clearly demarcated. Probably written in the postexilic period, like the books of Ezra and Nehemiah, the books of Chronicles see faithfulness to the Torah and separation from foreign influences as crucial means of preserving the integrity of Judah's faith and heritage.

Echoing Themes and New Ideas

Throughout these sacred narratives, important themes reverberate. One is that humans (including the people of Israel) sin; they fail to live up to God's demands. Second, God judges sin. God does not simply ignore evil; rather at times the Lord exercises judgment upon sinners. Third, however, Yahweh is gracious. God does not simply abandon humans (including Israel) to their sins or to the consequences of sin. The Lord acts, sometimes in mighty ways, to save the people from the oppression of enemies and from the plight of their own moral (or covenantal) failures. Over and over, these themes resound in the sacred narrative. They are seen in God's judgment and grace upon the first humans after their sin, in the watery judgment and new start for humanity through Noah, in the divine orchestration of unanticipated blessings in the story of Joseph, in the exodus from Egypt, and in the interplay of judgment and grace in the books of Joshua through Kings. In the Deuteronomistic History, a key pattern is repeated: the people falter in their commitment to God, foreign oppressors threaten them, the Lord raises up political/religious leaders to defend his people, and victory/salvation unfolds—then the cycle repeats itself (Judg 2:11–23). At the end of 2 Kings, this interplay between human sin, divine punishment, and divine grace is expressed. Because of a long history of covenantal unfaithfulness, Judah is judged by God and falls to the Babylonians. But hope glimmers. Recalling God's promise that David's dynasty would never end, the narrative informs its readers that an heir to David's throne (Jehoiachin) still lived in exile and was well treated by the king of Babylon (2 Kgs 25:27–30). In short, even in the face of Judah's destruction, hope for restoration through a Davidic king still lingered.

The themes of the grand narrative of the Old Testament are sometimes reinforced or augmented in other literature of the Hebrew Bible. For example, often the prophetic literature assumes the Deuteronomic principle that faithfulness to the covenant leads to blessing and that unfaithfulness ends in judgment. And frequently such judgment is manifested in political disasters that befall God's people. Thus, the prophets warn their audiences to repent and obey the covenant lest divine judgment overtake them through foreign oppressors; or they explain political hardships (including the falls of Israel or Judah) in terms of divine retribution. In turn, not infrequently, prophets offer hope for restoration to divine favor (including national autonomy) after military devastations have transpired. Often such divine refurbishment is tied to promises of a reestablished Davidic king and kingdom (Jer 29:8–9; Ezek 37:21–27).

Another theme some prophets share with the Deuteronomistic narrative is emphasis on obeying God and not merely performing religious rituals. In a famous passage in Jeremiah, the prophet condemns the people of Judah for believing that merely participating in the temple rituals in Jerusalem guarantees divine favor and security (Jer 7:1–26). Jeremiah, however, announces that God expects not only ritual piety but also obedience to God's law. Thus, the prophet proclaims:

> Thus says the LORD of hosts, the God of Israel: Amend your ways and your doings, and let me dwell with you in this place. Do not trust in these deceptive words: "This is the temple of the LORD, the temple of the LORD, the temple of the LORD." For if you truly amend your ways and your doings, if you truly act justly one with another, if you do not oppress the alien, the orphan, and the widow, or shed innocent blood in this place, if you do not go after other gods to your own hurt, then I will dwell with you in this place, in the land that I gave of old to your ancestors forever and ever. (Jer 7:3–7)

Jeremiah goes on to warn the people that if they continue to disobey God, the Lord will bring judgment upon them. Similar sentiments are expressed in the book of Amos, where the prophet portrays God as despising hollow religious rituals to the neglect of righteousness and justice: "I hate, I despise your festivals, / and I take no delight in your solemn assemblies. / Even though you offer me your burnt offerings and grain offerings, / I will not accept them / . . . / But let justice roll down like waters, / and righteousness like an ever-flowing stream" (Amos 5: 21–24).

Comparable perspectives are found in the Writings. For example, the book of Proverbs affirms that those who obey God's precepts prosper, while those who ignore divine wisdom falter: "Therefore walk in the way of the good, / and keep to the paths of the just. For the upright will abide in the land, / and the innocent will remain in it; / but the wicked will be cut off from the land, / and the treacherous will be rooted out of it" (2:20–22). Again, "But the path of the righteous is like the light of dawn, / which shines brighter and brighter until full day. / The way of the wicked is like deep darkness; / they do not know what they stumble over" (4:18–19; compare 6:12–15).

Or again, "A scoundrel and a villain / goes around with crooked speech, / winking the eyes, shuffling the feet, / pointing the fingers, / with perverted mind devising evil, / continually sowing discord; / on such a one calamity will descend suddenly; / in a moment, damage beyond repair" (6:12–15).

While the prophets and writings often echo and supplement principles articulated in the grand narrative of the Old Testament, sometimes they offer new ideas or even challenge perspectives voiced in those narratives. For example, both Jeremiah and Ezekiel dispute (or at least rescind) the notion of corporate responsibility—the idea that a whole family or people group can be held responsible for the actions of a member or segment of that group. The principle of corporate responsibility is manifested in the book of Joshua when a whole family is executed for the sins of one of its members (7:10–26), and in the book of Exodus when the Lord declares that for the sins of one generation, divine wrath will befall the next four generations (20:5). Such a view also is implicit in the Deuteronomistic Historian's assumption that all the people of Israel and Judah were punished due to the sins of some (but not all) of the people. Countering such a principle, Jeremiah and Ezekiel affirm a notion of personal responsibility. Each individual is responsible for his or her own sins. Ezekiel proclaims:

> The word of the LORD came to me: What do you mean by repeating this proverb concerning the land of Israel, "The parents have eaten sour grapes, and the children's teeth are set on edge"? As I live, says the Lord GOD, this proverb shall no more be used by you in Israel. Know that all lives are mine; the life of the parent as well as the life of the child is mine: it is only the person who sins that shall die." (Ezek 18:1–4)

Similar ideas are expressed in the book of Jerimiah.[10]

Other principles of the grand narrative, likewise, are sometimes challenged. The prophet Habakkuk puzzles over how God can use the Babylonians to exact judgment upon Judah when the Babylonians are even more evil than the people of Judah had been (Hab 1:1–13). The book of Job questions whether it always is the case that the righteous prosper and the wicked flounder in this life. And the book of Ecclesiastes wonders whether there truly is a difference in the rewards of the righteous life versus the evil life, or the life of wisdom versus the life of folly—for all lives end in death (see Eccl 2:12–16; 3:16–22; 5:13–17; 6:1–6). Similarly, portions of the Old Testament challenge the survival-strategy offered by Ezra and Nehemiah (the strategy of Jews excluding themselves from marital and other social interactions with Gentiles). Some near contemporaries of Ezra and Nehemiah endorse a more inclusive approach, proposing that Jews are to be light to the nations (Isa 49:6) and

---

10. "The days are surely coming, says the LORD, when I will sow the house of Israel and the house of Judah with the seed of humans and the seed of animals . . . In those days they shall no longer say: 'The parents have eaten sour grapes, and the children's teeth are set on edge.' But all shall die for their own sins; the teeth of everyone who eats sour grapes will be set on edge" (Jer 31:27–30).

are to bring Gentiles into the fold of God's covenant. Such ideals are expressed in works such as Ruth, Jonah, and Isa 56:3–8.

The Persian and Early Hellenistic Eras

The grand narrative of the Hebrew Bible ends with Ezra and Nehemiah (430s BCE), and only scanty information about Judah's history thereafter can be garnered from later sacred and secular literature. While the broad history of the ancient Near East is told in various sources, information about the people of Abraham is piecemeal at best. In this section, we explore the history of the Persian and early Hellenistic eras, from 538 BCE to roughly 198 BCE. We begin by describing the board historical context of the time and then piece together scattered information about the Jewish people.

We start with Cyrus the Great. After his conquest of Babylon and his subsequent release of Jews to return to their homeland, Cyrus ruled until his death in 530 BCE. He died in battle, fighting resistant tribes in Afghanistan. Cyrus was succeeded by his son Cambyses (reigned 530–522), who conquered Egypt in 522, among other places, bringing the land of the Nile into the Persian fold. Unfortunately, shortly after this victory, Cambyses learned of a rebellion in Babylon and (apparently) took his own life en route to Mesopotamia. Stepping into the power gap, Cambyses's general, Darius I, (reigned 520–484) proclaimed himself king and soon faced and gradually overcame numerous uprisings throughout the empire. Over several years of conflict, Darius solidified his power and ruled with considerable skill, setting up the famed satrap system (a system of provincial governors) to oversee his realm. By 490, Darius I felt confident enough to attempt to attack Greek lands across the Aegean Sea. He met the Athenians in battle at Marathon but was defeated and forced to retreat to Asia Minor. Darius I was followed by his son Xerxes I (reigned 486–464), who attempted to over-run the Greeks in 480. Xerxes overcame mixed forces in Thermopylae, then marched to and razed Athens. The Athenian navy, however, escaped, and near Salamis handed the Persian fleet a sound defeat. Xerxes I, like his father, was forced to return to Asia. A year later, in 479, the Persian armada suffered an even more stunning loss near Samos at the hands of Athenian sailors; this essentially ended Persian attempts to conquer Greece and the Aegean. For the remainder of the fifth century BCE, Persian rulers kept the Greeks at bay by bribing and goading rival parties among them. The Peloponnesian War occupied Sparta, Athens, and their respective allies for much of the latter half of that century (c. 459–404).

Xerxes I was succeeded by Artaxerxes I (reigned 465–424), who ruled during the eras of Ezra and Nehemiah and sanctioned their activities. Troubles with the Greeks and Egyptians plagued his rule. But Persia remained relatively stable. Artaxerxes I was succeeded briefly by Xerxes II in 424, but Xerxes II was usurped by Darius II (reigned 423–404). As the Peloponnesian War continued, Darius II was able to regain territories in Asia Minor. Artaxerxes II came to the throne in 404 and ruled until 358.

But his rule was plagued with troubles. Egypt revolted and won its freedom in 401, remaining independent until the 340s. The brother of Artaxerxes II attempted to commandeer his throne but was killed in battle. Later, several western satraps (governors) attempted to secede. While the king quelled their insurrection, the power of Persia was waning. Artaxerxes III came to the throne in 358 BCE (reigned 358–338). He brutally cut down all his rivals but virtually decimated his own dynasty in the process. Fighting insurgencies along many fronts, Artaxerxes III managed to reconquer Egypt, returning it to Persian control. Artaxerxes III was murdered and succeeded by his son Arses (reigned 338–336), who in turn was assassinated and replaced by Darius III (reigned 336–331). Darius III was last of the Persian emperors, meeting the unwelcome fate of facing the onslaught of Alexander the Great.

Even as Artaxerxes III was brutalizing his family and forcing Egypt back into the Persian fold, Philip II of Macedon (reigned 359–336 BCE) was accruing power throughout Greece, squashing opposition from various Greek states and Greek alliances. By 339, Philip controlled most of the Hellas, but he was murdered in 336, bringing his twenty-year-old son, Alexander IV, to the forefront of history. Alexander (the Great) was a brilliant military tactician, whose bravery and skills brought immense admiration from his troops. Not long after his accession to the throne, Alexander set his sights on Asia Minor, hoping to regain former Greek possessions there. In 334, he crossed the Hellespont and easily defeated Persian troops at Granicus. Having mastered his father's use of the phalanx as well as cavalry, Alexander soon swept through much of Asia Minor. In 333, Darius III marched out to meet the young Greek commander at Issus and there received a thorough defeat. Darius III fled the battle, leaving his wife, mother, and family to be captured. Alexander now aimed to control Persia. Throughout 333 into 332 BCE, Alexander marched along the eastern coast of the Mediterranean, conquering first Phoenicia, then Palestine, then Egypt. Many of these populations offered little resistance, often welcoming the new conqueror in hope of a better life. Tyre resisted and was decimated. Egypt gladly received Alexander, giving him the quasi-divine title of Pharaoh. Then in 331, with his flanks secured, Alexander marched into Mesopotamia. Meeting Darius III at Gaugamela, he again overcame a massive army. Darius III fled, but was killed by one of his satraps. With the defeat of Darius III, the governors of eastern Persia capitulated to Alexander's rule. Alexander took time to shore up his new possessions, but eventually (in 327–326), he marched an army to the Indus River, seeking to further expand his possessions. But many of his troops, some who had been with him from the beginning, pleaded for Alexander to end his expansionist pursuits. Alexander conceded to their desires and returned to Babylon. Three years later, in 323, Alexander died in Babylon due to persistent complications from war injuries. He was just shy of thirty-three years old.

After Alexander the Great's death, his empire soon was divided among his commanders. War broke out between Antigonus and four other former generals of Alexander. When the dust had settled, Lysimachus commandeered Thrace, Cassander took Macedon and Greece, Ptolemy I claimed Egypt, and Seleucus I controlled Syria, Mesopotamia, and much of Persia and Media. The latter two houses vied for control of Palestine, with the Ptolemies ruling there until 198 BCE, at which point Antiochus III (the Great), of the Seleucid dynasty, took control (reigned 222–187 BCE) after defeating the armies of the child Ptolemy V (203–181) at Panium.

The history of the Jews during the late Persian and early Hellenistic periods is spotty at best.[11] Broadly, we know that in addition to Jews in Judah, there were Jewish communities spread throughout the Near East, including especially in Babylon, Egypt, and Syria. But little is known about their daily lives, economic activities, and political intrigues. Scraps of information speak of a governor of Judah named Bagoas[12] in the late fifth century BCE. During his tenure, some maneuvering unfolded between the high priest (Johanan) and the priest's brother (Joshua). Apparently, Joshua tried to usurp his brother's office and wound up dead. Because of these events, Bagoas mandated heavy sanctions against Judah. We know that Bagoas was in office in 407, but the precise dates of his tenure are unknown. Further, we know nothing of his successors or of those who served as high priests after Johanan.

Ironically, some of the most detailed information of the late Persian period comes from a tiny Jewish community in Elephantine in Egypt. This was a military outpost with ties to Persian overlords. In a communique from the late fifth century, Elephantine leaders asked for aid from fellow Jews in Samaria and Judah to rebuild their temple to Yahweh. The temple likely had been destroyed by what today we might call anti-Persian Egyptian nationalists. Eventually, monies were received from worshipers of Yahweh in Samaria, under the auspices of Persian authorities in the Levant. But no such aid was sent by Jews in Judah, who were under the authority of the high priest Johanan. Johanan's refusal likely reflects the long-standing influences of Ezra's and Nehemiah's reforms, which included holding to the belief that there is only one valid Jewish temple—namely, the one in Jerusalem. Interestingly, these data also tell us that some individuals both in Samaria and in the diaspora saw themselves as worshipers of Yahweh but did not accept many of the restrictions mandated by the Jewish community in Judah. For this reason (likely in the late Persian or early Hellenistic era), Samaritans built their own temple to Yahweh at Mount Gerizim, near the city of Shechem.

11. Largely due to the books of Ezra, Nehemiah, and Chronicles, some information about Judah in the early Persian period is available. For example, we know that Cyrus the Great commissioned Sheshbazzar and company to return to Judah (Yehud) to restore a community there. Darius I ruled when Zerubbabel and the high priest Joshua rebuilt the temple. Given the political unrest of Darius's early reign, it is not hard to imagine that if rumors of messianic hope in Zerubbabel reached his ears, the king would have been inclined to shut down such aspirations. Although we do not know what happened to Zerubbabel, it is worth noting that after him there is no record of another member of David's house being commissioned by the Persians to govern Judah.

12. A Persian name.

Beyond these slight details, very little is known of Jewish history during the late Persian era. Similar ignorance holds regarding the early Hellenistic period. Few particulars are known about Jewish life, politics, and practices, whether in Judah or in the diaspora. Significantly, we do know that during the Ptolemaic reign, the population of Jews in Egypt grew immensely, especially in Alexandria (founded in honor of the great conqueror in 332). Apparently, Ptolemy I brought thousands of Jewish refugees from his military campaigns in Palestine to populate Egypt, and those numbers greatly increased over the ensuing centuries—with perhaps as many as a million Jews living in Alexandria by the first century CE.

Perhaps more significant than the details of politics are the broad cultural shifts that occurred for Jews in the Persian and early Hellenistic eras. Persian influence is especially seen in the language shift from Hebrew to Aramaic that transpired in Judah and throughout much of the Near East. This shift began in north Palestine with the victory of the Assyrians over Israel in 722 BCE, and it continued in Judah with the triumphs of the Babylonians and Persians in the sixth century. As the centuries flowed thereafter, Aramaic became the language of commerce and politics throughout the Near East. Certainly, a myriad of local dialects still peppered the landscape (including Hebrew), but often Aramaic tied the whole region together. And with Aramaic came the transfer of cultural assumptions often embedded in vocabulary and syntax.

Another Persian cultural influence on Jewish ways was a notable set of religious/ metaphysical perspectives. Many of these ideas were expressed by the Zoroastrian religion, which likely emerged in Persia in the sixth century BCE. Scholars are unsure whether Zoroastrianism fostered these ideas or absorbed them from other sources. Further, historians debate to what degree Jewish thinkers learned such concepts from Persia, and to what degree these ideas were present in the general religiocultural environment. What is clear is that ideas not expressed in earlier Hebrew works began to appear in Jewish literature during and after the Persian hegemony in the Near East. Among these ideas were beliefs in heaven and hell, life after death, resurrection of the body, and cosmic warfare between powers of good (including God) and fundamental principles of evil (including demons, devils, and Satan). The concept of Satan appears only in the latest writings of the Hebrew Bible and only three times—namely, in Zechariah (3:1–5), Job (1–2), and Chronicles (1 Chr 21:1). Other ideas, such as resurrection from the dead, spiritual warfare, and end-time judgment materialized in various later Jewish works—including the book of Daniel (likely completed in the Maccabean era; see Dan 12:2) and various works of the Apocrypha (Deuterocanon). Not all Jewish responses to Persian influences were positive. Writings such as Tobit and Judith (both in the Apocrypha and likely written in the late Persian or early Hellenistic era) wrestle with how to live faithfully as Jews in the context of foreign domination.

Hellenistic culture also impacted the Jewish mind, not least through the Greek language. Alexander the Great not only conquered with armies but also with ideas and a language (through which to express ideas). After Alexander, Greek became the language of commerce and statecraft for his empire. Enhancing this influence was Alexander's deliberate integration of Greek and Near Eastern populations through colonization and programed intermarriages between Greeks and denizens of the Persian Empire. Greek colonies were established throughout Palestine and beyond—including in the Negev, Philistia, the Transjordan, Galilee, and Phoenicia. With these towns came accoutrements of Greek life—gymnasiums, theaters, racetracks, and temples. By the second century BCE, the Decapolis (the league of ten Greek towns in northeast Palestine) was flourishing. The Hellenists brought with them new ideas: the geometry of Euclid (d. 285 BCE); the plays of Sophocles (497–406 BCE); the political ideas of Pericles (495–429 BCE); the metaphysics and ethics of Socrates (d. 399 BCE), Plato (424–348 BCE), Aristotle (384–322 BCE), and Epicurus (341–270 BCE). The Greeks also brought mores and lifestyles often shocking to traditional Hebrew perspectives. One particularly important impact of Hellenistic culture upon Jews was the translation of the Hebrew Bible (and other religious texts) into Greek. The development and use of the Septuagint (and other works) in the centuries just before Christ helped convey Jewish religious ideas to the broader world.[13]

The Jewish reaction to Hellenistic culture was mixed. Often the response was negative. As we shall see in the next section, the interaction especially was hostile during the reign of the Seleucid king Antiochus IV. His repressive reforms brought (understandable) vitriolic rejoinders from religious conservatives, including condemnation of Hellenistic idolatry, of sexual promiscuity, and of cultural arrogance. For many Jews, the answer to Greek cultural intrusion was abject separation from Hellenistic ways for the sake of faithfulness to Yahweh. Such reactions were echoes of Ezra's and Nehemiah's proposals of an earlier time. Expressions of this distaste for Hellenism and delight for Mosaic tradition are articulated in several Jewish religious texts of the period including the books of 1 and 2 Maccabees (in the Apocrypha) and Daniel (in the Hebrew Bible).

While the Jewish response to Hellenistic culture and control was often negative, many Jews welcomed features of Greek life, especially among the elite in Judah (and in the diaspora). Some segments of Jewish society gladly accepted the insights and advantages of Hellenistic culture, and hoped to reshape Jewish backwater ways to suit new political and social realities. Others, while not fully accommodating Greek ways, sought to intermingle the best Greek insights into the broad Hebrew religious perspective. The book of Wisdom (in the Apocrypha) is among such works. A much later (and fuller) example of such an amalgamation was the philosophy of Philo of Alexandria (c. 25 BCE—50 CE), who sought to integrate key insights from Greek philosophy with the core ideas of the Yahwist tradition.

---

13. The same might be said of the works of the New Testament—all of which were written in Greek. This literature, likewise, helped promulgate broadly Jewish religious perspectives upon the ancient Western world.

The Maccabean and Early Roman Period

As noted in the previous section, the Ptolemaic dynasty ruled Palestine until 198 BCE, at which point Antiochus III, of the Seleucid house, prevailed over Egyptian armies and came to possess these lands. These events were precursors of hard times about to befall the Jews of Judea (the Greek name for Judah). Unfortunately, after his success in Palestine, Antiochus III soon overstretched his reach, attacking Greece in 192 and bringing the wrath of Rome upon him. Rome declared war and conquered Antiochus in battle at Thermopylae and then again at Magnesia in Asia Minor. Antiochus III was forced to pay a huge indemnity, give up key territories in Asia Minor, and hand over several refugees of war (including Rome's great enemy, Hannibal).[14] Thus began the decline of the Seleucids, now harassed by Roman (and Parthian) expansionism. Antiochus III was succeeded by his son Seleucus IV (reigned 187–175), who was forced to search for revenue wherever it might be found, including through heavy taxation and through looting his subjects' temples—Jerusalem's temple among them.

Seleucus was murdered in 175 and succeeded by his brother Antiochus IV Epiphanes (reigned 175–163). Antiochus IV's kingdom was threatened by the Parthians in the east, the Ptolomies in the south, and the Romans in the west. Not surprisingly, like his predecessors, Antiochus IV was strapped for cash and resorted to heavy taxing and looting to shore-up his holdings. He also gladly sold offices to the highest bidders. Such was the case in 175, when Antiochus IV was offered a bribe from a Judean named Joshua (who preferred the Greek name Jason). Jason longed to take the place of his brother, Onias III, as high priest in Jerusalem. Antiochus IV accepted the bribe, empowered Jason, and set a wildfire of unrest. Jason fanned the flames by imposing measures intended to Hellenize the city and people of Jerusalem—a goal in keeping with Antiochus's hope to homogenize the culture of his kingdom. Jason built a gymnasium in Jerusalem (with all the trappings of the pagan culture and deities), and he encouraged Judah's elite to join. Apparently, many did; some young men even had their circumcisions surgically reversed to appear Greek when competing in the games. Protests broke out among the pious. Making matters worse, in 172 Antiochus deposed Jason, replacing him as high priest with a higher bidder—a man named Menelaus (of uncertain but nonpriestly origins). In a series of cumbersome events, tensions only grew as both Menelaus and Antiochus demonstrated little concern, and later utter contempt, for Jewish religious-sensitivities. Menelaus continued many of his predecessors' attempts to Hellenize the region. And both he and Antiochus ransacked the Jerusalem temple when revenue ran low.[15]

14. Hannibal, however, briefly escaped but later was captured and killed.

15. Shortly after taking office, Menelaus confiscated several precious items from the temple to pay his bribe to the king. In 169 and again in 168, Antiochus—largely to pay for expenses incurred in military campaigns in Egypt—pilfered expensive wares from the Jerusalem temple, including the gold overlay from its walls.

When armed rebellion began to surface in the region, Antiochus swiftly responded. In 167, he sent troops to quell the unrest, apparently indiscriminately slaughtering many residents of Jerusalem. A citadel was built, a garrison was placed in the city, and a Greek colony was established in the heart of the city. In turn, perhaps becoming convinced that Judea's unrest was due to religion, Antiochus imposed a crushing ban upon Jewish spiritual practices. With the threat of execution looming over practicing Judeans, temple sacrifices were ended, Sabbath gatherings forbidden, circumcision of infants prohibited, and adherence to kosher rules banned. Further, an image of Zeus was placed in Jerusalem's temple and swine were sacrificed there.[16] Shrines to Greek deities likewise were erected throughout Judea, and large numbers of pious Jews were arrested, many tortured and killed.[17]

It is not surprising that under such conditions armed resistance arose throughout Judea and other territories of Palestine. What is shocking is that eventually the rebellion succeeded.[18] The Jewish revolt was led by the Hasmonean family—first by a priest named Mattathias and then in succession by his sons Judas Maccabeus (the hammer), Jonathan, and Simon. In his old age, Mattathias inspired a nation when he stoutly resisted a Syrian official's demand that he sacrifice to a foreign deity. Mattathias responded by cutting down the emissary where he stood (as well as a fellow Jew who complied with the king's demands). Soon, Mattathias and his sons fled to the hills near their home in Modein, and they sparked a revolution. In 165 BCE, the temple in Jerusalem was liberated by Judas's forces and purged of its pagan defilements—an event celebrated in the annual feast of Hanukkah. In 142 BCE, through the military leadership of Simon, Judea gained independence from the Seleucids and established a new royal dynasty—the Hasmoneans—which ruled from 142 to 63 BCE. The exploits of the Hasmonean family and the war against the Seleucids are recorded in the books of 1 and 2 Maccabees. Key players in the Maccabean war were individuals known as Hasidim ("pious ones"), most of whom were tenaciously committed to the Mosaic law and fought with a zeal fueled by righteous indignation. In many ways, these individuals were the forerunners of two sectarian groups of the New Testament era: the Pharisees and Essenes.

Unhappily, many of the most religiously zealous Jews who fought for freedom from the Seleucids became disappointed as the years of Hasmonean rule unfolded. Family squabbles, compromises with foreign powers, attrition to Hellenistic ways, and plays for power soon tarnished the once noble (pious) heritage of that house. Many of the Hasidim complained that the Hasmoneans were not of Davidic lineage and thus

16. The book of Daniel (which almost certainly was written around the time of these occurrences) calls this event the "abomination of desolation" (Dan 9:27; 11:31; 12:11).

17. Second Maccabees describes several (perhaps legendary) examples of Antiochus's atrocities. A particularly heinous scene occurs when seven brothers are tortured and fried alive as their mother is forced to watch, because they refuse to eat pork (2 Macc 7:1–42).

18. The success of the rebellion was due in no small part to the growing political conundrum faced by the Seleucids, who were hard-pressed by Rome in the west and by the Parthians in the east.

were not legitimate heirs to the throne of Judah. Circumstances deteriorated further when King John Hyrcanus I (reigned 134–104), son of Simon, declared himself to be not only king but also high priest of Judah. For many of the faithful, the office of high priest was reserved only for members of the house of Zadok. Thus, John was a double usurper, not rightly qualified to be either king or high priest. The details and intrigues of the Hasmonean dynasty cannot detain us here. Suffice it to say that after a nearly one-hundred-year reign first with quasi-autonomy (from c. 142 to 116) and then with near complete autonomy (from 116 to 63), the Hasmonean kingdom became a protectorate of the Romans at the hands of Pompey.[19]

After Rome's victory, John Hyrcanus II ruled Judea (as ethnarch) until 40 BCE, at which point another family rose to ascendency—the dynasty of the Herods. The Herods hailed from Idumea, south of Judea.[20] Over time, a key leader among them— named Antipater (c. 100–43 BCE) gained favor with Rome so that in 40 BCE the Romans handed power over Judea to Antipater's son Herod, who became known as Herod the Great. To help appease Hasmonean sensitivities, Herod married into that family, wedding Mariamne—the great-granddaughter of John Hyrcanus II. (Herod eventually had her and their children murdered to secure is own "purer" dynastic name). Herold ruled Judea from roughly 40 BCE until 4 BCE. The New Testament informs us that Jesus of Nazareth was born during Herod's rule. Herod—whose favor with Rome allowed him to become immensely wealthy and to be granted control over most of Palestine—patronized several expensive public works, including the refurbishing and expansion of the temple compound in Jerusalem. The bulk of the New Testament history unfolds under the reigns of Herod's progeny, who after his death (under Roman supervision) divided rule of his lands.

Jewish Life and Faith at the Turn of the First Century CE

By the turn of the first century of the Common Era, the sacred story of Israel had grown in depth and complexity. Vines sprouting from diverse soils over centuries matured and intermingled into intricate patterns. Still, at the risk of oversimplification, we can identify a handful of common trends active in Jewish life by the beginning of the new millennium. First was a lingering commitment to Yahweh. Perhaps originally conceived as a tribal and later as a national deity, Yahweh came to be envisaged (especially during the epoch of foreign occupation) as the sole God of the universe— creator and sovereign of all. Long before the first century CE, at the center of Jewish

---

19. Ironically, the Romans (who long had desired to control the eastern Mediterranean) were invited by two factions of the Hasmoneans to intervene on their behalf. The Romans sided with the elder brother, John Hyrcanus II, against his younger brother, Aristobulus II. Rome defeated the latter's armies and declared John to be the rightful high priest. However, they did not recognize John as king but as ethnarch—a designation that effectively ending his independence and making him a vassal of Rome.

20. These were peoples known as Edomites in the days of ancient Israel. The Idumeans formally converted to the Jewish faith when John Hyrcanus I conquered their lands decades earlier.

faith was the Shema, expressed in Deuteronomy: "Hear, O Israel: The LORD our God is one LORD; and you shall love the LORD your God with all your heart, and with all your soul, and with all your might (6:4–5). Holding Yahweh to be the one and only God, this faith forbade the worship of other deities. This is evidenced by the outrage of pious Jews at Antiochus IV Epiphanes's attempt to honor Zeus in Jerusalem's temple. By the second century BCE exclusivist monotheism was a common and virtually irrevocable principle for most adherents of the Jewish tradition.

A second common theme of Judaism at the start of the Common Era was commitment to the laws of Moses. Originally formed over centuries out of diverse moral and ritual practices, the Torah (law/instruction) came to be codified and understood as the central focus of Jewish life, virtually synonymous with Israel's covenant with God. Thus, obedience to this law (however diversely such obedience might be interpreted within Judaism) became a clear mark of Jewish identity. Spread throughout the Near East—whether in occupied Judah (Yehud/Judea) or in diverse communities of the diaspora—Jews found commonality in their commitment to keeping the law.

When combined with the loss of an autonomous state and royal line, the affirmation of law helped generate a third characteristic of the Jewish faith. This was the increased prestige and power of priests in the Jewish community. This especially was the case in Judah proper. As the key functionaries in the animal sacrifices prescribed by Mosaic law, priests exercised great influence upon those who identified themselves as Jews (as followers of God's Torah). During the Persian, Hellenistic, and early Roman eras, Judah's priests (especially the high priests) often served as liaisons between the people of Judah and occupying powers, overseeing both sacred and secular affairs. The priesthood was hereditary so that, as time passed, aristocratic priestly families controlled more and more property, thus enhancing their influence upon the affairs of religion and state. Related to the rise of powerful priests was the revivification of Jerusalem's temple. Rebuilt in the days of Zerubbabel, the temple became the bedrock of the Jewish religion during the years of foreign occupation. While many Jews both in Palestine and beyond could not routinely (if ever) visit the temple in Jerusalem, many looked upon it and its chief priests as the center of Jewish religious practice.[21]

A fourth characteristic of Judaism at the turn of the Common Era was it growing emphasis on written scriptures and, subsequently, on the need for translators, interpreters, and teachers of the law. The postexilic era generated earnest attempts to collate and codify the Jewish sacred writings. Some of the latest redactions of the Hebrew Bible took shape during the late Persian period at the hands of priestly editors. In turn, during that time, the Torah's supreme canonical authority came to be recognized, being honored above all other sacred texts. Not far behind the affirmation of the Torah was acceptance of other writings, including the Former Prophets (Joshua through Kings) and the Latter Prophets, including Isaiah, Jeremiah, Ezekiel

---

21. For this reason, often the period between Zerubbabel and the temple's fall at the hands of the Romans in 70 CE is referred to as the era of Second Temple Judaism.

(also called the Major Prophets) and the Twelve (also called the Minor Prophets). Recognition of the Writings came more slowly, some perhaps as late as the first century CE. Through it all, however, the Torah (Greek: Pentateuch) received the greatest honor among sacred texts. The production and recognition of these authoritative writings, in turn, helped reshape the texture of the Jewish faith.

Almost certainly, the emergence of these authorized texts—along with the postexilic emphasis on heeding God's law—helped generate the need for and the proliferation of teachers, interpreters, and sometimes translators of the Scriptures. Scholars today are uncertain of when guilds of scribes first appeared in Jewish life. These were individuals trained in reading and interpreting the Hebrew Scriptures—especially the Torah. Certainly, by the first century BCE such scholars were found throughout Palestine as well as in various communities of the diaspora. In some contexts, scribes were needed to translate the ancient Hebrew writings for those whose familiarity with Hebrew was waning if not utterly lost. This especially would have been true of Jews of the diaspora, but also of many Jews in Palestine, where Aramaic and later Greek became most common. The need for scribes also grew due to the complexities and tensions found in the Hebrew scriptural traditions. Considerable nuance was needed to navigate the diverse elements of such writings. Indeed, even the scribes disagreed with one another on many points, and competing schools of interpretation arose among them.

Closely tied to the rise of written scriptures (and their scribes) was a fifth trend of Judaism in this era—namely, the emergence of synagogues. These were gatherings of Jewish faithful for worship and fellowship. At the center of these meetings was the hearing and exposition of the Scriptures—again, especially the Torah. The origin of synagogues likewise is uncertain. Some suspect that even before the fall of Judah in 586 BCE, the religious faithful (many of whom lived too far from Jerusalem to routinely visit the temple) often met in local gatherings to worship Yahweh and to share insights regarding God's laws. Such practices almost certainly increased during the exile, when the temple no longer existed and Jerusalem was far away. In turn, even after the return to Judah and the building of the Second Temple, many faithful (some in Palestine and many throughout the Near East) sought to honor God's Sabbath by meeting to hear precepts from the law. Obviously, also, such assemblies helped salve the need for companionship and mutual support. By the turn of the Common Era, synagogues were present in virtually every municipality in the Near East (and beyond) where Jews resided.

A sixth common feature of Jewish faith at the turn of the first century CE was a renewed interest in messianic hope. While hope for Davidic kings perhaps never completely left the Jewish faith, it seems to have been invigorated by the Maccabean victories. Unfortunately, for many faithful Jews messianic expectations were disappointed as the Hasmonaean era unfolded when these kings did not live up to the ideals promised in the Tanak—not the least of which failing to be from David's line. These messianic hopes were all the more challenged (but not vanquished) when the Romans brought political servitude back to Palestine. Messianic expectations came in many forms in the early Common Era. Sometimes such views were straightforward anticipation of this-worldly military victory over Roman occupiers. At other times, such hopes were mixed with apocalyptic visions of divine intervention, crashing into this world of evil and righting its wrong in grand displays of heavenly power. Tied to such hopes were other apocalyptic images, including resurrection from the dead, end-time judgment, and postdeath life in heaven or hell.

These diverse understandings of messianic hope were displayed by differing Jewish religious factions in the first century CE. Zealots often called for military insurrections against the Romans, hoping a messiah would rise up among them to ward off the hated occupiers. Many Zealots believed that faithfulness to God's law was a key to divinely sanctioned military success. Another group, the Essenes, also often looked for a military solution, living in a state of constant preparedness for war, but also exhibiting especially strict lives of faithfulness to the Mosaic law. Many Essenes looked for God's apocalyptic inbreaking into history, destroying the enemy in a grand show of cosmic power, and ushering in a new era of divine rule on earth. Often Essenes looked for two messiahs, one of Davidic linage to rule as king and another from Aaron's line to serve as a truly faithful high priest in Jerusalem. Other Jewish factions were far less likely to look for military solutions or divine intervention in the affairs of state. This was the case with the priestly clans and Sadducees. Most of these individuals called for caution when dealing with Roman occupiers, seeking compromise whenever possible. Sadducees were committed to the laws of Moses as expressed in the Torah but questioned the religious authority of the Prophets and Writings; they often saw these latter works more as commentary than authoritative. In turn, Sadducees typically rejected newer doctrinal perspectives not clearly present in Moses' law, including apocalyptic ideas such as resurrection from the dead, heaven and hell, and divine final judgment.

Another prevalent Jewish religious faction by the turn of the first century CE was the Pharisees. Pharisees were often open to a wider canon of literature than were the Sadducees, affirming the authority of the Prophets and the Writings, and also being open to the "oral torah." The oral torah was ongoing interpretation of God's law offered over the decades—and eventually centuries—by various rabbis (teachers) and scribes. As the name suggests, much of this commentary on the law was passed down orally, but as the years progressed, such discussion was preserved in writing, eventually forming what would become known as the Mishnah (and still later the Talmud). Pharisees often called for all Jews—laypersons as well as priests—to live by all the regulations of the Torah, including the priestly codes. Because of this, at times, Pharisees expressed harsh attitudes toward persons (including Gentiles) who did not live by the stricter principles they deemed to be essential. Pharisees also were open to later, apocalyptic, doctrines such as life after death, resurrection, and divine end-time intervention in history. Many looked for God's mighty hand to raise up a messiah to defeat Israel's enemies and inaugurate Yahweh's rule upon the whole world.

Conclusion

Christianity is grounded in at least four important foundations: a sacred text, a sacred history, a sacred person, and a sacred community. In this chapter, we have discussed the first two of these bases—the Bible and the story of Israel. In Chapter 2, we consider the other two foundations, namely, Jesus (the sacred person) and the church (the sacred community).

2

Sacred Person and Sacred Community

CHRISTIANITY IS GROUNDED IN four foundations: a sacred text, a sacred history, a sacred person, and a sacred community. In Chapter 1, we explored the sacred history of Christianity—namely, the story of the ancient Hebrews/Israelites/Jews. We also examined the sacred text of Christianity—the Bible—including the Old and New Testaments. In this second chapter, we turn to consider the other two foundations of Christianity—namely, Jesus (who is the sacred person) and the church (which is the sacred community). We begin by exploring the story, person, and work of Jesus.

Sacred Person

For Christians, sacred history reaches its crescendo in Jesus of Nazareth. Jesus was born into the world of Roman-occupied first-century Palestine, born into the heritage and hope of ancient Judaism. It was a context of religious and political factions, where opinions varied over how best to serve God, relate to Gentiles, and understand the divine promises of a glorious future for Israel, which many Jews closely associated with a promised messianic figure. From the perspective of a historian, Jesus was a first-century Jewish religious teacher or prophet whose activities aroused the ire of both Jewish and Roman authorities, and whose life culminated in his execution by crucifixion. But soon after his death, Jesus' followers began claiming that he had been raised from the dead and that God had authorized his teachings and deeds.

The Story of Jesus

A sacred history about Jesus developed—core narratives about his life and significance. Initially passed down orally by his early followers, many of these narratives eventually were written down. The Christian church ultimately canonized four of these accounts—the Gospels of Matthew, Mark, Luke, and John. While theologians and historians bicker over the historical accuracy of these narratives,[1] and while

1. For fuller discussion of the history of Jesus, see Robinson, *Christianity: A Brief History*, chapter

the details of these Gospel accounts vary—in some cases significantly—the central story line runs as follows.[2]

Jesus was a descendant of King David, miraculously born to a virgin named Mary; he grew up in a town called Nazareth in the region of Galilee. Somewhere between the ages of thirty and forty, Jesus was baptized by a prophet named John (the Baptizer). John was a fiery preacher who echoed many of the apocalyptic themes of his era, warning of a coming divine judgment and calling his countrymen to repent of their sins and to prepare for the coming of God. Soon Jesus likewise was preaching and ministering in and around Galilee. Many found Jesus' messages intriguing and flocked to him. He spoke with uncommon authority, often through tantalizing (and sometimes cryptic) parables as well as through short, pithy wisdom sayings. Jesus also performed wonders: healings, exorcisms, acts of great power. He healed the blind, the fevered, the disabled, and persons with leprosy; he miraculously fed five thousand with five loaves of bread and two fish (Matt 14:13–21; Mark 6:30–44; Luke 9:10–17; John 6:1–15); he calmed a storm with a spoken command (Mark 5:35–41), walked on the sea (Mark 6: 45–51), and even raised the dead (Mark 5:35–43; John 11:1–46).

The core of Jesus' message was that the kingdom of God (or heaven) was near, and that people needed to repent. Likely transcending John's message, Jesus encouraged his audiences to believe the good news (or gospel) of God's kingdom. Apparently for Jesus, the notion of the kingdom of God had multiple meanings. At root, it referred to God's rule or reign, and derivatively it referenced the domain governed by God. Often Jesus spoke of God's kingdom as a time when God would break into history to judge the wicked, reward the righteous, and establish a divinely ruled kingdom on earth. Involved in this inbreaking was something like God's rule within the hearts of individual believers—an inner change of perspective, an earnest commitment to God, a transformation of spirit.

For Jesus, genuine righteousness (and evil) flows from who a person is, not from mere conformity to external rules (Mark 7:14–23). Thus, as the fruit of a tree is produced by the inner nature of a tree, so righteousness (and evil) arises from the inner person (Matt 7:15–20). For this reason, Jesus sometimes was harsh toward his religious rivals (including Pharisees and scribes), accusing some of them of following God outwardly through public (even garish) displays of piety, while inwardly being motivated by pride, greed, a desire for recognition, and a self-righteous disdain toward others (Matt 6:2–6; Mark 7:1–13; 12:38–40). According to Jesus, one's motive for serving God must be love—love for God and love for fellow humans. These are the two greatest commandments (Matt 22:36–40). Part of Jesus' indictment against some religious teachers was that they cared more about keeping human regulations than about the loftier elements of God's law, including calls for justice, mercy, and care for the (spiritual and physical) needs of others (Matt 12:1–14; 23:23–24; Mark 7:

2.

2. This outline especially follows the story line expressed in the Synoptic Gospels.

1–13). According to Jesus, the command to love one's neighbor extends not only to faithful Jews but to sinners (Mark 2:17; Luke 15), Gentiles (Luke 10:25–37), personal and political enemies, and even persecutors (Matt 5:21–26, 43–44). Jesus also held a special place for the politically, socially, and religiously ostracized—for the poor, sick, hungry, and vulnerable (Matt 25:31–46; Luke 4:16–19; 14:12–14), and for persons despised by the religious elite (Mark 2:13–17).

None of these teachings alone likely would have gotten Jesus in trouble with authorities. But there seems to have been another element of Jesus' demeanor that caused concern among some religious leaders. According to the Gospel accounts, Jesus often expressed a high regard for his own role in the divine economy. He assumed authority to forgive sins (Mark 2:8–11; Luke 7:48). He proclaimed that in his actions the kingdom of God had come. That is, he claimed that in his ministry, scriptural promises were being fulfilled—promises tied to the coming of the messiah and to the outpouring of God's Spirit (Matt 11:2–6; 12:22–32; Luke 4:16–21). Indeed, Jesus saw himself and his mission as uniquely related to God and to the divine purpose. Thus, using the title "Son" in reference to himself, Jesus said, "he who rejects me rejects him who sent me . . . All things have been committed to me by my Father. No one knows who the Son is except the Father, and no one knows who the Father is except the Son" (Luke 10:16, 22). In a similar vein, Jesus called for absolute commitment to himself and his mission. Jesus demonstrated a lofty esteem for himself and his mission by calling for absolute and resolute commitment. Thus, he declares:

> If any want to become my followers, let them deny themselves and take up their cross and follow me. For those who want to save their life will lose it, and those who lose their life for my sake, and for the sake of the gospel, will save it. For what will it profit them to gain the whole world and forfeit their life? (Mark 8:34–38; compare Matt 16:24–28 and Luke 9:23–27)

In another context, Jesus said: "Whoever loves father or mother more than me is not worthy of me; and whoever loves son or daughter more than me is not worthy of me; and whoever does not take up the cross and follow me is not worthy of me" (Matt 10:37–38; Luke 14:25–33). Clearly (for the Gospel writers), Jesus highly esteemed his mission and his role in that cause.

The Gospel writers note that Jesus' conduct and teachings raised the ire of some Jewish political and religious leaders. His disregard for Pharisaic traditions, his association with sinners, his openness to Gentiles, his harsh words toward religious rivals, his seemingly arrogant self-appraisal, all led some to loathe him and to conspire against him. But even these actions likely did not trigger Jesus' ultimate arrest and execution. Rather, the catalyst for his condemnation seems to have been his activities during a Passover celebration in Jerusalem during what became the last week of his life. On the first day of that week, Jesus boldly entered Jerusalem riding on a donkey to the praises of a crowd chanting, "Hosanna! Blessed is the one who comes in the name of the Lord! Blessed is the coming kingdom of our ancestor David!" (Mark 11:9–10; see also 1 Macc 13:49–53; Zech 9:9; Matt 21:1–11). The messianic (and thus revolutionary) overtones of such actions apparently were obvious to the powers that be, raising suspicions of insurrection among the Romans and fear of Roman reprisal among Jerusalem's political elite.

Making matters worse, Jesus soon started a ruckus by overturning tables of money changers in the Jerusalem temple and by attacking persons buying and selling sacrificial animals there. Jesus' motives are not completely clear. But he seems to have been challenging the authority (or integrity) of the temple hierarchy (priests and Sadducees) and possibly criticizing the sacrificial system itself. During this turmoil, Jesus is recorded as quoting snippets of two Hebrew prophets, Isa 56:7 and Jer 7:11, declaring "My house shall be called a house of prayer for all the nations. But you have made it a den of robbers" (Mark 11:17). In Mark 11:7, the first passage Jesus quotes (Isa 56:7) voices concern over the exclusion of Gentiles and other undesirables from worshiping in God's temple; the second passage Jesus quotes (Jer 7:11) highlights the need for covenantal faithfulness over against the false security of religious institutions. According to the biblical accounts, while some conspiring against Jesus already had begun, after these events, the scheming became more pronounced (Mark 11:18; 12:12). Throughout the remainder of the Passover week, various religious-political factions deliberately attempted to ensnare Jesus in theological and partisan conundrums—all to no avail as Jesus cunningly addressed their questions and avoided their traps. By midweek a plot unfolded (involving one of Jesus' closest associates—Judas Iscariot) to arrest Jesus on Thursday night, try him, and swiftly condemn him for blasphemy and political sedition. At the trial, Jesus was condemned for blasphemy—for hoping to tear down the temple and for claiming to be the messiah (Mark 14:53–65). The next morning, Jesus was hauled before the Roman governor Pilate and soon condemned for treason (for claiming to be king of the Jews). He was swiftly crucified that same morning, and dead and buried by late afternoon (Mark 14:60–64; 15:1–15; John 18:33–37; 19:12–16).

The Resurrection of Jesus

The story of Jesus, however, does not end at his death. Each of the Gospels also declares that Jesus was raised from the dead. Thus, the Gospel of Mark says that on the first day of the week, after Jesus' death the previous Friday, faithful women came to his grave only to find the stone of his tomb rolled away. Inside, a man dressed in white declared to them, "Do not be alarmed; you are looking for Jesus of Nazareth, who was crucified. He has been raised; he is not here. But go, tell his disciples and Peter that he is going ahead of you to Galilee" (Mark 16:6–7). Matthew expands on Mark's narrative, noting that the women ran from the tomb intent on telling Jesus' disciples of his resurrection when "suddenly, Jesus met them and said, 'Greetings!'

And they came to him, took hold of his feet, and worshipped him. Then Jesus said to them, 'Do not be afraid; go and tell my brothers to go to Galilee; there they will see me'" (Matt 28:9–10). Soon thereafter, in Galilee, Jesus' disciples also saw him and received a commission to tell the news to and share his teachings with the world. Luke adds new elements to the story, including that Jesus' disciple Peter came to the empty tomb on Sunday, saw Jesus' burial clothes, and was dumbfounded. Later, Jesus appeared to Peter as well as to two disciples as they walked to the town of Emmaus. Still later that day, Jesus appeared to his closest disciples along with others gathered with them who were hiding in a house in Jerusalem. Jesus showed them his execution wounds, ate with them, and taught them from Scripture how his suffering and resurrection were long a part of God's plan (Luke 24:1–53).

Because of the diverse elements of these accounts and the late dating of the Gospels, historians sometimes question the veracity of every detail of these resurrection accounts. Less debatable, however, is that early followers of Jesus were convinced and were proclaiming that Jesus had been raised from the dead. Evidence for this is found in portions of the New Testament written earlier than the Gospels. For example, the apostle Paul (who likely turned to the way of Jesus in the mid-30s CE and who wrote many of his epistles in the late 40s to mid-50s) clearly affirms Jesus' resurrection from the dead. This is evident in two of his earliest letters, 1 Thessalonians and Galatians (see Gal 1:11–12; 1 Thess 1:3; 3:13; 4:13–18). Particularly significant, in 1 Corinthians, Paul declares:

> For I handed on to you as of first importance what I in turn had received: that Christ died for our sins in accordance with the scriptures, and that he was buried, and that he was raised on the third day in accordance with the scriptures, and that he appeared to Cephas, [Peter] then to the twelve. Then he appeared to more than five hundred brothers and sisters at one time, most of whom are still alive, though some have died. Then he appeared to James, then to all the apostles. Last of all, as to one untimely born, he appeared also to me. (1 Cor 15:3–8)

This passage is significant for several reasons. First, it points to some of the central components of Paul's own faith—including that Jesus was resurrected from the dead and thereafter appeared to several believers. Second, Paul himself had experienced or seen the risen Christ. His faith (including his belief that Jesus was risen) was not based solely on the testimony of others (compare Gal 1:12). Third, Paul was not the first to believe these things or to bear witness to them. Rather, Christians earlier than Paul also affirmed these claims (including that Jesus had been raised from the dead) and had passed them on to him. Indeed, some of these believers apparently witnessed the resurrected Jesus themselves. Finally, many scholars believe that in 1 Cor 15:3–8 (above) Paul is presenting a kind of creedal statement that likely was common among the congregations with which he was associated: thus, these beliefs (including that

Jesus was raised from the dead) were core elements of a formalized faith predating Paul. Similar affirmations and creed-like statements are found in the book of Acts where Jesus' resurrection is presented as a core aspect of the faith of early believers (Acts 2:24, 30–31; 4:2, 33; 17:18, 31–32).

Clearly, New Testament writers—including Paul—believed Jesus had been raised from the dead. Equally important, however, is the significance they attributed to this event. For many of these authors, Jesus' resurrection vindicated fundamental beliefs they held about who Jesus was and what he accomplished. As we will explore more fully below, early Christians ascribed numerous titles to Jesus, attempting to identify who he was. Among these titles were Christ (Messiah), Son of Man, Son of God, Servant, and Lord. In turn, often Christ's resurrection was presented as vindication of the belief that such titles properly apply to him.[3] The apostle Paul ties Jesus' divine sonship, messiahship, and lordship to his resurrection, stating that Jesus "was declared to be Son of God with power according to the spirit of holiness by resurrection from the dead, Jesus Christ our Lord" (Rom 1:4). In a similar way, in 1 Cor 15, Paul associates Jesus' resurrection with his exaltation by God (vv. 20–28). In the Letter to the Philippians, Paul quotes with approval likely an early hymn of the church, which proclaims that because of Jesus' humble obedience to God, God "highly exalted him and [gave] . . . him the name that is above every name, so that at the name of Jesus every knee should bend, in heaven and on earth and under the earth, and every tongue should confess that Jesus Christ is Lord to the glory of God the Father" (Phil 2:9–11). While this hymn does not explicitly mention Jesus' resurrection, the idea almost certainly lingers in Paul's mind as he writes. Comparable sentiments about the significance of Jesus' resurrection are also expressed in the book of Acts, in which Peter is depicted as connecting Jesus' resurrection to his messiahship, lordship, and exaltation (Acts 2:32–36).

Regarding what Jesus accomplished, several New Testament passages link saving benefits for believers to his resurrection. The most obvious benefit was that believers too would be raised from the dead. In both 1 Thessalonians and 1 Corinthians, Paul proposes that because of one's faith in Christ (or spiritual union with Christ) a believer can expect to be raised to life after death even as Christ was. Thus, Paul writes, "For since we believe that Jesus died and rose again, even so, through Jesus, God will bring with him those who have died" (1 Thess 4:14). In a similar manner, Paul says in 1 Corinthians:

> Now if Christ is proclaimed as raised from the dead, how can some of you say
> there is no resurrection of the dead? If there is no resurrection of the dead,
> then Christ has not been raised; and if Christ has not been raised, then our
> proclamation has been in vain and your faith has been vain . . . But in fact
> Christ has been raised from the dead, the first fruits of those who have died.

3. Some passages even suggested that Jesus' resurrection made him (or caused him to) be these things.

> For since death came through a human being, the resurrection of the dead has also come through a human being; for as all die in Adam, so all will be made alive in Christ. (1 Cor 15:12–22)

In these passages, Paul plainly connects the Christian hope for life after death with Christ's resurrection.

But Paul does not simply relate the believer's physical life after death with Christ's resurrection. He also associates Jesus' resurrection with the Christian faith itself, including the hope of forgiveness of sins and personal righteousness. In 1 Cor 15:17, Paul says: "If Christ has not been raised, your faith is futile and you are still in your sins." Paul's exact meaning is not clear, but it is not too much to read him as proposing that without Christ's resurrection, there is little reason to believe that Jesus is who Christians say he is—namely, Lord, Christ, Son of God, and so forth. In turn, if this is the case, there is little rationale to believe Jesus' death brings forgiveness of sins. In short, Christ's resurrection linked not only to the believer's hope in life after death, but also to the hope of forgiveness of sins. In light of these nuances, it is not surprising that Paul also associates Christ's resurrection with the Christian ultimate victory over sin. In the book of Romans, Paul notes:

> Do you not know that all of us who have been baptized into Christ Jesus were baptized into his death? Therefore, we have been buried with him by baptism into death, so that, just as Christ was raised from the dead by the glory of the Father, so we too might walk in newness of life. For if we have been united with him in a death like his, we will certainly be united with him in a resurrection like his. We know that our old self was crucified with him so that the body of sin might be destroyed, and we might no longer be enslaved to sin. But if we have died with Christ, we believe that we will also live with him . . . The death he died, he died to sin, once and for all; but the life he lives, he lives to God. So you must consider yourselves dead to sin and alive to God in Christ Jesus. (Rom 6:3–11)

For Paul, Jesus' resurrection points both to who Jesus is and to what he accomplished for believers.[4]

Similar ideas are expressed in the book of Acts. Acts 4:2 indicates that Jesus' disciples taught that "in Jesus there is resurrection from the dead." That is, faith in Jesus brings to believers resurrected life after death. Further, after proclaiming that God raised Jesus from the dead and "made him both Lord and Messiah," the apostle Peter calls his audience to "repent and be baptized . . . in the name of Jesus Christ so that you sins may be forgiven" (Acts 2:32–38). Comparable ideas are found throughout the New Testament. In these and other passages New Testament writers

---

4. Obviously, for Paul, Jesus' resurrection signifies more than this, including the inauguration of a new and final age, and a new covenant that accompanies that age. See my comments in the text below.

assert that Jesus' resurrection points not only to who Jesus is but also to the benefits he makes possible to those who believe.

Who Was/Is Jesus?

As the New Testament unfolds, it becomes clear that more was at issue (for those early Christian writers) than what Jesus taught or did. Indeed, often Jesus' words and deeds were interpreted as signs of something deeper; namely, they were indicators of who Jesus was/is. Jesus taught with great authority, but what was the source of this authority? Jesus performed healings, exorcisms, and great wonders, but what made such displays possible, and what did they say about the one producing them (see Mark 1:21–28)? Jesus rose from the dead, but what did this say about who he was? In answering these questions, the Gospel writers assigned several titles to Jesus, and with these designations came fundamental interpretations of Jesus' nature. Among those titles were Christ (Messiah), Son of Man, Son of God, Servant, and Lord. We turn to consider the meaning of these titles.

Jesus is referred to as Christ throughout the New Testament. In many instances the term is used as a proper name for him. The word *Christ* is the Greek rendering of the Hebrew word *messiah*, which means "one who is anointed." For ancient Hebrews, this word especially was used to reference the kings of Israel. The great prophet and priest Samuel anointed Israel's first king, Saul, as well as Israel's next and great king, David (1 Sam 9:25—10:1; 16:1–13). Many of the psalms are celebrations of Israel's anointed ones—that is, their kings (Pss 2, 18, 20, 110, 132). A tradition arose that the dynasty of David would reign forever (2 Sam 7:12–16). And, indeed, over all of Judah's long history, a Davidic king reigned (from c. 922 BCE to 586 BCE). But this rule ended in 586 BCE when the Babylonians conquered Judah, decimated Jerusalem, destroyed the Lord's temple, deported the bulk of its population, and executed its last king, Zedekiah (2 Kgs 25:8–12). After these events, Judah's exiles faced a theological dilemma—namely, how could the Lord be faithful to his promises to both Abraham and David? To Abraham God had promised a land; to David the Lord promised a never-ending dynasty. Both covenants had seemingly ended with the destruction of Jerusalem.

Glimmers of hope, however, broke through the darkness in the oracles of various prophets; expressed in their pronouncements was hope both for Israel's return to its homeland and for the reestablishment of the rule of David's house. The first of these restorations came through the edict of Cyrus the Great of Persia, who allowed groups of Jewish exiles to return to Judah. The second restoration never eventuated, as no Davidic king ever came to rule Judah again. Indeed, the promise to Abraham—the promise of a land of their own—never truly materialized either for the Jewish people under Persian rule. Rather, Judah remained only a vasal state, ruled by governors appointed by the Persian kings. Similar circumstances transpired during the hegemony of Alexander the Great and his successors. Judah gained freedom for only a brief period after the Maccabean Revolt, under the reign of the Hasmonaeans. But even then, no Davidic king ruled. And even this brief era of "national" autonomy soon ended at the hands of the Romans beginning with Pompey's victories in Palestine in the 60s BCE. As noted at the end of Chapter 1, from the fall of Judah to the reign of the Romans, hope for an autonomous Jewish state and for a restored Davidic-messianic ruler lingered and morphed, developing into diverse versions and expectations. When Jesus came on the scene, numerous and differing messianic expectations abounded, running the gamut from the Zealots' hope for a concrete military leader who would arise and overthrow foreign occupiers to more apocalyptic visions of God miraculously breaking into history, conquering Israel's enemies, and thereafter establishing by divine fiat an ever-ruling Messiah. According to this latter perspective, especially, the Messiah also would bring an era of abiding faithfulness to the demands of Yahweh's Torah.

Many early followers of Jesus saw him as the Christ. But strangely, he did not meet the criteria many first-century Jews expected in a messiah. He did not come with conquering armies or calls for revolt. Instead, he taught love for one's enemies, prayer for those who persecute, forgiveness even for those who seemed unforgivable. Further, Jesus was arrested by the Romans, tried, beaten, and executed. He died without attempting to overthrow Roman rule. What is more, Jesus did not bring staunch-obedience to the Torah. Instead, he disregarded many of the traditions of the Pharisees. He fraternized with persons of questionable religious repute—sinners, publicans, prostitutes, and Gentiles; he expressed seemingly haughty views of his own religious significance, and he died accursed upon a wooden cross (Deut 21:23, Gal 3:13). Jesus hardly fit the profile of the long-expected messiah. This likely explains, in part, why his movement and its messianic claims were rejected by most Jews of his era. These circumstances also created a theological puzzle for his earliest followers: How could Jesus be the Christ if he did not fulfill many of the messianic expectations?

To answer this question, the writers of the New Testament affirmed two stages of Jesus' messiahship that together met many of the messianic hopes. In the first stage, during his earthly ministry, Jesus fulfilled promises about a messiah who would teach righteousness. Jesus taught a new way to walk with God. Like other ancient rabbis, Jesus called his disciples to follow in his way of covenant-righteousness. This new way involved exercising faith in Jesus, loving God and others, and seeking divine empowerment by the Spirit of God. At the end of the first stage, amazingly, Jesus provided an atonement for sin through his death on a cross. His death was sacrificial, in some way replacing the sacrificial system of the ancient Hebrew tradition. The second stage of Jesus' messianic work involved his reign as a mighty messianic king. This second phase has only partially been fulfilled and will not be fully accomplished until later. Currently, Jesus is ascended in heaven and exalted by God to the highest place of honor (Acts 2:32–33; Phil 2:9–11). Thus, Jesus already is the king of all. But one day, the full impact of this reality will be demonstrated when Jesus returns in power to right the wrongs of this world—to reward the faithful, punish the wicked, and restore peace forever (Mark 13:1–37; 1 Cor 15:50–56; 1 Thess 5:1–11; 2 Thess 1:5–12; 2 Pet 3:8–10). In sum, then, one of the core titles ascribed to Jesus by his earliest followers was Christ.

Another title often given to Jesus in the New Testament is Son of Man. This phrase especially is used of Jesus in the Synoptic Gospels. At times, the Hebrew Bible employs this phrase to speak of humans per se, emphasizing their mortal, vulnerable, nature. But another Old Testament handling of the phrase speaks of an obscure divine-like being who one day will come to earth with great power. This portrayal of "Son of Man" is found in Dan 7:13–14, which declares:

> I saw in the night visions, and behold, with the clouds of heaven there came *one like a son of man*, and he came to the Ancient of Days and was presented before him. And to him was given dominion and glory and a kingdom, that all peoples, nations, and languages should serve him; his dominion is an everlasting dominion, which shall not pass away and his kingdom one that shall not be destroyed. (ESV; italics added)

The original meaning of this text is disputed; however, certainly some first-century Jews associated the title Son of Man with a divine-like figure who—through God's power—would break into history to right the wrongs of the evil age and bring an era of heavenly rule over earth. Sometimes, Jesus spoke of the Son of Man in a similar manner—that is, as one coming in great power to judge the world (Matt 25:31–46; Mark 8:38; 13:26; 14:62; Luke 12:8–9). At other times, Jesus talked about the Son of Man as one of humble status who heals, teaches, and forgives sins (Matt 13:37; Mark 2:1–12; 23–28; Luke 19:10). And in still other contexts, Jesus presented the Son of Man as one who must suffer and die as a ransom for others (Mark 8:31; 9:12; 10:45; 14:41). Most significantly, Jesus identified himself as the Son of Man. Jesus was the one who would one day come in power. Jesus was the one of humble status who taught, healed, and forgave. Jesus was the one who had to suffer and die for others. In short, Jesus was the Son of Man.[5]

The Gospel writers often artfully intermingle the concepts of Christ and Son of Man. This is perhaps understandable since each title envisions someone who will bring divine justice and righteousness to the world. The Gospel of Mark describes a particularly critical moment in Jesus' career, when Jesus asks his disciples who they

---

5. Scholars debate how well the Gospel writers preserve the teachings of "the historical Jesus." We briefly discuss these debates below. Suffice it to say here that at very least the Gospel writers themselves depict Jesus as identifying himself as the Son of Man. Indeed, interestingly, even some very skeptical scholars suspect that Jesus referred to himself as the Son of Man, since none of the Gospels mentions others referring to him as such. Rather, references to Jesus as the Son of Man are found only on the lips of Jesus himself. This has led some to speculate that "Son of Man" was Jesus' favored form of self-identification.

think he is. Peter responds, "You are the Christ," at which point Jesus begins teaching that "the Son of Man must undergo great suffering, and be rejected by the elders, the chief priests, and the scribes, and be killed" (Mark 8:29, 31). In short, Mark blends the roles of Christ and Son of Man. Similar melding happens in the other Gospels as well. Such mergers allowed the Gospel to emphasize the apocalyptic nature of Jesus' messiahship over a mere political understanding. Jesus (as Son of Man) was a divine-like figure whose messianic reign was delayed until a time when he would return with great power to overthrow evil, reward righteousness, and rule the world. In the meantime, in his earthly ministry, Jesus came to teach, heal, and lay down his life as a ransom for others. After his death and resurrection, Jesus ascended on high, to the right hand of God, to await his return in power.

An additional moniker given to Jesus is that of Son of God. This idea also is found in the Hebrew canon. Sometimes the construct speaks of the creaturehood of all humans (Mal 2:10); at other times it references the people of Israel, who are in a special covenant relationship with Yahweh (Exod 4:22); and in other cases the phrase designates the kings of Judah (2 Sam 7:14; Ps 2:7). Nevertheless, the New Testament writers apply the designation Son of God to Jesus in ways not clearly found in the Old Testament: New Testament writers often image him as intimately and uniquely God's Son. Often these depictions are subtle in the Synoptic Gospels but bolder in the Gospel of John. They also are clear in Paul's writing.

Mark's Gospel leads the way, announcing that its content concerns "the beginning of the good news of Jesus Christ, the Son of God" (1:1). Interspersed throughout the text are declarations of Jesus' divine sonship. At Jesus' baptism, for instance, a voice from heaven (God's voice) proclaims of Jesus, "You are my Son, the Beloved; with you I am well pleased (Mark 1:11; see also Matt 4:17 and Luke 3:22–23). In Mark 9, when Jesus is transfigured into a character of dazzling brightness, a divine voice proclaims, "This is my Son, the Beloved; listen to him" (9:7). Yet again, at his trial, Jesus is asked whether he is "the Christ, the Son of the Blessed." Jesus replies yes. The phrase "Son of the Blessed" almost certainly is a synonym for the expression Son of God.[6] Finally, in Mark 15, upon seeing Jesus die, a centurion overseeing the crucifixion proclaims: "Truly this was God's Son!" (15:30). Obviously, Mark wants his readers to know that Jesus is the Son of God.

Mark also alludes to Jesus' sonship in more subtle ways. For example, during his last week in Jerusalem, Jesus tells a parable about a vineyard-owner who leases his land to tenant-farmers to tend and harvest his crop. When the owner sends servants to collect his share of the produce, the tenants mistreat them and refuse to pay. Finally, the landowner sends his own son to collect the share. But the tenants kill him, at which point the landowner brings wrath upon them. Mark informs his readers (12:12) that key leaders in Jerusalem rightly understood Jesus to be speaking

6. Indeed, Matthew records the high priest as commanding Jesus to tell if he is the "Son of God" (Matt 26:63).

against them, and after this they looked for a way to arrest and kill him (14:1). The analogy making such an interpretation possible is this: Jesus is the son in the parable, who would be killed; God is the landowner in the parable, whose wrath might follow; and those seeking to kill Jesus are the unfaithful tenants in the parable (Mark 12:1–12). Again, Jesus is displayed as the Son of God.

The distinctiveness of Jesus' role as God's son is highlighted in the Gospel of Matthew, where Jesus proclaims:

> I thank you Father, Lord of heaven and earth, because you have hidden these things from the wise and the intelligent and have revealed them to infants; yes, Father, for such was your gracious will. All things have been handed over to me by my Father, and no one knows the Father except the Son and anyone to whom the Son chooses to reveal him. (Matt 11:25–27; compare Luke 10:16, 22)

With these words, Jesus claims to be matchlessly authorized by God to speak for God, who is uniquely Father to Jesus his Son.

The Gospel of John is even bolder in its proclamation that Jesus is God's Son. John informs his readers at the end of the Gospel that his purpose has been that individuals might believe that "Jesus is the Christ, the Son of God" (20:31). Throughout the Gospel, John emphasizes Jesus' sonship to God the Father. As Son of God, Jesus is sent by the Father (3:17, 4:34, 5:36, 38), knows the Father intimately (6:47, 10:15), speaks with unique authority for the Father (5:19, 8:26–28, 10:32, 14:8–12, 24), and is profoundly loved by the Father (5:20, 10:17, 15:9). Other New Testament writers proclaim Jesus to be the Son of God as well. Paul regularly refers to Jesus as God's Son or God's "own Son" (Rom 1:3–4, 9; 8:3, 32; 2 Cor 1:19; Gal 2:20). As Son, Jesus was sent by God (Rom 8:3; Gal 4:4). Through the death of God's Son, believers are reconciled to God (Rom 5:10). Christians have entered into the fellowship (1 Cor 1:9) and the kingdom of the Son (Col 1:13), and they have received the Son's spirit (Gal 4:7). One day, Jesus, as God's Son, will return from heaven in power (1 Thess 1:10). According to the author of Hebrews, Jesus—the Son of God—is "the reflection of God's glory and the exact imprint of God's very own being" (1:2–3). The New Testament writers make clear that, for them, Jesus is uniquely the Son of God.

A fourth title ascribed to Jesus in the New Testament is servant. This label is not as prominent as some of the others, but it is quite significant. In identifying Jesus with God's servant, the New Testament writers pull themes from the book of Isaiah. In several key passages, Isaiah describes a servant of God, who suffers for others (42:1–4; 49:1–7; 50:4–9; 52:13—53: 12). For instance, Isa 52:13—53:8 declares:

> See, my servant shall prosper; / he shall be exalted and lifted up / . . . He was despised and rejected by others; / a man of suffering and acquainted with infirmity; / . . ./ he was despised, and we held him of no account. // Surely he has borne our infirmities and carried our diseases; / yet we accounted him stricken, / struck down by God, and afflicted. / But he was wounded for our

transgressions, / crushed for our iniquities; / upon him was the punishment that made us whole, / and by his bruises we are healed. / All we like sheep have gone astray; / we have all turned to our own way, / and the LORD has laid on him the iniquity of us all. // He was oppressed, and he was afflicted, / yet he did not open his mouth; / like a lamb that is led to the slaughter / . . . / By a perversion of justice he was taken away / . . . / Who could have imagined his future? / For he was cut off from the land of the living, stricken for the transgression of my people . . . // Yet it was the will of the LORD to crush him with pain. / When you make his life an offering for sin, / he shall see his offspring, and shall prolong his days; / through him the will of the LORD shall prosper.

For many early Christians these words prophetically referred to Jesus, foreshadowing especially his death and its significance. First Peter makes this connection plainly when it declares of Jesus: "He himself *bore our sins* in his body on the cross, so that, free from sins, we might live for righteousness; *by his wounds you have been healed.* For you were *going astray like sheep*, but now you have returned to the shepherd and guardian of your souls" (2:24–25; italics added). The words italicized in this quote echo ideas expressed in Isa 53.

Similar associations are made elsewhere in the New Testament. For example, in Mark's description of Jesus' baptism, a voice from heaven declares: "You are my Son, the Beloved, with you I am well pleased" (1:11). This quote combines two Old Testament texts: One that speaks of a king of Israel called Yahweh's son (Ps 2:7). The other tells of a servant with whom the Lord is well pleased, who brings justice even in dire circumstances (Isa 42:1–4). The book of Acts also identifies Jesus with Isaiah's servant. In Acts 8, as a man from Ethiopia ponders the meaning of a passage from Isaiah 53 which speaks of a servant who was led like a sheep to the slaughter, a Christian leader named Philip interprets this for him in terms of "the good news about Jesus" (Acts 8:35). While not always explicitly identifying Jesus with the servant of Isaiah, several other New Testament writers refer to Jesus as God's servant (Acts 3:13; 4:27). One of the more significant ascriptions of this title to Jesus appears in Mark 10, where Jesus asserts that "the Son of Man came not to be served but to serve, and to give his life a ransom for many" (v. 45). Here Mark ties servanthood to another title of Jesus— namely, Son of Man. Jesus' declaration in Mark's Gospel occurs in the context of a story about two disciples asking to be seated in places of great honor with Jesus when he comes into his glory. Jesus explains to them that "whoever wishes to become great among you must be your servant, and whoever wishes to be first among you must be slave for all" (10:35–44). According to Jesus, then, his disciples should follow his example of servitude by being servants to each other.

A fifth New Testament affirmation is that Jesus is Lord. Sometimes, when applied to Jesus, the word "Lord" is used only as a polite form of address, like "sir" or "madam" (Matt 8:8, 21; 15:27; Mark 7:28; Luke 7:6). This especially is the case in the Gospel of Mark, and to a lesser degree in the Gospels of Matthew and Luke. In many contexts, however, the meaning of Lord as applied to Jesus is much deeper. This especially is the situation in Paul's Epistles. For Paul, the affirmation that Jesus is Lord was a fundamental confession of the Christian faith (2 Cor 4:5). In confessing this truth, salvation could be attained. Thus, Paul declares, "If you confess with your lips that Jesus is Lord and believe in you heart that God raised him from the dead, you will be saved" (Rom 10:9). Twenty-eight times Paul speaks of "our Lord Jesus Christ"; nine times, he writes of "our Lord Jesus."[7] For Paul, Jesus clearly is Lord, and because of this, salvation is found in him. The book of Acts offers a similar perspective. There, the apostle Peter is depicted as proclaiming that "this Jesus God raised up, and of that all of us are witnesses . . . Therefore, let the entire house of Israel know with certainty that God has made him both Lord and Messiah" (Acts 2:32, 36). Further, reception of "salvation" is tied to affirming the lordship of Jesus. To the question, "what must I do to be saved?" Acts 16:31 proclaims, "Believe on the Lord Jesus, and you will be saved, you and your household" (Acts 16:31). As in Paul's Epistles, so in Acts Jesus is Lord, and salvation is somehow tied to this truth. Similar views are expressed in the General Epistles. (See Heb 7:14; Jas 1:1; 2:1; 1 Pet 1:3.) Other grand claims are coupled with the proclamation that Jesus is Lord. For example, because Jesus is Lord, he has been granted the highest place of power and honor (Acts 2:33); every being will one day recognize him as "Lord of all" (Acts 10:36) and will bow before him (Phil 2:9–11). And all reality has come into existence through Jesus the Lord (1 Cor 8:5–6).

The early Christian use of title Lord for Jesus was especially significant because the word Lord (*kyrios*) was often used in the Septuagint to translate the Hebrew word *Yahweh*, the name of the God of Israel. Hence, when calling Jesus Lord, the New Testament writers drew near to calling him the God of Israel. This becomes even more apparent when one considers how closely New Testament phrases about Jesus parallel expressions used to speak of Yahweh in the Hebrew canon. For example, in the Old Testament, one reads of the "fear of the LORD," "word of the LORD," "Spirit of the LORD," "glory of the LORD," and "day of the LORD," while the New Testament writers use similar phrases to speak of Jesus (Acts 9:31; 11:16; 16:32; 1 Cor 1:8; 2 Cor 2: 1, 14; 3:17–18; 2 Thess 2:2). In turn, Yahweh is called "the Lord of glory" in 1 En 22:14 and 25:3, while Jesus is named "the Lord of glory" in 1 Cor 2:8 and Jas 2:1. Yahweh comes with his saints (Zech 14:5); Jesus comes with his saints (1 Thess 3:13). Those who call upon Yahweh will be saved (Joel 2:32); those who call upon Jesus will be saved (Rom 10:9–11). Every knee bows and tongue swears to Yahweh (Isa 45:23); every knee bows and confesses that Jesus is Lord (Phil 2:10–11). Examples could be multiplied. Such affirmations about Jesus are particularly astounding when one considers that most of these New Testament writers were from an ancient Jewish background, which predisposed them to affirm the distinctiveness and singularity of Yahweh.

7. Ladd, *A Theology of the New Testament*, 415–16.

Other titles were ascribed to Jesus in the New Testament. But the ones mentioned above will suffice for now. Another issue, however, arose for the earliest Christians—namely, what did Jesus accomplish? To this question we now turn.

What Did Jesus Accomplish?

At the center of early Christian teaching about Jesus was concern over how evil might be overcome—both personal evil and systemic evil. Early Christians agreed with the broad Hebrew tradition that humans are sinful, and that often something is wrong with human social structures. Adam and Eve sinned (Gen 3). Cain murdered Abel (Gen 4). Humanity became horribly violent by the days of Noah (Gen 6–9). Abraham believed God, but he also faltered in faith along the way (Gen 12). The Patriarchs all stumbled. The Israelites entered a covenant with God, only to break it—both before leaving Mount Sinai and also as they wandered in the wilderness (Exod 19–35). Once in the land of promise, the tribes of Israel routinely fell into sin, only to be rescued over and over by God's judges (who themselves also often sinned—see the books of Joshua and Judges). The kings of Israel and Judah alike floundered in their faithfulness to Yahweh, including David himself. God's prophets condemned the people for their personal unfaithfulness and their social injustice. Even after returning from Babylonian exile, the people of Judah wavered in their commitment to the Torah. And all the while, individuals and nations outside Israel and Judah proved again and again to be set against God and the divine ways. For the Tanak tradition, evil—both personal and systemic—was a perennial problem of humanity, one in need of a divine remedy.

The flip side of this Old Testament concern over personal and systemic evil was a vision of how things ought to be. This image essentially entailed hope for human harmony with God, with each other, and with the created order. Numerous metaphors are used in the Hebrew Bible to capture this vision. For convenience, we will refer to these as metaphors of salvation.[8] *First* is the idea of *divine blessing*. In Gen 12, God promises to make Abraham's name great, to give him many descendants, and to bless all nations through him. Throughout the centuries, these promised blessings formed a core of Israel's hope in God. Even after Israel's and Judah's sins brought decimation by foreign conquerors, a sliver of hope persisted: God would keep his promises to Abraham and would bless the people of Israel (Isa 10:20–23; Jer 31; Hos 11:8–11). Another metaphor for salvation is *liberation* or *deliverance*. In Exodus, God delivers the Hebrews from Egyptian servitude. And like the Abrahamic blessings, this rescue echoes as a symbol of hope in Old Testament thought. Typically, the notion of deliverance has to do with rescue from concrete physical threats—such as from enslavement, military conquest, or personal enemies.

---

8. The notion of salvation is one of many metaphors utilized in the New Testament to describe the work of Christ. While many other images are employed, the idea of salvation is one used throughout much of the New Testament, especially in Luke-Acts, John, and the Pauline literature.

A third image of salvation is *covenant,* especially as expressed in the books of Exodus through Deuteronomy. Often Christians have interpreted God's covenant with Israel as a *means to receiving* divine blessing. But a closer examination suggests that the Sinai covenant is best understood *as divine blessing* per se. The covenant is God's gift to Israel. It describes the blessed life and is a response to deliverance already received. To live by this covenant is to live in divine blessing. Related to the covenant is a fourth Old Testament metaphor for salvation, namely the *presence of God.* In the Priestly tradition, God's glory visits the people, first in the tabernacle and wilderness wanderings (Exod 40:34–38) and later in the Jerusalem temple of (1 Kgs 8:10–13; Isa 6; Hab 2:20). Understandably, the destruction of Judah's temple by the Babylonians in 586 BCE generated a crisis of faith for Judah, because in that demolition the chief symbol of God's presence with the people was lost. In hope, the prophet Ezekiel assured the exiles that God's spirit had moved from Jerusalem to Babylon to be with them (11:16), and one day God's spirit would reinhabit a restored Jerusalem temple (43:2–5; 44:4). In like manner, postexilic religious leaders sought to rebuild the temple so that God might properly bless the people (Ezra 3:8–9, 5:1–2, 16; Hag).[9] Also associated with the covenant is a fifth Old Testament image of salvation, and that is *atonement.* Scholars debate whether Old Testament sacrifices functioned primarily to purify mundane things so that God might properly be worshiped, or whether such sacrifices also brought forgiveness of sin. Most researchers believe that both were intended results of Old Testament sacrifices. If so, *atonement* for sin is yet another Old Testament metaphor for salvation. A primary example of such atonement is found in Lev 16 where Israel's high priest enters the Holy of Holies once a year to atone for the sins of the nation as a whole.

A sixth Old Testament picture of salvation is *promised land.* God promised Abraham a land for his people. Taking and keeping this land was a central concern in the books of Joshua through Kings; and returning to and keeping the land was a deep hope of the exilic and postexilic biblical literature. Through the idea of promised land, a practical need for living the covenant life was met, for righteous living requires an environment where such life might unfold (2 Sam 7:9–10). The hope of a right environment expands in later Jewish literature. Israel's prophets often envision God's rule extending over all nations (Zech 14:9). And during the intertestamental period, when hopes of God's concrete earthly rule through Judah floundered, many looked for God to supernaturally intervene in history, right the wrongs of the world, and bring divine rule. Connected to the idea of a promised land was a seventh image of salvation— namely, the notion of a *messianic ruler and kingdom.* These hopes were rooted in Yahweh's promise to King David that his dynasty would be everlasting (2 Sam 7:11–17).

9. Yahweh's presence with the people was a source of great hope and an awesome honor; but it came with obligations and potential danger. Many of the Torah's rituals (including sacrifices) prepared individuals and the nation as a whole for the advent of God. But failure to follow appropriate religious procedures could be deadly (Num 4:15; 2 Sam 6:6–7), and stubborn disobedience of God's moral expectations could lead to judgment (Num 15:27–31; Jer 7).

After Israel and Judah divided, and as external threats mounted, optimism over the Davidic house continued (Isa 9:2–7; 11:1–5; Mic 5:2). Even after the fall of Judah and the murder of its king, hope in the Davidic line continued, into the Persian era (2 Kgs 25:27–30; Hag 2:23; Zech 3:8; 6:9–15).

Eighth and ninth Old Testament depictions of salvation are those of *a new covenant* and of *the outpouring of God's Spirit*. Often the two are interconnected. After long centuries of Israel disobeying Yahweh's covenant, Jerimiah declares:

> The days are surely coming, says the LORD, when I will make a new covenant with the house of Israel and the house of Judah. It will not be like the covenant that I made with their ancestors when I took them by the hand to bring them out of the land of Egypt—a covenant that they broke . . . But this is the covenant that I will make with the house of Israel after those days, says the LORD: I will put my law within them, and will write it on their hearts; and I will be their God, and they shall be my people. No longer shall they teach one another, or say to each other, "Know the LORD," for they shall all know me, from the least of them to the greatest says the LORD; for I will forgive their iniquity, and remember their sin no more. (Jer 31:31–34)

In a similar manner, during Judah's exile in Babylon, the prophet Ezekiel speaks of a time when God will place "a new heart" within the people and will give them a "new spirit." Through that spirit, the people will follow the divine laws (36:26–27). Other prophets make similar promises about a future outpouring of God's spirit (Joel 2:28–29; compare Isa 11:2–3).

Second Temple Judaism reiterated and augmented these Hebrew scriptural views about the problems of evil and the promises of divine salvation, often kneading apocalyptic themes into them. Apocalyptic thinking especially added the notions that a grand cosmic battle is unfolding between the forces of God (good) and evil, and that the human world is wrapped up in this conflict and cannot disentangle itself from it without divine aid; instead God must, one day, wondrously intervene in history to overcome the evil of the world. By the arrival of Jesus, some first-century Jews emphasized overcoming the evil of political oppression through military rebellion. Others called for military efforts alongside earnest personal, covenantal righteousness. Still others called for strict adherence to divine laws with less emphasis on military action, but they often hoped also for divine inbreaking to overcome the political evil of the world. Some believed that God would only bring an apocalyptic solution if Yahweh's own people would first demonstrate earnest righteousness.

Many of these Old Testament and apocalyptic metaphors of salvation are used and transformed by New Testament writers. Often Jesus is depicted as fulfilling promises given to Abraham, promises to bless Israel and all peoples. Jesus is declared to be the Savior, one who liberates from sin and its oppression. Through his death and resurrection, Jesus wins victory over the demonic forces of evil. Further, Jesus faithfully fulfills God's previous covenant and establishes a new covenant, written on human hearts (as foretold by Jeremiah; see also Heb 8:7–13; 9:15–20; 10:9–18). Jesus preaches the coming of God's kingdom, echoing Old Testament metaphors of Yahweh as King (and Lord) and of God's rule over a promised land and kingdom. The title Christ, applied to Jesus, points to this messianic and divinely blessed rule. To first-century Jewish audiences, the idea of God's kingdom generated hopes of peace and justice (Isa 9:2–7), liberation from political, economic, and spiritual oppression (Isa 58:6–9; 61:1–2), fellowship with God (Isa 25:6–9), divine forgiveness and righteousness (Jer 31:33–34; Ezek 36:26–27; Mic 7:18–20), endless life (Dan 12:1–2), and resurrection (Isa 26:19). Jesus' death served as a sacrifice of atonement for sin, thus mirroring the Old Testament sacrificial system. Jesus also brought the outpouring of the Holy Spirit (promised by Joel; see also Acts 2:14–24), and in him the very presence of God is manifested, echoing the hopes of the priestly tradition.

To these metaphors of salvation the New Testament adds numerous others, some more directly allusions to Old Testament ideas than others. Among these are concepts such as justification (Rom 3:24, 28; 5:16–18), sanctification (John 17:19; 1 Cor 6:11), glorification (Rom 8:30), renewal/regeneration (Matt 19:28; Titus 3:5), rebirth (John 3:3, 7; 1 Pet 1:23), reconciliation (Rom 5:11; 2 Cor 5:18), adoption into God's family (Matt 5:9; John 1:12–13; Rom 8:14, 17), union with Christ (1 Cor 1:2; 1:30; Col 1:27), participation or fellowship with Christ (1 Cor 1:9; 2 Cor 13:14; 1 John 1:3), baptism in Christ and in the Spirit (Acts 1:5; 2:38; 11:16; 1 Cor 1:13), ransom/redemption (Mark 10:45; Eph 1:7; 1 Tim 2:6; Heb 9:12), new creation (2 Cor 5:17; Gal 6:15), a new self (Rom 6:6; Eph 4:22–24), resurrection (Luke 14:14; John 11:24–25; Rom 6:5), eternal life (Mark 10:30; John 3:15–16, 36), the image of and conformity to Christ (Rom 8:29; 2 Cor 3:18; Col 3:10), the heavenly city (Heb 11:16; 12:22), heaven (2 Cor 5:1; Phil 3:20), and so forth. All these metaphors provide insights, if not complete clarity, into the New Testament understanding of Christ's work. All these images may point to an experience or encounter or mystery not fully describable. Still they provide sufficient light to help articulate a vision of God's saving work in Christ.

With these metaphors in mind, a relatively consistent model of the process of salvation emerged in New Testament literature. This model is observed in the writings of the apostle Paul. Paul envisioned all humans as plagued with personal sin (Rom 3:23) and as trapped in a cosmic order (which includes human social structures) controlled by supernatural forces of evil (Rom 8:18–25; 1 Cor 15:24–28; Gal 1:4; Phil 3:21; compare Eph 6:10–12). In turn, Paul saw Jesus as the solution to these dilemmas. Through Jesus, past sins can be forgiven, present righteousness can be attained, and future reward (and victory) can be assured. Jesus died as an atoning sacrifice for sins so that faith in him brings divine redemption, forgiveness, justification, and reconciliation with God (Rom 5:1–11; 1 Cor 1:18–23; 15:3; 2 Cor 5:17–18; Gal 2:15–16; 3:13–14; 4:15; Col 1:14). No longer do God's people need to perform the sacrifices of the Torah for forgiveness (or cleansing). Rather, somehow,

Jesus is the one sacrifice (Rom 3:19–26). Through him, past sins can be forgiven. In turn, living the righteous life in the present is possible through union with Christ and his Spirit. Believers are "in Christ" and Christ is "in them"; and the Spirit of God indwells followers of Jesus, aiding them now in living lives of love and righteousness (Rom 8:1–13; Gal 5:16–17, 22–26).

Connected to Paul's idea of a self-changing union with Christ was his exhortation to live according to the dictates of love rather than merely according to external rules (Rom 13:8–10; 1 Cor 13:1–13; Gal 5:13–15). Paul also expressed belief in Christ's ultimate lordly victory over cosmic and worldly evil, so that the apostle proclaims that Jesus is Lord, and that one day all creation will be brought under his rule, and all beings will acknowledge his authority (Rom 1:4; 1 Cor 15:20–28; Phil 2:9–11). Part of this culminating conquest is the resurrection of human beings, the defeat of death, and moral purification of believers (1 Cor 15:42–58; 1 Thess 5:23). Clearly for Paul, then, Jesus' lordship and messiahship entail victory over both personal and structural evil. Through Jesus, an individual's sins can be forgiven, righteousness can be lived, and the ultimate victory of good over evil will be manifested.

The Gospel of John endorses a similar schema. Humans are sinners and live in an evil world—a world of darkness (John 1:5; 3:19), stubborn ignorance (1:10; 3:20–21), and unbelief (3:19). Human are condemned because of their unbelief (John 3:18; 8:24) and face the wrath of God (3:36). They are destined to death, judgment, and destruction (3:16, 36; 5:29). But God sent Jesus into the world to achieve the divine purposes (4:34; 5:17, 19–30; 7:28–29; 17:3–4). Critical components of Christ's mission were to save the world (John 3:17; 10:9), to take away its sins as the Lamb of God (John 1:29), and to provide a means to eternal life (John 3:15–16, 36; 4:14; 5:24; 6:40, 68). Those who believe in Christ have been born "from above" and of the Spirit (3:3–8), and they have been transformed from darkness to light (8:12; 12:35–36). In turn, in the present, Jesus' spiritual presence within Christians enables them to live for God—to bear righteous "fruit" (John 15:1–11). Jesus provides abundant life now (10:9–10), living water welling up within a believer's being (4:11–14), spiritual "food" that satisfies one's inner hunger and quenches one's inner thirst and (6:35). Indeed, in some sense, those who believe in Christ already have eternal life and never truly die (John 11:25–26); they have become children of God (John 1:12–13) and have been freed from sin (8:34–36). Also, the Spirit of God aids Christians in the present, in the physical absence of Jesus (who has ascended into heaven). This Holy Spirit is the Advocate and Spirit of truth, who abides in believers, teaches them truth and righteousness, reminds them of what Jesus taught, and helps them not to stumble morally (John 14:15–26; 15:25—16:15). In turn, like Paul, John calls Christ's followers to love one another; by such love, others will know they are Jesus' disciples (13:33).

Finally, for John, one day Christ will return in glory.[10] For John, Jesus always was glorious. Jesus was the incarnation of the Logos (Word) of God (1:14), who was with

10. An interesting feature of John's theology is that, for him, Jesus' glory especially was demonstrated

God in the beginning (John 1:1–2), through whom all things were created (1:3), who came down from heaven on mission for God (John 3:13–14; 3:17; 4:34; 5:30; 7:16, 28–29; 17:3–4), who uniquely was and is God's Son (John 1:49; 3:16; 5:25–26), who uniquely reveals God (John 3:34; 14:5–7), and who is over all things (3:31; 17:1). Jesus is Lord (John 20:13, 18, 20, 25, 28), perhaps especially in light of his resurrection.[11] Still, after his resurrection, Jesus left this world to be with the Father. But he will return. And when he does, the dead will be raised—some to life and some to condemnation (6:39). In turn, Christ's followers will go to a place that he has prepared for them, with the Father (14:1–3). And judgment will come (5:25–29).[12] Thus, as Paul Epistles do, so the Gospel of John also sees Jesus as the remedy for the problem of evil. Jesus (somehow) "takes away" human sin (as the Lamb of God), aids in right living (through his spiritual presence), and eventually will bring an end to the systemic evil of this evil world.[13] Similar—although often not identical—ideas about forgiveness, righteous living, and Christ's ultimate victory are found in other New Testament texts.

We might summarize the basic New Testament perspective about the process of salvation as follows. Jesus—who is Christ, Son of Man, Son of God, Suffering Servant, Lord, and (in John's Gospel) Logos of God—was sent by God the Father to fulfill the divine mission. The core of this mission was to reveal the divine nature and to save the world. Salvation includes many factors. First, it involves a changed status for the saved:

---

through Christ's death on the cross (3:14–15; 8:28; 12:23, 32). For this purpose, Jesus was born (18:37), and in dying on the cross, Jesus fulfilled God's mission (17:1–5; 19:28–30). At the same time, John also seems to endorse the notion that one day Jesus' full glory will be revealed when he returns.

11. Another interesting characteristic of John's Gospel is that, of the eighteen times Jesus is referred to as Lord, all but three occur in the last two chapters, after Jesus' resurrection.

12. Echoing his idea that Christ is glorified in the cross (see note 10 above), John also suggests that the world was judged by and the evil rulers of the world were driven out by Jesus' death (12:31).

13. None of this is to say that John's theology perfectly matches Paul's views or the perspectives of other New Testament writers. For example, unlike Mark, Matthew, or Paul, John does not clearly allude to Christ's death being a ransom or redemption for sin, nor does he directly state that Christ's death was a sacrifice (although the image of "Lamb of God" suggests this). Also, John does not record Jesus, on the night before his death, identifying bread and wine with his body and blood, or connecting these with a covenant of blood—as do Mark (14:23–24), Matthew (26:26–27), Luke (22:14–20), and Paul (1 Cor 11:23–26). In chapter 6, John does allude to ideas like those found in the Synoptic Gospel and Pauline accounts of the Lord's Supper. In John 6, Jesus claims, "I am the bread of life" (v. 35) and then says: "Unless you eat the flesh of the Son of Man and drink his blood, you have no life in you. Those who eat my flesh and drink my blood have eternal life, and I will raise them up on the last day" (6:53–54) John may have deliberately skipped the account of the Eucharist at the last supper (as told by the Synoptic writers and Paul) in order to add a unique twist to the Eucharist-tradition—wishing to emphasize the perennial spiritual presence of Christ in believers (metaphorically expressed in terms of "eating" his flesh and "drinking" his blood) rather than stress Christ's death as a sacrifice. It remains unclear precisely in what sense John thought that Christ's death "took away" the sins of the world. Also, unlike Paul and the Synoptic writers, John tones down the emphasis upon the future return of Christ in power, preferring to accent instead Christ's ongoing presence in the lives of believers in the here and now. He does affirm that one day believers will be raised from the dead (5:26–29), but his focus seems to be on believers living for Christ in the present world and realizing that they already have eternal life in Christ.

divine forgiveness of sins, reconciliation and peace with God, and redemption or ransom (from something). Often this altered status is associated with Jesus' death on the cross. Somehow Jesus' death was "for sinners," an atoning sacrifice, a sign or reification of a new covenant. In some way, Christ's death brought reconciliation, redemption, forgiveness, peace with God, and so forth. Second, salvation involves ongoing faithfulness toward God—righteous living. For Paul, this righteous living is aided by (or made possible through) the ongoing activity of God's Spirit in believers, guiding them toward righteousness, as well as through (or by) believers' spiritual union with Christ. Through this mysterious union with Christ, the Christian has become something new—a new self, a new creation (2 Cor 5:17). In a similar manner, for John, right living comes by (or is assisted by) believers becoming united to Christ (as branches are connected to a vine) or through the inner guidance of the Holy Spirit. Also, for John, believers have been changed, born anew, born of the Spirit. And they already have eternal life—a new life now present, but also one yet to come.[14] Finally, salvation references a future state, in which justice, righteousness, and resurrected life prevail. Paul along with the Synoptic Gospel writers especially speak in terms of Jesus' glorious return and future reign. John endorses these ideas too but tends to stress the believer's current possession of such an eternal state, divine presence, and victory.

Puzzles with the New Testament View of Salvation

Several ambiguities arise from this broad New Testament vision of salvation in Christ. One question concerns precisely what happened on the cross of Christ. As noted above, both Mark and Matthew declare that Jesus gave his life as a ransom for many, and that his death (in some way) was (or was like) a blood sacrifice poured out for the sins of others, forming a new covenant. Paul also calls Christ's death a sacrifice of atonement that redeems those who believe. John's Gospel is a bit vaguer about the meaning of Christ's death, claiming (without much clarification) simply that Jesus was "the Lamb of God who takes away the sin of the world" (John 1:29). The book of Hebrews is perhaps the most precise of all—declaring that Jesus was both the heavenly high priest who offered a once-for-all sacrifice to God, and the sacrifice itself (Heb 8:1—9:28). Interestingly, the companion works of Luke and Acts are somewhat cagey about the effects of Christ's death. The author of these works, whose gospel often duplicates Mark's account, does not mention Jesus being a ransom; nor does he, in his descriptions of the earliest Christian preaching (in Acts), mention any atoning significance to Christ's death.[15] Thus, while overall the New Testament affirms that Jesus' death functioned

---

14. Such notions are similar to the ideas in the Synoptics that the kingdom of God has already come and is yet to come.

15. This is not to say that the author of Luke-Acts does not see Jesus as the means to salvation, for he does. He identifies Jesus as the Christ and Savior (Luke 2:11), declares that Jesus came to bring forgiveness to the house of Israel (Luke 1:77), and insisted that salvation is found in no other name than

as a means for human salvation and as a ransom or sacrifice, the precise mechanics of this occurrence is not clearly stated. It would be left to postbiblical Christians to explore diverse models of Christ's "atonement."

Another ambiguity about the New Testament vision of salvation concerns the relationship between faith, righteousness, and the divine law. The apostle Paul contends that humans inevitably sin, and that without divine aid they cannot faithfully follow God. He insists that "no human being will be justified in . . . [God's] sight by deeds prescribed by the law [of God]" (Rom 3:20; brackets added). This is the case because "all have sinned and fall short of the glory of God" (Rom 3:23). Since (and possibly because of) Adam's sin, all humanity has been "made sinners" (Rom 5:19) and stands condemned. Although the law of God is good, it can only condemn humans rather than bring life to them because of their sinful tendencies. The law only shows humans what they should do (3:24) but it does not enable them to do it (Rom 7:11; Gal 3:12–13). Thus, no person can be justified (made or declared righteous) by performing (or trying to perform) the "works of the law" (Gal 2:15–16; 3:11). Instead, a person is "justified by faith in Jesus Christ" (Gal 2:15). Christ came "to redeem those who were under the law" (Gal 4:5). And this redemption comes through faith in Christ. The Pauline Epistle to the Ephesians captures these ideas well when it says:

> But God, who is rich in mercy, out of the great love with which he loved us even when we were dead through our trespasses, made us alive together with Christ . . . For by grace you have been saved through faith, and this is not your own doing; it is the gift of God—not the result of works, so that no one may boast. (2:4–9)

Several puzzles arise within Paul's perspective about faith and works of the law. First, one might wonder whether his perspective implies that a believer is free to behave any way he or she wishes. That is, if following the law does not bring righteousness, is sinning an acceptable option? Paul himself anticipates and rejects this suggestion. He argues that Christ set believers free from sin, and it would be folly to fall back into the bondage and curse of the sinful life. Instead, Paul urged individuals to live by the Spirit—that is, follow the urging of the Spirit—and one would not conform to the sinful nature. Paul also encouraged Christians to live by the principle of love, alleging that abiding by the dictates of love entails conformity to God's core commands (Gal 5:13–26; compare Rom 6:1—8:17).

A related problem, however, arises for Paul's claims about faith, righteousness, and the divine law. Precisely, what does *faith* mean? Is faith in Christ merely a flippant affirmation of some claim, like "Jesus is Lord," with little commitment to follow Jesus? Or is faith something deeper? Is it more like *faithfulness*—a life-changing commitment,

---

Jesus (Acts 4:12). Further, he seems to endorse the notion that Christ's death was some type of sacrifice in Luke 22:14–20, especially v. 20, and in Acts 20:28 where he describes the church as those "obtained with the blood of . . . [God's] own Son."

dedication, and loyalty to the lordship of Jesus? The Synoptic Gospels emphasize the costliness of following Christ. In Mark, Jesus says to a crowd and to his disciples:

> If any want to become my followers, let them deny themselves and take up their cross and follow me. For those who want to save their life will lose it and those who lose their life for my sake, and for the sake of the gospel, will save it . . . Those who are ashamed of me and of my words, in this adulterous and sinful generation, of them the Son of Man will also be ashamed when he comes in the glory of his Father with the holy angels. (8:34–38)

In a similar vein, Mark records Jesus as proclaiming, "Truly, I tell you, there is no one who has left house or brothers or sisters or mother or father or children or fields, for my sake and for the sake of the good news, who will not receive a hundredfold now in this age . . . and in the age to come eternal life" (10:29–30). In Matthew, Jesus declares, "Whoever loves father or mother more than me is not worthy of me; and whoever loves son or daughter more than me is not worthy of me; and whoever does not take up the cross and follow me is not worthy of me. Those who find their life will lose it, and those who lose their life for my sake will find it" (10:37–39; see also Luke 12:51–53). These verses call for extreme dedication or faithfulness to Christ and his cause.

Paul himself exemplifies this kind of dedication to Christ, persevering in his commitment to Christ and his message through numerous hardships—including, threats, beatings, imprisonment, and (according to tradition) ultimately execution. But all this raises questions about Paul's doctrine of justification by faith rather than through works of the law. How much faith (or faithfulness) is required? Is such dedication to Christ obligatory in order to be saved? And if so, how is this different than calls to be faithful to God's covenant or to heed moral demands of the law? Can a person perennially falter in commitments to Christ and still be saved? And if not, how is this different from being commanded to live by the precepts of the law? Similar ambiguity arises from Paul's appeal to following the guidance of the Spirit or the dictates of love. How is the Christian community to respond to persons who consistently ignore the guidance of the Spirit or fail to live according to the principles of love? Indeed, how is one to know what love demands or what the Spirit urges without some set of guidelines to aid in such discernment? None of this is to say that legitimate differences cannot be recognized between on the one hand heeding the call to discipleship or living by love or following the Spirit, and on the other hand obeying "works of the law." Rather, the precise differences are not clearly marked out in the New Testament literature. As we shall see, attempts to demarcate the differences have long puzzled generations of Christians since the first century. We will discuss some of these matters later.

Sacred Person: Summation

For Christians, Jesus is the apex of God's sacred history with humans. Jesus is the promised Messiah of Israel. He is the Son of Man who came from heaven to earth in humility, has now ascended into heaven with God the Father, but will one day return in great power to rule the universe. Indeed, in a certain sense, Jesus already rules. His victory is assured. Jesus is Lord, virtually identical to Yahweh (the God of Israel) and now reigns supreme with God, and will demonstrate this lordship upon his return. Jesus also is Son of God, somehow intimately connected to God's mission and uniquely attuned to the will and thoughts of God (the Father). Thus, Jesus uniquely reveals who God is and what God desires of humanity. Jesus also provides the way to salvation. Somehow, through his death, human sin is atoned for so that those who believe in him are spiritually united to him, empowered by him (or his Spirit) to live for God, and one day will reap the full rewards of eternal life—including resurrection from the dead and ultimate victory over personal sin. Further, upon Jesus' return, the whole universe will see a reversal of the curse of social and comic evil.

Sacred Community

In addition to a sacred text, a sacred history, and a sacred person, a fourth foundation of Christianity is its sacred community. During Jesus' lifetime, crowds often followed him, and some in these crowds became earnest disciples. The exact number of his most committed disciples is not known; however, the Scriptures often speak of an inner-circle of twelve who were handpicked by Jesus, and who helped in his ministry campaigns. Among these twelve, three were especially close to Jesus—namely, Peter, James, and John. There also were several women who followed Jesus, some of whom contributed significantly to funding his ministry. Upon occasion, Jesus sent out larger groups of disciples to minister in his name throughout Palestine. Interestingly, there is little evidence in the New Testament that Jesus attempted to establish a separate community around him during his lifetime. Rather, typically he and his closest disciples worshiped at various local synagogues as they travelled from town to town.

After Jesus' death and resurrection, however, communities soon gathered in his name—perhaps first in Galilee (see Matt 28:7, 16), but not long after in Jerusalem as well (Acts 1–3). Initially, the first followers of Jesus (later called Christians) did not see themselves as separate from the broader Jewish faith-community. Rather, believing Jesus to be the Messiah, they saw themselves as faithful Jews. According to the book of Acts, initially, believers in Jesus in Jerusalem continued going to the temple to worship. They also gathered in each other's homes to hear the teachings of the apostles, to break bread together, to fellowship, to witness various wonders, and to pray (Acts 2:42–44). In turn, outside of Jerusalem, Christians often gathered in one another's homes as well. As time passed, however, attempts to remain within the broader Jewish worshiping community waned as tension between adherents of the traditional Jewish faith and Christians grew.

Through missionary efforts, followers of Jesus eventually spread from Palestine to other regions of the Roman Empire and beyond. There is evidence of Christians in Samaria, Caesarea, Damascus, Egypt, and Mesopotamia by the end of the first-century. The book of Acts especially focuses on the spread of Christianity into Asia Minor (modern Turkey), Greece, and Rome. By the mid-40s CE, a vital Jewish-Christian community arose in Syrian Antioch where—according to the book of Acts (11:26)—followers of Christ were first given the name "Christians" (little Christs). Paul was an especially active missionary for the new faith. Originally, Paul opposed this new sect. But after a profound experience with the resurrected Christ, Paul became convinced of the messiahship of Jesus and of the truth of the Christian gospel. Through the 40s and 50s CE, Paul sought to spread the good news of Christ throughout Asia Minor and Greece, eventually landing in Rome. Through those years, Paul found success especially among Gentiles and saw himself as an apostle (one sent) to them. Evidence of his ministry is displayed in the many letters of the New Testament.

As Christianity spread, tiny communities of Christians formed wherever the message was received. Soon Christians referred to these groups as *ecclesia*. The core meaning of this Greek word is "assembly," and the word is often is translated "church" in English. In the Hellenistic world, *ecclesia* often referred to gatherings of citizens for various town meetings. So, at one level, Christian churches were simply the gatherings of persons committed to the lordship and mission of Jesus Christ. But at a deeper level, Christians themselves were "the church." That is, the church was not simply a *gathering* but more it was the *people* who (occasionally) assembled. And who were these people? At one level, the answer is simply those people who gathered in Jesus' name, or perhaps those who claimed to follow Christ. But at a deeper level, the New Testament seems to say the church is something more. It is the beneficiaries of Christ's saving work—those Christ saved, or was saving, or will save. Further, they were coworkers with Christ who sought to share the blessings of Christ with each other and with those not yet familiar with him.

These two understandings of the church (those gathered versus those saved) generate some tension. The New Testament often recognizes the possibility that some who gather in Christ's name are not truly part of the church, or perhaps are in danger of losing their status as part of the church. In the Gospel of Mark, Jesus warns of false prophets who might arise at the end times and lead the faithful away from Christ—perhaps prophets from within the believing community itself (Mark 13:6, 21–23). Elsewhere, Jesus tells the story of a man who planted wheat, but whose enemy came after him and secretly planted weeds. To avoid uprooting the wheat, the farmer waited until harvest to weed-out the weeds from the crop. The moral of the story seems to be that God will wait to the end of days to sort-out the faithful from the unfaithful (Matt 13:24–30). Several New Testament writers likewise warn of false-prophets and promoters of false doctrine (1 Tim 1:3, 6:2; 2 Pet 2:1; 1 John 4:1). And the book of Hebrews cautions of the possibility of some who follow Christ falling away before the end.

These passages seem to alert Christians of the need to discern between true believers and false believers within the church. Later theologians would distinguish between the visible and invisible church to acknowledge these two understandings of the church. The former refers to those who concretely gather in Christ's name, whether or not they sincerely believe in or follow him. The latter references those who truly are committed to Christ and thus are actually saved. According to these later theologians, only God knows who is in the invisible church (those who are saved). The membership of the *visible* church is discernible by empirical observation—by looking to see who claims to be Christ's followers or who gathers in his name. The New Testament does not directly address these differences, but (as noted above) some passages seem to assume something like this dichotomy.

Whichever way one might resolve this dilemma regarding the visible and invisible church, there certainly seem to be some New Testament passages that support the notion that the church is those who truly are (or will be) saved by Christ. This seems to be the perspective of the book of Ephesians. There, the Pauline author addresses "the saints who are in Ephesus" (1:2). "Saints" was a common term used by Paul and others to speak of Christians (or of the church: see Acts 9:13, 32; 26:10; Rom 1:7; 8:27; 1 Cor 1:2; 6:2; 16:15; 2 Cor 1:1; Phil 1:1).[16] The author of Ephesians effectively declares that these saints are the recipients of Christ's saving work. They are blessed "with every spiritual blessing" (1:3), chosen by Christ to be holy and blameless (1:4), destined to adoption (1:5), redeemed through Christ's blood (1:7), forgiven (1:7), granted an inheritance (1:11), recipients of "the gospel of . . . salvation" (1:13), and "marked with the seal . . . of the Holy Spirit," who "serves as a pledge of redemption for God's own people" (1:13–14). Clearly, the author of Ephesians sees the church (here called saints) as the recipients of the benefits of salvation. Indeed, the writer claims that for the sake of the church Christ was given lordship over all (1:22–23). Further, Christ is the Savior of the church (5:23) and "gave himself up" for the church (5:25). Plainly, the author of Ephesians sees the church as the recipients of Christ's saving work. Similar ideas about the church—perhaps not as thoroughly stated—are found in other New Testament writings (see 1 Cor 5:7; 7:23; Col 1:1–14, 18, 24; 2:13–14; 3:12).

Now all of this brings up another interesting question regarding the nature of the church—a dilemma addressed by later Christian thinkers. The dilemma is that sometimes biblical passages speak of the church as local congregations, and at other times the Bible speaks of the church as a whole. For example, in several cases Paul refers to the church as local assemblies or as Christians in a given area. Paul writes

16. For the New Testament writers, all Christians are saints. This word essentially means "holy-ones" or "those set apart for God." Later Christian generations would come to speak of saints as individuals *especially faithful* to God/Christ and duly recognized by official canonization.

of "the church of God that is in Corinth" (1 Cor 1:20), or the church that meets in the house of Prisca and Aquila (Rom 16:5), or again "the churches in Galatia" (Gal 1:2), or "the churches of the Gentiles" (Rom 16:4; see also 1 Cor 16:19; Col 4:15). In these passages, the apostle seems to have in mind separate congregations in various locales. But at other times, Paul (and other writers) seems to mean by "church" all followers (or all *genuine* followers) of Christ everywhere and of all times. This seems to be the case, above, when the author of Ephesians says that Christ is the Savior of *the church* and gave himself up for it. This usage of *church* suggests that Christ is the Savior of not only local congregations, but the church writ large—the church as the whole of those who are or will be saved. Similar usages of the word *church* are found in the book of Acts (9:31; 20:28). Again, later Christian thinkers would attempt to resolve this tension by distinguishing between the local church and the universal church. Obviously, the former entails individual congregations in concrete locales. The latter entails the church as a whole, in all places and at all times. (We will discuss the notions of the invisible versus the visible, and the local versus the universal, church more fulling in Chapter 6).

The notion that the church (as a whole) includes those who receive Christ's saving benefits leads to an interesting observation about salvation. Often, especially in the modern era, Christians think of salvation as primarily about individual persons. This is not utterly inappropriate. Certainly, places within the New Testament emphasize individual salvation (Mark 8:34–38) and call followers to discipleship in Christ even if it means separation from their normal social community (Matt 10:34–39). Still, it is important to keep in mind that for ancient and modern Christians alike, salvation has an essential corporate aspect. Through Christ, God seeks to save a community. Humans are not meant to be isolated from one another but to live in loving communion. Part of the brokenness of humanity can be seen in our hatred of, our violence toward, and our jealousy, and distrust of one another. Ideally the church is that community that loves not only God but also its "neighbors," including especially fellow believers.

The New Testament uses several metaphors to speak of the church. Many of these apply especially to the universal church. And often these images point not only to the idea that the church is the recipient of Christ's saving work but also to the truth that the church (in some sense) shares in his ministry. One of these metaphors is *the people of God*. The connection between Christians and *the people of God* may have been a core reason behind Christians identifying themselves as the *ecclesia* ("church"). The word *ecclesia* was after all the keyword in the Septuagint for the assembly of the people of Israel. Thus, by identifying themselves as the *ecclesia*, early Christians connected themselves with the house of Israel. The apostle Paul refers to Christians as heirs of Abraham (Gal 3:29), beneficiaries of God's promised blessings (Gal 3:14), a holy people (Rom 1:7), those circumcised in heart (Rom 2:29), and God's elect (Col 3:12). The First Epistle of Peter describes Christians as the elect of God (1:1), a royal priesthood, and a holy nation (2:9). Each of these phrases is used to speak of the people of Israel in the Hebrew Bible. In turn, like Israel, the church is both the recipient of divine blessings and the body of those called to share these blessings with one another and with the nations.[17]

Another New Testament image for the church is *the body of Christ*. As noted above, Paul and Pauline writers speak of Christians as being in Christ and Christ being in them. Extending this notion, these authors speak of the church (as a whole) as the body *of* Christ (1 Cor 12:27; Eph 4:12), the body *in* Christ (Rom 12:5), or *his* (Christ's) body (Eph 1:22–23). These authors use this metaphor to make several points. One is to stress the spiritual union of the church with Christ. The church is the body of Christ because it is spiritually in Christ and Christ is in the church.[18] Another point of the metaphor is to emphasize the collective church's sharing of one faith, one hope, one Spirit, one baptism, one God (Eph 4:4–6), and one set of ministerial goals. A third implication of the church being *the body of Christ* is that the church is a union in diversity: it is a singularity composed of many parts, just as the human body is a single body made up of many members. The church is many individual members yet makes up a whole.

This union in diversity means first that each member of the church is intrinsically valuable and is to be treasured and loved by the whole membership. Paul writes:

> If the foot would say, "Because I am not a hand, I do not belong to the body," that would not make it any less part of the body. And if the ear would say, "Because I am not an eye, I do not belong to the body," that would not make it any less a part of the body . . . But God has so arranged the body . . . that there may be no dissension within the body, but the members may have the same care for one another. If one member suffers, all suffer together with it; if one member is honored, all rejoice together with it. (1 Cor 12:14–26)

Further, because of the church's union in diversity, each member of the church has an important role to perform within the collective. Each member has been given a "manifestation of the Spirit for the common good" (1 Cor 12:7). Some members are given wisdom, some knowledge, some faith, some the gift of healing. Some are called to be apostles, some prophets, some teachers (see 1 Cor 12:8–11, 27–31; compare Rom 12:4–8; Eph 4:11–13). Finally, all these gifts and callings are for the common good.

But what is the common goal? What does God seek to achieve through the ministries of the diverse members of the church? The answer is complex, but in sum it seems to be to become a certain kind of people—a people who is like Christ. Thus, the author of Ephesians declares that the purpose of God's gifting the members of the church is "to equip the saints for the work of ministry, for the building up of the

---

17. The exact relationship between Israel and the church is not utterly clear in the New Testament. For, at times, the authors of the New Testament still refer to the people of Israel as God's people as well. (We will discuss the relationship between the church and Israel later in the book.)

18. The same can be said of the church's union with the Spirit of God. The church is one because each member of the church has received the one Spirit (1 Cor 12:13; Eph 2:16–18).

body of Christ, until all of us come to the unity of the faith and of the knowledge of the Son of God, to maturity, to the measure of the full stature of Christ" (4:12–13; compare Eph 5:1–2). The goal of church ministries is to become Christ-like. Like the image of the church as the people of God, the image of the church as the body of Christ suggests that the church includes both those who are saved (or will be saved) and those who share in his ministry.

The Christian community—the church—is a fourth great foundation of Christianity. The church is those people who gather in the name of Jesus in various concrete locales. More profoundly, the church is all those who are saved (or will be saved) through Christ, who likewise share in his mission and ministry to each other and to the world. We will say more about the nature and mission of the church in Chapter 6.

Conclusion

In Chapters 1 and 2, we have discussed four key foundations of Christianity. These groundworks include a sacred text, a sacred history, a sacred person, and a sacred community. No doubt other foundations could be named; further, our discussion hardly exhausts what could be said about these four fundamental aspects of Christianity. Still, this preliminary examination will suffice to introduce the basics of the Bible, the story of Israel, Jesus, and the church. In the next five chapters, we investigate some of the key teachings of Christianity.

Part Two: **Christian Theology**

3

Revelation, God, Creation, and Providence

In the previous two chapters, we examined four foundations of the Christian faith. In this third chapter, we turn to consider some of the central teachings of Christianity. Often the subject at hand is called theology, which involves attempts to define the nature of God and God's relationship with reality. Among the central topics and questions addressed by Christian theology are these:

1. Revelation and Authority (How are God and religious truths known?)

2. God (What is God's nature?)

3. Creation and Providence (How does God relate to reality as a whole?)

4. Humans (What is the nature of humans?)

5. Sin (What is the core human dilemma?)

6. Christ (What is Christ's nature and work?)

7. Salvation (How is God resolving the human dilemma?)

8. The Church (What is the nature and function of the church?)

9. Last Things (What is the destiny of created reality, especially of humans?)

Often four broad types of theological study are recognized. These are

1. Biblical Theology—the examination of the basic theological claims of the Bible

2. Historical Theology—the study of the teachings of Christians throughout the ages

3. Systematic Theology—the inspection and construction of Christian teachings with a view toward creating a coherent system of beliefs and communicating to a contemporary audience

4. Philosophical Theology—the study of theology using the tools and systems of philosophy

In this chapter, we focus primarily on systematic theology and address the first three theological topics.

Sometimes a distinction is made between *theology* and *dogma*. Dogma is the officially sanctioned teachings of church leadership about the topics or questions mentioned above. Theology is only proposed teachings about these topics or questions, offered by Christian thinkers, but not necessarily formally endorsed by church leadership. Not all Christians recognize the distinction between dogma and theology, for some do not acknowledge a central office establishing doctrine (teachings) for all believers. Often such Christians distinguish between what they see as authoritarian *creeds* that inappropriately purport to speak for all Christians and mere *confessions of faith* that express only the views of a local church.

Constructing theology often involves appealing to several basic sources. One fundamental source is *divine revelation*. Many theologians argue that God and religious truths remain a mystery unless God reveals such matters to humans. So, God is the ultimate source of knowledge about the divine being and about God's relationship to reality as a whole. Two broad forms of revelation often are noted: general revelation and special revelation. The former is that revelation available to all people of all times. The latter is revelation only available to particular persons. Closely tied to revelation is a second source of theology, namely, the *Christian Scriptures*. The Bible often is seen as the primary witness to God's revelation to humanity—and, for some the Bible itself is a form of revelation. A third source of theology is *Church Tradition*. Christians often believe that God's Spirit indwells, communes with, and leads the church. And the Holy Spirit aids God's people in understanding the content of Scripture. Thus, often it is assumed that the formal teachings and interpretations of Christians down through the ages hold considerable authority for Christian theology. Roman Catholics have tended to affirm the official teachings of the church to be virtually equal in authority to the Bible. Protestants, on the other hand, have tended to affirm the Bible as either the sole or clearly the primary source of authority over postbiblical church teachings. A fourth source for theology may be *individual Christian religious experiences*—especially when understood as the inner testimony of the Holy Spirit. (In fact, some writers point out that ultimately both the Bible and postbiblical tradition essentially emerge out of the living experiences of individual Christian believers.[1]) A fifth and

---

1. The appeal to individual religious experience certainly has its limitations. No person is an island. Interpretations of religious experiences often must be vetted through the broader Christian community, and various religious writers and communities have warned again utterly individualistic interpretations of faith based on personal experiences/encounters with the divine. Indeed, at a basic level, even "individual experiences" are not utterly unique since nearly always individuals must interpret their experiences through language, which itself is largely a construct founded on (often tacit) social agreements. Nevertheless, at times individuals do have powerful religious encounters or experiences to which others are not directly privy. And these encounters (while often filtered through the broader interpretive framework of community) often serve to impact how theology is interpreted. A classic example of this is Paul's encounter with the resurrected Jesus in Acts 9, or Peter's vision of unclean animals in Acts 10. Each of these experiences was eventually filtered through the broader

somewhat controversial source of theology is the *physical world* itself, along with the *broad resources of human history and culture*. Some Christians contend that through serious rational reflection genuine religious truths can be gleaned from nature itself and from the philosophical, psychological, political, socioeconomic, and religious movements of human history. Even Christians who are reluctant to acknowledge reason and human culture as legitimate sources of theology often admit that these resources impact Christian theology as it attempts to create a coherent worldview and to communicate to contemporary people.

Discussion of the sources of theology raises a related issue: What is the relationship between revelation, reason, and faith? Four broad approaches are often identified. First, a minority of Christian thinkers have proposed that *reason alone is the source of religious knowledge*. Eighteenth-century deists are perhaps the most pronounced example of this perspective. Many of them believed that a rational case for God's existence can be made, but they also insisted that claims for special divine revelation fall short of the demands of genuine knowledge. At the other extreme, a considerable number of Christian thinkers have proposed that *faith alone in divine revelation or in church authorities is the primary route to gleaning religious knowledge*. Tertullian (c. 155—c. 220 CE) is often interpreted as teaching (at least in some of his writings) that the only sure source of religious knowledge is what he called "the Rule of Faith." This rule of faith was a set of propositions based on the scriptural and apostolic traditions of his day. Tertullian did allow that as long as the essence of the Rule was not disturbed, there is room for discussion and dialogue. But even this is not necessary or even wise. For Tertullian, the best policy was simply to assent to the truth of the Rule. Tertullian summarized his views in the famous phrase: "What has Jerusalem to do with Athens, the Church with the Academy ?"[2] In other words, philosophy and natural reason lead to error; faith in Christian teaching leads to truth. A third approach holds that *reason precedes but is enhanced by faith in revelation*. Thomas Aquinas (1225–1274) proposed that reason is the starting point for establishing religious truth. Through reason fundamental truths about God can be established. Nevertheless, reason is limited. Some religious truths are beyond reason's grasp. These truths can be learned only through divine revelation, and reception of that revelation requires faith–especially intellectual assent to revealed truths (*fides*). A fourth and similar perspective contends that *faith in revelation is primary but is enhanced by reason*. Augustine of Hippo (354–430) insisted that religious faith is a precursor to truly exercising reason. Once one submits to God in faith, one is able to exercise reason in an appropriate manner. In an attitude of faith, one seeks through reason to better understand what one already affirms through faith. Indeed, there is some room for changing beliefs—especially those beliefs that are not central to one's basic commitments, or those that are not coherent with central

Christian community; but arguably each likewise was (or elements of each were) at first an individualist experience.

2. Tertullian, *Prescription against Heretics*, 7.

Christian teachings. In a sermon on the Gospel of John, Augustine famously commented: "Understanding is the reward of faith. Therefore, do not seek to understand in order to believe, but believe that thou mayest understand."[3] The majority of Christian theologians have endorsed some form of these last two approaches to revelation, reason, and faith.

Discussions about revelation, reason, and faith interface with concerns over the relationship between Christian teachings and contemporary knowledge. The Jewish and Christian faiths arose out of the ancient world and its outlooks. Hence, early devotees assumed many of the beliefs and values of their ancient cultures. Unsurprisingly, these assumptions often found their way into the Bible which, in turn, influenced the changing perspectives of new generations of Christians. Christian thought, however, did not evolve simply through reading Scripture and restating what previous Christians have thought. Each new generation adds nuances to the faith while attempting to be loyal to the fundament insights of their ancient heritage. Believers have done this not only to clarify ideas expressed in the ancient Scriptures but also to better interpret the Christian message for new generations.

The same is true in our own era. Contemporary theology attempts to convey the truths of Christianity to present-day audiences, and often this involves interpreting the faith in light of the presumed truths of the current generation. As was the case in the past, this does not mean making a complete compromise of Christian principles to ideas incongruent with the faith. But often it does require reevaluating what is essential to the faith and what is tangential (or historically limited). Discerning the difference between these two often is not an easy chore; disputes are inevitable. Still the task of interpretation also is unavoidable. Often in the following discussion of Christian doctrines, differences of opinion will be cited between various theological perspectives. Some of these disputes emerge from the clash between more or less liberal and more or less conservative theologians of the present era.[4] This is to be expected since each of these broad camps is attempting to express the Christian faith in light of the ideological changes that have arisen in our own time. Among these changes are especially viewpoints generated by contemporary philosophy, science, and historical studies. Still not all the quarrels come from disagreements between so-called liberals and so-called conservatives. Many theological disagreements reflect conflicts between Christians throughout history who, like contemporary theologians, hoped to make the faith intelligible in their own eras.

3. Augustine, *Gospel of John*, 29.6.

4. For a brief introduction to the development of liberalism and conservativism, see Robinson, *Christianity: A Brief History*, 352–58.

Revelation and Authority

The doctrine of revelation attempts to answer how God and religious truths can be known. The English term "revelation" comes from the Latin *revelatio*, which in turn translates the biblical Greek word *apokalysis*, meaning "unveiling." Thus, the essential meaning of the term "revelation" is the disclosure of something previously veiled or hidden. The Bible does not systematically articulate a doctrine of revelation. Like God's existence, the existence of divine revelation is assumed in the Bible. Two major categories of divine revelation are usually distinguished:

1. General Revelation, which refers to divine disclosures that are in principle available to all persons, at all times, through media such as the physical universe and human nature.

2. Special/Particular Revelation, which refers to divine disclosures to particular people at particular times and places through media such as visions, dreams, miracles, auditory experiences, inner religious experiences, and so forth.

General Revelation

The doctrine of General Revelation teaches that God has provided means for knowing religious truth that are in principle available to all people. Various media of General Revelation have been proposed. Here are four:

1. Revelation in and through the physical universe

2. Revelation in and through the general patterns of history

3. Revelation in and through the nature of human beings

    a. Human minds

    b. Human moral consciences

    c. Human religious consciousness

4. Revelation in and through the idea of God

The first three media appeal to knowledge gleaned from the senses. Essentially, one argues that by rationally reflecting on some aspect of nature, a person can discover truths about God's existence and nature. The fourth medium appeals to reason alone, contending that the logic of the idea of God rationally demonstrates and necessitates God's existence.

Disagreement arises concerning the content of General Revelation and whether this content can be acquired or known by humans. That is, what does general revelation reveal about God, and can humans grasp this revelation? There are at least two main traditional views about this. First, some theologians insist that through general revelation a relatively thorough *natural theology* can be developed. That is, without a previous commitment to Jesus Christ and without relying on other authoritative sources of Christian theology, one can—through rational reflection—demonstrate religious truths, especially truths about God. Several arguments for God's existence and nature have been offered. Here are some examples: *Cosmological Arguments* contend that the physical world needs an explanation, and that God is the best explanation. Thomas Aquinas (1225–1274) offered at least three versions of this:

1. The argument from movement to an unmoved mover.

2. The argument from events that are caused to a first, uncaused cause.

3. The argument from contingent things to a necessary being.[5]

Teleological Arguments insist that the order of the universe implies a divine designer. Aquinas propounded a version of this argument as well. He essentially argued that in nature things move toward goals, and often do so routinely. Such routine movement toward goals implies an intelligent designer. William Paley (1743–1805) offered a similar argument, contending that the universe is like a human artifact (such as a watch), which implies a wise and powerful designer.[6] More recently, mathematician William Dembski and microbiologist Michael Behe have argued for the existence of irreducibly complex systems in the universe, ones that cannot readily be explained by chance and natural laws.[7] They conclude that it is highly probable that such systems were intelligently designed. *Ontological Arguments* insist that the very idea of God implies that God exists. Anselm (c. 1033–1109) and René Descartes (1596–1650) each constructed arguments to this effect. Descartes argued that he had a concept of a "perfect being," and then pointed out that "existence is a perfection" so that anything that failed to exist would not be perfect. Descartes concluded that his concept of a perfect being—God—implies that God necessarily exists. *Arguments from Moral Conscience* propose that the existence of the moral conscience in humans is best explained in terms of a moral God who gives ontological grounding to such a conscience. C. S. Lewis, in *Mere Christianity,* offers this argument.[8] *Arguments from Religious Experience* insist that various religious experiences are evidence of a transcendent being that causes these experiences. Rudolf Otto proposed this in *The Idea of the Holy,*[9] as did William Alston in *Perceiving God.*[10]

While many theologians affirm that knowledge of God can be gleaned from general revelation, others disagree. Many theologians insist that truths about God

---

5. Thomas Aquinas, *Summa Theologica*, 1.2.2

6. Paley, *Natural Theology*.

7. Dembski, *No Free Lunch*; Behe, *Darwin's Black Box*.

8. Lewis, *Mere Christianity*.

9. Otto, *The Idea of the Holy*.

10. Alston, *Perceiving God*.

are objectively available in and through creation, history, and human nature, but that sin prevents humans (especially nonbelievers) from subjectively receiving these truths. This is a perspective often endorsed by the Protestant, especially the Reformed, tradition. This was the view of Martin Luther (1483–1546) and John Calvin (1509–1564). For these writers, human sin has disabled the human capacity to discover and accept the truth objectively revealed in nature.

A related issue about general revelation is this: Does general revelation give sufficient knowledge to save a person from sin and bring an individual into a right relationship with God? Many Reformed theologians, including John Calvin, insist that while the information objectively conveyed in general revelation *could* in principle lead a person to a right relationship with God, human sin prevents the sinner from receiving such information (or responding to it). Humans willfully continue being sinners and thus willfully suppress the knowledge of God that could be theirs through general revelation. In practice, then, general revelation brings only condemnation to humankind. Only through special revelation (and divine grace or aid) can salvation occur. Other theologians propose that general revelation provides sufficient information to bring a person to salvation, and some people positively respond to it and are saved. Justin Martyr (d. 165 CE) taught that all knowledge is a product of the divine Logos, the Word of God. Thus, wherever truth is found, some revelation also is present and some pagan philosophers likely were saved.[11] Huldrych Zwingli (1484–1531) affirmed absolute divine predestination. God saves whomever God wants to save. Hence, those whom God wants to save can be saved by whatever mechanism God chooses, including general revelation.[12]

A final comment about general revelation is warranted. It is not abundantly clear what role faith plays in general revelation. At times, advocates of *natural theology* and of the saving potential of general revelation leave the impression that the reception of general revelation is primarily a matter of reason, having little to do with the exercise of faith. That is, at least some knowledge of God (including possibly saving knowledge) can be gleaned by rational reflection on nature, on human nature, or even on the implications of the concept of God. On the other hand, for some theologians, such a perspective is simply unacceptable. For them, all knowledge of God, especially saving knowledge, must come from faith alone.

Special/Particular Revelation

Special or particular revelation refers to God's disclosure to particular people, at particular times and places. But what is the nature of this disclosure? If we assume that particular revelation occurs as an event in human history, what kind of event is it?

11. Justin Martyr, *First Apology*, 46; Justin Martyr, *Second Apology*, 10, 13. See McGrath, *The Christian Theology Reader*, 4.

12. Zwingli, *Sermon, August 20, 1530*, quoted in González, *A History of Christian Thought*, 3:69.

1. Is it an external event objectively present for several people to perceive?

2. Is it solely an inner or subjective event that can only be mentally experienced?

3. Is it a verbal event (external or internal) that often conveys information?

4. Is it solely a nonverbal experience that requires human interpretation?

5. Is the event of divine revelation self-authenticating? When a person experiences it, does the person automatically know that it is a revelation from God? Or can a person experience it but not know that it is a revelation?

6. What role does faith play in the reception of a particular revelation?

Several answers to these questions have been proposed.

One model of special revelation contends that special revelation is both *verbal and nonverbal.* In this view, numerous historical events (many now recorded in the Bible) have been divine revelations. Among these events might be (1) mighty acts of God, such as the parting of the Red Sea,[13] the resurrection of Jesus, the empowering of the church at Pentecost, and so forth; (2) historical patterns among the Israelites, when common events were interpreted as divine acts: Victories over or defeats by Israel's enemies, exiles into Assyria and Babylon, the return from Babylonian exile, and so forth; (3) inner, nonverbal experiences of the divine presence, such as the spiritually burning hearts of the travelers to Emmaus (Luke 24:13–35) or the testimony of the Spirit (Rom 8:16); (4) the preaching and teaching of the prophets; (5) the life, teaching, death, and resurrection of Jesus; and (6) the life, experiences, and writings of the early church. This verbal-and-nonverbal theory of special revelation was the dominant perspective throughout church history. Theologians such as Augustine, Thomas Aquinas, Martin Luther, and John Calvin all seem to have endorsed something like this. And many contemporary writers still do. In this model, faith is required in order to perceive that such events and words are revelation. Further, faith is required to gain salvific benefit from them. That is, on the one hand, a person must acknowledge the truth of revealed statements; on the other hand, an individual must personally trust the God who is disclosed in these verbal and nonverbal events.

A second model of special revelation contends that special revelation is *only nonverbal events.* There are many versions of this view, but two broad streams are these. One version insists that God is revealed in both nonverbal external events and nonverbal internal events. G. Ernest Wright, in *God Who Acts*, emphasizes God's revelation in key acts of history, particularly in biblical history. He insists that the Bible is not so much the word of God, but a human record of the acts of God in history. God acts in external and internal nonverbal events, and then humans verbally interpret these events, drawing inferences from them. These inferences are not necessarily correct, and so God's revelation comes primarily through nonverbal events. For this paradigm, examples of revelatory events might be mighty acts of God, historical patterns among

13. Also called the Sea of Reeds.

the Israelites, inner, nonverbal experiences of the divine presence, the resurrection of Jesus, and so forth.[14] Less clear in this model of special revelation is whether events like the *teachings* of the prophets, of the apostles, or of Jesus are divine revelation. In this view, faith is necessary in order to know that these events are divine revelation. Faith also is required to interpret the meaning of these events.

Another version of the nonverbal theory insists that particular revelation comes exclusively through inner religious experiences and not through external events. Examples of theologians who affirm this perspective are Friedrich Schleiermacher (1768–1834), Albrecht Ritschl (1822–1889), and Wilhelm Herrmann (1846–1922).[15] These authors stress an inner sense of communion with God, asserting that such an inner awareness was particularly acute in Jesus of Nazareth, and is available in principle to humans today. These writers tend to reject that outward events can serve as divine revelation, but they admit that external events can be catalysts for inner revelatory experiences. Thus, the primary examples of divine revelation in the Bible are events like the spiritually burning hearts of the travelers to Emmaus (Luke 24:13–35), or the inner testimony of the Holy Spirit that Christians are children of God (Rom 8:16). Ultimately, faith is required in order to know that such experiences are divine revelation. However, there is a tendency in this view to think of such inner experiences as self-authenticating. That is, in having these inner experiences, a person simply knows that she has encountered God.

Closely tied to verbal-versus-nonverbal theories of revelatory events is a question about the basic content of revelation. Specifically, what is being revealed through divine revelation? Two broad options are often cited. Many theologians have emphasized the *propositional* content of special revelation. Here the content is a set of truth claims or propositions or doctrines. This view was emphasized in medieval Catholic theology, especially by Thomas Aquinas. Aquinas emphasized faith as *fides*—that is, as intellectual assent that a proposition is true. Many Protestant groups, likewise, have emphasized this aspect of special revelation. This is especially the case among various conservative writers, such as B. B. Warfield (1851–1921)[16] and Carl F. H. Henry (1913–2003).[17] Like Thomas Aquinas, these writers emphasize the need for intellectual assent that a proposition or doctrine is true. These conservative writers, along with Thomas, recognize the importance of faith as *fiducia* (personal trust in God), especially for coming to salvation. But they tend to insist that such trust is not possible without *fides*, intellectual affirmation of key truths or doctrines. For Protestant writers, the Bible is the primary source for these revealed doctrines. In the Catholic tradition, the Bible is acknowledged as the primary source of revealed doctrines, but the Church (in its formal teachings) is the primary interpreter of these doctrines.

14. Wright, *God Who Acts*.

15. Dulles, *Models of Revelation*, 68–83

16. Warfield, *Revelation and Inspiration*; and Warfield, *The Inspiration and Authority of the Bible*.

17. Henry, *God Who Speaks and Shows, Part 2*, 248–303.

Contrary to those who emphasize the propositional content of revelation, many contemporary theologians have stressed the *personal* nature of revelation. They insist that the content of revelation is *not* primarily a set of doctrines; rather it is God. In other words, revelation essentially is a personal encounter with God. An analogy might be this: when a child is kissed by her mother, the child knows her mother through this experience in a personal way, and not primarily through affirming a set of propositions. While that experience and that knowledge might be partially captured in words or propositions, the encounter is deeper than that and cannot be fully apprehended by words or propositions. According to this model of revelatory content, revelation is primarily a personal and mysterious encounter with God.

A variety of theologians have endorsed this *personal* view of the content of revelation, including Friedrich Schleiermacher, Albrecht Ritschl, Karl Barth (1886–1968), and Emil Brunner (1889–1966). Many of these writers see Martin Luther as endorsing this perspective. Classic liberalism, represented by Schleiermacher and Ritschl, tended to reject a strong distinction between general and special revelation. Liberal theologians insisted that all humans have an innate capacity to encounter God, and all humans to some degree do encounter God in this way. The role of the Bible and of church teaching and preaching is to help evoke these personal revelatory encounters with God. But the Bible and church teaching and preaching are *not* such revelation itself.[18] Neo-orthodoxy, represented by Karl Barth and Emil Brunner, tended to reject the classic liberal view that humans have an innate capacity to encounter God. Instead, these writers insisted that God alone chooses if, when, and how persons receive revelation as divine encounter. Thus, God can (and often does) choose to use the Bible, preaching, and church teaching as opportunities to reveal God's self in a divine-human encounter. But neither the Bible, nor preaching, nor church teaching is revelation proper. For Barth, the words of the Bible and of church teaching and preaching can "become" the Word of God when God sovereignly chooses to use those human expressions to reveal God's self.[19]

Revelation and the Bible

As the discussion above shows, the precise relationship between the Bible and special revelation is disputed among theologians. Is the Bible a form of divine revelation? Or is it merely a human witness to more fundamental forms of revelation experienced in the past? A chief problem for verbal and propositional theories of biblical revelation is the following: What happens when scriptural claims contradict one another or conflict with truths known through science or history?[20] Does the

18. Dulles, *Models of Revelation*, 68–83.

19. Dulles, *Models of Revelation*, 84–97. Also see Brunner, *Revelation and Reason*.

20. For a discussion of the tensions between some biblical passages and science, see Chapter 14, below.

presence of such contradictions imply that God has revealed claims that are not true? Part of the motive for nonverbal theories of revelation and for understanding the content of revelation as personal rather than as propositional is the desire to avoid such problems. Advocates of these theories propose that the Bible is only human testimony about revelation and, thus, is subject to inaccuracies; but genuine (personal-encounter) revelation is not subject to error.

A primary difficulty for nonverbal or personal-encounter theories of revelation is this: How can one know that the human interpretations of wordless, divine revelations or of divine personal encounters are correct? How can one know that prior religious believers have rightly understood the meanings or implications of those wordless personal events? (Another way to ask this question is, why should someone believe these human testimonies since they are not divine revelation per se?)

Out of such concerns, and in an attempt to ensure the trustworthiness of the Scriptures and the accuracy of core teachings of Christian theology, some theologians associated with the verbal and propositional theories of revelation have advocated for the *inerrancy* of the Bible. This theory insists that everything the Bible *teaches* is true. The inerrantist scholar's task is to interpret the Bible so that whatever it teaches is true. Apparent contradictions within the text or between the text and other disciplines cannot be genuine incongruities. Rather, the inerrantist interpreter must show how disparate claims can be harmonized.[21]

Contrary to this *inerrantist* approach and in an effort to avoid strained interpretations of the biblical text, many biblical scholars maintain that the Bible need not be inerrant to be *sufficiently reliable*. Certainty is not available to religious believers; the human element of the Scriptures is unavoidable, and acceptance of the *overall* trustworthiness of the scriptural testimony is sufficient for religious belief. Proponents of this view find it ironic that inerrantists argue that to trust the Scriptures, one must believe—as an act of faith based on insufficient evidence—that the Bible is inerrant. In turn, proponents of sufficient-reliability ask, why not—admittedly based on insufficient evidence—simply exercise faith in the general trustworthiness of scriptural testimony from the start while admitting that there are some errors in the text? In the end, faith is required for both approaches; but in the view of *noninerrantists*, their approach is simply more honest about the nature of the scriptural text and its human limitations.

---

21. Conversations regarding the doctrine of inerrancy are complex and sometimes controversial. The doctrine of biblical inerrancy has many supporters, including the following: Lindsell, *The Battle for the Bible*; Henry, *God Who Speaks, Acts and Shows: Fifteen Theses*, 129–242; Erickson, *Christian Theology*, 188–209. For extended conversations about the elements of and controversies over the doctrine of inerrancy and of scriptural authority per se see Achtemeier, *Inspiration and Authority*; see also Mohler et al., *Five Views on Biblical Inerrancy*.

God

The doctrine of God is a central component of Christian theology. It emerged from the ancient Hebrew and early Christian religious traditions, and later blended with Greek-Roman philosophical speculation. The Hebrew and early Christian perspectives are captured in the Old Testament, Apocrypha, and New Testament writings. These traditions often are narrative in quality, describing Israel's and early Christians' corporate and individual encounters with God. This narrative structure itself is theologically significant, for it presumes that God *acts* in history and at times *interacts* with humans. Further, it suggests that God's *nature* is learned through what God does and not just through what God says or what others say about God. The philosophical sources of the doctrine of God arise from rational musings about the nature of ultimate reality. These speculations help produce notions of God as an unchanging, perfect being who explains all but is unaffected by anything.

God in the Old Testament

The Old Testament tradition bears testimony about several core divine attributes. First, God is **personal**. The terms "person" or "personal" are not explicitly applied to God in the Hebrew Scriptures. But that God is a person is implied by many texts. Several person-like qualities are ascribed to God: God loves, repents, knows, speaks, expresses wrath, shows mercy, is wise, wills, plans, acts intentionally, and so forth. Further, personal pronouns and personal titles are used of God: *he, his, me, mine, Lord, king, shepherd*, and so forth. In turn, God is portrayed as entering into personal relations with humans. Yahweh makes promises and enters into covenants (Gen 9:8–16; 15: 1–21; 26:1–6; Exod 19–20). A second divine property set is **holiness and righteousness**. Covenant relationship with Yahweh is not always a pleasant or easy affair. It typically involves a call to obedience and commitment. This is most obvious in the covenant of God with the nation of Israel, where obedience in the form of right worship and right social and personal behavior is demanded, and where punishment and ruin are promised if the covenant is broken. Throughout the Old Testament, concern is expressed over both right worship and right moral practices. Often these commands are seen as reflecting something about Yahweh—namely, (1) Yahweh is morally righteous and demands right actions from others, and (2) Yahweh is deserving of unique honor or worship. These ideas are sometimes captured in the descriptor *holy*. The core meaning of the term is "to be cut off" or "to be separated out." Thus, God is said to be "separated out" from other things. Over time, the word seems to have come to mean both that God is utterly different from other things (and thus deserving of unique honor, glory, or worship) as well as that God is separated from sin (that is, morally different from sinful human beings).[22] God is holy and righteous, and thus demanding.

A third set of related attributes ascribed to God in the Old Testament are these. God is *faithful, trustworthy, loving, merciful, just, and electing*. God is faithful to divine promises and covenants; thus, God is trustworthy (Gen 15:1; 50:24; Deut 7:9, 12). Often God's motive for keeping the covenant and protecting his people is love (Exod 2:23–24; 3:7–8), and frequently tied to this love is concern for the oppressed (Deut 10:16–19). In turn, divine compassion provides a motive for Israel's own social responsibilities and laws, and often Israel is condemned for failing to show compassion to the oppressed around them (Amos 5:21–24; Isa 58: 6–9). Even in judgment, however, God's love can dampen the divine wrath so that the deity recoils from bringing utter destruction upon Israel (Hos 11:8–11). Nevertheless, God's love also is mysterious. This mystery is exemplified in Yahweh's election of Abraham and of the people of Israel. In Gen 12:1–4, no explanation is given for God's choice of Abraham; God simply chooses. In like manner, Deuteronomy indicates (in more than one place) that it was not because of the merits of the Israelites that God chose them or blessed them. Rather, it was because of God's love and free choice (7:7–8).

Closely tied to Yahweh's covenant faithfulness is a fourth attribute set: God is *almighty and sovereign*. It is precisely because Yahweh is powerful that he can keep his promises, protect Abraham and his descendants, deliver Israel from slavery, fight for Israel in the conquest of the promised land, and return his people from Babylonian captivity. (See Gen 15:1, Exod 7:5, 8:10, 22; 9:14–16, 29; Josh 3:10; 1 Sam 17:26, 36; Isa 43:3–5, 13, 14; Jer 10:10). Yahweh's power is especially demonstrated in the divine creation of and sovereignty over nature (Pss 89:8–13; 135:5–7). God's power is also shown in his dominion over the kingdoms of the earth (Pss 22:27–28; 47:8–9). In light of such claims, often God is referred to as God Almighty or El Shaddai (Gen 17:1; 28:3; 35:11; Deut 10:17; Isa 6:3). A fifth ascription is that God is *a wise creator*. The classic texts for God's creating are Gen 1 and 2. As already mentioned, God's acts of creation and rule over nature demonstrate the divine power; but they also demonstrate God's knowledge and wisdom (Pss 19:2; 44:23; 73:11; 94:11; 103:14; 139:6; Prov 3:20; 8:22–31; Job 21:22; 38:4ff). While Yahweh/God alone acts in creation, the Old Testament at times cryptically speaks of a sort of council with God at the act of creation through which (in some sense) creation occurred. Specifically, some passages speak of the Spirit, Wisdom, and Word of Yahweh present at creation (Gen 1:2; Pss 33:6; 104:24; Prov 3:19; 8:22–31; Jer 10:12; 51:15; Wis 9:1–2; Isa 40:13–14). Sixth, God is *everlasting*—presumably never beginning or ending (Pss 41:13; 90:2; 102:27; Isa 40:28; Neh 9:5). Seventh, God is *not physical*. Yahweh cannot be represented by any created things. Exod 20:4–6 disallows the making and worshiping of idols, explaining that Yahweh is a jealous God. Deut 4:15–20 explains the prohibition against idols on the grounds that Yahweh has

---

22. Many of these ideas—moral obligations, devotional obligations, covenant obligations—are captured in Deut 30:11–18 and Josh 24.

no physical form, and thus any such figures either misrepresent Yahweh or implicitly represent something that is not God or is only a creature of God. Many scholars see Exod 20:4–6 as a command from an early period in Israel's history to worship no other gods because, even though there are other gods, Yahweh is jealous and demands exclusive devotion. In turn, Deut 4 is from a later perspective—one that forbids idol worship because Yahweh is not physical, and thus any physical representation cannot be of Yahweh but only of some element of the created world.[23] An eighth attribute set ascribed to God in the Old Testament is that Yahweh is **unique and uniquely worthy of worship**. Throughout the Old Testament one reads that there is none like Yahweh. Such claims are found in Exod 8:10; 15:11; Deut 3:24; 4:35; 33:26; Pss 71:19; 86:8; 89:6; and Isa 40:18; 42:8; 46:9. In these verses and others, different divine attributes are used as evidence of Yahweh's uniqueness.

God in the New Testament

New Testament writers endorsed these (and other) Hebrew scriptural claims about God. But their understanding of the deity was affected profoundly by their encounter with Jesus. Eventually, orthodox Christians came to teach that Jesus is completely human and completely God in one being, and that he is a member of the divine Trinity. But such claims were not unambiguously taught in the New Testament. From the earliest period, some Christian writers were making grand claims about Jesus' nature and significance.[24] The earliest affirmations of Jesus' lordship, messiahship, and divine sonship seem to have been linked to his resurrection from the dead (Acts 2:32, 36; 5:31; 13:32–33; Rom 1:3–4). By the 50s CE, the apostle Paul was employing titles such as Christ, Lord, and Son of God to point to Jesus' transcendent nature and existence prior to his birth (Rom 1:4; 10:9; 1 Cor 15:24–28; 2 Cor 8:9; Phil 2:6–11). By the 60s CE, the Gospel of Mark linked the titles Lord, Son of God, and Messiah (Christ) not only to Jesus' resurrection, but to his earthly ministry as a whole. And by the 70s and 80s CE, the Gospels of Matthew and Luke offered birth narratives that pronounced Jesus'

---

23. The Bible is full of anthropomorphism—descriptions of God with human characteristics, including both human physical/bodily characteristics (Gen 2:7; 3:8; 11:5; Ex 31:18, 23; 2 Chr 16:9, etc.) and human personality traits such as life, love, thought, will, judgments, etc. Generally, theologians insist that while God transcends complete human comprehension, ascriptions of personality-traits to God often are appropriate since God is more like a person than a non-person (although the doctrine of the Trinity may imply that God transcends singular-personhood *per se*). On the other hand, theologians typically insist that attributing physical (bodily) characteristics to God is inappropriate for God is a spirit not a physical entity (John 4:24; Luke 24:39; Acts 17:24). Sometimes a distinction is made between God's essential nature and certain *theophanies* that occur, wherein God appears in some (physical) form to reveal God's self to a human. But such theophany, as the name suggests, involves God appearing to someone in a certain way (so the person can somewhat understand God) without revealing the intrinsic nature of the deity—which is invisible (John 1:18; 1 Tim 1:17; 6:15–16).

24. For a discussion of these developments see Brown, *An Introduction to New Testament Christology*.

heightened status as Messiah, Son of God, Savior, and Emmanuel ("God with us") from his conception (Matt 1:18–2:23; Luke 1:5–2:40). Further, the late-first-century Gospel of John pushes the moment of Jesus' heightened status back to before Jesus' conception to the creation of the cosmos itself. Identifying Jesus as the incarnate Word (*logos*, rationality) of God, John proclaims that this Word was with God from the beginning, and that through this Word all creation came into being (1:1–3). A handful of other later New Testament writings likewise acknowledge the exalted status of Jesus prior to the creation of the world (Col 1:15–17; Heb 1:2–3).

In addition to these varied claims about Christ, the New Testament makes interesting claims about the Spirit of God. Often the Spirit implicitly or explicitly is identified with the Spirit of Yahweh from the Hebrew Bible, whose outpouring was promised by the prophet Joel (2:28–29; see Acts 2:16–17), and who inspired the prophets of Israel (Acts 4:25; 28:25–27; Heb 3:7–11). Sometimes, the Spirit is spoken of in abstract terms, almost as a synonym for divine activity (Luke 1:35; Acts 10:45). But in other places, the Spirit is referenced with personal pronouns (Acts 13:2; 15:28). Paul saw the Spirit as intricately involved in the life of the Christian community. The Spirit guides Christians toward action (Gal 3:5), ensures redemption (2 Cor 1:12), and empowers service (1 Cor 12:11). The Gospel of John emphasizes the role of the Spirit in drawing persons to Christ (16:13–15) and in aiding Christians in bearing witness to their faith (15:26).

Throughout the New Testament, a close association is made between God (sometimes called Father), Jesus (Lord or Son), and the Spirit (or Holy Spirit). Several New Testament formulas depict the three together in an underdefined interrelationship. Examples of passages that do this are the benediction in 2 Cor 13:14, the confession in Eph 4:4–6, and the baptismal formula in Matt 28:19. The exact relationship between God or the Father, the Lord or the Son, and the Holy Spirit is unclear in the New Testament. Both Jesus and the Spirit are said to be from God (John 15:26; 1 Cor 2:12; 6:19) and to have access to the thoughts or will of the Father (Matt 11:27; 1 Cor 2:11). Further, a mutual dependence exists between the Son or the Lord and the Spirit. While the Spirit is sent by the Son (John 15:26; Gal 4:6), the Son relies upon the Spirit too. Jesus was conceived by the Spirit (Matt 1:20; Luke 4:18), uttered words of God through the Spirit (John 3:34; 6:63), healed the sick and cast out demons by the Spirit's power (Matt 12:15–21, 28; Luke 4:14; 5:17). This parity between the Spirit and the Son or the Lord is found in many New Testament formulas (Acts 9:31; Rom 9:1; 15:30; 1 Cor 6:11, 15, 19; Phil 2:1; 3:3; Heb 10:29; Rev 2:18, 20). Evidence from the New Testament suggests that these associations between Father, Son, and Spirit emerged out of the religious experiences of early Christians. Somehow religious encounters, influenced by experiences with or traditions about Jesus and filtered through categories found in the Hebrew tradition moved early Christians to express their burgeoning faith in terms of a mutually interdependent relationship between a father-like God, a resurrected Lord or Son, and a holy Spirit. Still the precise nature of these interrelationships was not clarified in the New Testament and was left to later Christian speculation.

The Doctrine of the Trinity

Debates about the nature of God emerged in the early centuries of Christianity. Often Christians were clearer about what the relationship between Father, Son, and Spirit *is not* rather than on what it is. Early on, several heretical positions were identified and rejected. One of these views was *unipersonalism*—the theory that God is a singular person and Christ is not part of the deity. Second-century *dynamic monarchianism* held that Jesus was merely a man in whom dwelled an impersonal power (Greek: *dynamis*) from God. Theodotus of Byzantium (190s) taught that Jesus was endowed with this divine power at his baptism. Paul of Samosata (200–275), bishop of Antioch, taught that the Logos or the Son and the Spirit were attributes of a unipersonal God. Arius (c. 255–336), presbyter in Alexandria, taught that God's essence cannot be shared or communicated, and that the Logos or Son is a creature of God, created prior to the creation of the universe. The Logos, of its own nature, is subject to corruption and sin, but God (the Father) gave him grace not to sin. Arianism was rejected at the Council of Nicaea (325) and again at the Council of Constantinople (381).

A second Trinitarian heresy was *modalistic monarchianism*, from the second and third centuries. This theory affirmed the deity of the Father, Son, and Holy Spirit, but denied any personal or *hypostatic* distinctions (see below) between Father, Son, and Holy Spirit. Rather, it insisted that these titles refer to differing offices or modes of being found in the one God. Noetus of Smyrna (late second century) taught that God the Father submitted to human birth, became the Son, suffered, and died. Noetus's views were condemned for affirming *patripassianism* (Father-suffering or -passion). Orthodoxy taught that Jesus Christ alone suffered, and only in his human nature, not in his divine nature. Sabellius (third century) referred to God as *huiopator* or "son-father." For him, God is one; Father, Son, and Spirit are modes within the single-person deity. Sabellius used the term *prosopa* to describe the modes of the Trinity, by which he meant "role" or "mask." In his view, Father, Son, and Holy Spirit are roles played or masks worn by the one true God. A third trinitarian heresy is *tritheism*—the belief that Father, Son, and Spirit are not one God but three separate deities.

A moment of clarity about the nature of God emerged in a formula proposed by Tertullian (c. 155—c. 220), which states that God is one substance and three persons (Latin: *una substantia et tres personae*). That is, Father, Son, and Spirit are three persons in one substance. A similar moment of clarification came in the Nicene Creed. This creed was produced by the Council of Nicaea in 325 and was reaffirmed (with some emendations) at the Council of Constantinople in 381. In essence the creed confesses that the Father, Son, and Holy Spirit are three *hypostases* in one being (Greek: *tres hypostaseis, mia ousia*). In Tertullian's (Latin) and Nicaea's (Greek) formulae, the church avoided direct contradiction in its claim that God is both three and one. In essence, the church asserted that God is one in one sense, but three in another sense. But the precise meaning of these formulae was (and sometimes still is) a matter of dispute. The terms *substantia* (Latin) and *ousia* (Greek) were sufficiently alike not to generate major controversy.

But the varied meanings of (Latin) *persona* and (Greek) *hypostasis* (both singular nouns) produced some problems. The Latin word *persona* did not convey the idea of an individual self that our contemporary English term *person* does. Rather, *persona* was a theatrical term. It expressed the idea of a role or of a mask. It referred to the role that an actor plays in a drama, or the mask an actor wears during a play. Thus in theological contexts, the term could be interpreted as saying that God is a single being who plays three different roles—of Father, Son, and Holy Spirit. Such a view was denied by the broad Christian community. It is unlikely, however, that Latin-speaking Tertullian intended this understanding of the term *persona*. He insisted that the Father, Son, and Spirit were simultaneous *personae* (persons) within the Trinity. Still, the connotation of the word *persona* with a mask or role made many Greek-speaking, Eastern theologians uncomfortable. On the other hand, the Greek singular noun *hypostasis* conveyed several meanings. Sometimes it was used synonymously with another Greek word, *ousia*, meaning "being" or "essence." This was Origen's understanding of the *hypostasis*, as well as the meaning employed in the original Nicene Creed. At other times, *hypostasis* meant "that which stands under a given set of properties." Thus, it conveyed the idea of a mode of being. Finally, sometimes *hypostasis* referred to an individual being. Gradually, the Latin *persona* and the Greek *hypostasis* came to be accepted as virtual synonyms, and the Western and Eastern Trinitarian formulations were thought to say essentially the same thing. But the precise meaning of these formulae periodically still generates theological controversy among Christians.[25]

Further controversies arose between Eastern and Western perspectives of the Trinity. One of these tensions was over the interrelationship between Father, Son, and Spirit. Eastern thought was deeply influenced by three thinkers from Cappadocia. These writers are often called the Cappadocian Fathers and include Basil of Caesarea (c. 329–398), Gregory of Nyssa (c. 335–395), and Gregory of Nazianzus (c. 329–389). The Cappadocian Fathers provided an influential model for understanding the relationship between the members of the Trinity—a model that especially became characteristic of the Eastern Church. While defending the full deity, equality, and unity of the three members of the Godhead (that the three have the same *ousia* or "essence"), the Cappadocians also emphasized key distinctions between the Three. They began by emphasizing the priority of the Father as the source or fountainhead (*monarchia*) of the Trinity. For them, the reality of the Father is imparted to the Son and the Holy

---

25. Much of the controversy over these varied terms flowed from the disconnect that often occurs when translating from one language to another. Eastern religious leaders were predominantly Greek speakers while religious authorities from the West primarily spoke Latin.

Spirit. While the Father is unbegotten, the Son is begotten by the Father, and the Spirit proceeds from the Father. Thus, while the three are all one *ousia* ("essence"), they are distinctive in their derivations. The Father is unbegotten, the Son is begotten of the Father, and the Spirit proceeds from the Father.

To avoid the objection that these claims makes the Son and Spirit creatures of the Father, Gregory of Nazianzus (basically following Origen [c. 184—c. 253]) argued that the Son is *eternally* begotten by and the Spirit *eternally* proceeds from the Father: thus, there never was a time when either did not exist. The Cappadocian formula of the Trinity was essentially affirmed in the Nicene Creed of 381, in which the Son is said to be begotten of the Father, and the Spirit is said to proceed from the Father. Partly in an attempt to avoid the charge of tritheism (affirmation of three gods), Gregory of Nyssa insisted that the actions of the Father, Son, and Spirit are unified or identical. Thus, whenever one acts, all three are acting too. This perspective eventually was endorsed by the church as a whole. It was expressed in terms of two concepts: *perichoresis* and *appropriation*. The Greek *perichoresis* is often translated into English as "mutual inter-penetration." The idea is that the three persons of the Trinity share the same life, share a communion of being. While each is a distinct person, each penetrates the other two and is penetrated by them. *Appropriation* refers to the action of all three persons in every act of the Godhead: any act by one member of the Trinity is simultaneously an act by all three. Emphasizing *perichoresis* (mutual interpenetration) can be seen as an attempt to avoid tritheism (the heresy of three gods); emphasizing *appropriation* (an act of one is an act of all three together) is more or less an attempt to avoid modalism (the heresy of one god with three separate modes or offices).

The Cappadocian formula differed from what would become the Western model of the Trinity in two key ways. First, it emphasized an *interpersonal* rather than an *intrapersonal* understanding of the Trinity. That is, the Cappadocians envisioned the Trinity more as a society of three persons and less as three aspects of one individual. By contrast, Augustine of Hippo (in the West) offered a more intrapersonal model of the Trinity—one based on the inner-workings of the human mind. In *De Trinitate (On the Trinity)*, Augustine wrestled with several analogies for the Trinity, but he found most helpful the analogy of the human mind as it directs its awareness upon God. According to Augustine, this analogy involves remembering, knowing, and loving God. Thus, Father, Son and Spirit are like the equal and interpenetrating faculties of a particular human's memory, understanding, and will (or love), as these faculties are directed toward God.[26] The Cappadocian interpersonal model became dominant in the Greek-speaking, Eastern Church while Augustine's intrapersonal model tended to dominate the Latin-speaking West.

The second difference between the Cappadocian formula of the Trinity and the Western formula has to do with the relationship between the Son and the Holy Spirit. The Cappadocians emphasized the role of the Father as the fountainhead of the Trinity,

26. Kelly *Early Christian Doctrines*, 276–78; and Kaiser, *The Doctrine of God*, 89

stressing that the Son is begotten by the Father and the Spirit proceeds from the Father. Augustine, however, perhaps innocently, endorsed the notion that the Holy Spirit proceeds both from the Father and the Son. He expressed this with the Latin phrase *filioque* which translates "and son." This seemingly subtle difference eventually generated a major controversy between the Eastern and Western Churches in the eleventh century, when Eastern leaders noticed that Western versions of the Nicene Creed had added the phrase *filioque* to the original creed. For Eastern theologians (then and now), such an addition undermined the unique role of the Father as the source or fountainhead of divinity. For Western writers, the Eastern formula failed to recognize that the Spirit is also called the Spirit of Christ in the New Testament, and it failed to recognize an intimate connection between Son and Spirit.

Philosophical Influences

A cursory examination demonstrates that Christian teachings about God have been influenced by philosophical speculation. Plato (428/427 or 424/423—348/347 BCE) argued that a truly perfect being cannot change because change involves becoming better or worse. A perfect being cannot get better (since it already is perfect), and it cannot be subject to the degradation of getting worse. Further, Plato argued that the greatest reality cannot be physical, for physical things can change, but perfect being cannot change. Also, the highest form of reality must be timeless. Since it undergoes no change, whatever it is, it always is. Consequently, perfect reality must exist in a singular, eternal moment, without temporal duration. In a similar manner, Aristotle (384–322 BCE) insisted that as the uncaused cause of all other things, God is pure actuality with no potential for change. Whatever the deity is, it simply is, always.

Such reasoning undergirds several Christian attributions to God. For example, many theologians have asserted that God is immutable (unchanging), impassible (not subject to suffering), *a se* (literally "of self"; that is, not affected by anything external to God), and eternal (timeless). Related attributes are these: God is *omnipotent* (all-powerful), *omniscient* (all-knowing), *omnipresent* (present everywhere), and perfectly good. Sometimes these various traits are summarized by saying that God is the most perfect Being. God is the ultimate, the very best and greatest that can be. Saint Anselm spoke of God in these terms. Others have summarized God's characteristics by saying that God is *infinite*. There is no limit to God's perfections and greatness. In addition to these traits, another attribute sometimes ascribed to God, not so much to summarize God's characteristics as to explain the deity's self-existence, is the attribute of *necessity*. That is, God's existence and core attributes are necessary. God is not a contingent being, but one that necessarily exists and necessarily has certain great-making qualities.

Creation and Providence

Christian theology claims God is Creator of all things that are not God. Further, God sustains all that is, perpetuating created reality (including our universe) in its ongoing existence. God also is sovereign over all. God has a plan and has the power and wisdom to work out that plan in the created order.

Creation

Several biblical passages point to God's creative activities (Gen 1:1—2:4a; 2:4b–25; 14:19, 22; Prov 8:22–31; Isa 40:28; 42:5; 45:12; 18; John 1:3; Acts 4:24; 14:15; Col 1:16–17; Heb. 11:3; Rev 4:11). The first two accounts in the book of Genesis (both creation accounts) have played especially important roles in the development of the doctrine of creation. The first narrative describes the creation of the universe in six days as God simply commands "Let there be . . . ," and what the deity commands comes into being. Among the creatures created by God are humans, who are said to be made in the image of the divine. The second story especially focuses on the creation of humans. Each text offers variances not easily reconciled with the other. Throughout history, these narratives often have been taken to be literal descriptions of events in cosmic history, although Jewish and Christian interpreters have long recognized poetic and symbolic components in these writings. Below we discuss some of the problems faced by a literal, historical interpretation of these passages in the light of modern science.

A central claim of the Christian doctrine of creation is that God created out of nothing (*creatio ex nihilo*). God used no preexisting substances to bring the universe (in its initial state) into being. God simply willed or commanded, and the universe came into being. Such a view appears to have come gradually to the ancient Hebrew mind. The influential account of God's creating in Gen 1, where God forms and fills the earth in six days, does not explicitly state that God creates from nothing. Indeed, many biblical scholars see in that text vestiges of a common ancient notion that God created out of preexisting stuff. Still while the idea of *creatio ex nihilo* is not clearly stated in Gen 1, some Jewish and Christian thinkers feel that the doctrine is implied in the overall texture of the Old Testament Scriptures—particularly in the notion that God is the Creator of everything. If God creates everything, there is nothing from which this everything derives except God. The notion of *creatio ex nihilo* is first explicitly affirmed in the Apocryphal book of 2 Maccabees, chapter 7 and verse 28: "I beg you, my child, to look at the heaven and the earth and see everything that is in them, and recognize that God did not make them out of things that existed." The notion of creation out of nothing seems to be assumed by Rom 4:17 and Heb 11:3, and possibly by 2 Cor 4:6.[27]

---

27. There have been some dissenting voices throughout Christian history regarding creation out of nothing. Contemporary process theology has affirmed the primordial existence of the world *with*

In addition to claiming that God creates from nothing, the biblical use of the word "create" (*bara*) suggests that creation entails the continuing fashioning of the universe. Several Old Testament passages speak of God's creating events in and through the natural order. God creates individual humans (Ezek 21:30), people groups (Ps 102:18), individual animals (Ps 104:24–30), the nation of Israel (Isa 43:1, 7, 15), and so forth This usage suggests that while in an ultimate sense God created out of nothing, God's creative activities also apply to events occurring through natural processes. God is, in some sense, immanent in the processes of the world. Augustine highlighted this view, affirming what he called "rational seeds" that God "implanted" in the original creation, which gradually emerge over time.[28] An idea closely associated with the doctrine of continuing creation is that God sustains the universe. Perhaps the clearest statement of this view appears in Heb 1:3: The Son "is the reflection of God's glory and the exact imprint of God's very being, and he sustains all things by his powerful word." Thus, while the created order is distinct from and quasi-independent of God, it is utterly subject to God's will for its continued existence. Once created, the created order is not now a reality or force out of God's control or divorced from God's direct activity. God's action is necessary for the continued existence of the created order.

A typical affirmation of the Christian doctrine of creation is that God created freely. God's creative acts are not necessary. They do not follow necessarily from God's nature, nor is the deity externally compelled to create. Creation is a free act of God's will. A further claim of the doctrine of creation is the created order is essentially good. Contrary to some forms of metaphysical dualism that affirm an eternally evil world-substance that God molds or shapes, the Christian doctrine of creation typically insists that the existence of all things ultimately comes from God, and since God is good, all that God creates is good (at least initially). This seems to be implied in the Gen 1 account in God's judgements about the various phases of creation. After each step of creation, God declares that what was made is good (Gen 1:4, 10, 12, 18, 21, 25, 31). Indeed, Augustine,[29] Aquinas[30] and others argue that all that God has created remains intrinsically good even after the emergence of sin among creatures. That is: to exist, to have being, is good. Evil is a privation of being, a lack of being. Moral evil is understood as loving or favoring a lesser reality more than a higher reality. Of course, God is the highest Being.

An interesting question that arises from the doctrine of creation is, what kinds of beings has God made? Clearly, the scriptural tradition holds that God created the physical universe and the beings of that world. God created the sun, moon,

---

God. See Cobb and Griffin, *Process Theology*, 65. But the major Christian tradition has been to affirm *creatio ex nihilo*.

28. Augustine, *De Genesi ad litteram*, 6.5.8 (quoted in Copleston, *Mediaeval Philosophy, Part 1*, 91).

29. Augustine, *Concerning the Nature of Good, Against the Manichaeans*.

30. Thomas Aquinas, *Summa Theologica*, 1.5.3; 1.48.1–5.

stars, plants, animals, humans, and so forth. But the overall texture of the biblical materials also suggests that God created nonphysical (purely spiritual) beings as well—such as angels, demons, and the devil. The precise origin, nature, number, and kinds of spiritual beings are not clearly described in the scriptural tradition; and these have been the topic of much speculation among Christian (and Jewish) theologians. We cannot entertain these discussions here. Suffice it to say that a general consensus has emerged in Christian thought that God, as creator of all, created whatever spiritual beings there are—including angels and malevolent beings such as the devil and demons. The consensus also has formed that when God first created beings like the devil or demons, they were intrinsically good but became morally evil by somehow turning away from God.

The Doctrine of Creation and Contemporary Knowledge

Can the Christian doctrine of creation be reconciled with modern science? Answering this question partly depend on how one understands the dilemma. For some the issue is whether there is any room for supernatural influence in the natural world. Some philosophers insist that the universe is a closed system, and that every event that occurs is explainable exclusively in terms of natural physical causation. There simply is no room for divine causality is such a system. Most Christian theologians reject such claims. Rather, they assume that God causally influences the cosmos. Of course, opinions vary over when, where, and how divine influence occurs. Eighteenth century deists rejected the idea that God causally influences natural processes after the initial creation, but they believed the deity brought the universe into existence. Many classic liberals hesitated to say God truncates natural processes to miraculously intervene in history. But most of them believed, not only that God created the universe, but that the deity's sway is *immanent within* cosmic processes. Conservative theologians tend to believe, not only that God created the universe, and that God's influence is inherent in cosmic processes, but also that occasionally the deity interrupts natural processes and miraculously affects the physical world. Thus, if by the opening question of this section one means, Is divine causal influence upon the cosmos possible? most theologians would say yes.

But there is a second possible interpretation of the question, is the doctrine of creation compatible with modern science? One may mean, Is the *description* of divine creation in the Bible, especially Gen 1, compatible with modern science? Or more precisely, Is the description of the age and chronological development of the universe in Gen 1 harmonious with the current scientific understanding of that evolution? Certainly at first glance, the two accounts are significantly different. Contemporary scientific cosmology holds that the universe is about ten to fifteen billion years old, developing to its current state over many millennia. With this assessment comes a complex understanding of the chronological development of the universe. Astrophysics argues that the universe emerged from a huge cosmic explosion that spewed atomic particles into an expanding time-space nexus. As these particles cooled, atoms formed and eventually coagulated into vast systems of swirling gases, which eventually formed stars, and eventually solar systems; over billions of years, various forms of life developed on this planet from relatively simple biological systems to progressively complex structures. When compared with the Gen 1 account, the scientific explanation is quite different. When read as a straightforward historical and chronological description of creation, Gen 1 leaves the impression that the universe, earth, and life upon the earth were created over a relatively short period of time (six days). Further, the Genesis narrative suggests a rather different chronological order of development from the scientific understanding. For example, according to Gen 1 the earth was created before the sun, moon, and stars. (Compare Gen 1:2, 3 with Gen 1:14–19.)

These differences have fostered diverse responses from theologians. Some attempt to interpret the biblical perspective so that it more or less fits with the main teachings of science. For example, *the age day theory* proposes that the six days of Genesis 1 represent great expanses of time rather than literal twenty-four-hour periods; during these expanses God gradually developed the universe as is purported by science. (One problem with such an approach is it fails to do justice to an historical-grammatical reading of the Genesis text.) Other Christians endeavor to interpret the scientific evidence so that it somehow supports the cosmic age and development implied in the biblical narrative. Proponents of this view, sometimes called *scientific creationists* allege that the scientific data confirm a six-literal-day creation. Most scientists (and theologians) disagree, and they believe the creationist theory plays loose and fast with the empirical evidence.

Most theologians opt for a different approach to solving the incongruities between Gen 1 and science. They insist that the biblical and the scientific accounts simply represent two different kinds of explanation. Science looks for and offers explanations of things in terms of *efficient cause*, answering questions like What physical events caused other physical events? And, when did various events occur? On the other hand, the Genesis 1 account, as a religious narrative, offers explanations in terms of *final causation*, answering questions like For what purpose did the universe come into existence? And, what is the ultimate meaning of human and cosmic existence? Hence, the two explanations (scientific and religious) are answering dissimilar questions.[31]

This difference is analogous to the distinction between (on the one hand) describing the physiology of the brain and nervous system when two people fall in love, and (on the other hand) describing this same event using the language of romance. The ancient writers did not have the tools of science necessary to study and describe the various physical and biological processes that brought about the world they knew, but they did possess the linguistic tools (and personal experiences) needed to express the value and the meaning of life in light of their ancient understanding of natural

31. One progenitor of this view is Gilkey in *Maker of Heaven and Earth*.

processes. Often their ancient "scientific" beliefs were inaccurate, but their under-standing of the significance and meaning of life was essentially correct. For example, some biblical texts ascribe mental life to the kidneys (Jer 11:20; Rev 2:23) or love to the bowels (Phil 1:8). Contemporary science attributes the physical production of such experiences to the brain and nervous system. Even though the ancient writers were incorrect in placing the origins of such mental states in bodily organs, these writers were correct about the value and meaning of these emotions in a person's life and in a person's relationship with God and others. In a similar manner, the ancient writers may not have understood the details of the processes of cosmic evolution, but they may have fully comprehended that whatever the processes are, their meaning and value is grounded in God. (Indeed, the only way they could have talked about natural processes was in terms of the "science" of their day. Otherwise their contemporary audiences would not have understood what they were saying about nature or about God.) Through the images of their day, these writers were (and perhaps God was) able to convey the deeper truths about the natural world—namely, that the world has come from God and finds its meaning in God. Thus, according to this approach, a contemporary reader must not interpret Gen 1 as a set of scientifically informative truths but rather as a poetic account that conveys religious truths—truths concern-ing the ultimate source and purpose of the universe and of humans, as well as truths concerning ultimate values and ethical obligations.

Obviously, this third approach to reconciling the scriptural and scientific accounts of cosmic development offers many advantages to theologians; indeed, it is a perspec-tive that this author tends to favor. But a number of problems with this tactic can be cited. One drawback is that it is not clear that religion and science are totally different realms of thought, or that they have no impact on each other. On the one hand, it is not obvious that information about natural processes or natural events has no bearing on religious viewpoints. For example, unlike ancient writers, we do not now consider the heart to be the literal source of thought or emotion. Rather, we understand the connection between the heart and emotions (and thoughts) to be metaphorical, due to contemporary science's understanding of the nervous system and its connection to emotions. On the other hand, it is not apparent that core religious claims in no way influence one's interpretation of natural processes or natural events. At the core of the Christian faith is the claim that Jesus Christ was raised, bodily, from the dead. This often is understood to be a claim about a natural, historical, physical event. But if this is correct, one has an example of a religious claim that also is a profound claim about natural processes—namely, that a physical event transpired that is highly unusual and grossly outside typical natural processes. The relationship between science and the Christian faith is highly complex, and its many puzzles cannot be resolved here. In Chapter 13 of this book we examine some of these matters in greater detail. But even there we can only scratch the surface of the issues.

Providence

The doctrine of providence affirms that God *sustains* the created order in its existence from moment to moment, and effectively *governs* that world toward the purposes God intends. As pointed out in our discussion of the doctrine of creation, Christian theology often affirms that God sustains the ongoing existence of the created order through time. Created reality is completely subject to God's will that it continues to exist and to God's power of maintaining its existence from moment to moment. The doctrine of divine sustenance helps differentiate Christian theology from deism, which often says that God created the universe but then "stood back" and allowed it to run on its own natural power. Rather, typically Christian theology teaches that God perennially sustains the universe's existence.

In addition to claiming that God sustains the universe, the doctrine of providence also teaches that God has a plan for how the events of creation-history are to unfold and deliberately moves creation toward those goals. Portions of the Bible seem to teach that God's plan is all-inclusive. The divine plan includes events that happen to whole people groups (Isa 37:26) and to individuals (Ps 139:16), including to the wicked (Prov 16:4; Matt 26:24; Mark 14:21). Further, God's plan is efficacious. What God plans, comes to be. It cannot be circumvented (Isa 14:24, 27; 46:10). Further, the doctrine of providence typically insists that God governs the created order so that God's plan is fulfilled. Portions of the Bible also seem to teach that God's governing pertains to every detail of the created order—for example, to events in nature (Ps 135:5–7; Matt 5:45), to the actions of animals (Ps 104:21–29), to national events (Isa 10:5–12; Dan 2:21; Acts 17:26), to the fortunes of human life (1 Sam 2:6–7; Ps 31:14–15), to the choices made by humans (1 Sam 24 ; Prov 19:21), even to evil events (2 Thess 2:10–12).

The doctrine of God's all-inclusive plan and governance generates three interrelated problems. These are the problem of creaturely freedom, the problem of creaturely responsibility, and the problem of Creator-creature interactions. If God's plan and governance are all-inclusive, and if created entities cannot in any way circumvent God's plan and control, it is difficult to explain how creatures are free. Created beings cannot do other than God plans and controls. In turn, if creatures are not free, it is difficult to see how or why they are responsible for their actions. Further, if creatures are not responsible for their actions, who is? The only truly free agent appears to be God. Hence, God appears to be responsible for all human action, including sin. Finally, if God's plan is all-inclusive, and if this plan was envisioned by God prior to any creature existing, then it is difficult to understand how God and creatures genuinely interact. For example, if prayer can affect what God does, it seems that the divine plan is not all-inclusive after all. On the other hand, if God's plan is unchanging, then it is hard to understand how prayer in any way can affect God's actions.

God Alone Causes Events

Several theological theories have emerged attempting to explain divine-creaturely interaction. Some theologians have argued (or at least seem to imply) that God is the only true cause of all that happens. Medieval *occasionalism* argued that there are no genuine causal connections between creaturely events, but that from moment to moment God directly causes objects to move so as to appear to be in causal relations.[32] These motions are occasions for God's direct causal action on the world. Some interpretations of Calvinism border on saying that God alone is the cause of all that happens. Jonathan Edwards (1703–1758) affirmed what he called *creatio continua*—the notion that God creates all things new from moment to moment. Such a theory seems to imply that God is the only genuine cause of creaturely events.[33] John Calvin's own position on these matters is less clear. Calvin held that God decides or ordains all that happens, including what creatures think, will, and do. Concerning salvation, Calvin insisted that God decides prior to and without regard to the actions of creatures who will be saved and who will not be saved. According to Calvin, faith is a God-given grace and not a human action. Thus, the believer believes only because God enables him or her to believe. In turn, divine foreknowledge of creaturely events is based on God's will. Because God's will determines what creatures do, in knowing God's own will, God also knows (by determining) what creatures will do. Many see Calvin's view as ultimately leading to the notion that God is the sole actor.[34] A problem with such views is that they deny human freedom and responsibility, and they imply that God is the direct cause of evil and sin. Further, these views effectively deny genuine Creator-creature interaction. God seems to be the only acting agent.

Double Agency or Concurrence (God and Creatures Cause Events)

A number of theologians have taught that God's actions and creaturely actions concur with one another so that any given event in the created order appropriately may be ascribed both to God and creatures. In other words, any event in creation is caused both by God and by an element or agent within the created order. Thomas Aquinas seems to have endorsed something like this view. He argued that God knows all possibilities, and that God chooses to actualize one set of these possibilities, thus causing a particular history of the created order to unfold. Nevertheless, in knowing all possibilities, God also knows the creaturely causes necessary to bring about the actualities that God wants. And so, in willing a set of possibilities to be actualized, God also

---

32. One author of this view was Nicholas Malebranche (1638–1715).

33. Edwards writes: "God's upholding created substance, or causing its existence in each successive moment, is altogether equivalent to an immediate production out of nothing, at each moment . . . So that this effect differs not at all from the first creation, but only circumstantially" (Edwards, *Original Sin*, 402).

34. Calvin, *Institutes of the Christian Religion*, 1.15–18; 2.1–3.

wills the creaturely causes necessary to produce these events. As these events unfold, both God and creatures cause what happens in creation-history. God is the primary cause; creaturely elements and agents are the secondary causes. Thomas further asserts that among the creaturely causes that God wills are free agents who freely choose to actualize certain events. By labeling an event and agents as free, Thomas means that such an event cannot be predicted based on previous events. In other words, an event is free if it is undetermined by previous causes. There is tension in Thomas's system. On one hand, Thomas insists that it is not possible to know with certainty what a free creature is going to do until after the creature has acted. This is because a free event is one that is not completely determined by previous events. On the other hand, Thomas assumes that in choosing a set of possibilities to actualize, God knows with certainty what a free creature will choose.[35] But this contradicts his belief that one cannot know with certainty what a free creature is going to do until after the creature has done it. Thus, Thomas's view of freedom seems to undermine his explanation of divine-creaturely concurrence.[36]

God Sustains and Creatures Cause Events

Yet another set of theories about divine-creaturely interactions insists that God is not the direct cause of creaturely events; rather God simply sustains creatures in their existence, while creatures themselves exercise their God-given powers of self-action and will. One such theory is Molinism. Molinism arose out of the thought of Luis de Molina (1535–1600).[37] Followers of Molina argue that God's creative actions do not influence the human will directly. Instead, God only sustains the created agent per se, allowing that agent to willfully act in diverse ways. In other words, God sustains a creature in its existence, enabling it to exercise its own powers freely. According to Molinism, freedom is the ability to choose between contrary desires, and not merely to choose what one most strongly desires. That is, freedom is the capacity to be self-determined rather than determined by previous causes.

A problem immediately arises for Molinism: How does God ensure that the divine will and plan are accomplished? Molinism attempts to answer this question by introducing the concept of *middle knowledge*. Molinism insists that in addition to knowing all possibilities, God also knows all conditional truths. That is, God knows the truth of every proposition that begins with the word *if*: If such and such a circumstance occurs, then such and such a consequence or event will follow. Hence God knows not only what could happen (possibilities), but what would happen given any particular set of circumstances (middle knowledge). According to Molinism, middle

35. Thomas Aquinas, *Summa Theologica* 1.14.

36. For a further discussion and critique of Thomas's approach to divine providence, see Robinson, *Eternity and Freedom*, 48–62.

37. Molina, *On Divine Foreknowledge*.

knowledge combined with knowledge of God's own will gives God a perfect knowledge of the future and complete control of future events. Nevertheless, Molinism claims that creatures remain free because God's middle knowledge is not based on previous causes; rather it is simply an intuitive knowledge that God has. A key problem with Molinism is that it cannot clearly explain how God is able to have middle knowledge. How can one know with complete certainty what a genuinely free creature will choose in any given circumstance? At best, Molinism must appeal to the mystery of God's knowledge. At worst, Molinism may be judged to be incoherent.[38]

Arminianism is another theory that claims that God merely sustains creatures while creatures exercise their own free will. Arminian theologians agree with Molinism that God simply sustains creatures in their existence, and that creatures act with their own genuine power. Arminians, however, describe differently how God plans and governs. They insist that God simply approves those events that God foreknows are going to happen. Thus, God's plan is based on God's foreknowledge. Concerning salvation, Arminians insist that those whom God foreknows will believe in Jesus are those whom God wills to save. In like manner, those events that God knows are going to happen in the future are those that God wills to occur. God simply acquiesces to these events. Since God knows the whole future, God is able to will or approve all that is going to unfold.[39] A central problem with Arminianism is that while it makes room for creaturely freedom and responsibility, it does not clearly affirm God's total control over creation. One is left wondering: How can God ensure that God's plan and will are going to be accomplished in each moment of creation-history? God does not seem to ensure that the divine will is done, but only seems to accept whatever is going to happen.

A third theory affirming that God merely sustains while creatures freely cause their own actions is one that rejects that God foreknows or predestines the future. According to some writers, God's providence may be likened to human governing and planning. God knows what God intends to do. God has a good idea of how to implement the divine plan. And as time passes, God works out the details of that plan in an active interplay with genuinely free creatures. Among theologians affirming such a view are process theologians Charles Hartshorne,[40] David Griffin, and John Cobb Jr.[41] Also, nonprocess theologians such as Peter Geech,[42] Richard Swinburne,[43] Clark Pinnock, William Hasker, and John Sanders[44] affirm similar

---

38. For a brief critique of Molinism, see Robinson, *The Storms of Providence*, 212–29.

39. See Arminius, "A Declaration of the Sentiments of Arminius."

40. Hartshorne, *The Divine Relativity*; and Hartshorne, *A Natural Theology for Our Time*.

41. Cobb, *God and the World*.

42. Geach, *Providence*.

43. Swinburne, *The Coherence of Theism*.

44. See, Pinnock, et al., *The Openness of God*. See also Hasker, *God, Time, and Knowledge*; and Sanders, *The God Who Risks*.

views. This approach to providence faces a number of puzzles, including the following: While such views affirm creaturely freedom, responsibility, and interactions with God, they do not clearly handle what seems to be the biblical affirmation of both divine foreknowledge of and divine planning and control over all events. Countering this criticism, proponents of these views insist that traditional affirmations of a complete, all-inclusive divine plan or of exhaustive divine foreknowledge are not necessarily taught in the Bible. One writer notes:

> As it actually functions in the Bible, prophecy is primarily an expression, not of divine knowledge, but of divine agency. Its major purpose is not to provide information about the future, although it may indeed do that. Rather, its major purpose is to express God's intentions to act in certain ways and to assure people that God is directly involved in their lives. Accordingly, when God makes a prediction, his perspective is not that of a passive observer, but of an active participant. He states that certain things will happen because he intends to bring them about.[45]

Detractors of this view, however, contend that the Bible in fact teaches that God knows the future and not just that God knows the divine intentions.

Appeal to Mystery

A final theory concerning divine-creaturely interactions insists that the relationship between divine and creaturely actions is simply a mystery. G. C. Berkouwer argued that the Christian must simply affirm in faith that God is in complete control of all that happens and that humans are genuinely free.[46] Beyond this one cannot go. For many, the problem with such an approach is that it is rationally dissatisfying.

Conclusion

Christianity is grounded in four core foundations: a sacred story, a sacred text, a sacred person, and a sacred community. From these foundations, Christians have formed many of their central teachings. These teachings often are called doctrine or theology. In this third chapter, we have discussed four important doctrines of Christian theology: revelation, God, creation, and providence. In the next four chapters, we consider Christian teachings regarding humanity, sin, Jesus Christ, salvation, the church, and last things.

---

45. Rice, "Divine Foreknowledge," 134–35.
46. Berkouwer, *The Providence of God*, 133–41.

4

Humans and Sin

IN THE PREVIOUS CHAPTER, we examined four chief teachings of Christianity—the doctrines of revelation, God, creation, and providence. In the next four chapters we explore Christian beliefs about humanity, sin, Jesus Christ, salvation, the church, and last things. Before addressing these latter doctrines separately, it will be helpful to show how they are interconnected. Christians believe that as the Lord created the cosmos as a whole, God also created humans. Humanity faces a great dilemma. In spite of the fact that humans have been created by God and are intrinsically good, evil has emerged from them. They have sinned and have become sinners (beings prone to sin); as a result, they have been alienated from God's good intensions for them. Worse still, humans are incapable of overcoming their sinful tendencies and their alienation from God. But God has not left them to their own devices. In love, the deity has devised a plan for overcoming human sin and its consequences, and now is operating that plan toward fruition. Central to God's plan is Jesus Christ. Through Christ, God has accomplished core elements of the divine plan to save humanity. The nature of this salvation is multifaceted and mysterious, involving changes both to the moral and to the ontological character of humans. Among these altered characteristics are life everlasting and the propensity to be good. This salvation is not merely individualistic; it includes the formation of a community of persons being re-formed by God—namely, the church. The church is both the product and an instrument of God's saving activities. That is, it is both the community saved by God and a means by which God brings others to salvation. The doctrine of last things (often called *eschatology*) points toward the end-game of God's plan for humanity. It describes the fulfillment of divine salvation—including the formation of renewed individuals, a renewed community, and (ultimately) a renewed world. In this fourth chapter, we examine the Christian doctrines of humanity and of sin. In the following section, we begin by examining core Christian teachings about human beings.

Humans

As we have seen, the doctrine of creation holds that God creates all that is not God. Thus, God creates whatever exists, including physical and spiritual realities. Among the creatures are humans.

Humans as Creatures of God

From the claim that humans are creatures of God, several important implications immediately arise. *First, humans are dependent beings.* Humans are not necessary. We could have failed to be. Ultimately, we exist only because God freely has willed it. Further, we are not self-sufficient. Even after we come into existence, we continually depend on God for our existence. Indeed, we depend on many things in order to continue existing. We depend on air to breathe, food to eat, the laws of physics to function. And ultimately all of these depend upon God. Humans (like the rest of the created order) are dependent beings. *Second, humans have a purpose.* Some philosophies deny purpose to the universe and to humanity. For example, the ancient Greek philosopher Democritus (c. 460—c. 370 BCE) taught that reality is tiny chunks of matter (called atoms) that randomly move through space and combine to form larger objects. Atoms have always existed and have always been moving, and there is no particular reason for their existence or movement. Consequently, there is no ultimate purpose or explanation for the universe or for humans. Similar ideas are expressed by the nineteenth-century philosopher Friedrich Nietzsche (1844–1900):

> In some remote corner of the universe, poured out and glittering in innumerable solar systems, there once was a star on which clever animals invented knowledge. That was the haughtiest and most mendacious minute of "world history"—yet only a minute. After nature had drawn a few breaths the star grew cold, and the clever animals had to die . . . One might invent such a fable and still not have illustrated sufficiently how wretched, how shadowy and flighty, how aimless and arbitrary, the human intellect appears in nature. There have been eternities when it did not exist; and when it is done for again, nothing will have happened. For this intellect has no further mission that would lead beyond human life.[1]

Christianity denies these negative conclusions. The universe, including humans, has a purpose. It has been created by a personal and purposeful God. In turn, God decides what the purpose of the universe and of humans is.

A third implication of the claim that humans are created by God is that humans are essentially good. The conclusion of Gen 1 is that after God had created human beings, he declared not only that what was created is good, but that it is very good. Somehow

---

1. Nietzsche, "On Truth and Lies," quoted in Jones, *Kant and the Nineteenth Century*, 243.

the existence of human beings contributes to making a world that was already good even better. Even though humans are sinful (as we discuss below), humans are fundamentally good in at least two ways. First, what we are made of is good. Whatever components go into making us (the things that we are) are essentially good, including our material bodies. Second, how we are made is good. There is a beauty and craftsmanship to human beings that adds to and perhaps even surpasses the beauty and craftsmanship of the rest of the universe. As the psalmist says, we are "fearfully and wonderfully made" (139:14 KJV)

A fourth implication of the claim that humans are created by God is that the fundamental nature of humans is determined by God. There has been a long-running debate in theology about whether humans are free or not, whether God determines every aspect of our lives or not. Some traditions (such as Calvinism) hold that every aspect of our lives is determined by God—every thought, every action. Consequently, what we are is totally decided by God. Other traditions (like Arminianism) insist that some aspects of our lives are determined by us, by our free choices. Consequently, what we are is partially determined by God and partially determined by us. But even if we are free, and thus partly define ourselves, God determines our *fundamental nature*. That is, God creates us as the free beings that we are. And God sets the limits of our freedom. As pointed out earlier, all of us depend on things like air to breathe, food to eat, the laws of physics. None of us, by the power of his or her legs, can jump to the moon. We are finite and dependent beings. Even in our freedom, God determines our fundamental nature and limits of our freedom.

A fifth implication of humans being creatures of God is that humans are not the ultimate source of truth and value. Some philosophers contend that humans determine what is true and false, right and wrong, beautiful and ugly, significant and insignificant. The ancient Greek philosopher Protagoras (c. 490—c. 420 BCE) claimed that "man is the measure of all things,"[2] that humans determine what is and is not true. Friedrich Nietzsche contended that value is whatever the individual chooses to value; right and wrong is what the individual says is right and wrong.[3] But Christian theology maintains that humans are not the final arbiters of truth or value. There are claims that are true even if no human believes them; there are actions that are wrong, even if every human says they are right. Further, Christian theology contends that God is the final judge of truth and value. At very least, God knows what is true and what is valuable (even when we do not). And in many situations, God determines what is true and valuable.[4] *A sixth implication of humans being created by God is*

---

2. As quoted by Plato in *Theaetetus.*

3. Nietzsche, *Thus Spoke Zarathustra,* and *Beyond Good and Evil.*

4. The precise relationship between God, truth, and value is a philosophical puzzle. *Concerning value* (especially right and wrong), one may ask, Is something good because God loves it, or does God love it because it's good? (Plato asked this question; see *Euthyphro* in Plato, *Euthyphro, Apology, Crito, Phaedo.*) In other words, does God simply decide what is good, or are things simply good and God recognizes this? *Concerning truth*: Are some truths independent of God? Is logic something that

that the appropriate human response to God is gratitude: gratitude for our existence, goodness, nature, and purpose.

Humans as the Image of God

It is one thing to say that as creatures of God, humans have a nature and a purpose; it is another thing to describe what that nature and purpose are. Regarding these issues, a central claim of Christian theology is that humans are created in the *image of God*. But what does this mean? Several biblical passages speak of humans as image or likeness of God. The Old Testament literature especially uses the Hebrew words *selem* ("image," "shadow," or "statue") and *demut* ("likeness"). In Gen 1:26–27, God declares "Let us make humankind in our image (*selem*), according to our likeness (*demut*) . . . So God created humankind in his image, in the image of God he created him; male and female he created them." Gen 9:6 says, "Whoever sheds the blood of a human, by a human shall that person's blood be shed; for in his own image God made humankind." The New Testament often uses the word *eikon* ("image," "likeness"). Second Corinthians 3:18 states, "And all of us, with unveiled face, seeing the glory of the Lord as though reflected in a mirror, are being transformed into the same image from one degree of glory to another." Rom 8:29 proclaims, "For those whom he foreknew he also predestined to be conformed to the image of his Son." And Col 3:9–10 charges, "Do not lie to one another, seeing that you have stripped off the old self with its practices and have clothed yourselves with the new self, which is being renewed in knowledge according to the image of its creator." In a similar vein, using the Greek word *homoiosis* ("likeness," "image"), Jas 3:9 asserts that humans are "made in the likeness of God."

All the Old Testament passages mentioned above suggest that the divine image and likeness are things that humans have or are. Gen 9:6 particularly suggests that because of being made in God's image, humans have a special kind of dignity. Murder is condemned and capital punishment affirmed because humans are made in the divine image. Two of the New Testament passages above, 1 Cor 11:7 and Jas 3:9, also refer to the image or likeness as something humans have or are simply due to their creation. But 2 Cor 3:18, Rom 8:29, and Col 3:10 apparently refer to image as something toward which Christians are moving.

In the light of these passages, several interpretations of the image of God have been proposed throughout Christian history. A number of theologians have maintained that the divine image in humans refers to some essential property that all humans possess or are. In the Middle Ages, many theologians differentiated between "image" and "likeness" in Gen 1:6. For some, the *image* of God refers to key properties of human beings, such as reasoning and free will. *Likeness* refers to moral character

---

God must conform to, or does God create logic? Can God do the logically impossible? Or does logic restrict what God can do? For example, can God create a married bachelor or a square circle?

or actual moral righteousness. According to various medieval thinkers, the divine likeness was lost at the fall of humankind (see below). But the divine image was kept, though perhaps in a diminished form. Irenaeus (130–202 CE) was one of the first to make this distinction. He taught that image refers to human reason, moral freedom, and moral responsibility. Likeness, however, refers to the actual righteousness that humans had prior to the fall into sin.[5] *Augustine* associated image with reason, insisting that part of the image was lost, and part was retained after the fall.[6] *Thomas Aquinas* understood image as mind and free will, and likeness as virtue. He insisted that likeness was lost at the Fall; image was retained. Likeness was lost due to sin but can be regained through human effort.[7] A problem with this medieval view is that it strains the biblical evidence. Most modern biblical interpreters reject any strong dichotomy between *selem* ("image") and *demut* ("likeness") in Gen 1:26. Rather, the two terms seem to be a Hebrew parallelism. That is, they are essentially synonyms that have been placed together for emphasis.

During the Reformation a different interpretation of divine image emerged. In this view, image and likeness are essentially the same concept. In turn, the divine image (likeness) in humans is simply original innocence or moral perfection possessed prior to the fall of humankind in the garden of Eden. In other words, the divine image refers to our moral standing before God. The first humans were morally pure. But when they sinned, all humanity lost its innocence or righteous standing before God. Now only through Christ can that standing be restored. *Martin Luther* denied that sinful humans are free. Sin has enslaved us, and we cannot freely choose right or God. Luther insisted that the original divine image and likeness were lost through sin. Intellect and will remain, but they are *impaired* by sin. The divine image is being restored through Christ.[8] *John Calvin* essentially agreed with Luther. He affirmed the original moral perfection of Adam and insisted that the divine image was lost after the first sin. Perhaps inconsistently, Calvin also claimed that a remnant of the divine image still exists in humans. For Calvin, the image is being restored in individuals through Christ.[9] This view seems to fit well with Paul's use of the term "image" (Rom 8:29; 2 Cor 3:18; Col 3:10). But it does not fully comply with Gen 9:6 or perhaps Jas 3:9, where divine image or likeness seems to refer to something that humans still have or still are.

In the twentieth-century, neo-orthodox theologian *Karl Barth* added a new spin on the idea of divine image. Barth proposed that divine image refers to the unique human capacity to enter into interpersonal (I-Thou) relationships. According to Barth, this is the primary point of the male-female distinction and its connection to the concept of image of God (Gen 2:18–24). Barth sees the human male-female relationship

---

5. Irenaeus, *Against Heresies*, 5.6.1.

6. Augustine, *On the Trinity*, 14.4.

7. See Cairns, *The Image of God in Man*, 114–20. Also see Simango, "The Imago Dei."

8. Luther, *Lecturers on Genesis*, 1:60–70; 2:141.

9. Calvin, *Institutes of the Christian Religion*, 1.1.

as an analogy to the I-Thou relationship between the members of the Trinity. Thus, the primary importance of the male-female human distinction is not sexual but interpersonal.[10] While Barth offers interesting insights, it is not abundantly clear that interpersonal relationship captures all that the idea of divine image entails.

Another twentieth-century neo-orthodox theologian, *Emil Bruner*, distinguishes between the formal and material image of God in humanity. The formal image is the human capacity to be responsible before God. This aspect was not lost when humans sinned, and it is common to all humans. It is that aspect especially emphasized in the Old Testament. The material image refers to the actual moral character of humans. This actual moral conformity to God's moral-likeness is somehow lost to humans and can only be restored through Christ.[11]

A number of contemporary theologians retain the basic medieval idea that divine image refers to some essential property or properties that humans possess or are. Often these newer interpretations reject that medieval idea that image and likeness are different concepts. Rather, they simply recognize diverse aspects of the general concept of divine image or likeness. For example, *W. T. Conner* suggested that image refers to humans as "spiritual beings," which means we have the power of (a) intelligence and self-consciousness, (b) self-determination, (c) love, (d) moral consciences, and (e) "affinity for God." *Millard Erickson* affirmed what he calls a structural view of divine image in humans. Image describes what a human is rather than something that a human has or does. Erickson insists that the divine "image is the power of personality which make man like God, capable of interacting with other persons, of thinking and reflecting, and of willing freely."[12] A criticism of these various contemporary views of divine image might be that they are not fully compatible with Paul's writings on image as something that must be *restored*.

We may conclude this discussion of the divine image in humans by noting that no definitive consensus exists among Christians (especially Protestants) concerning the precise meaning of the term *the image of God*. Still, we may identify some important themes that this biblical concept seems to support. First, the divine image seems to refer both to something that humans are (or possess) and to something that humans should be, hope to be, or are becoming (in Christ). This follows from diverse biblical passages that imply one or the other of these ideas. Second, the divine image (especially in the New Testament) is closely related to moral righteousness—to right actions, attitudes, and thoughts. And this connection (between divine image and righteousness) may imply several truths both about what humans are and about what we should be (or are becoming) in Christ. *Regarding what humans are*, the connection of divine image to moral righteousness suggests that humans must have basic

10. Barth, *Church Dogmatics*, III/1, 184, 197–98.

11. Brunner, *Doctrine of Creation and Redemption*, 55–57, 60, 105–6.

12. Erickson, *Christian Theology*, 470. For further discussion of these models of divine image see Erickson, *Christian Theology*, 460–74.

characteristics that in principle allow us to be morally righteous. Among these basic characteristics are the following:

1. The ability to exercise free will. This is a controversial claim among Christian theologians. But many contend that the capacity for moral actions requires the ability to perform or refrain from performing the moral act in question. In short, to be capable of morality, humans must be free to choose between good and evil.

2. The ability to reason. In order to make decisions concerning right and wrong, humans must have a level of intelligence sufficient to deliberate over the choices to be made. A considerable degree of abstraction is needed in order to consider which action is best—including which action likely will bring about the greatest value.

3. The ability to relate interpersonally. While some moral decisions involve actions toward nonpersons (such as cutting down a tree, or marring a beautiful landscape), the most significant moral decisions involve actions toward other persons (such as physically wounding someone, stealing from another, lying to another, or breaking a covenant). Consequently, the connection between divine image and righteousness fits well with the notion that humans have the ability to interrelate with other persons, including God. To enter into personal moral relations with others may involve a number of things, such as caring for the needs and interests of the other, desiring what is best for the other, communicating with or seeking to communicate with the other, seeking like goals with the other and mutually working toward those goals, acknowledging the intrinsic value of the other, and so forth. Underlying all this is the assumption that humans are persons and that God is personal. Further, it is assumed that persons are intrinsically valuable, and that generally persons are more valuable than nonpersons. While all reality may be intrinsically valuable, persons have a value that generally transcends the value of nonpersons.[13]

4. The ability to exercise responsibility. Closely tied to the idea of moral freedom and idea of interpersonal relationships is the notion that humans are responsible for the moral choices that they make. Our choices are in some sense *responses* to the demands that moral righteousness makes upon us. Likewise, our choices are personal responses to the demands of a righteous, gracious, and personal God. Because God freely and graciously has created us, because God continues to bless us, because God does what is right, and because God is intrinsically the highest good, we are morally obligated to respond to God in a positive way. That is, we are obligated to do what God demands for two kinds of

---

13. Admittedly, the precise nature of being a person is not easy to characterize. Presumably, it involves some combination of the following traits: (1) consciousness and self-consciousness, (2) knowledge, (3) ability to communicate, and possibly (4) ability to experience emotion.

reasons: (1) because what God demands is right, and (2) because it is this good and benevolent God who demands it.[14]

Regarding what humans should be or are becoming, the connection of divine image to moral righteousness may also suggest that humans have a specific purpose and destiny. That purpose or destiny is that we become morally righteous. To say that humans have certain basic characteristics that could allow us to be morally righteous is not the same as saying that we *are* morally righteous. In fact, Christian tradition teaches that humans are not actually morally righteous. Humans sin and in fact are sinners. But through Christ human beings are becoming morally righteous. This is our purpose and destiny. Furthermore, it is important to notice that to be morally righteous does not simply mean doing what is right, doing good acts. Ultimately it means becoming good (or morally righteous) within ourselves—that is, becoming beings who freely and intrinsically choose what is right. Again, this is our purpose and our destiny. Finally, being morally righteous ultimately involves being in righteous personal relationships with other persons, including God. Being righteous is not simply freely choosing abstract good acts to perform, but freely choosing to be in a right relationship with other persons, including God.

The Components of Human Beings

In addition to proclaiming that humans are made in the image of God, Christian theology also wrestles with differing ideas concerning the composition of human beings. What are the basic parts of humans? Several biblical terms are used to describe the nature of humans. Among these words are the Hebrew *nepes* ("breath," "soul," "life"), *ruah* ("wind" or "spirit"), *basar* ("flesh" or "muscle"), and *leb* or *lebab* ("heart," center of thought and will); and the Greek *psyche* ("soul" or "life"), *pneuma* ("spirit," "wind," "breath"), *sarx* ("flesh"), *soma* ("body"), *kardia* ("heart," seat of thought, will, and decisions), and *nous* ("mind," "will," "intellect"). Such words

---

14. Something of a dilemma arises from the claim above that humans must possess certain core characteristics (such as free will, reason, capacity for interpersonal relations, and aptitude for responsibility) that allow them to have the potential to act morally and to be moral beings. The problem is that, de facto, many humans do not possess all these characteristics, and some possess them in lesser degrees than others. This partly is due to the fact that such abilities seem to be closely related to conditions of the human body (brain development especially)—so that humans whose bodies do not function in certain ways do not or cannot possess these abilities. Two broad responses are sometimes made to this quandary. One reply is that every human, as a soul/spirit being, *innately has these abilities* but simply *cannot manifest them* because of debilitating conditions of the body. Such is the view of Moreland and Rae in *Body and Soul*. Another response is to grant that because of certain conditions of the body, some humans neither possess nor manifest these characteristics. Nevertheless, each human ultimately has the *potential* to have these and manifest them either in this life through natural bodily growth or through God's ultimate granting of these abilities in some future state. This view is defended in Robinson, "Divine Image, Human Dignity, and Human Potentiality"; and Robinson, "Human Potentialism and Bioethics."

appear to have been used in nontechnical ways and were not placed in the context of well-thought-out theories of human nature.

Nevertheless, Christian history developed several basic theories of the human constitution. *Trichotomism* holds that humans consist of three main aspects: body, soul, and spirit. The body is physical and is an element shared by animals, plants, and humans. The soul involves the "psychological element." It is the seat of reason, emotions, and personal interrelations. Some animals have a "rudimentary soul," and by this are differentiated from plants. The human soul is more developed than the souls of animals. The spirit is a unique religious and moral element of humans and sets humans apart from both plants and animals. *Dichotomism* teaches that humans consist of two basic aspects: the body and the soul/spirit. The body is physical or material. The soul or spirit is immaterial, and it is immortal or at least capable of immortality. Dichotomists insist that the terms *soul* and *spirit* are essentially synonyms. Dichotomism was affirmed by the Council of Constantinople in 381 and was the primary view of the church throughout history. A third theory is *monism*. Monism affirms that humans are essentially a unity of a body and soul. Therefore, human nature cannot be divided. In monism, humans are complex and compound, but soul and body are essentially inseparable. According to this view, the biblical terms "body," "soul," and "spirit" simply reflect different perspectives on (or descriptions of) a singular entity or self. Thus, to be human is to be a body, and there is no disembodied human existence. Eternal life may be understood as either resurrected (bodily) life, a metaphor for existence in the memory of God, or some less tangible notion. A number of theologians, especially in modern times, have endorsed this monist understanding of the human constitution. Their motive partly stems from the growing scientific awareness of the close connection between thought life and the brain. Other writers insist that while human nature ultimately is a unity, it is possible for the spiritual aspect of humans to exist without the body until the two are united by God at the second coming of Christ (see the discussion below).

The Origin of the Soul

In addition to examining the elements that constitute humans, an important question remains concerning the origin of the soul. Several views have been affirmed by Christian theology. Influenced by Greek philosophy in the early centuries of the church, some theologians taught that the human soul is eternal. The soul has always existed and always will exist. Plato taught the doctrine of *recollection*—the notion that the human soul knows innate concepts (forms) by remembering these ideas from previous bodiless existence.[15] Thus, the soul exists prior to the birth of an individual. Following Plato, Origen of Alexandria (c. 184—c. 253) taught that the human

15. Plato, *Phaedo* and *Meno*, 108–76.

soul preexists an individual's body; at conception God connects the soul to a human body. Unlike Plato, however, Origen believed that the soul is created. It has always existed but only as the result of God's creative activity from all eternity. Origen's views regarding the soul's infinite past existence were rejected by most Christian believers.[16] Another, more widely accepted outlook, called *creationism*, claims that while the human body is a product of natural physical reproduction, the human soul is directly created by God at the moment of conception. Irenaeus,[17] Pelagius (fl. c. 390–418),[18] and Thomas Aquinas[19] taught this. A third perspective teaches that both the human body and human soul are generated at the moment of conception by natural physical reproduction. Thus, one's soul (as well as one's body) derives from one's parents. Tertullian as well as others endorsed this perspective. Each of these three theories of the origin of the soul assumes a dichotomy between soul and body; hence, for thinkers who endorse monism (see above) none of these theories captures the truth that an individual human is a psychosomatic whole.

Science and the Antiquity of Humanity

In addition to questions concerning the image of God and the constitutional nature of humans, the doctrine of humanity must wrestle with the age of the human race. A candid reading of Genesis suggests that Adam and Eve were historical figures, the first two humans to populate the planet. Further, the genealogies of the early chapters of Genesis suggest a relatively short period between Adam—the first human—and later human cultures, including ancient Israel. All of this is compounded by what appears to be an avowal by the apostle Paul that Adam was "the first human" (Rom 5:12–21; 1 Cor 15:21–22, 45). These affirmations seem directly to conflict with the present-day anthropological and geological understanding of the age and chronological development of the human species. Contemporary anthropology places North American Indian cultures as far back as 25,000 BCE, Cro-Magnon humans[20] back to 40,000 BCE, and Neanderthals from about 30,000–200,000 BCE. Cro-Magnons clearly used stone tools and produced art. Neanderthals buried their dead and showed other evidences of religious practices. Which of these life-forms were human? Were some of them human and others not? If so, who were the humans? And when and how did they emerge? All of this is complicated by the fact that the Genesis account attributes Neolithic practices to Adam, Eve, Cain, and Abel—that is, practices of agriculture,

---

16. Origen, *De Principiis*, 2.9.1. For commentary on Origen's views on these matters, see Wassen, "On Preexistence."

17. Irenaeus, *Against Heresies* 2.33.5.

18. See Garrett, *Systematic Theology*, 509. Pelagius, *Libellus fidei*, 9.

19. Thomas Aquinas, *Summa Theologica*, 1.90.3.

20. Often referred to as anatomically modern humans or early modern humans.

advanced tool making, shepherding, and so forth. But evidence for such activities only dates to about twelve thousand years ago.

A variety of solutions has been proposed to this tension between archeology and the biblical account, each proposal facing difficulties. Some so-called *scientific creationists*[21] reject the consensus of the scientific community regarding the antiquity of humans and attempt to reinterpret the empirical data to show that the data in fact support the late origins of the universe, of the earth, and of life on the planet, including of human beings. Obviously, such a scheme is not convincing to the majority of scientists.

A number of conservative Christian interpreters have endorsed a different theory sometimes called *pre-adamism*. This perspective accepts the scientific consensus that the universe is quite ancient and that life, including humanoid life, has long existed on earth. But this model proposes that many of the early human-like fossils are of species not fully human. Only the latest fossils, perhaps Cro-Magnons or a subgroup of them, constitute humans in the biblical sense. Pre-adamism takes various forms. One proponent of this view, Victor Pearce, identified the Adam of Eden with new Stone Age humans. Prior human-like forms were not fully human. But Adam and company were fully human, and (as the biblical narrative suggests) they were farmers and breeders who (as the fossil record suggests) arose only in the late Stone Age. Pearce believed that pre-adamic human-like creatures died out prior to the divine creation of Adam from the dust of the ground.[22] In a similar manner, Evangelical theologian Millard Erickson advocates for a form of pre-adamism in which God created humans by divine fiat roughly thirty thousand years ago, at which point the broad story of Genesis 2–4 unfolds. For Erickson, human life did not properly emerge until the ascendency of language, which Erickson places around 30,000 BCE. According to Erickson, human-like creatures prior to this were not fully human, apparently including those beings that made tools and buried their dead from two hundred fifty thousand to fifty thousand years ago.[23] Pearce's and Erickson's theories face numerous problems. One problem is this: It is difficult to understand the burial activities of groups like Neanderthals, if they were not religious in nature. And if Neanderthals and their practices were religious, how could God justly exclude such beings from a divine-human relationship? Further, there now is evidence of interbreeding of the various forms of pre-Cro-Magnon humans, interbreeding that is echoed in modern human DNA encoding.

Both Pearce and Erickson see the creation of modern humans as a direct, miraculous, act of God: to their way of seeing things, the emergence of humans was significantly severed from the natural evolutionary process—that is, human derivation was disconnected from descent from earlier animal and humanoid life. Other pre-adamist

---

21. Discussed further in Chapters 3 and 13.

22. Pearce, *Who Was Adam?*

23. Erickson, *Christian Theology*, 448–51.

Christian writers see the arrival of modern humans (those created in God's image) as arising from natural evolutionary processes—so that humans biologically descended from earlier forms of prehuman animals. But even here, differences appear in the degree of divine intervention in the natural processes. Early twentieth-century Baptist theologian Augustus Strong proposed that modern humans descended through natural evolutionary processes from prior prehuman animals; nevertheless, at their arrival, God implanted a distinctive human soul within them so that they might be uniquely the image of God.[24] Other writers—including Earnest Messenger,[25] Emil Brunner,[26] and C. S. Lewis[27]—propose that humans evolved through natural processes from prior prehuman forms, and that at a key point in this evolution God set them apart as beings made in the divine image. Often this moment of distinction is associated with the natural emergence of self-awareness.[28] God did this without supernaturally infusing some extra feature into them—such as a uniquely designed human soul.

A third theological approach to the question of human antiquity is to insist that the biblical and the scientific accounts of the emergence of humans simply represent two different kinds of explanation. Science gives explanations in terms of *efficient cause*; the ancient biblical narrative offers explanations in terms of *final causation*. Thus, the accounts of the creation of humans (and of the fall of humanity into sin) cannot be taken as descriptions of literal historical events, but as poetic narratives designed to express profound insights regarding the spiritual or religious nature and propensities of all humans. The stories of Adam, Eve, Abel, Cain, and other protagonists of Genesis 1–11 are metaphorical descriptions of what effectively happens to all humans throughout history. There is often is overlap between this perspective and those mentioned in the paragraph immediately above. Obviously this third interpretation echoes the one discussed in Chapter 3, an interpretation that seeks to reconcile science and the biblical narratives about general creation.

Sin

We turn now to examine Christian beliefs regarding sin. The doctrine of sin is one of the more complicated (and at times controversial) sets of teachings in Christian theology. Christianity assumes that humans sin. Indeed, Christians typically teach that all humans sin.[29] From such simple (almost obvious) claims, several deeper questions surface, including these:

24. Strong, *Systematic Theology*, 466–67.

25. Messenger, *Evolution and Theology*.

26. Brunner, *The Christian Doctrine of Creation and Redemption*.

27. Lewis, *The Problem of Pain*.

28. See Ramm's comments in Ramm, *The Christian View of Science and Scripture*, 319.

29. Several biblical passages lend weight to this idea: Gen 6:5; Ps 53:1–3; 143:2 Prov 20:9; Eccl 7:20; Isa 53:6; Rom 3:22–23; 5:12; and Eph. 2:3.

1. What is the nature of sin?

2. What is the origin of sin?

3. If all humans sin, why?

4. What are the consequences of sin?

5. Why does God tolerate sin (and evil in general)?

The Nature of Sin

We begin by examining the nature of sin. The Bible does not give a precise definition of *sin*. Rather, several words describe it, each giving a different insight into sin's
character. These concepts may be grouped in various ways. Here is one schema. *First,
several biblical terms for sin imply a breach of God's law or standards*. The most common words for this are *hata'* in Hebrew and *hamartanein* in Greek, each meaning
"missing the mark." In this context, the idea is that humans (deliberately or unintentionally) miss the mark of God's standards. Related words are *'avar* in Hebrew[30]
and *paraptoma* in Greek.[31] Often these words are translated "transgressions," the core
idea being crossing over or deviating from a standard. Two other important Greek
concepts are *anomia*[32] (lawlessness—pointing to a general disregard for the divine
law) and *adikia*[33] (unrighteousness). *A second set of words depicts sin as breach of
covenant or trust*. Several Hebrew words emphasize this aspect of sin: *parar*[34] ("to
break off"), *'avar* ("to pass over God's covenant relation"), and *ma'al*[35] ("to break faith
with the divine covenant"). In the New Testament the Greek word *parapiptō* serves
a similar purpose (see Heb 6:6). A central concern of the Old Testament is that God
entered into a covenant relationship with Israel, but Israel was unfaithful. In both the
Old and New Testaments, this concern over a covenant breach becomes a tool for
conceptualizing more generally the tension between God and humanity. God calls
humans to an interpersonal, covenantal relationship, but humans are unfaithful to
that call. *A third set of biblical terms speaks of sin as rebellion*, including the Hebrew
words *pasha'* (2 Kgs 12:19; Isa 1:2), *marah* (Isa 1:20), and *marad* (Ezek 2:3), and the
Greek word *apostenai* (Luke 8:13; Heb 3:12). Finally, an interesting insight into sin is
suggested by the occasional use of the Hebrew word *'awah* ("bent" [Gen 4:13; Prov
12:8]), implying perhaps a person is warped by his or her own sin. Often the uses of

---

30. See Num 14:41–42; Deut 17:2; Hos 6:7; Jer 34:18; and Dan 9:1.

31. See Matt 6:14–15; Mark 11:25; Rom 4:25; 5:15–18, 20; 11:11–12; 2 Cor 5:19; Gal 6:1; and Eph
1:7; 2:1.

32. See Matt 7:23; 13:41; 24:12; 2 Thess 2:1–12; and 1 John 3:4

33. See Rom 1:18, 29; 2:8; 3:5; 2 Thess 2:10, 12; Heb 8:12; and 2 Pet 2:13, 15.

34. See Lev 26:15–16; Deut 17:2; 31:20; Isa 24:5; 33:8; and Jer 31:32; 33:20.

35. See Num 5:12, 27; and Josh 7:1; 22:20.

all these concepts of sin carry with them the idea of a personal affront against God, and not merely the breaking of some arbitrary moral standard. The sinner is undermining an interpersonal relationship with God.

Several terms are used to speak of sin in the Bible. But what is the essence of sin? A number of suggestions have been made. Not surprisingly, one view is that sin primarily is the breaking of divine commands, including especially the breaching of a covenant relationship with God. As just noted, many of the words used to describe sin in the Bible point to the breaking of a divine command or the breach of an interpersonal covenant with God. An immediate problem with such a definition of sin, however, is that it seems to assume some knowledge of God's laws or of God's covenant. A typical assumption of moral thought is that persons should not be held culpable for disobeying moral rules if they do not know those rules or have no means of knowing them. And it appears that many humans (indeed most) have not heard the divine law or the covenant as found in the Old or New Testaments. So how can such persons be accountable for their disobedience?

One proposed answer is that the law of God (or covenant of God) somehow is "written on their hearts"—that is, all humans have an intrinsic awareness of what God expects and thus are accountable for when they circumvent those expectations. Such a theory is suggested by the apostle Paul in Rom 2:14–16 and has been developed by theologians such as Thomas Aquinas[36] and Joseph Butler (1692–1752).[37] But the validity of such theories is not obvious to everyone. Another problem with defining sin's essence as disobedience (or as a breach of covenant) is that even if breaking divine commands is a critical element of sin, it may not explain WHY humans overstep such commands. What is it about humans that motivates them to disobey? In light of this question, the search for the essence of sin often involves attempting to identify those inner (psychological) traits that often lead to overt acts of sin. Many of the following theories attempt to answer this question.

Eastern Orthodoxy has traditionally interpreted the core of sin as *sensuality*. This view is suggested in the writings of Clement of Alexandria (150–215) and Origen of Alexandria.[38] Friedrich Schleiermacher (1768–1834) expresses a similar ideology.[39] This perspective sometimes interprets the apostle Paul's warning in Rom 7–8 against living "according to the flesh" to mean that the root of sin is human bodily sensuality. In Rom 7, Paul alludes to the law of the mind and to the law of sin; and he notes that he serves the law of mind with his mind and the law of sin with his flesh. Also, in Rom 8, Paul says that to set one's mind on the flesh means death and hostility to God. Further, in chapter 8, Paul differentiates between being "in the flesh" and being "in the

36. Thomas Aquinas, *Summa Theologica*, Ia. q. 79, a 13; and Thomas Aquinas, *Summa Theologica*, I-II. q. 91.

37. Butler, *Sermons*.

38. Kelly, *Early Christian Doctrines*, 178–83.

39. Schleiermacher, *The Christian Faith*, 271–73

Spirit." From these verses, some writers have taught that sensuality is the root sin. Two problems with identifying sin with sensuality are these. First, many sins are not particularly related to carnal desires. Thus, sins like pride, ingratitude, and unbelief seem to be overlooked in this account of sin. Second, this perspective does not fit well with other passages of Paul's writings where the apostle speaks positively about the human body.[40] For instance, in Rom 12:1, Paul encourages early Roman Christians to make their "bodies" living sacrifices to God. In 1 Cor 6:19–20, Paul says that "your body is a temple of the Holy Spirit within you," and that you should "glorify God" in your body. Many commentators argue that Paul's use of the term "flesh" in Romans, and elsewhere, has a technical and nonphysical meaning. It refers to the sinful tendency or nature of humans, rather than the physical, sensual aspects.

Another candidate for the essence of sin is *pride*. Augustine endorsed this perspective. For him, humility before God is a basic virtue of the Christian life and is essential to a right relationship with God; lack of humility (pride) is the failure to exude this primary virtue.[41] Closely related to pride is selfishness. A number of theologians have suggested that the essence of sin is *selfishness*—the "choice of self as the supreme end which constitutes the antithesis of supreme love to God."[42] In this view, sin is the decision or tendency to love one's self above all others, including God. Thomas Aquinas seems to affirm this interpretation of sin's essence.[43] A problem with declaring selfishness (or pride) to be the essence of sin is that some sins involve loving something other than oneself. For example, one might love another person, or an ideology, more than one loves one's self or God. In light of this, several theologians have proposed that the heart of sin is *idolatry*—the displacement of God. In short, fundamentally sin is loving anything in the place of God. This idea is suggested by important texts in the Old and New Testaments. One of the hallmarks of the Ten Commandments is the command to have no other gods than Yahweh (Exod 20:3). In a similar vein, the Gospel traditions depict Jesus as proclaiming (or agreeing) that the greatest command is to love God with the fullness of one's being (Mark 12:30). In light of such considerations, a number of theologians have taught that the essence of sin is idolatry. Among those affirming this view are Martin Luther (1493–1546),[44] John Calvin (1509–1564),[45] and Millard Erickson.[46]

40. This view also does not cohere with the scriptural teaching (mentioned earlier) that the created order is intrinsically good. In some interpretations, this theory virtually declares that sensuality per se is wrong, rather than that sensuality leads to wrong thoughts or behaviors; but this may suggest that something is askew with the corporal nature or sensuality per se.

41. Augustine, *City of God*, 12.6 and 14.13. Reinhold Niebuhr makes a similar claim regarding the center of sin being pride. See Niebuhr, *The Nature and Destiny of Man*, 1:186–207.

42. Strong, *Systematic Theology*, 567. See also, Hovey, *Manual of Christian Theology*, 160.

43. Thomas Aquinas, *Summa Theologica*, I, II, q. 77, art. 4.

44. Luther, *Large Catechism*.

45. Calvin, *Institutes of the Christian Religion*, 1. 11–13.

46. Erickson equates idolatry with creaturely attempt to displace God. Erickson, *Christian*

Two other candidates for the essence of sin are *ingratitude* and *unbelief*. The apostle Paul hints at the former of these when he declares that humans were condemned because they knew God but did not offer thanks to God (Rom 1:21). The Gospel of John alludes to the latter when it says that those who do not believe in Christ are already condemned (3:18). And some biblical passages especially indict deliberate refusals to believe or trust God or Christ (Mark 3:28–30; Heb 6:4–6). Not surprisingly, like other attempts to define sin's essence, these last two proposals also face difficulties. While each is a relatively clear example of sin, it is not obvious that either captures all that sin is.

We may sum up our discussion of sin as follows. No consensus exists among Christians regarding the essential nature of sin. At the end of the day, perhaps sin is simply multifaceted and cannot be reduced to a singular principle. A similar conclusion may be drawn from the story of Adam and Eve in Gen 3. Traditionally, this narrative has played a pivotal role in the Christian understanding of the nature, origin, and consequences of sin. Here we focus on its implications for the nature of sin. In the Genesis 1 narrative, Adam and Eve are instructed by God not to eat the fruit of "the tree of the knowledge of good and evil" on penalty of death. Tempted by a serpent, Eve eats the forbidden food, as does Adam, who is with her. Immediately, they become aware of a change within them or at least of a change in their relationship with God. When God visits them, they hide out of fear; and God knows they have eaten the forbidden fruit. Divine curses ensue. In Gen 3:3–6, the serpent counters Eve's (and God's) claim that upon eating the forbidden fruit, she and her husband will die. Instead, says the serpent, God knows if they eat it they will become like God, able to distinguish good from evil. Upon looking at the fruit, Eve sees that it is good for food, pleasant to the eye, and desirable for becoming wise, like God. And so, she takes it and eats it, and gives some to Adam who also eats. Here several images describe sin and its allure. The couple is tempted to doubt the trustworthiness of God, to desire to be god-like themselves, to throw off God's command in favor of their own designs, and to do what appears beautiful and pleasant in their own eyes. In short, in these verses the nature of sin as pride, sensuality, idolatry, selfishness, doubting and disobeying God are all insinuated along with the notion that sin partly arises from human ignorance, finitude, and frailty. One need not interpret this account to be literal history to glean numerous insights about the nature of sin.[47]

Theology, 530.

47. The account is highly symbolic, filled with literary devices that evoke reflection without necessitating presuming that the story is literal history. Among the literary devices are names with generic meanings. The name Adam is the Hebrew word for "human" or "humanity"; Eve means "living"; Able means "mist"; Cain perhaps means "spear." Some theologians still wish to take the account as history, but they face puzzles similar to those discussed in the previous chapter regarding interpreting Gen 1 as a literal description of the emergence and chronological development of the physical universe.

Sins and Sinfulness

Many biblical passages speak of sin as individual acts of sinning. But some texts depict sin as a state of being, as a characteristic or disposition of an individual. Rabbinic literature recognized two forms of sin. First, there are specific acts of sin. Second, there is "evil imagination"—sin as a state of being (Gen 6:5, 8:21). The New Testament expresses similar ideas. First, at times New Testament writers list and condemn individual sins (Rom 1:29–31, Gal 5:19–21). But at other times, they speak as if sin is a state of being. Thus, the Gospel of Matthew depicts Jesus as emphasizing the motives for sinning and not just overt acts of sin (Matt 5:21–44); further, Jesus is pictured as teaching that individual sins flow from a person's inner being (Matt 5:15; 7:17). The Gospel of Luke speaks of "sinners," which suggests not simply that people do evil acts but that (some or all) people are intrinsically evil or prone to evil. In a similar manner, the apostle Paul speaks of human bondage to the fleshly nature and contrasts such a state with living by the Spirit of God (Rom 5–8; Gal 5:16–18, 22–23). In turn, Paul (or a Pauline writer) speaks of putting off the old self corrupted with deceitful desires and putting on a new self that is created in God's image (Eph 4:22–24). In light of these biblical perspectives, Christian theology often recognizes the existence of individual acts of sin as well as (and more fundamentally) the human state of being sinful (a sinner).

The Origin and Transfer of the Sinful Nature, and Human Responsibility

Christian theology often assumes that humans have a sinful nature and that from this nature particular acts of sin arise. But what is the cause of this sinful state? Where did it come from? Why do humans now have it? Further, do humans have any choice in the matter? Did we choose to be sinful beings, or do we have this trait whether we want it or not? Further still, does God hold humans responsible for this nature? Are we condemned only for our specific sins or for our sinful nature as well? Several theories have been proposed that attempt to answer these questions. Most of them wrestle with two key New Testament passages from the apostle Paul: Rom 5:12–19 and 1 Cor 15:21–22. Thus, we will take a brief look at these passages before examining various theories of the origin and transfer of the sinful nature.

Romans 5:12, 18–19

> Therefore as sin came into the world through one man and death through sin, and so death spread to all men because all men sinned—. . . Then as one man's trespass led to condemnation for all men, so one man's act of righteousness

leads to acquittal and life for all men. For as by one man's disobedience many were made sinners, so by one man's obedience many will be made righteous."

1 Corinthians 15:21–22

For as by a man came death, by a man has come also the resurrection of the dead. For as in Adam all die, so also in Christ shall all be made alive.

These verses assume that the story of Adam and Eve in Gen 3 describes the *origin* of human sin. In turn, these passages assert some sort of a connection between Adam's sin and the sins, death, and condemnation of all humanity. The precise nature of this connection is subject to diverse interpretations.

Augustine of Hippo (354–430), whose view has dominated Western Christian theology) understood these verses to mean that when Adam sinned, all humans (1) literally sinned "in him," (2) became guilty of Adam's sin, (3) became subject to divine condemnation, and (4) received a sinful nature and tendency to sin. Augustine interpreted the last phrase of Rom 5:12 ("because all of have sinned") to be saying "in him" (in Adam) "all have sinned." Augustine likely got this translation from early Latin translations of the New Testament in Greek. Not all have agreed with Augustine. Most modern commentators concur that the Greek of Rom 5:12 does not say "in him all have sinned," but should be understood as saying "because all have sinned." (This is reflected in the translation given above.) Nevertheless, controversy still rages over precisely what the phrase means, especially in light of verses such as 5:18 and 19, which seem to affirm a close connection between Adam's sin and the sin and condemnation of all humans.

Some theologians insist that the last phrase of Rom 5:12 is asserting that death comes to all people because in fact all people commit individual acts of sin. But others insist that this does not take into account the close tie between Adam's sin and the sin of humanity, a tie suggested in vv. 18 and 19. One contemporary biblical commentator has proposed that Rom 5:12 should be understood to say that death comes to all because all have sinned, but also to say that all people sin because all people have a corrupt nature that has come upon them due to the sin of Adam.[48] Another contemporary commentator insists that in fact Paul is simply ambiguous, perhaps deliberately ambiguous, about the connection between Adam's sin and the sins, sinfulness, and condemnation of all humans. Paul is attempting to hold in tension two paradoxical notions: (1) that humans are responsible for their sins, and (2) that the sinful tendency is something that humans cannot fully control.[49] Still other theologians have insisted that the story of Adam and Eve, and the alleged connection between contemporary humans and these first humans must be understood as myth, as story designed to convey religious and

48. Cranfield, *Romans*, 1:278.
49. Dunn, *Romans 1–8*, 290, 298.

existential truth about the human condition and not to be taken literally. In particular, the story of Adam and Eve, and Paul's connecting Adam's sin to the sin of all, expresses the paradox that humans inevitably sin and yet also are responsible for their sins. This was the view of Reinhold Niebuhr.[50]

At any rate, with these biblical passages in the background, several theories have been proposed throughout history that attempt to answer questions about the origin of human sin, sinfulness, and responsibility. Augustine's rival, *Pelagius*, held that humans are born innocent and are able to obey God without internal, supernatural divine aid. In short, humans do not have a sinful nature, and thus are not responsible for that nature. Rather, they are held accountable for only the actual sins they commit. Obviously, since humans do not have a corrupt nature, they do not choose such a nature. Humans do not sin because of some innate sinful tendency; however, they do *learn* how to sin from one another. Hence, for Pelagius, the chief impact that Adam's and Eve's sin had on humans is to serve as a bad example. Another theory about human sinfulness was proposed by *James Arminius*. He taught that humans innately have a corrupt, sinful nature. This nature somehow has been inherited from Adam. Nevertheless, humans are not held responsible for this corrupted nature. Rather, God's prevenient grace abolishes the legal consequences of Adam's sin and of our sinful nature. Humans are only responsible for the actual sins they commit. Arminius apparently tacitly denied that humans choose their corrupt natures. (However, he might have allowed that humans acquiesce to their corrupt nature once they become aware of it.)

The *realist theory* teaches that humans have an innate corrupt nature, and this nature is "biologically" inherited through Adam. Further, God holds us responsible for our corrupt nature as well as for our individual acts of sin. This view attempts to justify the divine condemnation of humans (for their inherited corrupt nature) by saying that the common human nature existed in the first human, Adam. Thus, God imputes the guilt of Adam upon all humans because all were germinally, biologically in Adam. The realist theory is related to the *traducian* view of the origin of the human soul, which affirms that the soul is a product of parents through biological reproduction, and not through direct creation by God.[51] The realist theory appears to deny that individual humans choose their sinful nature. However, it might be compatible with the notion that humans acquiesce to their sinful nature once they become aware of it.

According to the *federal theory*, humans innately have a corrupt/sinful nature and are held responsible for their corrupt nature as well as for individual sins. But humans have not biologically inherited the sinful nature from Adam. According to the federal theory, God appointed Adam as the representative of the human race. God made a covenant of works with Adam, and thus with all humanity. On the condition of obedience, humankind could have eternal life. On the condition of disobedience,

---

50. Niebuhr, *The Nature and Destiny of Man.*

51. Interestingly, Augustine seems to affirm the realist theory while also holding the contrary so-called creationist view that each human soul is directly created by God at conception.

humankind would become subject to guilt and death. When Adam sinned, all humanity was condemned. God imputed upon each human the guilt of Adam's sin. Further, because all humans "legally" participated in Adam's sin, all have inherited a corrupt nature with its tendency to sin. The federal theory is tied to the *creationist* view of the origin of the soul. Although our souls are not directly, biologically connected to Adam, we are connected by way of a covenant made between God and our representative, Adam. The federal theory denies that humans directly choose our sinful nature. But it may be compatible with the idea that humans acquiesce to that state once we become aware of it.[52]

Evangelical theologian Millard Erickson rejects both the federal and the realist theories because he believes they imply that guilt is imputed upon human infants; and this, in turn, implies that unrepentant and unbaptized babies are doomed to eternal condemnation (a view that Augustine endorsed). Erickson argues that some willful choice is required in order for guilt justly to be imputed upon persons (infants). Thus, Erickson insists that through Adam humans somehow inherit an innate sinful nature, but only have a conditional guilt because of this nature. This guilt is not held against us until we become aware of our sinful nature and *acquiesce* to it. At some moment—often around adolescence—humans become aware of their sinful nature and willfully approve of it. At that moment, humans become guilty of the sin of Eden without directly committing that sin because we tacitly approve of our own sinful tendencies.[53]

With the exception of Erickson's comments, all of these theories of human sinfulness developed prior to the rise of modern science and the growing scholarly perspective that the Old Testament stories of origins (including accounts of creation and of primordial humans) cannot be taken as literal history.[54] In light of this, several contemporary theologians have proposed more figurative interpretations of Paul's theology of sin and of his interpretation of Gen 3. One such interpretation is offered by Baptist theologian Dale Moody, who tries to stay faithful to the Pauline doctrine, while also augmenting it in the light of current views of natural history. Moody proposes that a person is "guilty before God because of his [or her] personal sin, not because he [or she] has inherited an alien guilt that goes back to the first man and first woman."[55] Moody interprets 1 Cor 15:22 (which says, "For as in Adam all die, so in Christ shall all be made alive") to mean that "just like Adam died because of his willful sin against God, so all other humans die because of their willful sin against God." Moody points out that the text does not say, "in Adam all die." Rather it states "as in Adam," which Moody interprets to mean "as in Adam's case, so in everyone else's case, sin leads to

---

52. Numerous summaries of the Pelagian, Arminian, realist, and federalist theories have been made. See Strong, *Systematic Theology*, 597–634; Erickson, *Christian Theology*, 575–83; Garrett, *Systematic Theology*, 1:562–69.

53. Erickson, *Christian Theology*, 582–83.

54. As noted elsewhere, the literature in Gen 1–11 is highly symbolic.

55. Moody, *The Word of Truth*, 289. Brackets added.

death."[56] Moody interprets Rom 5:12 in a similar manner. It reads: "Sin came into the world through one man, and his sin brought death with it. As a result, death has spread to the whole human race because everyone has sinned." Again, Moody insists that the text does not say that all die "because Adam sinned"; rather it says "all die because everyone has sinned."[57] Moody maintains that "we take the correct approach to this problem when we see the experience of the first man and the first woman as pictures of what happens to every man and every woman."[58] Just like Adam and Eve, all sin and are guilty before God for the individual acts of sin that they perform. Moody argues that "Paul saw this pattern in his own experience when he said: 'I myself was once alive apart from the law; but when the commandment came sin sprang to life, and I died'" (Rom 7:9). In other words, Paul experienced the emergence of sinful acts in his own life when he became aware of God's law; and through the emergence of sinful acts, Paul became guilty before God.[59]

Moody contends that his view does not deny "inherited sin." He argues that all humans are in a state of sin, having inherited "tendencies that . . . lead to actual transgressions."[60] But these inherited tendencies are not subject to judgment. Only the actual act of transgression that results from the tendency to sin makes humans culpable before God. Moody believes that Rom 5:19 (which Moody translates, "just as all people were made sinners as the result of the disobedience of one man, in the same way they will all be put right with God as the result of the obedience of one man") does not support the idea that all are sinners in Adam. Rather, the verse means that "the obedience of Jesus Christ puts all people right with God who *respond in the obedience of faith*, and the disobedience of one man makes all people sinners *when they respond in the disobedience of unbelief*."[61] According to Moody, humans do have an inner, innate sinful nature, but he leaves open the possibility that this nature may be passed in differing ways: biologically, psychologically, or socially.

Following reasoning similar to Reinhold Niebuhr's, Moody denies the historical existence of Adam and Eve as the first two humans, interpreting the story of the fall as a picture of what happens in all humans. He contends that humans are not held responsible for their sinful nature but only for those sins that they actually commit. He believes, however, that humans do all fall and become guilty before God. It is not clear whether Moody holds that humans choose their sinful nature or not. If it is biologically transmitted, then we probably do not choose it. But if it is socially or psychologically transmitted, it may be partly chosen. In either case, there

---

56. Moody, *The Word of Truth*, 286.
57. Moody, *The Word of Truth*, 286–87.
58. Moody, *The Word of Truth*, 287.
59. Moody, *The Word of Truth*, 287.
60. Moody, *The Word of Truth*, 290.
61. Moody, *The Word of Truth*, 287 (italics added).

would be room to affirm that perhaps humans acquiesce to their sinful nature once they become aware of it.

Except for Pelagius's view, most of the theories mentioned above speak of the sinful nature as if it were a substance—a reality whose nature is to sin. Although traditional theologies typically deny that *human nature* is essentially sinful, many insinuate that *current "fallen" human nature* is sinful. Over against this, some theologians propose that the human proneness to sin is better understood as a condition that arises out of more basic features of human existence, features that per se are not sin or sinful. One example of this interpretation is found in the writings of Reinhold Niebuhr. For Niebuhr, human sin arises inevitably out of freedom and finitude. As free beings, humans can aspire to unlimited power, knowledge, and accomplishments. But as finite beings, humans cannot attain such heights. The clash between aspiration and limitedness generates anxiety and provokes the yearning to transcend one's creaturely status, effectively generating longing to take the place of God. While neither freedom nor finitude is sin per se, the two predictably lead to sinful acts. Thus, humans sin, not because they have or are a sinful nature, but because they are finite and free beings who inevitably (statistically but not causally necessarily) sin.[62]

A similar theory is proposed by Frederick Tennant, who sees sin arising from the tension between fundamental animalistic instincts and awareness of moral requirements. Animal instincts are vestiges of the human decent from earlier life-forms. In such animals, these instincts are not sin per se. Rather they often help preserve individual organisms in hostile environments and allow their species, and ultimately descendant species, to survive on the planet. As humans progressed, they became increasingly aware of moral ideals. And with the coming of moral sensitivities, an inevitable conflict of conscience arose in humans between higher sensitivities and baser animal instincts. Moral insights call for care of others while baser instincts seek personal survival and the attainment of basic desires. The collision of these propensities inevitably led to acts of sin.[63]

Both Niebuhr and Tennant contend that humans are responsible for the individual acts of sin that arise out of these natural conditions, even while insisting that the conditions themselves are not sin. For some theologians, theories like Niebuhr's and Tennant's are welcome because they help the Christian doctrine of sin fit more smoothly with what current scientific theory suggests about the emergence and development of the human species. These paradigms also help theologians avoid a substantival understanding of human sinfulness. Instead, the inevitability of human sinning is explained by common features of human beings arising out of the evolutionary process and not in terms of an alleged substance-like reality called the sinful nature. But many theologians do not find these models helpful. For many, these

---

62. Niebuhr, *The Nature and Destiny of Man*.

63. See Tennant, *The Origin and Propagation of Sin*. Similar views are expressed in Berkhof, *Christian Faith*, 202–8.

theories effectively underestimate the severity of human sin and the need for divine intervention. Instead, these paradigms imply that in principle humans on their own could overcome their baser instincts (Tennant) or their anxiety rising from freedom (Niebuhr), and could reach self-attained sinlessness. According to many theologians, only God can bring such a change to human life, and this is because a fundamental alteration of (sinful) human nature itself must occur.[64]

The Consequences of Sin

Granting that sin is multifaceted, and that humans sin and are prone to sin (perhaps even have a sinful nature), what are the consequences of sin? We begin this discussion by returning to the Gen 3 account. According to that narrative, once Adam and Eve sinned, divine curses followed. Specifically, thereafter, the serpent would slither on the ground and would experience enmity between his kind and humankind. The woman would endure pain in childbirth and would be ruled by her husband. And the man would struggle to produce food from the ground, only to return in death to that dust from which he was formed (vv. 14–19). Again, one need not take these curses literally to see the author's (or the redactors') intent to speak symbolically about some of the effects of sin. At least five costs are suggested. *One is a broken or strained relationship between humanity and God.* Before sin, the human couple trusts, obeys, depends upon, and fellowships with God. The Lord regularly visits them in the garden. Following sin, the two are expelled from the food-giving garden, bereft of fellowship with God, and dependent upon their own toil to survive. Further, in the act of their sin, the couple doubts and disobeys God. *A second consequence of sin is injured human relationships.* In vv. 11–12, when the Lord asks the man whether he had eaten from the forbidden tree, Adam replies the woman (whom God had given him as a companion) had given the fruit to him, and he ate. In short, Adam tries to deflect his culpability by pointing out the blameworthiness of Eve (and of God!). In a similar manner, tension is seen in the relationship between the man and woman when God announces that now the woman will be lorded-over by her husband (v. 16). The relationship of mutual companionship degenerates into a relationship in which the man wields power over the woman.[65] *A third impact of sin is a negative relationship with the created world.* God had placed the man and woman in the garden and had provided for them. But now they must struggle to survive in an unfriendly environment (vv. 17–19). *A fourth result of sin is death.* The text does not directly assert this. But it does suggest a strong tie between sin and death. First, God warns that if the two ate the fruit, they would die (2:16–17). Upon eating the fruit, they do not die immediately, but they are expelled from the garden so

64. See Erickson, *Christian Theology,* 537, 547.

65. Sometimes the notion that Eve was to be ruled by her husband is used to support the dominance of husbands over their wives. What is interesting about the Genesis text is that such rule is described as a curse, as a negative consequence of sin, not as a divinely sanctioned ideal.

that they may not eat from "the tree of life" and thus live forever (vv. 22–24). Further, God's curse upon the man is that he will return to the dust from which he came (v. 19). *A final consequence of sin is a change within Adam and Eve themselves.* After sin, they fear God and choose to hide from the Lord. They make excuses for their actions, thus demonstrating an awareness of their own guilt. And (as noted above) they attempt to deflect blame upon others, suggesting both an awareness of guilt and a desire for self-protection even if at the expense of others (vv. 11–19).[66]

Similar assessments of the effects of sin are found throughout Christian Scriptures. For example, at the core of biblical ethics is the insistence that humans be right with God and with their fellow humans. The first four of the Ten Commandments demand right relations with God (Exod 20:1–11; Deut 5:6–15). The last six mandate right interconnections with others (Exod 20:12–17; Deut 5:16–21). Further, the constant refrain of many of the Old Testament prophets is that Israel or Judah are to manifest both faithfulness to God and social justice. These themes are reiterated by Jesus when he asserts, based on Old Testament passages, that the two greatest commands are to love God and to love one's neighbor (Matt 22:37–40; Mark 12:28–34; Luke 10:25–28). A consistent motif of much of the Bible is that sin results in broken relationships between God and humans, and between humans. It should be noted that more than merely broken fellowship with God is expressed. Because of sin, humans are said to be alienated from, even enemies of, God (Gen 3:23; Rom 5:10; 8:7; Eph 4:18), in rebellion against the deity, and under divine wrath and judgment (John 3:18–36; Rom 1:18–2:16).

Less abundant than passages dealing with broken divine and human relationships, there are nonetheless some biblical texts that address sin's negative effects upon the created world as a whole, to return to the third consequence of sin articulated above. Perhaps the clearest statement of this is in Rom 8:18–22, where Paul says:

> I consider the sufferings of this present time are not worth comparing with the glory about to be revealed in us. For the creation waits with eager longing for the revealing of the children of God; for the creation was subjected to futility, not of its own will but by the will of the one who subjected it, in hope that the creation itself will be set free from its bondage to decay and will obtain the freedom of the glory of the children of God.

Following themes found in Jewish apocalyptic literature, Paul assumes that in the current age the created order is ensnared by evil supernatural forces. But through Christ,

---

66. The text also highlights the fact that after sin, the man and woman became aware of their own nakedness (2:25; 3:7, 10–11). "Their eyes were opened" (3:7). The precise connection of this awareness of nakedness with sin and guilt is not precisely explained. Perhaps the connection hints at the awkwardness felt among humans at pubescence about their own nakedness and sexual awareness. It may also involve an etiology for explaining the relatively odd fact that humans (unlike other animals) wear clothes. The awareness of nakedness may also suggest an uncomfortable awareness of one's own vulnerability before God, fellow humans, and nature. See Sailhamer, *Genesis*, 48–49.

God is overcoming the current era and one day will subjugate all reality to the divine will and authority (see Rom 12:2; 1 Cor 15:24–28; Gal 1:4; Phil 3:21). Part of God's victory will include an end to decay and death in the created world (see Rom 8:2; 1 Cor 15:26; compare Isa 11:6–9; 65:25). Similar visions are offered in the book of Revelation. Echoing ideas found in the book of Isaiah (Isa 65:17–25), the author of Revelation declares that at the end of this age God will create a new heaven and a new earth, and will dwell with the faithful in a new Jerusalem. There will be no more death or pain or sorrow; and all things will be made new (Rev 21:1–5). All these point to a broken created order and to the divine intent to heal that system.

Next, to circle back to the fourth consequence of sin that we listed earlier (death), several biblical passages connect sin to death. As noted above, portions of Gen 2 and 3 insinuate this, and other texts are even more explicit, including Ezek 18:4, Rom 6:23, and 1:15. The meaning of death in these passages is somewhat obscure. Are these verses speaking of physical death or of some other kind of demise? Theologians often differentiate between three kinds of death in the biblical tradition: physical death (the death of the body), spiritual death (separation from right relationship with God), and eternal death (never ending separation from God). These definitions are not precisely spelled out in the Bible. But some such distinction seems likely. Obviously not everyone who sins immediately physically dies. And some scriptures state that those who are not presently "in Christ" are already dead in their sins and trespasses, even though they are not physically dead (Eph 2:1–6; Col 2:13–15). Further, in passages that connect death with sin, the opposite of such death often is identified as "eternal life," not simply ongoing physical life (see John 3:16, 11:25–26; Rom 5:18–19; 6:23; Eph 2:5–6; Col 2:13–14). In spite of this, the apostle Paul clearly connects the end of physical death with God's remedy for sin through Christ in 1 Cor 15:12–23. In light of all this, Christian theology often identifies all three types of death (physical, spiritual, and eternal) as ultimate consequences of sin.

Puzzles especially emerge regarding the relationship between sin and physical death. First, as just noted, not everyone who sins immediately dies. Further, Christian tradition typically asserts that Christ was without sin and yet clearly also teaches that he died on a cross. So, if physical death happens because of sin, how can Jesus die if he is sinless? Moreover, contemporary science makes plain that death was a common feature of animal life long before humans came on the scene. These considerations have led many theologians to propose that while humans were created for everlasting life, such life was not natural to their being. Such life could only happen by God's ongoing sustaining of their existence. Were we humans left to our own devices, death would be our natural end, as it is for all animal life. Interestingly, such an interpretation is suggested by the Gen 3 narrative, where after their sin, Adam and Eve are barred from Eden and the "tree of life" and therefore cannot live forever (vv. 22–24).

Finally, the fifth set of consequences for sin that we listed above has to do with changes within the human person. Sin impacts the individual sinner. With sin comes a sense of guilt (Rom 2:14–15) and perhaps a degree of self-deception as a person attempts to justify or exonerate oneself (Gen 3:11–13; Jer 17:9). Sin brings with it not only a subjective awareness of guilt but an objective state of being guilty before God. Several biblical passages speak of being in bondage or servitude to sin, as if one has become a slave to sin. In the Gospel of John, Jesus says, "Everyone who commits sin is a slave to sin" (8:34). In Rom 6:16, Paul makes a similar comment, and Paul often speaks of being freed from sin through Christ's Spirit (Rom 8:2; Gal 5:1, 13, 16–18). A long dispute persists among theologians over the degree to which humanity is in "bondage" to sin. Pelagius taught that humans are capable of not sinning, and that some indeed have avoided sin.[67] Augustine insisted that prior to the fall Adam and Eve had the power not to sin,[68] but after the fall they only had power to sin. Augustine tried to retain some degree of freedom, however, by asserting humans remain free, but free only to choose among diverse evil actions.[69] Similar views were expressed by Martin Luther and John Calvin. James Arminius likewise insisted that without divine grace, humans cannot not sin. But he tempered this claim by also asserting that God offers a prevenient grace that empowers sinners to freely (of their own power) believe in Christ. Eastern Orthodox writers, on the other hand, have long maintained that humans are capable of not sinning, even though in fact all humans sin. A number of contemporary theologians endorse the notion that humans are free and capable of not sinning, but the overall context of human existence makes sin inevitable although not ontologically or causally necessary.[70] We will discuss these matters in more detail under the topic of salvation.

The Mystery of Sin

A final observation about the doctrine of sin is needed. Whereas the Scriptures are clear that humans are morally culpable for their sins, there also is something of a mystery about sin and responsibility. This mystery is symbolically seen in the serpent's temptation in the garden. The serpent's origin, arrival, and precise meaning are unexplained. Even if—as some propose—the serpent represents animalistic desires, Christian theology must puzzle over why such desires must be faced by humankind in the first place. Over time, the serpent's role in Christian Scripture and theology expanded so that it became synonymous with dark forces of evil at work in God's world, including with words and concepts such as the Hebrew *satan* (meaning "accuser"), the Greek *diabolos* or "devil" (meaning "opponent"), and the Greek *diamōn* (meaning

67. Much of Pelagius's writing is lost to modern readers. A helpful source for his views is Pelagius, *The Christian Life and Other Essays.*

68. Augustine, *City of God*, 12.21; 13.3

69. Augustine, *Against Two Letters of the Pelagians*, 1.5.

70. For a discussion of many of these themes, see Robinson, *The Storms of Providence*, chapters 2 and 3.

"demon"). In whatever way these concepts are interpreted (whether as literal super-natural evil beings or symbols of an evil that transcends humans alone), they suggest there is something pitiful about human sin. Even though humans are responsible for the evil they perform, other factors are involved in the human submission to tempta-tion and sin. A kind of ignorance (Luke 23:34) or frailty (Pss 78: 38–39; 103:11–14) or deception (Gen 3: 1–5, 13) is at work when humans sin. And while these factors do not exonerate humans, they may explain, in part, why God actively pursues human redemption. In Chapter 13 of this work, we will explore one of the deep conundrums of the faith—namely, the origin of evil and why God tolerates it.

Conclusion

At the root of the Christian faith is the claim that humans are created by God in the divine image. As such, humans are of immense value with grand potential. Never-theless, human beings also have fallen into sin; they have become prone to sin and unable (from their own resources) to overcome this sinful state and sinful ways. In this fourth chapter, we have examined many of the components of these important doctrinal claims. In Chapter 5 we discuss two further cardinal teachings of the Chris-tian faith—namely, the doctrines of Christ and of salvation.

5

Christ and Salvation

IN CHAPTERS 3 AND 4, we explored the doctrines of revelation, God, creation, providence, humanity, and sin. In this fifth chapter we examine Christian teachings regarding Christ and salvation. According to Christian thought, humans have fallen into sin, and dire consequences have befallen individual humans and human society. In turn, in ways not utterly clear in the Scriptures, the cosmos itself has been negatively impacted by evil. For Christians, the doctrines of Christ and salvation describe God's primary answer to the dilemma of sin and evil. We turn first to the doctrine of Christ.

Christ

In our explication of the doctrine of God, we examined the notion that Christ is a co-equal member of the divine Trinity. That prior discussion focused on Christ's intrinsic nature, divorced from his role in the divine plan of salvation. Here we explore the import of Christ for salvation. Often such expositions divide into conversations (1) about the nature of Christ as the incarnate God and (2) about the work unto salvation that Christ accomplished in his incarnation. In many ways this division is arbitrary, for the two topics frequently meld into one. At the center of Christian teachings about Christ's incarnate nature is that he was fully human and fully God in a singular, undivided unity of being. Regarding Christ's work unto salvation, Christian theology has noted various roles played by Christ but especially has concentrated on his death on the cross. We begin by discussing Christ's incarnate nature.

The Person of Christ

Christian theology insists that Jesus was fully human and fully God in a singular, undivided unity of being. Thus, central to Christian theology is the claim that Jesus Christ was a *human being*. Several biblical considerations lend weight to this claim. Jesus was born (Luke 2:7, 11), grew (Luke 2:52), hungered (Matt 4:2), thirsted (John 19:28); he endured pain (Heb 5:8), loneliness (Mark 14:32–42), fatigue (John 4:6), and emotional anguish

(Matt 26:37; Mark 15:34). He expressed amazement (Luke 7:9) and limited knowledge (Mark 9:21; Mark 13:32). He worshiped (Luke 4:16) and prayed (Luke 22:41–44; John 17). And he died (Mark 15:37; Luke 23:46; John 19:30). Jesus was a human being. Christian tradition insists that Jesus was like other humans in every way, except that he did not sin. Several New Testament passages support the notion that Jesus was sinless (2 Cor 5:21; Heb 4:15; 7:26–27; 9:14; 1 Pet 2:22; 3:18; 1 John 3:5).

As Christian theology developed in the postbiblical period, two heresies were recognized and condemned for denying the full humanity of Jesus. One was *docetism*. Docetism derives its name from the Greek word *dokeō*, meaning "to appear." Docetism insisted that Jesus only appeared to be a human. He was not really a body or flesh at all. He was more like a ghost or apparition. This view held that the material world is inherently evil, and that God, who is spirit, could not possibly inhabit something material. Thus, Christ's body must have been a phantasm. Docetism was affirmed by the gnostics of the second century and by the Manicheans of the third and fourth centuries. In his early years, Augustine of Hippo endorsed Manicheanism because he believed it solved the problem of evil, asserting that there are two basic realities—spirit (good) and matter (evil). Second John 7 seems to challenge an early expression of Docetism when it declares: "Many deceivers have gone out into the world, those who do not confess that Jesus Christ has come in the flesh; any such person is the deceiver and the antichrist."

A second heresy denying Jesus' full humanness was Apollinarianism. Fourth-century bishop Apollinarius reasoned that if Jesus were God and man, he would have to have both a human *nous* ("mind"/"soul") and a divine *nous*. Apollinarius felt this was impossible. Thus, he proposed that Jesus was a "compound unity," a unity of a human body with a divine *nous* or *pneuma* ("spirit"). Apollinarius understood John 1:14, "the Word became flesh," to mean that the divine mind/spirit took on or entered a human body. Writers such as Gregory of Nazianzus rejected Apollinarius's perspective on that grounds that only those aspects of humanity assumed in Christ can be saved. Thus, if Christ did not have a human mind (*nous*), that aspect of humanity cannot be saved. The Council of Constantinople (381 CE) condemned Apollinarius's teachings.[1]

Various charges have been made against the doctrine that Jesus was a human being. One difficulty sometimes posited is whether Jesus could be truly human and yet also not sin. Is not moral error a common human trait? Traditional Christian orthodoxy often replies to this charge that while all other humans do in fact sin, sinfulness is not an essential attribute of humanity. It is an acquired characteristic, and one that in fact diminishes our true humanity. In this sense, then, Jesus was not less human than other humans due to his lack of sin; rather, he was more human than any of us.

---

1. Apollinarius's doctrine was subtle. He argued that the ideological archetype of humanness eternally exists in God so that human nature preexists in the deity. Thus, Christ's *nous* was somehow both divine and human. In light of this, some wonder to what degree Apollinarius disagreed with what came to be orthodoxy. For a brief discussion of the context of the Apollinarian debates see Robinson, *Christianity: A Brief History*, 163–68.

Another criticism sometimes raised regarding Jesus' humanity arises from feminist concerns. In Daniel Migliore's words, "can a male be the savior of women, or does the particularity of Jesus' sex preclude him from being a universal savior? This question . . . grows out of the history of oppression that women have experienced and that has all too often been supported in the church by direct or indirect reference to the maleness of the one who is said to be the norm of full humanity. If true humanity is by definition masculine, then women must always be less than fully human."[2] Migliore, however, offers a helpful reply to this dilemma by noting that

> a response to this concern must emphasize, as a number of feminist theologians do, that the New Testament sees the full humanity of Jesus not in his maleness but in his shocking love, his prophetic criticism, his inclusive freedom for God and for others . . . The theological significance of the humanity of Jesus resides not in his masculine gender but in his unconditional love of God and his . . . inclusive love of others. This alone makes the life and death of Jesus a radiant expression of the eternally self-giving, other-affirming, community-forming love of the triune God.[3]

Similar arguments could be given concerning Jesus' cultural, racial, or ethnic particularities. These are not what make Jesus uniquely most human.[4]

In addition to affirming the humanity of Jesus, Christian theology traditionally has affirmed his *deity* as well. In previous chapters we discussed the biblical and post-biblical developments of belief in Christ's deity. We will not rehearse that discussion here, except to say that the growing consensus of the Western Church was that Christ was not only human but also God and an equal member of the Trinity. Two heresies are often condemned for their denial of the deity of Christ. First, Ebionism (of the second century) insisted that Jesus was only a man, not divine. Jesus was born of the natural sexual relations of Mary and Joseph. Jesus did have a special relationship with God through "the Christ" (or "the Spirit"), which came upon him at his baptism. Just prior to his death, however, the Christ left Jesus. A second heresy that denied the deity of Christ was Arianism of the fourth century (endorsed by the presbyter Arius). Arianism insisted on the absolute uniqueness and transcendence of God the Father, claiming that God alone is uncreated. Jesus was united to the Logos or Word of God. But the Word was merely a creature. Thus, Jesus (in whom the Word was incarnate) was not God but a creature. Arians pointed to biblical passages that emphasize the subordination of the Son to the Father (John 14:28) and that speak of the limitations of Jesus' knowledge (Mark 13:32). They insisted that such passages imply that Christ was a being different from God. While Origen and other orthodox theologians stressed the eternal generation (begotteness) of the Son from the Father, Arius and

2. Migliore, *Faith Seeking Understanding*, 147.

3. Migliore, *Faith Seeking Understanding*, 148.

4. For further discussions of these matters, see Chapter 10, below, on feminist ethics.

his supporters affirmed the temporal emergence of the Son from God out of nonexistence. Arianism was rejected by the Council of Nicaea of 325.[5]

Christian theology traditionally also affirms that Jesus is God and human in *a singular unity*. There is no direct biblical statement to the effect that Jesus was both fully God and fully human in a singular united being. Rather, this unity seems to be implied in biblical claims that speak of Jesus as a singular person while simultaneously ascribing both human and divine attributes to him (John 1;14; Rom 1: 1–4; 9:5; Gal 4;4–5; 1 John 1:1–3; 4:2–3). The most telling statement concerning the unity of the divine and human in Jesus Christ is the Definition of Chalcedon of 451. This creed states:

> Following, then, the holy fathers, we unite in teaching all men to confess the one and only Son, our Lord Jesus Christ. This selfsame one is perfect [*teleiōn*] both in deity [*theoteti*] and in humanness [*anthrōpoteti*]; this selfsame one is also actually [*alēthōs*] God and actually man, with a rational soul [*psyches logikes*] and a body. He is of the same reality as God [*homoousion to patri*] as far as his deity is concerned and of the same reality as we are ourselves [*homoousion hēmin*] as far as his humanness is concerned; thus like us in all respects, sin only excepted. Before time began [*pro aiōnon*] he was begotten of the Father, in respect of his deity, and now in these "last days," for us and on behalf of our salvation, this selfsame one was born of Mary the virgin, who is God-bearer [*theotokos*] in respect of his humanness [*anthrōpoteta*].[6]

Four main heresies often are identified as denying the unity of Christ. The first of these is Nestorianism. As patriarch of Constantinople, Nestorius (386–451) was asked to rule concerning the use of the term *theotokos* when applied to the Virgin Mary. The term meant "God-bearer." Nestorius was uncomfortable with the word because it seemed inappropriate (and inaccurate) to state that God had a mother. At best, he believed that if the word *theotokos* were used, it should be accompanied by the term *anthrōpotokos*, meaning "human-bearer." Nestorius preferred to think of the two natures of Christ as conjoined rather than as a unity. But many Christian leaders of his day believed that to deny that Mary was mother of God was to reject the full unity of the divine and human in Christ. Nestorius formally consented to the Chalcedonian formula of unity. But some of his followers did not. They denied the unity of the divine and human in Jesus, affirming instead a conjunction of the two in Jesus.

A second theory condemned for its denial of the unity of divinity and humanity in Jesus was Eutychianism. Eutyches (375–454) denied the existence of two natures in Christ, claiming that Jesus had only one nature—that of "God made flesh and become human." His theory was unclear, but he seems to have affirmed that Christ had two natures before the incarnation and only one after it. A school of thought rose up around Eutyches that taught that the humanity of Christ was virtually nullified in its absorption

---

5. For a discussion of the core issues involved in the Arian debates see Robinson, *Christianity: A Brief History*, chapters 4–5.

6. Leith, ed., *Creeds of the Churches*.

into his deity. Indeed, Eutyches himself described the absorption of Christ's humanity into his deity as analogous to a drop of honey (human nature) being mingled with the ocean (divine nature). For many pro-Chalcedonian theologians of the time, Eutyches's doctrine denied the true unity of the human and divine in Jesus, or it even verged on Docetism. The labels *Monophysites* or *Miaphysites* were applied to those who endorsed Eutyches's views, for they affirmed only one nature in Christ.

A third heresy that denied the unity of the person of Jesus is *adoptionism*. Adoptionists taught that Jesus was only human in his early life, but eventually he was adopted by God as the divine Son and, in that moment, he became divine. In other words, rather than claim that in Christ God became human, adoptionism affirmed that a human became God. Appealing to various New Testament passages, adoptionists often claim that Jesus was adopted and deified at the moments of his baptism (Mark 1:11) or his resurrection (Rom 1:4). A fourth view allegedly[7] denying the unity of deity and humanity in Jesus is *kenoticism*. This theory became popular in the nineteenth century. Phil 2:7 claims that Jesus "emptied himself" (from the Greek *kenoō*—"to empty") and became a human servant. Based on this passage, kenoticism asserts that the Logos, or second person of the Trinity, emptied himself of his uniquely divine attributes and put on only human qualities. Gottfried Thomasius (1802–1875) proposed that the Logos gave up great-making attributes such as omnipotence, omniscience, and omnipresence, but kept key moral characteristics such as holiness and love.[8] Wolfgang Gess (1819–1891) asserted that the Logos yielded up all such divine attributes and became a mere human, but regained the divine attributes over time as his human life progressed.[9] Kenosis theory hoped to affirm that ontologically Christ remained God while also giving up some (or all) divine attributes in order to endure the limitations of human life. This theory has been criticized on several grounds, including that it denies the genuine union of God and human in Jesus Christ, teaching instead that the second person of the Trinity was God, then became human, only to become God again.

What is the significance for Christian theology in claiming (insisting) that Christ was fully human and fully divine in a singular, inseparable unity of being? The Scriptures do not explicitly explain this. As time progressed, however, several Christian writers became convinced that if Christ had not been both human and divine, human salvation would not be possible. As we see below, Anselm helped solidify this notion in the twelfth century. But these ideas were expressed long before Anselm.

---

7. Not all theologians see the kenotic theory as heretical or as going as far as did Thomasius and Gess. Roger E. Olson, for example contends that this theory is an option for mainstream orthodox Christians, so long as they do not "go so far as to say that the heavenly Logos/Son gave up his attributes of deity in order to become human" (Olson, *The Mosaic of Christian Belief*, 240).

8. Thomasius, *Christi Person und Werk*.

9. Gess, *The Scripture Doctrine of the Person of Christ*.

The Work of Christ

In addition to claiming that in his incarnation Christ was fully God and fully human, Christian theology insists that Jesus played a central role in God's plan of salvation. But what did God accomplish through Christ? A helpful breakdown of Christ's work, originating in Eusebius of Caesarea (260/265—339/340 CE) and greatly developed by the Reformed tradition, is to divide Christ's achievements into three main functions. These roles are tied to three key offices in the Old Testament tradition: prophet, king, and priest. Seventeenth century Reformed theologian Francis Turretin (1623–1687) expressed this breakdown as follows:

> The threefold misery of humanity resulting from sin (that is, ignorance, guilt, and the oppression and bondage of sin) required this threefold office. Ignorance is healed through the prophetic office, guilt through the priestly, and the oppression and bondage of sin through the kingly. The prophetic light scatters the darkness of error; the merit of the priest removes guilt and obtains reconciliation for us; the power of the king takes away the bondage of sin and death.[10]

Although this division of Christ's offices is somewhat arbitrary, it is helpful in identifying important elements of Jesus' work. These components include Jesus' revealing God to humanity, ruling over creation, and mediating between God and humans. In the New Testament, Jesus often is recognized as a prophet (Matt 13:54–57; 16:14; Mark 6:1–5, 15; Luke 7:16; 13:31–33) and, like the Old Testament prophets, Jesus revealed the will and nature of God (Matt 11:25–27; John 8:26–28). Indeed, Christ often is described as the fullest revelation of God (John 14:8–12, 24; Heb 1:2–3). In turn, Jesus often is portrayed as ruler. The title Christ obviously points to this kingly role, as does the title Lord. Even the designation Son of Man suggests ultimate cosmic rule (Dan 7:13–14; Matt 25:31–46; Mark 8:27–33,38; 14:26, 62; Luke 12:8–9) . Further, numerous New Testament passages point to Christ's all-inclusive authority over creation (Matt 28:18; Acts 2:32–36; 1 Cor 15:24–28; Phil 2:9–11).

While the first two roles as prophet or revelation and of king or ruler are important components of the doctrine of salvation, Christ's function as priestly mediator especially is highlighted in the story of salvation. In the Old Testament, priests were mediators between God and Israel, offering sacrifices of purification and atonement so that God might bless the nation with the divine presence. In a similar way, in the New Testament, Jesus is portrayed as an intercessor between God and humanity, offering purification and atonement so that believers might be brought into the presence of God. But unlike the Old Testament priests, Jesus not only offered sacrifices; he *was* the sacrifice that brings atonement. His death was sacrificial (Rom 3:21–26, esp. 25; Heb 8:1–9:14). This sacrificial aspect of Christ's work is explicitly stated in several New Testament texts and is implicit in several others. It is presupposed in Paul's emphasis on Christ's cross as the

---

10. Turretin, *Institutes of Elenctic Theology*, 14.5 (quoted in McGrath, *Christian Theology*, 332).

shocking and ultimate wisdom of God (1 Cor 1:18–24), in the Synoptic Gospels' focus on the last passion-filled week of Jesus's life, and in John's identifying Christ's glory with his death (John 8:28; 12:32–33). For the writers of the New Testament, Christ's death on the cross was a pivotal moment in salvation-history.

But what precisely happened on the cross for the sake of human salvation? Here the New Testament gives several hints but not abundant clarity. As just noted, one of the strongest interpretive images of Christ's cross is that of sacrifice. Paul speaks of Jesus' death as a "sacrifice of atonement" (Rom 3:25),[11] as a sin offering (Rom 8:3), and of Jesus as a "paschal lamb" that was sacrificed (1 Cor 5:7). Further, Paul sees Christ's death as being "for us" (Rom 4:25; 8:3; 1 Cor 15:3; Gal 1:4) and "for sins" or "for our sins."[12] At one place, Paul even speaks of Christ, who knew no sin, as being "made sin" for our sake (2 Cor 5:21). Similar notions of Christ being a sacrifice for sins (or for our sins) are found throughout the New Testament.[13] In the Old Testament, the significance of sacrifices is not precisely explained, but does involve a sinner's sins being expunged and forgiven (Lev 4–5). In turn, the imagery suggests that somehow the sacrificial animal (which was innocent and unblemished) represents the offender and perhaps even dies in his or her place (Lev 1:4; 16:2; compare Num 27:18; Deut 34:9). In a similar manner, the apostle Paul and other New Testament authors see Christ as representing and dying for sinners, and as somehow removing (or making possible the removal of) their sins.[14] Scholars debate whether Christ's sacrifice is best described as an *expiation* of sin or as a *propitiation* of divine wrath. *Expiation* speaks (rather vaguely) of a removal of sin and its penalties, while *propitiation* indicates the placating of God's righteous indignation. Commentators also puzzle over to what degree Christ serves as a substitute for sinful humans. Does Christ take on the very guilt of sin or only its negative consequences? Does Christ receive the punishment of our sins or only shield us from that punishment? Answers to these questions are not transparent in the Scriptures, and we cannot entertain these disputes here.

Granting the image of the cross as sacrifice, we may ask further, what was accomplished through this event? Here the New Testament offers numerous metaphors, all informative yet also ultimately indefinite. One image is that of justification. Through the cross, the sinner gains acquittal before the divine court (as it were); or perhaps more accurately, as the primary partner of the divine-human covenant, God declares believers' breach of the agreement ended (Rom 8:3; Gal 1:3). Another picture of the effect of Christ's death is that of a financial transaction. The sinner is ransomed or redeemed as a slave's freedom might be purchased or as a debt might be paid (Mark 10:45; Rom 3:24; 1 Cor 6:20; Gal 3:13; Eph 1:7; Col 1:14; 2:14; 1 Tim 2:6; 1 Pet 1:18). A third image of the cross's effect is a victory over military foes. Through Christ's death

11. Or "mercy seat"—the place of atonement in the Old Testament tradition.

12. Rom 5:6–8; 8:32; 2 Cor 5:14–15, 21; Gal 2:20; 1 Thess 5:9–10.

13. Matt 26:28; Heb 8:11–15; 1 Pet 2:24; 1 John 2:2; 4:10.

14. See Dunn, *The Theology of Paul the Apostle*, 218–23.

(and often resurrection) the forces of evil, sin, and death are conquered (Phil 2:6–11; Col 1:13; 2:15; Heb 2:14).

Drawing from these varied biblical metaphors, several models of Christ's atonement have been proposed throughout the history of the church. One paradigm is the *ransom theory* or the *Christus Victor* (Christ the Victor) model. In this theory of the atonement, Christ's death (in some sense) paid a ransom to free humans from bondage to sin and to the devil, and simultaneously provided victory over the forces of sin and evil. Here the New Testament's financial and military metaphors of Christ's work are mixed. Origen was an early proponent of this view. Puzzling over the biblical notion that Christ died as a ransom, Origen wondered to whom the ransom was paid. He did not think God could be the recipient, since through Christ God was paying the ransom. Rather, Origen mused that the devil must be the beneficiary. In some sense, Satan owned or had a right to rule humans due to sin. For the sake of justice, God refused to steal humans back from Satan but chose to pay for their return instead. The devil demanded Christ's life and death in exchange for all humanity; God accepted the terms; Christ died, and believing humanity was freed. But the devil overestimated his own power to retain Christ, and Jesus burst the bonds of sin and death through his resurrection.[15]

Origen's ideas were developed further by other writers. Basil of Caesarea emphasized the need for Christ to be both human and God in order for the ransom strategy to work. So Christ had to be human in order to justly stand for the rest of humanity, and Christ had to be God in order to overcome the forces of the devil. Gregory of Nyssa highlighted the hiddenness of Christ's deity in the incarnation. In pride, Satan greedily accepted the sinless Christ in exchange for the rest of humanity; but Satan did not realize that Christ was God and thus could not be controlled. Gregory spoke of Christ as bait that the devil foolishly swallowed only to be impaled on the fishhook of Christ's deity.[16] Rufinus (344/345–411), Augustine of Hippo, and Peter Lombard (1096–1160) spoke of the cross as a mousetrap that ensnared Satan. Augustine, however, avoided the notion that God somehow deceived Satan by veiling Christ's deity. Rather, the bishop argued that in greed, the devil accepted Jesus as a ransom but overstepped his rights since Christ was sinless and, hence, not subject to Satan's dominion. Consequently, Satan lost control of all humanity but also had no rightful claim on Jesus.[17]

Not all ancient theologians endorsed the ransom theory. Gregory of Nazianzus rejected the notion that God could owe anything to the devil, as well as that God could be the recipient of Christ's death as ransom. John of Damascus (b. 675 or 676) augmented the theory by denying that Christ was a ransom *to the devil*; rather, Christ was a ransom to *death*. Death had captured humanity due to sin. Christ gave himself over to death;

15. Origen, *Commentary on Romans Books 1–5*, 2:13; and Origen, *Commentary on Matthew*, 13:28.

16. Gregory of Nyssa, *Great Catechism*, 22–26.

17. Augustine, *On the Trinity*, 13.12–14.

humanity was freed; but since Christ was sinless, death could not hold Christ either. The ransom theory had many advocates throughout the Middle Ages but fell into disfavor over time. It was criticized by Anselm of Canterbury (1033–1109) for its portrayal of God as deceptive, for its failure to address the enmity between God and humans, and for its inability to explain the need for Christ's incarnation.[18]

In light of his discomfort with the ransom theory, Anselm offered another model of Christ's atonement, one that eventually came to greatly influence Christian theology. This theory is sometimes called the *satisfaction theory*, for it portrays the cross of Christ as satisfying something in the nature of God. The ransom theory focuses on the human need to be freed from some power other than God—the devil, or death. But for Anselm, and for those who expanded his theory, a more basic problem required mending—namely, the human and divine interrelationship. Due to sin, God and humanity are at odds; an implicit (covenant-) relationship is broken; and divine forgiveness is needed. All of this insinuates that something in the nature of God must be addressed to overcome the divine-human antipathy. But what aspect of God might that be?

Anselm's answer is honor. God created humans to be morally righteous and faithful. By sinning, humans have failed to render the righteousness and obedience due God and thus have insulted the divine honor. To atone for this insult, humans must be punished, or some other form of *satisfaction* must be offered to God. But humans have no means of producing the requisite satisfaction. To atone for their insult, humans would have to give back to God not only what they owe—namely, their lives lived obediently—but also a further reparation for dishonoring God. Obviously, humans cannot give more than their very lives; consequently, they cannot recompense for their insult to God's honor. Complicating matters is Anselm's further contention that only humans can offer reparation since they are the ones who dishonored God. Graciously, however, God has devised a way for the insult to be erased, short of punishing humans. This is through Christ, who uniquely is both God and human. As a human, Christ was appropriately obliged to offer the requisite satisfaction; as God, he was able to render it. Christ's sinless obedience to God, even to the point of death, endowed him with merit sufficient to satisfy God's injured honor. Indeed, for Anselm, this is precisely why God the Son became incarnate. For Anselm, the incarnation was (in some sense) necessary in order to restore the divine honor, while also saving humans from divinely deserved punishment.[19]

The essentials of Anselm's theory were adopted and augmented by other theologians. Among them was John Calvin. Like Anselm, Calvin believed that the cross of Christ addresses something in the nature of God. But unlike Anselm, Calvin did not identify this feature as divine honor. Rather, it is God's righteousness and justice. As an essentially good being, God is opposed to sin. In turn, as a just entity, God cannot simply overlook sin or leave it unpunished. Sin must be rightly opposed and justly

18. See comments in Erickson, *Christian Theology*, 723–27.
19. Anselm, *Cur Deus Homo*.

punished. Further, because all humans are sinners, all deserve punishment. But God did not abandon human beings to the punishment they deserve. Rather, the deity allowed Christ to be a substitute for them. On the cross, Jesus received the punishment all sinful humans merit. For Calvin, this is the meaning of New Testament phrases such as Christ died "for us" or "for our sins." Thus, Calvin writes: Christ "took upon himself and suffered the punishment that, from God's righteous judgment, threatened all sinners," and "by this expiation he [Christ] made satisfaction and sacrifice duly to God the Father" and "appeased God's wrath."[20] Or again Calvin notes, "Christ was put in the place of evildoers as surety and pledge—submitting himself even as the accused—to bear and suffer all the punishments that they ought to have sustained."[21] Similar to Anselm, then, Calvin believed that God graciously devised a means by which the divine nature might be satisfied, without humans being punished. The Trinitarian God brought it about that the punishment of sin required by divine justice was fulfilled through Christ's death. Christ voluntarily stood in the place of sinners and submitted to the punishment due them. For this reason, Calvin's version of the satisfaction theory is often called the *penal substitutionary* theory.

In addition to the dissimilarities already mentioned, two further differences between Anselm's and Calvin's views are notable. First, Calvin tacitly rejects Anselm's notion that the human breach with God can be repaired by penitence-like *satisfaction* rather than by punishment. For Calvin, punishment is required. But apparently how such punishment is exacted is at the divine discretion. Second, Anselm explained the human inability to satisfy the demands of divine honor in terms of humans' not being able to give more than an obedient life to God. But Calvin, endorsing Luther's doctrine of salvation by grace alone,[22] interpreted the human inability to meet the demands of divine justice in terms of a complete human incapacity to do any truly righteous acts, at least not without divine aid. In spite of these differences, the overarching structure of the two theories is very similar. Like Anselm, Calvin insists that human salvation can come only through Christ, who is both God and human. As a human, Christ rightly assumed the human obligation to satisfy God's justice and condemnation of sin. As God, Christ was able to destroy death, overcome sin, and defeat the powers of evil.[23] As a person who was both God and human, Christ was able to live a sinless, obedient human life and to satisfy the divine demands for humanity and, consequently, stand in its place before God.[24]

Several objections have been raised against Calvin's penal substitutionary theory. One criticism is that it "seems to set God in contradiction to Godself. It . . . brings mercy and justice into collision . . . Grace is made conditional on satisfaction. But is conditional

20. Calvin, *Institutes of the Christian Religion*, 2.16.2.

21. Calvin, *Institutes of the Christian Religion*, 2.16.10.

22. For further discussion of this idea, see the section below on Salvation (pages [x-ref]).

23. Calvin, *Institutes of the Christian Religion*, 2.12.1–2.

24. Calvin, *Institutes of the Christian Religion*, 2.16.5

grace still grace?"[25] A second objection is that the scenario proposed by the model is still not just. How can the innocent Christ *justly* suffer for the guilty?[26] Even if Jesus gave up his life willingly, and even if in Christ the Trinitarian God took upon itself the penalty of human sin, one might wonder whether this was truly just. And if not, how can a just God tolerate it? One might reply that it is not just, but it is mercy. But then the question remains: Are God's holiness and God's love and mercy at odds?

A third set of theories of Christ's atonement, often called *moral influence theories*, focus on the subjective effects of his death on humans. Two broad versions of this theory are often recognized. One stresses how Christ's death provides an example to live by. The other emphasizes how the cross demonstrates God's love for humanity and thus motivates us to love and obey God. Faustus Socinus (1539–1604) endorsed the first of these.[27] For various reasons, including the two mentioned in the previous paragraph, Socinus rejected the idea of vicarious satisfaction—the idea that Christ's death somehow "satisfied" God's wrath against humanity. Rather, he emphasized 1 Pet 2:21: "For to this you have been called, because Christ also suffered for you, leaving you an example that you should follow in his steps." Socinus concluded that Jesus' death fulfills two human needs: First, it gives an example of how humans are to love God—totally, in full obedience, without reservation. Second, it shows that such love for God is humanly possible. Horace Bushnell (1802–1876) affirmed the second version of this theory. According to Bushnell, God is love. Thus, humans need not fear divine justice or punishment. The basic problem of humans is not that we have disobeyed God's law or deserve punishment. The basic problem is our attitude toward God. If we would repent of our disobedience, we would be forgiven. God is ready to forgive. The death of Christ, then, makes us aware of, demonstrates, God's love for us.[28] It shows us God's love "in such a compelling way that we are constrained to respond in wonder and gratitude";[29] Hastings Rashdall (1858–1924) held similar views.[30] Peter Abelard (1079–1142) is often credited with developing the moral influence theory, although he also simultaneously affirmed more traditional views of Christ's death as a sacrifice.

Various criticisms are offered against moral influence theories. Positively, they highlight the genuine subjective impact the story of Christ's death often has on hearers. Christians long have found in Christ's cross both an example of faithfulness to God and a picture of the divine love for humankind. But moral influence theories stop short of the full biblical testimony about Christ's death. They ignore or unduly quell scriptural references to Christ's death as ransom, as a sacrifice, as sin-bearing for us. Further, they tend to sentimentalize God's love and underestimate "the power and

25. Migliore, *Faith Seeking Understanding*, 153.

26. Strong, *Systematic Theology*, 755.

27. See Socinus, *Racovian Catechism*.

28. Bushnell, *The Vicarious Sacrifice*.

29. Migliore, *Faith Seeking Understanding*, 153–54.

30. Rashdall, *The Idea of Atonement in Christian Thought*.

tenacity of evil."[31] Finally, one might question whether the tragedy of Christ's death is appreciated in these views. Was Christ's death the only way God could have demonstrated love? Would no other, less bloody example have done the job? In other words, to allow oneself or someone else to be killed in order to demonstrate love for another hardly seems to display love *unless* such a death were (in some sense) necessary for bringing great benefit or avoidance of terrible harm to the one loved. Otherwise, the death would be a tragic waste, and allowing it might be more a sign of bizarre or twisted affections than of deep love.

While articulating the precise nature of Christ atoning work on the cross faces problems, a core claim of Christian theology is that somehow through Christ's death a fundamental element of human salvation was achieved. Perhaps each of these theories offers some insight into the nature of Christ's atonement without capturing fully the mystery of God's work in Christ.

Salvation

At the center of Christian theology is belief that God is seeking to save humans from sin and its impact on life. As we have seen, the doctrine of sin announces that people sin against God and (in some sense) are sinful (prone to evil). Sin, in turn, brings negative consequences. It generates enmity, breaks down fellowship with God, and strains relations among humans. Sin also negatively impacts the cosmos and produces undesirable consequences for individuals. Among these unwanted personal costs are guilt, divine condemnation, bondage to sin, and death. In many ways, the goal of salvation is to undo human sinfulness and its consequences, so salvation entails making fundamental changes to the cosmic order. Said more positively, the goal of salvation is to bring humans into a right relationship with God and with each other, to restore humans to the kind of beings God intends them to be, and to make the created order whole.

Biblical Metaphors for Salvation

In Chapter 2, we noted several metaphors employed in the Bible to depict the notion of salvation. Each of these adds texture to the Christian understanding of what God has done in Jesus. All these metaphors may point to an experience or encounter or mystery not fully describable. Still they provide sufficient light to help articulate a vision of the Christian understanding of salvation. Readers might wish to review these metaphors before continuing to the next section. Among the metaphors (previously discussed) are the following: divine blessing, liberation or deliverance, covenant, the presence of God, atonement, a promised land, a messianic ruler and kingdom, a new covenant, an outpouring of God's Spirit, justification, sanctification, glorification, renewal or

---

31. Migliore, *Faith Seeking Understanding*, 154.

regeneration, rebirth, reconciliation, adoption into God's family, union with Christ, participation or fellowship with Christ, baptism in Christ and in the Spirit, ransom or redemption, a new creation, a new self, resurrection, eternal life, the image of Christ and conformity to Christ, the heavenly city, and heaven.

Two Questions about Salvation

Keeping in mind these multiple biblical metaphors of salvation, we consider different models of salvation. That is, we ponder diverse ways the salvation process has been construed. Assuming that salvation involves undoing sin and its consequences, two interrelated questions arise for the doctrine of salvation. *First, which aspect of sin, if any, must be remedied first?* Historically, most theories of salvation have presumed that the impact of sin on the individual must be tackled first. Each person's sin produces guilt and enslavement to sin, which in turn generates a broken relationship with God and with fellow humans. Thus, the sin of individuals must be cured before other features of sin can be resolved. Or at least no complete resolution can occur without the change of individual sinners. A few models of salvation, however, propose that the systemic characteristics of sin must be dealt with before genuine change for individuals can transpire. Individuals live in social structures (i.e. economic, political, and ideological systems) that often define them and control their lives. Such arrangements can unjustly exploit persons or groups even when no single individual breaks moral rules within such systems. Thus, individuals can live justly within such systems but still participate in unjust structures that exploit others. In light of such systemic injustice, some theologians insist that only when social systems are changed can the deeper problems of sin be addressed.

The first of these approaches was favored by the majority of the New Testament's authors. Neither the Gospel writers nor Paul called for radical changes to the Roman Empire's social structure. To do so would have meant annihilation. Rather, they called for changes in individual lives and expressed belief that such changes could better society. Even more, most New Testament writers assumed that social changes would fully come only through God's supernatural inbreaking into world history. They looked for Christ to return in power to correct the systemic wrongs of their societies. Most orthodox writers of the second and third centuries endorsed similar views. With the delay of Christ's return, the ascendancy of Emperor Constantine I, and the steady emergence of a Christianized Rome, ideological shifts occurred. Gradually, anticipation of Christ's apocalyptic return diminished (without utterly fading) as theologians began to think of the church and empire as the primary instruments of God's reign on earth. Through these institutions the systemic ills of humanity might be saved. Even in these contexts, however, there was a general recognition that God's complete reign was not fully present and was yet to come. Perhaps not until the musings of nineteenth-century classic liberal theology did the notion of salvation through systemic social changes come to full fruition. Many of these theologians hoped for the improvement of human life through natural social progress, which they saw directed by an immanent divine providence. Echoes of the classic liberal emphasis on salvation through social changes are found in some forms of contemporary liberation theology, although liberation theologies are prone to see such changes less as inevitable (or peaceful) progressions and more as radical transitions from current immoral systems.

A second question about the nature of salvation is this. What roles do God and humans play in the salvation-process? Does God alone act? Do humans in any way contribute to the process? Pelagius believed that humans play the fundamental role in their own salvation. They are free to follow God and to not sin, and they can do these things by their own efforts. God primarily supplies external aids to assist individuals in their moral journeys toward personal righteousness. And through personal moral changes, the human world as a whole can be improved. Many classic liberals, likewise, saw humans playing a primary role in the salvation process. Through human agency, individuals and social structures can and will be changed. Granted, these human efforts are the outworking of an immanent divine providence; nevertheless, they also are fully natural events in time and space, and there is little need for supernatural intervention in human history.

Traditional Catholic and Protestant theology has tended to reject the idea that humans are the primary agents in salvation history. Rather, God is the principal actor. Only by God's direct action upon the inner being of individuals can salvation come. God must alter the sinful person, changing his or her intrinsic nature. Two contrary trajectories occur in traditional theology. Some theologians *virtually* make God the sole actor in salvation, while others make room for divine-human interplay. The Protestant Reformers Martin Luther and John Calvin verged on the first of these approaches. Each held that God predestines who will be saved; the deity accomplishes this preordination by supernaturally giving faith and spiritual change to those divinely chosen. Those not ordained to salvation cannot exercise faith and cannot alter their spiritual condition. God alone determines who receives inner spiritual changes and who does not. Protestants James Arminius and John Wesley (1703–1791) represent the second view. They insisted that the act of faith is a freely chosen human feat. In turn, based on that free act of faith, God changes the spiritual nature of persons, affectively dealing with the sinful nature. Arminius and Wesley, however, were cagy. Neither one wanted to commit the perceived error of Pelagius—making salvation dependent on human effort. Rather, each proposed that even the act of faith is made possible by a divinely given grace, which allows all humans—if they so choose—to freely respond to God in faith. This grace is prevenient—that is, given to all humans—so that all are free to choose for or against God. Thus, Arminius and Wesley sought to retain the primacy of divine agency in salvation while granting some human contribution. Roman Catholic tradition uncomfortably houses both of these approaches to salvation. Augustine favored the former of the two; Pope Gregory the Great and Erasmus leaned toward the latter. As we will see below and in the next chapter, a chief difference between traditional Roman Catholic and Protestant views of salvation has to do with how each interprets the role of the church and its sacraments in the workings of individual salvation. Virtually all traditional models of salvation, however, endorse the primacy of divine agency, and many models attempt to make room for human freedom in the salvation process.

Traditional Protestant Theology of Individual Salvation

We turn to examine two key traditional models of individual salvation. We begin with conventional Protestant theology. According to this view, the primary problem facing humans is individual sinfulness. From personal sinfulness flow many, if not all, the unwanted consequences of sin, including broken relationships with God and with fellow humans, guilt, divine condemnation, and bondage to sin. The initial goal of salvation, then, is to change human nature from sinful to righteous. And given this change, many of the negative consequences of sin can be undone. In positive terms, this transformation of the individual is described as becoming like Christ or being conformed to the image of Christ. As Christ was free from sin, guilt, and divine condemnation, so redeemed humans are to be free from sin, guilt, and condemnation. As Christ loved God and his fellow humans, so humans are to love God and their fellow humans. As Christ obeyed God and stood in a right relationship with God the Father, so humans are to obey God and be in good standing with God the Father. As Christ was raised from the dead and entered into glory, so humans one day will be resurrected and enter into glory.

Critical to the salvation of individuals is the work of Christ. Christ provides prophetic revelation, kingly rule, and priestly intercession. But for traditional Protestant theology, Christ's death on the cross is particularly significant. His death somehow atoned for the sins of humanity. The precise nature of this atonement is subject to dispute; we have discussed some interpretations of it above. Also significant to the traditional Protestant understanding of salvation is the notion of spiritual union with Christ. This New Testament expresses this idea in diverse ways, including in Paul's concepts of Christ being "in" believers (Gal 2:20; Col 1:27) and believers being "in" Christ,[32] as well as in notions like the indwelling of the Spirit or of the Spirit of Christ. For Protestant theology, Christ's atoning death and spiritual presence provide the core benefits of salvation. From these emanate forgiveness of sin, redemption, justification, sanctification, reconciliation, rebirth (renewal or regeneration), glorification, and so forth.

Most Protestants agree that personal salvation occurs in phases. It has a beginning phase, a middle period, and a final state. Often included among the elements of the *beginning phase* are repentance and faith. Whether these two are parts of salvation

---

32. 1 Cor 1:4–5; 2 Cor 5:17; Eph 1:3–4, 6–8; 2:10; 1 Thess 4:16.

proper or preliminary to salvation is a matter of debate. The biblical concept of repentance conveys the idea of change or turning. Often it involves turning from sin,
or turning to God, or both. The biblical notion of faith, in turn, often carries both the
idea of believing core truths and trusting God. Often in the New Testament, humans
are asked to repent of sin and believe in Christ (or the gospel). Likewise, in the New
Testament, repentance from sin and faith in Christ are portrayed as interconnected
ways to reap the benefits of salvation.

In addition to the preliminary acts of repentance and faith, often included in
the first phase of salvation are events such as union with Christ, spiritual rebirth
(regeneration), justification, reconciliation, and adoption into the family of God.
As noted above, union with Christ is often seen as the primary cause of these other
aspects of salvation. Regeneration refers to a spiritual change in the individual,
transforming the person from a state of bondage to sin to one of freedom to begin
living a righteous (Christ-like) life. Most Protestants do not see regeneration as actually making a person sinless. Rather, regeneration is the initial spiritual change
that enables a person to begin moving toward righteousness. One theologian has
referred to regeneration as the reception of a new ruling disposition that enables
a person to freely do what it right.[33] As we will see below, some Protestants use the
term *regeneration* to refer to the ongoing movement toward righteousness in the
Christian's life. *Reconciliation* is restoration to a right relationship with God. And
adoption refers to a believer's being grafted into the family of God.

Justification is a very important concept in the Protestant theology of salvation.
Protestants typically understand justification as God's declaring a believer to be righteous, even though that individual is not literally righteous. It is a forensic judgment
something like acquittal or forgiveness. Martin Luther and his younger colleague
Philip Melanchthon (1497–1560) taught that salvation is a gift from God. Humans
do not gain salvation by being righteous but by being declared righteous by God.
Christians are not literally righteous; they are still sinners. But God declares that they
are righteous and imputes to them (credits to them) Christ's righteousness as if it were
their own. Drawing from the apostle Paul, Luther and Melanchthon referred to this
divine declaration that humans are righteous as *justification*.

The *middle period* of individual salvation involves movement toward actual moral
conformity to God's will. Like the beginning aspects of salvation, this movement is
made possible by the believer's spiritual union with Christ (and by the indwelling of the
Holy Spirit). This growth toward actual righteousness is *sometimes called sanctification*.
John Calvin refined Luther's understanding of justification. At issues was precisely how
justification as a forensic or legal declaration of righteousness relates to the actual process of becoming righteous in the life of the Christian. Luther had declared that good

33. Strong, *Systematic Theology*, 809. Many Protestant theologians believe that regeneration in fact
is an ongoing process throughout the Christian life, so it is more or less synonymous with sanctification. Even so, most would agree that its inception is at the beginning of a believer's life.

works flow from the gratitude and freedom of the Christian whom God had graciously declared righteous. But Luther did not clarify the role played by God in this process. Calvin sought to resolves these issues by focusing first on the Christian's spiritual union with Christ, a union that occurs as a result of a person's (God-given) faith in Christ. For Calvin, "faith unites the believer to Christ in a 'mystic union.'"[34] Further, Calvin contended that because of and through this mystic or spiritual union with Christ, the believer is both justified (declared righteous) and, subsequently, led toward a life of actual righteousness or Christ-likeness. Thus, it is the Christian's spiritual union with Christ that causes both justification and eventual growth toward righteousness. Calvin refers to this movement toward actual righteousness as *regeneration*. Many Protestants prefer the term *sanctification*.[35] Most Protestants, including Calvin and his spiritual descendants, do not think that one can ever attain moral perfection in this life; but a few Protestants have taught that virtual moral perfection is possible in this life.[36] The *final stage* of individual salvation sometimes is called *glorification*, which includes personal resurrection, moral perfection, and eternal life. (We will say more about the final state of salvation in Chapter 7 when we discuss eschatology).

A critical question for salvation theology is, how does one receive the benefits of salvation? For Protestants, the answer is relatively simple. One receives salvation through faith in Christ. This does not mean that faith somehow *causes* salvation. Rather, faith is simply accepting what God offers through Christ, recognizing one's own inability to achieve what God has made possible in Christ. Faith is trusting God. Like many "simple" doctrines, the doctrine of salvation through faith alone can be quite complicated. Part of its complexity arises from Luther's contention that humans cannot exercise faith on their own. Indeed, they cannot even desire to love or to obey God. Rather, as indicated in our discussion above, God must give sinners the requisite desires to love and to obey, and must provide the power to believe.

John Calvin and many of the Reformed tradition endorsed Luther's insights at this point. Indeed, many of these writers believed that God's influence upon the believer is so great that he or she cannot fail to exercise faith in Christ and, subsequently, cannot fail to be saved. The divinely given urge to believe ensures that the one so empowered will accede to that inner desire. In light of this, many Protestant theologians distinguish between a general divine call to salvation and a special or effective call to salvation. The former is offered to all people, but the latter is only extended to those predestined to salvation by God. Not everyone responds in faith to the general call, but all who are specially or effectively called do respond in faith and are saved. Not all Protestants agree with Luther and Calvin on these various points. They prefer the notion that God offers a prevenient grace that empowers all humans to make a *free* choice. Whether persons choose to have or not have faith in Christ is up to them.

34. McGrath, *Reformation Thought*, 112.
35. McGrath, *Reformation Thought*, 112.
36. Wesley, *A Plain Account of Christian Perfection*.

Often this later group of theologians insists that there is only one call to salvation, a general one extended to all persons.

Another puzzle regarding the doctrine of salvation by faith concerns how faith and regeneration interrelate. The dilemma may be expressed as follows: Does a person become regenerated (spiritually changed) because of faith, or does a person exercise faith because he or she has been regenerated (spiritually changed)? Writers such as Arminius and Wesley favor the first of these options. Many Reformed writers prefer the second option. A problem with the former perspective is some biblical texts suggest that only those God chooses to save can positively respond to Christ (Matt 22:14; John 6:44; Rom 8:29–30). A difficulty with the latter view is that many New Testament passages assert that salvation (including spiritual change) results from a person's faith in Christ (John 3:16; 11:25–26; 20:30; Acts 16:31; Rom 1:16–17; 10:5–13). To resolve this dilemma, some (who endorse that only those God so empowers can exercise faith) distinguish between regeneration and "effective calling." They claim that regeneration only occurs after faith; however, divinely given faith comes only to those whom God has chosen and effectively called to have faith.[37]

A third problem for the doctrine of salvation by faith arises when one ponders when a person is able to exercise faith. Many of the early Reformers—including Luther and Calvin—continued the Catholic practice of baptizing infants, and they maintained that such infants are saved. But if faith is the precursor to salvation, in what sense could babies exercise faith in Christ? We will discuss this dilemma below when we examine the doctrines of the church and baptism. In anticipation, we may note that the question of infant faith led some Reformers to conclude that only individuals sufficiently mature to exercise faith can be baptized. But this led to another problem: What happens to infants and children who die prior to being mature enough to exercise personal faith in Christ? Are they damned? Are they saved and, if so, how?

Traditional Catholic Theology of Individual Salvation

So much then for the basic Protestant doctrine of individual salvation. We turn now to consider the broad Catholic vision of such salvation. Catholic theology shares much with traditional Protestantism, including emphasizing the need to cure the sinful nature of individuals before resolving the problems of human interrelationships and cosmic disorder. As in Protestant thought, so in Catholic theology individual salvation depends on the work of Christ, especially his atoning death and his spiritual union with the believer. From this atonement and spiritual empowering the other benefits of salvation flow. Like Protestantism, Catholicism recognizes a temporal flow

37. Millard Erickson endorses this last perspective, claiming that regeneration follows faith, but such faith follows from an irresistible call. See Erickson, *Christian Theology*, 863–64. For a defense of the traditional Arminian perspective see Wiley, *Christian Theology*. For the more traditional Calvinistic interpretation, see Murray, *Redemption, Accomplished and Applied*.

in individual salvation. There are beginning, middle, and culminating phases in salvation. Among the elements of the initial phase are repentance from sin and faith in Christ. Following these, other aspects of the beginning period of salvation unfold, including mystical union with Christ, regeneration, justification, reconciliation, and divine adoption. In turn, a period of moral development follows this initial phase, ideally trailed by an ultimate culmination of the individual's salvation.

While Catholicism and Protestantism agree on the basic structure of individual salvation, they disagree on several details. One difference concerns the nature of justification. Luther and other Protestants taught that justification addresses the legal standing of believers before God. As sinners, humans stand condemned by God, but through Christ believers are declared to be righteous even though they are in fact still sinners. They are acquitted because the righteousness of Christ has been *imputed* (credited) to them, even though they are not literally righteous. Thus, believers have an "alien righteousness" attributed to them, one that is not literally in them. Following Augustine of Hippo, on the other hand, Catholic leaders at the Council of Trent (1545–1563) insisted that justification is more than this. They agreed that justification involves a change of legal status before God; it includes divine forgiveness and a declaration of right standing before God. But it also includes an *infusion* of actual righteousness into the believer. The Christian receives inwardly the righteousness of Christ. Thus, believers become literally righteous, even though this righteousness is not of their own doing.

In addition to differences about imputation versus infusion of Christ's righteousness, Protestants and Catholics disagree over the preconditions necessary for the reception of salvation, including justification. For Catholics, Christ's righteousness is conveyed to believers by faith *through* the sacraments, especially the sacrament of baptism. The sacraments do not *cause* the righteousness of Christ to flow into the believer. God is the ultimate cause of this mystery. But the sacraments are the primary, divinely chosen precondition for conferring this gift upon believers. Protestants, on the other hand, tend to reject the notion that the sacraments convey (either by imputing or infusing) the righteousness of Christ upon believers. Instead, as noted above, whatever benefits of salvation the Christian receives are given by God in light of the believer's faith in Christ. Similar to Catholics, Protestants reject the idea that faith *causes* salvation (including justification). Ultimately, God causes this. Rather, Protestants hold that God sovereignly chooses faith as a precondition for receiving the benefits of salvation. Like Protestants, Catholics face puzzles about the relationship between faith and the salvation in infants and children. Often Catholic theologians speak of the sacraments as activated by or as signs of inner faith; but in what sense can infants or young children exercise faith? We will discuss these issues in the next chapter when we examine the doctrine of church sacraments.

Beyond these distinctions, Catholics and Protestants also disagree over the extent of justification. As noted above, often Protestants distinguish between justification as an instantaneous event at the beginning of salvation and sanctification as an ongoing process through life. Further, and adding to the confusion, some Protestants see *regeneration* as a synonym for *sanctification*, while others see regeneration as a once-for-all event at the start of the salvation process. Catholics, on the other hand, tend to blend the initial and ongoing phases of salvation into a singular process, seeing justification, sanctification, and regeneration as virtual synonyms, or as all three involving past, present, and future aspects. This ambiguity between Catholic and Protestant usages of the terms *justification*, *sanctification*, and *regeneration* amplified, if not in some cases generated, the disagreements between the two camps. Such circumstances exemplify how tangled thinking can produce unnecessary disagreements. Both groups agree that salvation involves a magnanimous act of divine forgiveness of sin at the beginning of the salvation process, a forgiveness that cannot be earned and is by sheer grace. Both in turn believe that through the working of Christ and the indwelling of the Spirit, Christians should (and perhaps must) move toward real personal righteousness in life, otherwise the claim that an individual is being transformed by God is a sham or a self-delusion. And both camps agree that ultimate salvation from sin and its consequences comes after this earthly life. This is not to say that genuine disagreements do not exist between Catholic and Protestant theologies, but some of the disagreements might be (and in some cases are being) resolved by dialogue.

Here is a final note on Catholic theology of individual salvation: Traditional Roman Catholic theology insisted that the Roman Church is the only channel of God's grace. God's grace is conferred only through the sacraments of that Church. Thus, anyone outside of the Church was thought to be doomed, without grace. Catholic theology has changed over the last century. The Second Vatican Council (1962–1965) recognized three types of saved people: (1) Catholics within the church; (2) non-Catholic Christians "linked" to the church, and (3) non-Christians who are "related" to the church. This last group refers to those not in any church who are nevertheless not separated from God's grace. Such individuals are brought to God through the cosmic Christ, the Logos who enlightens all humans. Thus, Catholic theology has become open to the possibility of salvation outside of the Catholic Church, including for persons from other Christian traditions and even for some who are not affiliated with Christianity at all.[38]

The Role of the Holy Spirit in Individual Salvation

The Spirit (or breath or wind) of God played a vital role in the theology of the ancient Israelites. In the Hebrew Bible, the Spirit/Breath of God is associated with the creation (Gen 1:2; Job 26:12–13; Ps 33:6),[39] sustenance (Job 33:4; 34:14–15; Ps 33:6),

38. Many Protestant writers likewise are open to the salvation of persons outside formal connection to a Christian church per se. See Chapter 13, below, for further discussion.

39. Ps 33:6 may emphasize more the notion that God's creation of the world is by divine

and future renewal (Isa 32:13) of the world and of life. The Spirit of God, likewise, is depicted as giving to some servants of God various practical skills, such as leadership and military acumen (Exod 31: 31:3–5; 35:31; Num 27:18; Deut 34:9; Judg 3:10; 6:34; 14:6, 19; 15:14–15 1 Sam 11:6).[40] The Spirit also plays an important function in influencing and empowering the prophets and their prophecies. In early Hebrew biblical literature, such gifting often was portrayed as a kind of manic possession (Num 24:2; 1 Sam 10:6, 10; 19:24). The preexilic classic prophets (Amos, Hosea, Isaiah, and Micah) tended to stress the word of the Lord more than the work of the Spirit in their ministries; nevertheless, they believed that their messages *came from* Yahweh (Hos 6:5; 9:8; 12:10; Isa 3:2). Postexilic biblical literature underscored the Spirit's influence in the ministry of the prophets, including in the messages and writings of the prophets (Isa 48:16; 61:1; Ezek 2:1–2; 3:12; 8:3; Zech 7:12).

A critical element of the Hebrew Bible's testimony about the Spirit of God is the Spirit's role in returning Israel from its fallen state. Often tied to this renewal were hopes of the restoration of Israel to the land and to political autonomy; but typically combined with this was anticipation of *restored righteousness* before God. Ps 51 captures this latter hope for the individual follower of Yahweh. The Psalmist pleads:

> Create in me a clean heart, O God,
>
>> and put a new and right spirit within me.
>
> Do not cast me away from your presence,
>
>> and do not take your *holy spirit* from me.
>
> Restore to me the joy of your salvation,
>
>> and sustain in me a willing spirit (vv. 10–12; italics added).

Here, in one of only three passages in the Hebrew Bible that refer to God's spirit as "holy," the author requests a right and willing spirit. Implicit is the desire to be personally faithful to Yahweh; further, a connection is made between righteousness and God's holy spirit.

In a similar manner, several Old Testament passages tie the future restoration of Israel's faithfulness to the outpouring of God's Spirit. Isa 34 indicates that the fallen nation of Israel will only be reestablished when "a *spirit* from on high is *poured out*" (Isa 34:14; italics added). In Isa 44:3, the Lord promises to restore the land of Israel by pouring out "water on the thirsty land" and pouring out the divine spirit on the descendants of Israel. Ezek 36 describes Yahweh as promising the people of Israel,

> I will take you from the nations, and gather you from all the countries, and
> bring you into your own land. I will sprinkle clean water upon you, and you
> shall be clean from all your uncleannesses, and from all your idols I will

---

breathed- out command (Heron, *The Holy Spirit*, 11).

40. In many instances, it is unclear whether these abilities are from birth or given in a miraculous dispensation (Heron, *The Holy Spirit*, 13).

cleanse you. A *new heart* I will give you, and a *new spirit* I will put within you
. . . I will put *my spirit* within you, and make you follow my statutes and be
careful to observe my ordinances (Ezek 36:24–27; italics added).

Similar to the psalmist in Ps 51 (above), Ezekiel here insists that—in the context of a
restored land—God will give to the people of Israel a new heart and new spirit, one
that allows them to be faithful to God's laws. In turn, this new heart and spirit are
linked to God's depositing of the *spirit of God* within the people. In all these verses, we
see a connection between the outpouring of God's Spirit and the moral uprightness/
faithfulness of a restored Israel.

Another important theme in the Hebrew Bible regarding God's Spirit is Joel's
affirmation of a future outpouring of the divine Spirit upon the general population of
Israel (not just upon appointed spokespersons), which, in turn, will lead to visions and
prophetic messages. In Joel 2:28–29, the Lord proclaims:

Then afterward
  I will pour out my *spirit on all flesh*;
your sons and your daughters shall prophesy,
  your old men shall dream dreams,
  and your young men shall see visions.
Even on the male and female slaves,
  in those days, I will pour out my spirit (italics added).

Related to these themes regarding the outpouring of God's Spirit are similar
promises regarding the coming of a great Davidic *messiah* ("anointed one").

A shoot shall come out from the stump of Jesse,
  and a branch shall grow out of his roots.
The *spirit* of the Lord shall rest on him,
  the *spirit* of wisdom and understanding,
the *spirit* of counsel and might,
  the *spirit* of knowledge and the fear of the LORD . . .
with righteousness he shall judge the poor,
  and decide with equity for the meek of the earth;
he shall strike the earth with the rod of his mouth,
  and with the breath of his lips he shall kill the wicked.
Righteousness shall be the belt around his waist,
  and faithfulness the belt around his loins (Isa 11:1–5; italics added).

Upon the Davidic messiah will rest the spirit of the Lord; this messiah will be just,
righteous, and faithful; and his rule will bring justice, righteousness, and faithfulness
to Israel. In like manner, Isa 42 speaks of a servant of the Lord upon whom God's spirit

is placed, who will bring justice to the nations (vv. 1–4). Many of these trends found in the Hebrew Bible were echoed and augmented in the intertestamental literature of Second Temple Judaism. The writers of this literature often credited the inspiration of Scriptures to the work of God's Spirit and emphasized the future outpouring of the *Holy* Spirit upon the faithful in the coming days of the Messiah.[41]

New Testament writers, likewise, developed these various themes of the Hebrew biblical and intertestamental literature. They attributed the inspiration of prophecy and of scriptures to the Spirit of God (see Acts 1:16; 2 Pet 1:21). More profoundly, these early Christian writers saw in Jesus the fulfillment of many prophetic promises from the Hebrew Bible—including especially the advent of a Messiah in whose wake also came the outpouring of the Holy Spirit and of righteousness. The writers of the Gospels saw the advent and activities of Jesus as closely related to the work of the Spirit of God.[42] Jesus was conceived by the mysterious work of the Holy Spirit (Matt 1:18, 20; Luke 1:35). At his baptism, the Spirit descended upon Jesus (Matt 3:6; Mark 1:10; Luke 3:22; John 1:32). Immediately after Jesus' baptism, the Spirit led him (*compelled* him according to Mark) into the wilderness to be tested (Matt 4:1; Mark 1:12; Luke 4:1–2). "And Jesus returned in the power of the Spirit into Galilee" (Luke 4:14), and there began his public ministry. Luke depicts Jesus inaugurating his ministry in a synagogue in Nazareth by reading from Isa 61. Luke renders Isaiah this way:

> The *Spirit of the Lord* is upon me,
>> because he has anointed me
>> to bring good news to the poor.
> He has sent me to proclaim release to the captives
>> and recovery of sight to the blind,
>> to let the oppressed go free,
> to proclaim the year of the Lord's favor. (Luke 4:18–19; italics added)

Clearly, Luke wanted his readers to understand Jesus' ministry as one commissioned and empowered by the Spirit of Yahweh. Indeed, each Synoptic Gospel comments that a critical purpose of Jesus's ministry was to baptize people with the Holy Spirit (Matt 3:11; Mark 1:8; Luke 3:16). Further, Jesus performed various ministries, including especially exorcisms, through the power of the Spirit; thus, when some religious leaders accused him of casting out demons through the prince of demons, Jesus warned them they were in danger of blaspheming against the Spirit of God (Matt 12:22–32). The

---

41. Heron, *The Holy Spirit*, 23. See Psalms of Solomon, 17:32–39 and Testament of the Twelve Patriarchs 18:6–12. It should be noted that Second Temple Jewish expectations varied. Not all Jews of that era were looking for a messiah. See Wright, *The New Testament and the People of God*, 302, 307–8.

42. In the New Testament, numerous locutions are used for God's Spirit: Spirit of the Father (Matt 10:20), Spirit of his Son (Gal 4:6), Spirit of Jesus (Acts 16:7), Spirit of Christ (Rom 8:9), Spirit of life (Rom 8:2), Spirit of Sonship (Rom 8:15), Spirit of grace (Heb 10:29), Spirit of truth (John 14:17), Spirit of wisdom (Acts 6:3, 10), and Paraclete (John 14:16). See Heron, *The Holy Spirit*, 39.

book of Acts suggests that Jesus' whole life reflected the influence of God's Spirit. In Acts, the apostle Peter notes that the story of Jesus had been heard throughout Galilee and beyond, namely, the tale of "how God anointed Jesus of Nazareth with the Holy Spirit and with power; [and] how he went about doing good and healing all who were oppressed by the devil, for God was with him" (10:38 brackets added). God and God's Spirit were with Jesus throughout his ministry.

In turn, this empowering of Jesus became the mechanism by which his followers were baptized in the Spirit. In his Pentecost sermon, having witnessed the spectacular influence of the Holy Spirit upon the early church and upon Jewish pilgrims in Jerusalem, Peter notes: "This Jesus God raised up, and of that all of us are witnesses. Being therefore exalted at the right hand of God, and having received from the Father the promise of the Holy Spirit, *he has poured out* this that you both see and hear" (Acts 2:32; italics added). Indeed, Peter interpreted these events as the fulfillment of Joel's ancient prophecy regarding the outpouring of the Spirit (mentioned above; compare Joel 2:28–29 and Acts 2:17–18). In light of passages such as these, Alasdair Heron rightly comments: "This is the message that sets the New Testament apart from the Old, and from the intertestamental writings. The Messiah has come; the age of the Spirit has opened; the Spirit itself is the power of the divine purposes centered in Jesus Christ, and radiating from him."[43] Heron further notes: "The Spirit came on him [Jesus] from the Father; it comes to his [Jesus'] followers *through him*. So the activity of the Spirit is intrinsically bound up with Jesus Christ himself, and this double pattern of his reception and bestowal of the Spirit is constitutive of the whole fresh understanding of the matter in the New Testament."[44]

In light of all this, the role of the Holy Spirit (as depicted in the New Testament) is pivotal in the workings of human salvation. The Gospel of John suggests that the Spirit of God plays a vital part in convicting humans of sin and warning them of divine judgment (John 16:7–11). A similar idea is suggested in Jesus' warning not to blaspheme against the Spirit of God, suggesting that sometimes persons (including some in Jesus' day) can hold views or exude attitudes that at some level they know are counter to the inner testimony of God's Spirit (Matt 12:22–32). The Spirit also is instrumental in what above we have called *regeneration*, changing the inner being of persons so that they might live for God. Such an idea is suggested in John 3 where Jesus insists that "truly, I tell you, no one can see the kingdom of God without being born from above," and "no one can enter the kingdom of God without being born of water and Spirit" (vv. 3, 5). In a similar manner, the book of Titus states: "When the goodness and loving-kindness of God our Savior appeared, he saved us, not because of deeds done by us in righteousness, but in virtue of his own mercy, by the washing of *regeneration* and *renewal in the Holy Spirit*, which he poured out upon us richly

---

43. Heron, *The Holy Spirit*, 39.

44. Heron, *The Holy Spirit*, 42.

through Jesus Christ our Savior" (3:4–6; italics added). Clearly, the Spirit is involved in the process of regeneration and renewal.

The Holy Spirit also is active in what theologians often call *sanctification*—the ongoing movement of the believer toward righteous living. This role of the Spirit is suggested in Rom 8, where Paul insists that through "the law of the Spirit," believers have been freed from sin and death (v. 2) and now live "according to the Spirit" so that "the just requirement of the law might be fulfilled" in them (v. 4). The Spirit of God dwells within such believers and leads them so that they might put to death evil deeds[45] and thus live righteously (vv. 9–14). In a similar manner, Paul encourages Christians in Galatia to "live by the Spirit . . . and do not gratify the desires of the flesh" (5:16). The term "flesh" was a code word for Paul to speak of sinful tendencies in general, and not merely sins involving physical desires or actions. Paul's point is that by living in and through/by the Spirit's guidance, the Christian can live righteously. One can follow the precept of loving one's neighbor as one's self (Gal 5:14). And through the Spirit of God, one can receive key moral virtues or dispositions. Paul refers to these as "the fruit of the Spirit." He writes:

> The fruit of the Spirit is love, joy, peace, patience, kindness, generosity, faith-fulness, gentleness, and self-control. There is no law against such things . . . If we live by the Spirit, let us also be guided by the Spirit. (Gal 5:22–25)

It is likely that Paul did not see this list as exhaustive but as exemplars of the kind of influence the Spirit manifests in persons' lives.

Related, although perhaps not identical, to the Spirit's aid in developing and living a moral or righteous life, the Spirit also is accredited with assisting Christians in witnessing for Christ (Acts 1:4–5), in understanding spiritual truths (John 16:13), and in praying to God (including when words are inadequate; Rom 8:26); the Spirit also intercedes for God's people as they pray (Rom 8:27) and offers Christians inner assurance of their faith (John 15:26; Rom 8:23; 2 Cor 1:22; 5:5; Eph 1:13). Finally, the Holy Spirit is recognized as gifting Christian with various abilities (*charisma*), all designed (according to Paul) to edify the Christian community and its ministries (1 Cor 12:4–7; Eph 4:12). Among these are prophecy, ministry, teaching, exhortation, generosity, leadership, and mercifulness (Rom 12:6–8); also, there are gifts of wisdom, knowledge, faith, healing, working of miracles, discernment of spirits, speaking in tongues, and interpreting such utterances (1 Cor 12:8–11). Additionally, given by the Spirit are key office-like gifts—that is, God gifts some people to be apostles, prophets, evangelists, and pastor-teachers (Eph 4:11). The book of Acts likewise associates the Spirit and the baptism of the Spirit with several phenomena, including speaking in tongues (at least some of which are foreign languages: 2:4; 10:46; 19:6), praising God (10:46), proclamation (2:11; 4:8; 4:31), Christian prophecies (2:17–18; 11:28; 20:23;

---

45. Literally, "deeds of flesh."

21:4; 21:11), visions (7:55), divine guidance (8:29; 10:19; 11:12; 13:2), and guidance through church ministers (13:4; 20:22; 20:28).[46]

Similar to the doctrine of the believer's union with Christ, a central component of the Spirit's role in human salvation is the Spirit's mysterious union or communion with believers (Rom 8:11, 15–17; 1 Cor 2:9–13; 3:16). In this context, Heron again is helpful when he notes that "the Spirit is the inner dynamic of the life of faith, life which . . . at its inmost core is formed by participation in a movement of God himself. It is the hidden centre of our own identity, the reflection and actualization in us of Christ's relation of sonship to the Father."[47] According to many theologians, this union with the Holy Spirit (who likewise is the Spirit of Christ) is the most fundamental element of human salvation.

Excursus: The New Perspective on Paul

Over the last half century, something of a renaissance has occurred in New Testament Pauline studies. This renaissance—often referred to as the "New Perspective on Paul"[48]—grows out of a desire to rightly interpret Paul's writings within the context of first-century Judaism and out of a concern that some earlier interpretations fell short of this goal. One result of this movement has been challenges to some traditional (even venerable) interpretations of Christian doctrine, not the least of which is the Protestant doctrine of justification. The New Perspective is colossal in its scope and hardly homogenous; there are multiple disputes among its proponents. Here we can only give a general account of the movement and its import for theology. We begin by describing the core claims of one of this movement's pivotal (and more conservative) advocates: N. T. Wright.[49]

According to Wright, Paul's theology is couched in the broad first-century Jewish understanding of sacred history—the story of Israel. A fundamental aspect of this history is God's covenant with Israel, which itself is grounded in Yahweh's covenant with Abraham. Many first-century Jews saw themselves and their people as still living in the era of exile under foreign occupiers. In turn, many believed—as the Deuteronomistic Historians had before them—that this period of exile was somehow due to Israel's failure to keep its end of the covenant bargain. Further, many religious Jews of the first century hoped that God would restore Israel to its former state of divine blessing, which would include victory over its enemies, national

---

46. See Heron, *The Holy Spirit*, 43.

47. Heron, *The Holy Spirit*, 49–50. See also comments in Pinnock *Flame of Love*, 152–55.

48. The use of the phrase "the new perspective" is somewhat dated now since these views have been much discussed since the 1970s.

49. N. T. Wright's scholarly output is immense. The following summary of his thought on the "new perspective" is largely from his book *Justification*, especially 55–108. I also have relied upon a much shorter article of his: Wright, "New Perspectives on Paul." A much fuller description of his interpretation of Paul is found in Wright's two-volume work called *Paul and the Faithfulness of God*.

autonomy, and (most importantly) restoration to a proper and faithful status in God's covenant. And some first-century Jews even hoped for the wide-ranging rule of Israel's Messiah over the nations of the world.

Further, for many pious Jews of the first-century, Israel's victory,[50] while ultimately dependent upon God's grace and intervention, was partly reliant upon Israel's return to faithfulness to the divine covenant—that is, to following the Torah. Many first-century Jews practiced what has been dubbed "covenant nomism." This is the idea that while God's covenant relation with (and covenant blessings for) Israel is grounded in divine initiative and grace, *remaining in this covenant* (with its blessings) is partly facilitated by Israel's corporate (and individual) faithfulness and obedience to the covenant law. Thus, many pious first-century Jews vigorously sought to follow the law in hope of the divine restoration of Israel.

For first-century Jewish believers, however, Israel's hope was not utterly dependent upon human faithfulness. Ultimately, it was contingent upon God's faithfulness. Often in the Hebrew Bible and in the literature of Second Temple Judaism, God's covenant-faithfulness is referred to as "God's righteousness." While Israel's covenant-faithfulness (righteousness) had faltered, God's covenant-faithfulness (righteousness) had not. And part of the divine righteousness included God's commitment to restoring divine blessings upon Israel, which included a revival of Israel's own covenant-faithfulness. In other words, Israel was not alone. God was active in aiding Jews in returning to covenant-faithfulness and to receiving divine blessing.

For N. T. Wright (and many other proponents of the New Perspective on Paul), it is at this point that Paul's insights regarding salvation through Jesus the Messiah emerge. Paul—in many ways—saw himself as a faithful Jew whose eschatological hopes for Israel (and the rest of humankind) had been met in Jesus, the Messiah. For Paul, Jesus accomplished what Israel had not (and could not), namely, covenant-faithfulness. Jesus met the demands of God's covenant—not so much by fulfilling every mandate of the divine law but by being faithful to God and God's demands. This faithfulness of Jesus Christ especially was demonstrated in his submission to death on the cross. This act was one of obedience but also of faith toward God—faith here understood both as trust in and faithfulness to God. Jesus accomplished what corporate Israel could not—namely, covenant-faithfulness to Yahweh. Therefore, Jesus accomplished what God had all along planned to do through Israel: that is, to restore (or make possible the restoration of) all humanity to a right standing with God (as promised to Abraham in God's covenant with him [Gen 12:1–3]). This right standing essentially meant Gentile incorporation into the covenant of God, integration into God's family. Further, as a result of Jesus' faithfulness, God exalted Jesus above every name, proclaiming him Lord of all and ensuring his ultimate victory over cosmic and human evil. Also, through Christ, victory had come for those who unite with him in faith. According to Wright (and other advocates of the New

---

50. Often expressed in terms of "return from exile."

Perspective), Jesus serves as a representative of Israel and thus of all humanity (since Israel itself was such a representative of humanity). Through Christ, the blessings of the covenant can be received. Those benefits include, especially, forgiveness of sin and spiritual empowerment to live righteously.

The New Perspective on Paul has generated several new insights about Paul's theology, and some of these viewpoints contest traditional interpretations of Christian theology—especially about the doctrine of salvation. Among the more significant challenging-insights of this new view are the following. First, the New Perspective offers a reevaluation of first-century Judaism's understanding of the doctrine of salvation. (Sometimes this new discernment is referred to as "the New Perspective on Judaism"). The issue arises in light of Paul's claim that a person is justified by faith, not by works of the law (Rom 3:28; Gal 2:16). Martin Luther evoked this principle to challenge a merit-based understanding of salvation prevalent in the late medieval church. The medieval view asserted that a person is saved by God's grace and by the accruing of actual merits before God—either by personal acts of righteousness or by receiving merits from others (like saints and Christ).[51] Unfortunately, Luther also projected something like a worth-based understanding of salvation upon the Judaism of Paul's day (and ultimately upon Judaism in general). That is, Luther—and many Christians after him—presumed that Judaism was a works-righteousness approach to salvation as well. According to the New Perspective on Paul (and Judaism), however, such an interpretation is inaccurate (and at times has contributed to anti-Semitic rhetoric). Rather, the ancient Jewish faith too was a religion of grace, affirming that God's invitation to Israel to enter into covenant/salvation was a sheer act of grace. Further, the laws of the covenant were not means to receiving divine blessing but were loving responses to God's grace and were ways of staying in the covenant-relationship. Additionally, even in cases when the covenant was breached, there were mechanisms for restoring the covenant affiliation—namely, repentance and sacrifices. Thus, the Jewish faith did not teach a merit-based means of obtaining divine blessing (salvation), contrary to some (especially Lutheran) teachings.

All this leads to a second challenging insight from the New Perspective on Paul. The question arises: What was Paul rejecting when he proclaimed that justification is *not by works of the law*? Does this not imply that the apostle was countering a merit-based approach to salvation of some sort? Proponents of the New Perspective on Paul say no (at least initially). According to them, Paul was rejecting the alleged obligation for believers in Christ (especially Gentiles) to follow certain codes of the Jewish law that were designed to distinguish and separate Jews from Gentiles—regulations like circumcision, refraining from unclean foods, and keeping weekly Sabbaths. Such laws tended to generate a kind of religious-ethnic pride by which

---

51. It is not clear that such a merit-based approach was officially sanctioned by the Church, but practices of that era—especially the lucrative sale of indulgences—indicate that such a view was (at the very least) willfully tolerated.

one group (law-abiding Jews) saw itself as better than the other (Gentiles). Essentially, Paul was proclaiming the equality of Jewish and Gentile Christians, opposing Christian believers who were insisting that Gentiles must practice Jewish separatist customs in order to follow Christ. For Paul, Gentile adherence to such laws created an inappropriate division between believers, generated a religious pride from one group over another, and failed fully to appreciate that all along—from the days of Abraham onward—God's plan was to include Gentiles in the blessings of the divine covenant. Thus, Paul denied that justification is by works of the law, contending instead that justification is by faith in Christ only.

For proponents of the New Perspective on Paul, this interpretation of Paul's understanding of "works of law" is reinforced by the fact that the apostle often spoke approvingly of many of the Old Testament laws—especially moral rules (do not steal, do not lie, do not commit adultery, avoid sexual misconduct, love one another) as well as fundamental religious proscriptions (do not worship idols).[52] Paul saw many of these regulations as important aspects of living the Christian life. Indeed, in several places, the apostle proclaims that in the final judgment before God, individuals (including Christians) will be judged *by their works* (Rom 2:1–16, 14:10–12; 2 Cor 5:10). In fact, in one passage, Paul even asserts that persons will be *justified* by their deeds in God's judgment (Rom 2:13). (As we will see below, this last point will play a significant role in the New Perspective's understanding of *justification*).

A third important insight of the New Perspective on Paul is its interpretation of the Greek phrase *dikaiosynē theou*, "the righteousness of God." In Greek, this expression can mean "the righteousness *from* God" or "the righteousness *possessed* by God." The former of these interpretations is evidenced in the New International Version's translation of Rom 3:21–22, which says: "But now a righteousness *from* God, apart from law, has been made known, to which the Law and the Prophets testify. This righteousness *from* God comes through faith in Jesus Christ to all who believe."[53] This understanding of "the righteousness of God" fits well with conventional Protestant and Catholic interpretations of justification. Traditional Protestant interpreters have understood this phrase to reference a righteousness that God has *imputed* upon believers—a righteous not intrinsic to them. On the other hand, standard Catholic interpreters have understood this idiom to point to a righteousness God has *infused* into the believer—a righteousness that is not produced by but is somehow intrinsic to the believer. In both cases, the divinely given righteousness is "from" God; indeed, it somehow is God's (or Christ's) own righteousness imputed to or infused into the Christian. Proponents of the New Perspective, however, (typically) favor the second interpretation of "the righteousness of God"—a righteousness possessed by God. Such an interpretation is rendered by the Revised Standard Version of these same verses: "But now, apart from law, the

52. See Rom 3:31; 8:4; 1 Cor 7:19; Gal 5:14.

53. Emphasis added. As we are about to see, there is considerable controversy regarding the translation "faith *in* Jesus Christ" as well. We will discuss this debate in the next paragraph.

righteousness *of* God has been disclosed, and is attested by the law and the prophets, the righteousness *of* God through faith in Jesus Christ for all who believe."[54] According to advocates of the New Perspective, the meaning of this phrase flows from its usage in the Hebrew Bible and in the literature of Second Temple Judaism. Specifically (as mentioned in my summation of Wright's views), it refers to God's covenant-righteousness, the Lord's faithfulness to the covenant with Israel.

A fourth insight of the New Perspective concerns the Greek phrase *pistis Christou*. This expression can be translated "faith *in* Christ" or "faith (faithfulness) *of* Christ." This difference can be seen in how the Revised Standard Version translates Rom 3:21–22 as opposed to how the (Old) King James Version renders it. The Revised Standard Version says, "But now, apart from law, the righteousness of God has been disclosed, and is attested by the law and the prophets, the righteousness of God through *faith in* Jesus Christ for all who believe." Here, *pistis Christou* is translated "faith *in* Jesus Christ." But the (Old) King James Version says, "But now the righteousness of God without the law is manifested, being witnessed by the law and the prophets; Even the righteousness of God which is by *faith of* Jesus Christ unto all and upon all them that believe."[55] In this translation, *pistis Christou* is rendered "faith *of* Jesus Christ." For many advocates of the New Perspective on Paul, this difference makes much difference. For them, Paul is saying that due to Jesus Christ's faithfulness to God's covenant-demands, salvation has been made possible for those who believe in him. In turn, as noted above, because of his faithfulness, Jesus became the representative of Israel and of all humanity, fulfilling the stipulations of the divine covenant, so that all who believe in him are spiritually and representationally "united to him," thus receiving the blessings promised by God.[56]

A fifth and particularly contentious plank of the New Perspective is its nuanced interpretation of *justification*, including a rejection of both Reformed and Catholic notions—respectively—of "imputed" and "infused" righteousness. Regarding the rejection of transferred righteous, Wright agrees with traditional views that justification is essentially a legal concept that denotes the moment when a judge declares (reckons) that a defendant (or a plaintiff) is "righteous" (vindicated or acquitted) before the court. But Wright rejects any notion that such a judgment involves the transfer of the judge's (or anyone else's) righteousness upon the guilty party.[57] For

54. Italics added. Also, the same issue over the translation "faith in Christ" arises here as did in the previous quote.

55. Italics added.

56. One of the first writers to make an extended case for interpreting *pistis Christou* as "faith (or faithfulness of) Christ" was Richard Hays in his work *The Faith of Jesus Christ*. Wright and many others have endorsed this perspective as well. Interestingly, Dunn does not accept this interpretation, even though he endorses the notion that Jesus serves as a representative of humankind before God and thus fulfilled the divine covenant for them. Dunn, *The Theology of Paul the Apostle*, 379–385.

57. Wright argues that when a judge declares someone is acquitted (justified), the judge's own righteousness is not attributed to the defendant. Thus, the very logic of the traditional understanding

N. T. Wright, such an interpretation misunderstands Paul's use of the concepts of "God's righteousness" and of "the faith of Christ," as if such phrases mean that the righteousness of God, of Christ, or of both is somehow credited to (imputed to) or mysteriously implanted (infused) into the believer. Instead, according to Wright, the believer simply is declared righteous by divine judgment.

James Dunn, another advocate of the New Perspective, also rejects the notion that righteousness is imputed to or infused into the believer. He argues that a correct understanding of "the righteousness of God" (as God's covenant-faithfulness) undercuts the need for and the logic of such claims. Righteousness as covenant-faithfulness nullifies the ideas of imputation or infusion because it denies that righteousness is a moral or legal standard (over and above God) that the deity must heed. Such an understanding of righteousness is more a Greek or Roman understanding of righteousness and less a Hebrew one. The Hebrew notion is personalistic, dealing with the interpersonal relationship between covenant partners. Underlying the Augustinian and Reformed doctrines of imputed and infused righteousness is the concern that an injustice would unfold if God simply justified sinners (declared them righteous) when in fact they did not have righteousness. Thus, by teaching that God's righteousness is somehow imputed or infused into believers, traditional theologians attempted to avoid the legal impropriety of claiming that sinners were righteous when they were not. But according to Dunn, such a breach of moral or legal protocol is overcome if one understands that God's acquittal is not about dealing with some abstract principle of justice but rather is an issue of the Lord's faithfulness to the covenant-promises—specifically, to the divine pledge to save humanity through Abraham's progeny. Dunn writes:

> God . . . justifies the ungodly . . . This is no abuse of legal process or a legal fiction . . . For here . . . the distinction between Greek and Hebrew concepts of "righteousness" . . . becomes relevant . . . [I]n the law court, strictly speaking, there is no place for forgiveness; the due processes of the law must take their course. But where the issue is more of mutual obligation between partners in a relationship, there it is for the injured party to determine whether the relationship is to be ended because of the other's breach of faith or sustained despite it. It is the latter course which God in his grace follows in justifying the sinner.[58]

For James Dunn, understanding "the righteousness of God" as the divine faithfulness to the covenant undermines the need for and logic of imputation and infusion.

These rejections of imputation and infusion are problematic enough for many traditionalists. But the plot thickens. For N. T. Wright goes on to propose that justification is not merely an event that occurs at the moment a believer believes. It also involves God's judgment at the end of time when a final verdict regarding the believer

---

of imputation or infusion breaks down. Wright, "New Perspectives on Paul."

58. Dunn, *The Theology of Paul the Apostle*, 385–86.

is handed down. And this final justification is based on works (as Paul seems to say in Rom 2:13 and elsewhere). Wright envisions two phases of justification. The first is God's original declaration of the believer's right-standing at the moment that person received Jesus as Lord and Savior. This is "the anticipation in the present of the verdict which will be reaffirmed in the future."[59] The second moment of justification is at the final judgment when God declares the believer is vindicated—that is, righteous. For Wright, this declaration is not a legal fiction. The believer truly *is* righteous at the end. And this is the case, not only because God legally declares it, but because the believer has truly become righteous. But how? According to Wright, this righteousness is made possible (over time) through the believer's spiritual union with Christ and through the indwelling and leading of God's Spirit. Wright states:

> The point of *future* justification is then explained like this. The verdict of the last day will truly reflect what people have actually done. It is extremely important to notice . . . that Paul never says Christians *earn* the final verdict, or that their "works" must be complete and perfect . . . They are seeking it, not earning it. And they are seeking it through that patient, Spirit-driven Christian living in which—here is the paradox at the heart of the Christian life which so many have noticed but few have integrated into Paul's theology of justification!—from *one point of view* the Spirit is at work, producing these fruits (Galatians 5:22–23), and from *another point of view* the person concerned is making the free choices, the increasingly free (because increasingly less constrained by the sinful habits of mind and body) decisions to live a genuinely, fully human life which brings pleasure . . . to God in whose image we human beings were made.[60]

In another place, Wright explains:

> The "works" in accordance with which the Christian will be vindicated on the last day are not the unaided works of the self-help moralist. Nor are they the performance of the ethnically distinctive Jewish boundary-markers (Sabbath, food-laws and circumcision). They are the things which show, rather, that one is in Christ; the things which are produced in one's life as a result of the Spirit's indwelling and operation.[61]

Dunn offers a similar understanding of final justification. He writes:

> Justification is not a once-for-all act of God. It is rather the initial acceptance by God into restored relationship. But thereafter the relationship could not be sustained without God continuing to exercise his justifying righteousness with a view to the final act of judgment and acquittal.[62]

59. Wright, "New Perspectives on Paul."

60. Wright, *Justification*, 191–92 (italics original). Wright cites the following passages as exemplifications of this paradox: Col 1:29; 1 Cor 15:10. See also Wright, *Justification*, 105–7, 190–93.

61. Wright, "New Perspectives on Paul."

62. Dunn, *The Theology of Paul the Apostle*, 386.

Again:

> In terms of Paul's theology of justification, the decisive beginning has to be worked out until and in the final verdict. The relationship with God must be sustained by God to the end.[63]

For Dunn, this final vindication (justification, including actual righteousness) is accomplished in and through the believer's union with Christ and the empowering aid of the indwelling Spirit of God within the believer. Dunn states:

> The interrelationship between the divine grace and the obedience of faith . . . lies in the recognition that Paul's gospel is only partially expressed through the forensic metaphor of justification. The gospel is also expressed in terms of the gift of the Spirit. But also in terms of identification with Christ . . . The point, then, is that Paul envisaged salvation as *a process of transformation* of the believer, not simply the believer's *status*, but of the *believer* as such. Final judgment will be the measure of that transformation. Central to the process is the believer's moral determination and obedience. Fundamental to the process is the enabling, in motive and doing, of the Spirit. But the transformation is "in Christ," "into Christ," "with Christ" . . . If it is true that Christ alone had/has the "native ability" to measure up to God's pattern for humanity, then it is by becoming like Christ that those "in Christ" will satisfy the final inspection. Not solely by having righteousness imputed as an "alien righteousness." And certainly not by Pelagian or semi-Pelagian self-effort. But by a progressive transformation into Christ's likeness.[64]

Both Dunn and Wright see themselves as endorsing the essential insights of the Reformation, including especially Calvin's emphasis on the believer's union with Christ and the indwelling of the Spirit as sources of ultimate righteousness. But these authors feel that Paul's doctrine of justification is more complex than imagined by the Reformers; it involves more than a forensic declaration of righteousness, including also the movement toward a final vindication. In turn, Dunn and Wright reject the notion that divine righteousness per se is imputed to or infused into the believer, insisting instead that the righteousness that emerges at the end-time is that of the believer per se. But even here Dunn and Wright echo the Reformation (especially Calvin's) principle that such righteousness is not possible except through union with Christ and the directing influence of the Holy Spirit. Not surprisingly, many traditionalists balk at the New Perspective's rejection of imputation of God's/Christ's righteousness and question the double-layered understanding of justification as involving an initial and final state. Thus, whether these writers sufficiently conform to the Reformed perspective remains an ongoing dispute.

63. Dunn, *The Theology of Paul the Apostle*, 493.

64. Dunn, *The New Perspective on Paul*, 93–94; see also Dunn, *The Theology of Paul the Apostle*, 487–88.

Much ink has been spilled debating the virtues and vices of the New Perspective on Paul. Many of these disputes are beyond the scope of our inquiry. Some positive contributions of the movement include

1. A better understanding of first-century Judaism's affirmation of divine grace and of "covenant nomism."

2. A better grasp of the dynamics of Paul's theology in light of his historical, theological, and cultural context, including his use of the phrases "righteousness of God" and (possibly) "faith of Christ," as well as his employment of Hebrew covenant theology to explain the notion of justification.

3. A fuller appreciation of the Christian call for social and ethnic equality in Christ and in the church. This (arguably) emerges from a better understanding of Paul's own concern over "works of the law."

4. A fuller grasp of the corporate nature of salvation. (For Wright especially, Christ's death and resurrection make possible the incorporation of Gentiles—as well as Jews—into the divine covenant—into the family of God).

A concern with this movement over the relationship between faith and faithfulness lingers. The problem arises in light of the New Perspective's claim (mentioned above) that end-time justification is based on actual righteousness—specifically, on the righteousness of the believer. For many traditionalists, this assertion smacks of a return to "works-righteousness," that one is saved by becoming moral, doing good, or heeding God's commands. Such an assertion seems to be a direct contradiction of the notion that justification is *not by works of the law, but by faith alone*. As noted above, Wright and Dunn attempt to remedy this problem by appealing both to the believer's spiritual union with Christ and to the indwelling of the Spirit of God within the believer. In essence they insist that while final justification is based on actual righteousness, this righteousness itself is the result of the ongoing activity of God's Spirit in the believer and of the believer's union with Christ.

However, the question remains—both for traditionalists and advocates of the New Perspective: How exactly do faith in Christ and the call to faithfulness interrelate? As noted in Chapter 2, this seems to be a perennial problem for Christian theology. The relationship between faith and faithfulness, between trusting God and obeying God, is (upon examination) vague in the overarching New Testament testimony. Even a writer like Paul—who expressly stresses the role of grace and faith over works—still urges Christians to live by various principles of the law. And even N. T. Wright admits his own solution is "paradoxical."[65] It is unlikely that these debates over faith and faithfulness will be solved anytime soon.[66]

65. Wright, *Justification*, 192

66. It would appear these questions persist within the Hebrew Bible and in Second Temple Judaism. Critics of the new perspective on Paul (and Judaism) are quick to point out that even if ancient

Social Salvation

As noted above, the doctrine of salvation is concerned not only with individual salvation but also with social salvation—that is, with the undoing of various broken relationships among humans due to sin. Here Christian theology links with social ethical theory and with the study of various social structures, including political, economic, institutional, and family configurations. Various theological approaches have been proposed for dealing with diverse social ills. A fuller account of these approaches will be given in Chapters 8–10 when we examine Christian ethics. For now, examination of one such system will have to suffice. We might refer to this view as socioeconomic liberation theology.

This form of liberation theology insists that a basic problem of humanity is the repression and exploitation of weaker social classes by dominant ones. Thus, while salvation addresses many human problems, a core aspect of God's redeeming work involves liberating humans in weaker classes from oppression. Some key tenets of this liberation theology are

1. The Bible, and thus God, explicitly sides with the oppressed.

2. Salvation concerns not just individual life after death but creating just political and economic systems in this world. Eternal life and the kingdom of God include participation in God's culmination work in the present (in this world and history) and not merely being plucked from history. God's goal is to save people from all forms of oppression, including social and economic abuses.

3. Capitalist economic and political systems tend to be intrinsically corrupt and inequitable so that affluent nations and classes tend to prosper through the exploitation or neglect of poorer nations and classes. In turn, as these trends progress, the poor and oppressed find it harder to improve their lots in life.[67]

Liberation theology has been criticized on at least two points. First, it may unduly bias God toward the poor and oppressed and hence mitigates against the universal

---

Judaism saw Israel's initial entrance into covenant with God as an act of divine grace, the ongoing call to obey the precepts of the law in order to remain in that covenant ultimately implies another form of works righteousness. Presumably there comes a point when a person's failure to abide by the law ends in exemption from divine blessing. This seems to be the case in the Deuteronomistic tradition's explanation of Israel's and Judah's falls. In turn, a close examination of the sources of Second Temple Judaism indicates that many Jews of the era saw obedience to the law as essential to gaining the blessings of the coming age. (See Carson et al., eds, *Justification and Variegated Nomism*, vol 1, *The Complexities of Second Temple Judaism*.) Similar comments hold true about Paul's Christian antagonists in Galatians. As one commentator notes: Once the keeping of separatist regulations "becomes a requirement, it has clearly become a condition for salvation and is not merely something that you can do if you please." Thus, the "seeds" of a merit-based notion of salvation were implicit in the views of Paul's opponents. (See Marshall, *New Testament Theology*, 212, note 8.)

67. For a brief survey of liberation theology, see Boff and Boff, *Introducing Liberation Theology*. For a quick synopsis and critique of this perspective, see Erickson, *Christian Theology*, 829–32.

appeal of divine salvation. In reply, liberation theologians insist the Bible shows the same bias to the poor and oppressed in many places. Further, as Daniel Migliore comments: "Rightly understood . . . the theme of God's solidarity with the poor is an expression of inclusivity, not exclusivity. It is the poor who are being unjustly excluded, and thus it must be the poor who are first and explicitly included in the salvific activity of God."[68] No doubt Migliore is correct concerning the exclusion of the poor and oppressed from political and economic arenas. It is less clear, however, that these groups are any more or less ensnared by the deep problems of private and personal sin.

A second criticism is that liberation theology has too-narrow concepts of sin and salvation. It sometimes focuses too exclusively on social liberation and not on private enslavement to sin and sins. Migliore again insists, however, that when rightly conceived, liberation theology can include both political and private sin.

> Liberation [theology] . . . underscores the corporate, political dimension of sin and salvation. This emphasis is a response to the entrenched and damaging privatization of sin and salvation . . . There are corporate structures of sin and injustice. Jesus did not simply come up against sinful individuals but a sinful structure of life. Similarly, salvation is not just the rescue of isolated souls to fellowship with God. Jesus proclaimed and inaugurated the rule of the gracious and righteous God that encompasses the whole of life.[69]

At worst, then, liberation theology may simply be an attempt to cure the ills of humans through political structural changes and outward moral changes without dealing with the problem of the individual human sinful nature and sins. At best, however, liberation theology may be a helpful corrective for too narrow a focus on private sins and sinfulness, and not enough on the inherent evil of human political and social structures.

Cosmic Salvation

The Christian doctrine of salvation also is concerned with reversing the damage done by sin to the cosmos as a whole. Unfortunately, the precise impact of sin on the cosmos and the exact nature of the divine renewal of the created world are ambiguous in the biblical tradition. In turn and obviously, the complete cosmic renewal (whatever that may mean) appears to be beyond the pale of human ability. At best, only incremental improvements might be made by humans, even if we knew what changes were needed. The Bible and church tradition typically depict such renewal as occurring through an end-time, transcendent divine breaking into history to make anew the broken cosmos. Thus, we will reserve discussion of these matters for Chapter 7, where we address eschatology. However, there is one aspect of cosmic

68. Migliore, *Faith Seeking Understanding*, 157.

69. Migliore, *Faith Seeking Understanding*, 157.

renewal that might be addressed prior to end-times. This is concern over the earth's ecosystem and the human overuse (exploitation) of earth's resources. Certainly this is a human concern, since currently (and perhaps permanently) humans are dependent upon the earth for their (physical) existence.

Conclusion

At the center of Christian theology is concern over the realization of God's plan of salvation for the created order. This salvation involves divine restoration of individual humans, of human social systems, and of the cosmos as a whole to divinely intended ends. At the center of God's saving activity is the person and work of Jesus Christ, whose being, life, death, resurrection, and ongoing spiritual presence provide the foundations through which individual humans, humanity, and the cosmos are being restored. Discussion of these matters has been the focus of this fifth chapter. In Chapter 6, we turn to consider the nature of the community that God's salvific plan is forming and the institution that God graciously chooses to employ (at least in part) to bring about divine salvation—namely, the church.

6

The Church

IN THE PREVIOUS THREE chapters, we discussed the following core topics of Christian theology: revelation, God, creation, providence, humanity, sin, Christ, and salvation. In this sixth chapter we turn to the doctrine of the church. Three questions help direct the Christian understanding of the church: What or who is the church? What is the church's purpose? How does the church achieve its purpose? (That is, what practices does the church engage and who performs these?)

The Nature of the Church

We turn first to consider the nature of the church. Following insights from Daniel Migliore,[1] we offer the following preliminary definition of the church: The church is a community drawn together by the spiritual presence of Christ, called to minister in various ways, including by proclaiming the Word of God, providing resources for bringing salvation to individuals and to the world's social structures, all in the context of an intimate interpersonal fellowship with one another and with God. Like most definitions, this one has flaws and is incomplete. But it serves as a springboard for discussing the nature of the church. With this definition in mind, let us consider the following questions about the church:

1. Is the church a community or an institution?

2. Who are the members of the church community?

3. What are the essential structures and practices of the institutional church?

4. Are there additional core characteristics of the church and what are they?

5. What is the relationship of the church and the kingdom of God?

1. See Migliore, *Faith Seeking Understanding*, 192–200. Drawing from Avery Dulles, Migliore identifies five models of the church. The first model emphasizes the church as an institution of salvation. A second paradigm sees the church as the herald of good news. A third pattern characterizes the church as an intimate spiritual community. A fourth model of the church pictures the church as a servant. A fifth type sees the church as a sacrament of salvation. See also Dulles, *Modes of the Church*.

156

6. What is the relationship of the church and Israel?

7. What is the relationship of the church to other world religions?

Community or Institution?

We begin our discussion of the church's nature by noting that it is both a community and an institution. That is, it is a group of persons in communion with one another *and* an institution whose activities achieve some purpose(s). Sometimes these two aspects of the church are played off each other so that one is deemed central and the other secondary. Differing traditions (at different points in their history) have stressed one of these features over the other. The medieval church gravitated toward accentuating the institutional nature of the church, emphasizing its role—especially its sacraments—as the means by which persons come to salvation. The claims of Cyprian of Carthage (210–258 CE)—that outside of the church there is no salvation and that the church is the mother of those saved—fit well with an institutional understanding of the church. Writers like Robert Bellarmine (1542–1621) and Adolphe Tanquerey (1854–1932) likewise accentuated the institutional nature of the Catholic Church. John Calvin—and through him the Reformed tradition—also stressed the institutional nature of the church. He defined it as the "external means or aims by which God invites us into the society of Christ and holds us therein." In turn, like Cyprian, Calvin spoke of the church as the "mother of all the Godly."[2]

Free church traditions, on the other hand, have tended to see the essential nature of the church as community. Sometimes called *congregationalism*, this view insists that "the true church essentially is people standing in voluntary covenant with God."[3] Baptist theologian Stanley Grenz (1950–2005) explains:

> By asserting that the church is formed through the covenanting of its members, congregationalists reversed the order of priority. No longer did the corporate whole take precedence over the individual as in the medieval model. On the contrary, the congregationalists viewed the church as the product of the coming together of individual Christians rather than the individual Christian being the product of the church.[4]

This understanding of the church appears to be correct: the church is both an institution and a community. Even if one feature is more basic than the other, neither the institutional nor communal nature of the church can be neglected.

This dual role of the church is implicit in the various biblical images of the church discussed in Chapter 2. *Ecclesia* is a called and gathered community. But this

---

2. Calvin, *Institutes of the Christian Religion*, 2.4.1.

3. Grenz, *Theology for the Community of God*, 649.

4. Grenz, *Theology for the Community of God*, 649.

community congregates around the lordship of Christ and his saving benefits, and it seeks to fulfill the will of its Lord both for its members and for the wider world. As the *people of God*, the church is a community individually and corporately in covenant with God, seeking to keep its covenant obligations to God and to one another. As the *body of Christ*, the church is a community spiritually connected through Christ, yet also tasked with sharing its gifts with one another and ultimately with the world as a whole. Part of this body's goal is to minister to and build up one another (1 Cor 12:1–31; Eph 4:15–16). As the *temple of the Spirit*, the church as a whole and each member of the church is filled by God's Spirit, but like the Jerusalem temple, the church also provides means for drawing the faithful to God and his saving benefits. The church is a community and an institution.[5]

The Church as Community

Who, then, is the church? Who are its members? As noted in Chapter 2, the New Testament suggests that ultimately members of the church are beneficiaries of Christ's salvation—those who are or will be saved. The Epistle to the Ephesians especially highlights that the church is those who are saved (or being saved) by Christ.[6] Similar pictures of the church are found throughout the New Testament.[7] The church then is those who are saved. But further clarification is needed. Also noted in Chapter 2, New Testament usage suggests that each local congregation is part of a larger whole; or better, each local church is the instantiation, in a specific locale, of the one church. This has led many theologians to distinguish between local churches and the church as a whole—the universal church. Further, the New Testament recognizes that not all those who claim to be followers of Christ truly are. Some are false believers, liars, or fallen away. Presumably, those who are disingenuous or utterly unfaithful are not saved. In light of this second set of New Testament considerations, several Christian thinkers have distinguished between the visible and invisible church. The visible church is those physical persons who gather in various locales throughout the world—some of whom are saved, some of whom are not. The invisible church, on the other hand, is those persons who are saved.[8]

---

5. See comments in Berkhof, *Christian Faith*, 343; and in Grenz, *Theology for the Community of God*, 471–72.

6. See the discussion in Chapter 2, above (pages [x-ref])

7. See Rom 1:7; 8:1–2; 1 Cor 1:2, 8; 2.

8. Distinctions between the visible and the invisible church, and between the universal church and local churches, have been made (with varying degrees of clarity) throughout Christian history, including in the writings of Augustine, Luther, and Wycliffe. Calvin especially makes this distinction, as do several Protestant confessions after him. See Calvin, *Institutes of the Christian Religion*, 4.1. See also the Augsburg Confession, articles 7 and 8, and the Westminster Confession, chapter 25, section 1. Both confessions are found in Leith, ed., *Creeds of the Churches*.

In light of these distinctions, we may differentiate two ways of thinking about church members: (1) the true (or invisible) church and (2) the empirical (or visible) church.[9] The true church is persons who are saved. This church can be thought of holistically or in terms of its parts. Holistically, the true church is a single overarching community made of *all* saved persons. We might call this the *true universal church*. Broken into parts, the true church is multiple groups of saved persons scattered in differing locales. We might call each of these communities a *true local church*. The empirical church, on the other hand, is observable human communities that gather in Christ's name, manifest various organizational structures, and engage in diverse visible activities. Considered individually, each of these visible gatherings constitutes a *local empirical church*. Considered collectively, the *universal empirical church* is all local empirical churches combined, forming the *universal empirical church*. It should be kept in mind that some persons in the empirical church are saved and some are not. In other words, some in the empirical church are part of the true church; others are not.[10]

At times, the true church and the empirical church are conflated. Roman Catholic ecclesiology sometimes does this—understanding the Roman Church and its hierarchy as the one true universal church. In doing so, Roman Catholic thought fuses the true church with the empirical church.[11] But for many Protestants such an understanding of the universal church runs afoul of the invisible nature of salvation. It simply cannot be known whether each member of every Catholic congregation (or any other congregation) truly is saved.[12] Further, such a definition of the universal church seems to imply that denominations outside the Catholic Church are not genuine churches; obviously, this is a perspective with which other denominations disagree.

9. I have chosen the designations true and empirical over invisible and visible for the following reason: In the traditional schema one faces the (often confusing) oddity of speaking of the visible church as containing within it the invisible (the saved) church. But then one wonders what to call that part of the visible church that is not saved. The solution chosen here is to speak of the true church (the saved church) and the empirical (observable) church, which contains members of the true (saved) church within it.

10. See, Erickson, *Christian Theology*, 957.

11. The Second Vatican Council asserts that the visible church and the invisible church "form one interlocked reality" so that the "Church constituted and organized in the world . . . subsists in the Catholic Church, which is governed by the successor of Peter and by the bishops in union with that successor." The Council attempts to soften this perspective by speaking of Protestant groups as "linked" to the Roman Church and "honored with the name of Christian" even though they "do not profess the faith [of the Catholic Church] in its entirety or do not preserve unity of communion with the successor of Peter." Still, the Council ultimately identifies the empirical Roman Church with the true church. See Vatican Council II, *Dogmatic Constitution of the Church[: Lumen Gentium]*, chapter 1, section 8 and chapter 2, section 15, in Leith, ed., *Creeds of the Churches* (brackets added).

12. The Council of Trent seems to admit this when it notes that a sacrament conveys saving grace "*on those who place no obstacles in its way.*" In other words, a sacrament is efficacious only if the participant does not act in ways that undermine its effectiveness. See "The Canons and Decrees of the Council of Trent," Session 7, Canons on the Sacraments in General, Canon 6, in Leith, *Creeds of the Churches*, 426 (italics added).

Who then is the church? Who are its members? Which community is it? The true church is all persons saved—of all times. The empirical church, which includes members of the true church, consists of some who are and some who are not members of the true church.[13]

Core Structures and Practices of the Institutional Church

We turn now to consider the core structures and practices of the institutional church. Obviously, the church (or churches) manifests a wide variety of activities and organizational structures. Most traditions allow for flexibility regarding many such matters. We will discuss some of these activities below. But here the question is, What structures and activities are *fundamental* to the institutional church? Two broad answers have been proposed in Christian history.

First, in the Catholic tradition (especially before the Second Vatican Council), the center of church structure is the episcopacy (bishops), and the defining practice is the administration of the sacraments. The sacraments mysteriously convey God's saving grace upon those receiving them. And bishops have the God-given power to administer the sacraments—the means of salvation.[14] In turn, bishops can transfer aspects of their power to lesser functionaries—specifically, to priests. Episcopal authority is grounded in apostolic succession—an (alleged) unbroken chain of ordination (and transfer of authority) running back to the first-century apostles. Shades of the notion that the sacraments convey saving grace are found throughout church history.[15] Not surprisingly, then, for the Catholic tradition the episcopacy (bishops) is an indispensable office of the church, and the administration of salvation *through* the sacraments is the church's fundamental activity. In light of these considerations, one can understand Cyprian of Carthage's claim that "outside the church, there is no salvation."[16] The church and its administration of the sacraments through the episcopacy is essential to salvation.[17]

---

13. Of course, this definition does not inform us of which specific persons are members of the true church, for the saved status of each is not definitely knowable in this life.

14. As noted in Chapter 5, Catholic tradition does not claim the sacraments *cause* salvation. Rather, salvation is caused *by God* but the sacraments are a divinely sanctioned prerequisite for God's saving action.

15. Ignatius spoke of the Lord's Supper as "the medicine of immortality" (Ignatius, *The Epistle to the Ephesians*). Ambrose claimed that baptism "effects the reality of regeneration" (Ambrose, *On the Mysteries and the Treatise on the Sacraments*). The Council of Trent condemned those who teach that "the sacraments . . . do not contain the grace that they signify, or that they do not confer that grace" (The Canons and Decrees of the Council of Trent," Session 7, Canons on the Sacraments in General, Canon 6, in Leith, ed., *Creeds of the Churches*).

16. Cyprian, *Letters 72*.

17. The Eastern Orthodox tradition likewise holds a perspective similar to the one described in this paragraph.

The sixteenth-century Reformers offered a different perspective on the fundamental structure and practices of the institutional church. For Martin Luther, the institutional church is found wherever the proclamation of God's Word is heard and received in faith. For him, the sacraments do not covey salvation. Rather, salvation comes by positively responding to the Word of God—the saving gospel of Jesus Christ. In turn, Luther endorsed the "priesthood of believers," contending that any Christian (in principle) could rightly interpret the Scriptures, proclaim the gospel to others, and (with the Spirit's aid) lead others to faith and thus to salvation in Christ. Hence, bishops (or other duly sanctioned clergy) are not *necessary* for the reception of salvation. First, salvation does not come via receiving the sacraments per se; it comes through faith in God's promises. Second, any believer can proclaim the gospel and can lead others to faith in Christ—that is, to salvation.

Luther did recognize the role of persons specially called by God (through the church) to perform key ministries of the church—especially, preaching and teaching the Word of God and administering the sacraments, and he contended that normally (especially in public worship venues) these individuals perform these tasks. But such ministries were extensions of the church as the body of believers (priests), not an authority independent of and above believers. Luther writes:

> For although we are all priests, this does not mean that all of us can preach, teach, and rule. Certain ones of the multitude must be selected and separated for such an office. And he who has such an office is not a priest because of his office but a servant of all the others, who are priests. When he is no longer able to preach and serve, or if he no longer wants to do so, he once more becomes a part of the common multitude of Christians. His office is conveyed to someone else, and he becomes a Christian like any other. This is the way to distinguish between the office of preaching, or the ministry, and the general priesthood of all baptized Christians. The preaching office is no more than a public service which happens to be conferred upon someone by the entire congregation, all the members of which are priests.[18]

Thus, while all Christians can minister the Word of God and even (when needful) the sacraments, the norm is that duly appointed members of the church do so.[19]

All the Reformers agreed that salvation comes through faith, not through receiving the sacraments. But puzzles arose regarding the utility of sacraments. If sacraments do not covey the grace of salvation, what do they do? Are they even needed? None of the Reformers (in Lutheran, Reformed, or free churches) were willing to give up these practices. But why perform them? A variety of functions are ascribed to the sacraments by Protestants. According to early Reformed leader Huldrych Zwingli, sacraments serve as *human pledges* of allegiance to God, depicting *their* faith in God's

18. Luther, *Selected Psalms II*, 332.

19. For a discussion of these matters, see Klug, "Luther on Ministry," especially 303.

promises. Luther and Melanchthon preferred to think of sacraments as *God's pledges* to those who participate in them; thus, sacraments strengthen faith by reassuring Christians of the promises depicted by them.[20] Another benefit of the sacraments is that they serve as signs separating Christians from other peoples. The Reformed Westminster Confession identifies all three of these functions.[21]

Thus, while sacraments do not covey salvation, they are important activities of the church for they aid Christians in their faith in various ways. Indeed, for both the Lutheran and Reformed traditions, administration of the sacraments remains a central function of the church, even though they are not necessary for salvation.[22] As we will see below, while most Protestants agreed that the sacraments are core features of the church (even though salvation is not conveyed through them), other disagreements arose between Protestants regarding the meaning, function, and practice of the sacraments.

Other Key Characteristics of the Church: The Four Marks

Having discussed the nature of the church as a community and the core practices and structures of the institutional church, we turn to consider other important defining characteristics of the church. Four identifying marks are ascribed to the church in the Nicene Creed, and are often used to speak of the church's nature. These are oneness, holiness, catholicity, and apostolicity. Different meanings of these attributes have been proposed throughout Christian history, often varying from one tradition to the next.

Often in the Catholic tradition, the church is perceived as the means to salvation, so that church unity is grounded in persons being formally part of the visible institutional church. This means being led by and receiving saving ministries from officially sanctioned ministers of the church whose authority has been handed down

---

20. The Augsburg Confession captures these ideas when it says that sacraments are "signs and testimonies of God's will toward us *for the purpose of awakening and strengthening our faith*" (Augsburg Confession, article 13, in Leith, ed., *Creeds of the Churches*, 72 [italics added]). Compare this with Philip Melanchthon, who says, "the use of the sacraments is a reminder and a testimony of the gracious will of God and the promise of grace, and is a pledge and application to him" (Melanchthon, *Melanchthon on Christian Doctrine*, 203 [chapter 19]).

21. "Sacraments are holy signs and seals of the covenant of grace, immediately instituted by God, to represent Christ and his benefits, and to confirm our interest in him: as also to put a visible difference between those that belong unto the Church and the rest of the world" (Westminster Confession, chapter 27, in Leith, ed., *Creeds of the Churches*).

22. The Augsburg Confession states that the true church is those "among whom the Gospel is preached in its purity and the holy sacraments are administered according to the Gospel (art. 7). Reformed theologian John Calvin states that "we have laid down as distinguishing marks of the church the preaching of the Word and the observance of the sacraments" (*Institutes of the Christian Religion*, 4.1.10). The Westminster Confession asserts that the true church has "been given the ministry, oracles, and *ordinances* [sacraments] of God." And individual churches are "more or less pure according as the doctrine of the Gospel is taught and embraced, *ordinances administered*, and public worship performed" (chapter 25, in Leith, ed., *Creeds of the Churches* [italics and brackets added]).

from the apostles of Christ. Thus, in the Catholic tradition, the church's *oneness* means being under the authority of the Roman Church's hierarchy and receiving salvation through its ministries. For Protestants, typically the oneness of the church is thought to be invisible, grounded in each Christian's spiritual union with Christ, which is fostered by a shared faith in Christ. There are, however, outward signs that point to this inner union. These signs vary among Protestant groups but often involve affirming core doctrines, participating in church sacraments, and fellow-shipping with a local church-community. John Calvin perceived the genuine visible church to be those congregations that rightly proclaim the Word of God and rightly administer the sacraments. Thus, for him (and many who followed him), the church's invisible unity is somewhat visibly manifested in correctly teaching God's word and faithfully administering the sacraments. In modern times, the ecumenical movement (following Ignatius of Antioch's notion that "where Christ is there is also the church") has attempted to define the church's oneness in terms of all those who gather in Christ's name, thus reducing the requirements for being a church and, consequentially, allowing greater diversity within the one church.

Biblically, the notion of holiness refers both to God's setting the church apart for divine purposes and the personal righteousness of the church's members. The ancient Donatist crisis generated controversy over this mark of the church. For several centuries, Christians of North Africa insisted that church members must be personally righteous to remain in the church. This was especially true for priests and bishops sanctioned to administer the sacraments. For Donatists, those clerics who failed to be faithful to Christ during times of persecution had permanently lost their authority to administer Christ's sacraments. Augustine, and the majority of Christians of his era, insisted that there must be room for forgiveness for such sins in the church, and that the church is a mixed body of both sinners and saints (righteous persons). In turn, Augustine insisted that the efficacy of the sacraments was in no way denigrated by the moral status of a priest or bishop. As long as such persons had been duly sanctioned to administer such rites, the sacraments themselves were efficacious. Further, Augustine insisted that the church's holiness is that of Christ, not that of humans. It is Christ's holiness and unity with Christians that makes the church holy, not its human officials or members. Magisterial Reformers such as Luther, Calvin, and others endorsed a similar view of the church's holiness. Some in the Anabaptist traditions, however, saw personal, actual righteousness as a necessary quality of church members. Some congregationalists endorsed this perspective as well but some did not.[23] Many Baptist confessions (especially those influenced by Reformed theology) tended to affirm that the church's holiness ultimately is found in Christ. For most of these Protestant groups, all members of the true church will be made personally righteous

---

23. The later Wesleyan and Holiness traditions took this Anabaptist noting of actual righteousness even further, contending that (in principle) a pious Christian could attain holiness in this life, through the ongoing work of the Holy Spirit. See Wesley, *A Plain Account of Christian Perfection*.

through Christ at the end of time, as Augustine taught; but all church members currently living in this world fall into sin, even those earnest in their faith, and thus they too await their final salvation from sin in the world to come.

The mark of *catholicity* in some sense refers to the church as a whole. But its precise meaning has varied through history, and often a single author will endorse multiple meanings of it. Sometimes the term has been used to speak of how the church is physically spread throughout the whole world. At other times, it references the notion that the church teaches the full range of correct doctrine. At still other moments, *catholicity* has been used to speak the church's outreach or ministry to all peoples, nations, and ethnicities—so that the whole world is subject to its ministries. In the Catholic traditions, the mark of *apostolicity* especially came to reference the Catholic Church's historical and authoritative link to the apostles of Christ through the process of episcopal succession. For many Protestant churches, who reject the Catholic Church's claim of apostolic succession, apostolicity especially has to do with the church's faithfulness to the New Testament apostles' teachings.

Relation of Church to Kingdom of God

We turn now to consider the relationship of the church to the kingdom of God. As noted in Chapter 2, the Kingdom of God was a central theme of Jesus' preaching. Throughout church history, diverse understandings of the church's relation to the kingdom have been proposed. Often the church has been equated with God's kingdom. Borrowing from and perhaps misappropriating Augustine's distinction between the City of God and the City of Mankind, the medieval church virtually equated the visible (institutional) church with the kingdom of God. In this view, the Roman Church—with its authority to administrate the instruments of salvation (the sacraments)—is the kingdom of God. Several Protestant thinkers made a similar move, equating the kingdom of God with the invisible (rather than the institutional) church; thus, for them, the kingdom is the community of the saved. Broadening this idea, some liberal theologians equated the kingdom of God with all virtuous persons.

Other theologians have separated church and kingdom of God, seeing each as a distinct movement in the divine plan. A unique perspective about the relationship between church and God's kingdom is offered by a conservative form of Protestantism called *dispensationalism*. For dispensationalists, the church refers to those who are saved, while the kingdom references the political (and ethnically distinct) kingdom of Israel that God will restore at Christ's return. This kingdom of Israel will be ruled by its Messiah—Jesus—and will reign over the whole world for a thousand years before God's final judgment. The dispensationalists' distinction between the church and God's kingdom is based on the following reasoning. While in and through the church God has fulfilled many of the divine promises of the Old Testament, other prophetic promises have not yet been fulfilled—including especially those that pledge a full restoration of the kingdom of Israel to its land, political dominance over the world, and righteousness before God. For dispensationalists, these promises will be fulfilled when Israel is restored as a dominant political kingdom, when it is ruled by its Messiah (Jesus), and when a mass conversion of Jews to faith in Christ has unfolded at the end-times. Many dispensationalists see the restoration of the modern state of Israel as a portent of the imminent return of Christ.

Many theologians reject equations of the (visible or invisible) church with the kingdom as well as the dispensationalists' separating of the two. Baptist theologian Stanley Grenz speaks of the church as the "sign of the Kingdom."[24] That is, the church is not identical with God's kingdom, but it represents (or expresses) elements of that kingdom and points toward—promises—the future, end-times appearance of that kingdom. According to Grenz, the kingdom of God is both God's right to rule and God's actual rule. As Creator of all that is, God has the right to rule all and ultimately is in control of all; but the actualization of such rule is not fully manifested (due to human sin and perhaps other evil forces). Yet through Christ's and the Spirit's activities in the church, God's kingdom (God's rule) is now partially manifested and will fully be seen in the eschaton. Even so, the kingdom (including God's rule) is not identical to the church. First, the kingdom's scope is broader, for God's right to and actual rule runs through the whole of reality and thus does not depend on the church. Second, the church itself is a product of and thus is dependent upon God's kingdom.[25]

Relation of Church to Israel?

Another issue for Christian theology is how is the church related to the people of Israel.

As noted above, one New Testament image of the church is that of *people of God*. But this expression originally was applied to the people of Israel. The earliest followers of Christ thought of their faith not as a rejection of Judaism but as a fulfillment of Jewish hopes. And they saw themselves as faithful Jews. For them, the long-awaited kingdom of God had come with all of its blessings, ushered in by Jesus the true Messiah. Israel's redemption had come, along with the outpouring of God's Spirit, forgiveness of sins, renewal of righteousness, reconciliation with God,

24. Grenz, *Theology for the Community of God*, 472.

25. Grenz, *Theology for the Community of God*, 472–79. Grenz's view is similar to that of New Testament scholar George Eldon Ladd. Ladd argues that "the Kingdom is primarily the dynamic reign or kingly rule of God, and derivatively, the sphere in which the rule is experienced . . . The church is the community of the Kingdom but never the Kingdom itself" (Ladd, *A Theology of the New Testament*, 111). Ladd further insists that none of the New Testament discussions of the kingdom equates Jesus' followers with the kingdom. Rather, most texts suggest that the church is created by the kingdom. In turn, the church bears witness to and is an instrument of the kingdom through its preaching (Acts 8:12; 19:8; 20:25; 28:23) and other ministries. Further, the church is the custodian of the kingdom, providing the means by which persons enter the kingdom—primarily through proclaiming the gospel. See Ladd, *A Theology of the New Testament*, 105–19.

and eventual restoration of Israel to political autonomy (Acts 1:8). Included in these end-time blessings was salvation for Gentiles as well.

For these reasons, the apostle Paul spoke of the followers of Jesus as Abraham's descendants.[26] The book of 1 Peter ascribes to Christians characteristics once attributed to ancient Israel, stating, "You are a chosen race, a royal priesthood, a holy nation, God's own people, in order that you may proclaim the mighty acts of him who called you out of darkness into his marvelous light" (2:9). Other ascriptions are given to the church elsewhere.[27] For early Christians, the church was in some sense the descendants of Abraham—that is, the people of God.

But an uncomfortable realization soon arose for the early church: most Jews were not turning in faith to Jesus as their Messiah. Indeed, many offered staunch resistance, and some even persecuted followers of Jesus. In light of these circumstances, some New Testament writers spoke harshly of Jewish opponents for their rejection of Christ, suggesting that divine punishment would befall them. In an early letter, the apostle Paul castigates those Jews who killed Jesus as well as those who at the time were persecuting Christians, claiming that "the wrath of God has overtaken them" (1 Thess 2:16). The Gospel of Matthew warns Jewish leaders that "the kingdom of God will be taken from you and given to a people that produces the fruit of the kingdom" (21:43). It is unlikely that either Paul or Matthew intended to say God rejects Jews. Each writer, himself, was of Jewish decent, and each commonly addressed congregations filled with Jewish (as well as Gentile) Christians. Their animus was focused on those who rejected Jesus and others who persecuted Christians.

Indeed, Paul was unnerved and grieved that more of his contemporary Jews (that is, more of the people of Israel) failed to accept Jesus as their Messiah (Rom 9:1–2). And he pondered whether their refusal implied that God's promises to Israel somehow had failed. Paul insisted they had not. The apostle offered several reasons for this conclusion, some clearer than others. For example, he argued that reception of God's promised blessings never was a matter of mere physical descent from Abraham; rather it always depended on believing God's promises (Rom 9:6–8). Further, Paul pointed out that the Hebrew prophets realized that not all Israel would be saved but only a faithful remnant; and there certainly were a number of Jews in the church of Paul's day (Rom 9:27;10:3–13). Perhaps most profoundly, however, Paul contended that God's promises to Israel are irrevocable, so that ultimately God will not abandon Israel but will one day draw them to himself. Paul speculated that one reason much of Israel was rejecting Jesus in his day was so that Gentiles might receive the good news of Jesus. But

---

26. In Gal 3:29, the apostle declares that "if you belong to Christ, then you are Abraham's seed, and heirs according to the promise." In Rom 2:28–29, Paul explains that a person is not a Jew outwardly by circumcision, but inwardly by "circumcision of the heart," which is a spiritual state. In Rom 4, Paul says that Abraham was declared righteous due to his faith, so that he is the ancestor of all who believe in Christ. In Rom 8:14, Paul asserts that persons are children of God not by the flesh but by the promise of God.

27. Compare Hos 2:34 and Rom 9:24–25, and Joel 2:28 and Acts 2:17.

the apostle also insisted that the time would come—namely, when the "full number of Gentiles has come in"—when Israel would accept Jesus as their Messiah and be saved (11:11–32).[28] A running assumption for Paul, then, was that persons can only be saved through faith in Jesus Christ, and he took for granted that rejection of Jesus entails condemnation. But because Paul believed in God's faithfulness and that ultimately Yahweh would save the Israelites, Paul also contended that one day Jews would accept Jesus as Messiah. But what of Israelites prior to the advent of Jesus? What of individuals like Abraham, Moses, David, and others? Were they not saved because they did not know who Jesus was? For Paul the obvious answer was that such persons likewise were saved. They were saved through their trust in God's promises, for such faith implicitly was in Jesus, who was the fulfillment of those promises.

Paul's core assumptions have often been endorsed by Christian thinkers throughout history, leading to a broad consensus about the relationship between the church and Israel. Theologians frequently taught that the Jewish faithful prior to Jesus were saved by their implicit faith in Jesus as they trusted God's promises, but theologians also often held that after Jesus all individuals—including Jews—must profess faith[29] in Jesus to be saved. Since often Jews refused to affirm Jesus as Messiah and Savior, Christian writers typically assumed that Jews were not saved and thus not part of the church. In light of these suppositions, patristic writers like Melito of Sardis (d. 180 CE) and Hippolytus of Rome (179–235 CE) spoke of the Christian church as the *new* people of God and of the Israelites as the *old* people of God, suggesting that after Jesus something new had emerged, making the older obsolete.[30] As the medieval church developed, and as emphasis fell more and more on the Roman Church as the institution through which salvation (by means of the sacraments) is dispensed, the perceived gap between Israel before and after Jesus widened. The ancient Jews had faithfully anticipated the coming of Christ and were saved, but some of Jesus' contemporaries had rejected him and were damned. In turn, Jews thereafter who continued to deny Jesus also were not saved.

The Protestant Reformers of the sixteenth century echoed these ideas. Philip Melanchthon claimed that many ancient Israelites "received forgiveness of sins, and were justified; that is, they were pleasing to God, received the Holy Spirit, and were made heirs of eternal blessedness *for the sake of the promised Savior, through faith in the promised Savior.*"[31] Thus, many Jews prior to Christ were saved by their implicit faith in Jesus. But Melanchthon also insisted that with the coming of Christ, the old way dissipated, and those who failed to have faith in Christ (and attempted to attain

---

28. Compare Eph 2:11–22.

29. Either explicitly, or implicitly through Christian baptism. This view was not held by all in the church. Some early theologians of the church seem to have affirmed some form of universalism. See discussions of this issue in chapter 7.

30. Pannenberg, *Systematic Theology*, 3:470–71.

31. Melanchthon, *Melanchthon on Christian Doctrine*, chapter 16 (italics original).

salvation by sacrifices or moral living) were not saved, including (those he named) the "godless Jews."[32] Similar sentiments are expressed in the Westminster Confession of the Reformed tradition, which declares that God gave "to the people of Israel, as a Church under age, ceremonial laws, containing . . . ordinances . . . prefiguring Christ."[33] In turn, these laws "were *for that time* sufficient and efficacious, through the operation of the Spirit, to instruct and build up the elect in faith in the promised Messiah, by whom they had full remission of sins and eternal salvation."[34] Again, faithful Jews prior to Jesus were saved by their implicit faith in Christ. But with the coming of Jesus, the only way to salvation was through faith in him.[35] And presumably direct rejection of Jesus as Christ led to condemnation. In sum, following the apostle Paul, Christian thought often has assumed that before Christ, faith in God's promises brought salvation to many descendants of Abraham, but after Christ, failure to accept Jesus as Messiah, or flat rejection of him, leads to condemnation. Hence, in some sense the former way (which once was efficacious) is now obsolete, having been replaced by a new way that more precisely recognizes and honors Jesus as the long-awaited Messiah and Savior.

Sometimes this traditional perspective is accused of *supersessionism*, the view that God has forsaken his former people (the Jews) and has replaced them with a new people of God (the Christian church). Such a charge is particularly distressing in the context of Western Christian civilization's long history of political oppression of Jews. In late antiquity and through the Middle Ages, Christian animosity toward Jews morphed into sheer anti-Semitism, resulting in Jews being depicted as the killers of Christ and blamed for a plethora of social ills. Often New Testament texts, taken out of the context of the struggles of their era, were later employed to justify such ethnic hatred and abuse of Jews. Further, as the connection between church and empire, and later between church and Christendom grew closer, Jews often were perceived to be enemies of the state. The Protestant Reformation did not always help. Initially, Martin Luther saw Jews as potential allies and recipients of the gospel;[36] but when many of Jewish decent did not turn to Jesus as Messiah, Luther's disposition turned vile.[37] These tendencies came to a horrible crescendo when Hitler's Third Reich attempted to exterminate ethnic Jews throughout Europe in the mid-twentieth century. In such a context, supersessionism seems like yet another way to degrade and denounce Jews and Judaism per se as well as the heritage of Christianity.

Defenders of the traditional perspective on church and Israel admit that their system has been misused so as to denigrate Jews and their legacy. But these authors

---

32. Melanchthon, *Melanchthon on Christian Doctrine: Loci communes 1555*, chapter 16. Presumably by "godless Jews" Melanchthon meant non-Christian Jews since the days of Jesus.

33. Westminster Confession, art. 19, sec. 3.

34. Westminster Confession, art. 7, sec. 5 (italics added).

35. Westminster Confession, art. 7, sec. 5; art. 11, sec. 2; art. 14.

36. See Luther, "That Jesus Christ Was Born a Jew."

37. See Luther, *On the Jews and Their Lies.*

quickly contend that such abuses are not inherent in their system. When rightly understood, affirming the messiahship of Jesus is an outgrowth and fulfillment of God's covenant with ancient Israel; for in Christ, many of the divine promises to Israel have been fulfilled, and God has ushered in a means to salvation long-promised by God to Jews as well as to Gentiles. This fulfillment is based on God's faithfulness to the covenant rather than on the faithfulness of God's human covenant partners. With the New Testament writers, then, proponents of the traditional viewpoint on the relation of ancient Israel to the church contend that faith in Jesus the Messiah is not a rejection or suspension of the ancient covenant with Israel but its fulfillment.

While the above doctrine has been typical of many Christian traditions, there have been dissenters. A principal example of this is dispensationalism. Dispensationalists contend that the church on the one hand and national, political, and ethnic Israel on the other are different entities, and God deals with each in different ways. Especially, there are multiple divine promises in the Hebrew Bible addressed exclusively to the nation of Israel, and not to the church. Among these promises are vows to one day restore Israel as a kingdom, to grant them rule over all nations, and to bring them back to faithfulness to God. For many dispensationalists, when political Israel rejected Jesus in the first century, God temporarily postponed fulfilling key prophecies for political Israel and ushered in the era of the church instead. But the time will come when God will renew his dealings with national Israel, restore them as a kingdom (ruled by Jesus the Messiah) and fulfill many of the promises not yet met. Often tied to this perspective is the belief that in the end-times Christ will rule over the world through the restored Israel for one thousand years (for a period often called the millennial reign) before the final judgment.

Dispensationalism has had tremendous influence especially among conservative separatist Christian traditions. One of its greatest contributions has been to remind Christian theology of the apocalyptic and eschatological nature of the Christian message. Jesus' first-century followers earnestly believed in and expected the apocalyptic intrusion of God in history, and they saw Jesus and the coming of the Holy Spirit as initial phases of this inbreaking.[38] Further, dispensationalism has to some degree helped challenge the implicit supersessionism that sometimes lingers in Christian ecclesiology. Dispensationalists can deny that the church has superseded Israel, insisting instead that the period of the church is temporary and that soon God will again "focus" on Israel proper.[39] Nevertheless, dispensationalism faces various criticisms. One is that it does not do justice to New Testament passages that closely tie (even identify) the church with the true spiritual descendants of Abraham. Further, it is not abundantly

38. Stanley J. Grenz notes, "By reintroducing the eschatological dimension to ecclesiology dispensationalism has served an important purpose" (*Theology for the Community of God*, 478).

39. Jürgen Moltmann writes, "Whatever we think about this modern salvation-history apocalyptic, it has vanquished anti-Judaism by vanquishing ecclesiastical absolutism" (*The Church in the Power of the Spirit*, 139–40).

clear that dispensationalism ultimately avoids the charge of supersessionism any better than traditionalism: like traditionalism, dispensationalism holds that in the end-times the Jewish people will convert to Jesus Christ en masse, a conviction that still suggests that the current Jewish faith is incomplete or insufficient.

In light of these varied problems faced by dispensationalism and the traditional perspective alike, some theologians have suggested that as was the case for the faithful of Israel prior to Christ, perhaps even now those of the Jewish religion who place their faith in God's ancient promises are implicitly believing in God's ultimate fulfillment (without realizing that it is Jesus) and thus are tacitly members of the true church. Such a suggestion is tempered by the fact that contemporary Jewish hope often includes an explicit rejection of Jesus as Messiah, and such denials are often met with condemnation in the New Testament literature (see John 3:18). Nevertheless, God's grace has surprised humankind in the past. However one might attempt to deal with these puzzles, one immediate value of discussing the relationship of the church and Israel is a healthy reminder that the current state of affairs is only temporary, and that God is not finished with either Israel or the church. Many divine promises from both the Hebrew Bible and the New Testament have not yet been fulfilled.[40] And the full revelation and salvation of God has not yet arrived either for Israel or for the church.

The Church and Other Religions

A final question about the nature of the church is this: Are there any members of the true universal church who are not members of the empirical church? Some writers insist (or at least imply) that the local empirical church is the sole concretization of the true church. In other words, while not everyone in the empirical church is saved, no one outside it is saved. And so, outside the empirical church there is no salvation. Others would argue that the empirical church is the primary but not exclusive instantiation of the true church. Thus, while many individuals outside the empirical church are excluded from the true church, some are included; some are saved. As observed in Chapter 3, some theologians maintain that general revelation gives sufficient knowledge to bring persons to salvation. Opposing these views, other theologians insist that while the information objectively available through general revelation *could* save a person, it does not because human sinfulness keeps sinners from receiving or positively responding to the information in general revelation.

---

40. Many advocates of the traditional perspective recognize (with their dispensationalist counterparts) that several prophecies about Israel have not yet been fulfilled. Thus, they too look to a time when such divine promises will be fulfilled, including Paul's claim that one day Israel will turn to Jesus. Examples include contemporary theologians as diverse as Erickson (*Christian Theology*, 964–66), Wolfhart Pannenberg (*Systematic Theology*, 3:470–77), Jürgen Moltmann (*The Church in the Power of the Spirit*, 136–50), and Henrikus Berkhof (*Christian Faith*, 261–65, 339–45), as well as writers from previous eras such as Charles Wesley and Charles Spurgeon.

Only through special revelation and the urging of the Spirit of God can persons receive the Gospel and positively respond to it in faith.[41]

There is some ambiguity here, however. For the relationship between the local church and special revelation is vague. What of persons who do not hear the message of special revelation through a living member of the church, but do hear it (so to speak) by reading the Bible? Here is a case where one receives the content of special revelation but not through the living community of a church. Some theologians respond to the quandary by noting that in hearing the message of the Bible, a person is already receiving the message *from the church*—for members of the ancient church composed the Bible. Thus, still only through special revelation has salvation come.

The Purpose or Mission of the Church

We turn now to the second major question of the doctrine of the church, and that is: what is the church's purpose? We may speak of seven broad purposes of the church. These are (1) to participate in and facilitate God's plan of salvation, (2) to glorify God, (3) to worship God, (4) to evangelize the world, (5) to edify its membership, (6) to serve as Christ served, and (7) to appreciate and promote all that is good.

To Participate in and Facilitate God's Plan of Salvation

In a sweeping way, we may say the church's purpose is to participate in and help facilitate God's plan of salvation. That is, that church is to receive God's salvation and help bring it to others. As noted in Chapter 5, biblically God's saving work includes salvation of individuals, social structures, and ultimately the universe itself. There is, of course, controversy among Christians regarding which of these is fundamental and whether the latter two are even realistic, practical goals of the church. Still, thinking holistically about salvation, we might speak of the church's purpose as participating in and facilitating each of these aspects of divine salvation

In terms of participation, individually, the church participates in God's salvation as each member is reconciled to God through Christ and moves toward Christ-likeness (toward that divine image originally intended for humans) through the inner workings of the Holy Spirit. Socially, the church participates in God's salvation by building a loving interpersonal community (the church) that (ideally) reflects the loving communion of the Triune God. *In terms of facilitating salvation,* individually, the church calls others to be reconciled with God in Christ and to move toward Christ-likeness. Socially, the church facilitates salvation by working for and encouraging social systems that reflect God's visions for justice, peace, interpersonal communion,

---

41. Examples of those affirming salvation via general revelation are Justin Martyr and Huldrych Zwingli. John Calvin held an opposing view. See Chapter 3, above (page 69). Also, see Chapter 14, below, for discussions of the relationship of Christianity and other religions.

and so forth. Regarding the cosmos, the church calls for and works for thoughtful stewardship over nature. Another way we might sum up this first broad purpose of the church is to say its goal is to participate in and facilitate God's kingdom.

To Glorify God

Another purpose of the church is to glorify God. Often theologians—especially from the Reformed tradition—insist that the ultimate purpose of the church is to glorify God. This certainly seems to be an accurate assessment. The book of Ephesians suggests this:

> In him [Christ] we were chosen, having been predestined according to the plan of him who works out everything in conformity with the purpose of his will, in order that we who were the first to hope in Christ, might be for the praise of his glory. (1:11–12)

Ultimately, the church's purpose (and the purpose of all creation) is to bring glory to God. The question, however, is, what about the church glorifies God? According to the perspective proposed here, the church glorifies God especially when individual humans conform to the image of Christ, and when human social systems reflect the loving interpersonal relations within the Trinity. As Stanley Grenz notes, that which glorifies God is consistent with the divine character, so that God especially is glorified when the church conforms to the moral and communal nature of God.[42]

To Worship God

A third central purpose of the church is to worship God—to recognize, announce, and celebrate the divine worthiness and grandeur. A continual attitude of joy, thanksgiving, and praise should attend the Christian's lifestyle (Phil 4:4, 1 Thess 5:16–18). Ideally, every action should be done in an attitude of praise. Thus, Col 3:17 declares, "And whatever you do, in word or deed, do everything in the name of the Lord Jesus, giving thanks to God the Father through him." In addition to a general life of praise, a special place is reserved for corporate worship. The church is to be a community that gathers for worship (1 Cor 14:26; Heb 10:25). In corporate worship the church focuses on cognitively, affectively, and emotively giving glory to God. Thus, the New Testament is full of images of the church gathered and engaging in a variety of activities to worship God (Acts 2:42–47; 1 Cor 14; Col 5:15–17). In its corporate worship, the church mimics the worship rendered to God in heaven (Rev 4).

42. Grenz, *Theology for the Community of God*, 489.

To Evangelize the World

A fourth purpose of the church is to evangelize the world. Evangelism essentially means to share good news. So, a prime task of the church is to speak the good news (the gospel). But what is the content of this news? Jesus came preaching the good news of God's kingdom. The long-awaited rule of God on earth was near. The proper response to this news was to repent of sins and believe the good news. Soon, however, it became apparent to Jesus' earliest followers that Jesus himself played a crucial role in the coming of the kingdom. Through him, God's rule on earth had been inaugurated, and the blessings of the kingdom were being made available to Israel and to humanity as a whole. Ever since, part of the church's purpose has been to spread this good news. In going to the world with this news, the church mimics God's own activities toward the world. As Jürgen Moltmann points out, the nature of the church as a missionary church derives from the nature of God as a missionary God. As the Father sends the Son and the Son sends the Spirit, so the church is sent to share the good news of the kingdom.[43]

In large measure, evangelism involves telling others the wondrous news of God's salvation in Christ, calling persons to receive the reconciliation with and forgiveness of God that Christ makes possible (Matt 24:14; Rom 10:14). It also entails discipling persons in the way of Christ—teaching them of him, of the salvation that has come through him, and of the way of life to which he calls persons. The call to discipleship is classically captured in what often is called the Great Commission, found in Matt 28:19–20, where Christ says: "Go therefore and make disciples of all nations, baptizing them in the name of the Father and of the Son and of the Holy Spirit, and teaching them to obey everything I have commanded you." Here, the church's task is to reach all nations—all people groups—with Christ's call to discipleship. Evangelism also involves living the gospel, being what Grenz calls the presence of God's kingdom in the world. In so doing, the church not only lives the principles of the kingdom (valuable in itself) but also presents to others a life that draws them toward the kingdom. This living of the kingdom demonstrates what personal and corporate life is to be.[44]

To Edify Its Membership

In the church's attempt to disciple the world, it soon finds itself discipling itself, for the church is those who have been called out of the world to God.[45] The notion of *discipleship* implies edification (1 Cor 14:4–5; Eph 4:11–12). Millard Erickson suggests that evangelism focuses on teaching the world (non-Christians). Edifying emphasizes

---

43. Moltmann, *The Church in the Power of the Spirit*, 50–56.

44. Grenz, *Theology for the Community of God*, 503.

45. This is part of the meaning of *ecclesia*.

activities aimed at the church.[46] Three activities are especially implied in edification. The first is teaching. Edification means diligently educating the church toward fuller understanding of and obedience to Christ. Here both preaching and instruction are useful (Rom 10:14–17; 12:7; Eph 4:11; 2 Tim 2:2; 3:16–17). Second, edification implies purification. As the church seeks to become more faithful to Christ, it must discipline itself (Matt 18:17). Discipleship implies mutual accountability (1 Pet 2:12), correction from error, and movement toward holiness and Christ-likeness. Finally, the notion of edification denotes fellowship, both in the sense of mutual service to and participation with one another. Thus, the church reaches inwardly, to itself, in an effort to generate mutual encouragement and sympathy (Rom 12:16). The church willingly bears the burdens of its constituency and lovingly shares its goods and services. Such fellowship also involves fostering a sense of oneness and singularity of vision/mission (Rom 12:3–6; 1 Cor 12:4–13, 4:12–16).

To Serve as Christ Served

A sixth purpose of the church is to serve as Christ served (Mark 10:32–45). This service is rendered by individuals in the church to others of the church (1 Cor 12). It also is rendered by individuals or the church as a whole to persons outside the church, especially those in deepest need—the poor, the disenfranchised, the oppressed, the alien. Obviously, care for spiritual needs is a part of this service. Evangelism and edification are parts of this ministry. But care for physical, social, political, and psychological needs also is demanded. Jesus came to be a servant to cure the spiritual ills of persons—somehow serving as a sacrifice for sin and bearing human sin in himself (Mark 10:45; Rom 3:21–25; 1 Pet 2:23–25; compare Isa 53:5–12). But Jesus also brought healing to the sick, sight to the blind, exorcism for the demon-possessed. (Matt 11:2–6; Luke 7:18–24), and he called his followers to do the same. He called them to care for the poor, the downcast, the religiously unacceptable. The church now equally is called to be servants—to one another, to the lost, and to the socially, economically, and politically downcast (Matt 25:31–46; Luke 1:46–48, 52–53; 12:13–21; 16:19–31; 18:18–21; Jas 2:1–17).[47]

Some Christian leaders have protested servicing the political or social needs of the poor on that grounds that the church has limited resources and must focus on spiritual needs first, or on the grounds that to address such matters can make persons blind to the deeper need to reconcile personally with God. Countering these views, Stanley Grenz rightly notes that

---

46. Erickson, *Christian Theology*, 964–66.

47. For much more on Christian outreach to those socially and economically outcast, see Chapters 8, 9, and 10 below.

the involvement of the church in social action is crucial regardless of its relationship to evangelism. It is a natural extension of Jesus' own ministry as entrusted to us. Hence, in embarking on a ministry of service, the church is simply continuing the mission of Jesus himself . . . Involvement in service . . . arises out of a wholistic conception of the gospel. Those who deny a connection between evangelism and service articulate a gospel directed only to one dimension of the human predicament. For them the good news is for the individual, and it facilitates . . . reconciliation with God . . . The biblical gospel, however, is explicitly social. It focuses on reconciliation with God, of course. But reconciliation is a social reality, for we are in a right standing with God only as we are likewise being brought into right relationship with others.[48]

In closing, we might add that the mandate to care for the poor or disenfranchised does not mean that such persons are better than others or that their spiritual need for reconciliation with God is either greater or lesser than that same need in the socially advantaged. Outreach to the disadvantaged follows from the biblical emphasis on care for the needy and from the sheer logic that the neediest are the ones who most urgently need attention.

To Appreciate and Promote All That Is Good

A final function of the church is to appreciate and promote all that is good. Like its mission to glorify God, this goal of the church envelops the totality of life. God is creator of all, so that all that is good reflects something of the divine nature. The natural world declares God's glory (Ps 19; Rom 1:19–20), and humans are fearfully and wonderfully made (Ps 139:14). The wonders and effects of nature are signs of God's glory: the songs of birds, the elegance of deer, the majesty of trees, the grandeur of mountains, the power of the sea, the splendor of the night sky. All these creations and more speak of God's greatness. In turn, the handiwork of humans likewise manifests God's goodness, wisdom, and power: music, art, literature, poetry, science, and technology. These capacities too are gifts from God. Sin and natural evil are parts of this world and often taint these varied beauties, but they cannot fully mute their goodness and wonder. Because of this, the Christian life is one that first celebrates the created beauties and capacities. Christians also participate in the production of these glories, all the while recognizing that the abilities to envision and create such beauties are themselves gifts from God.

Of course, a central aspect of the appreciation and promotion of the good is an admiration, sponsorship, and performance of moral (or righteous) actions, especially in the context of interpersonal relations. The potential to do good is a divine gift, engrafted into the essence of humans. Indeed, the ability to act morally in the context of interpersonal relationships is perhaps the greatest divine gift given to

48. Grenz, *Theology for the Community of God*, 507–8.

humanity. In giving these potentials, God has made humans themselves most like God of any creature, creating humans in the divine image, so that individually and corporately humans might reflect God's moral and interpersoal nature. The great tragedy at the heart of the Christian story is the loss of humankind's ability to act rightly in interpersonal love. But the grandeur of the Christian gospel is that through Christ and through the empowering of the Holy Spirit, God is restoring these abilities and relationships to humanity. While Christians appreciate and promote all that is good, they especially celebrate moral righteousness for in such goodness they see God's love and glory most stunningly manifested.

The Ministries, Ministers, and Governance of the Church

We turn at last to consider how the church accomplishes its purpose(s). As the church attempts to perform its varied tasks, diverse persons (ministers) within the church engage in differing services (ministries) to achieve those goals. Therefore some mechanisms for making decisions and for orchestrating ministries also are needed. In light of these realities, three broad topics arise about the practices of the church: (1) What are the church's ministries? (2) Who are the church's ministers? and (3) What forms of governance and administration does the church employ?

Church Ministries

The earliest Christians engaged in a myriad of ministries. Over the span of Christian history, a host of other ministries have also arisen. In a sense, there are as many ministries as there are activities of church members. Every kind act, every loving word, aids in accomplishing the first, second, and last broad goals of the church (discussed above)—namely, participating in and facilitating salvation, glorifying God, and promoting all that is good. Some ministries are well suited to enhance the church's worship, and many ministries more narrowly focus on facilitating the third, fourth, and fifth purposes of the church: evangelizing the world, edifying members, and rendering service. The apostle Paul mentions a number of gifts especially focused on edifying the church (Rom 12:3–8; 1 Cor 12:7–11). And the writer of Ephesians speaks of office-like gifts whose purpose is to "prepare God's people for works of service, so that the body of Christ may be built up" (4:12 NIV).

Various lists have been drawn up in discussions about the main ministries of the church. Here we discuss five core ministries. These are (1) meeting together, (2) worshiping God, (3) doing acts of service, (4) proclaiming and teaching God's Word, and (5) administering the sacraments (which are sometimes called ordinances). As will become apparent, distinct interpretations of these church practices have arisen among ecclesial traditions. Some of the greatest differences between Protestant groups have emerged over the sacraments of the church.

The first core ministry of the church is *meeting together*. In the New Testament, groups of Jesus followers often were known as *ecclesia*, assemblies—those called out and gathered by God. This term echoed the practices of ancient Israel, who assembled as God's people to worship the Lord. Reformed theologian Hendrikus Berkhof identifies meeting together as one of the ministries of the church. This is the case in part because in these assemblies many of the other ministries of the church are performed. But more profoundly, in the community's gathering per se, something of God's grace is conveyed. The wholeness of the human-community-restored is (at very least) depicted and, hopefully in some measure, is realized. In such meetings, a community of mutual affection, fellowship, and purpose, united by their love for God and for one another, is manifested. Such gathering is a sign of eschatological hope, of what God intends to bring to all humankind. In addition to this, the gathered community offers and helps facilitate a corporate encounter with God. Its liturgies—calls to worship, public prayers, congregational responses, readings from Scriptures, testimonies, songs of praise, homilies, and sacraments or ordinances—all encourage collective and individual encounters with God.

A second major ministry of the church is *worshiping God*. A central purpose of Christian gatherings is to express corporate praise and thanksgiving to God. One of the great sins of humanity is its sheer failure to be thankful to God for the many divine blessings (Rom 1:21). While personal and private praise often is heard in the New Testament, the praise and worship of the church body also is noted (Luke 1:46–55; Heb 13:15; Jas 5:13;). Many of these practices echo the worship of ancient Israel as expressed in the Psalms. The theme of God's and Christ's worthiness especially is found in the book of Revelation (4:11; 5:9–12; 7:12; 19:5). As noted above, a core purpose of human salvation and of the church is for the praise of God's glory (Eph 1:11–12).

A third ministry of the church is doing is *acts of service*. As noted above, serving as Christ served is a core purpose of the church, and among Christ's ministries was care for the needs of others, including physical needs. This commitment to practical needs flows from the biblical concept of salvation itself. As Hendrikus Berkhof notes:

> Salvation not only concerns man's heart in its relation to God, but from that center it touches all of his life as well as that of humanity. Salvation is total; it is the answer to man's double estrangement: from God and from himself; that is, it is the answer to man's guilt and his need. Now that in Christ God's kingship has come near and we are made to share in it by the Spirit, this should also become clear in what happens to the concrete forms of need and guilt of man's existence in the world. Otherwise the comprehensive purpose of God's salvation has still not become clear.[49]

For this reason, the church has long cared for the needy (Matt 25:31–46; Acts 6:1–8; 20:1–5; Rom 15:25–32; 1 Cor 16:1–4, Jas 2:1–17). And that call now continues.

49. Berkhof, *Christian Faith*, 369.

A fourth key ministry of the church is *proclaiming and teaching of the Word of God.* The notion of the Word of God conveys numerous meanings. In its most profound sense, the Word of God is *Jesus,* who is the Word of God incarnate (John 1:1–3, 14). In him, the fullest revelation of God is given (Col 2:8–10; Heb 1:1–4). In many ways, then, the proclamation and teaching of the Word is the announcing and describing of Jesus himself—his life, ministry, mission, atoning death, resurrection, and very being. For this reason, the heart of the New Testament is the four Gospels, for there we read about this fullest expression of God—namely, Jesus the Christ. In a secondary way, however, ministry of the Word refers to proclaiming the stories, teachings, demands, and invitations of holy *Scriptures,* for there we learn of the Lord's activities among humankind and of Christ's lordship and saving mission. In the Scriptures, we also hear God's invitation to come and participate in salvation and blessings. As we have seen, proclaiming and teaching God's Word were central tasks of the first-century church.

Proclaiming and teaching the Word of God takes wide-ranging forms. It includes evangelistic preaching, preaching sermons to the faithful, instructing new converts, leading Bible studies, and even holding conversations among church members about theology and about living the Christian faith. Evangelistic calls to faith in Christ and to conversion to his way of life have always played some role in Christian life, even though such efforts waned somewhat during the Middle Ages, when membership in the church became a virtual birthright of Western civilization. Preaching was revitalized, however, by mendicant orders in the late medieval era, and soon returned to center-stage thanks to the sixteenth-century Protestant Reformers. For Luther and Calvin, a true sign of the church is its proclamation of God's Word, which includes calling humans to faith (and thus to salvation) in Christ. For Luther, preaching essentially is a sacrament—that is, a means by which God conveys grace. For him, however, reception of such grace is not automatic, for it requires a response of faith.[50] Evangelistic preaching became a hallmark of the eighteenth- and nineteenth-century revivalist movements in England and America where altar calls routinely were given, asking individuals to repent of sin and receive Christ as Savoir. In the twentieth century, these practices became entrenched in many fundamentalist and Evangelical church-services; and they continue in the twenty-first century.

In addition to evangelism, which is directed toward nonbelievers, often preaching is directed to the faithful. Such preaching comes in what we call *sermons* or *homilies.*[51] This kind of preaching seeks to edify and instruct church members. Often two elements are involved in such sermonizing. The first element is exposition and interpretation of scriptural texts. The second element is application of scriptural teachings to daily life. Each component is important for guiding church members in the life of faith.

Instructing new converts also has a long-history in the church. A typical practice of churches in the second and third centuries was to require a formal process of

---

50. Luther, however, also believed that human faith itself is a gift from God.

51. Although sermons and homilies can be evangelistic as well.

training prior to baptism. Candidates (often called *catechumens*) were introduced to the basic teachings of the faith and were tested to ensure compliance. In later centuries, as infant baptism became more prevalent, and as the rite of confirmation came into vogue, young adults were taught the basics of the faith through instruction manuals (*catechisms*) before their confirmation into the faith. Even Luther, whose calls to *sola scriptura* (Scripture only) caused him to criticize the teaching-manuals of the Catholic Church, later developed Lutheran catechisms for the instruction of young and old alike. Individual and collegial Bible studies and discussions were hallmarks of the Pietist movement of Philipp Jakob Spener (1635–1705) in the seventeenth century and were echoed in the Methodist movement of John and Charles Wesley (1707–1788) in the eighteenth century and by the Sunday school movement of the nineteenth and twentieth centuries.

The Ministry of the Sacraments

A *fifth* important ministry of the church is the *administration of the sacraments or ordinances*. Because of the complexity of this ministry, we have placed commentary on it in a separate section. The (Latin) term *sacramentum* or "sacrament" has been used in various ways throughout history. In the classical Roman period, it was employed to speak of monies set aside for religious purposes or of the sacred military oath taken by soldiers vowing their allegiance. The term was coopted by Christians to translate the Greek word *mystērion* from the Greek New Testament into Latin. As time progressed, "sacrament" came to designate certain core rituals of the church. Considerable differences exist between Christian traditions regarding how many sacraments there are, what sacraments do, who receives them, and who may officiate over them.

We begin by examining the Roman Catholic perspective on the sacraments. Over time, the Catholic Church came to endorse seven sacraments. These are *baptism, the Eucharist, penance, confirmation, holy matrimony, holy orders*, and *extreme unction*. We already have mentioned baptism and the Lord's Supper (the Eucharist), and we will say more momentarily. Penance is a formal mechanism for absolving postbaptismal sins. Confirmation refers to the act of an adolescent or adult believer formally and consciously confirming his or her commitment to the Christian faith, and receiving the Holy Spirit to aid in this commitment. Since often persons were baptized in infancy, the ritual of confirmation was understood as the way young adults could confirm the faith implicit in their earlier baptism. Extreme unction is the act of anointing with oil believers near death, absolving them of past sins, and preparing them for life after death. *Holy matrimony* refers to marriage officially sanctioned by the Church; and *Holy orders* denotes ordination into the clergy.[52]

---

52. These sacraments were formally endorsed by the Fourth Lateran Council of 1212.

Roman Catholic tradition tends to affirm an *instrumentalist* understanding of the sacraments, contending that through these rites divine grace (and thus salvation) is infused into participants. Ignatius of Antioch (d. c. 108/140) spoke of the Lord's Supper as "the medicine of immortality."[53] Ambrose of Milan (340–397) claimed that baptism "effects the reality of regeneration."[54] Augustine of Hippo insisted that the sacraments produce the saving effect of which they also are signs. The Council of Trent condemned those who teach that "the sacraments . . . do not contain the grace that they signify, or that they do not confer that grace."[55]

While seven sacraments are recognized in the Catholic Church, typically baptism and the Lord's Supper are thought to be the most important. This is the case both because of their clear use in New Testament times and because of the relatively late development and recognition of the other five sacraments. Baptism is understood as the sacrament through which salvation initially is received; through it one obtains remission of sins, baptism of the Spirit, and admission into the church. Baptism may be received only once in a person's life, but this may happen at virtually any age, including in infancy. Early in the second century, some Christian leaders voiced the opinion that only one grievous postbaptismal sin can be forgiven. This led Tertullian (c. 155–240) to propose that baptism ought to be postponed late into life out of fear that one might commit grievous (and unforgivable) sins after baptism.[56] Concerns over postbaptism sins helped generate the doctrine of penance. Penance is a formal mechanism by which fallen Christians may repent and receive forgiveness after baptism. Cyprian of Carthage (208–258) argued for the practice of penance on the grounds that without forgiveness of sins after baptism, there would be little incentive for fallen Christians to return to Christ.[57] Ironically, contrary to Tertullian, Cyprian advised that infants be baptized as early as possible out of fear that they might die before receiving the saving waters of baptism. His concerns were founded in part on his affirmation of original sin—the notion that each human, from conception, is born with a sinful nature. (Augustine also adopted this view of sin and baptism.) Over time, concern for unbaptized infants fostered belief in limbo, a place where unbaptized babies go upon death. Limbo is not heaven, but neither is it a place of torment. Thomas Aquinas speculated that it was a place of happiness—but not the bliss of heaven.[58] The doctrine

---

53. Ignatius, *Epistle to the Ephesians*.

54. Ambrose, *On the Mysteries*.

55. "The Canons and Decrees of the Council of Trent," Session 7, Canons on the Sacraments in General, Canon 6, in Leith, ed., *Creeds of the Churches* (italics added).

56. Both the Shepherd of Hermas and the Didache of the late first or early second centuries taught that only one grievous post-baptismal sin could be forgiven.

57. Cyprian, *Letters*, 51.17; Cyprian, *On the Lapsed*, 34.

58. Thomas Aquinas, *Summa Theologica*, Supplement, q. 71, art. 7.

of limbo was never formally endorsed by the Roman Church. In 2006, Pope Benedict XVI formally denied the validity of the doctrine limbo.[59]

The Lord's Supper is the second of the two major sacraments of the Catholic Church.

First-century Christians memorialized Jesus's death through a ritual meal, sometimes referring to it as the Lord's Supper (1 Cor 11:20–21) or the Eucharist (1 Cor 11:24). It is unclear whether the authors of the New Testament saw the bread and wine of this meal as somehow becoming the literal flesh and blood of Jesus, or whether they understood the elements of the meal as together composing a material analogy to a Christian's spiritual participation in the life of Christ. Also uncertain is whether first-century Christians thought partaking of this meal produced saving benefits or only reminded participants of the salvation that had come through Christ's death. By the second century, however, many Christian writers seem to assume that the elements of the Lord's Supper were the very body and blood of Jesus and that by partaking of the meal itself participants received the saving benefits Christ's death.[60] By the second and third centuries, many writers also were teaching that the Eucharist was a form of sacrifice, a reenactment of Christ's sacrifice on the cross.[61]

These tendencies to see the elements of the Lord's Supper as transformed into the body and blood of Jesus and to understand the meal as a sacrifice became more prominent in the ensuing centuries. In 1212, the Fourth Lateran Council officially endorsed the doctrine of *transubstantiation*—the view that upon being blessed by a priest, the Eucharistic elements of bread and wine become the very body and blood of Christ. The council also validated the notion that the Eucharist is a sacrifice that mysteriously reenacts the very sacrifice of Christ on the cross. These views were reaffirmed at the Council of Trent (1545–1563). Formally, the doctrine of transubstantiation claims that while the *attributes* of the bread and wine remain the same, the *substance* of these elements are changed into the very body and blood of Christ. In turn, this doctrine insists that such transformation only occurs through the consecrating and blessing of a duly authorized priest of the Church.

One further note regarding the Catholic understanding of the sacraments is its insistence that the saving power of the sacraments is not diminished by the immorality or unfaithfulness of presiding bishops or priests. As long as a priest has been duly sanctioned through apostolic succession to consecrate the various sacraments, these sacraments are effective regardless of the officiant's lack of moral character or faithfulness. This issue arose, especially, in the fourth century during the Donatist controversy, wherein members of that party insisted that the ministries of morally lapsed bishops and priests no longer were valid, including their administration of the

---

59. International Theological Commission, "The Hope of Salvation."

60. Ignatius, *Letter to the Smyrnaeans*, 6; and Ignatius, *Epistle to the Ephesians* 13, 19–20; Justin Martyr, *First Apology*, 66.

61. Justin Martyr, *Dialogue with Trypho*, 41; Irenaeus, *Against Heresies*, 4.17.5.

sacraments. Donatists affirmed the principle of *ex opere operantis*—that the validity of the sacrament is due to the faithfulness and moral purity of the one who oversees it. On the other hand, Augustine, whose view came to dominate Catholic thought, affirmed the principle *ex opere operato*, insisting that the potency of the sacraments was due to the ritual itself, not due to the one administering it.

Sixteenth-century Protestant Reformers challenged many of these Catholic teachings about the sacraments. Virtually all Protestants denied that the Eucharist is a sacrifice, or that by a priest's announcement the elements of the Lord's Supper are transubstantiated into the very flesh and blood of Christ. Further, all disallowed that the sacraments infuse divine grace (righteousness) into participants. Additionally, Protestants reduced the number of sacraments from seven to two. The only sacraments they recognized were baptism and the Lord's Supper. Reformers rejected these sundry practices for various reasons. But at the heart of disagreements between Reformers and Roman Catholics was the Reformers' denunciation of what they perceived to be a works-righteousness system of salvation in the Roman Church.

By the fifteenth century, Catholic doctrine understood justification as a person's becoming morally righteous through the sacraments and through merits. Ultimately, salvation was given when a person became truly righteous. Baptism transmitted righteousness to a person, but acts of penance in this life and purification in purgatory after death restored righteousness lost due to sins committed after baptism.[62] Also, for Catholics, venial (that is, lesser) postbaptismal sins were forgiven through the perennial sacrifice of Christ at the Lord's Table. Luther, and other Reformers, rejected many of these ideas. For them, humans can never become righteous through self-effort; in this life, humans are always sinners. Further, actual righteousness is not transferred to persons through the sacraments, as if God's grace were a commodity that could be transported and infused through a ritual.[63] Rather, for the Reformers, grace is a divine temperament: it is God favoring sinners in spite of their evil. Instead of mysteriously giving people actual righteousness, God graciously declares sinners righteous, crediting Christ's righteousness to them. God justifies individuals, not by works, but based on their faith (trust) in Christ, whose once-for-all sacrifice atoned for all sins. In short, salvation does not come by doing righteous deeds or being righteous, or by participating in the sacraments. Righteousness (and thus salvation), by a sheer act of divine grace through the atonement of Christ, is attributed to those who place their trust in Christ.

With these rationales in the background, Protestants rejected various Catholic practices that they thought supported or relied upon a "works-righteousness"

---

62. Out of such ideas, the theory of indulgences also arose. Allegedly, there was a great well of merits stored up that struggling Christians might tap into to reduce their (or loved ones') penance or time in purgatory. These merits were those of saints from the past, including Mary and of course Jesus. Such merits could be obtained in various ways, including by donating funds to the church. In many ways, the doctrine of indulgences was the catalyst that set the Reformation in motion.

63. And righteousness certainly could not be earned by financial donations.

approach to salvation. Thus, the Reformers denounced the Catholic notions that sacraments *infuse* righteousness into participants, or that priestly pronouncements empower sacraments to do this. Reformers also denied that postbaptismal sins must be redressed by acts of penance or trial in purgatory, perpetual sacrifices of Christ through the Mass.[64] For the Reformers, all such practices were undermined by justification by grace through faith. Supporting this range of Protestant claims was a renewed appreciation for the authority of Scripture over postbiblical church traditions. Luther and fellow Protestants often appealed to *sola scriptura*—the Scripture only—in their defenses of various practices and denials of others. For example, a core reason for their rejection of all but two sacraments was the absence of clear New Testament teachings regarding the other five.

In spite of these many Protestant agreements about sacraments, there were several disagreements between Protestant groups. We first consider differences concerning baptism. While Luther claimed that salvation is by faith in Christ alone, he also taught that baptism remits sin and imparts salvation. For Luther, faith in Christ essentially is trusting in the promises of God. These promises are presented in God's word, but they also are pictured in the sacraments, including baptism. Thus, when a person is baptized, he or she implicitly is accepting (trusting) God's promise to save through Christ.[65] In this sense, baptism *strengthens* faith by painting a picture of the gospel, which, in turn, solidifies and encourages a person's preexisting faith. As noted earlier, baptism presents *God's pledge* to save, and this reassures participants. But more profoundly, for Luther, baptism also *awakens* faith. It generates faith within a baptized person. For Luther, faith is God-given, not human-produced. When a person hears the gospel, God creates faith in that individual; in like manner, when someone is baptized, God awakens faith within him or her. In this way, Luther defended infant baptism. Luther justified infant baptism by insisting that baptism not only strengthens faith but actually (perhaps mysteriously) generates faith. He proposed that faith need not precede or immediately accompany baptism, for faith itself is not a human act but God's work upon the sinner. Luther even suggested that infants may have a rudimentary faith due to baptism. Thus, baptism can be given to a passive infant, for it awakens faith in the child, thus bringing salvation.

Not all early Reformers were impressed with Luther's views on baptism. Among his detractors were the Anabaptists or Radical Reformers. Most of these reformers rejected the notion that baptism remits sin or brings salvation. Only faith in Christ saves; and this faith must be exercised by a deliberate choice. Like Luther, Anabaptists believed that hearing and positively responding to the word of God is key to salvation. But unlike Luther, they did not see participation in baptism as virtually synonymous with accepting

64. The term *mass* is yet another name for the Lord's Supper, though for Reformers the word also entailed the Catholic notion of sacrifice. Thus, many Reformers, including Zwingli, rejected this name for the meal.

65. See Luther, *Luther's Small Catechism* (1529), art. 4.

the divine promises. Rather, one must make a conscious choice to believe in order to be saved. In turn, these Radical Reformers rejected infant baptism, for babies are incapable of performing deliberate acts of faith. Further, many of these Radical Reformers proposed that persons who had been baptized as infants (when they had been unable to willfully choose it) needed to be baptized again when they were old enough to decide for themselves. For this reason, these reformers became known as *Anabaptists* (rebaptizers). Initially, Anabaptists faced considerable persecution at the hands of Catholics and other Protestants. Over time, however, repression diminished, and their numbers grew. Today, several denominations endorse this perspective, among them are Mennonites, Brethren, Baptists, and Pentecostals.

One particularly sticky theological problem for such groups concerns salvation of persons who die without becoming old enough (or rational enough) to consciously (or deliberatively) choose to believe in Christ. Many of these Radical Reformers believed in *original sin*, the idea that all humans are conceived with a sinful nature and thus need salvation from the moment of conception. But does this mean that infants or young children who die prior to being capable of choosing Christ are bound for hell?[66] Few Radical Reformers were willing to answer yes to this question. Instead, they developed the notion of *the age of accountability*.[67] This theory proposes that God does not hold individuals responsible for their sinfulness until they have reached an age when they can be held responsible for their choices for or against Christ. Until that time, individuals are granted salvation and are ushered into heaven at death. Critics contend that such a view lacks biblical support and seems to assume that persons can be saved without faith in Christ. Differing ages have been proposed for when the *age of accountability* arises in a person; many speculate it is somewhere around early adolescence.

While many Protestants disagreed with Luther, they likewise did not accept the views of the Radical Reformers. Among these were Huldrych Zwingli, John Calvin, and the Reformed churches that they helped spawn. We must be cautious here, however, for Zwingli endorsed many of the Anabaptist interpretations of baptism. Indeed, it is more accurate to say that many of the Anabaptists accepted several of Zwingli's opinions; for Zwingli was among the first to deny that baptism saves, that baptism primarily is *God's pledge* to humans, and that baptism is a kind of surrogate of the gospel that activates faith. Instead, Zwingli believed that only faith in Christ saves, and that such faith is awakened by the Word of God but not really by baptism. In turn, Zwingli insisted that baptism is primarily a *human pledge* of faithfulness to God rather

66. This is not unlike a dilemma faced by Roman Catholics about unbaptized infants. Catholic lore (if not dogma) attempted to solves such a problem with the concept of limbo. But most Protestant groups reject such a notion. The Catholic Church formally rejected the doctrine of limbo in 2007. See International Theological Commission, "The Hope of Salvation."

67. The notion of an *age of accountability* was not unique to Protestants. The Catholic faith had long postponed the sacrament of confirmation until later in life, until what was sometimes designated the age of reason—sometimes set as early as age seven.

than the other way around. That is, baptism is a sign or expression of human faith in Christ. Obviously, then, Zwingli and the Radical Reformers had much in common. But Zwingli vehemently opposed the Anabaptists' rejection of infant baptism and their calls for rebaptizing Christians baptized in infancy. Rather, Zwingli supported infant baptism, although his rationale for the practice was distinct from Luther's. He saw infant baptism as a pledge of unity not only with God but also with the church. For him, baptism was analogous to circumcision in the Old Testament; it solidified one's membership in the community of God's people.

John Calvin merged aspects of Luther's and Zwingli's views, while also denying other features of each. Calvin defined a sacrament as "an outward sign by which the Lord seals on our consciences the promises of his good will toward us in order to sustain the weakness of our faith; and we in turn attest our piety toward him."[68] Following Augustine, Calvin also defined a sacrament as "a visible sign of a sacred thing," or "a visible form of an invisible grace."[69] Like Zwingli, then, Calvin saw the sacraments—including baptism—as *human pledges* of allegiance to God and to the church. They "attest our piety." But like Luther, Calvin also recognized sacraments as *God's pledges* to humanity. They encourage and evoke faith by reminding persons of the divine promises. Or more precisely, through the sacraments (and the Word of God) the Holy Spirit arouses faith and thus saves.[70] While Calvin agreed with Zwingli that the sacraments attest to faith, he criticized his fellow Swiss Reformer for failing to acknowledge that the sacraments—including baptism—display the gospel and thus evoke faith and salvation. It is less clear to what degree Calvin disagreed with Luther about the effects of the sacraments. Calvin does clearly reject what he calls a "magical" view of sacraments—which he attributes to Catholics of his day—that teaches that the sacraments in themselves save; some see Calvin's criticisms here as leveled at Luther as well.[71] Calvin accuses his opponents of failing to distinguish between the visible signs (sacraments) and the matter these signs represent. The matter is Christ and his redemptive work; it is he, not the sacrament, that saves.[72]

Regarding baptism specifically, Calvin insists it is a visible sign "of the initiation by which we are received into the society of the church, in order that, engrafted into Christ, we may be reckoned among God's children."[73] Like other sacraments, baptism both strengthens and evokes faith and also attests one's faith. Baptism is a token or seal to assure believers that they have been cleansed of sin, have died and been raised to life in Christ, and have been spiritually united to Christ.[74] Calvin

---

68. Calvin, *Institutes of the Christian Religion*, 4.14.1.

69. Calvin, *Institutes of the Christian Religion*, 4.14.1.

70. Calvin, *Institutes of the Christian Religion*,.4.14.11–14, 17.

71. González, *A History of Christian Thought*, 3:150–51.

72. Calvin, *Institutes of the Christian Religion*, 4.14.14–16.

73. Calvin, *Institutes of the Christian Religion*, 4.15.1.

74. Calvin, *Institutes of the Christian Religion*, 4.15.1, 5–6.

teaches that even though baptism is the normal pattern for Christians and should be followed when possible, it is not necessary for salvation. Ultimately, salvation comes through faith in the divine promises.[75] Unlike Catholic teaching, which says that baptism remits only past sins and original sin, Calvin maintains baptism points to the cleansing of all sins—past, present, and future.[76] With Catholics (and contrary to some Anabaptists), however, Calvin agrees that the authenticity of baptism does not rely upon the merit of persons administering it.[77]

Against Anabaptists, and with Luther and Zwingli, Calvin endorses infant baptism. His reasoning is similar to Zwingli's. Calvin argues that the covenants of the Old Testament and of the New Testament are essentially the same one; each promises divine salvation by grace through faith in Christ. The Old Testament anticipates Christ's fulfillment of God's promise to save; the New Testament experiences that fulfillment. Each covenant, in turn, has sacraments associated with it, designed to remind and assure participants of God's promises and faithfulness. Baptism is analogous the Old Testament sacrament of circumcision, which assures of one's membership in the covenant community. By analogy, since infants were initiated into the community by circumcision in the Old Testament era, infants are brought into the church through baptism in the Christian epoch.[78] Calvin admits that he cannot explain precisely how infants, who have no knowledge of good and evil, and who cannot repent or believe, can be saved through faith. But he insists that "God's work, though beyond our understanding, is not annulled."[79] Calvin also suggests "that infants are baptized into future repentance and faith, even though these have not yet been formed in them," and that "the seed of both lies hidden within them by the secret working of the Spirit."[80]

One final note is needed regarding the sacrament of baptism. Throughout the centuries varied modes (ways of performing) baptism have been used. Three major forms are performed; these are sprinkling, pouring, and immersion. Many traditions practice more than one of these, and they consider all or most acceptable. Some groups, however, insist on only one proper form. Baptists often insist on immersion as the only genuine mode, contending this is the core meaning of the biblical term.

More could be said about Protestant perspectives on baptism. But let us turn to their varied views on the Lord's Supper. As noted above, Protestants rejected the notions that the sacraments infuse grace, that the Eucharist is a sacrifice, or that by priestly utterance the elements of the Supper transubstantiate into the body and blood of Jesus. But there were considerable variances among Protestants on other matters regarding the Lord's Supper. Luther rejected transubstantiation, but he affirmed the

75. Calvin, *Institutes of the Christian Religion*, 4.15.20. Compare 4.14.14.

76. Calvin, *Institutes of the Christian Religion*, 4.15.3–4.

77. Calvin, *Institutes of the Christian Religion*, 4.15.16.

78. Calvin, *Institutes of the Christian Religion*, 4.16.5

79. Calvin, *Institutes of the Christian Religion*, 4.16.17.

80. Calvin, *Institutes of the Christian Religion*, 4.16.20.

real presence of Christ's body and blood in the meal. (According to the Catholic doctrine of transubstantiation, upon being consecrated by the priest, the bread and wine of the Eucharist do not remain bread and wine but rather become Christ's body and blood.) Luther renounced transubstantiation for its Aristotelian philosophical underpinnings, claiming that such a theory was idle speculation and that the church should not be held captive to such musings. Further, the theory claimed that the bread and wine no longer were bread and wine but had become Christ's body and blood. But Luther found such a claim scripturally unwarranted and rationally unacceptable. Nevertheless, Luther insisted (in the face of resistance from several other Protestant groups) that in the Eucharist Christ's body and blood really are present "in, with, under" the bread and wine. Luther refused to speculate over how this is possible, only that it is taught by Scripture and thus is true. Like other Reformers, Luther denied that the Eucharist was a sacrifice or that by a priest's pronouncement the bread and wine are transformed. Luther contended that God brings Christ's presence to the table how and when God chooses.

Huldrych Zwingli disagreed with Luther especially about the real presence of Christ's body and blood in the Eucharist. Instead, he taught that Jesus' statements in Matt 26:26–28, "This *is* my body" and "This *is* my blood," are metaphors to be understood as "this *represents*" or "this signifies" my body and blood. Thus, the Eucharist represents Christ's blood and body; it is not literally these things. In turn, the Eucharist primarily is a remembrance of what Christ did on the cross for sinners (Luke 22:19; 1 Cor 11:25–26). And, as baptism does, so the Eucharist serves as a *human pledge* of alliance to Christ and his church. Zwingli's views on these matters essentially were accepted and amplified by various Radical Reformers of his day and by later Protestant groups such as the Brethren, Baptists, and others.

John Calvin taught that, like baptism, the Lord's Supper is a pledge from God designed to reassure believers of the divine promises. It also acts as a testimony of a Christian's faith. Unlike baptism, which initiates the believer's life in Christ and occurs only once, the Lord's Supper is repeated as a regular reminder of God's salvation and assurance to the faithful. Calvin (in spite of lengthy discussions) is unclear regarding the precise nature of Christ's "presence" in the Supper.[81] A standard interpretation of him in Reformed churches is that "he denied the bodily presence of the Lord in the sacrament, but . . . he insisted on the *real*, though spiritual presence of the Lord in the Supper."[82] This interpretation is affirmed in the Westminster Confession, which states: "Worthy receivers, outwardly partaking of the visible elements in this sacrament, do then also inwardly by faith, really and indeed, yet not carnally and corporally, but spiritually, receive and feed upon Christ crucified, and all

81. At times, Calvin speaks of Christians participate in the body and blood of Christ through the elements of the Supper, while also saying of this participation and these realities are "spiritual" and "invisible."

82. Berkhof, *Systematic Theology*, 646 (italics original; brackets added).

benefits of his death."[83] In spite of ambiguities in his thought, Calvin clearly rejected the claim that participating in Christ's body and blood are mere metaphors for faith in Christ.[84] He also repudiated the notion that the bread and wine transubstantiate into Christ's body and blood, and thus cease being bread and wine.[85] Further, he denied Luther's contention that the body and blood of Christ are present "in," "with," or "under" the bread and wine, for this would require that Christ's spatial body was somehow ubiquitous—that is, in all spaces. Rather, Calvin insisted that through the Holy Spirit, individuals consuming the Lord's Supper partake of Christ's body, which is currently ascended into heaven with God the Father.[86]

Church Ministers

Obviously, if the church engages in ministries it must have persons (ministers) who facilitate those ministries. But who are the ministers of the church? As Daniel Migliore notes, Christian theology often recognizes two understandings of church ministers, each coexisting with the other and equally valid. The first is a broad understanding of church ministry that identifies all Christians as ministers. Such a perspective is an important insight of the sixteenth-century Protestant Reformation—an insight that stressed what Luther and others called "the priesthood of believers." This idea was not invented by the Reformers but echoes an inherent tenor of New Testament teaching. This understanding of ministers is suggested by the apostle Paul's claim that each Christian is gifted by the Spirit for the good of the church (Rom 12; 1 Cor 12; Eph 4) and by 1 Peter's declaration that Christians are "a royal priesthood" (2:9). According to this broader view, each Christian is a priest or minister of God. A second understanding of ministers is narrower; it speaks of those members of the church who are set apart for administrating especially critical ministries of the church—including especially leadership, preaching and teaching, and the sacraments.[87] We briefly address each of these concepts of ministers.

The dynamic between the communal and institutional aspects of the church is seen in the doctrine of the priesthood of believers. As understood by Protestants, this teaching asserts first that every believer is in an immediate relation with God through the sacrifice of Christ and the appropriating power of the Holy Spirit. Through no other person must someone go to receive forgiveness and grace. Nonetheless, in spite of the immediacy of this relationship, the doctrine of the priesthood of believers also recognizes each Christian is a kind of mediator between God and other humans. In this sense, each member of the church is a priest for all other members (and possibly for all

83. Westminster Confession, art. 29, sec. 7.
84. Calvin, *Institutes of the Christian Religion*, 4.17.5–7
85. Calvin, *Institutes of the Christian Religion*, 4.17.13–15.
86. Calvin, *Institutes of the Christian Religion*, 4.17.16–33.
87. Migliore, *Faith Seeking Understanding*, 227.

humanity). As Donald Bloesch notes, "In the New Testament church . . . one becomes a priest by being united through faith in the one Mediator, Jesus Christ. Because we are his brethren, we share in his priestly role."[88] As priests, individual Christians testify to of the salvation in Christ, offer intercessory prayers, and seek to minister in a host of ways to the church (and the world) through the gifts of the Spirit.

The New Testament also recognizes a narrower understanding of ministers. It speaks of persons called out to lead and teach the church. In the earliest New Testament literature, church offices and structures were fluid.[89] Still, there are hints in Paul's Letters of growing church structures and offices. In 1 Thessalonians, Paul encourages congregants to respect those who "rule" or "manage" them (*proistamenoi*; 5:12), suggesting a leadership-structure in the congregation. In his Letter to the Romans, Paul speaks of a deacon named Phoebe (16:1). And in Philippians, he addresses the bishops or overseers (*episcopoi*) and deacons (*diaconoi*) of that church (1:1). In later Pauline letters, the ministerial structures of churches seem to solidify. The author of 1 Timothy speaks of bishops, deacons, *and* elders (*presbyteroi*),[90] often applying to these offices the same descriptors employed in 1 Thessalonians to speak of persons who rule or manage—derivatives of *proistamenoi*.[91] From the literary context, it is clear these are leaders of the local church. First Timothy also identifies core characteristics and duties of bishops or overseers (3:1–7) and of deacons (3:8–12). Among the responsibilities assigned to overseers are teaching, managing, and taking care of God's church. Similar duties are assigned to elders in 1 Tim 5:17–19, namely, ruling, teaching, and preaching. Deacons appear to have served as assistants within the church and are especially (but not exclusively) associated with ministries to the needy (Acts 6:1–5). In the Letter to the Ephesians (4:11), another term is used to speak of local church leaders. This is the word "pastor" or "shepherd" (*poimenes*). The text combines into one role shepherd and teacher so that the ministry at issue is that of the shepherd-teacher.

Scholars dispute whether the offices of bishop, elder, and pastor are one office or separate offices. Sometimes the New Testament denotes one bishop of a church but several elders. This suggests that the offices were different. On the other hand, in the book of Acts, the roles of overseer, elder, and pastor seem to be combined. Paul calls the *elders* of the church of Ephesus together (Acts 20:17) and says to them: "Keep watch over yourselves and over all the *flock*, of which the Holy Spirit has made you *overseers*, to *shepherd* the church of God that he obtained with the blood of his own son" (20:28; italics added). The highlighted words above reveal the combining of the titles and tasks

88. Bloesch, *Essentials of Evangelical Theology*, 2,:106.

89. The apostle Paul addresses most of his epistles to congregations as wholes rather than to formal officers of the church. And in his lists of spiritual gifts, Paul names ministry-enabling gifts available to all Christians, not just leaders.

90. Paul does not use the term "elder" (*presbyteros*) in his earliest (and undisputed) letters.

91. Bishops (1 Tim 3:4), deacons, (1 Tim 3:12), and elders (1 Tim 5:17) manage the church. Compare 1 Thess 5:12. See Ladd, *A Theology of the New Testament*, 532.

of the three offices mentioned—elder, bishop or overseer, and pastor or shepherd. In like manner, in the book of Titus, *bishop* and *elder* are used as synonyms (1:5–9).

In addition to these varied offices of the local church, the New Testament sometimes speaks of ministers who transcend single congregations. Eph 4:11 speaks of apostles, prophets, and evangelists. And in 1 Corinthians, Paul speaks of apostles and prophets (12:28). The exact nature of prophets and evangelists is disputed by scholars, but many believe these individuals traveled and ministered to multiple congregations in diverse regions. While the term "apostle" (*apostolos*) is often used to speak of the twelve disciples handpicked by Jesus (Acts 1:2, 15–26), the word apparently designates others as well. Occasionally, Paul used the title to describe himself and his ministry (1 Cor 9:1; 2 Cor 1:1; Gal 1:1), and on occasion he distinguishes the twelve apostles from other apostles (Rom 16:7, which speaks of a woman named Junia as an apostle; 1 Cor 15:5, 7).

Whatever the precise relationship between elders, bishops, pastors, and deacons may have been in the first century, it was not long before clear distinctions were made between these terms or roles. By the second century, a three-pronged system of ministerial offices arose, where the offices of bishop, presbyter (priest), and deacon were plainly separated. Ignatius of Antioch (c. 50–110) promoted such a system, insisting that bishops hold primary authority over local or regional churches; in turn, presbyters and deacons are subservient to the episcopal office. It is perhaps no coincidence that Ignatius also advanced an instrumental understanding of the Eucharist, referring to that meal as "the medicine of immortality"[92] and, thus suggesting that individuals receive eternal life by partaking of the Lord's Supper. These tendencies continued into the third century. Cyprian of Carthage (210–258) taught that "the bishop is in the Church and the Church is in the bishop; and if anyone be not with the bishop he is not in the Church."[93] This brash assessment was fueled by an increasingly instrumentalist interpretation of the sacraments (especially baptism and the Eucharist). These rituals were said to produce—through God's grace—the benefits of salvation so that without them individuals could not be redeemed. In turn, because only duly ordained bishops (and those they appointed) could rightfully dispense the sacraments, bishops were (for all intents and purposes) the fountains of salvation. Not surprisingly, as time progressed, the functions of bishops also increased. Through them, sins were forgiven, reconciliation with God occurred, clergy were ordained, doctrines were protected, and the life-giving sacraments were given.[94] While presbyters had similar functions to those of bishops, these capabilities were granted only through the episcopacy. The growing power of bishops and the instrumentalist understanding of the sacraments also helped drive a wedge between clergy and laity (nonclergy), undermining any

---

92. Ignatius, *Epistle to the Ephesians*, 20.2.

93. Cyprian, *Epistle 51*, 68.8.

94. Hippolytus, *The Apostolic Tradition*, 3. 4–5.

strong sense of the priesthood of believers and diminishing egalitarian understandings of the church for church members.

As time passed, the role and prestige of bishops continued to blossom. An elaborate hierarchy of ecclesiastical leadership arose. Priests were charged with ministering to local congregations in territories called *parishes*. Several parishes, in turn, came to make up a *diocese* and were overseen by a *diocesan* (or *ordinary*) *bishop*. Several dioceses were under the watch and care of even more powerful and honored bishops called *metropolitan archbishops*, who ruled territories called *provinces*. And over several provinces were high-ranking bishops called *patriarchs*, who ruled their *patriarchates* from one of the great cities of the Roman Empire. The cities with the greatest clout were Jerusalem, Antioch, Alexandria, Rome, and eventually (after Constantine) Constantinople. The patriarch of Rome (often referred to as the pope) was generally held in the highest esteem, in no small part due to his residing and ruling from the capital of the Roman Empire. While most of the ancient patriarchs recognized the pope as a first among equals and thus due special honor, they did not see the Roman bishop as having jurisdiction over their territories. After the fall of Rome and the gradual split of the Roman Empire into East and West, popes claimed more and more authority especially in the West and often attempted to assert this power in the East. The end result, in the West, was a church hierarchy with diverse levels of bishops, ruled by the highest-ranking patriarchs and overseen by the pope.

As the medieval era unfolded, the power of the papacy increased. Often this authority was founded upon the instrumentalist understanding of the sacraments. On occasion, popes used their power over the sacraments as political tools to control secular kings and provinces. Seeking to gain or retain political or religious compliance, popes would threaten civic leaders (through excommunication) or whole populations (through interdictions) with separation from the church and its sacraments—thus imperiling their salvation. The late fifteenth-century selling of indulgences flowed in large measure from this grand understanding of church ministry-structure.

The Protestant Reformation of the sixteenth century brought changes to the understanding of church ministerial offices. Seeing the hierarchical structure of the Catholic Church as part of the cause of church abuses and looking back to scripture, Reformers such as Luther and Zwingli concluded that there is only one basic ministerial office—namely, the pastor, which they saw as synonymous with bishop and presbyter, priest, or elder. This conclusion flowed partly from New Testament usage but also from Protestant understanding of the church proper. For them, ultimately the visible church is found in local congregations, not in an ecclesiological hierarchy over and above the local church. In turn, the church is not grounded in its pastors or leaders, as Cyprian taught; rather, the church is the congregation, each member of which is a minister or priest. Hence, the pastorate is grounded in the body of believers; they (through God's guidance) recognize and call pastoral ministers. As we will see in below, the exact mechanisms for selecting church leaders vary among

Protestant groups. Still, the central assumption of most Protestants is that the local church (guided by God's Spirit) possesses the authority to call (or at least approve) its own leaders. Further, traditionally for Protestant churches, the primary ministers of the church are all the church's members, who, in turn, recognize and call some to be overseers, elders, pastors.[95] Following the Scriptures, many Protestant groups also recognize deacons as distinctive ministers in the church. A central job of the pastor is to lead the church in correct doctrine and practices, to proclaim the gospel, and administer the sacraments. Likewise, as Eph 4:11–12 suggests, a core role of the pastor/elder is to "equip the saints for the work of ministry."

Church Government

We turn now to consider how the church governs itself. How does the church make decisions or establish policies? Three broad governing approaches have emerged among churches over the centuries. These are the *episcopal*, *presbyterian*, and *congregational* approaches.

The first of these styles is exemplified by the Roman Catholic system, as well as by the Anglican and Orthodox Churches.[96] At the heart of these administrative structures is the *episcopacy*. According to this approach, Christ authorized the apostles, who authorized bishops after them, who in turn commissioned other bishops through a long history of successors. Bishops, thus, mediate the authority of Christ on earth. For many centuries, pivotal church decisions were made by councils (synods) of bishops from various locales. Sometimes such synods were only regional. But at times attempts were made to gather bishops from all regions. These gatherings were often called *ecumenical* councils—meaning, assemblies of "the whole earth." Over time, the pope (that is, the Roman bishop) came to be recognized as the ultimate authority within the Western church. This interpretation emerged gradually and not without conflict. Even when his ultimate authority was generally recognized, however, often the expectation was that the pope's decisions should coordinate with the views of the general council of bishops. Papal power reached its zenith in the nineteenth century at the First Vatican Council (1869–1870) when the pope was formally recognized as the chief authority in the Roman Catholic Church, with power to overrule episcopal councils and even offer infallible teachings when officially (*ex cathedra*) pontificating doctrine. Technically, the English monarch is the head of the Anglican Church, but typically major decisions are

95. Perhaps de facto if not de jure, many Protestant believers think of the pastors (and other church leaders) as *the* ministers of church and think of congregants as mere recipients of ministry from these ministers. But at least theoretically most Protestant churches still affirm the priesthood of believers and the notion that all Christians are ministers of Christ.

96. The Episcopal Church in the United States offers a form halfway between the episcopal and representative forms of governing. This system is overseen by a general convention composed of laypersons and clergy, but these representatives must be confirmed by the House of Bishops and by the House of Deputies (made up of laypersons and priests from each diocese).

made by a college of Anglican bishops overseen by the archbishop of Canterbury. Each of these systems emphasizes the office of bishops, seeing the episcopacy as distinct from the presbyter or priest, which is interpreted to be a lesser office. It is bishops who establish church policies, clarify doctrine, ordain ministers, and ensure proper management of church business and ministries. The Eastern Orthodox Church is a community of regional churches, each self-governed by a synod of bishops who elect their own ruling bishop called a patriarch.

The presbyterian or representative model of church governance is found especially among Reformed and Presbyterian churches. The focus of this approach is on delegates elected to represent local congregations and on associations of congregations. It is these representatives who make the key decisions of a local church or of groupings of churches. These delegates often are called *presbyters*, in this case meaning "elders" or leaders of the church. Presbyters or elders include ordained ministers as well as lay leaders. Indeed, typically in Reformed and Presbyterian polity, both ordained and lay elders are deliberately selected to represent local congregations and groups of congregations. Several levels of decision-making assemblies set policy in Reformed and Presbyterian churches. For local congregations, elders (both lay and ordained) meet in *sessions* or *consistories*. Multiple churches in a region are represented by elected delegates in assemblies called *presbyteries* or *classes*. Again, in such gatherings, both ordained and lay representatives participate. Even broader assemblies are manifested in gatherings called *synods* and *General Assemblies*. In all these governing bodies, the primary decision makers are elders selected to represent various local and regional congregations. Through the assemblies of these elders the fundamental decisions of the churches are made.

The congregational or independent model of church rule manifests in various Protestant denominations, including among Mennonites, German Baptists, Amish, and Hutterites (all from Anabaptist roots); also functioning congregationally are the Religious Society of Friends (Quakers), Congregationalists, Baptists, Churches of Christ, Disciples of Christ, and many forms of Pentecostalism. At the root of this form of ecclesiastical governance is the autonomous congregation, which collectively sets policy for the local body of believers. In such churches, every member has a say in church affairs. Ideally, decisions are made by mutual consent. But often majority rule is the norm. Frequently the congregationalist model is defended as being implicit in the doctrine of the priesthood of believers. Among the most important decisions made by the church collective is selection of church officers, including especially the pastor. It is not uncommon for churches with this style of governance to enter into association with like-minded congregations, but such connections are considered strictly voluntary and may be disjoined by each independent congregation.[97]

---

97. With perhaps a touch of irony, a number of Protestant groups—often with heritages of congregational governance—have over the last several decades been moving toward more authoritarian styles of church government wherein congregations have very little say in church decision-making.

Different scriptural texts can be cited to defend each of these models of church governance. The episcopal system is suggested by Jesus' selection of the apostles with no clear consultation with other disciples.[98] In turn, Acts 14:23 indicates that on occasion Paul selected elders for churches he had founded. The presbyterian model is most compatible with the fact that often in the New Testament the offices of elder and bishop are essentially equated (Acts 20:25–28; Titus 1:5–7), so that any attempts to interpret bishops as higher-ranking than elders seem to be incorrect. The congregational model is undergirded by several instances in the New Testament where local congregations as a whole make critical decisions about church ministries, discipline, and leaders (Acts 1:15–26; 13:1–4; 15:2–3; 1 Cor 1:10). Each model has some modicum of scriptural support.

No doubt, each model has attractive features. In general, a positive aspect of both the episcopal and presbyterian models is that they help produce (though they do not ensure) theologically informed decisions because they include clergy, who (ideally) are trained in such matters. Also, at times, the episcopal and presbyterian systems can bring about more streamlined decision-making processes, for they often involve fewer voices. A positive feature of the congregational model, however, is that it (ideally) values every member's opinion and seems to be most consistent with the spirit of the priesthood of believers. Of course, each system has its problems as well. The episcopal model is subject to authoritarian abuses while both the presbyterian and congregational paradigms can fall prey to petty rivalries and to the tyranny of the majority.

Conclusion

As we have observed in this sixth chapter, the Christian doctrine of the church is complex. It involves several layers and nuances. This complexity is, perhaps, not surprising for it is in and through the church that much of the Christian faith is lived out. In this chapter, we have discussed the central issues surrounding the nature, purpose, and activities of the church. In the next chapter, we examine the Christian doctrine of Last Things—the Christian vision of God's culminating activities with humankind.

Several Baptist churches, as well as various freestanding megachurches, have moved to elder systems of governance, in which church members (or church attenders in congregations with no membership) have no direct input into church decision-making or polity. The irony of this situation is that these congregations often hail from theological traditions whose followers once cherished (and even died for) congregational authority and independence.

98. Although, Acts 1:15–26 suggests that the congregation in Jerusalem played a role in selecting someone to replace the fallen Judas.

7

Last Things

WE TURN NOW TO discuss the doctrine of *eschatology* or *last things*.[1] Among its many gifts to the world, the Hebrew tradition brought with it a linear concept of time. Unlike many ancient cultures that saw the world unfolding in an endless series of repeating cycles, the ancient Israelites understood cosmic history as having a beginning, an end, and a transitional period between these. Through this middle period, humanity and the cosmos now travel, moving toward culmination.

The basic narrative of this time line is familiar. In the beginning, with beautiful intensions and set purpose, God created the universe and humanity. But something went wrong. Evil entered the cosmos, expressed particularly in human sin but also in other aspects of creation. Hence, God's loving design was challenged and distorted. For individual humans, sin brought guilt, death, a distorted character, and enmity with God. It also generated strained relationships with fellow humans. Further, the universe itself somehow was affected for the worse. But God did not abandon creation or humanity. God seeks to redeem the created order, including especially human beings—restoring them to their divinely established purpose. The doctrine of *last things* describes the culmination of this divine salvation in human and cosmic history. It tells of God's transformation of humans into the image of God and of the renewal of fellowship with God, among humans, and with the universe. But the doctrine divulges more than this. It also addresses the state of those who—for whatever reason—are not (or refuse to be) restored by God.

Biblical Hope

Eschatology is grounded in the hope of the Hebrew tradition and in its primary fulfillment in Jesus Christ. At the core of this hope is God's promise to Abraham to bring blessing to his descendants and through them benefit to all nations. These promises were voiced in the context of the pervasiveness of human sin and its individual, corporate, and cosmic consequences. Through Abraham, God (the faithful covenant

1. "Eschatology" is derived from the Greek word *eschata*, meaning "last."

partner) would remedy sin and its aftermath. Through Abraham, God likewise called the people of Israel—Abraham's descendants—to receive the divine remedy for sin and to be an instrument through which salvation might come to all nations. God also established a royal dynasty—the dynasty of David—to defeat Israel's enemies, to secure Israel's borders, to reign justly, and to both exemplify and enforce God's righteous ways. But Israel—like humanity as a whole—was unfaithful to God; Israel did not righteously keep the covenant; its kings and people often disobeyed God, worshiped idols, and ignored personal and social righteousness. Thus, judgment befell them. The kingdoms of Israel and Judah fell to foreign powers.

But embers of hope remained. Promises of a restored kingdom composed of remnants of fallen Judah (and Israel) were foretold by Yahweh's prophets. In 538 BCE, a remnant indeed returned from Babylonian exile. But problems persisted. The province of Judah was perpetually ruled by foreign nations. And no Davidic messiah arose to overthrow the oppressors. But hope still smoldered. Over time, various images were envisioned of divine restoration of Israel—images often drawing from older Hebrew scriptural traditions and from burgeoning apocalyptic themes. In the air lingered promises of military victories over Israel's enemies, hopes of reestablished faithfulness to God's Torah, and dreams of an overwhelming and cataclysmic divine intervention into cosmic and human processes. Also, there were hopes of an autonomous Israel ruled by a faithful Davidic king and possibly of Israel ruling all nations.

Into this ethos of eschatological hopes, Christianity was born, often assuming, manipulating, and reinterpreting many of themes of Israelite and later Jewish faith. According to early Christians, Jesus was the Messiah (Christ), the Son of Man, the Suffering Servant, the Son of God, and Lord; all of these concepts are from the Hebrew tradition, augmented in varying ways by apocalyptic thinking, and adopted and adapted by Christian writers. As Messiah, Jesus will one day meet the expectations of that promised office. As noted in Chapter 2, early Christians divided Jesus' messianic fulfillment into two phases: (1) his earthly ministry wherein the means of righteousness before God was made possible, and (2) his future return in glory and power when he will right the wrongs of the world, overcome the forces of evil, reward the righteous, punish the wicked, and bring peace, justice, divine presence, and divine rule.

Eight Major Biblical Eschatological Themes

Naturally, the contemporary Christian doctrine of eschatology is deeply influenced by these ancient Jewish and early Christian traditions about the end-times. Several New Testament concepts inform the doctrine of eschatology. We begin by discussing eight major eschatological ideas in the New Testament. *First* are the notions of *sin*, *evil*, *suffering*, and *death*. While not uniquely eschatological themes, these concepts play a crucial role in New Testament thinking. For ancient Hebrew and early Christian thought, each of these realities is a problem to be resolved in human and cosmic life. Humans sin, bringing ruin upon themselves and upon their relationships with one another and with God. But human sin is a symptom of a larger, cosmic problem. In this world there are spiritual forces standing against God. The rebellion of certain supernatural beings helps explain cosmic evil. Further, somehow flowing from sin and evil are suffering and death. Suffering and death plague human life but also impact the life of animals and the character of the cosmos as a whole. At the heart of the biblical narrative is God's design to atone for and uproot sin, evil, suffering, and death.

Related to these four problems is a *second* major eschatological theme of the New Testament, namely, the notion of *two ages*: (1) a present evil age (of sin, suffering and death) and (2) a future age (when God will fully reign, and these troubles will be vanquished). The idea of two ages was pivotal to the apocalyptic thinking of many practitioners of Second Temple Judaism and of most first-century Christians.[2] Related to the notion of two ages is a *third* eschatological theme, namely, *the kingdom of God*. In many ways, the idea of the kingdom of God is a synonym for the age to come—the period when God's rule will be thoroughly manifested.[3] However, as noted in Chapter 2, Jesus preached the *nearness* of God's kingdom, teaching in his own words and deeds that the kingdom and its benefits were already dawning. Likewise, while conceiving the kingdom as not fully realized, the apostle Paul taught that in Christ aspects of the kingdom already had come: salvation had come (Gal 1:4; Col 1:13; 2:14), the Spirit of God had been given (Rom 8:1–17; Gal 3:1–5; 5:13–26; Eph 1:13–14), and for believers a new age and new selves had begun (2 Cor 5:17). In short, the early Christian understanding of the coming age and of the kingdom of God differed from mainstream Jewish thought of the era. While typical Jewish thought looked forward to the new age and reign of God on earth, early Christians saw the coming age and kingdom as already partially manifested in Jesus and in his followers.

A *fourth* eschatological theme in the New Testament was the *return of Christ*. As noted above, first-century Christians expected Christ to return in power and glory to bring the full realization of the new age and kingdom of God upon the earth. Often New Testament writers speak of this as the day of the Lord, or the day of the Lord Jesus Christ, or they employ other similar phrases.[4] They seem to have drawn from the Hebrew scriptural tradition, which often spoke of the day of the LORD.[5] The apostle Paul used several expressions to describe the return of Christ. He wrote of Christ's *parousia* or "arrival" (1 Cor 16:17; 2 Cor 7:7; Phil 2:2), *apokalypsis* or "unveiling" (Phil 2:10–11

2. See 1 Cor 2:6–8; 3:18–21 ; Gal 1:4; ; Eph 1:21; 2:2.

3. In God's kingdom, death will be overcome (1 Cor 15:50) and wickedness will be excluded (1 Cor 6:9; Gal 5:27; Eph 5:5).

4. Acts 2:20; 1 Cor 1:14; 5:5; Phil 1:6; 1 Thess 5:2; 2 Thess 2:2; 2 Pet 3:10; .

5. Sometimes this expression in the Hebrew Bible denoted God's impending judgment upon Israel and Judah (or others) through the existing kingdoms of the ancient world, such as the Assyrians (Isa 2:12; 7:17–25; Amos 5:18) or Babylonians (Jer 46:10). In other instances, the day of the Lord referenced a more universal and culminating event when God would establish the divine kingdom, reward the faithful, and judge the wicked (Joel 3:14–21; Zeph 1:14–18; Zech 14:1–21).

1 Cor 1:7; 2 Thess 1:7), and *epiphaneis* or "appearing" (1 Thess 2:8). Whatever phrasing was used, for several New Testament writers, the return of Christ will bring multiple end-time events, including revelation of Christ's glory (Matt 24:27; Tit 2:13), resurrection of the dead (1 Cor 15:23; 1 Thess 4:13–18), and the destruction of evil (1 Thess 2:19; 3:13; 4:15; 5:23; 2 Thess 1:7–8; 2:8). It also will bring the full revelation of Christ's lordship and the defeat of all forces opposed to him, including death (1 Cor 15:24–28; Col 2: 9–10, 15). Further, in some sense, through Christ all things in heaven and on earth will be restored to right order (Eph 1:10; Col 1:20).

A *fifth* end-time topic is the general *resurrection* of the dead. By *general resurrection* one means the raising of all the dead, not just Christ's resurrection. Only the slightest hints of resurrection are found in the Old Testament literature—for example, see Isa 26:19 and Dan 12:2. Hope of resurrection became much more pronounced in the era of the Second Temple; but even in the days of Jesus not all Jewish sects affirmed that the dead would rise (most notorious for their denial of resurrection were the Sadducees). Nevertheless, an end-time resurrection is assumed by the writers of the New Testament. Surprisingly, little is said of the general resurrection in the Synoptic Gospels, although much is said of Jesus rising from the dead. Luke records Jesus commending secretive generosity and teaching that such acts will be repaid "at the resurrection of the righteous" (14:14). John's Gospel speaks of a general resurrection on a couple of occasions (5:28–29; 11:25), and this in spite of its emphasis that believers in Christ already have eternal life (e.g., 3:36; 4:14, 36; 5:24; 6:47; and so forth). Most telling in the Gospel of John, Jesus says, "The hour is coming when all who are in their graves will hear his [the Son of Man's] voice and will come out—those who have done good, to the resurrection of life, and those who have done evil, to the resurrection of condemnation" (5:28–29; brackets added). Here, John writes of the resurrection both of good and evil persons. Paul speaks more of the final resurrection than any other New Testament writer. In Rom 6:5, he ties believers' future resurrection to their union with Christ's resurrection (see also Phil 3:10–11). In 1 Cor 15, Paul argues passionately for the resurrection of the dead against those who reject such teaching. And in 2 Tim 2:18, the author rebukes two teachers who allege that the general resurrection has already happened. There is some dispute over whether Paul taught the resurrection of the righteous only, or of both righteous and wicked. In his undisputed letters, Paul mentions only the righteous in connection with the general resurrection. The author of Acts, however, asserts that Paul taught the resurrection of both the just and unjust (24:15). Paul also clearly taught that the final resurrection would occur at the return of Christ (1 Thess 4:13–18).[6] The book of Revelation speaks of two resurrections of the dead (Rev 20:5, 12)—a view not clearly endorsed elsewhere in Scripture.

A *sixth* major theme of New Testament eschatology is divine *judgment*. On numerous occasions, the Gospel of Matthew warns of "the day of judgment," when human

6. Such an understanding likewise is expressed in the Matt 24:30–31, 1 Cor 15:23, and 1 John 5:28–29.

sin will be revealed and condemned (7:2; 10:15; 11:22, 24; 12:36, 41, 42). In chapter 25, Matthew speaks of the coming judgment of the Son of Man, who will condemn those who maltreat or ignore needy "brethren" (25:31–46). John's Gospel proclaims that the Son of Man has been given authority to execute judgment (5:27), and that humans will be judged by how they respond to Jesus' word (12:48). John also insists that those who believe in Christ already have life, and those who do not are condemned already (3:17–18). Paul makes a similar comment in 2 Thessalonians (2:12). Paul in turn speaks of the judgment seat of God (Rom 14:10) and of Christ (2 Cor 5:10), and he declares that Christ will judge the wicked at his appearing (2 Thess 1:7–8; 2 Tim 4:1). In Romans, Paul insists that through Christ, God will "judge the secret thoughts of all" (2:16; compare 1 Cor 4:5). In several places, Paul intimates that while Christians too will be judged, they have safekeeping in and hope of acquittal in Christ (Rom 3:21–26; 5:1–11; 8:1, 33–34; 1 Cor 3:10–15; Gal 5:5).

The notion of judgment leads to a *seventh* set of biblical images of the eschaton.[7] We might call these images of the *final state* of humans (as well as of other creatures). For convenience, we refer to these as *heaven* (the final state of the righteous) and *hell* (the final state of the wicked). (The use of these terms is somewhat problematic since the Scriptures use diverse concepts to describe the final circumstances of the redeemed and unredeemed alike.) It should be noted that judgment need not bring punishment alone; judgment also involves acquittal and reward. So what we are calling heaven and hell each may result from divine judgment. A starting point for this discussion is to return to Matt 25:31–46 (a passage mentioned in the previous paragraph). There, we see depicted the fates of both the faithful and the unfaithful. To the faithful, the Son of Man (depicted as the end-time judge), says, "Come, you that are blessed by my Father, inherit the kingdom prepared for you from the foundation of the world" (v. 34). Later, this group is called "the righteous," who enter "eternal life" (v. 46). Next, the Son of Man says to the unfaithful, "You that are accursed, depart from me into the eternal fire prepared for the devil and his angels" (v. 41). These individuals enter "eternal punishment" (v. 46).[8] While Matt 25:31–46 is a parable and thus calls for cautious interpretation, it points to several common features of the New Testament understanding of the final state. First, it points to the Son of Man (ultimately identified as Jesus in New Testament materials) as the final arbiter of judgment. Second, it depicts the final condition of the faithful (called "the righteous") as an eternal state of blessedness and life. Third, it

---

7. *Eschaton* simply refers to the circumstances that unfold in the end-times.

8. There is some dispute over how best to translate *aionios*, translated above as "eternal" in Matt 25:46. David Bentley Hart recently has argued that this term is best interpreted as "of the Age," "age-long," or "for an extended period." He thus rejects its translation as "eternal" (everlasting or never-ending) and dismisses the notion of eternal or everlasting punishment. See Hart, *That All Shall Be Saved*, especially 121–28. Traditional translations and many modern exegetes (so far) side with something like "eternal" or "everlasting." For a brief critique of Hart's views, see McClymond, "David Bentley Hart's Lonely, Last Stand."

describes the circumstances of the unfaithful as accursedness, eternal punishment, and fire. This same destiny is appointed for the "devil and his angels."

The New Testament uses a number of concepts to describe the final state of the faithful. One of these is heaven. The word *heaven* is used in several ways in the New Testament. Sometimes it denotes the physical sky and that which is beyond it (Matt 5:18; 24:29; compare Gen 1:1). Occasionally it is employed as a synonym for God or God's power (Matt 21:25; Luke 15:18, 21; John 3:27). And frequently it denotes the abode or kingdom of God. In the Lord's Prayer, Jesus invokes "our Father in heaven" (Matt 6:9). Heaven is the place where God's will especially is performed (Matt 6:10). It is where God's angels are (Luke 22:43) and from where Jesus came (John 3:13, 32, 6:42). Further, from heaven, Christ will come again (John 14:2–3; 1 Thess 1:10; 4:16). Heaven also may be where the saved will be one day. Texts such as Matt 6:19–20, Col 1:5, and 1 Pet 1:4–5 often are interpreted to teach this. According to these verses, heaven is where the inheritance of the faithful is secure and never-fading. The book of Revelation speaks of the coming of a new heaven and new earth wherein the faithful will dwell with God (Rev 21:1–3) and where there will be no more death, sorrow, or pain (22:4). Of note, it will be a place where the faithful will be called God's people and God's children, pointing to the importance of corporate as well as individual salvation (vv. 3, 7). Paul declares in his Letter to the Romans that current suffering is unworthy of comparison to the glory that will be revealed to the faithful in the end (8:18).[9]

The final state of the unfaithful or wicked is depicted in disturbing, even horrifying, images. It is described as an everlasting[10] punishment (Matt 25:45) and fire (Matt 25:41; Mark 9:43, 48), as a place of deep darkness, weeping, and gritting of teeth (Matt 8:12, 13:42, 50; 22:13; 24:51; Luke 13:28). Paul speaks of it as a place of "eternal destruction" and of separation from the presence of the Lord and his glory (2 Thess 1:9).[11] He also sees the punishment of evildoers as the product of divine wrath (Rom 2:5). The book of Revelation speaks of a lake of fire—which also is called the second death—wherein the host of evildoers are thrown. Such images are disconcerting indeed. Sometimes the final state of the wicked is referred to as hell, which translates the Greek word *Gehenna*. Gehenna was literally the name of a garbage dump south of Jerusalem where perpetual burning occurred. In the days

9. Clearly, various texts speak of heaven as a place where God, angels, and treasures of the faithful are. It is less clear, however, that all New Testament writers thought heaven is where God's faithful ultimately will *abide*. A close examination of the texts above shows that another interpretation is available—namely, that the faithful will be on a restored earth. The above text from Revelation seems to assert that, in fact, the redeemed of God will dwell on the new earth where God also will be. In turn, even 1 Thess 4:17 does not say that believers will join Christ in heaven but only that they will meet him in the air and will forever be with the Lord. This could mean that they will join him only to return to a restored earth.

10. See note 8 above for a different rendering of *aionios*.

11. Matthew also suggests the notion of separation from God when he depicts Jesus as saying to the wicked, "I never knew you; go away from me you evildoers" (7:23) and when Matthew has the Son of Man saying to the wicked, "Depart from me" (25:12).

of the prophet Jeremiah, in this valley (translated Hinnom), the people of Judah engaged in vile practices, including child sacrifices, that disregarded divine law. Jeremiah condemned the valley, naming it the "valley of slaughter" (7:32; 19:6) As time passed, this valley (and its garbage dump) was associated with the perpetual burning of divine judgment. One final note about the final state of the wicked: Paul at times uses the terms "death" or "perishing" to describe the final condition of unbelievers. While acknowledging the reality of some existence for the wicked beyond death, Paul occasionally equates death with their ultimate status. Sin brings death (Rom 6:13, 33) so that sinners in some sense are already dead, already perishing. And ultimately, for some, such a state persists beyond the grave (Rom 6:16–23; 7:10–11; 8:6; see also 1 Cor 1:18; 2 Cor 2:15; 2 Thess 2:10; Eph 1:1–2).

An *eighth* critical theme of New Testament eschatology is that of the *renewal of the cosmos*. This idea is expressed in Revelation's description of the coming of a "new heaven and new earth" (Rev 21:1–2), where God will dwell with his people, and there will be no more death, mourning, crying, or pain (vv. 3–4). It also is assumed in Paul's words, when he writes:

> For the creation waits with eager longing for the revealing of the children of God; for the creation was subjected to futility, not of its own will but by the will of the one who subjected it, in hope that the creation itself will be set free from its bondage to decay and will obtain the freedom of the glory of the children of God (Rom 8:18–22).

Paul sees the created order yearning for release from its current subjugation to death and decay; in a similar way, believers in Christ yearn for resurrection—"the redemption of our bodies" (8:22–23). And here, Paul evokes the great eschatological theme of hope: hope for salvation founded in the love of God in Christ (8:24–25, 37–39). Such hope for cosmic renewal echoes expectations expressed in some Old Testament passages. For instance, Isa 11:6 speaks of a messianic time when the wolf will live peaceably with the lamb, the leopard with the kid, and the calf with the lion, and when all will be led by a small child. Isa 65:25 envisions an era when the wolf and lamb will eat together, and when lions will eat straw like oxen. Hosea imagines God making a covenant with the wild animals, in a time when bow, sword, and war are abandoned (2:18; see also Ezek 34:25). All these scriptural passages (including similar New Testament passages) are vague at best, but they suggest some sort of future alteration of the physical world, including changes to animal life and the ecosystem (see e.g., Rom 8:18–25; 1 Cor 15:24–28; Rev 21:1–4).

Ten Minor Biblical Eschatological Themes

In addition to the eight major eschatological themes above, the New Testament names some less prevalent ideas about end-times. These concepts are minor in the sense that they are less frequently mentioned in the Scriptures and often are not well defined or developed. Among these happenings are

1. Israel's initial rejection of Jesus as the Christ

2. The destruction of Jerusalem's temple

3. The scattering of the Jewish people

4. Various woes and persecutions, especially upon the followers of Christ

5. Worldwide evangelism of Gentiles

6. The occurrence of "the desolating sacrilege"

7. The rise of a "man of lawlessness" against Christ and Christians

8. The ultimate conversion of Israel to Jesus as Christ

9. The intermediate state between death and resurrection

10. The millennial reign of Christ

The first nine of these notions concern events that *precede* the return of Christ, the establishment of his kingdom, and the culmination of all things. The tenth item seems to happen after Christ's return but before the culmination.

The first of these minor themes is expressed in various parts of the Gospels, often in the context of eschatological ideas, so that, in some sense, Israel's turning from Jesus during his ministry is interpreted to be a precursor to or element of the end-times. As Jesus inaugurates the kingdom of God, Israel's rejection of him is an element of the last days.[12] Items 2–6 above are addressed in the Synoptic Gospels in what often is called Jesus' Olivet Discourse. This is a discussion between Jesus and his disciples on the Mount of Olives during the week ending in his crucifixion, on a day when they had earlier visited the Jerusalem temple. This discourse (with variations of content) is found respectively in Matt 24, Mark 13, and Luke 21. In all three Synoptic Gospels, the dialogue unfolds after Jesus comments that not one stone of the temple complex would be left standing (Matt 24:2; Mark 13:2; Luke 21:6). Naturally, some of his disciples implore: "Tell us, when will this be, and what will be the sign that all these things are about to be accomplished?" (Mark 13:4). Matthew adds to this question, "and what will be the sign of *your coming and of the end of the age*?" (24:3; italics added). That is, Matthew makes clear the concern is "the sign" (the indicators) of when Christ's return and the end of the age will happen. A twofold question is being asked: When will the temple fall, and what will be the sign of the return of Christ and the end of the age?

In Mark 13, Jesus warns his followers not to be misled (apparently in times to come), for many will come, says Jesus, claiming to be Jesus himself (or the Messiah or the Son of Man), but their claims will be false (vv 5–6). Jesus then informs his disciples that when they hear of wars and rumors of wars, this is to be expected,

---

12. Matt 11:20–24; 23:31–36; Luke 10:13–15; 13:34–35; 19:41–42.

but it will not automatically mean the end has come (v 7). For it will be common for nations and kingdoms to rise and fall and fight, and there will also be various natural calamities; but all of this is simply "birth pangs" before the end (v. 8). In turn, Jesus' disciples can expect to be persecuted—handed over to councils, beaten in synagogues, tried by government officials, because of their witness about Christ (v. 9). Jesus also claims that apparently before the end, "the good news must first be proclaimed to all nations" (v. 10). Jesus adds that "the one who endures will be saved" (v. 13). Jesus further predicts that a "desolating sacrilege" will unfold, at which time persons in Judea will need to flee into the mountains, because "in those days there will be suffering such as has not been from the beginning of the creation," nor ever will be again (vv 14, 19). At that time, warns Jesus, persons should not listen to others claiming to be or alleging someone is the Messiah, for various false messiahs and false prophets will arise (v 22). Then, after the time of suffering, great cosmic events will unfold, and "the Son of Man" will be seen descending in the clouds with great power and glory (vv 25–26); and he will gather the elect (v 27). Ironically, Jesus concludes by warning that no one knows the day or the hour of these events, not even the Son of Man himself. Rather, Jesus encourages his followers to "keep awake," to be prepared, for the Son of Man will come suddenly (vv. 32–37).

Matthew and Luke offer similar accounts of the Olivet Discourse, often duplicating Mark's report word for word. At times, however, they offer differing phraseology, and sometimes they make significant alterations. Matthew adds that when persecution comes, many Christians will fall away, lawlessness will run rampant, and love will grow cold (24:11–12). Matthew also supplements Mark's report by noting that the Son's appearing will be obvious to all: it will be as plain as lightening flashing across the sky from east to west (vv 27–28). Matthew also greatly extends Mark's warning to be prepared because no one knows for sure when Christ will return: Matthew offers several parables reinforcing the call to be prepared (24:36—25:46). Luke also offers changes to Mark's Gospel. Perhaps most significantly, he does not use the phrase "desolating sacrilege" but writes instead about the fall of Jerusalem—of armies surrounding the city and of wrath falling upon its people, who will either fall by the sword or be enslaved (21:20, 24). Luke also adds an interesting phrase when discussing the fall of Jerusalem, saying Jerusalem will be under the control of Gentiles "until the times of the Gentiles are fulfilled" (v 24).

With all this in mind, we note the following. In the Olivet Discourse, all three Synoptic writers affirm items 2–4 listed above: the destruction of the temple,[13] the scattering of the Jewish people, and woes and persecutions. Mark and Matthew speak of points 5 and 6: evangelizing of Gentiles and "the desolating sacrilege" (Matt 24:15; Mark 13:14). Mention of "the desolating sacrilege" clearly echoes the book of Daniel, which describes a time when Gentile overlords disallowed sacrifices in the Jerusalem temple (8:13; 9:27; 11:31; 12:11). Apparently, Mark and Matthew saw or

13. Also see Mark 13:2; 14:58; 15:29; Luke 23:27–31.

foresaw something similar happening in the end-times. Luke does not directly use the phrase "the desolating sacrilege." However, many commentators believe Luke was not denouncing this notion; rather, he was explaining it in terms that Hellenistic audiences unfamiliar with the Hebrew tradition would understand. Thus, arguably for Luke, the phrase "the desolating sacrilege" essentially refers to Jerusalem's fall to Gentiles. That is, many commentators see Luke's phrase "until the times of the Gentiles are fulfilled" as referring to a period when the gospel of Jesus is proclaimed to Gentiles—essentially restating something like Mark's and Matthew's notion that the gospel must be preached to all nations. Certainly, Luke endorsed the view that the church was to be Christ's witnesses "to the ends of the earth" (Acts 1:8; compare Luke 24:47). Indeed each of these Synoptic authors saw these various events as preceding (and possibly as signs) of Christ's return.

But what of items 7–10 above: the man of lawlessness, the conversion of Israel, the intermediate state between death and resurrection, and Christ's millennial reign? The man of lawlessness is referenced in 2 Thessalonians. There, the author attempts to alleviate the fears of ancient readers who had heard that the day of the Lord had already come (2:1–2). To counter this anxiety, the writer insists that that day "will not come unless the rebellion comes . . . and the lawless one is revealed" (2:3). The lawless one will exalt himself as an object of worship, attempting to usurp God's rightful place. In turn, this one will only emerge after that which now "restrains" lawlessness is removed. Since these events have not happened, Christ has not yet returned. In further comments, the writer notes that the coming lawless one will be empowered by Satan; also, this individual will be quickly destroyed by the Lord Jesus at his return (2:4–9). Second Thessalonians does little to clarify these ideas, leaving all but perhaps the first readers uncertain of their meaning. A similar shadowy figure, called "the antichrist," is mentioned in 1 and 2 John. The writer warns that this one is coming, and because of this his readers "know that it is the last hour" (1 John 2:18). In short, the antichrist is tied to end-time events. However, the author of 1 John also speaks of many antichrists (2:18) and of the "spirit of the antichrist" already present in the world (4:2–3), suggesting that "antichrist" is as much a principle as a concrete individual. Again, insufficient data are given to describe clearly this concept or the details surrounding it.[14] Finally, the book of Revelation speaks of two beasts—one a false prophet (13:11–12; 19:20), the other (Rev 13:1–2) matching some of the characteristics ascribed to the man of lawlessness (from 2 Thessalonians) and of the antichrist (from 1 and 2 John)—namely, political power and blasphemy (Rev 3:4–5, 13–15).

Item 8 above, the end-time conversion of Israel, is avowed by the apostle Paul in Romans. There Paul writes especially to Gentile believers:

14. The notion of antichrist is similar to and may be borrowed from the Synoptic Olivet Discourses that speak of false messiahs (Matt 24:24; Mark 13:32). The concept of antichrist might also derive from Old Testament passages that speak of a blasphemous human ruler (Ezek 38:1; 39:6; Dan 8:25; 2 Macc 9:12; 2 Esd 5:6–13).

> I want you to understand this mystery: a hardening has come upon part of
> Israel, until the full number of the Gentiles has come in . . . [A]s regards elec-
> tion they are beloved, for the sake of their ancestors; for the gift and the calling
> of God are irrevocable. Just as you were once disobedient to God but have
> now received mercy because of their disobedience, so they have now been dis-
> obedient in order that, by the mercy shown to you, they too may now receive
> mercy. (11:25–31)

While the logic of Paul's argument might be questioned,[15] his core point is clear: he
believes Israel eventually will turn to Jesus as their Christ. In Rom 11:12, Paul uses an
interesting phrase, which echoes Luke's mention, in the mouth of Jesus, of "the full
number of Gentiles." Paul speaks of the "full number of Israel." In each case, the same
Greek word is employed. In Romans 11:12, Paul says especially to Gentile readers:
"Now if their [Israel's] stumbling means riches for the world, and if their defeat means
riches for Gentiles, how much more will their full [*pleroma*] inclusion mean!" Paul
then seems to think that even though now God is working to bring in the full number
of Gentiles, God also is concerned with the salvation of the full number of Israel.
Hints of these ideas are expressed in the Synoptic Gospels as well. As noted above,
Luke comments that Jerusalem will be under Gentile control "until the times of the
Gentiles are fulfilled" (21:24). Some see here something like Paul's view that after the
era of the Gentile conversion, Israel too will turn to Jesus.[16]

A *ninth* minor New Testament eschatological topic is the intermediate state between death and resurrection. What happens to those who die before the end-time
resurrection of the dead? The Old Testament offers only glimpses of life immediately after death. Strands in that literature suggest that individual life simply ends at
death, and the only hope for life after death comes through one's progeny. But other
materials point toward a kind of wispy, gloomy postmortem existence in a place
called Sheol. Sheol is a dark and foreboding habitat beneath the earth (Ps 63:9; Ezek
32:18) where the dead—the *rephaim* (shadow-like figures)—dwell in a powerless,
ephemeral state. Synonyms for the locale of the dead are "the Pit" (Isa 4:15; Ps 88:6;
Ezek 28:8) and "the heart of the sea" (Ezek 28:8). Isa 14::9–11 offers a typical picture
of this existence. It reads:

> Sheol beneath is stirred up
>> to meet you when you come,
> it rouses the shades [*rephaim*] to greet you,
>> all who were leaders of the earth;

15. It is unclear why the disobedience of Israel is needed for Gentiles to turn to Christ, and vice
versa.

16. See Ladd, *A Theology of the New Testament*, 200–201. There is considerable ambiguity in Paul's
statements here. Does he mean all ethnic Israelites will turn to Christ, even those not practicing the
faith? Does he include persons who have become Jewish but not by race? For that matter, does he
mean every single Gentile also will believe?

it raises from their thrones

   all who were kings of the nations.

All of them will speak

   and say to you:

'You too have become as weak as we!

   You have become like us!'

Your pomp is brought down to Sheol,

   the sound of your harps;

maggots are the bed beneath you,

   and worms are your covering.

The Hebrew concept of Sheol is much like the notion of Hades in classical Hellenistic thought—which often is depicted as a place of powerlessness and shadow-like existence. Indeed, the Greek term *hades* often is used to translate the Hebrew word *sheol* in the Septuagint.

Normally, in the Old Testament, no distinction is made between the righteous and unrighteous dead; both go to Sheol. Further, there is no clear indication that in Sheol the righteous are better off than the wicked. Occasionally, some hope is expressed that the Lord will not abandon the righteous to Sheol; but these passages are few and may only reference temporary escape from death (See Ps 9:17–18; 16:8–11; 73:24; Hos 13:14). In the era of Second Temple Judaism, however, some views about life after death changed. Affirmation of resurrection became more prominent. And periodically the wicked dead were said to go to a place of torment called Hades, while the righteous go to a place of blessing called *paradise* (meaning "the park" or "the garden"). (See also 1 En 22–23; 4 Ezra 7:75–78).

Similar ideas are expressed in a parable of Jesus found in Luke 16:19–31, where Jesus speaks of the after-death plights of an unnamed rich man and a poor beggar named Lazarus. The rich man ignored Lazarus in life, failing to care for Lazarus's dire physical conditions. At death, each man found himself in a different state. The poor man was with Abraham in a place of blessing. The rich man was in "hades," a habitat of fiery agony and thirst. For many ancient and modern Christian writers, Luke's account authorizes the notion that immediately after death, the disembodied spirits of the redeemed go to a place of blessing while the bodiless souls of the unredeemed go to a state of torment, each group awaiting the resurrection of their bodies at Christ's return. Some interpreters, however, reject this exposition of Luke's parable, insisting that caution is needed in interpreting this story. This is the case because the predominant New Testament understanding of the afterlife affirms the resurrection of embodied humans rather than of life as disembodied souls. These commentators note that Jesus' (and Luke's) main point was to teach that even if someone rose from the dead, people currently living would not necessarily believe that person's testimony

(vv. 27–31). In light of this, some writers propose that Jesus only adopted this parable from popular lore to make his basic point without, in turn, endorsing every element of the story, including the idea that prior to resurrection the dead exist as disembodied spirits. Other interpreters believe that implicit in this parable is affirmation of the consciousness of humans after death prior to resurrection. Similar arguments are made regarding Luke 23:43–44 where Jesus informs the thief dying on the cross next to him "Truly I tell you, today you will be with me in Paradise." Note that the term "paradise" is used, which in late Second Temple Judaism is sometimes employed to speak of the place where the righteous dead go prior to resurrection (See En 60:7, 23; 61:12). Again, such nomenclature suggests belief in disembodied existence immediately following death but prior to resurrection.

Another text often cited for addressing the intermediate state between death and resurrection is 2 Corinthians 5:1–10. There, the apostle Paul notes that while "we are at home in the body we are away from the Lord" (v 6); but we "would rather be away from the body and at home with the Lord" (v. 7). All of this suggests that persons (or at least believers) can exist without a body while in the presence of the Lord. The precise nature of this existence is not described by Paul. Indeed, commentators are unsure whether Paul here is speaking of some kind of disembodied life after death prior to resurrection or simply describing the resurrected life proper. Some affirm the latter interpretation in light of Paul's remark that in this world "we groan, and long to put on our heavenly dwelling, so that by putting it on we may not be found naked. For while we are still in this tent, we sigh with anxiety; not that we would be unclothed, but that we would be further clothed, so that what is mortal may be swallowed up by life" (vv. 2–4). Paul here may simply refer to the loss of our mortal body and the reception of an immortal, resurrected, body. Similar ambiguity exists in Philippians 1:22–23, where Paul comments that he longs to "depart and be with Christ" rather than remain "in the flesh," again suggesting some sort of life with Christ independent of the body. But again, the precise nature of such an existence is not described.

The *tenth* and final "minor" theme listed above—the millennial reign of Christ—is attested in the book of Revelation, specifically Rev 20:4–7. It says (italics added):

> Then I saw thrones, and those seated on them were given authority to judge. I also saw the souls of those who had been beheaded for their testimony to Jesus and for the word of God. They had not worshipped the beast or its image and had not received its mark . . . They came to life and reigned with Christ a *thousand years*. (The rest of the dead did not come to life until the thousand years were ended). This is the first resurrection. Blessed and holy are those who share in the first resurrection. Over these the second death has no power, but they will be priests of God and of Christ, and they will reign with him a *thousand years*. When the *thousand years* are ended, Satan will be released from his prison.

This quote essentially makes the only mention of Christ's *millennial* reign in the New Testament. It likely attempts to capture Hebrew scriptural promises regarding the reign of the Messiah (Ps 2; Isa 2:2–7; 11:1–9; Zech 9:9–10) and of the faithfulness of God (see Dan 9:7, 22). It also may reflect ideas prevalent among some Jewish writers of Second Temple Judaism. For example, the book of 4 Ezra (also called 2 Esdras) speaks of an end-time *four-hundred-year* reign of the Messiah immediately preceding the age to come.[17] As we will see below, the notion of Christ's millennial reign and its relation to other eschatological themes has been the matter of considerable theological speculation throughout the ages.

The Imminent Return of Christ

There is evidence in the New Testament that Jesus' earliest believers expected his return and the culmination of history in their lifetime. In 1 Thessalonians, Paul seems to assume the real possibility of Christ's return before Paul's death (4:13–18). And a line from the Synoptic Gospels' Olivet Discourse leaves the impression that its authors believed Christ's return was imminent; they report Jesus saying—after he has described the coming of the Son of Man in power—that "truly I tell you, this generation will not pass away until all these things have taken place" (Mark 13:30; Matt 24:34; Luke 21:32).[18] The nearness of Christ's return also seems to be presumed in 2 Thessalonians where it is reported that some church members feared that Christ already had come, and they had missed it (2 Thess 2:1–3).

Along with this suspicion that Christ's return was imminent, several New Testament passages admit (with some concern) that Christ's second advent was delayed. In the Olivet Discourse, Jesus tells his disciples that even after several future dire circumstances have unfolded, the end would not immediately follow (Matt 24:6; Mark

17. "For behold, the time will come, when the signs which I have foretold to you will come to pass, that the city which now is not seen shall appear, and the land which now is hidden shall be disclosed. And every one who has been delivered from the evils that I have foretold shall see my wonders. For my son the Messiah shall be revealed with those who are with him, and those who remain shall rejoice four hundred years. And after these years my son the Messiah shall die, and all who draw human breath. And the world shall be turned back to primeval silence for seven days, as it was at the first beginnings; so that no one shall be left. And after seven days the world, which is not yet awake, shall be roused, and that which is corruptible shall perish. And the earth shall give up those who are asleep in it, and the dust those who dwell silently in it; and the chambers shall give up the souls which have been committed to them. And the Most High shall be revealed upon the seat of judgment, and compassion shall pass away, and patience shall be withdrawn; but only judgment shall remain, truth shall stand, and faithfulness shall grow strong. And recompense shall follow, and the reward shall be manifested; righteous deeds shall awake, and unrighteous deeds shall not sleep. Then the pit of torment shall appear, and opposite it shall be the place of rest; and the furnace of hell shall be disclosed, and opposite it the paradise of delight" (4 Ezra 7:26–36).

18. One solution to the dilemma of Christ not returning before his first-century generation passed away is to understand the events referenced by Jesus (in the passages just cited) to be the destruction of Jerusalem, which did occur in 70 CE. See further comments on these matters below.

13:7). In turn, Jesus cautions that no one knows the day or the hour of the coming of the Son of Man, "neither the angels in heaven, nor the Son, but only the Father" (Matt 24:36; Mark 13:32). Other passages from the Synoptic Gospels likewise hint at a delay in Christ's return (see Matt 25: 5, 19; Luke 17:22; 18:1–8). And John's Gospel, while affirming the future resurrection, emphasizes the resurrection's power already present in believers (11:25–26). In turn, the notions that the gospel must be preached to Gentiles and that a "lawless one" must appear also point to attempts to explain the delay of Christ's return. The book of 2 Peter addresses the issue head-on when it notes that scoffers ask, "Where is the promise of his coming?" To this, the author replies:

> But do not ignore this one fact, beloved, that with the Lord one day is like
> a thousand years, and a thousand years is like one day. The Lord is not slow
> about his promise, as some think slowness, but is patient with you, not want-
> ing any to perish, but all to come to repentance. (2 Pet 3:3, 8–9)

While the postponement of Christ's return did not destroy the early Christian faith, it did affect it. The clarion call to evangelize the world along with the harsh reality of persecutions that confronted the first-century church were interpreted as precursors of Christ's return. Each of these ideas finds precedence in the Hebrew tradition. Various scriptures and religious texts of Second Temple Judaism point to promises of both end-time Gentile conversion and horrible persecution of the faithful. When Gentiles began coming to the Christian faith and when persecutions befell the church, these seemed to be echoes of promises and warnings long a part of Jewish tradition and (partial) explanations for the delay of Christ's return. The full number of Gentiles and of Israel had not yet come, nor had persecution run its course. Persecution in particular seems to fuel the concerns of Mark and Matthew, each likely writing after the fall of Jerusalem and after various persecutions befell the church—including Nero's suppression of Christians in 64 CE. The book of Revelation also seems especially concerned with the ill-treatment of Christians and with the promise of divine retribution upon the enemies of God and reward for the faithful. Many scholars suspect that Revelation was written around the era of emperor Domitian (ruled 81–96 CE) in a time when local governors in Asia Minor[19] felt it politically expedient to urge citizens to offer homage to the imperial- and emperor-cult, at times enforcing stiff penalties—even death—upon those who refused to comply.

Issues of Interpretation

Having surveyed the broad New Testament teaching about eschatology, several questions arise regarding how best to interpret these varied ideas. One question concerns

---

19. The book of Revelation is addressed to seven churches in Asia Minor (Rev 1–3) and is said to be written by a Christian prophet named John, who had been expelled to the island of Patmos in the Aegean Sea (Rev 1:9).

the supernatural assumptions of the literature. The writers of the New Testament were children of their era; they believed they were living in an evil age, influenced not only by malicious human political and economic forces but also by hostile spiritual beings—Satan, the devil, demons, and other powers. They believed, at some level, that such supernatural beings cause diseases, mental illness, and other human suffering, and that these entities play a role in the catastrophes of human history—including the suppression of Israel by foreign rulers. These early Christians also believed in God's overarching sovereignty in human and spiritual affairs, that one day God would break into history, defeat the forces of evil (both physical and spiritual), and establish the divine kingdom on earth as it is in heaven. These Christians also believed in a future resurrection of the dead. But can modern readers, trained in the empirical sciences and historical method, take such notions seriously? To be a follower of the Christian way, must one believe in such supernatural entities and events? Some religious writers of the modern era have said no, arguing that the Christian eschatological message must be reshaped for modern sensitivities.

A second question of interpretation concerns the intended meaning of the biblical texts themselves. Even if one grants the existence of both natural and supernatural realities, how does one distinguish between ancient authors' attempts to describe literal (real) supernatural and natural realities and their deliberately employing metaphorical language to describe such events or entities? The book of Revelation—like other apocalyptic literature of the ancient world—uses symbols to speak of various concrete realities. But how does one know where the symbolism begins and ends, and where literal interpretations are called for? For example, in the end-times, is there a literal beast that rises from the sea to persecute followers of Christ (Rev 13:1–4), or is this a metaphor for something else, such as a human ruler who arises against the church? Or again, is the one worshiped in heaven literally a lamb that was slain (Rev 5:6–14)? Or was this—almost certainly—a metaphor for Christ? But if these are metaphors, what about the thousand-year reign of Christ (Rev 20:4–7), or the new Jerusalem coming down from the sky (Rev 21:2, 9–27), or the lake of fire (Rev 20:14–15)? Where does symbolism end and concrete reality begin?

A third question of interpretation concerns the chronological order of the events envisioned in various New Testament eschatological narratives. Even when one presumes some physical and supernatural events literally occur, the precise sequence of these events is often unclear. Which events occur first? Which next? Which are last? And, how much time elapses between them?

Related to all these questions are several ambiguities that arise over the precise nature of some eschatological events or entities. What is the nature of resurrected life? Are there truly resurrected bodies, or is the notion of resurrection primarily a metaphor for some other sort of existence—for example, bodiless spirits? On the other hand, if there will be resurrected bodies, what is their nature? Of what are they made? Can they be harmed? Do they ingest food? Do they need food to exist?

Or again, what is the nature of heaven? Is it a physical (that is, a temporal, spatial) place? Is it really made of pure gold with walls of jasper surrounding it (Rev 21:18, 21)?[20] What is the nature of hell? Is it a place? If it is a place, is it a place of torment, fire, physical and spiritual harm?

Much ink and has been spilled and much imagination has been spent by Christians attempting to answer these sorts of questions. We cannot offer a thorough discussion of such topics but can only touch on some of the most relevant issues. In the discussion that follows, we offer a brief systematic analysis of key components of the contemporary Christian doctrine of last things. In this examination, we often presume a more or less literal understanding of the existence of supernatural beings as well as natural entities. This perspective was prevalent among Christians at least until the Enlightenment era, and still is dominant among Christians today. Periodically, however, we will note the views of those who attempt to interpret Christianity without appeal to (various features of) supernaturalism.

Contemporary Eschatological Themes

Not surprisingly, contemporary Christian eschatology is deeply influenced by the multiple themes of the biblical end-times tradition. It also is influenced by theological ideas developed after the New Testament era, throughout church history. In broad strokes, traditional Christian eschatology involves the following core ideas. First, this theology assumes that God is Creator of all, and ultimately is in charge of all that happens. Nothing occurs that is not at least permitted by God—such as sin.[21] Nevertheless, in spite of ultimate divine sovereignty, the world is not as God would have it. Evil, sin, suffering, and death have penetrated and permeated the created order, so that humans now live in an evil, sinful, and death-ridden world. But God is not finished with the cosmos. The Lord intends to redeem this fallen world, rectifying the wrongs done, rewarding the faithful, punishing the wicked, and restoring human nature—along with the rest of the created world—to God's original benevolent purposes. Sadly, according to the broad stream of Christian thought, this restoration will require the destruction, punishment, or both, of some of the wicked—those unwilling to conform to the good that God has ordained. Their fate is largely due to their own recalcitrance, to their own evil. (As we will see below, however, there long has been a minority opinion among Christians that possibly all humanity will eventually be saved).

Sometimes two broad types of eschatology are distinguished; these are *historical or cosmological eschatology* and *personal eschatology*. Historical or cosmological eschatology wrestles with the culminating events of human and cosmic history. It addresses the completion of God's designs for the created order as a whole. Personal

20. Strictly, these verses speak of the New Jerusalem that may be understood as on a restored earth. Still the nature of heaven remains a puzzle.

21. Some Christians say that nothing happens that God does not cause, including sin.

eschatology addresses the fate of individual human beings. On a cosmic and world-historical scale, the divine end-time restoration involves the following core events: (1) the atonement of sin through the death of Christ, (2) the reception of Christ's benefits by those willing (by divine grace) to respond positively to his saving lordship, and (3) the outpouring of God's Spirit to aid believers in their loving faithfulness to God through Christ. According to the New Testament, in these (and other) events God's promised end-times have begun. But these are only the beginning. Now is the time for persons (including Gentiles, not just Jews) to turn to God through Christ and receive his freely given salvation.

But this era of redemption is not of endless duration. A time is coming when God's plan for the cosmos, for human history, and for human salvation will be culminated. Key elements of this consummation are (1) the return of Christ in glory and power, (2) the resurrection of both the redeemed and the unredeemed to face divine judgment, resulting respectively in eternal reward or eternal punishment, (3) the reign of Christ, and (4) the establishment of a renewed heavenly and earthly order, ruled by God, wherein evil and its consequences are overcome and God's good will for creation is accomplished. From the perspective of individual or personal eschatology, the culminating events include (1) personal physical death, (2) an intermediate period between physical death and resurrection, (3) individual resurrection, (4) divine or messianic judgment, and (5) the establishment of and perpetuation of a person's final state.

Precursors of Christ's Return

Numerous puzzles arise for the broad picture of cosmic or historical eschatology and personal eschatology. One question concerns the nature and timing of events leading up to Christ's return. As noted above, the Olivet Discourse describes many of these occurrences, including

1. The destruction of Jerusalem's temple

2. The scattering of the Jewish people

3. Various woes and persecutions, especially upon the followers of Christ

4. Worldwide evangelism of Gentiles

5. A "desolating sacrilege"

Other New Testament passages point to

6. The rise of a "man of lawlessness" against Christ and Christians

7. The ultimate conversion of Israel to Jesus as Christ

Many writers have attempted to decipher the precise content and arrangement of these events. Even if organizing such an account were possible, it is beyond the scope of our project to tease out its details.

Suffice it to say that many theologians believe that items 1–3, and 5 refer to events that unfolded in the first century when Roman armies decimated Jerusalem and scattered its inhabitants. Such an interpretation helps explain Jesus' comment that "this generation will not pass away until all these things have taken place" (Matt 24:34; Mark 13:30; Luke 21:32). Thus, according to this perspective, the persecutions and woes described in the Synoptic Gospels likely capture various struggles that befell Jerusalem's and Judea's inhabitants of that time, including many followers of Christ. And the "desolating sacrilege" (which clearly echoes events from the book of Daniel) likely referenced some single religious horror or multiple horrors that befell Jerusalem—including perhaps Rome's destruction of the temple per se. While many Christian writers see the events named above as having occurred in the first century, some theologians attempt to connect these predictions to events far in the future (from the time they were announced), so that ultimately the end-times (more or less) repeat and transcend the turmoil the befell the generation of Jesus' day.

Regarding other precursors of Christ's return, the apostle Paul's reference to the rise of the lawless one, as well as John's use of the term "antichrist" and Revelation's depiction of the "beast," are more enigmatic. They may serve primarily as symbols of lawless and irreverent political power, often manifested in particular political rulers, rather than as allusions to a single concrete human being. Indeed, there is reason to suspect that Revelation's beast was a not-so-veiled reference to Emperor Nero, whose name or title—when converted to numbers—is 666 (see Rev 13:18). But even if Nero was being referenced, he may only have served as an archetype of anti-Christian political leadership in general. Of course, not all Christians have accepted such metaphorical interpretations of "the man of lawlessness" or "the beast." Throughout history, Christians have assigned the title "antichrist" to numerous political and religious leaders, or they have looked for the concrete manifestation of such a person, in anticipation of Christ's imminent return. In turn, often based on questionable guesswork and strained calculations, numerous dates for Christ's parousia have been forecast throughout history, none of which (thus far) have proved to be accurate. Perhaps for good reason, Jesus warns in the Synoptic Gospels that no one but the Father knows the precise time and date of his return.

The eras of worldwide evangelism (item 4 above) and of Israel's ultimate conversion (item 6)—endorsed respectively by the Synoptic writers and by Paul—seem to have been thought of as events still in the biblical writers' (not too-distant) future. Sometimes pious Christians express concern over what appears to be an errant belief of the Gospel writers or even of Jesus himself, namely, the expectation that the glorious appearing of the Son of Man would occur within their lifetimes. And often (sometimes arduous) exegesis is employed to deny this. One possible solution to this dilemma is to

note that often the Old Testament prophetic literature conflated predictions of immediate occurrences with more distant ones, with little concern that this somehow made
such predictions false. Rather, such intermingling of imminent and distant futures
may indicate only that the precise timing of divine fulfillment was not clear to either
Israelite prophets or the writers of the New Testament. Further, authors of prophetic
literature—whether in the Hebrew Bible or Christian Scriptures—may have seen many
of their prophecies as paradigms of end-time events that sometimes repeat through
history as God exercises his plans for the world.[22]

Christ's Reign and the Millennium

In addition to questions about the precursors of Christ's return, puzzles over the
nature and timing of Christ's reign also arise, including issues having to do with
the nature of the millennium. In the second and third centuries, the concrete realities of periodic regional and sometimes empire-wide persecution helped keep alive
hopes of an imminent appearance of Christ to right the wrongs of world history.
Evangelism too was stressed as missionaries spread throughout the empire with the
story and faith of Christianity; many saw such missions as antecedents to Christ's
return. In this context, most early post-first-century Christians held onto central
elements of New Testament eschatology: the resurrection of Jesus, his ascension to
the Father in heaven, and his ultimate return to earth to resurrect the dead and to
judge the world.[23] In turn, some early postbiblical writers also endorsed the *millennial reign of Christ*. Because affirmation of Christ's one-thousand-year reign
emerged relatively late in the first-century Christian literature—appearing (so far as
we know) only in John's Revelation—support for this doctrine was not unanimous
among Christian writers of the second and third centuries. Among those endorsing
a literal one-thousand-year reign of Christ were Justin Martyr (d. 165), Irenaeus (c
130–202), the writer of the Epistle of Barnabas (early second century), and Tertullian (c 155—c 240). These writers are sometimes called *premillennialists* (or *historic
premillennialists*),[24] for they claimed that Christ's return will inaugurate (and thus
predate) his thousand-year reign. According to these writers, after the millennium
Christ will judge the world, determining the final fate of each human. Premillennialists tend to be pessimistic about the world and about the church's ability to
change it; thus, like Jewish apocalypticists, Christians living after the first century
but still in the period that historians call late antiquity looked for a dramatic divine

---

22. See Travis, *I Believe in the Second Coming of Jesus*, 35–37.

23. Each of these is a teaching of the Apostles' Creed, dated perhaps as early as 150 CE.

24. Historic premillennialists, who both grace Christian history and are counted among present-
day believers, are to be distinguished from dispensational premillennialists, who follow a more modern form of premillennialism. For more on this distinction, see Stiver, *Life Together in the Way of Jesus
Christ*, 461–72; and Grenz, *The Millennial Maze*, 91–147.

inbreaking to right the wrongs of the world. These Christian premillennialists were deeply influenced by the book of Revelation; consequently, they often endorsed two resurrections: the first of the righteous prior to the millennium, and the second of the unrighteous after the millennium and prior to judgment.

With the rise of the first Christian emperor, Constantine I (272–337), and the subsequent demise of anti-Christian persecution, eschatological theology shifted its focus. Eusebius of Caesarea (c. 260–334) rejected premillennialism and floated the idea that Christ's reign was manifested through the Christian Roman Empire. While he did not quite equate church and state, his notion of the empire ruling in God's stead anticipated later views that Christ's reign might be expressed through some human institution, either empire or church. Augustine of Hippo (354–430) interpreted the millennial reign of Christ in terms of the historical rule of the church. For Augustine, the church and its ministries are the concrete materialization of Christ's victory over Satan. Augustine, however, rejected the idea of a Christianized empire ruling in Christ's stead. Augustine's views came to dominate medieval Christian thought about Christ's reign. His perspective is sometimes called *amillennialism*, which more of less means belief in no millennium. For Augustine, the image of Christ's one-thousand-year reign in the book of Revelation (20:4–7) is merely symbolic of the Messiah's rule through the church. Even the number 1,000 is for Augustine emblematic of an indefinite temporal era. The transition from earlier premillennialism to amillennialism may be explained (in part) by two factors. First, as the centuries passed with no appearance of Christ, it became difficult to maintain the premillennialist belief that Christ's return was imminent. Second, the pessimism of premillennialism about the world and the church's ability to change it, which was in no small measure reinforced by the dire straits faced by many Christians prior to Constantine, did not match the new optimism that arose with and after his accession.

Augustine's views prevailed throughout the Middles Ages. But some dissent arose, especially in the twelfth and thirteenth centuries. Some writers began predicting the emergence of a political leader who would unite Christian Europe, whose empire would reign for many glorious centuries before the Antichrist would arrive (only to be defeated with the return of Christ). A less political, more spiritual vision of a millennial age arose in the writings of Joachim of Fiore (c. 1132–1202). Joachim envisioned three ages—the age of the Father, the age of the Son, and the age of the Spirit—each lasting over a thousand years. According to Joachim, the last stage was about to dawn, in 1260 CE. It would be an era of great spiritual awakening, when peace would reign and the world would convert to Christ. This period would be inaugurated by the coming and the defeat of the Antichrist and would end with the glorious return of Christ.

Views somewhat like these twelfth-century theories emerged in the nineteenth and early twentieth centuries. Many Christians of the late nineteenth century affirmed that through Western civilization and its Christian heritage, a grand era of peace, prosperity, health, and education was dawning. This entailed a period of worldwide evangelism, thus fulfilling the biblical commission to convert the world to Christ. It also included extending Christ's love to an economically, politically, and socially deprived world, through the benevolence of Western Christian achievements, including medical and scientific technology. Many Christians believed this era would end with the glorious return of Christ. These models of the millennium (including those from the twelfth century mentioned in the previous paragraph) are sometimes called *postmillennialism*, for they propose that Christ's return will occur after a time of Christian advancement.[25] All of these postmillennial paradigms are more optimistic than their premillennial relatives about the influence of the church upon the world.

In the nineteenth century and through the twentieth century, a resurgence of premillennialism arose; it has become known as *dispensational premillennialism*. In their own ways following after Joachim of Fiore, dispensationalists divide world history into diverse eras of divine activity. The current phase is one of grace, when God offers salvation to all nations. But the time soon is coming when God will refocus primarily on the nation of Israel. Dispensationalists see Christ's return occurring in several phases. First, God will *rapture* the (largely) Gentile church from the great end-time tribulation, leaving behind all those who do not believe in Christ to endure tremendous hardship at the hands of the Antichrist, the Beast, or both. Many dispensationalists believe this rapture will occur before the great end-time tribulation (these Christians are called *pretribulationists*), but a few, labeled *midtribulationists*, contend that the church will be raptured halfway through that time of tribulation. During these end-times, many of Israel will turn to Christ and face hardships. But after this period of trouble, Christ will return in power and will rule over all nations for a thousand years; he will reign from Jerusalem and from the restored kingdom of Israel. During Jesus' millennial reign, Satan will be bound and forbidden to interfere in human affairs; but after the millennium, Satan will be released and will rally forces against Christ, only to be swiftly and finally defeated. Then will occur the final judgement and the internment of persons to their final states of hell or the "new heaven and new earth" (see Rev 21:1)

Historical premillennialists and dispensational premillennialists share common beliefs, but these also differ in key ways. Unique to dispensationalists is belief that the church will be "raptured" *from* tribulation. Most historical premillennialists believed that the church would endure such tribulation—and they held this view in no small measure because they already were experiencing grievous persecutions. Dispensationalists draw much of their doctrine of rapture *from* tribulation from Matt 24:36–44, which compares the coming of the Son of Man to the days of Noah when the flood swept away the inhabitants of the earth. At the coming of the Son of Man, says Jesus, "two men will be in the field; one is taken and one is left. Two women will be grinding

---

25. It is not abundantly clear that these postmillennial theories differ that much from Augustine's views, since he too looked forward to the return of Christ *after* the era of the church. For this reason, some label Augustine's perspective postmillennial as well.

at the mill; one is taken and one is left" (vv. 40–41). Dispensationalists take this passage to mean that unbelievers will be left behind to face tribulation while sincere believers will be taken away to be with the Lord, thus avoiding tribulation (or much of it). Some Bible scholars and theologians throughout history (prior to dispensationalism) understood Matthew's verses (and others like them) to be warning Christians of the persecutions *they would face* (and encouraging Christians *already being maltreated*). Another interpretation of these verses is that those taken are persons who have been unfaithful to Christ, who must then face divine judgment, as happened to those who were unfaithful to God during the days of Noah's flood.

Both dispensational and historical premillennialists—following Rev 20—often affirm two resurrections from the dead: one before the millennium (so that those who have died in Christ might be raised and rule with him) and one after the millennium (so that those who died without Christ might face the final judgment). But unlike historical premillennialists, who affirm only one return of Christ, dispensational premillennialists essentially affirm two returns of Christ. The first reappearance is dubbed *the rapture*, and its occurrence will be hidden from most of the world. The second is Christ's arrival in power, visible for all to see, to begin his millennial reign. Most contemporary versions of Christ's millennial reign take some form of premillennialism, amillennialism, or postmillennialism.

The Afterlife

Another set of eschatological questions arise concerning the status of persons after death—both before and after resurrection. What are the conditions of persons immediately following death? And what is the nature of resurrected life? As already indicated, the Hebrew understanding of the state of the dead seems to have gone through several phases. The earliest biblical literature says little to nothing about life after death, and finds hope in descendants, not after-death personal existence. Later Old Testament materials speak of a shadowy, unsavory postmortem subsistence in Sheol, noting no real distinction between the righteous or unrighteous there. Later Jewish literature moved toward belief in a pleasant existence for the righteous in the afterlife and an unpleasant one for the unrighteous; this literature also endorsed the resurrection of the dead. The New Testament clearly advocates resurrection from the dead and hints at existence immediately after death.

As history unfolded, postbiblical Christians began to speculate further about the state of the dead—both immediately after death and after resurrection. Discussions of these matters throughout church history often have been influenced by Greek—especially Platonic—philosophy. Plato affirmed the intrinsic immortality of the soul. For him, and many who followed him, humans are immortal souls who have no beginning or end; they exist everlastingly. Humans *are* souls *in* bodies, who, when their bodies die, continue to exist as conscious but bodiless beings. For Plato, death is in some ways welcomed, for it entails the soul's release from the limitations of the body. Plato's view can be described as *spiritual monism*, for at the end of the day, Plato saw the soul as the identifying marker of human beings, whereas the body is only a temporary and (in many ways) unwelcome imposition upon the human soul.

Elements of Plato's thought are found throughout Christian doctrine. Most Christians have rejected Plato's notion that souls have always existed, affirming instead that souls are created by God. Nevertheless, for many Christian writers, once created, souls exist everlastingly. Therefore, death is death only of the body, not of souls. For many Christians then—contrary to Plato—the soul's everlasting existence is not natural but the result of God's gracious granting and perpetuating of life. Further, Christians typically (although not always) have rejected Plato's disparagement of the human body. While acknowledging fleshly temptations and weaknesses, the Christian tradition typically has affirmed the value of the human body, seeing salvation as a matter of God redeeming both soul and body. Predominantly, then, Christianity has affirmed a kind of mind and body *dualism*, one which recognizes two aspects of human nature—both body and soul.

Not all Christians have endorsed human dualism. Some theologians teach that humans are a psychosomatic (soul-body) unity wherein soul and body cannot be separated. According to this view, a human is a living (animated) body. In recent years especially, many scholars have become convinced that such a unified understanding of human nature was assumed in the ancient Hebrew and early Christian biblical traditions.[26] This is why resurrection of the body was stressed by many in Second Temple Judaism as well as by most New Testament Christians. In the New Testament, unlike in Plato, the salvation of the body is critical, and the death of the body is a tragedy, not a welcome comfort for the bodiless soul.[27] Proponents of this holistic position often note that contemporary neuroscience seems to support the notion that humans are psychosomatic entities—that personality, thought, emotions, and so forth are causally tied to the human body. It is a matter of dispute whether this understanding of human nature is pure materialism or is something more (since it attempts to envision body and mind as a singular whole). For convenience, we will refer to this view of human nature as *holism or monistic holism*, and we will leave it to others to determine whether this is sheer materialism or not.

As we are about to see, these two perspectives on human nature—dualism and holism—greatly influence how one conceptualizes postdeath existence. In the discussion that follows, we first will look at different Christian views of existence between death and resurrection, and then we turn to the nature of resurrected life.

26. See Cullmann *Immortality of the Soul or Resurrection of the Dead?* Also see Brunner, *The Christian Doctrine of the Church, Faith, and Consummation*, 383–85, 408–414.

27. In most biblical literature, there is no hint of an immortal soul, and especially no notion of a naturally immortal soul. Rather, all life is created by and dependent upon God. Aristotle held a similar view of human nature, contending that the soul is simply the form (the defining characteristics) that make humans the kind of physical beings they are. They are a hylomorphic (form-matter) whole.

Between Death and Resurrection

Plato's broadly dualistic understanding of human nature (as souls with bodies) has greatly impacted Christian thought about the state of the dead, both before and after resurrection. At least two dualistic models of human existence between death and resurrection have been envisioned. One proposal is that after death, bodiless, conscious souls continue to exist, awaiting resurrection from the dead. This (Platonically informed) perspective has been endorsed by many mainstream Christian writers, including Augustine, Thomas Aquinas,[28] Martin Luther, and John Calvin. Many contemporary theologians still favor this perspective.[29]

Often associated with this understanding of postdeath, preresurrection existence is a (sometimes elaborate) vision of the living conditions (so to speak) of such bodiless, conscious, souls. Often such conditions are described as a state of blessedness for the redeemed and woe for the unredeemed (similar to the image in Luke 16:19–31). Irenaeus (c. 140—c. 202) taught that the souls of martyrs go immediately to be with Christ, but less faithful believers must await resurrection to be with Christ. Clement of Alexandria (150–215) asserted that the souls of the faithful must face some remedial suffering before entering heavenly bliss. By the fourth century, Ambrose (337–397) and Augustine (354–430) were endorsing the notion of purgatory—a place of remedial suffering for those souls destined for heaven. Meanwhile, writers such as Cyril of Jerusalem (313–386) and John Chrysostom (d. 407) affirmed the value of praying for the dead with a view toward aiding them in their ascent to heaven. By the late Middle Ages, a grand system of postdeath existence was envisioned. In this vision, at death all souls immediately receive *particular judgment*, wherein is decided their inalterable eternal fate—some are destined to heaven and some to hell. Before resurrection, however, those destined to hell exist in a state of horrendous agony awaiting even greater and eternal suffering in hell after the final judgement. Those souls already perfect, the saints, will go immediately to heaven to be with Christ. Most of the redeemed, however, must face remedial suffering in purgatory so that the lingering effects of their venial sins might be cleansed. At the resurrection, these varied souls will face *the final judgment* and be consigned to their respective ultimate conditions of heaven or hell. Not all persons, however, go either to heaven or hell. Some—specifically Old Testament saints, who could not directly express faith in Christ, and unbaptized infants, who never personally sinned but were guilty of original sin—go to limbo. According to Thomas Aquinas, limbo is a place of happiness, not suffering; but it still pales before the glory experienced by those in heaven.[30]

28. Even though Aquinas endorsed Aristotle's understanding of the soul as the form of a physical body, he also taught that at death, the human soul exists without the body until resurrection. For Aquinas, although the human soul can and does exist without the human body, this is not its natural state of body-soul, which occurs again at resurrection.

29. See for example Erickson *Christian Theology*; and Davis, *Risen Indeed*.

30. In 2007, Pope Benedict XVI eliminated the concept of limbo from Catholic teaching.

Not all advocates of postdeath conscious souls endorse the full range of Catholic doctrine about the afterlife prior to resurrection. Protestants typically have rejected the doctrines of purgatory and limbo. Often they discard the doctrine of purgatory because of what they perceive to be in it a works-righteousness approach to salvation: Protestants hold that salvation comes solely by divine grace through faith in Jesus Christ and not through various remedial forms of suffering or contrition. Sixteenth-century Reformers especially opposed the practice of selling indulgences so that one might be saved from eons in purgatory. Still, many Protestants have endorsed belief in conscious, bodiless souls after death, including John Calvin[31] and the authors of the Westminster Confession.[32] Contemporary author Millard Erickson represents this group when he affirms that the souls of the righteous go to paradise prior to resurrection, while the souls of the unrighteous go to hades. At the resurrection and final judgment, the righteous go to heaven and the unrighteous go to hell.[33]

Various criticisms are leveled against this traditional dualist vision of the afterlife. Not surprisingly, Christian holistic monists reject this dichotomist perspective on the grounds that it does not fit the biblical understanding of human nature. Further, according to holistic monist Stanley Grenz, this view elevates the soul over the body, essentially making it the true center of human nature; the dualistic view thus minimizes the New Testament emphasis on resurrection. Why is resurrection needed if existence as a soul alone is possible?[34] Finally, some question whether the traditional view makes the final judgment redundant. If particular judgment unchangingly seals the fate of persons, why bother with a final judgement?

A second dualistic model of the state of persons after death and before resurrection claims that the soul simply sleeps during this interim. That is, the soul continues to exist but in an unconscious state. Martin Luther seems to propose this view when he states, "Just as a man who falls asleep and sleeps soundly until morning does not know what has happened to him when he wakes up, so we shall suddenly rise on the Last Day; and we shall know neither what death has been like or how we have come through it."[35] Similar views are expressed by Athenagoras of Athens (133–190),[36] William Tyndale (c. 1494–1536),[37] and various Anabaptist writers. Soul sleep is formally endorsed

31. Calvin, *Institutes of the Christian Religion*, 3.25.6; see also Calvin, *Institutes of the Christian Religion*, 1.5.5 and 1.15.2.

32. Westminster Confession, chapter 32, in Leith, ed., *Creeds of the Churches*.

33. Erickson, *Christian Theology*, 1084–85.

34. Grenz, *Theology for the Community of God*, 592.

35. Cited in Althaus, *The Theology of Martin Luther*, 414. There is debate about whether Luther endorsed soul sleep per se or whether he wished to describe the experience of individuals inducted into divine eternity only at the point of death.

36. "Those who are dead and those who sleep are subject to similar states, as regards at least the stillness and the absence of all sense of the present or the past, or rather of existence itself and their own life" Athenagoras, *On the Resurrection of the Dead*, 16.

37. Tyndale, *An Answer to Sir Thomas More's Dialogue*.

by Seventh-day Adventists and Jehovah's Witnesses. Often soul sleep is defended based on biblical passages that refer to death as sleep (1 Kgs 2:10; John 11:11; Acts 7:60; 1 Cor 15:6, 18, 20, 51; 1 Thess 4:13–15). It seems likely, however, that such verses use "sleep" as a euphemism for death, and not in reference to a sleeping, unconscious soul. Numerous problems are alleged against the doctrine of soul sleep. One difficulty is that some New Testament passages hint at some form of consciousness between death and resurrection (Luke 16:1–10). Second, it is difficult to differentiate "soul sleep" from nonexistence. Philosopher René Descartes famously distinguished two components of human beings, namely spatial bodies and nonspatial, experiencing, thinking souls or minds. (This is a perspective many dualists seem to endorse.) But if a human has no body (which disintegrates at death) and thus is only a thinking soul, in what sense can we speak of a nonthinking, nonconscious thinking soul? How would a nonthinking, nonexperiencing soul differ from a nonexistent soul?

Dualists do not hold a monopoly on theories of conditions between death and resurrection. Monistic holists offer scenarios as well. One holist paradigm proposes that at death human persons simply cease to exist. Thus, end-time resurrection involves God creating persons anew. This is the perspective of John Hick (1922–2012). Hick argued that at resurrection, God creates a replica of the previous person, creating (from preexisting materials or from nothing) a living body (a psychosomatic whole) with essentially the same attributes as the person who died (and no longer exists). For Hick, such an exchange would be similar to moving software from one computer to another.[38] Hick's model is similar to the dichotomist "soul sleep" scenario, except instead of saying the soul is unconscious between death and resurrection, this theory asserts the human person (the soul-body unit) simply does not exist.

A common criticism of Hick's viewpoint is that such a perspective makes it difficult, if not impossible, to claim that the resurrected person is the *same* individual as the one who died. Identity often is established based on some shared history. In the case of a body, even if changes occur in the material making-up that body, as long as those changes are gradual and involve overlapping of shared stuff over time, we typically think the body at an earlier time is the same as the one at a later time. For example, most adults consider themselves to be the same being as they were when they were children even though considerable physical changes have occurred over time. This is partly because the changes were gradual and involved overlapping materials (the gradual discarding of old cells and their replacement with new ones). In like manner, in the case of a fellow human person's soul or mind, even when thoughts, emotions, attitudes, experiences, knowledge, and dispositions change for that person, we typically think of him or her as the same person undergoing changes so long as the fluctuations are gradual and involve overlapping mental states. (Often these states are said to be connected by memories and conscious experience as a whole.) But, according to critics of this monist model, shared history would not exist between a

38. See Hick, *Death and Eternal Life*, 278–288.

person who has died (and no longer exists) and one who later comes into existence with similar characteristics. Intuitively, this seems especially true if great expanses of time pass between the death of the first and the emergence of the second. According to these detractors, this monist model describes the production of a replica of the previous person, not the person herself.[39]

A second holist theory of the state of the dead before resurrection proposes that resurrection occurs immediately after death. Erickson calls these theories "instantaneous resurrection" models.[40] These paradigms attempt to explain postmortem consciousness without appeal to disembodied souls. Instead of saying that after death a bodiless, cognizant soul persists, these models propose that a sentient, psychosomatic person comes into being. In turn, this emergence results from "resurrection." An obvious question arises: In what sense does resurrection occur at death if the corpse is still in the tomb? Proponents of instantaneous resurrection reply that resurrection does not involve the use of elements from the deceased's body. Rather, it entails the divine production (creation?) of a psychosomatic person who is fitted for eternal life.[41] Advocates of instantaneous resurrection draw inspiration from 1 Cor 15:44, where Paul distinguishes between a physical body and a spiritual body, noting that the spiritual body is "raised in power." For this reason, these models are sometimes called *spiritual resurrection theories*, for they endorse the resurrection of a psychosomatic person fitted for the spiritual world. Such theories also find support from 1 Cor 15:50, where Paul declares, "What I am saying, brothers and sisters, is this: flesh and blood cannot inherit the kingdom of God, nor does the perishable inherit the imperishable," and in 2 Cor 5:8 where Paul claims that "we would rather be away from the body and at home with the Lord." The first verse suggests that the physical body, per se, cannot enter God's kingdom. The second intimates that believers will be with Christ immediately after death and will not have to wait until Christ's return.[42] Extrapolating from these verses, some monistic holists propose that resurrection does not involve the physical body, but it does occur immediately after death.[43]

---

39. Dan Stiver notes this problem in Hick's position. See Striver, "Hick against Himself," 162–72. Erickson voices a similar concern. See, *Christian Theology*, 1080.

40. Erickson, *Christian Theology*, 1083–84.

41. Notice this is the generation of a body-soul unit, not just a raised body. This is a critical point for the monist.

42. According to W. D. Davies, when Paul wrote 1 Corinthians, he assumed that resurrection would happen at the return of Christ, but later (when writing 2 Corinthians and puzzling over the state of believers who die prior to Christ's return) Paul came to believe that the dead in Christ instantly receive resurrected bodies—ones fitted for eternity. See Davies, *Paul and Rabbinic Judaism*.

43. Catholic holists also draw insight from Pope Benedict XII, who in 1336 declared in a papal bull that the souls of the righteous experience heavenly vision instantly following death, and that the unrighteous immediately face the fires of hell at death.

Several theologians endorse instantaneous spiritual resurrection. Among them are Karl Rahner (1904–1984),[44] Gisbert Greshake,[45] W. D. Davies (1911–2001),[46] Hans Küng (1928–2021),[47] Dan Stiver,[48] Stephen Travis,[49] and Donald G. Bloesch (1928–2010).[50] Rahner taught that body and soul are inseparable so that resurrection entails the emergence of an embodied person. Rahner also insisted, however, that resurrection does not involve the resuscitation of the dead physical body, for such bodies are not fit for transcendent existence. Instead, at death a glorified whole person is brought to life "in the presence of God," not in the temporal-spatial world. Indeed, Rahner insisted that Jesus' resurrection likely did not involve his corpse; rather, it was a real, but transcendent spiritual event. Protestant theologian Donald Bloesch affirmed that at death resurrected bodies arise fitted for paradise where they, in turn, await complete resurrection at Christ's return. Some of these writers depict instantaneous resurrection as occurring in God's eternal frame of reference so that from the perspective of the resurrected individual, resurrection occurs immediately at death *as well as* at the end-time return of Christ. Thus, while for persons still alive in earth's temporal frame of reference there is a temporal gap between a loved one's death and resurrection, there is no gap for the resurrected person.[51] Other holists, including Stiver and Bloesch, prefer to think of instantaneous resurrection bringing persons into temporal frames of reference distinct from earthly time, but still temporal rather than atemporal. In this way, resurrected participants still await final resurrection in the last days.

Various criticisms have been leveled against these holist views of instantaneous resurrection. Joseph Ratzinger (who reigned as Pope Benedict XVI from 2005 to 2013) and Stephen Davis see an incoherence to the theory of so-called spiritual resurrection. On the one hand, its proponents seek to ensure the singular psychosomatic nature of humans by repudiating separation of soul and body at death. On the other hand, they deny that the earthly body of the person is raised to life. But Ratzinger and Davis ask: If the earthly body is not raised from the dead, how is this so-called spiritual resurrection a redemption of *the person* who has died, who allegedly was synonymous with his or her physical body?[52] Millard Erickson offers another criticism of instantaneous resurrection, complaining that the theory does not fit the biblical testimony, which teaches that a person's actual physical body is transformed, not

44. Rahner, *Foundations of Christian Faith*.

45. Greshake, *Aufersthung der Toten*; Greshake and Kremer, *Resurrectio Mortuorum*.

46. Davies, *Paul and Rabbinic Judaism*.

47. Küng, *On Being a Christian*, 351.

48. Stiver, *Life Together in the Way of Jesus Christ*.

49. Travis, *I Believe in the Second Coming of Jesus*.

50. Bloesch, *The Last Things*.

51. Travis, *I Believe in the Second Coming of Jesus*, 175.

52. Pope Benedict XVI, *Eschatology*, 108–9. Stephen T. Davis notes that instantaneous resurrection implies that a replica of the person has been created, but the person himself or herself (who for the monist is identical to his or her body) is not "raised" at all. See Davis, "Eschatology and Resurrection."

some spiritual duplicate of it (see John 5:25–29; Phil 3:20–21; 1 Thess 4:16–17).[53] In a similar critique, Ratzinger notes that the Scriptures teach that Jesus rose *on the third day*, not immediately after his death—contrary to the spiritual-resurrection theory. Finally, Ratzinger questions the coherence of claiming that human beings—who are intrinsically temporal—can be swept up into the divine, atemporal eternity.[54]

The Resurrected Life

In addition to these models of existence between death and resurrection, Christian theologians offer varied visions of resurrected life. Four of these we have already discussed. One is the holist theory just mentioned—namely, that embodied persons are resurrected immediately at death. A second is the holist notion that the deceased cease to be at death but are resurrected at the consummation (or at least duplicates of them are made). A third theory is the dualist affirmation that the conscious souls of the departed reunite with their resurrected bodies at Christ's return. And the fourth model declares that unconscious souls of the dead are awakened and reunited with their resurrected bodies at Christ's return. Given the different conceptions just presented of the intermediate period between death and resurrection, each of these theories nevertheless endorses a similar picture of what ultimate resurrected life is like. For most it is an eternal existence in a body fitted for such an existence. The chief difference is dualists think souls can exist without bodies (albeit, temporarily), while holists insist that human existence is always embodied—so that body and mind cannot be disconnected.

But what is the nature of this resurrected embodied being? Here the biblical clues are sparse. Some theologians see in the accounts of Jesus' appearances something of what resurrected life will be like. Thus, like his resurrected body, bodies in the general resurrection will be related to the earthly bodies that have died. This is, in part, the point of the empty-tomb narratives of the Gospel writers.[55] These authors wished to show that Jesus' body was no longer decaying but somehow brought into glory. In turn, several New Testament writers stress the quasi-physical nature of Christ's resurrected body as well as its similarity to his pre-death body. John's Gospel especially seeks to show the physical nature of Christ body by depicting the resurrected Jesus as eating with his disciples (21:9–13) and displaying his wounds from crucifixion (20:26–28). In a similar manner, in the Gospel of Luke, the resurrected Jesus encourages his disciples to look at and touch his hands and feet, and know it is he and not an apparition (24:36–40). In turn, Jesus eats with them (24:41–43). Given all this, the Gospel writers also let it be known that Jesus' resurrected body also was different from the pre-death one. While Jesus appeared to his disciples in physical form, he was not always

---

53. Erickson, *Christian Theology*, 1084.

54. Pope Benedict XVI, *Eschatology*, 109. Similar concerns cause Stiver, who endorses instantaneous resurrection, to reject the notion that the person raised enters into a timeless existence.

55. All the Gospels declare that Jesus' tomb was empty.

immediately recognized. In Luke's Gospel, Jesus walks with two disciples to Emmaus, but not until he breaks bread with them do they recognize him (24:13–32). And John informs his readers that Jesus appeared to his disciples by somehow entering a room whose doors were locked (20:19–23). His body was before them, but it was different from the preresurrection body. While these narratives offer hints of resurrected life, they leave much undisclosed. Paul, likewise, offers only hints of what the resurrected life might be. In 1 Cor 15, Paul compares the relationship between earthly or physical bodies and resurrected bodies to the relationship between a seed and a full-grown plant. The latter two are quite distinct, yet also related. So, the resurrected body will be different than the mortal body, but also like it and perhaps also somehow related to it or from it (vv. 35–38). Paul also notes that unlike our mortal bodies, resurrected ones will be "imperishable" (v. 42). Obviously, the precise nature of the resurrected body remains a bit mysterious for Christian theology.

While the notion that resurrection involves the generation of an embodied entity is the dominant view in Christian theology, it is not the only game in town. Some writers propose that resurrection is a metaphor for purely spiritual or bodiless existence, and that the body does not literally rise from the dead. Notice that this theory is essentially an extension of the theory that between death and resurrection conscious souls exist. Sometimes Origen of Alexandria defended resurrection will entail the raising up of physically embodied persons. But in much of his writing he affirmed that the spatial body will be replaced by a "spiritual body" fitted for existence in a spaceless, contemplative realm with God. In a similar manner, several nineteenth-century Protestant liberals favored the notion of the continued existence of the human soul beyond death while rejecting the resurrection of spatial-temporal bodies.[56] Twentieth-century philosophers H. H. Price (1899–1984) and H. D. Lewis (1910–1992) each famously made cases for the possibility of nonphysical human life. Price in particular attempted to make room for interactions between purely nonphysical entities through mental images and ideas based on prior experiences of the physical world. This would allow sensory-like (but not physical) interactions between nonphysical souls.[57] Lewis offered several extended arguments for the reality of souls.[58] These theories face a number of problems, not the least of which is the rather strong biblical support for the end-time resurrection of physical bodies (John 5:25–29; Phil 3:20–21; 1 Thess 4:16–17) as well as the claims that Jesus' tomb was empty and his resurrected body was tangible. Some critics even go so far as to assert that bodiless existence is impossible, but Christian writers must be cautions about such claims for they could lead to the conclusion that God must be spatial-temporal. Nevertheless, in light of the biblical testimony, many

---

56. For example, see Fosdick, *The Modern Use of the Bible*, 98–104. Fosdick writes, "I believe in the persistence of personality through death, but I do not believe in the resurrection of the flesh" (Fosdick, *The Modern Use of the Bible*, 98).

57. Price, "Survival and the Idea of 'Another World'"; and Price, "What Kind of Next World?".

58. Lewis, *The Self and Immortality*.

Christians throughout history—and even more in recent times—have assumed some sort of *physical*, embodied resurrected existence.

The Final State: The New Creation and Heaven

A last set of puzzles for contemporary eschatology concerns the final state of the cosmos and of human beings. The Christian Scriptures paint a dire picture of the impact of sin and evil upon God's creation. Sin has alienated humans from God; distorted human relations; brought guilt, condemnation, and death to individuals; and (somehow) decay, fracture, and disquiet to the cosmos as a whole (see Chapter 4, above). Further, as we have seen in this chapter, eschatology deals with the realization of God's saving purposes for individual humans, human history and community, and the cosmos as whole. Various images are used to speak of the divinely renewed world, including a new age (1 Cor 2:6–8; 3:18–21; Gal 1:4; Eph 1:21; 2:2), the kingdom of God (Matt 6:10;), the messianic kingdom, the new Jerusalem (Rev 21:2), God's city (Heb 11:10, 16; 12:22), a heavenly country (Heb 11:16), a new heaven and new earth (Rev 21:1), and heaven (1 Thess 4:16–17; Col 1:5). In 2 Cor 5:17, Paul speaks of Christians as being "a new creation" in Christ. The old has passed away; something new has come. Elsewhere, Paul writes of putting on the new self or new nature, created to be like God (Eph 4:24). In a similar manner, the book of Revelation pictures God saying at the end-times, "See, I am making all things new" (21:5). So, another image of the final state is that of "new creation," both of humans and of the cosmos as a whole. The meanings of these images often are mixed and metaphorical. But they point to the Christian hope of a new environment where the wrongs and sorrows of this present era will be undone, and where God's good will for the created order (including humans and their social systems) will be manifested.

The precise nature of this new order is vague, and often only pictorial language can describe it. Among the varied characteristics of this new world are the following. First it will be a place where God is present and experienced. After describing the eschaton as a new heaven, a new earth, and a new Jerusalem (Rev 21:1–2), the book of Revelation declares:

> See, the home of God is among mortals.
> He will dwell with them;
> they will be his peoples,
> and God himself will be with them (21:3);

Further, in Rev 21:7 God says, "Those who conquer will inherit these things, and I will be their God and they will be my children." These are familial images of communion with God. The old dilemma of anthropomorphic language haunts these descriptions. Will God, who is spirit, somehow be visibly manifested? For that matter, what will the nature of human bodies be? And how will humans interact with God? Whatever the literal meaning of these images, they convey the sense of familial intimacy, community, communion, interaction with God.

Perhaps in such a context uncertainties regarding God's existence or kindness toward humanity melt away; the sense of isolation from, failure before, and enmity with the divine dissolve in the presence of this one whose reality, favor, and love cannot be doubted. The intimacy of the garden of Eden—long lost—is restored, so that humans again walk with God (compare Gen 3:8). For New Testament writers, something of this intimacy is already experienced in the indwelling of God's Spirit in believers and in the incarnation of God in Jesus Christ. But they looked forward to an even fuller and persistent experience of this in the eschaton.

A second characteristic of the new environment will be the removal of all that undermines God's original good purpose for humans and the created order. The story of the fall of humanity in Gen 3, echoed throughout Scripture, pictures humans now estranged from each other and from their better selves. Individuals are burdened with feelings of guilt and objective culpability before God. And they are ensnared by their own sins—pettiness, selfishness, defensiveness, lust, and pride. Such guilt and enslavement will be removed in the age to come. In turn, the enmity between humans will cease. As there will peace with God, so there will be peace among humans. And more than peace, there will be fellowship, kindred-spirit, community. God values each person and thus is concerned with individual salvation. But God also values the human community and interpersonal love. A number of theologians emphasize the communion of love among the members of the Trinity. And many New Testament passages note, in turn, that the human community is to echo this divine loving interrelationship (see John 13:35; 1 John 4:20).

With the elimination of sin and sinfulness will also come an eradication of the debilitating consequences of sin. Rev 21:4 says that in the new era God

> will wipe every tear from their eyes.
> Death will be no more;
> mourning and crying and pain will be no more,
> for the first things have passed away.

Here we see the removal of humankind's greatest enemies: sorrow, remorse, suffering, and the last and greatest—death (compare 1 Cor 15:26). With these in mind, heaven also is a place of rest. It is the welcome repose from hard labors performed and sorrows endured (Rev 14:13).

A third characteristic of heaven is celebration and service. While at times heaven is depicted as a place of rest, it is also seen as a place of activity. One of Jesus' favorite images of God's kingdom was that of a grand banquet (Matt 22:1–14; Luke 14:15–24). Heaven is a place of celebration, and this rejoicing is over the salvation God has rendered. In Luke's Gospel, Jesus describes the father of the prodigal son (who also is the picture of the heavenly Father) declaring upon his son's return:

> Bring quickly the best robe, and put it on him; and put a ring on his hand, and
> shoes on his feet; and bring the fatted calf and kill it, and let us eat and make
> merry; for this my son was dead, and is alive again; he was lost, and is found.
> (Luke 15:22–24)

Heaven is a place of celebration. It also is a place of service. The images of heaven as a community, a city, a nation, a fellowship—all point to an era of action and interaction. Love is not inactive. It does; it works; it serves. As Stephen Travis notes, the language of love is meaningless without active "self-giving to God and to others in relationship."[59]

A final characteristic of heaven is the worship of God. The book of Revelation captures several scenes of worship in heaven. In them one gets some idea of the celebration of God's glory and grace in the new heaven and earth to come. In Rev 4, John of Patmos describes his heavenly vision:

> Around the throne, and on each side of the throne, are four living creatures . . .
> Day and night without ceasing they sing,
>> "Holy, holy, holy,
>> the Lord God the Almighty,
>> who was and is and is to come."
> And whenever the living creatures give glory and honor and thanks to the one who
> is seated on the throne, who lives forever and ever, the twenty-four elders fall before
> the one who is seated on the throne and worship the one who lives forever and ever;
> they cast their crowns before the throne, singing,
>> "You are worthy, our Lord and God,
>> to receive glory and honor and power,
>> for you created all things,
>> and by your will they existed and were created." (4:6b–11)

Then later, John describes a vision of the Lamb of God:

> Then I looked, and I heard the voice of many angels surrounding the throne and the
> living creatures and the elders; they numbered myriads of myriads and thousands of
> thousands, singing with full voice,
>> "Worthy is the Lamb that was slaughtered
>> to receive power and wealth and wisdom and might
>> and honor and glory and blessing!"
> Then I heard every creature in heaven and on earth and under the earth and in the
> sea, and all that is in them, singing,
>> "To the one seated on the throne and to the Lamb
>> be blessing and honor and glory and might
>> forever and ever!" (5:11–13)

Among other characteristics, the final state will involve worship of God.

59. Travis, *I Believe in the Second Coming of Jesus*, 180.

The Final State: Hell

While there are questions about the final state of those redeemed by God, there are even more troubling queries regarding the fate of the unredeemed. As we have seen, the Bible (at least as traditionally interpreted) offers various alarming pictures of the final state of those who do not conform to God's will and do not receive the salvation offered in Christ. Among these images are utter darkness, weeping and gnashing of teeth, exclusion from God's kingdom, removal from God's presence, eternal fire, and a lake of fire. Inspired by such images, Christians through the ages have concocted even more horrendous visions of the plight of "the damned." A Christian work of the second century, the *Apocalypse of Peter*, offers disturbing images of the plight of the wicked after Christ's return. Varying degrees and kinds of punishment are envisioned, each fitted to redress evils done. Women who lured men with their wiles hang by their hair in a fiery cavern; mothers who aborted their babies are dowsed in flaming feces while the spirits of their murdered children torture them; unfaithful husbands are strung up by their genitalia as their bodies are roasted over an eternal flame.[60] Peter's Apocalypse was counted as scripture according to some canonical lists of the patristic era. Similar pictures of the plight of the wicked are imaged by the renowned Latin theologian Tertullian, of the late second century. And many of these visions became common features of medieval Christian theology and religious art. Dante's *Inferno* is a classic expression and interpretation of such themes.

As Jonathan Kvanvig notes, the traditional Christian view of hell typically endorses four theses. (1) The purpose of hell is to render divine punishment; (2) hell cannot be escaped; (3) there will be some persons in hell; and (4) existence in hell will be never-ending.[61] To this list we might add (5) hell will involve horrendous anguish and suffering. Several criticisms of this understanding of hell have been leveled. First, many argue that eternal punishment runs counter to the loving nature of God. If God is love, if God yearns for all to be saved, God would not allow persons to suffer endlessly. Further, if God is inexhaustibly wise and powerful, God could find some way to draw all recalcitrant sinners to himself. A second criticism of eternal punishment is that it is not just. Justice often is construed either as retributive or remedial. In the first case, justice is rendering what is due—"just deserts." In the second instance, justice tries to reform a perpetrator, to bring him or her into conformity with the good. But according to critics, hell fails to be just in either of these senses. First, it miscarries at retributive justice, for finite crimes cannot justly be met with infinite (eternal) punishment. Second, it flounders at remedial justice, for it offers no hope of reform for the sinner or of reprieve from punishment once in hell. At best, say critics, eternal punishment is crude vindictiveness if not gleeful sadism.

60. See the Apocalypse of Peter; see also Harris, *The New Testament*, 438–39.
61. Kvanvig, "Hell."

In place of the traditional view of hell, several theories of the final state have been offered. One proposal is that all persons (ultimately) will be saved. This perspective is often called *universalism*. Obviously, universalism challenges (3) above. It says, eventually, there will not be any persons in hell. Universalism can be construed to mean that at death a person immediately is transported into the presence of God and is transformed into the kind of moral being intended by God. More often, universalists assume that some remedial process will transpire so that a person moves toward being the kind of individual desired by God. Origen of Alexandria (c. 184—c. 253) taught a version of universalism, contending that ultimately even Satan would return to God.[62] John Hick proffered a version of universalism, proposing that individuals transmigrate through numerous life cycles, ultimately choosing to be reconciled to God.[63]

More recently, Orthodox theologian David Bentley Hart has defended universalism, finding it implicit in many New Testament passages and anchored in several key early theologians of the church (including Origen, Gregory of Nyssa, Isaac of Nineveh, and Maximus the Confessor).[64] Hart contends that the broad sweep of New Testament teaching points to universal salvation rather than eternal punishment. Among such New Testament passages, Hart cites (with his own translations) Rom 5:18–19; 11:32; 1 Cor 15:22; 2 Cor 5:14, 19; Eph 1:9–10; Col 1:27–28; 1 Tim 2:3–6; Titus 2:11; and many others.[65] Following especially Gregory of Nyssa, Hart proposes that "the cosmos will have been truly created only when it reaches its consummation in the 'union of all things with the first Good,' and humanity will have truly been created only when all human beings, united in the living body of Christ, become at last the 'Godlike thing' that is 'humankind according to the image.'"[66] According to Hart, when confronted by scriptures that warn of divine punishment in the afterlife and others that point toward universal salvation, the Christian interpreter should see these as

> two different moments within a seamless narrative, two distinct eschatological horizons, one enclosed within the other. In this way of seeing the matter, one set of images marks the furthest limit of the immanent course of history, and the division therein . . . between those who have surrendered to God's love and those who have not; and the other set refers to that final horizon of all horizons, 'beyond all ages,' where even those who have traveled as far from God as it is possible to go, through every possible self-imposed hell, will at last find themselves in the home to which they are called from everlasting, their hearts purged of every last residue of hatred and pride.[67]

---

62. Origen, *De Principiis* 3.6.5. Origen also was open to the idea that another fall might transpire, resulting in a replay of salvation history.

63. Hick, *Philosophy of Religion*, 120–41.

64. Hart, *That All Shall Be Saved*, 68.

65. Hart, *That All Shall Be Saved*, 92–102.

66. Hart, *That All Shall Be Saved*, 68.

67. Hart, *That All Shall Be Saved*, 103–4.

Seemingly, for Hart, divinely sanctioned post-death suffering (depicted in the biblical literature) serves ultimately as a means toward assured reconciliation with God and not as gleefully imposed divine retribution. Many writers endorse universalism on the grounds that ultimately God's love wins and will not allow consigning persons to hell. Further, for reasons given above, these writers insist that eternal punishment would not be just.

Criticisms of universalism include, first, that it does not sufficiently account for those scriptural passages that warn of divine punishment. While the Scriptures teach that God does not want persons to perish, they also warn that some will be destroyed.[68] Second, arguably, universalism fails to take seriously the importance of human freedom. According to many traditionalists, out of love, God has granted human freedom to love or not love. But assuming such freedom, it seems possible that persons might eternally reject God. Of course, the universalist might retort that God could force the most recalcitrant persons to love him. But traditionalists counter that it is unclear that forced love is truly love. God might be able to force someone to do something; but it is not clear God can force someone to *freely* do something, including love. In turn, to force such actions would undermine God's good purpose in granting freedom to humans in the first place.[69]

At this point, however, the traditional view seems to be hampered by its claim that once in hell persons cannot escape; such persons are permanently consigned to hell (point 2 above). Traditional theology teaches that at death an individual's final state is unchangingly determined by *particular judgement*. And the same is true of *final judgment*. This seems to mean there is no way in hell (literally) to repent and turn back to God. But some critics insist that limiting the period for receiving grace to this present, earthly life alone is at best arbitrary and at worse unjust—especially if one understands justice as remedial. In light of such reasoning, some nontraditional writers propose there may be singular or multiple post-death opportunities to turn to God and be saved. We might refer to this view as the *post-death-opportunities model*. This model need not lead to universalism, for free beings might eternally choose not to turn to God. This seems to be C. S. Lewis's assumption in *The Great Divorce*.[70] On the other hand, while Origen and Hick agree that in principle persons might eternally reject God, they seem to assume that such a scenario is highly (perhaps infinitely) unlikely. In short, the post-death-opportunities model is not incompatible with universalism.

Several criticisms have been leveled at the post-death-opportunities model. One problem is this: The New Testament seems to stress that persons need to decide

---

68. As noted above, universalists often interpret these passages as pointing toward temporary punishment or purging, while traditionalists understand them to be denoting never-ending states. This debate likely will not be resolved any time soon.

69. Hart offers another universalist counter to the traditionalist appeal to freedom, arguing that it is incoherent to suppose that "a rational agent in full possession of his or her faculties could, in any meaningful sense, freely reject God absolutely and forever" (Hart, *That All Shall Be Saved*, 18).

70. Lewis, *The Great Divorce*.

for Christ in this life, and it does not suggest or encourage holding out until after death. Heb 9:27 declares: "It is appointed for mortals to die once, and after that the judgment." For many traditionalists, this suggests that now is the time to decide, for there will be no post-death opportunities. Jonathan Kvanvig offers a second interesting criticism of the universalist view, particularly of those (like Origen and Hick) who also affirm human freedom and multiple post-death chances. Kvanvig notes that the universalist contends that God's goodness demands (perhaps necessitates) that if God creates creatures subject to moral failure, God must somehow ensure their salvation. But given freedom, such beings can fail to come to salvation. And according to traditionalists, some do fail to come to salvation. But now the dilemma arises for the universalist who endorses human freedom. For he or she must admit—given freedom—that some creatures *could* choose against salvation, even though in fact (in the end) they do not chose against it. But this, in turn, implies that God's goodness (God doing and being good) is contingent upon the choices free creatures make. If they chose for salvation, God is good. But if they chose against salvation, God is no longer good. But most theists—whether traditionalists or universalists—do not wish to claim that God's goodness somehow depends on human choices. According to Jonathan Kvanvig, the universalist (who seems to be committed to the notion that humans *could have chosen* against salvation) is not any better off than the traditionalist (who says that some humans in fact do choose against salvation). In turn, Kvanig contends that it simply is better to reject the universalist supposition that in order to be good God must ensure the salvation of all creatures.[71]

A third alternative model of hell is called *annihilationism*. The core idea of this theory is that the plight of the wicked—those who refuse to align with the divinely intended good—is termination of existence. Often this model is associated with *conditional immortalism*, which holds that the human persons is not intrinsically immortal but requires divine empowering to live everlastingly. This interpretation can work for either dualistic or monistic views of human nature. For the former, a human is body and soul, and both body and soul require divine aid to exist everlastingly. For the latter, the human is an inseparable body-soul unity that requires God's energizing to continue subsisting. In either case, annihilationism declares that sometime after judgment God extinguishes the life of unredeemed persons. Like universalists, annihilationists reject the traditional doctrine of hell because they see it as an affront to divine love and justice. For them, annihilation of the wicked is far more just than perennial torture. To torment endlessly would serve no remedial purpose, would be punishment far exceeding the crime, and would be vindictive and sadistic. Annihilationist Clark Pinnock (1937–2010), writes:

> The God revealed in Christ is boundlessly merciful, not a cruel and sadistic torturer . . . Moral intuition, if raised in the school of Jesus, agrees that this

71. Kvanvig, "Hell," 417–18.

is intolerable. It revolts us when God is pictured as acting like a bloodthirsty monster who maintains an everlasting Auschwitz for his enemies whom he will not even allow to die. One could fear such a God, but I do not know how one could love and respect him.[72]

Defenders of annihilationism cite several biblical texts that (while not directly teaching this view) comport well with it. Ps 37 speaks of the wicked fading like grass and ceasing to be (2, 9–10). Mal 4:1–2 depicts evildoers burned up in an oven. Jesus speaks of malefactors being cast into hell (Gehenna) and consumed by its fire (Matt 3:10, 12; 13:30, 42, 49–52). Jesus also warns against one who can destroy both body and soul in hell (Matt 10:28). Paul and other epistle writers speak of the destruction of wrongdoers (1 Cor 3:17; Phil 1:28; Heb 10:39; 2 Peter 2:1, 3). For annihilationists, these passages suggest utter destruction of the wicked. Biblical texts that speak of eternal fire or eternal punishment (Matt 25:46; 2 Thess 1:9; Heb 6:2) address the *permanence of the result* of punishment and not the duration of punishment per se. Pinnock identifies a number of ancient theologians who endorsed annihilationism, including Clement of Rome (d. 99 CE), Ignatius of Antioch (d. 108/140 CE), and Irenaeus of Lyon (130—c. 202 CE). Modern proponents of this view include John Stott (1921–2011), John Wenham (1913–1996),[73] and Stephen Travis.[74]

Detractors question annihilationists' interpretations of biblical texts that speak of eternal burning (Matt 18:18; 25:1; Jude 7), torment (Rev 20:10), or punishment (Matt 25:46), contending the more natural reading of these passages is that the unfaithful endure everlasting states. Matt 25:46 is especially telling, for it offers a parallel between eternal punishment and eternal life, declaring "And these will go away into *eternal punishment*, but the righteous into *eternal life*" (italics added). Annihilationists wish to retain the claim that the righteous live forever but attempt to deny that punishment also is everlasting. Detractors insist this breaks the parallelism of the text. According to traditionalists, the natural reading is that both life and punishment are eternal. (As was the case in discussion of universalism above, the meaning of *aiōnios* is critical here. Traditionalists are correct if the best translation of this word is "eternal." But if the word is better understood as denoting an "extended but limited period" then—as was the case for universalism—there may be some warrant for the annihilationist's notion that the punishment or torment of the unfaithful is limited—although the consequences—of annihilation—may be permanent).

Jonathan Kvanvig offers a second criticism of the annihilationist perspective. He notes that the force of their position is grounded on the assumption that the biblical images of torment, fire, and darkness are to be understood as literal, physical tortures. But if these images are understood as metaphors for mental, emotional anguish in

---

72. Pinnock, "Annhilationism," 470.

73. Pinnock, "Annhilationism," 467.

74. Travis, *I Believe in the Second Coming of Jesus*, 198–99

persons eternally separated from the goodness and blessing that is God, then the horror of hell becomes more about one's awareness of what has been lost than about vindictive torments imposed. Kvanvig sees this as a legitimate interpretation available to traditionalists, allowing them to retain the claim that the wicked live eternally but not in tortures imposed but in self-imposed exile from God.[75]

Jonathan Kvanvig's own position on hell is that the traditionalist claim that hell is punishment should be dropped. For Kvanvig and others, a more accurate understanding of the consignment of the unredeemed to hell is that it results from divine love. In granting humans freedom, God has made it possible for them to reject eternal fellowship with him. God's motive for granting such freedom is love. God wants humans to be creatures who can enter into loving relationships, and to do so they must be free. But if free, they also can reject God eternally, which is precisely what hell is. So, God consigns humans to hell, for this is what they want. And God's motive for this is love.[76]

Conclusion

Christianity is multifaceted. Grounded in the foundations of a sacred story, a sacred person, a sacred community, and a sacred text, Christianity affirms a broad set of teachings attempting to describe the nature of God and God's relationship with reality. Among the questions these teachings attempt to answer are these:

1. How are God and religious truths known?

2. What is God's nature?

3. How does God relate to reality as a whole?

4. What is the nature of humans?

5. What is the core human dilemma?

6. What is Christ's nature and work?

7. How is God resolving the human dilemma?

8. What is the nature and function of the church?

9. What is the destiny of created reality, especially humans?

With these questions in mind, several doctrines of the church have emerged—specifically: (1) revelation, (2) God, (3) creation and providence, (4) humanity (5) sin (6) Christ, (7) salvation, (8) the church, and (9) last things. In Chapters 3 through 7, we have explored many of the core elements of (and puzzles surrounding) these doctrines. In the next three chapters, we examine another important feature of Christianity—namely, ethics.

75. Kvanvig, "Hell," 417.
76. Kvanvig, "Hell," 419–21.

Part Three: **Christian Ethics**

8

The Foundations of Christian Ethics

IN CHAPTERS 1 AND 2, we discussed the foundations of Christianity which include the Bible, the story of Israel, the person and work of Jesus, and the Christian Community. In Chapters 3 through 7, we examined the core doctrines of the Christian faith. Chapters 8, 9, and 10 will explore another critical aspect of Christianity—namely its ethics. In this eighth chapter, we explore the general features of ethics as well as the basic contours of Christian ethics. We also investigate the rudimentary aspects of biblical ethics. Let us turn first to general ethics.

General Ethics

Ethics may be defined as the study of theories of right and wrong, virtues, and how we should live. At its core, ethics wants to know: How should we (or I) live? The ancient Greeks often asked the question, what is the good life? Unfortunately, this question is ambiguous. For some, it is interpreted to mean, what life will be the most satisfying, fulfilling, pleasant? For others, the question is asking, what life *ought* persons live, regardless of how satisfying, fulfilling, or pleasant, that life might be? Ethics also is concerned with discerning *which actions* are right and which are wrong. Stanley Grenz (1950–2005) speaks of this dimension of ethics as the "ethic of doing," for it concerns what persons *do*—how they act. A central question for the ethics of doing is what makes an *action* right or wrong? That is, what justifies the claim that an action is right (or wrong)? By contrast, ethics also is concerned with *virtues*—those characteristics that make an individual a good person. Grenz refers to this as the "ethic of being," for it addresses what kind of person someone should be, or what makes *a person* good.[1]

Another concern of ethics—not identified in the definition above—is which actions are obligatory and which are not required? There are many actions that are good, but no one is obliged to do them. (For example, it may be good to pick up all the nails in the streets of a town. But, typically, we do not believe individuals are obligated to remove them all.) Some philosophers also distinguish between the concepts of right

---

1. Grenz, *The Moral Quest*.

versus good. Others see these concepts as essentially synonyms. Often this chapter uses the terms "good" and "right" interchangeably. Finally, some philosophers distinguish ethics from morals. According to some writers, ethics refers to a systematic and theoretical study of ethical concepts; morals refer to practicing the moral life, living it out. Not all philosophers agree with this last distinction either.

Key Questions in General Ethics

A variety of questions arises in the general study of ethics. First, what makes an act right or wrong? Second, do ethical norms change or vary? Third, what makes a virtuous person? Fourth, how do we know what is right? Fifth, how should we (or I) live? That is, what is the good life? Sixth, what do ethical sentences mean? Seventh, what is the grounding of morality?

What Makes an Act Right or Wrong?

There are two broad theories answering the question, what makes an act right or wrong? First, *teleological* (or *consequentialist*) theories insist that an act is right *if it brings about* a good or valuable result. The word *teleological* comes from the Greek word *telos*, which means "end, purpose, or result." The most straightforward form of teleological theories simply asserts that a deed is right if it produces a *good state of affairs*. In this case, *good* is understood to be an intrinsic attribute of the circumstances that have come about. However, many teleological theories attempt to avoid saying that an action is right because it brings about a good result. Rather, these theories try to ground good in some more basic reality—namely, in some state of affairs *valued* by the human community.[2] An example of a teleological theory that seeks to define good in terms of *valuable consequences* is one that asserts that an action is right if it brings *pleasure* or absence of pain to an individual or a group. In this case, a deed is deemed right if it brings about some valuable nonmoral consequence or a balance of valuable nonmoral consequences to someone or some group—namely, pleasure or absence of pain.

A variety of ultimate (good-making) values or goals have been proposed through the centuries. *Hedonism* holds that pleasure is the essence of good or is the highest good. The pleasure of an individual or of a group is the ultimate criterion for determining whether an act is good.[3] *Eudemonism* proposes that wholeness, happiness, or well-being is the essence of good or are the highest good. The happiness, well-being, of an individual or a group is the ultimate criterion for determining whether an act

2. Essentially, this latter set of teleological theories attempts to avoid saying that an action is right because it is right (or good or moral). Allegedly, such a definition would be circular. Rather, according to these proposals "right" must be defined by some more basic reality. And this more basic realty is something valued by some in the human community.

3. *Hedonism* comes from the Greek word *hēdonē*, meaning "pleasure."

is good.[4] *Appetitism* asserts that the essence of good or the highest good is found in those acts that humans desire or approve of. An act is good because it is approved of or desired by humans.[5] *Volitionalism* asserts that the essence of good or the highest good is found in those acts that humans choose to value. An act is good because individuals or groups choose to value it.[6] In addition to hedonism, eudemonism, appetitism, and volitionism, other proposed right-making values or goals have been proposed, including power, self-fulfillment, and self-preservation.

There are several types of teleological ethical theories. Among them are *subjectivism*, *cultural relativism*, *egoism*, and *utilitarianism*. Each of these models declares that an act is right if it generates a valuable, nonmoral, consequence. *Subjectivism* asserts that an act is right if it brings about the individual's approval, or if it is willed by the individual. *Cultural relativism* claims an act is right if it is approved by a given culture. *Egoism* insists that an act is right if it benefits an individual. Often benefit is defined in terms of bringing pleasure or happiness or self-fulfillment to the person. At least, three types of ethical egoism may be discerned. *Individual ethical egoism* asserts that all persons should act so as to benefit me. *Personal ethical egoism* claims that I should always act so as to benefit myself, but others may not be obligated to act for my benefit. *Universal ethical egoism* declares that each individual should act so as to benefit himself or herself.[7] *Utilitarianism* asserts that an action is good if it brings benefit to the majority of people. Again, often benefit is defined in terms of pleasure or happiness or self-fulfillment. Two forms of utilitarianism frequently are mentioned. *Act utilitarianism* teaches that an act is good if in *this particular instance* it brings about some valuable consequence for most people. *Rule utilitarianism* claims that an act is good if it *generally* brings about some valuable consequence for most people.

Distinct from teleological theories are *deontological (nonconsequentialist) ethical theories*. According to these models, some actions simply are intrinsically good, regardless of their consequences. In other words, the consequences do not determine whether the action is right or wrong. It does not matter whether the action brings pleasure, happiness, power, self-fulfillment, or self-preservation to someone; it does not matter whether a person or persons approve of it or choose it. Rather, the act simply is right (or wrong). Typically, deontological theories emphasize *duty*, *moral obligation*, and *moral law*. The idea is that certain actions in and of themselves simply are good. The term *deontological* comes from the Greek word *deon*, which means "it is necessary or due."

---

4. The term *eudemonism* comes from the Greek verb *eudaimeo*, which means "to be happy" or more literally "to have a good spirit."

5. *Appetitism* captures the essence of a number of theories that emphasize ethics as grounded in desire or feeling. The name is based on the Latin term *appetitus*, which means "desire."

6. *Volitionalism* captures some of the insights of certain existentialist and social contract theorists. The name is based on the word *volition*, which means "will" or "choice."

7. Thiroux and Krasemann, *Ethics*, 38.

Sometimes deontological theorists attempt to explain why an action is intrinsically right or good (or is one's duty). One explanation for why an action is right is *primary ethical realism*. According to this perspective, good is a basic category of reality, a brute fact. Acts are good because they have the basic quality of goodness. They are ontologically intrinsically good. Plato (428/427 or 424/423—348/347 BCE) seems to have affirmed this view. According to him, an action is good because it participates in the idea of goodness. In other words, an act simply has the quality of goodness.[8]

Not all deontologists affirm primary ethical realism. Some claim that while an action is intrinsically good, its goodness is established by a more basic kind of reality. Thus, an action is intrinsically good because it is prescribed by or logically entailed by some other, more basic, reality. We might call this *secondary ethical realism*. There are at least two versions of this perspective. First is *rational ethical realism*. This model asserts that an action is intrinsically good because it logically follows from or is prescribed by reason. Immanuel Kant (1724–1804) endorsed something like this. He argued that an action is good if it performs a duty that has been prescribed by reason. A second form of secondary ethical realism proposes that an action is intrinsically good because it logically follows from the nature of God or is prescribed by God. This view often is called *divine command theory*. It asserts that an action is good because it performs a command that has been stipulated by God. Various theistic philosophers and theologians affirm this view.

In addition to these distinctions between primary and secondary ethical realism, some ethicists distinguish between *act-deontological theories* and *rule-deontological theories*. Act-deontological theories assert that there are no general moral rules in ethics. Rather, there are "only particular actions, situations, and people about which we cannot generalize. We must approach each situation individually as one of a kind."[9] In turn, a particular act is good in and of itself, within a specific situation, but no general rule can be stated or developed concerning this action.

Rule-deontological ethical theories insist that an act is good if it follows a rule that prescribes actions that are good in and of themselves. In other words, an act is good because it conforms to a rule of action that is good in and of itself. An example of a rule-deontological theory is the divine command theory. This theory proposes that an action is good because it conforms to a moral rule given by God. Allegedly such rules are to be obeyed regardless of the consequences. Kant's theory is another example of a rule-deontological ethical theory. For him, an act is good if it conforms to a moral rule given by reason.

---

8. In the *Republic*, Plato attempts to show that the just life is a balanced, internally contented life. Thus, in some ways he attempts to justify the just life because it brings about a valuable consequence. Nevertheless, Plato ultimately seems to endorse the notion that an action is good because it intrinsically manifests the form of goodness.

9. Thiroux and Krasemann, *Ethics*, 56.

Do Ethical Norms Change or Vary?

Another key question of ethics is, do ethical norms vary? Two basic options are possible. *Absolutism* holds that ethical norms do not vary from person to person, culture to culture, or time to time. Deontological theories tend to be absolutist. They normally assert that ethical norms do not change. Primary ethical realism asserts that if an action is intrinsically right, it is always right. If an action is intrinsically wrong, it is always wrong. Secondary ethical realism often assumes that if an action is prescribed by reason or by God, it is always good. Contrary to absolutism, *relativism* holds that ethical norms differ from person to person, culture to culture, or historical period to historical period. Many teleological theories assume that ethical norms vary. For example, ethical egoism asserts that what may benefit me may not benefit you, and so what is right for me may not be right for you. Or again, ethical egoism might claim that an act that would benefit me today may not benefit me tomorrow; thus, the act is right today but not tomorrow.

What Makes a Virtuous Person?

The first two questions addressed above are concerned with the ethics of doing, with right *actions*. But what of the ethics of being? In addition to theories that emphasize moral acts, ethics examines the *characteristics that make a good person*. These characteristics are often called *virtues*, virtues that constitute a good character. At issue is (1) what virtues (characteristics) makes a person good, and (2) how does one acquire these virtues. Throughout history, different virtues have been identified as defining characteristics of a good person. Plato spoke of four key virtues: wisdom, courage, temperance, and justice. Plato saw these virtues as arising from when a person and a state live according to the precepts of reason. Aristotle (384–322 BCE) spoke of virtue as means between two extremes. Thus, for Aristotle, a virtuous person is one who is well-balanced, not prone to act in the extreme. An example virtue is courage. For Aristotle, a courageous person is one who is neither foolhardy nor cowardly, but somewhere between these. Aristotle defined a virtue as a habit of action or as a proneness to act in a certain way. He believed that such virtues must be taught and learned. He also contended that these virtues reflect that which is the most reasonable course of action. Stanley Grenz distinguishes between deontological and teleological theories of virtue. *Virtue deontological models* assert that some "character traits are intrinsically good," whereas *virtue teleological models* insist that a character trait is virtuous if it tends to bring about desirable results.[10] A number of contemporary philosophers have endorsed virtue ethics, including Alasdair MacIntyre,[11] Stanley Hauerwas,[12] and

10. Grenz, *The Moral Quest*, 42.

11. MacIntyre, *After Virtue*.

12. Hauerwas, *The Peaceable Kingdom*.

Carol Gilligan.[13] These writers often affirm the important role of community and of tradition as grounding for ethical norms and in the development of virtuous persons.

How Do We Know What Is Right?

A fourth key question for general ethics is, how do we know what is right or wrong? How do we know which *acts* are right or wrong? How do we know which *virtues* make a good person? Several answers have been proposed. Some writers assert that knowledge of good and evil comes through *intuition*. We just know, through some inner awareness, that some acts are right or wrong, and that some character traits are good or evil. Joseph Butler (1692–1752) affirmed the existence of a moral conscience in all humans. He appealed to Rom 2:14–15 as scriptural evidence for this. Henry Sidgwick (1838–1900) also affirmed knowledge of morality through intuition.[14] Other writers claim that knowledge of good and evil comes from the basic structures of *reason*. It simply is rational to be ethical, and people can be shown this via reason. Immanuel Kant affirmed this as did Thomas Aquinas (1225–1274). Many writers claim that knowledge of good and evil has been *revealed* to humans by some higher spiritual reality—such as God. Revelation may be a direct, inner experience (something like Butler's view of conscience) or may be indirect through a written record of some original historical revelation (such as the Bible or some other scripture). Appeal to revelation as a source of ethical knowledge is common in Christian ethics. Still other writers claim that knowledge of good and evil occurs through a conscious *choice* on the part of the individual or group. We know that something is good or evil because we chose to affirm it as such. Our choice makes us aware that it is good or evil. This seems to be the view of certain existentialist and social contract theorists.

How Should We Live? What Is the Best Life?

A fifth question for ethics is: how should we (or I) live? Or what is the best life? As noted above, this is a central concern of ethics. (As will be apparent below, this question is closely tied to that of what makes an act right or wrong). Often two broad answers are given to the questions, how should we live or what is the best life. One answer is, live so as to bring about a valued result. A variety of good-defining qualities (valued-states) have been proposed. (These proposed qualities essentially mirror those given above describing what—allegedly—makes an action right.) *Hedonism* proposes the good life is the one that brings a balance of pleasure over pain in one's life. *Eudemonism* suggests that the good life is one that bring happiness or contentment to someone. *Appetitism* asserts the good life is the one that most fully fulfills human

13. Gilligan, *In a Different Voice*.

14. For summaries of Butler's and Sidgwick's views, see Denise et al., eds., *Great Traditions in Ethics*.

desires or accomplishes what humans approve of. *Volitionalism* claims that the good life is the one humans deliberately choose. A second theory of the best life holds that the good life entails doing good or being good, or both. It involves performing good acts and (perhaps more importantly) being a good person. Often this view presumes that goodness cannot be defined by something else. Goodness is a property intrinsic to some actions or some character traits.

What Do Ethical Sentences Mean, and What Is the Grounding of Morality?

A sixth important question for general ethics is, what do ethical sentences mean? For example, precisely what am I saying when I state, "It is wrong to murder"? Closely related to this question is the further concern: What is the grounding of morality? In other words: What establishes the truth of ethical statements? To answer these questions, it is helpful to consider two important issues. First, what functions do ethical sentences perform? Language philosophy discerns several different sentence-functions—several distinct ways sentences work. Among these functions are

1. Interrogative sentences

   These are sentences that ask questions (for example, Why is the sky blue?).

2. Informative or cognitive sentences

   These sentences assert that something is true or false. They convey information. In logic, such sentences are often called propositions or claims (for example, The sky is blue).

3. Directive/imperative sentences

   These sentences issue a command (for example, Make the sky stop being blue).

4. Expressive sentences or terms

   These sentences or words express emotion (for example, Ouch! Yuck!).

Other functions of sentences also have been noted. A key question, then, in determining the meaning of ethical sentences is, what kind of sentence-function do ethical sentences play? Are they informative? Do they state a proposition that is true or false? Or are ethical sentences more like interrogative, directive, or expressive sentences or words? When I say, "Murder is wrong," am I attempting to convey information, attempting to make a claim that is true or false? Or am I really asking a question, stating a command, or expressing an emotion?

A second important issue to consider in attempting to discern what ethical sentences mean is, what grounds ethical claims? That is, to what do ethical terms refer? When I say, "Rover is a dog," there is a thing (object) to which the term Rover refers. I can point to something that I can sense and say, "That is Rover." But when I say, "Murder is wrong," to what does the term "wrong" refer? Can I point to it? Can I sense it? Where is it or what is it?

Several responses to these questions are possible. One answer is that the term *wrong* refers to nothing. There literally is no object, no thing, to which the term refers. A second reply might be that the term *wrong* refers to some mental experience. For example, the word *wrong* may denote some feeling of disgust that I experience when I think about murder; or again, it may signify the pain that someone experiences while being murdered; or again, it may refer to my desire or the desire of others to avoid being murdered; or again, it may mean some belief that I hold. A third answer might be that the term *wrong* refers to some metaphysical object or reality—a reality that somehow resides in or is possessed by the action of committing murder.

In light of these preliminary questions (and possible answers), several theories of meaning for ethical sentences and terms have been proposed. *Cognitive theories* hold that ethical statements convey information; they are either true or false. In turn, these theories insist that the *truth* of ethical claims is grounded in reality in some way. That is, ethical statements are true or false, and there is some explanation for why they are true or false. There are two types of cognitive ethical theories. First, *objectivism* insists that ethical statements are informative; they are true or false. Further, ethical terms refer to some *objective* reality, some reality beyond human opinions, ideas, or beliefs. A second type of cognitive ethical theory is *subjectivism*, which asserts that the truth of ethical claims is grounded in some inner experience of an individual or a group.

There are two types of objectivism. *Naturalistic objectivism* insists that ethical statements convey information; they are either true or false. Further, ethical terms refer to some objective reality in the natural world. And the truth of ethical statements is grounded in that objective reality of the natural world. Brooke Moore and Robert Stewart distinguish two types of naturalistic objectivism: reductive naturalism and nonreductive naturalism. *Reductive naturalism* "attempts to reduce ethical facts to empirical facts. For example, the claim that 'goodness' can be defined as 'pleasantness' is a reductive claim because it involves the assertion that goodness is the same thing as the empirical property of being pleasant."[15] In other words, according to a form of reductive naturalism, the good refers to the empirical experience of pleasure. *Nonreductive naturalism* avoids reducing ethical facts to empirical facts. It would not claim that the good is identical to some empirical property. Rather, it asserts that the good is inseparably *related* to some empirical fact. For example,

> a nonreductive naturalist might argue . . . that a person's good is determined by certain universal needs that have a biological basis or that normally develop in social interaction . . . One's own good, moral virtue, and morally right action

15. Moore and Stewart, *Moral Philosophy*, 22.

can be linked in these ways with empirical facts. These facts about human nature and society determine moral facts even though the moral facts cannot be reduced to empirical facts by any definitions.[16]

Hedonism, eudemonism, and appetitism are more or less naturalistic, objectivist theories. They claim that goodness refers to some natural objective event—namely, to the experience of pleasure, or of contentment (happiness), or to the experience of having desires fulfilled. In turn, these theories insist that the truth of an ethical statement is determined by whether or not pleasure or happiness or satisfaction is experienced (by someone) as a result of taking or not taking an action. For example, if someone says, "Murder is wrong," this statement is true if, for someone or for a group of people, the act of murder results in a lack of pleasure or a lack of contentment or generates a desire to avoid murdering someone or a group of people.

A second type of objectivism is *metaphysical or transcendent objectivism*. This view asserts that ethical sentences are informative; they are either true or false. Further, ethical terms refer to some transcendent (nonnatural or supernatural) objective reality. In turn, the truth of ethical statements is grounded in these nonnatural objective realities. Primary ethical realism is an example of this perspective. According to primary ethical realism, the term *good* refers to some indefinable, basic quality of reality. Hence, an ethical statement is true if it accurately conveys information about this basic quality. For example, if someone says, "Murder is wrong," and if murder in fact has the quality of wrongness, then the statement is true. Secondary ethical realism is another example of nonnatural objectivism. According to secondary ethical realism, the good refers to some quality that has been prescribed by reason or by God. And so, an ethical statement is true if it accurately conveys information about this quality. For example, if someone says, "Murder is wrong," and if murder in fact has been forbidden by reason or by God, then the statement is true.

Subjectivism insists that ethical sentences are informative; they are either true or false. Further, ethical terms refer to the beliefs of individuals or societies. In turn, the truth of ethical statements is grounded in these beliefs. Thus, when one says. "murder is wrong," and if in fact the act of murder is believed to be wrong by someone or by a group, then the statement is true. Volitionalism is more or less a subjectivist theory. Something is wrong because an individual or a group believes it is wrong or choose to make it wrong.

Noncognitive theories insist that ethical sentences are not informative. They are neither true nor false. Further, ethical terms have no reference; they do not refer to anything. Finally, according to these theories, nothing grounds the truth of ethical statements. This is the case because ethical statements are *neither true nor false*. There are at least three types of noncognitive theories of meaning. *Emotivism* asserts that ethical statements are essentially expressive. They communicate feelings so that they

16. Moore and Stewart, *Moral Philosophy*, 23.

are roughly equivalent to grunt-like expressions such as "Ouch!" When I say, "murder is wrong," I am expressing some sort of emotion, such as "Murder, yuck!" But I am not making a statement that is either true or false. *Imperativism* holds that ethical statements are essentially directive. They issue commands. Thus, when I say, "Murder is wrong," I am saying "Don't murder." I am not saying anything that is informative—true or false. *Prescriptivism* insists that ethical statements suggest or commend certain actions to others. Ethical sentences are not quite commands (directives) but more like suggestions or recommendations for action. When I say, "It is wrong to murder," I am saying, "I would suggest or recommend that you not murder."

General Features of Christian Ethics

So much then for the key features and questions of general ethics. We now turn to consider the broad characteristics of Christian ethics. Like general ethics, Christian ethics is concerned with discerning (1) which actions are right or wrong, (2) which character traits make someone a good person, and (3) how a person (or society) is to live the good (or righteous) life. Unlike general ethics, however, Christian ethics is more thoroughly bound to the theology and moral insights of the Christian tradition, especially as described in Christian Scriptures and as expressed in the life and teaching of Jesus. A wide variety of approaches and emphases is found in Christian ethics, so that believers answer the seven questions above in different ways.

Regarding the *meaning* and *grounding* of ethical claims, throughout history most Christians have assumed (often without directly saying) that key ethical sentences are informative; they convey information: they are either true or false. (Thus, ethical sentences are not merely questions or emotional outbursts.) Yes, many ethical sentences are commands, which are neither true nor false. The Ten Commandments are clear examples of this. But for most Christians, such commands are grounded in the *truth* that it *is* wrong to do the actions prohibited in the commandments.[17] And sentences asserting that something is wrong (or right) are informative: they are truth-claims.

Many Christians assume that ethical truths are grounded in something that transcends human conventions, beliefs, or acts of will. That is, most Christians reject a purely subjectivist interpretation of the meaning of ethical claims. They deny that human beliefs or choices make an action right or wrong. Rather, most Christian ethicists affirm some form of objectivism, assuming that ethical truths are based upon a reality independent of human beliefs or choices.

Indeed, most Christians endorse some form of *metaphysical or transcendent* objectivism. Specifically, Christian writers often insist that ethics is grounded in God. One way to express this belief is to say that ethics is founded upon God's will or commands; God demands that rational creatures do what is right and avoid

---

17. For example, it is wrong to murder, steal, commit adultery, and so forth.

what is wrong. Sometimes this perspective is called the *divine command theory*. But such a view faces an immediate puzzle: Is an action (or virtue) good because God commands it? Or does God command it because it is good?[18] The first alternative suggests that God's moral commands are arbitrary, that God could as easily command "You *shall* murder, lie, steal, or commit adultery" as command "*Do not* murder, lie, steal, or commit adultery." And if God should so command, then murdering, lying, stealing, or committing adultery would all be right rather than wrong, for it is God's will or command that makes actions right (or wrong). On the other hand, the second alternative seems to subjugate God and God's will to a reality that transcends the deity—namely, the good itself. Goodness per se mandates that God command certain actions because they are good. And such a circumstance seems to undermine the authority or sovereignty of God.

Some Christian writers attempt to soften the blow of this dilemma by insisting that good is grounded not simply in God's will or commands but in God's nature. God is good and, because of this, God commands what is good (and not what is evil). In other words, God's demands are not sheer acts of caprice. Rather, they flow from the *nature of God*, who is good. There is considerable warrant for such a claim. As we shall see below, several biblical passages suggest that God's commands flow from God's nature, which itself is good. It is a matter of debate, however, whether appeal to the good nature of God resolves the intellectual puzzle created by the above dilemma. One might still wonder whether appealing to God's good nature does not essentially imply that indeed God depends upon goodness to be who God is.[19] We will not attempt to resolve this long-running debate here.[20]

In addition to affirming moral objectivism, Christian ethics typically has recognized the importance of both deeds and character traits. That is, Christian writers have tended to affirm the need both to *do* the right thing and to *be* the right kind of person. As we will see below and in the next two chapters, the biblical writers, as well as authors from across Christian history, often blend these concerns, typically assuming that being good and doing good are mutually interdependent.

Furthermore, often Christian ethics stresses both teleological as well as deontological approaches to ethics. That is, often Christians emphasizes the need to perform certain actions for the sake of those acts (deontology) as well as to seek desirable (good) outcomes (teleology). Deontology is seen in Jesus' emphasis on doing the will of God. Followers of Christ are to perform acts commanded (or willed) by God. Thus, in the Lord's Prayer, Jesus instructs his disciples to pray "thy will be

18. Plato voiced this concern in the context of ancient Greece's polytheism. He asks: Do the gods love an action because it is pious, or is an action pious because the gods love it? Plato, *Euthyphro* in *The Dialogues of Plato*, 10a.

19. This was the conclusion that Plato wanted his readers to draw regarding the relationship between good and the gods in *Euthyphro*.

20. For discussions of these matters, see Linville, "Moral Particularism"; and Yandell "Moral Essentialism," both in Loftin, ed., *God & Morality*.

done" (Matt 6:10). Here one does an act for its own sake or, more accurately, for the sake of God's command to do it. On the other hand, Jesus also emphasizes seeking desirable outcomes (teleology). In the Lord's Prayer, Jesus also urges disciples to pray "thy kingdom come" (Matt 6:10). In this case, followers of Christ are to seek a good outcome—namely, the reign of God on earth. Apparently, for Jesus, some actions are performed for their own sake (because they are intrinsically good or willed by God), and some actions are done for the sake of generating or contributing to a good outcome (a good state of affairs).[21] A similar dual emphasis is found in other portions of Christian Scripture. Likewise, as we will see in the next two chapters, throughout Christian history, while writers sometimes stress either divine commands or divine outcomes, often Christian thinkers recognize the importance of both. And recognition of both commands and outcomes comes in no small measure because of these writers' attempts to be faithful to Scripture.

The Sources of Christian Ethics

A core concern of Christian ethics is, how do we know what is right? How do we know which *acts* are right or wrong? How do we know which virtues make a good person? As noted above, in general ethics, several answers to these questions are proposed—including intuition, reason, revelation, and human choice. Christians also appeal to diverse sources to discern what actions and virtues are right (and wrong). These include revelation, the Christian community, reason, conscience, and the Holy Spirit.

Special Revelation and the Bible

As we have seen in earlier chapters, many theologians insist that God is the ultimate source of information about theological matters, including knowledge of right and wrong. The Lord has revealed something of the divine nature and will to humans. Two forms of revelation often are recognized—namely, general revelation and special revelation. *General revelation* refers to truths accessible to all persons in all times and places. *Special revelation* alludes to truths revealed to particular persons at specific times and places. Key events in the history of Israel are considered moments of special revelation, including God's interaction with specific persons—Abraham, Moses, Samuel, Jeremiah, and so forth. In turn, for Christians, God's ultimate and most complete revelation came in Jesus of Nazareth.[22]

Granting the occurrence of special revelation, many Christian theologians also recognize that the essential content of this revelation is made available to contemporary Christians through the Bible. Indeed, in many ways, the Scriptures are now the

21. See Henlee H. Barnette's comments on these matters in Barnette, *Introducing Christian Ethics*, 5–6. See also Marshall, *The Challenge of New Testament Ethics*, 8–9.

22. For a fuller account of these ideas, see Chapter 3, above (pages [x-ref]).

principal source for knowing God's nature, will, and moral expectations. As noted in Chapter 3, the precise character of both special revelation and of the Bible is disputed among theologians. We will not rehearse those debates here. Suffice it to say that many Christians consider the Bible to be a primary source for knowing God and God's will—including the divine moral values and demands.

The Christian Community

In addition to special revelation and the Bible, Christians often believe that God's Spirit indwells and leads the church. The Spirit of the Lord aids the Christian community in interpreting the Bible. Drawing on these claims, several theologians presume that the formal doctrines and interpretations of Christians through history serve as important or even essential sources for Christian beliefs and ethical practices today. As noted in Chapter 3, the Catholic tradition at times has elevated the formal teachings of the post-biblical church to the status of near-equal authority to the Bible. On the other hand, Protestants have tended to acknowledge the Bible as the only certain source of moral teaching so that postbiblical Christian pronouncements are ever subject to revision in light of Scripture. Nevertheless, Protestants often recognize key postbiblical church teachings as having substantial authority. In turn, beyond the *formal* pronouncements of the church, the Christian community typically exercises influence upon the every-day, practical decision-making of Christians. As Roger Crook notes, "The individual believer lives within [the church's] fellowship, is taught by the fellowship, is prompted into action by the fellowship, and acts with concern for the fellowship."[23]

Reason

A third source of guidance for Christian moral decision-making is reason. A strong tradition among some Christian groups is that through reason one can construct a *natural moral law*. Thomas Aquinas endorsed this view, as do many in the Catholic tradition.[24] According to this perspective, in creating the universe, God established core moral norms that, in turn, can be learned through rationally reflecting on the nature of the world. From this moral reasoning, core moral principles arise. Not all Christian ethicists agree with this position. But even Christians who reject *natural moral law* per se still acknowledge the utility of reason for ethical decision-making. For example, even if one sees the Bible as the primary source of information about ethical truths, a person must exercise reason (1) to understand the nature of those norms and (2) to see how biblical ethical principles apply to contemporary issues not directly addressed by

---

23. Crook, *An Introduction to Christian Ethics*, 61.
24. See Chapter 9, below (pages [**x-ref**]).

Scripture. While some Christians affirm the utility of reason over Scripture, most see rationality as playing a subsidiary role in formulating ethical norms.

Conscience

A fourth source of ethical knowledge is moral conscience. The precise cause or source of moral conscience is disputed. Some people contend that moral conscience is purely the product of a person's social environment. Our families, traditions, and cultures generate the consciences that we have. Others, however, insist that while our societies obviously help shape our moral sensitivities, a conscience is also a product of some form of divine influence. Again, appeal to natural-law morality often assumes that humans have some (inkling of a) natural moral awareness—an awareness that may be innate or perhaps learned through rational reflection. Still others would tie the concept of moral conscience to the workings of the Holy Spirit. A classic biblical passage that speaks of divinely sanctioned moral conscience is Rom 2:14–15:

> When Gentiles, who do not possess the law, do instinctively what the law requires, these, though not having the law, are a law to themselves. They show that what the law requires is written on their hearts, to which their own conscience also bears witness; and their conflicting thoughts will accuse or perhaps excuse them.

The Holy Spirit

According to many Christians, a fifth source of moral knowledge is the Holy Spirit. The New Testament is full of descriptions of the Spirit's activity in the lives of Christians. In Luke 24:49, Jesus says to his disciples after his resurrection, "And see, I am sending upon you what my Father promised; so stay here in the city until you have been clothed with power from on high." In Acts 1:8, Jesus says, "But you will receive power when the Holy Spirit has come upon you; and you will be my witnesses in Jerusalem, in all Judea and Samaria, and to the ends of the earth." In Acts 2, the Holy Spirit falls upon the church with great power and is seen as the fulfillment of Old Testament prophecy. In John 14—16, Jesus speaks several times of sending the Holy Spirit, who will be a Counselor and Spirit of truth. This Spirit will remind the church of Christ's teachings and will convict nonbelievers of sin and of the ways of righteousness.

Throughout the ages, Christians have spoken of experiencing the presence of the Holy Spirit and of being guided by that Spirit. For example, the Religious Society of Friends (Quakers) speak of the Spirit in terms of an *inner light* that directs individuals and congregations in decision-making and conduct. Many Protestant Christians, while affirming the central authority of the Bible, endorse the *priesthood of believers* and assume that the Holy Spirit leads persons toward righteous living and right beliefs.

Crook is likely correct in asserting that the role of the Spirit is less that of directly giving information to persons (in words) and more that of prompting persons "to move in a specific direction" and of "convicting" persons that something should or should not be done.[25] That is, often the experience of the Spirit is a mysterious awareness of the divine presence urging one to act. Further, the Spirit not only works upon individuals but often manifests within the Christian community as a whole.[26]

Obviously, all these sources of guidance for moral decision-making face difficulties. A chief difficulty for each is the problem of verification. It does not seem possible to somehow verify (1) that the Bible has come from God, or (2) that the Spirit of God is in fact directing a person, or (3) that the Christian traditions or current Christian community correctly discern what is right, or (4) that the voices of conscience or reason in fact offer accurate descriptions of what one should do. Of course, in many ways, these difficulties are faced by any ethical theory.

Biblical Ethics

Christian ethics is deeply influenced by the ethics of the biblical literature. In those writings, one finds a broad theological narrative from which flow core moral insights. Among those insights are depictions of the kind of person one should be (ethics of being) and of what kinds of actions one should perform (ethics of doing). For Christians, at the center of the biblical story is the life and deeds of Jesus Christ. In him, one sees what kind of person to be and what kinds of actions to manifest. Of course, Christ is best understood in the context of the fuller biblical narrative flowing through the Old Testament into the New Testament.

Ethics and the Biblical Narrative

At the heart of the biblical story is the God of Israel. This God is creator of all. As creator, Yahweh is not only powerful but also good. God's good purposes are demonstrated in the creation of a good world and of humans whose existence makes the universe even better. God's goodness is manifested in the divine watch over and care of the created order. But God's benevolence most fully is shown in his creation of and relationship with humans. God is a personal being, and the Lord calls humans into interpersonal communion with him and with each other. The story of the garden of Eden points toward this idyllic God-human and human-human fellowship. There God walks and talks with the

---

25. Crook, *An Introduction to Christian Ethics*, 64.

26. A word of caution is often noted concerning the work of the Holy Spirit, and that is that the Holy Spirit will not contradict the core claims and example of Christ. This was a concern in the early church. In John 16:14–15, Jesus is recorded as saying, "When the Spirit of truth comes, he will guide you into all the truth; for he will not speak on his own, but will speak whatever he hears . . . He will glorify me [Christ], because he will take what is mine and declare it to you."

first humans, and they in turn commune with the Lord and with one another. Further, in the garden humans experience harmony with the created order.

Communion with God involved obedience to divine demands. God expected certain behaviors and forbade others. Within the ancient Jewish mind-set, God's commands were not given so that the deity might lord over creatures. Rather, these demands were proffered for human benefit. God's commands reflect the good nature of the Lord, and they bring life to those who follow them. Among other benefits, such commands bring peace among humans and with God. As Henlee Barnette remarks regarding the Israelite tradition, "fellowship with God is inseparable from the good life," and "obedience to God's will is a basic principle of Old Testament ethics."[27]

According to the biblical narrative, then, the Creator God is good. But something goes wrong with the created world. The first humans sin, and with that moral breach come human enmity with God, with their world, and with one another. Also, sin brought divine judgment. Judgment itself shows God's concern for the good. God cannot tolerate evil, including human sin, at least not indefinitely. From its opening narratives, then, the Hebrew Bible demonstrates concern over ethics and over human failure to be good. God calls humans to do what is right and humankind often fails.

At this point, another theme emerges in the narrative of Scripture. The God of Israel not only is creator but also redeemer. Out of goodness and love, the Lord sought to rectify the wrongs that arose from human sinfulness. God called Abraham, commanding him to go to an undisclosed land and promising to bless him, his family, and all humanity through them. Later, the Lord entered a covenant with Abraham, reinforcing his promises. Abraham believed God, and "the LORD reckoned it to him as righteousness" (Gen 15:6). In this arrangement, God essentially entered "into a covenant of kinship with Abraham, promising to redeem his descendants from their future captivity in Egypt just as if he were their nearest kin or their go'el ("kinsman with the responsibility of redeeming or rescuing from danger"; Gen 15:13–21; Lev 25:25).[28] Thereafter, in the narratives of the Torah, the Lord is said to be the God of Abraham and of Abraham's descendants (Gen 17:7; 24:7; 26:24; 28:13, 15; Exod 3:6). Further, Abraham and his offspring need not fear, for God is with them and will keep the divine promises (Gen 26:24; 46:3; Exod 3:12). Significantly, the Lord's commitment to the covenant with Abraham and his offspring is fueled by steadfast love (*chesed*)[29] and faithfulness (Gen 24:27; 32:9–11; Exod 34:6; Ps 57:3, 10; 136:1–26).

---

27. Barnette, *Introducing Christian Ethics*, 12–13.

28. Kaiser, *The Doctrine of God*, 4–5.

29. The Hebrew word *chesed* (also transliterated *ḥesed*) is notoriously difficult to translate. The Revised Standard Version (RSV) translates it as "steadfast love," given above. Others translate it as "kindness" (NIV), loving-kindness (ASV), and "gracious love" (ISV). Norman Snaith proposed the translation "covenant love" (Snaith, *Distinctive Ideas*, 118–66). Whatever way it is translated into English, many writers agree that *chesed* is closely associated with an emotion or attitude tied to covenant faithfulness. Thus, Dale Moody agrees that *chesed* is "the power which guarantees a covenant and makes it strong and durable" (Moody, *The Word of Truth*, 108).

Later, Abraham's descendants find themselves enslaved in Egypt, but faithfully keeping promises to Abraham, the Lord rescues the Israelites with a mighty hand. The same steadfast love and faithfulness that motivated God's watch and care over Abraham's immediate progeny now fuel the divine commitment to Abraham's more distant descendants. Exod 2:23–24 records: "The Israelites groaned under their slavery, and cried out . . . God heard their groaning, and God remembered his *covenant with* Abraham, Isaac, and Jacob" (italics added). In Exod 3:7–8 Yahweh declares: "I have observed the misery of *my people* who are in Egypt; I have heard their cry on account of their taskmasters. Indeed, I know their sufferings, and I have come down to deliver them from the Egyptians" (italics added). As the quotes above show, in the days of Moses, the theme God's covenant with Abraham was still operative, as was a strong familial identification of the Israelites as God's people. After freeing Abraham's descendants (the people of Israel) from bondage in Egypt, God entered into a covenant with them as well. The Lord promised to be their God, called them to be his people, and offered the stipulations of the covenant. Just like the Abrahamic covenant, the Mosaic covenant was ensured by God's steadfast love and faithfulness. Exod 34:6–7 proclaims that the Lord is "a God merciful and gracious, slow to anger, and abounding in *steadfast love* and *faithfulness*, keeping *steadfast love* for thousandth generation, forgiving iniquity and transgression and sin." The Lord remains the redeemer God in the era of the exodus.

But just as the Lord's covenant with Abraham had, so God's covenant with Israel called for obedience. Stipulations were laid down about right actions and attitudes. The redeemer God still was the good God of creation, demanding righteous living and calling persons to right relations with one another and with the divine. As we will see below, at the center of the Lord's expectations are the Ten Commandments, which draw out the core stipulations of the covenant. The redeemer God of the book of Exodus is still concerned with ethics, with who humans should be and how they should behave. For this reason, Exod 34:7 also declares that the Lord is a God "by no means clearing the guilty, but visiting the iniquity of the parents upon the children and the children's children, to the third and the fourth generation."

As time passed, Israel was unfaithful to the divine covenant. But God remained faithful. When Israel failed, God promised the blessings of the covenant to a remnant of the people, calling them to restored faithfulness. Sadly, this remnant also struggled to be faithful. But God's steadfast love and faithfulness did not falter. For the writers of the New Testament, Jesus Christ provided the ultimate fulfillment of the divine-human covenant and offered a way (as Israel's representative) for both Israel and other nations to fulfill the requirements of the covenant. Christ's death provides an atonement for sin. And God's Spirit extends spiritual empowerment to live righteously before the Lord, and to live in loving fellowship with God and with others. In Jesus Christ, the redeemer God was most fully displayed.

Being and Acting Like God

One best comprehends the ethics of the Bible from the vantage point of the broad biblical narrative noted above. This ethic includes an understanding of both what kind of people God expects humans to be, and how they are to act. At the heart of the biblical narrative is the call *to be like and to act like God*, for God is good and God does what is right.[30] Thus, in Lev 19, Yahweh commands the people of Israel to be holy, for he is holy (v. 2; compare Lev 11:44–45; 20:7). Immediately following this command is a list of moral mandates for the people, including care for parents, justice for the poor, truth-telling, fair business dealings, and so forth. For the biblical writers, these mandates are the demands of holiness and reflect the holy nature and actions of God. In a similar manner, the book of Deuteronomy declares:

> the LORD your God is God of gods and Lord of lords, the great God, mighty and awesome, who is not partial and takes no bribe, who executes justice for the orphan and the widow, and who loves the strangers, providing them food and clothing. You shall also love the stranger, for you were strangers in the land of Egypt. (Deut 10:17–19)

As God loves the stranger (or alien) in the land, so God's people are to love foreigners in the land of Israel. Similar sentiments are expressed in the New Testament. The First Letter of John declares, "We love because he first loved us" (4:19), intimating that in loving one another, Christians mimic God's love for them. Eph 5:1 instructs: "Be imitators of God." For the authors of the Bible, human ethics is grounded in the *nature and the actions* of the good God.[31]

Yahweh's and Christ's Moral Virtues and Behaviors

But what are the character traits and behaviors of this good God? Numerous divine virtues and moral actions are named throughout the Scriptures. Here are some of the most fundamental ones. Exod 34 offers what Dale Moody calls "the five points of Yahwism"—that is, five central virtues ascribed to Yahweh in the early biblical tradition and echoed throughout the Hebrew Bible. These are mercy, grace, patience, steadfast love, and faithfulness.[32] Exod 34:6–7a declares:

> The LORD, the LORD,

---

30. God also refrains from what is wrong.

31. Although one may intellectually abstract ethics of being from ethics of doing, realistically the two are inseparable. Ultimately, the moral person does what is right. Perhaps for this reason, often biblical texts mix demands to do what is right with calls to be a certain sort of person. As we will see, there are biblical passages that suggest that sometimes one can do good acts while not being good—that is, one can follow moral rules with false motives. Nevertheless, ultimately, truly good acts flow from the kind of person someone is.

32. Moody, *The Word of Truth*, 104–13.

> a God *merciful* and *gracious,*
>
> *slow to anger,*
>
> and abounding in *steadfast love* and *faithfulness,*
>
> keeping *steadfast love* for the thousandth generation,
>
> forgiving iniquity and transgression and sin. (italics added)

These five moral attributes of Yahweh resound across the pages of the Hebrew Bible, and often are repeated together. Routinely, God is depicted as "merciful" (Hebrew: *racham*—often translated "compassionate"),[33] "gracious" (Hebrew: *chen*),[34] and "slow to anger," "long-suffering," and "patient" (Num 14:18; Ps 86:15; Jer 15:15). Further, we have already seen the central roles played by divine steadfast love (*chesed*) and faithfulness (Hebrew: *emuhah*) in the biblical narrative. These two virtues describe God's nature and explain why the Lord stubbornly shows mercy, grace, and patience toward Abraham's descendants. God has covenanted with Abraham and with the people of Israel, and even though Israel falters, Yahweh remains lovingly and tenaciously faithful to the covenant.

Moody identifies a sixth important virtue of Yahweh, namely what Moody calls "election love" (Hebrew: *ahabah*). This is the love ascribed to Yahweh in Deut 7:7–8, where Yahweh declares to the people of Israel:

> It was not because you were more numerous than any other people that the LORD set his heart on you and chose you—for you were the fewest of all peoples. It was because the LORD *loved* [*ahabah*] you and kept the oath that he swore to your ancestors, that the LORD has brought you out with a mighty hand, and redeemed you from the house of slavery, from the hand of Pharaoh king of Egypt (italics and brackets added).

A similar idea is expressed in Deut 4:37–39, where the text says that the Lord chose Israel and called them out of Egypt because God *loved* (Hebrew: *ahabah*) their ancestors. Again, in Jer 31:2, Yahweh asserts, "I have *loved* you with an everlasting *love*; therefore, I have continued my faithfulness to you." According to Moody, this love "is prior to the covenant relation of *chesed* (steadfast love), for it answers the question as to why there was a covenant in the first place."[35] It is this love that motivated the election of Israel.

A seventh important divine moral virtue is righteousness (Hebrew: *tsedaqah*) In Ps 5:8 the speaker pleads, "Lead me, O LORD, in your *righteousness.*" In Ps 7:17 the speaker announces, "I will give to the LORD the thanks due to his *righteousness.*"[36] As noted in Chapter 6 in our discussion of the New Perspective on Paul, the Hebrew

---

33. See Deut 4:31 2 Chr 30:9; Neh 9:17, 31; Ps 37:26; 103:8; Joel 2:13; Jonah 4:2.

34. 2 Chr 30:9; Neh 9:17, 31; Ps 86:15; 103:8; 111:4; 112:4; Joel 2:13; Jonah 4:2.

35. Moody, *The Word of Truth,* 113.

36. See also 2 Chr 12:6; Neh 9:8; Pss 7:9; 103:17; 111:3; Jer 9:24; Dan 9:14; Zeph 3:5; Zech 8:8.

concept of righteousness is primarily a relational idea. It is not so much about conforming to an abstract moral principle that stands over against an individual or community. Rather, it is an interpersonal concept; it concerns meeting obligations laid upon persons due to a relationship they have entered. Thus, "Yahweh's righteousness is fulfillment of the demands of the relationship which exists between him and his people Israel, his fulfillment of the covenant which he has made with his chosen nation."[37] For this reason, the Lord's righteousness typically is expressed in terms of the divine faithfulness to the covenant with Israel. Yahweh is righteous in that he lives up to the terms of the agreement. Not surprisingly then, God's righteousness is often manifested in his saving of Israel in times of distress, for such protection is part of the divine covenant agreement.[38]

An eighth core moral character-trait of God is justice (*mišpāt*). God is just and desires justice be done (Pss 33:5; 37:28; 97:2; 99:4). Related to justice is that Yahweh shows no partiality (regarding wealth or class status) and demands that judges do the same (Deut 10:17; 2 Chr 19:7). Thus, Lev 19:15 commands: "You shall not render an unjust judgment; you shall not be partial to the poor or defer to the great: with justice you shall judge your neighbor."

A ninth moral virtue of God is *holiness*. As noted above, Lev 19 commands the people of Israel to be holy, *for the Lord is holy*. As discussed in Chapter 3, the root meaning of "holy" is "to be separate," so that scriptural writers often used the concept of holiness to capture God's utter distinctiveness from the created order and from human beings. There is no god like the God of Israel. Yahweh is unlike any other reality; all else depends on God, and nothing fully measures up to the divine grandeur. At least three implications flow form Yahweh's holy grandeur. First, God is good and demands that humans be righteous as well. As noted above, implicit in the divine command to Israel to be holy is that God is good and expects goodness from human beings. Israel is to mimic God's goodness.

A second implication of Yahweh's holiness is that God is morally distinct from human beings. While humans often fall into and languish in their sin, God is far removed from this shortcoming. For this reason, God's holiness evokes praise, for unlike humanity the Lord is morally worthy. This worthiness is contrasted with the unworthiness of sinful humans. In a classic description of encountering Yahweh, the prophet Isaiah envisions the Lord seated upon a throne in the temple, surrounded by seraphim who cry out: "Holy, holy, holy is the LORD of hosts; the whole earth is full of his glory." Upon experiencing this vision, Isaiah cries out, "Woe me! I am lost, for I am a man of unclean lips, and I live among a people of unclean lips; yet my eyes have seen the King, the LORD of hosts!" (Isa 6:3–5). Cognizance of Yahweh's glory results in Isaiah's awareness

---

37. Achtemeier, "Righteousness in the OT," 82.

38. Von Rad, *Old Testament Theology*, 1:372. Often "righteousness" is used as a synonym for "salvation" or "deliverance." See Isa 51:5; Mic 6:5,

of his own moral unworthiness and of the uncleanness of his people. Divine holiness is tied to God's moral worthiness and purity (see Ps 99:9; Rev 5:6–13).

A third implication of God's holiness is that ultimately, God cannot tolerate evil. Thus, Exod 34:6–7, which affirms the divine virtues of mercy, grace, patience, steadfast love, and faithfulness, also declares that the Lord in no way clears the guilty but instead visits "the iniquity of the parents upon the children and the children's children, to the third and the fourth generation" (v. 7). Exod 32 depicts Yahweh saying to Moses, after the Israelites sinned: "I have seen this people, how stiff-necked they are. Now let me alone, so that my *wrath* may burn hot against them and I may consume them; and of you I will make a great nation" (vv. 9–10; italics added). Deut 29 warns:

> It may be that there is among you a man or woman, or a family or tribe, whose heart is already turning away from the LORD our God to serve the gods of those nations. It may be that there is among you a root sprouting poisonous and bitter growth. All who hear the words of this oath and bless themselves, thinking in their hearts, "We are safe even though we go our own stubborn ways . . . [But] the LORD will be unwilling to pardon them, for the LORD's *anger and passion will smoke against them*. All the curses written in this book will descend on them, and the LORD will blot out their names from under heaven . . . [Indeed] all the nations will wonder, "Why has the LORD done thus to this land? What caused this great display of anger?" They will conclude, "It is because they abandoned the covenant of the LORD, the God of their ancestors, which he made with them when he brought them out of the land of Egypt. They turned and served other gods, worshiping them . . . , so the anger of the LORD was kindled against that land, bringing on it every curse written in this book. The LORD uprooted them from their land in anger, fury, and great wrath, and cast them into another land, as is now the case (vv. 18–28; italics added).

Although Yahweh is merciful, gracious, slow to anger, and abounding in love, the Lord also punishes sin. God does not tolerate evil indefinitely.[39]

Not surprisingly, as a close examination of the passages above (and others) shows, typically in the Hebrew Scriptures divine moral *acts* are associated with Yahweh's moral *virtues*. Because of Yahweh's love (*ahabah*), he is faithful to the covenant with Israel (Jer 31:2). Because of God's steadfast love (*chesed*), he forgives iniquity,

---

39. It is not uncommon for the divine moral virtues mentioned in the section above to be listed together in the Hebrew scriptures, perhaps as litanies or confessions. Isa 5:16 declares: "But the LORD of hosts is exalted by *justice*, / and the Holy God shows himself *holy* by *righteousness*." Ps 33:4–5 proclaims: "The word of the LORD is *upright*, / and all his work is done in *faithfulness*. / He loves *righteousness* and *justice*; / the earth is full of the *steadfast love* of the LORD." Jer 9:23–24 records "Thus says the LORD: Do not let the wise boast in their wisdom, do not let the mighty boast in their might, do not let the wealthy boast in their wealth; but let those who boast boast in this, that they understand and know me, that I am the LORD; I act with *steadfast love*, *justice*, and *righteousness* in the earth, for in these things I delight, says the LORD."

transgression, and sin (Exod 34:7). Because the Lord is just, he is impartial in judgments (Deut 10:17–18).

Many of the virtues and actions ascribed to God in the Old Testament are likewise attributed to God in the New Testament. And like the Hebrew biblical tradition, the New Testament often ties God's moral action to the divine moral nature. As in the Old Testament, so in the New, God is depicted as merciful,[40] gracious,[41] slow to anger (1 Pet 3:20; 2 Pet 3:9), steadfast in love,[42] faithful,[43] righteous,[44] just and impartial (Acts 10:34–35; Rom 3:5–6; 9:14), holy,[45] and as one who (ultimately) punishes sin (Matt 11:22–24; Rom 2:2, 5; 13:2; 14:10; 2 Thess 1:5). In turn, because God has these character traits, God acts accordingly: God performs merciful, loving, faithful, just acts. Obviously, the New Testament nuances many of these ascriptions to God in light of the early Christian experience of Jesus as Christ. One of the more distinctive New Testament contributions to ethics is its emphasis on divine love. The most common New Testament word for God's love is *agapē*.[46] This was a kind of unconditional and universal love. In the New Testament, *agapē* is a defining moral virtue of God. In turn, Jesus serves as the exemplar of what God is like, including what God's love is like.

Obviously, as is the case in the Old Testament, the New Testament makes plain that God's moral character is demonstrated in his righteous *actions*. Thus, God's love is shown in the sending and giving of Christ as a sacrifice for sin (John 3:16; 1 John 4:10). God's mercy is demonstrated by his granting salvation to sinners (Rom 5:8) and to Gentiles and Jews alike (Rom 11:25–32). God's grace, likewise, is manifested in drawing persons to salvation in Christ (Acts 11:19–23; Rom 3:21–25). Similar comments abound regarding the nature and actions of Christ. Christ is good, and Christ does good, and these righteous actions flow from his nature.

Here it is critical to reiterate the point made in the previous section—namely, that followers of God (indeed all people) are to be and to act like God. For Christians, this means, being and acting like Jesus. This principle is enunciated in several New Testament passages. In John 13:34, Jesus says, "A new commandment I give to you, that you love one another; *even as I have loved you*." In Philippians, Paul encourages his readers:

> Let the same mind be in you that was in Christ Jesus, who, though he was in the
> form of God, did not regard equality with God as something to be exploited,

40. God is depicted as merciful (Luke 6:36; Rom 11:32; Jas 5:11). Christians are to be merciful (Matt 5:7; 9:13; 18:33; Luke 10:37; Jas 2:13).

41. Acts 11:23; 20:24; Rom 3:24; 5:15; 1 Cor 1:4; Eph 2:8–9; grace of Christ: Acts 15:11; Rom 16:20.

42. See comments on *agape* above.

43. God is depicted as faithful (Rom 3:3; 1 Cor 1:9; 10:13; 2 Cor 1:18; 2 Thess 3:3).

44. God is depicted as righteous (Matt 6:33; Rom 1:17; 3:21–22, 25; 2 Cor 5.2:21).

45. God is depicted as holy (Luke 1:49). Note especially these references to the Holy Spirit: Matt 1:8; Mark 3:29; Luke 3:16, 22; John 14:26; Acts 1:2.

46. For example, see John 3:16, 1 Cor 13, and 2 Cor 5:14–15.

but emptied himself, taking the form of a slave, being born in human likeness. And being found in human form, he humbled himself and became obedient to the point of death—even death on a cross. (2:3–8)

Just as Christ was humble, obedient, and loving, so the Philippian believers were to be (Phil 2:1–3). In a similar manner, Paul says to Christians in Corinth, "Be imitators of me, as I am of Christ" (1 Cor 11:1). Eph 5:1–2 captures the dual call to Christians to be both like God and like Christ: "Therefore be imitators of God, as beloved children, and live in love, as Christ loved us and gave himself up for us, a fragrant offering and sacrifice to God." And again, in Matt 5:14, Jesus summarizes many of his moral teachings by saying, "Be perfect, therefore, as your heavenly Father is perfect."

Biblical Moral Precepts: Obedience and The Law of God

An important theme in the biblical narrative is obedience to divine law. God has laid down core regulations regarding how the covenant people are to act, as well as about the kind of persons they are to be. The story of the garden of Eden sets the tone for this emphasis on divine law by depicting Yahweh as commanding the first humans not to eat the fruit of the tree of the knowledge of good and evil, for in doing so they will die (Gen 2–3). Whatever the precise meaning of this symbolism is, entailed in the narrative is the notion of God as lawgiver. This idea is reinforced and clarified throughout the Hebrew Bible. In Exod 19 and 20, the Lord lays down the core covenant obligations expected of Israel. These include the Ten Commandments as well as other regulations. And the remainder of the Torah (Exodus through Deuteronomy) articulates a host of other rules imposed upon Israel. Often these laws are seen as expansion on and implications of the basic laws of the covenant.[47] The Israelites did not see these demands of Yahweh as arbitrary. Rather, like God, these commands themselves were deemed righteous (Ps 19:7–9).

In turn, Yahweh's righteous stipulations were not burdensome but life-giving. They enlivened individuals as well as expressed how Israel might live corporately as the people of God. Further, Israel's laws were not exclusively moral in nature. Many precepts involved regulations about correct worship and about how to come properly before Yahweh. Thus, the first four of the Ten Commandments address how properly to relate to God (Exod 20:1–11; Deut 5:6–15), while the last six address how to interact with other humans—especially with the covenant community (Exod 20:12–17; Deut 5:16–21). In a similar manner, the mandates in Lev 19 address both social and religious responsibilities.

The divine laws vary in the precision of their demands. Some commands offer exhortations regarding what kind of person to be or how one ought generally to behave.

47. As Elizabeth Achtemeier notes, to be righteous in the covenant relationship "Israel had to fulfill the demands of her relationship with Yahweh, and this included obedience to the law of the Lord" (Achtemeier, Righteousness in the OT," 81–82).

Appeals to God's character traits often evoke such broad demands. Israel was to be merciful, gracious, long-suffering, steadfast in love, faithful, loving, righteous, and so forth, for these are the characteristics of God. Such commands in themselves do not tell the hearer precisely what action to take, only to do those deeds that comport with the virtues in question.[48] In a similar manner, Jesus identifies as the two greatest divine commands the mandates to love God and to love others (Matt 22:34–40; Mark 12:28–34). Jesus' affirmation echoes core commands given respectively in Deuteronomy and Leviticus. Deut 6:4–5 declares: "Hear, O Israel: The LORD is our God, the LORD alone. You shall love the LORD your God with all your heart, and with all your soul, and with all your might." And Lev 19:18 commands: "You shall love your neighbor as yourself." Each of these passages identifies *ahabah* as the kind of love demanded by Yahweh.

While many biblical mandates are general in nature, some are more precise. Examples include the following commands from Exod 22:

> When someone steals an ox or a sheep, and slaughters it or sells it, the thief shall pay five oxen for an ox, and four sheep for a sheep. The thief shall make restitution, but if unable to do so, shall be sold for the theft. When the animal, whether ox or donkey or sheep, is found alive in the thief's possession, the thief shall pay double. If a thief is found breaking in, and is beaten to death, no bloodguilt is incurred; but if it happens after sunrise, bloodguilt is incurred. When someone causes a field or vineyard to be grazed over, or lets livestock loose to graze in someone else's field, restitution shall be made from the best in the owner's field or vineyard. When fire breaks out and catches in thorns so that the stacked grain or the standing grain or the field is consumed, the one who started the fire shall make full restitution. (Exod 22:1–6)

The biblical law contains both broad moral precepts and minutely detailed moral injunctions.

Old Testament Ethics

But what are the main moral principles and norms expressed in the divine law? As we have seen, at the core of the Old Testament ethic is affirmation of fundamental divine virtues. Among these virtues are mercifulness, grace, patience, steadfast covenant-love, faithfulness, righteousness, justice, and holiness—the last of which includes moral perfection and aversion toward (even intolerance of) evil. Often, Israel is called to possess these virtues and to act in harmony with them. In addition to appeals to various divine moral *virtues*, however, often the Hebrew tradition also articulates core moral *principles* and *rules* for the people of Israel to follow. As noted in Chapter 1, often the Hebrew biblical literature is divided into three main sections:

48. Often, however, concrete examples of what it means to exude such moral virtues are offered in the biblical text when calls to be like Yahweh are given. But obviously these examples do not exhaust what it means to display God's moral virtues.

the Torah, Prophets, and Writings. Various moral maxims are located in each of these sections of the Hebrew Bible.

Ethics of the Torah

We begin with the Torah. Scholars often identify three main sets of moral (and cultic) codes in the Torah tradition. These are the Covenant Code (Exod 20:22—23:33), the Holiness Code (Lev 17–26), and the Deuteronomic Code (Deut 12–26). The first of these is generally recognized as the earliest of the three. At the center of the Covenant Code (and of the biblical legal system in general) are the Ten Commandments. These state:

1. You shall have no other gods before me (Exod 20:3).

2. You shall not make for yourself an idol (Exod 20:4).

3. You shall not make wrongful use of the name of the Lord your God (Exod 20:7).

4. Remember the Sabbath Day, and keep it holy (Exod 20:8).

5. Honor your father and your mother (Exod 20:12).

6. You shall not murder (Exod 20:13).

7. You shall not commit adultery (Exod 20:14).

8. You shall not steal. (Exod 20:15).

9. You shall not bear false witness against your neighbor (Exod 20:16).

10. You shall not covet your neighbor's house; you shall not covet your neighbor's wife, or male or female slave, or ox, or donkey, or anything that belongs to your neighbor (Exod 20:17).

The first four commandments deal with Israel's relationship with Yahweh. The last six, on the other hand, deal with interrelations between human beings. The first command sets down the precept that only Yahweh is to be worshiped. The second forbids the making or worshiping of images of Yahweh or other deities. Two explanations are given for this mandate. Exod 20:5 explains that Yahweh is a jealous God and will not tolerate worship of other deities. Deuteronomy (likely written considerably later than Exodus) notes that Yahweh has no form, so it is inappropriate to depict Israel's God in a physical form (4:15–24). The third command calls for reverence for the Lord so that the faithful are not to use (literally "pick up") the divine name in a trifling way. While this command may entail not using the Lord's name in vulgar curses or profanity, its intent transcends this. Any trite use of God's name is prohibited. The fourth commandment calls for setting aside a day for worshiping Yahweh and for rest. Clearly for the Israelites, the seventh day was a day set aside (holy, separated out) for worshiping their God. But also, that day was to bring relief from the hard toils of life, so that Israel might rest from its labors. Exodus explains this day of rest in terms of the cosmic creation. Yahweh created in six days and then rested (20:11). So, Israel honors the splendor of God's creative power by resting weekly, on the seventh day. Deuteronomy, later, adds that God gave Israel a day of rest as a reminder of their redemption from slavery in Egypt (5:15). Thus, honoring the seventh day involves setting it aside both for worship and for rest.

The fifth mandate is to honor one's parents. Show them respect. This command seems especially concerned with preserving the people of Israel over time. They are a holy people whose welfare is in one another. Familial respect, including financial support in old age, is a cornerstone of a society's survival. The sixth command issues the demand not to murder. Often this text is translated "Do not kill," but its core intent was against murder. Israel's laws allowed for killing fellow humans in warfare and via capital punishment for egregious crimes. But the taking of innocent human life without just cause is forbidden. The seventh commandment denounces adultery and affirms the sacredness of marriage. Originally, the mandate was targeted especially against sexual relations with another man's wife. But over time, the Israelites' tradition prohibited sexual relations outside of marriage, including specifically marital infidelity, for both males and females (Lev 20:10). The eighth mandate is against stealing. Perhaps this command was initially especially a prohibition against kidnapping. But it soon entailed broader meaning. As Henlee Barnette remarks, implicit in forbidding theft is an affirmation of the right to private property. So, while Israel was a unified people, within that community individual ownership of assets was recognized and protected.[49] The ninth commandment forbids bearing false witness. This prohibition initially and especially concerned telling falsehoods in court. Such actions could bring unwarranted punishment upon defendants, as well as unfair settlements for plaintiffs with legitimate grievances. The principle entailed in this command, however, eventually was expanded to comprise avoidance of lying in general—including, keeping false records or inaccurate scales and making underhanded business deals. The final commandment is distinctive in its tone. While the other nine focus on commands against observable, outward, actions, this command prohibits an inner attitude—namely, covetousness (having an inordinate, compelling, desire for the possessions of others). While an explanation for this rule is not given, it is relatively clear that such a norm strikes at one of the core inner motives for human breaches of morality. Human desires for things not properly theirs often produce many illicit outward actions.

The Ten Commandments are examples of *apodictic* laws. These are commands stated in absolute form: "Do this! Don't do that!" Most ancient laws were expressed in *casuistic* (hypothetical) form: "If this happens, then the following should unfold." In addition to the Ten Commandments, the Covenant Code (Exod 20:22—23:33) includes several lesser rules, most in casuistic form. The quote above from Exod 22:1–6 exemplifies such decrees. To modern ears, many of these mandates are out-of-date,

49. Barnette, *Introducing Christian Ethics*, 23.

dealing with concerns such as livestock theft, obsolete farming techniques, and odd (even detestable) social structures (such as slavery, arranged marriages, and so forth). Acknowledging the datedness of many of these regulations, scholars nevertheless often recognize core ethical principles at work in many of these imperatives. There are prohibitions against theft, mandates for restitution of stolen property, protections against assault and slander, distinctions between intentional and accidental violations of law—including (effectively) differentiation between manslaughter and murder. Also, there are proscriptions against exploitation of the poor and the vulnerable, including against loansharking and against mistreating immigrants (Exod 21–23).

As Roger Crook notes, these laws reflect "a concern for persons and an interest in protecting the rights of individuals to life, to well-being, and to the ownership of property." They also give attention to "the protection of certain people who are often victimized in society: slaves, women, the poor, and orphans."[50] Many ethicists see active in these laws the affirmation of the principle of retributive justice—the notion that the punishment should fit the crime. This ideal is expressed in the famous line: "You shall give life for life, eye for eye, tooth for tooth, hand for hand, foot for foot, burn for burn, wound for wound, stripe for stripe" (Exod 21:23–25). Whereas this passage is sometimes taken to outline a particularly harsh vision of punishment, some scholars see in this principle an attempt to circumvent vengeance and punishments that might exceed the severity of the crime. Thus, this saying may have sought to emphasize *proportional* justice not *harsh* penalties.

The Holiness Code (Lev 17–26) is a second moral code in the Hebrew Bible. The Holiness Code is part of a larger piece of the Torah sometimes referred to as the Priestly Codes. This literature especially outlined principles laid down by Israel's priests in a twofold effort to guide the people in worshiping Yahweh and in remaining morally and religiously pure before God. As noted above, the root meaning of *holy* has to do with separation: the people of Israel were to be separate (distinct) from other people groups, as Yahweh was different from all other things and deities. The Israelites were to be a holy people, which included engaging both in proper worship practices and in appropriate moral behaviors. The Holiness Code manifests special concern for rites to keep Israel holy (separated from) its neighbors. Lev 19 and 20 capture many of the most germane moral principles of the Holiness Code. For example, Israelites were to honor their parents (19:3), not make idols (19:6), save portions of their harvests for the poor and for immigrants in their land (19:9–10), deal fairly with one another, speak truthfully (19:11–12) and not defraud one another in business transactions. They were to pay fair wages on time (19:13), render unbiased judgments in courts, and not steal (19:15). In a classic passage later emphasized by Jesus, the Israelites were instructed to love their neighbors (19:17–18) and foreigners in their land as they loved themselves (19:33–34). Interestingly, the Hebrew word for *love* in these passages, *ahabah*, is the same as the one employed to

50. Crook, *An Introduction to Christian Ethics*, 70.

speak of Yahweh's love for Israel (Deut 7:7) and of the love for God expected from Israel (Deut 6:5). The Levitical laws also prohibited child sacrifices (Lev 20:2) and forbade a variety of illicit sexual relations (20:10–21).

The third moral code of the Torah is the Deuteronomic Code (Deut 12–26). Many of the principles and precepts of the Covenant Code and Holiness Code are echoed in Deuteronomy, seemingly in updated forms, suggesting revisions based on differing social circumstances. Perhaps the most distinctive element of the Deuteronomic Code is its clear emphasis on love—on God's love for Israel and on Israel's call to love God. The Lord's love for Israel is demonstrated in divine saving acts; Israel's love for God is (ideally) an expression of gratitude to the Lord for his saving works.

Ethical Principles of the Prophets

In addition to the Torah, the prophetic tradition of the Hebrew Bible likewise features several important moral principles and ideals. The prophets were active during the long era of the divided kingdoms of Israel and Judah. According to the biblical narrative, during this period, Israel and Judah often slipped away from the ideals of the divine covenant, failing both to be faithful to Yahweh alone and to maintain personal and social righteousness. Many Israelites were tempted to follow other gods, often watering down their worship of Yahweh with practices associated with foreign deities. The people of God also often engaged in personal and social sins condemned by their covenant with the Lord. The prophets saw themselves as spokespersons for Yahweh, frequently introducing their messages with the phrase, "Thus, says the Lord." The prophets often called out for justice,[51] righteousness,[52] and love.[53] They called for fair business practices (Mal 3:5), fidelity in marriage (Jer 7:9–10; Mal 2:14–16; 3:5) temperance in lifestyle (Isa 3:18; Amos 6:1–14), and compassion for the poor. They renounced exploitation of the weak, the vulnerable, and foreigner (Isa 5:8; Amos 8:4–6). They cried against violence and hatred (Mic 3:1–3, 9). Often these spokespersons for God condemned what they perceived to be false piety based on an inappropriate sense of religious security—a piety that formally worshiped Yahweh but ignored the divine covenant. Amos cries out against the northern kingdom of Israel in the voice of Yahweh, saying,

> I hate, I despise your festivals,
>> and I take no delight in your solemn assemblies.
> Even though you offer me your burnt offerings and grain offerings,
>> I will not accept them;
> and the offerings of well-being of your fatted animals

---

51. Isa 1:17, 21, 27; 5:7, 16; 28:17; Jer 5:28; 21:12; 22:3; Amos 5:7, 15, 24; Mic 3:9; 6:8.
52. Isa 1:21, 26–27; 5:7, 26; 26:10; 42:26; Jer 22:3; 23:5; 31:23; Ezek 3:20; 18:21–24; Amos 5:24.
53. Isa 56:5–7; Hos 6:6; 10:12; 12:6; Amos 5:15; Mic 6:8; Zech 8:19.

> I will not look upon.
>
> Take away from me the noise of your songs;
>
> > I will not listen to the melody of your harps.
>
> But let justice roll down like waters,
>
> > and righteousness like an ever-flowing stream. (Amos 5:21–24)

Jeremiah, likewise, condemns the people of Judah and (especially) of Jerusalem for falsely believing that the Lord would protect them in spite of their failure to honor God or keep the divine moral prerogatives. Jeremiah proclaims:

> Thus says the LORD of hosts, the God of Israel: Amend your ways and your doings, and let me dwell with you in this place. Do not trust in these deceptive words: "This is the temple of the LORD, the temple of the LORD, the temple of the LORD." For if you truly amend your ways and your doings, if you truly act justly one with another, if you do not oppress the alien, the orphan, and the widow, or shed innocent blood in this place, and if you do not go after other gods to your own hurt, then I will dwell with you in this place, in the land that I gave of old to your ancestors forever and ever. Here you are, trusting in deceptive words to no avail. Will you steal, murder, commit adultery, swear falsely, make offerings to Baal, and go after other gods that you have not known, and then come and stand before me in this house, which is called by my name, and say, "We are safe!"—only to go on doing all these abominations? Has this house, which is called by my name, become a den of robbers in your sight ? (Jer 7:3–11)

As the passage above demonstrates, most of the ethical insights of the prophets flow from the core morality of the Torah covenant tradition. Above, Jeremiah essentially lists Judah's violations of the Ten Commandments.

During the era of the prophets, a significant shift of psyche began to unfold. This involved a growing awareness of the individual's value and responsibility before Yahweh. Both the literature of the Torah and of the Deuteronomistic Historians tended to emphasize the importance of the community of Israel as a whole and expressed less concern for individuals. The sins of the one were projected upon the whole community, and often the whole people were judged for the sins of some. Thus, in the book of Joshua, all of Israel is condemned for Achan's breach of the Lord's *cherem* upon Jericho (Josh 7).[54] And all of Judah fell to the Babylonians under God's judgment, even though some, presumably, were faithful to Yahweh. Scholars sometimes speak of corporate personality and corporate responsibility to capture this perspective. Although

---

54. Although it should be noted that Yahweh's wrath against the whole is appeased by the punishment of the individual (and his family). The word *cherem* has various and often uncertain meanings in the Hebrew biblical literature. One common meaning is that some action or object is banned or proscribed by God. Another related meaning is that some action or object is devoted to destruction or devoted to God.

individuals were important and were held accountable for their own sins, often in the early literature of the Hebrew Bible emphasis fell upon the value and responsibility of the people as a whole. And, in a sense, the individual person was subsumed into the personality of the whole community. But with the fall of Jerusalem at the hands of the Babylonians in 598 and 586 BCE, some prophets began to emphasize the culpability of individuals for their own sins and stressed less the notion of corporate responsibility. This is observed in the works of Jeremiah:

> The days are surely coming, says the LORD, when I will sow the house of Israel and the house of Judah with the seed of humans and the seed of animals. And just as I have watched over them to pluck up and bring evil, so I will watch over them to build and to plant says the LORD. In those days they shall no longer say: "The parents have eaten sour grapes, and the children's teeth are set on edge." But all shall die for their own sins; the teeth of everyone who eats sour grapes shall be set on edge. (Jer 31:27–30)

A similar view is expressed by Ezekiel (See Ezek 18:1–32). The precise reason for these shifts from emphasis on corporate to personal responsibility is uncertain. The exile to Babylon likely undermined tribal and extended-familial connections, requiring Jewish individuals and smaller family units, more and more, to fend for themselves economically and religiously. There may also have been a growing theological and ethical puzzlement about the rightness of condemning one set of persons for the sins of others.[55]

Ethical Principles of the Writings

These shifts from accenting corporate to emphasizing individual responsibility provide a bridge to the ethics of the *wisdom literature* of the Old Testament, for in these materials one also sees individual moral actions and responsibility stressed. Also like the Prophets, the Writings typically echo many of the moral and religious precepts enunciated in the Torah. For instance, Ps 1 declares that the wicked ultimately falter before the judgment of Yahweh, while the righteous prosper and are happy. Ps 112 praises those who are "gracious, merciful, and righteous" (v. 4), and who are generous, just, and freely give of their wealth to the poor (vv. 5, 9). Ps 15 commends those who "walk blamelessly," do what is right, and speak truthfully (v. 2), lend freely (5), and do not slander or bring harm to others (v. 3). Ps 119 honors those who are blameless, obey God's law, seek the Lord wholeheartedly (vv. 1–2), and "do no wrong" (v. 3).

The book of Proverbs echoes many of these moral insights of the Psalms. For these writers, "The fear of the LORD is the beginning of knowledge" (1:7). In the opening chapters of Proverbs, wisdom is personified as a virtuous woman whose teachings

---

55. Likely, a number of factors contributed to the emerging emphasis upon individual responsibility. See Barnette's comments in Barnette, *Introducing Christian Ethics*, 32–33.

bring life. A core element of wisdom's message is that the wise person heeds Yahweh's commands and thus is virtuous and does what is right. The Lord gives wisdom so that persons might be blameless, faithful, just, and righteous (2:6–9). Thus, the wise course is to "trust in the LORD with all your heart, / and do not rely on your own insight. / In all your ways acknowledge him, / and he will make straight your paths" (3:5–6). Many of the virtues and sins identified in the Torah and Prophets are reiterated here. Among those attitudes and actions denounced are quarrelsomeness (3:30), violence (3:31), haughtiness, lying, murder, bearing false testimonies, and sowing discord (6:17–19). Adultery is often condemned as particularly disruptive to one's life and community (6:23–35). Exploitation of workers and of the poor is condemned, as are deceptive and untoward business practices (11:1; 20:14; 22:16). On the other hand, employees are encouraged to work hard and earnestly for their employers (6:6–8; 10:26). Often in Proverbs, good and evil are described as flowing from the inner person, so that comparisons are made between those who are righteous, faithful, and blameless, and those who are wicked, crooked, and perverse (10:6–11). In a verse echoing the Torah's call to love God and others, and anticipating Jesus' similar affirmation, Prov 10:12 asserts: "Hatred stirs up strife, but love covers offenses."

At times the books of Proverbs and Psalms (as well as the Deuteronomistic Historian) leave the impression that the wicked always suffer and the righteous always prevail in this life (see Prov 11:17, 19). But some of the psalms challenge this notion. And the books of Job and Ecclesiastes especially question this claim. Ps 10 puzzles over the prosperity of the unrighteous. There, the speaker laments the deeds of the wicked, who often are boastful, greedy, filled with deceit, and who even deny God's existence (vv. 3–4, 7). These evil ones often persecute the poor (v. 2), scheming against them and seeking to take their meager properties (vv. 2, 9). Also, the wicked often are violent, even murderous (vv. 8, 10). Against such evil the psalmist pleads for divine aid and puzzles over the Lord's inactivity toward them. Finally, the psalmist expresses hope and belief that ultimately Yahweh will vindicate the righteous and the downtrodden (vv. 17–18).

The book of Job wrestles with the suffering of the righteous. The author seems to reject the notion that the righteous always prosper and the wicked always ultimately falter in this life. The protagonist, Job, seemingly is blameless and upright yet suffers greatly. The book of Job also ponders human motives for serving Yahweh. Do the Lord's people (including Job) obey God only for the blessings provided, and what happens when blessings no longer prevail? The book of Job responds that earnest obedience to God is not motivated by hope for divine blessing. In the process of struggling with these issues, the story of Job yields some insights about the righteous life. Job 31 especially articulates the kind of life Job himself lived as a righteous person. The righteous individual avoids adultery and sexual lust outside of marriage. Such a person is truthful, just to servants, generous to the poor and to the vulnerable, temperate with wealth, faithful in worshiping only Yahweh, and not gleeful when harm comes to an enemy.

New Testament Ethics

The Hebrew Bible offers many insights about morality and promotes several core ethical precepts. The same is true of the New Testament. At the center of the New Testament is the story of Jesus; in that narrative one finds several fundamental moral principles. Jesus often is depicted as a grand teacher, and at the core of his teaching is proclamation of the coming kingdom of God. This kingdom involves God's reign in the lives of individuals as well as ultimate divine rule throughout the world. A central element of the God's reign is the formation of a people, a community, mutually committed to God and to one another in love and faithfulness.

The Ethics of Jesus

According to the New Testament testimony, Jesus affirmed many of the fundamental moral principles of the Hebrew Bible, often shaping them with his own emphases. Like the Old Testament tradition, Jesus saw a close connection between theology and ethics. Morality is grounded in the nature of God, so that Christ's followers were to be perfect as God the Father is perfect (Matt 5:48; compare 1 Pet 1:15–16). Jesus also endorsed the essential assumption of the Hebrew biblical tradition that one should *obey* God, for Yahweh has given humans (especially the covenant people) life-giving moral principles by which to live. In turn, Jesus affirmed the basic precepts of the Ten Commandments (See Matt 19:16–20). He taught against murder (Matt 5:21–22), adultery (Matt 5:27–28), theft (Matt 19:18), and lying (Matt 5:33–37). He called for honoring parents (Mark 7:9–13). He presumed worship of Yahweh alone and personally kept the Sabbath (Luke 4:16). And there is no hint that Jesus in any way sanctioned the making or venerating of idols. Jesus also called for compassion for the poor, the downtrodden, and the vulnerable (Matt 19:16–26; Luke 4:18; 14:13; 16:19–31). All these principles are at the center of the Jewish religious ethic.

But Jesus often added his own nuances to these precepts. First, Jesus stressed the inner motives of persons. Murder begins with inordinate anger toward another (Matt 5:21–22). Adultery arises from inappropriate lust for someone (Matt 5:27–28). Ultimately, evil flows from our inner selves (Matt 7:15–20). Second, Jesus emphasized the value of individuals. This is not to say that Jesus disowned the importance of community or the value of life together. But Jesus also celebrated the value of each person. He taught that each self is more valuable than the world (Matt 12:12; Mark 8:36). He claimed that the Sabbath is made for humans, not humans for the Sabbath (Mark 2:27). He showed forgiving-compassion toward a woman accused of adultery (John 8:3–11). He encouraged his followers not to worry, for God values all creatures and cherishes humans even more (Matt 6:25–30). Third, Jesus stressed the importance of servanthood, teaching his disciples that if someone wants to be first, he or she must be last, becoming a servant to all (Mark 9:35). Indeed, Jesus himself practiced servanthood toward others (Mark 10:45). Fourth, as Barnette puts it, Jesus "manifested a genuine contempt for mere negative goodness."[56] People should proactively initiate good actions toward others. This is a core meaning of Jesus' saying, "Do to others as you would have them do to you" (Luke 6:31). Again, for Jesus, right behavior flows from one's own being; it is not merely a response to evade unwanted consequences or to avoid breaching a moral (divine) command. Doing good results from who one is good.

Finally, Jesus also stressed love as the deepest motive for doing what is right—love for God and love for others. Jesus states:

> You shall love the Lord your God with all your heart, and with all your soul, and with all your mind." This is the greatest and first commandment. And a second is like it: "You shall love your neighbor as yourself." On these two commandments hang all the law and the prophets. (Matt 22:37–40).

Jesus insisted that such love for one's "neighbor" applies to all persons, even those outside the Jewish community. Thus, when a scribe asked him, who is my neighbor? Jesus told a parable of a good Samaritan who shows mercy to a distressed Jewish traveler (Luke 10:25–37). Part of the point of the story was to show that the Samaritans (who often were despised by first-century Jews) likewise were neighbors. In a similar manner, Jesus countermanded what seems to have been a common notion: that a person should love his or her neighbor but hate his or her enemies. Instead, Jesus asserted, "Love your enemies and pray for those who persecute you" (Matt 5:44).[57]

With his emphasis on love, Jesus nuanced the Old Testament notion of obeying God. For Jesus, obedience to Yahweh is still a fundamental principle of morality. But he recognized and taught that earnest love for God and for fellows generates an ethic that transcends the requirements of God's law as it was understood by some of his contemporaries. Love calls for inner change, which also augments how one understands the requirements of the written law. Thus, Jesus said, "Do not think that I have come to abolish the law or the prophets; I have come not to abolish but to fulfill" (Matt 5:17). But Jesus also added to this: "Unless your righteousness exceeds that of the scribes and Pharisees, you will never enter the kingdom of heaven" (Matt 5:20). Jesus saw his teachings as endorsing the Old Testament moral precepts but also transcending how these principles were sometimes understood. In light of this conception

---

56. Barnette, *Introducing Christian Ethics*, 45.

57. As we have seen, the Hebrew biblical tradition also affirmed love as a central motive for obeying God and for doing right toward others. In some ways, then, Jesus was simply drawing from these scriptural insights. Nevertheless, most commentators agree that Jesus expanded and nuanced these principles in ways not fully manifested in the older traditions.

of Jesus' project, contemporary ethicist Roger Crook insists that Jesus' central moral imperative was "obedient love."[58]

Many of Jesus' core ethical teachings are found in Matt 5:1—7:29, in what often is called the Sermon on the Mount. There, Jesus begins by naming eight core character traits of those who follow his teachings. He claims that those who have these virtues are blessed; thus, this list often is called the Beatitudes. The basic idea is that those who exude these character traits are happy or fulfilled. The first virtue is *poorness of spirit*. Jesus said, "Blessed are the poor in spirit, for theirs is the kingdom of heaven" (Matt 5:3). ("Kingdom of heaven" is used by Matthew as a synonym for kingdom of God.) Thus, Jesus claims that the poor in spirit receive the kingdom of God. The phrase *poor in spirit* likely refers to those who are "spiritually humble,"[59] who are aware of their "spiritual bankruptcy before God" and of their utter dependence upon God's grace and aid.[60] Such poorness of spirit was demonstrated in Jesus' parable of the tax collector who prays fully acknowledging his unworthiness before God and his need for divine mercy (Luke 10:10–14). Such persons, claims Jesus, will participate in the very kingdom of God.

The second virtue extolled by Jesus in the Sermon on the Mount is *mournfulness*. Matt 5:4 states, "Blessed are those who mourn, for they will be comforted." The notion of mourning here references sorrow in general, not just anguish due to the death of a friend or loved one. Jesus did not explain what kind of sorrow or what kind of mourners he means. However, he may especially have had in mind those who sorrow over sin—their own sin and the evil of the world in general.[61] The third blessed trait Jesus mentions is *meekness*: "Blessed are the meek, for they will inherit the earth" (Matt 5:5). The terms *meek* and *meekness* do not describe persons who are weak or groveling. Meek persons are those who are submissive to God, those who are willing to obey God and accept divine discipline.[62] The quality of meekness may also characterize those who are nonviolent and humble, who surrender to the God of peace.[63] These persons—says Jesus—will inherit the earth. A fourth blessed virtue is that of *yearning for righteousness*. Matt 5:6 says, "Blessed are those who hunger and thirst for righteousness, for they will be filled." As noted above, in the Old Testament literature, righteousness especially involves meeting the demands of God's covenant, including faithfulness to covenant promises. Yahweh's own righteousness is often associated with the divine saving actions toward Israel—God's rescuing Israel from

---

58. Crook, *An Introduction to Christian Ethics*, 81.

59. Stassen and Gushee, *Kingdom Ethics*, 38.

60. Barnette, *Introducing Christian Ethics*, 52.

61. Stassen and Gushee, *Kingdom Ethics*, 39–40. See Amos 4:1–5 for its indictment against those who do not mourn over evil. Also see Isa 25:7–8 and Rev 21:4, where hope for an end to both death and mourning is anticipated.

62. Barnette, *Introducing Christian Ethics*, 52.

63. Stassen and Gushee, *Kingdom Ethics*, 40–41.

political bondage, oppression, unfair treatment, and the like. Often this divine righteousness is displayed *in spite of* Israel's unfaithfulness (unrighteousness) toward the covenant. With this background in mind, Jesus teaches that those who yearn for such covenant-righteousness will receive it. Such yearning may be synonymous with desiring the reality and benefits of God's righteousness; but more than likely Jesus here offers a blessing for those with a burning hunger for their own righteousness and for the fruits of divine righteousness in this world—including a calling to care for the oppressed and vulnerable.

A fifth core Christian moral characteristic is *mercifulness*. "Blessed are the merciful, for they will receive mercy" (Matt 5:7). As we have seen, mercy is one of the core moral virtues ascribed to Yahweh in the Hebrew Bible. No wonder then that Jesus sees this trait as critical to the Christian life. In a similar vein, in the Sermon on the Mount, Jesus teaches his disciples to forgive, warning them if they refuse to forgive, God will not forgive them (Matt 6:12–15). Other parables as well speak of the irony of persons who hope for mercy from God but are unwilling to show mercy themselves (Matt 18:23–35). Jesus, in turn, is understood to have shown the deepest mercy in his death on the cross for sinners (Luke 23:34). A sixth blessed virtue is *purity of heart*: "Blessed are the pure in heart, for they will see God" (Matt 5:8). Jer 17:9 famously says, "The heart is deceitful above all things and beyond cure. Who can understand it?" In the Sermon on the Mount, Jesus claims that those of an unalloyed commitment to God will see, dwell with, God. Here one might question whether anyone truly has a pure heart, a heart set fully and unabashedly upon love for and service to God. Indeed, Jesus spent much effort warning followers and detractors alike that good actions flow from the heart, so that it is not enough simply to do good deeds but to do them from the overflow of one's own internal commitments—e.g., from purity of heart (Matt 7:15–20). The apostle Paul likewise directly challenges the notion of an utterly pure heart but goes on to relay the promise that such can be given through the indwelling of God's Spirit (Rom 7–8).

A seventh core virtue is *peacemaking*. Matt 5:9 states: "Blessed are the peacemakers, for they will be called children of God." The virtuous person seeks peace. This may include the individual's acceptance of God's peace offering in Christ. It also may entail drawing others to a right relationship with God. But almost certainly Jesus also had in mind those who seek to bring peace to the world. God is said to be the God of peace (Rom 15:33; 16:20; Phil 4:9). Jesus likewise sought to bring peace (Luke 2:14; 19:38; Rom 5:1). And Jesus here calls his disciples, too, to engage in making peace. For him, to do so is to be recognized as the children of God.

An eighth blessed moral virtue is that of *being persecuted for the sake of righteousness*. In a remarkable reversal of common assumptions, Jesus says that blessedness befalls those who suffer for the sake of righteousness. In Matt 5:10–12 Jesus declares: "Blessed are those who are persecuted for righteousness' sake, for theirs is the kingdom of heaven. Blessed are you when people revile you and persecute you and utter all kinds of evil against you falsely on my account. Rejoice and be glad, for your reward is great in heaven, for in the same way they persecuted the prophets who were before you." Almost certainly, Matthew includes these words of Jesus to comfort his first-century community, who likely faced persecution at the hands of those opposed to the way of Jesus. Jesus here likewise encourages Christians that suffering for the sake of righteousness (which also usually means suffering at the hands of those opposed to righteousness) brings divine, heavenly reward. This is not suffering for suffering's sake. Nor is it suffering so that one might be rewarded. Rather, it is pains endured *for the sake of righteousness*. Suffering for righteousness here likely means simply doing so for the sake of good or for the sake of God's (and Christ's) cause.

In addition to promoting these eight character traits, Jesus's Sermon on the Mount also highlights important principles of *moral behavior*. In a series of sayings, Jesus compares and contrasts his moral precepts with some commonly assumed by his hearers. For example, in Matt 5:21–22a, Jesus comments: "You have heard that it was said to those of ancient times, 'You shall not murder'; and 'whoever murders shall be liable to judgment.' But I say to you that if you are angry with a brother or sister, you will be liable to judgment." Again, Jesus says: "You have heard that it was said, 'You shall not commit adultery.' But I say to you that everyone who looks at a woman with lust has already committed adultery with her in his heart" (5:27–28). Jesus also teaches:

> You have heard that it was said, 'An eye for an eye and a tooth for a tooth.' But I say to you, Do not resist an evildoer. But if anyone strikes you on the right cheek, turn the other also; and if anyone wants to sue you and take your coat, give your cloak as well; and if anyone forces you to go one mile, go also the second mile. Give to everyone who begs from you, and do not refuse anyone who wants to borrow from you. (5:38–42)

And further, Jesus states: "You have heard that it was said, 'You shall love your neighbor and hate your enemy.' But I say to you, Love your enemies and pray for those who persecute you" (5:43–44).

In these proposals one sees several trends of Jesus' moral disposition. The first two precepts point toward Jesus' tendency to emphasize inner motives for evil actions and not just outward behaviors. The third and fourth directives demonstrate Jesus' inclination to avoid acts of vengeance and to look for ways to challenge, even redeem, moral abuses. Rather than offer retributive justice or hate for one's enemies, Jesus calls for surprising acts of goodness toward perpetrators of injustice. Glen Stassen and David Gushee refer to these proposals as *transformative initiatives*. These actions (proposed by Jesus) are designed to transform the person who is harmed "into an active peacemaker," altering the circumstance from a moment of conflict and anger to a peacemaking process that can help to transform an "enemy into a friend."[64] A final trend observed in all four of these (and other) moral mandates of Jesus is the inclination

64. Stassen and Gushee, *Kingdom Ethics*, 135.

to value even the perpetrators of wrongdoing. Anger, lust, revenge, and hatred all tend to dehumanize persons, turning them into objects of contempt or of pleasure rather than recognizing them as potential members of God's family and kingdom. Perhaps no parable of Jesus depicts God's love for wrongdoers (and enemies) more than the story of the prodigal son. There a loving father gladly receives back into the family a repentant son who had dishonored him. Indeed, the father's love compels him to rejoice at his wayward son's return (Luke 15:11–32).

The Ethics of Paul

Much more could be said of Jesus' ethics. But let us move on to briefly describe the ethics of the apostle Paul. Paul offered ethical ideals similar to Jesus'. He emphasized love for and obedience to God and love for one's neighbor. Like Jesus, Paul saw the core of the Old Testament law summarized in the commands to love God and others (Rom 13:8–10; Gal 5:13–14). Paul writes: "The commandments, 'You shall not commit adultery; You shall not murder; You shall not steal; You shall not covet'; and any other commandment, are summed up in this word, 'Love your neighbor as yourself.' Love does no wrong to a neighbor; therefore, love is the fulfilling of the law" (Rom 13:9–10). Paul also taught that morality comes from within through the aid of God's Spirit. Paul led and followed the growing Christian consensus of his day that righteousness cannot come from obeying the Old Testament laws, but primarily through faith in Jesus Christ and through loving obedience to him empowered by the Holy Spirit. Paul notes:

> For those who live according to the flesh set their minds on the things of the flesh, but those who live according to the Spirit set their minds on the things of the Spirit. To set the mind on the flesh is death, but to set the mind on the Spirit is life and peace. For this reason the mind that is set on the flesh is hostile to God; it does not submit to God's law—indeed it cannot, and those who are in the flesh cannot please God. But you are not in the flesh; you are in the Spirit, since the Spirit of God dwells in you. (Rom 8:5–9)[65]

Paul saw the Christian life exemplified in several key virtues. In one place he names these virtues "the fruit of the Spirit," noting that "the fruit of the Spirit is love, joy, peace, patience, kindness, generosity, faithfulness, gentleness, and self-control. There is no law against such things" (Gal 5:22–23). The crowning Christian virtue, for Paul, was love (see 1 Cor 13).

---

65. Paul use of the term "flesh" needs some explanation. Most biblical scholars agree that the apostle does not use the term to speak primarily of sensual temptations, ones based on physical desires. Rather, Paul seems to use the concept to speak of the general human tendency toward sin. For this reason, a possible translation of Paul's of technical use of this word might be "carnal attitude" (see J. B. Phillips's New Testament [PHILLIPS]) or "sinful selves" (see *New Century Version* [NCV]).

As Paul ministered to various churches, he found it necessary to go beyond emphasizing merely the principles of love and loving obedience to God. At times, he listed sets of sins that Christians were to avoid, sins that often his congregations (and the communities around them) struggled with. Among those listed by Paul are these: envy, murder, strife, deceit, malice, gossip, slander, God-hating, insolence, arrogance, boastfulness (Rom 1:29–31), sexual immorality, impurity, debauchery, idolatry, witchcraft, hatred, discord, jealousy, fits of rage, selfish ambition, dissensions, factions, drunkenness, orgies, and the like (Gal 5:19–21).

New Testament Ethical Trends

Ideas similar to Jesus' and Paul's are found throughout the New Testament. We may summarize the broad sweep of New Testament ethics with the following observations. First, New Testament writers agreed with the Hebrew biblical tradition that God is good, and thus the Lord possesses numerous core moral character traits, including mercy, grace, patience, faithfulness, justice, righteousness, and holiness. Above all, however, God is loving; indeed, in some sense, God is love (1 John 4:16). In light of the Lord's character traits, humans (especially followers of Christ) should exude similar virtues. The greatest of these virtues is love. With Jesus and Paul, as well as with the broad Old Testament tradition, various writers of the New Testament saw love for God and for fellow humans as the greatest commands and the highest virtues.

First-century Christians also assumed that persons should follow the basic precepts of the Ten Commandments, which (as we saw in Paul) flow from love. That is, one should

1. Only worship the one true God

2. Not make, honor, or worship idols

3. Honor God

4. Worship God regularly

5. Honor parents

6. Not murder

7. Not commit adultery

8. Not steal

9. Not bear false witness or lie

10. Not covet

Followers of Christ also should manifest personal righteousness and seek social justice (including by caring for the poor and oppressed). Further, Christians should avoid sexual immorality, thus not following the looser sexual restrictions of the broader Greco-Roman culture. All these moral principles were to be tempered by a righteous inner life and a loving spirit.

Conclusion

More could be said about the general features of ethics and of Christian ethics, including the moral principles of the Old and New Testaments. But the discussion above illuminates many of the core features of these topics. In the next two chapters, we examine some important models of Christian ethics that have arisen in church history.

9

Christian Ethics in the Classical, Medieval, and Reformation Eras

IN CHAPTER 8, WE discussed the general nature of ethical studies, including the broad contours of Christian ethics. We also examined the fundamental tenets of biblical moral thought. In Chapters 9 and 10, we explore several important ethical models (and emphases) that emerged in Christian history. In this ninth chapter, we discuss key Christian ethical perspectives that arose in the classical, medieval, and Reformation periods.

Around the close of the first century, as the first generation of followers of Jesus passed-away, those Christians who immediately followed them continued to ponder the implications of their faith for moral living. Often, these second- and third-generation disciples appealed to the ethical insights of the Hebrew Bible and to the growing library of early Christian literature.[1] In turn, as Christianity spread into the Roman world (and beyond), many believers drew from the intellectual fountains of their broader culture, especially from the musings of the great Greco-Roman philosophers. To the ethical theories of these key philosophers we turn first.

Classical Greco-Roman Ethics

Among the pagan philosophical perspectives that influenced Christian ethics were the views of Plato (428/427 or 424/423—348/347 BCE), Aristotle (384–322 BCE), Epicurus (341–270 BCE), and various Stoic writers.[2]

---

1. This literature, obviously, included what would gradually become known as the New Testament.

2. For good summaries of these ethical perspectives, see Denise et al., eds., *Great Traditions in Ethics*. Other helpful sources are Jones, *The Classical Mind*; Grenz, *The Moral Quest*, 59–94, and Wogaman, *Christian Ethics*, 17–26.

Plato's Ethics

Like many Greek philosophers, a central question for Plato was, what is the good life? Plato's thesis was that the best life is one ruled by reason. Plato was convinced that heeding the dictates of reason would produce a harmonious, well-rounded person (soul) and society. When reason governs the desires and passions of an individual, a well-balanced personality arises. Further, when reason directs social relationships, an orderly society emerges. Plato used the term *justice* to speak of the harmony of the soul and of society. For Plato, justice is essentially a harmonious functioning of the parts of the soul or of a society. Plato seems to have assumed that the purpose of humanity is harmony or justice—a rational, biological, and emotional balance, where all aspects of life and all classes of society work together.[3] Plato taught that inner and outer harmony lead to genuine happiness (*eudaimonia*).

Plato also taught that human knowledge of particular objects is grounded in knowledge of universal ideas. We only know what an object of the senses is when we categorize it, when we recognize it as being in a general classification. For example, we do not know what Spot, Rover, and Fido are until we recognize that each is a dog. The term *dog* is a universal concept or universal *form*. Plato used his doctrine of universal forms to ground ethical rules objectively. He disagreed with the Sophists of his day, who claimed that ethical norms are relative, that ethical norms are based on the opinions of society, and that they are subject to change from person to person or culture to culture. Instead, Plato insisted that an act is either objectively good or objectively evil, but not both. An action is just if it participates in the universal idea of Justice. It is unjust if it does not participate in this idea. In turn, an act is good if it participates in the universal idea of the Good. Ultimately, for Plato, the most real thing (the highest form) is the idea of the Good. The idea of the Good is what all things strive for. This is what establishes their purpose, their *telos*.

Since humans are reasoning beings, the purpose of humans is to live a life directed by reason. That is, the good life for humans is the life conformed to reason. Plato believed that the human soul is composed of three distinct faculties: *reason, spirit, and appetite*. Reason is the rational part of the soul. Spirit is the seat of emotions within the soul, the part that leads to action. And appetite is the seat of desires, the animalistic part of the soul. Plato taught that individual happiness is possible only when these three aspects of the soul function in harmony with one another. Further, such harmony is possible only if reason is in control. If either of the other two faculties takes precedence, chaos results. Thus, to fulfill one's purpose and to be happy, one must let reason rule the spirit (emotions) and, in turn, allow reason and the spirit together to rule appetite (desire).

---

3. Plato's notion of justice involves the idea of "each getting its due." For Plato this means that each aspect of the human psyche (reason, emotion, appetite) and each aspect of society (rulers, military, workers) performs the roles best suited for it.

Plato correlated several key virtues with the proper functioning of these faculties. When reason rules the soul, a person displays or possesses the virtue of *wisdom*. When reason controls spirit (emotions), one displays or possesses the virtue of *courage*. And when the reason and spirit combine to control appetite (desires), a person possesses the virtue of *temperance*. When these three faculties function together, under the rule of reason, the virtue of *justice* results.

Plato saw the state (Greek: *polis*) as "the individual writ large." And so, the same basic relationships that make a properly functioning and happy soul also make a happy society. Plato insisted that society is made of three key types of social roles: *rulers*, *military*, and *workers* or *commoners*. According to Plato, the rulers should rule by reason; they should be philosopher-kings. In turn, rulers should be assisted by the military (persons of action) in controlling the commoners and in keeping society in harmony. Only when a society is ruled by reason can harmony occur. When the populace or military rule, chaos ensues. Thus, for Plato, a practical argument for justice can be made. Individuals and societies should be just (and ultimately good) because injustice leads to disharmony of both soul and state. And disharmony leads to unhappiness.

Plato seems to endorse both a deontological and a teleological view of ethics. On the one hand, his insistence that an action is good because it participates in the idea of the Good suggests a deontological view. An act is good because it participates in the reality of the Good. On the other hand, Plato justified living a good life by pointing out that such a life brings about harmony or happiness, and this sounds much like a teleological perspective. These deontological and teleological ideas might be melded by saying that for Plato the good of humans is to manifest our purpose or function (*telos*), and that function is in large measure defined by our status as rational beings. By achieving our own good (as rational beings), we find happiness or harmony (justice).

Aristotle's Ethics

As it was for Plato, the central question for Aristotle's ethics was, what is the good life? And like Plato's, Aristotle's thesis was that the life of reason is happiest and best. However, Aristotle's rationale for this thesis is different from Plato's and the meanings of his terms are distinctive. Aristotle begins by pointing out that there are many good things in the world. Indeed, every human art, science, and action aims to accomplish something good, some good purpose. However, there is a hierarchy of good purposes. Some goals are sought for the sake of other goals. And those goals that are sought for their own sake are higher than those sought for the sake of others. Ultimately, according to Aristotle, there must be a highest goal that all other goals and all human actions seek to attain. According to Aristotle, the highest goal is happiness (*eudaimonia*). Happiness is the one goal that is both final and self-sufficient.

By *final* Aristotle meant it is a goal that is chosen for its own sake and not for the sake of some additional goal. By *self-sufficient* Aristotle meant that happiness is a goal that by itself makes life desirable and lacking in nothing.

Aristotle was quick to point out, however, that the meaning of happiness is ambiguous. There are many opinions about what happiness is. Nevertheless, Aristotle suggests that the meaning of happiness may be attained by examining the function or purpose of human beings; for how good a thing is often is relative to its function. For example, a flute player is a good flute player if he or she plays the flute well. In a similar fashion, Aristotle proposes that a good human is one who performs the function of humans well.[4] Or to put it in terms of the great ethical question: the good (human) life is one that performs well the function of humans.

But what is the function of humans? According to Aristotle, it is not life, for many biological entities (including plants) are alive. Further, it is not perception or sensation, for many biological entities (such as animals) experience sensations. Rather, it is reason. Reason is the unique function of humans. Humans are rational animals. Here, Aristotle essentially agrees with his teacher, Plato, that reason plays a central role in determining what the good life is for humans. According to Aristotle, humans perform the function of reason in two key ways: one passive and irrational, the other active and rational. Passively and irrationally, we perform acts that conform to principles of reason. We do these acts without really thinking about the principles that they exemplify. We do them without engaging in reasoning per se. On the other hand, actively and rationally, we perform acts of reasoning itself. We think, contemplate, speculate, and so forth. According to Aristotle, the function of humans is to perform these various active and passive activities, all of which conform to reason (in some sense). And the good life is one in which we perform these actions well. Human good is reasoning well and performing, in an excellent way, acts that passively accord with reason.

Aristotle's distinction between two types of "acting according to reason" allowed him to differentiate between two types of virtues. First, there are *intellectual virtues*. These are acts of reasoning well. Or perhaps even better: these are dispositions to reason well. Wisdom is an example of an intellectual virtue. It is the act of reasoning well or the state of being predisposed to reason well. Second, there are *moral virtues*. These are acts of conforming to the principles of reason, or dispositions to act in accord with the principles of reason. Courage, temperance, and justice are examples of moral virtues. Each of these is a matter of acting in accord with reason or being disposed to act in accord with reason. We notice, then, that virtues are a matter of character, a matter of one's predisposition to act in a certain

---

4. Aristotle assumes that all things have a function or purpose (a telos). In turn, this purpose is established based on the kind of thing something is—its essential form. In turn, a thing is happy to the degree that it manifests the perfect form that it is. So, a human is happy to the extent that he/she manifests the form of humanness.

way, a matter of habit. If one is predisposed to reason well and to perform actions that accord with the principles of reason, one is virtuous.

Aristotle divided the intellectual virtues into two broad types: (1) *philosophical wisdom*: those predispositions (habits) that enable a person to attain knowledge of universal, fixed truths and principles; and (2) *practical wisdom*: those predispositions (habits) that enable a person to apply rational principles in daily actions. Intellectual virtues are learned through education and experience. They concern acts of reasoning per se. Thus, they are affected by conceptual learning. Moral virtues, on the other hand, are not a matter of reasoning per se. They are simply a matter of "blindly" acting according to the principles of reason. Thus, moral virtues may be learned by sheer force of habit. That is, moral virtues are learned by practice, by doing virtuous acts. Aristotle contended that intellectual virtues are higher than moral virtues, and that among intellectual virtues, philosophical wisdom is more important than practical wisdom.

A final question remains: What kind of actions conform to the principles of reason? That is, what actions do moral virtues predispose humans to do? According to Aristotle, in general, it is those actions that are the mean between two extremes. Every type of moral action is on a continuum. At one end is a complete failure to act in a certain way. At the other is to act in excess. For example, when confronting dangers, courage is the medium between foolhardiness (showing too little fear) and cowardice (showing too much fear). Thus, according to Aristotle, reason dictates that one should live by the *golden mean*, the mean between two extremes.[5] Further, the morally virtuous person is one who is disposed to choose those actions that reason recommends, namely, those that are a medium between two possible extremes. Aristotle insisted that there is no formula for discovering the precise mean in every situation. Rather he insisted that in a general way reason could discern what the best course of action is by seeking the means between extremes. Aristotle lists several important human virtues. Over time, classical Greco-Roman thought came to recognize four cardinal virtues that were believed to be the sources of all other virtues. These were *wisdom* (or *prudence*), *courage* (or *fortitude*), *temperance*, and *justice*.

Aristotle was not happy with Plato's theory of forms. Plato affirmed two realms of reality: the realm of perfect forms and the realm of particular objects. But Aristotle felt that this view overcomplicated the world. And so, he postulated a different relationship between universal forms and particular objects. Instead of claiming that particular objects "participate" in universal forms, Aristotle suggested that universal forms "participate" in particular objects. That is, Aristotle claimed that universal "forms" only exist in particular objects.

Subtle as these differences are, Aristotle's view of forms impacted his *approach* to ethics. For Plato, an act is good because it conforms to the universal Idea of the

5. This was Aristotle's version of the long-standing ancient Greek emphasis on the value of moderation.

Good, an idea that is supposedly innate within human minds. But for Aristotle, an act is good because it conforms to the general idea of Good that arises in the human mind as a result of observing various good acts of humans. In other words, the good acts of humans determine and demonstrate what the Good is. Thus, Aristotle's approach to ethics primarily was empirical rather than rational. He takes a *look-and-see* approach to determining what is right and wrong, rather than a *think-about-it* approach.

Aristotle's affirmation of happiness as the chief goal of humans places his ethics in the teleological tradition. For Plato, an act is good because it participates in goodness itself, in the idea of the Good, in a transcendent, nonempirical reality. This makes Plato's ethics deontological. (Although, as we have seen, there is tension in Plato's account between deonotology and teleology.) But for Aristotle, an act is good because it leads to some valuable empirical consequence, namely, to fulfillment of human *function* (living according to reason), which in turn leads to happiness. And this makes Aristotle's ethics teleological.

Sometimes this distinction between teleological and deontological theories is expressed by the terms *naturalistic* and *transcendental*. Aristotle's ethics is naturalistic rather than transcendental. Plato grounds the good in a nonnatural, transcendental object—namely, in the idea of the Good. But Aristotle grounds the good in the natural world. The good is that which brings about the valuable consequence of making people happy.

Aristotle's emphasis on happiness makes his ethics *eudaimonian*. For him the highest good is happiness or satisfaction. The highest goal is not performing an act that conforms to some transcendent, ontological reality called the good. More specifically, Aristotle's ethic is a form of rationalistic eudemonism. Aristotle insisted that the essence of humans is our ability to reason; this ability is what sets us apart from other beings. Thus, our chief function in life is to reason and to act in conformity with the principles of reason. In turn, the best way for us to be happy is to fulfill our basic function and to satisfy that part of ourselves that is at the core of what we are, namely, reasoning. An act is good if it leads to the fulfillment or satisfaction of our rationality.

Epicurus

Another important classical perspective on ethics was offered by Epicurus. A number of ancient Greek philosophers proposed that a life of pleasure and avoidance of pain is the best life. Among these thinkers were contemporaries of Plato named Thrasymachus (d. 399 BCE) and Aristippus (435–350 BCE). In Plato's *Republic*, Thrasymachus is presented as an antagonist of Socrates and as arguing that the best life is one of personal pleasure and power. Aristippus was a student of Socrates who, despite his teacher's views, affirmed sensual pleasure as the highest good. He taught that the good life is the pleasant life, and that the pleasant life is one filled with many intense pleasures. The goal in life, then, is to seek as many intense pleasures as possible. He recommended a life of control over others and over one's environment, so as to insure personal pleasure.

Epicurus was a student of Aristippus, but his views differed significantly from his teacher's. Epicurus emphasized "peace of mind," and "pleasures that endure." He believed that avoiding pain is more fundamental to happiness than obtaining of pleasures. In other words, as long a person's basic needs are met and one is not in pain, that individual will be happy. While fulfilling desires for intense pleasure is in itself permissible, it is also difficult to achieve. Usually the pain or frustration that result from striving to satisfy most exotic or intense desires outweighs the pleasure that one receives from eventual satisfaction. Thus, Epicurus recommended that persons seek those desires whose goals are easily attained, rather than struggle to fulfill the more exotic desires, whose ends are difficult to reach. Epicurus insisted that nature readily satisfies most basic human needs and desires, and that in meeting these needs a person can find happiness.

Epicurus believed that two anxieties especially prohibit human happiness. These are fear of death and fear of divine retribution. Epicurus insisted, however, that humans need not fear either of these. First, Epicurus denied the rationality of fearing death. He affirmed the "atomic theory" of Democritus (c. 460—c. 370 BCE), who taught that all physical reality is atoms in motion. Atoms are tiny, solid, indestructible, everlasting material bodies. According to Epicurus, the human soul as well as the human body is made of these atoms. Further, sensation is a material or physical phenomenon. It is the motion of atoms in the body and in the soul. Thus, when a person dies, the atoms of the soul and body disperse, and sensations cease. According to Epicurus, then, there is no need to fear death because there will be no more pain after death. Epicurus also argued humans need not fear divine retribution. He reasoned that highest god is blessed. And if truly blessed, such a being would not be concerned about or involved in the affairs of humans. If such a being were to be concerned with humans, such concern would bring an end to divine blessedness and serenity. It follows then, that humans need not fear divine retribution, for god is simply unconcerned and uninvolved in human affairs. The views of Thrasymachus, Aristippus, and Epicurus often are called *hedonistic egoism*, for they essentially recommend that an act is right if it brings pleasure or the avoidance of pain to the individual.

Stoic Ethics

Stoicism was founded by a Greek named Zeno from Cyprus (c. 336—264 BCE). Zeno came to Athens around 315 BCE and soon was influenced by the teachings of Socrates (c. 470–399 BCE). In 300 BCE, Zeno founded his own school in Athens, which became known as the Stoa or porch, for Zeno routinely taught from the porch (*stoa*) of one of the great building in Athens. Zeno was influenced by the Cynics, in particular by a Cynic named Crates (c. 365—c. 285 BC), who had been a friend and student of Socrates. Zeno was influenced by the Cynic emphasis on self-reliance and disdain for elaborate needs. Zeno was also impressed with Aristotelian epistemology—in particular with Aristotle's emphasis on sense-knowledge. Zeno and early Stoics taught that the mind is a blank page at birth and that through the senses the mind receives images that are impressed upon it like a stamp upon wax. The mind catalogues these impressions and from them derives general concepts. However, unlike Aristotle, who believed that general concepts have a real, substantial existence in the many particulars in which they abide, the Stoics insisted that universal concepts are only mental constructions. Stoics tended to be materialists. Indeed, most claimed, not only that god and the soul are material, but even that good and evil are somehow material realities. Because the Stoics rejected Plato's understanding of forms as realities that exist independent of particular physical objects, these writers seemed to be forced to conclude that only material things exist.

The lasting impact of the Stoics was in ethics. Following Aristotle's teleology, the Stoics insisted that all things have a natural *telos* or goal; and that humans have a natural *telos*. But this goal is not contemplation, as Aristotle had claimed. Instead, the *telos* of humans is to live in conformity with the *world order* or *cosmic logos*. Stoics taught that the universe is a fully rational, fully material, and fully deterministic system. All that happens in the world is determined by previous, material causes, and all that happens is in conformity with a rational *cosmic* plan. Further, Stoics taught that the world-system is divine. Thus, Stoics were pantheists.

From this basic metaphysical position, several ethical ideas emerged. First was the idea that each human has an element or spark of the divine within him or her. Since the universe as whole is divine, then the parts of the universe (including humans) are parts of divinity. Second, all humans are a part of a larger whole. Thus, Stoics emphasized the *cosmopolis*, the *world-city*. They insisted that there is a commonality shared by all humans, and that all humans are valuable. Third, all that happens in the universe is divine, rational, and determined. Fourth, the best approach to life is passive acceptance of the things that happen in the universe. (This view is found especially in the early Stoics.) Since all things are determined, and since no one can control the unfolding of the determined material world, the best way to be happy is to accept what happens and be apathetic to those things that one cannot control. Overt actions are of little consequence since all is determined. What matters is our *attitude* toward things and our *motives* for trying to do things.

Fifth, the Stoics emphasized *duty* as a chief moral concept. Aristotle had emphasized the consequences of actions. An action is good if it leads to ultimate human happiness. And while Plato had taught that an act is good if it participates in the form of goodness, he also emphasized the consequences of being good (in particular of being just). But the Stoics were among the first to emphasize doing acts for their own sake, *regardless of their consequences*. For the Stoics, one should perform the actions that reason dictates. For the early Stoics, this meant apathetically accepting whatever happened in the cosmic order. For later, Roman Stoics (such as Cicero and Marcus Aurelius), this often meant considering the needs of the cosmopolis as a whole over one's own needs or wants.

Sixth, Stoic emphasis on the rationality of the universe and the commonality of all humans as citizens of a cosmopolis led many to endorse the notion of *natural (moral) law*. This is the idea that beyond laws established by human conventions and governments, there exists a moral law dictated by the rational universe itself. According to many Stoics, this natural law trumps human conventions, grounds the dignity of all humans, and establishes moral principles for humanity as a whole to follow. Hints of these ideas are found in Aristotle. But the notion of natural law came to full fruition in the writings of the Stoics. As we will see, the concept of natural (moral) law, played an important role in Christian ethics ancient and medieval.

Christian Ethics in the Classical Era

Prior to the ascension of Emperor Constantine I (272–337) and his official sanctioning of the Christian religion, Christian voices varied considerably on the question of how best to live in a largely pagan society. Many believers found themselves at odds with the mores of the broader culture, often condemning aspects of that society as immoral even while attempting to assuage the fears of imperial rulers that Christianity was subversive. The ethical ideals of Christians in the first century emerged from principles taught in the Hebrew Bible, especially as understood by Jesus and his earliest disciples. Central to first-century Christian ethics were the commands to love God and to love fellow humans. In turn, righteousness and obedience to God were to flow from one's own inner being—empowered by God's Spirit. Formally, the earliest Christians endorsed the Ten Commandments, interpreted in light of Jesus' ministry and teachings. Thus, Christians worshiped the God of Israel only, gathered weekly to do so, and condemned veneration of idols. Christians likewise condemned lying, stealing, murder, and sexual misconduct. First-century Christians also sought to aid the poor and downtrodden. Concerns over living-up to these expectations were mollified by promises of God's willingness to forgive moral breaches through Christ's atoning death, and to aid believers in moral living through the Holy Spirit.

In the second and third centuries, Christians continued to affirm the moral precepts of their first-century brothers and sisters, but changes of emphasis began to surface; a degree of rigidity arose so that progressively righteousness was interpreted as following precise ethical rules. As Christians encountered their broader culture, many sought to apply their moral sensitivities to diverse contemporary practices. From prohibitions against violence and murder, Christians rejected the Roman practices of abortion, infanticide, and gladiatorial games; and many Christians declined to serve in

Rome's armies.[6] Against false worship, the church refused membership to sorcerers, astrologers, pagan priests, and even sculptors whose primary income came from crafting idols. Against sexual impropriety, there were church condemnations of prostitutes and even of actors (given the lewdness of theater). Indeed, prohibitions regarding sexual conduct became stricter in the second and third centuries than in New Testament times. So the author of the *Didache* warned against lustfulness and fornication. Ignatius of Antioch (d. 108/140) declared that adulterers will not inherit the kingdom of God. Clement of Rome (d. 99) warned against "impure embraces," "filthy lust," and "detestable adultery."[7] Same-sex relations likewise were typically condemned. Heterosexual couples were encouraged to marry, stay together in marriage, and be sexually faithful. And frequently in early Christian literature, celibacy was heralded as especially commendable.[8] Many Christians honored virgins, as well as widows who refrained from sex so that they might better serve Christ. And early on, bishops, priests, and deacons whose spouses died were expected not to remarry, and clergy who were unmarried when ordained were encouraged to remain that way.

Second- and third-century Christians also often called for charity toward the less fortunate. The rich were obligated to care for the poor. And the poor were to be earnestly grateful for the benevolence of the rich. Typically, care for the poor was expressed in terms of private morality. Such actions were expected of individuals; but little effort was made by Christians collectively to change the inequalities and injustices of the broader economic and political system of the Roman Empire. For example, no substantial effort was made by Christians to undermine the empire-wide practice of slavery. Christian attempts to change the system almost certainly would have meant persecution and possible annihilation of Christian communities throughout the empire.

The fourth and fifth centuries brought significant changes for Christians, as they went from a sometimes despised and persecuted sect to followers of the formal religion of the Roman Empire. These changes occurred rapidly thanks to Emperor Constantine I and those emperors who followed. Obviously, Christians of these centuries retained many of the core values espoused in the Hebrew and early Christian traditions. At the center of their ethics were the calls to love God and love their fellow humans, as well as affirmation of various dictates flowing from the Ten Commandments, including

6. There is no clear evidence of Christians serving in the Roman military prior to 170 CE. This is partly explained by the fact that membership in the imperial legions required a religiously charged oath of loyalty to Caesar that conflicted (in the minds of many Christians) with devotion to Jesus as Lord. Further, there is evidence that many early Christians endorsed a kind of pacifism that disallowed killing humans. Often early Christian writers encouraged fellow disciples to seek peace with all, to love one's enemies, to pray for persecutors, and to repay good for evil. Nevertheless, many early Christian authors likewise recognized the state's right to protect its citizens and borders, and to punish (genuine) evildoers. See Wogaman, *Christian Ethics*, 34–37.

7. Wogaman, *Christian Ethics*, 32.

8. Wogaman, *Christian Ethics*, 32–33.

faithfulness to the God of Christ alone, routine weekly worship, and prohibitions against, murder, theft, sexual immorality, lying, and so forth. Christians continued to condemn many of the practices of the broader culture, including the debauchery of the theater and the gore of gladiatorial contests. Through the second and third centuries, there had arisen among Christians special admiration for individuals who had died for their witness for Christ (martyrs) as well as for persons who, for the sake of Christ, exercised control over their desires by abstaining from sex.

These commitments were challenged when Christianity became the favored religion of Rome. Soon a multitude of former pagans flowed into the church, bringing with them values at odds with the faith. As a result, Christian clergy faced the monumental task of teaching vast numbers of citizens the basic tenets, mores, and attitudes of the faith. One result of this clash of cultures was the emergence and growth of monasticism. At the core of the monastic movement was concern over ethics. Practitioners of the monastic idea sought to live a genuine and upright life for Christ. Several central mores undergirded monastic morality. First was commitment to self-denial or self-mortification (death to self). Following Jesus' dictum that one must "deny himself, pick up his cross, and follow" Christ (Luke 9:23), many monks sought a life of self-control in which the spirit governs desires, thoughts, and actions. Through a regimen of prayer, meditation, and Scripture reading, an individual sought death to self and renewed life in Christ. The majority of monks took vows of chastity and poverty, hoping to control their bodily desires and enliven the life of the Spirit.

Another key precept of monasticism was detachment from the world. To avoid sin, many monks sought to isolate themselves both mentally and physically from the temptations of the world. Many removed themselves to deserts or wastelands, away from contact with the general population. At first this meant escaping non-Christian culture. But as the culture became more Christian (at least in name), many monks sought refuge from what they saw as morally compromised congregations and clergy. Some monks were individualistic, living alone (but often drawing crowds of admirers). Other monks gathered in communes, but still these groups tended to be isolated from the broader populace—all in an effort to live a life holier than the average Christian or pagan.

While monasticism germinated and grew, other Christian writers of the fourth and fifth centuries sought to communicate their faith with the broader society, often assimilating ideas and ideals at the root of Greco-Roman culture. A motive for such assimilation was a desire to help Christians and pagans alike better understand the Christian faith and ethic. Such was the case with writers like Clement of Alexandria (c. 145—c. 215) and his student Origen (182–251). Clement taught that there is no dichotomy between Christian faith and philosophical truth, for truth simply is whatever is true. Both the Christian religion and pagan philosophy (when properly reasoned) convey truth. Thus, pagan philosophers, to the degree that their reasoning leads to truth, can contribute much to the Christian perspective, both by adding insights not formally stated in Scripture or tradition, and by reinforcing truths explicit in the faith.

In a similar manner, following the Gospel of John, Origen identified the second member of the Trinity—the Son of God—with the *logos* (word) of God, insisting (with John's Gospel) that this divine *logos* enlightens all humans (1:1–9). In turn, Origen identified this logos of God with *reason* itself, proposing that whenever humans correctly cogitate, they demonstrate the presence of God the Son within them. Thus, for Origen, all (correct) reasoning flows from God's presence in humans. In turn, this divine rational principle allows persons to establish certain basic moral principles (*natural moral laws*) through reason alone, independent of special divine revelation. This is a law that transcends, sometimes overrides, and sometime confirms the laws established by human convention.[9] These moral norms are precepts demanded by rationality itself. In turn, according to Origen, such moral thinking allows Christians to draw ethical insights from non-Christian philosophers, who themselves discovered such principles through reason alone.[10]

Augustine

The most influential Christian writer of the classical era was Augustine of Hippo. Augustine was born in Numidia, North Africa in 354 CE. His father was non-Christian; his mother was Christian. For a number of years, Augustine taught rhetoric in Rome and endorsed Manichaean teachings. (Manicheanism was a dualistic system which affirmed the existence of two fundamental realities: matter and spirit. According to Manicheanism, matter is evil, and spirit is good.) In 386, Augustine converted to Christianity and was baptized on Easter Day 387. In 395 he was consecrated an auxiliary bishop of Hippo. In 396, he became ruling bishop of Hippo. Augustine died in 430 CE.

Like many theologians of the classical period, Augustine was informed primarily by the biblical tradition, but his theology also included often enough mixtures of Greco-Roman philosophical insights. Augustine affirmed the existence of only one God—the Christian God. This God is the most perfect and most real being of all. God is "a nature than which nothing more excellent or more exalted exists."[11] God is omnipotent, omniscient, and perfectly good. God is self-sufficient—that is, dependent on nothing. All things come from God, and God created all that exists ex nihilo—from nothing. God is also a Trinity—three *personae* (persons) in one *substantia* (being).

Humans are created by God and are made in the image of God. Originally, as a result of this image, humans were free to choose good or evil, and free to love God and others. Unfortunately, humans fell into sin. The first humans chose evil; they sinned

---

9. By affirming natural law, independent of human conventions, Origen mimics the insights of Aristotle and several Stoics.

10. Wogaman, *Christian Ethics*, 40–45.

11. Augustine, *On Christian Doctrine* 1.7.

and thus became sinners. In turn, all humans that came after them became sinners. Because of this, humans are no longer free not to sin. Humans now are predisposed to sin; they cannot not sin. Because of this proneness to sin, humans are subject to divine punishment, to eternal punishment.[12]

Augustine also believed that God is merciful. God has provided a means by which humans might avoid punishment and attain eternal life. Sin has been atoned for by the death of Jesus Christ, who is a member of the Godhead, and who became a human in order to provide an atonement for sin. Now eternal life can be obtained and eternal punishment avoided through spiritual union with Christ. Faith, love, and hope are necessary for this union. And faith, love, and hope result from God's power upon people. God gives humans the power to exercise faith, love, and hope. Thus, God chooses to save; humankind cannot choose to have faith in Jesus Christ; God predestines some to salvation.

Augustine's philosophy may be described as a Christianized Platonism or Christianized Neoplantonism. Like Plato, Augustine affirmed the existence of eternal truths. These are the Platonic *universal forms*. Augustine insisted that particular objects participate in the reality of these universal forms or in eternal truths. In turn, he claimed that we know particular things by categorizing them, by recognizing that they belong to or participate in a certain universal class. Further, like Plato, Augustine insisted that eternal truths are more real than particular objects and more real than the humans who come to know them. Our minds must conform to the truth of eternal truths and not the other way around. Augustine writes:

> When a man says that . . . seven plus three are ten, he does not say that it ought to be so; he knows it is this way, and does not correct it as an examiner would, but he rejoices as if he had made a discovery. If truth were equal to our minds, it would be subject to change. Our minds sometimes see more and sometimes less, and because of this we acknowledge that they are mutable. Truth, remaining in itself, does not gain anything when we see it, or lose anything when we do not see it. It is whole and uncorrupted. With its light, truth gives joy to the men who turn to it, and punishes with blindness those who turn away from it.[13]

For Augustine, humans come to know eternal truths through a divine inner revelation or inner light. God enlightens all human minds with eternal truths so that they might have knowledge—that is, so that they might know objects encountered by the senses and might be able to reason. Augustine also insisted that knowledge of truth ultimately

12. Augustine admitted that eternal punishment for earthly, temporal sins seems harsh and unjust. But he insisted that it only seems unfair to our weak, mortal condition. We fail to see the real travesty of the first sin. Augustine justified eternal punishment on the grounds that the first human "destroyed in himself a good which might have been eternal" and as a result "became worthy of eternal evil." Augustine, *The City of God* 21.12. Augustine also taught that with Adam's sin "the whole mass of the human race is condemned; for he who at first gave entrance to sin has been punished with his posterity who were in him as in a root" (Augustine, *City of God*, 22.22).

13. Augustine, *On Free Choice of the Will*, 2.12.134–35.

is knowledge of God because God is the source of truth, and indeed is Truth itself. In turn, according to Augustine, God has impressed the eternal moral law upon the human heart; in other words, God has enlightened human minds with an awareness of the moral law, in a way similar to the way the divine inner light gives us knowledge of theoretical universal and eternal truths.

Initially, the existence of evil proved to be a stumbling block for Augustine's conversion to Christianity. For many years, Augustine rejected the faith of his mother, for he could not comprehend how evil could exist if the singular ultimate reality was a good and all-powerful God. If such a deity existed, evil should not exist since God both could and would want to get rid of evil. For this reason Augustine endorsed the dualism of Manicheanism for some time. Eventually, however, Augustine's study of Neoplatonism provided a means by which the great theologian was able to overcome his intellectual dilemma. With the philosophers Plato and Plotinus (c. 204/5–270), Augustine argued that evil is the lack of reality; it is the privation of being. It is like darkness, which Augustine interpreted to be simply the absence of light. There is no substance to it. When humans choose or do evil, they simply choose or do a lesser good, a lesser reality, than what could (and should) be done. Indeed, in many ways for Augustine the will (of humans and perhaps other moral beings) is the ultimate grounding of evil. For no created reality per se is evil. Rather, evil emerges when one *wills* to do or to value a lower good over a higher one. And ultimately, since God is the highest good, evil arises when the will chooses any lower good over God—over God per se and over God's will. If one should wonder why the will chooses a lesser good, no clear answer can be given. The will's choice of lesser good itself is a privation of being; it is a misdirection of the will and ultimately is inexplicable (irrational).

Augustine's ethics was eudaimonian in the sense that he agreed with many ancient philosophers that the ultimate goal humans seek is happiness. However, Augustine denied that happiness can be attained in this world. Happiness in this world is always subject to change, always threatened. And the human heart or soul is in search of a happiness that endures, that can never be threatened. Augustine concluded that only eternally existing happiness is genuine happiness. In other words, "life eternal is the supreme good."[14] Closely tied to the idea that eternal life is the ultimate good is Augustine's assertion that God is our ultimate good and ultimate happiness. Augustine claimed that God is humanity's "chief good."[15] In turn, Augustine declared that "following after God is the desire of happiness; to reach God is happiness itself."[16]

But how does one *attain* God, and thus achieve eternal life and happiness? For Augustine, attaining God ultimately is a mystery. It is a spiritual union with God that is not fully explicable.[17] It is similar to the union with ultimate reality envisioned by

14. Augustine, *City of God*, 19.4.

15. Augustine, *City of God*, 22.29.

16. Augustine, *Of the Morals of the Catholic Church*, 11.18.

17. Augustine, *City of God*, 22.29–30.

Plotinus and other Neoplatonists. Nevertheless, Augustine indicates that this union results from loving God. And so, he writes: "If God is man's supreme good . . . it clearly follows . . . that to live well is nothing else but to love God with all the heart, with all the soul, with all the mind."[18] The lust (concupiscence) of the will for lesser goods can be overcome only by redirecting its complete affection toward God.[19] Thus, the ethical life arises from love for God. Love (for God) is the highest virtue. And from this virtue all other virtues spring. Temperance simply is love given entirely to God. Fortitude is love bearing all for God's sake. Justice is love serving God only and thus ruling all else well. Prudence is love distinguishing actions and goals that move one toward God rather than away from God.[20]

For Augustine genuine love of God involves obedience to God and conforming to the eternal moral laws that exude from God's nature. These laws are summed up in the divine commands to love God, love others, and love our selves.[21] Further, this love for God occurs only via faith and via divine grace. Because humans are tainted by sin, human effort is never sufficient to bring about a genuine love for or obedience to God. God must extend divine aid in order for us to love and obey God. Indeed, according to Augustine, a great fault of much of pagan ethics was its false belief that humans can attain good and happiness by their own powers—by their own moral virtues and efforts. Such achievements are only possible by divine aid.[22]

Medieval Christian Ethics

Medieval Christianity was deeply impacted by a growing sacramentalist understanding of salvation. *Sacramentalism* contends that the saving effects of Christ's atoning work are received through the sacraments of the true church. Through these rites, divine grace is *infused* into believers so that they might receive the saving benefits of Christ's work. Baptism affords the individual the initial infusing of this saving grace. Through the Eucharist, this infusion is maintained throughout life. And penance provides a means by which postbaptismal sins might be forgiven. Penance came to involve confession of personal sins and formal absolution by the church. Often between confession and absolution, the penitent believer was expected to demonstrate true remorse for sin through varied acts of contrition. Over time, these acts of contrition were seen as virtual punishments or penalties for sin designed to gain absolution on

18. Augustine, *Of the Morals of the Catholic Church*, 1.25.46, quoted in Copleston, *A History of Philosophy*, 2:97

19. For Augustine, "Concupiscence is that power which leads us from the contemplation of the supreme God to the contemplation of inferior and transitory realities" (quoted in González, *A History of Christian Thought*, 2:44).

20. Augustine, *Of the Morals of the Catholic Church*, 15.25.

21. Augustine, *City of God*, 19.14.

22. Kent, "Augustine's Ethics," 210. Also see, Augustine, *City of God*, 8.8–10.

earth and so avoid harsher penalties in the afterlife. Typically, the penance process was overseen by priests (or higher-ranking ministers) of the church.

The practice of penance (and the underlying theory of sacramentalism) led to the production of various confession manuals (confessionals), which listed various sins and the necessary penance for each. Early on, some sins were deemed more grievous than others, hence requiring more arduous penalties than lesser infractions. The Synod of Elvira (306) set the tone for these confessionals by listing numerous sins and their requisite acts of contrition. As time progressed, the confessional tradition grew, and elaborate manuals were produced throughout medieval history, many providing mind-numbing details about both sins and the penance required for each.

One consequence of confessionalism in the Middle Ages was a tendency to define morality in terms of what one should *avoid* rather than in terms of what proactively one should do and become. Another consequence was that moral contrition became objectified so that ethics was interpreted almost as a kind of economic transaction between God and penitent sinners, brokered by the church. These tendencies flowered (or decayed) in the late medieval period into the practice of commutation—that is, "the payment of money as a penalty or payment in lieu of some other penalty."[23] Such practices not only favored the rich over the poor, but also led to the abuse of indulgences—the virtual sale of forgiveness for cash.

Thomas Aquinas

One of the greatest theologian of the medieval church was Thomas Aquinas (1225–1274). Thomas affirmed Aristotle's basic understanding of reality and ethics. Aristotle believed that physical objects are a combination of matter and form. *Matter* is the stuff physical objects are made of. *Form* is what makes a particular object *the kind of thing* it is. (For example, Fido is a kind of thing, namely, a dog. *Dogness* is Fido's form. In turn, Fido is made of matter. Thus, Fido is matter in the form *dog*.) Aristotle also taught that all naturally occurring things have a form (their essence) that they inherently tend to move toward. That is, each natural substance has an inherent goal (*telos*) that it is driven to become. This inner impulse to change is like an innate desire (although this "desire" need not be conscious). A tadpole is naturally driven to become a frog (which is its essential form). A human infant, as a rational being, is driven to become an adult human that reasons and gains knowledge.[24]

According to Aristotle, many types of finite reality naturally, but *unconsciously*, move toward their essential forms. For example, tadpoles unintentionally become frogs. Aspects of human life likewise unconsciously move to their essential form; thus, human infants grow toward adulthood *without deliberation*. But because humans also

---

23. Wogaman, *Christian Ethics*, 84.

24. *Rational being* is the kind of thing (form) humans essentially are.

are rational, aspects of them *consciously* seek their essential goal—which is reasoning, knowing truth, and living according to the dictates of reason.

Thomas adopted many of these features of Aristotle's metaphysics. He affirmed that physical objects are matter in some form, and that all natural substances (including humans) inherently move toward becoming the kind of thing they are—their form. Often these movements occur innately and unintentionally. But in the case of a human's search for knowledge and attempt to live by the precepts of reason, deliberate choices must be and are made. Thomas essentially endorsed Aristotle's claim that the human good (*telos*) is reasoning well, gaining knowledge, and performing, in an excellent way, acts that passively accord with reason. In turn, Thomas agreed with Aristotle that attaining these things brings happiness to humans.

But distinctions soon emerged between Thomas and Aristotle. First, Aristotle taught that the highest happiness of humans is knowledge—especially, knowledge of the *first principles of nature*; but Thomas insisted that the highest happiness is *knowledge of God*. For Thomas, God is the highest reality and the ultimate Truth; and as rational beings, humans cannot be satisfied (happy) until they know God. For Thomas, such knowledge of God cannot be merely guesswork, or even based on philosophical reasoning[25] or faith. Ultimately, this knowledge must be a kind of direct awareness of God—what Thomas called the *beatific vision*—which ultimately comes to humans only through divine grace in the afterlife.

Another divide between Aristotle and Thomas is this. For Aristotle, the ability to gain knowledge (including some knowledge of God) is an *intrinsic aptitude* of humans. As rational beings, humans can naturally (even though deliberately) gain knowledge of the physical world and of God. Such information is obtainable by humans through their natural intellect. Thomas partly disagreed. Thomas granted that through the innate structures of human reasoning, humans can gain knowledge of the physical world and

25. Both Thomas and Aristotle offered rational arguments for God's existence. And both recognized that while such arguments demonstrate God's existence, they do not give direct or full knowledge of the nature of God. Aristotle believed that all naturally occurring substances are drawn toward (desire) some highest form—the utterly perfect reality. Aristotle claimed that this perfect form is unchanging because if something is perfect it cannot get better, nor can it be subject to the degradation of getting worse. In turn, if this perfect reality cannot change, it cannot be made of matter because matter intrinsically has the potential to take on (become) an infinite number of forms. In turn, since this perfect reality cannot be made of matter, it must be pure form. Aristotle called this pure, perfect form God (*theos*); he also called it the First Mover, for Aristotle believed the highest reality is the ultimate explanation for why there is any motion in the universe. Ultimately, all reality is driven (or desires) to be like God. In turn, Aristotle believed that often rational reflection leads individuals to yearn for and gain knowledge of God, who is the ultimate reality and the highest truth. Thomas affirmed Aristotle's notion that there must be some highest reality that all things are drawn toward (desire), namely God. For Thomas, this ultimate reality is the Christian God. God is pure form and the First Mover of all that is. Like Aristotle, Thomas maintained that humans innately but also consciously seek God, who is both the highest reality and the ultimate Truth (as well as the source of all truth). But like Aristotle, Thomas believed that knowledge of God based on rational argumentation or speculation does not render knowledge of God per se. For Thomas, such knowledge can come by divine grace in the afterlife.

some knowledge of God. But, Thomas insisted, deeper knowledge of God (in this life) is only possible through divine grace and revelation. Further, the deepest knowledge of God (the beatific vision) is only obtainable in the afterlife, which also is only possible by divine grace. Thomas agreed with the Christian tradition that since the first sin of Adam and Eve, humans are innately prone to sin and have a sinful nature. Thomas taught that after the fall, humans retained the *image* of God—which entails various *natural* abilities, including both rationality and will; but humans lost their *likeness* of God—which includes qualities supernaturally given to humans such as righteousness. Thus, humans cannot do what is right through their own natural abilities, nor can they come to deeper knowledge of God that way. Such righteousness and knowledge come by direct, divine aid—via revelation and infused grace.

With Aristotle, then, Thomas agreed that there are two sets of *natural virtues*, namely, intellectual virtues (which allow humans to correctly reason) and moral virtues (which involve habits that produce actions that passively conform to the dictates of reason). For Thomas, these human virtues flow from innate abilities resulting from being created as rational beings. In turn, Thomas followed Aristotle and the broader Greco-Roman tradition by identifying four *cardinal virtues*. These are prudence (wisdom), justice, temperance, and fortitude (courage). Also, in accord with traditions from the classical world, Thomas endorsed the notion of *natural law*—the idea that some moral precepts are discoverable through reason alone. According to Thomas, these cardinal virtues and natural moral precepts[26] are knowable by *natural* human abilities—unaided by supernatural grace or special revelation.

But beyond these habits and information available to natural human assets, there are virtues and knowledge only reachable supernaturally—by direct divine aid. Thomas identified three core virtues not accessible except through divine grace; these are faith, hope, and love.[27] Thomas referred to these as *theological virtues*—virtues directly given by God. According to Thomas, only through these divinely given virtues can a person attain humankind's ultimate *telos*—namely, rightly knowing God and living morally according to the dictates of reason. Further, ultimately one can attain full knowledge of God only by divine grace through beatific vision in the afterlife. In turn, only by gaining such eternal knowledge can a person be happy. Regarding the theological virtues, Thomas writes:

> Now man's happiness is twofold . . . One is proportioned to human nature, a happiness, namely, which can obtain by means of the principles of his nature. The other is a happiness surpassing man's nature, and which man can obtain by the power of God alone, by a kind of participation of the Godhead . . . And because such happiness surpasses the power of human nature, man's natural principles, which enable him to act well according to his power, do not suffice to direct man to this same happiness. Hence it is necessary for

26. Along with basic knowledge of God. See previous note.
27. Thomas drew these three from the apostle's comments in 1 Cor 13:13

man to receive from God some additional principles, by which he may be directed to supernatural happiness . . . Such principles are called *theological virtues*. They are so called, first, because their object is God, inasmuch as they direct us rightly to God; secondly, because they are infused in us by God alone; thirdly, because these virtues are not made known to us, save by divine revelation, contained in Holy Scripture.[28]

In addition to these differences between Thomas and Aristotle, one can also see some important variances between Thomas's and Augustine's ethics. Thomas agreed with Augustine that evil is the deprivation of being. But Thomas went further, insisting that evil also involves a substance's failure to obtain its natural purpose (*telos*). That is, evil includes a thing failing to manifest its essential form. Further, following Aristotle and somewhat contrary to Augustine, Thomas asserted that the natural end of substances can be discerned by natural reasoning—that is reasoning unaided by direct divine aid. And through such inherent reasoning a natural moral law is detectable. Hence, ethics partly is grounded in human reasoning alone (unaided by special divine influence), even though a complete ethic requires God's revelation and a supernaturally infused grace to enable frail (sinful) humans to come to a fuller understanding of and obedience to God.[29]

Thomas made some important distinctions in defining moral acts. He discerned three core elements contributing to the rightness of an action. These are the *end* (consequence) achieved by the act, the *motive* for performing it, and the overarching *circumstances* under which the act is performed.[30] For example, the act of saving a plant from being stepped on (the consequence), so that one might receive a monetary reward for one's effort (motive), under conditions requiring nothing more than moving a pot off the sidewalk (circumstance) seems to be morally less significant than saving the life of a child (the consequence), because one values human life (motive), under conditions that require placing oneself in great personal danger (circumstances). Thomas also emphasized the importance of the character of the moral agent performing an act. This is related to the notion of *motive*. A person who routinely does good for the right motives is a better person than one who only occasionally does good acts for the right motives. In turn, actions flowing from the person who routinely does good are better than those flowing from the person who occasionally does good, precisely because the first individual is habituated toward doing right while the second is not. In other words, acts performed by *virtuous* persons are better than acts performed by less virtuous persons.

At this point, one might ask: what ultimately makes an act good? As we have seen, Thomas partly answers this by saying that those actions are good that enable

28. Thomas Aquinas, *Summa Theologica*, 1–2, q. 62, a.1, answer 3.

29. Wogaman, *Christian Ethics*, 88–92.

30. Thomas Aquinas, *Summa Theologica*, 1–2, qq. 18–20 (quoted in Jones, *The Medieval Mind*, 261–63).

humans to attain their essential form. But matters are a bit more complex than this. Ultimately for Thomas, a good action is one that conforms with "the rational structure of the universe," which has been imagined and established by God in the creation of the world.[31] A good act is one that conforms with this structure; an evil act is one that does not so conform. Thomas referred to this divinely established rational structure as the *eternal law*. While humans do not have direct access to this eternal law (which essentially is the very mind of God) through reason, persons can nevertheless discern portions of the eternal law by rationally reflecting on the nature of the observed universe. From these reflections humans can grasp the *natural law*—that is, the moral law implicit in the created order. In turn, because of this access to the natural law, people (through natural reason without direct divine aid) can also know much about right and wrong; they can establish (as Aristotle did) the core intellectual and moral virtues. In turn, because of their access to the natural law, humans are morally responsible for performing its precepts, and they are culpable for not performing them. But because human reasoning is not perfect, and because the human will is prone to sin, the natural law alone is insufficient to lead humanity to the ultimate, supernatural good that is God. In order for humans to find the ultimate, supernatural good, a further moral law is needed—one revealed by God (in Scripture). Thomas calls this the *divine law*. Through scriptural revelation and both the moral requirements and the divine grace described there, persons can move toward moral living and the ultimate human goal of full knowledge of God.[32]

Late Medieval Challenges to Thomas's Ethic

Not all philosophers and theologians of the late medieval period agreed with Thomas's close tie of ethics to reason, even divine reason. Duns Scotus (1266–1308) emphasized the primacy of the divine will over all other principles. According to Scotus, for God to be truly sovereign (omnipotent), the divine decrees, including moral mandates, must be free; that is, no other principles outside of God's will can dictate what God commands, not even the dictums of reason. Thus, moral principles and laws—which are established by God—must be grounded in God's (free) will.[33] Scotus's view is sometimes referred to as *voluntarism*—the notion that moral mandates are established by the divine will.

William Ockham (1280–1349) held views similar to Scotus's but added further criticisms of Thomas's system. Ockham argued that natural human knowledge (of

---

31. Jones, *The Medieval Mind*, 264.

32. Thomas Aquinas, *Summa Theologica*, 1–2, qq. 91, 93–94, 98, 106.

33. Duns Scotus was subtle here, however, for he recognized that emphasis on divine will alone could lead to the dilemma that moral mandates are utterly arbitrary and that God just as easily could have commanded "Thou shalt murder" as "Thou shalt not murder." Thus, Scotus attempted to avoid this by arguing that while God's moral will often conforms to the dictates of reason, reason is not the *cause* of God's willful choosing of such mandates. See Jones, *The Medieval Mind*, 312–13.

ethics and of the world in general) is far more limited than envisioned by Aquinas (and Aristotle). These limitations follow from the notion of divine omnipotence. God can do anything that is logically possible. Thus, since it is logically possible for God to cause us to *experience* the *sensations* of a red, round, sweet "apple" without there actually being such an objective apple (as when we hallucinate or dream), then we cannot truly know the nature of the external world or the causal relationships within it. Further, we cannot draw inferences about the natural world based on sensations since our sensations themselves could be in error. Among the inferences about which we cannot be sure are conclusions about the characteristics of the natural world. In turn, we cannot draw reliable inferences about ethical principles based on nature either. In the end, says Ockham, God's will is inscrutable, and our natural knowledge (including knowledge of ethics) is severely limited. Thus, the only reliable source of knowledge—including of ethical knowledge—is divine revelation.[34]

The Reformation Era

The sixteenth-century Protestant Reformation likewise brought challenges to the medieval (especially Thomistic) consensus regarding ethics.

Martin Luther

A chief leader of the Protestant Reformation was *Martin Luther* (1483–1546). At the center of Luther's protest was the question, how can a person be righteous in God's eyes? By Luther's time, the medieval church had come to endorse the view that a Christian could become literally righteous by that person's own moral acts or by having Christ's own righteousness transferred into the believer through the sacraments. Baptism infuses (Christ's) literal righteousness into a person; confession, penance, and purification in purgatory restore this righteousness if it is lost due to sin after baptism. Luther (and many other Reformers) disagreed both that a person could be morally righteous by self-effort and that righteousness could somehow be infused into a person, as if righteousness were an element poured into someone. Counter to this, Luther insisted, all persons (including Christians) remain sinners (unrighteous) all their earthly lives, and righteousness cannot be transmitted from one person to another. Rather, God saves persons by imputing (crediting) Christ's righteousness to them on the basis of their faith or trust (Latin: *fiducia*) even though they are not literally righteous. According to Luther, this is the central meaning of the biblical (and Pauline) idea of justification. Believers in Christ are justified—that is, declared righteous—because of their faith in Christ even though they are not factually righteous.

---

34. Jones, *The Medieval Mind*, 317–19. Also see Grenz, *The Moral Quest*, 154.

But what are the implications of Luther's views of justification for ethics? Does his position lead to the conclusion that Christians need not perform righteous or good acts because they in fact cannot do so? According to Luther, the answer is no! Rather, right living proceeds from a grateful heart that has been set free from the burden of self-righteousness. The Christian ever acknowledges his or her perennial sinfulness and inability to be literally righteous by self-effort. Further, the believer recognizes and rejoices over the ever-present reality of God's acquittal of sin and declaration (through Christ) of the sinner's righteousness. From this fundamental state of having been graciously justified, the Christian is free to do good acts without the burden of trying to be morally perfect. Indeed, from this state, love spontaneously arises. Luther comments: "From faith flow forth love and joy in the Lord, and from love a cheerful, willing, free spirit, disposed to serve our neighbor voluntarily, without taking any account of gratitude or ingratitude, praise or blame, gain or loss."[35]

In a similar manner, Luther contended that right living proceeds from an inner, spiritual change—that is, from the emergence of a new self through the empowering presence of God's Spirit. Luther notes that righteousness does not come from doing good deeds; rather, good deeds flow from good persons. Thus, only when an individual has been transformed by God into a righteous person do good acts naturally emerge. For Luther, the fatal flaw in the medieval understanding of justification is that justification (allegedly) attempts to produce good persons by requiring them to first do good things (i.e., to take the sacraments). But for Luther, inner righteousness only comes from divine grace and God's alteration of the human spirit. It is a gift from God. Indeed, striving to be righteous by deeds is itself a kind of rejection of God's grace; it is an attempt to achieve that which only God can give. In a similar manner, Luther rebuffs Thomas's notion that through reason and through force of habit persons can develop natural virtues. For Luther, such a view fails to grasp the thorough depravity of human tendencies, which penetrates to and distorts even the human ability to reason. Like Duns Scotus and William of Ockham, Luther taught that ethics is grounded not so much in reason as in the divine sovereign will.[36]

For Luther, then, persons cannot be righteous or saved by attempting to live by the precepts of God's law. Nevertheless, the divine law does plays a fundamental role in ethics. First, the law demonstrates the inability of humans to faithfully obey God. And awareness of this helps evoke (by the Spirit's urging) a contrite yearning for divine grace. Second, the law helps restrain the amount and degree of evil in the world, as human governments (following the basic precepts of the law) restrict foul deeds "through the sword"—that is, through various punishments.

---

35. Luther, *Concerning Christian Liberty* (1520), quoted in Wogaman, *Christian Ethics*, 117.

36. In many ways, Luther affirmed Thomas's idea of natural law—the idea that the divine moral will is present in the structures of human society and nature. But Luther's anthropology—especially his view of innate human sinfulness—led him to deny that humans can truly grasp or especially do what that natural law demands.

All this sets up Luther's understanding of two distinct arenas of human life. The one is the kingdom of the world (of non-Christians); the other is the kingdom of God (of Christians). Each has its own set of moral expectations. The former is ruled by God's law and is kept in check by means of the sword—the threat of punishment. The latter is ruled by divine grace and faith, and it is stayed by the precepts of love, the teachings of the gospel, and the inner testimony of the Spirit. Individual Christians should show mercy, be ready to forgive personal slights, and even be willing to die rather than kill in self-defense. But Luther thought it would be foolish to attempt to rule secular affairs with such grace. Until all become Christians and hence do right because they are inwardly righteous, concrete political structures must be ruled by the precepts of law. Evil must be kept in check by the state; hence by the state, evildoers must be punished, and the innocent must be protected from theft, bodily harm, and death. Although individual Christians should not kill in self-defense, Christians acting as functionaries of the state (and for the sake of protecting innocents) may inflict harm and even use deadly force against perpetrators of evil. Indeed, such actions are motivated by love—love for the innocent whose lives, properties, or rights are threatened.

Here is one final note regarding Luther: The great Reformer endorsed *the priesthood of believers*. Each Christian is directly in communion with God through Christ and is commissioned by God to minister in Christ's name. Thus, each Christian can interpret the Scriptures, proclaim it to others, and (with the Spirit's aid) lead others to faith and to salvation. Bishops, and other formal clergy, do not possess exclusive power to bring God's salvation to others. In light of this, Luther stressed the value of each Christian's calling (vocation) from God. For Luther, the medieval bifurcation of regular service to God (from in ordinary laypersons) and extraordinary service to God (manifested in clergy and monks) is improper. All forms of work that bring benefit to humanity are service to (and callings from) God. Luther writes:

> To call popes, bishops, priests, monks, nuns, the 'religious' class, but princes, lords, artisans, farm-workers, the 'secular' class, is a specious device invented by time-savers . . . All Christians whatsoever belong to the religious class . . . Those who exercise secular authority have been baptized like the rest of us; therefore they are priests and bishops. They discharge their office as an office of the Christian community and for its benefit.[37]

This notion of divine calling elevated the significance of the daily work done by ordinary believers, allowing the Protestant tradition to recognize most human occupations as vocations from God, each worthy of celebration and each commissioned by God.

37. Luther, *Works*, 6:407, 10–15, 17, 22, quoted in White, *Christian Ethics*, 180.

John Calvin

John Calvin (1509–1564) agreed with the central teachings of Luther regarding salvation. Like Luther, he rejected the notions that the sacraments infuse divine righteousness into persons, and that through self-effort (or willful cooperation with God) humans can do good things. Rather, sin permeates all human endeavors, rendering autonomous human acts bereft of genuine righteousness. Salvation comes only by divine grace, by God calling persons and granting them saving faith. Through that divinely given faith, believers are justified; that is, righteousness is imputed (credited) to them even though they are not literally righteous.

Calvin also agreed with Luther that genuine righteous does not come through doing good things but by being (divinely) inwardly changed. Here Calvin enhanced Luther's notion of morality flowing from changed persons: he employed the concept of *regeneration* to speak of God's spiritual activity of moving persons toward inner righteousness—a righteousness that also generates right acts. Through spiritual union with Christ, the believer is inwardly moved toward becoming like the image of Christ and doing as Christ would do.[38]

Calvin also followed Luther's notion that the law performs two functions. First, the law demonstrates to humans their utter incapacity to meet God's moral expectations. Second, through governors empowered to punish, the law restrains human wrongdoers. Thus, like Luther, Calvin allowed for police actions, corporal punishment, and war as actions (regrettably) necessary to protect the innocent. But Calvin adds to Luther's musings a third important function of the revealed law; namely, it directs individual Christians and Christian societies toward right living. The law describes what right living is to be, and while no human can fully obey the law (and hence no one can be made righteous through it), the law still gives guidance to individual believers seeking to follow Christ's way. In turn, the divine law also offers models for civic life. Agreeing with Luther that the sinful nature taints the human ability both to discern and to actualize what is right, Calvin nevertheless believed that through divine revelation Christians have access to the basic moral precepts necessary for building a just society—precepts available (though in a veiled way) through reason. Thus, Calvin was far more proactive than Luther in seeking to construct a godly society.[39] In turn, Calvin—perhaps even more than Luther—recognized the value of all human work,

---

38. Later Reformed writers would speak of this aspect of salvation as sanctification. See Chapter 5, above.

39. Stanley Grenz comments, "The connection between natural law and biblical precept fostered a stronger social ethic among Calvinists than Lutherans . . . The convergence of the natural and the revealed law suggests that society ought to be ordered in accordance with Christian ethical guidelines, for such an ordering is in line with the nature of society as created by God. It is no accident, therefore, that Reformed Christians, more so than their Lutheran counterparts, have been transformationists. Calvinists have sought to mold human society in accordance with what they saw as Christian principles of human social interaction" (Grenz, *The Moral Quest*, 163).

seeing such endeavors as divine vocations (as God's own benevolence to the world) and recognizing those performing such activities as called by God.

Other Voices of the Reformation Era

Not everyone agreed with Luther's and Calvin's views of salvation and ethics. *Erasmus of Rotterdam* (1466–1536), for instance, challenged Luther's denial that the human will can make no contribution toward receiving salvation or living the Christian life. For Erasmus, such a denial undermined any sense that human actions are *moral* acts, or that human choices are responsible. Additionally, Erasmus wondered whether persons could find incentive to behave morally or fight temptation if they believed that they contribute noting to their ultimate eternal destiny. Countering Luther, Erasmus proposed that humans must (to some degree) freely cooperate with God's saving actions in order to live a moral life and move toward holy living. The Roman Catholic *Council of Trent* (1545–1563) likewise rejected Protestant notions that human free will plays no role in salvation or in the ethical life. Rather, the council insisted that the human will freely cooperates with God's call to salvation and helps a person prepare to receive justification. In turn, freely chosen moral acts also contribute to the Christian's ongoing growth in righteousness after baptism, even though such acts are ever aided by God.

Another set of reactions to Luther and Calvin were expressed by *Anabaptists*. Unlike their Catholic counterparts, Anabaptist writers affirmed the core of Luther's doctrine of justification—affirming salvation by grace through faith alone. However, many Anabaptists insisted that human free will must play some critical role in the act of believing in Christ. The believer must freely choose to believe. In turn, differing from both Luther and Calvin, Anabaptists insisted upon *believer's baptism*. That is, each person must make a conscious choice to believe in Christ and receive the rite of baptism. Again, free will plays a crucial function for many Anabaptists. Here, though, is a final caveat: Anabaptists often also emphasized the need for Christians to be earnest in their attempts to follow Christ. Often only those who gave evidence of their commitment to Christ were admitted into the fellowship of Anabaptist congregations, and sometimes persons whose actions demonstrated egregious disregard for Christ's moral principles were formally banned from and shunned by the believing community.

Post-Reformation Protestant Developments

The early Reformers—including Luther and Calvin—hoped to reform the medieval church. But their efforts resulted in splintering Western Christianity into a myriad of forms. The diversity of these ruptures and the complexity of their history are beyond our concern here.

Suffice it to say that one result of these disruptions was an undermining of the medieval consensus about religious and moral authority. No longer did Protestant Christians heed the prescriptions of the Roman Catholic hierarchy; rather, they sought moral and doctrinal authority primarily from Scripture, reason, and the inner testimony of the Spirit.[40] Often Protestant writers endorsed some blending of these three.

A key example of such a Protestant ethic is found in the perspectives of the *Puritans* of England and America during the sixteenth, seventeenth, and eighteenth centuries. Puritans sought a church with morals and practices more consistent with biblical ecclesiastical images. Many Puritans sought to stay connected to the Church of England, desiring only to change some of its practices from within. Other Puritans—often called Separatists—were convinced that the Anglican church was too far removed from biblical ecclesial practices or morality; so, they sought to disassociate with that church and form separate congregations. At times Puritans, such as many of those who moved to the American colonies, hoped to establish commonwealths that honored and exemplified the moral and social demands of Christian Scripture. Though diverse in many ways, Puritans often shared several core views regarding ethics. Many imbibed the Reformed tradition's affirmation of Christian vocation, encouraging members to celebrate diverse forms of employment as legitimate expressions of divine calling. They typically encouraged hard work, honest business practices, frugal lifestyles, and generosity toward those in need. Although Puritans often are thought of as overly stringent regarding personal and social mores, they often saw themselves as taking seriously biblical mandates to live holy lives. Typically, Puritans invoked Scripture and the inner testimony of God's Spirit as primary sources of moral precepts.[41]

A second example of post-Reformation Protestant ethical theory is that offered by Anglican Bishop *Joseph Butler* (1692–1752). According to Butler, the grounding of human knowledge of morality is *conscience*. Conscience is a reflective, rational faculty that discerns the moral characteristics of actions and prompts humans toward doing good or avoiding evil. Butler agreed with philosophers who claim that in principle ethical norms should be actions that humans are capable of performing. He also granted that actions are motivated by passions and appetites, and that often these impulses are strong. Butler insisted, however, that these impulses can be regulated by three principles of the human self—namely, self-love, benevolence, and conscience. Self-love regulates our passions so as to promote our own best interests. Benevolence regulates our appetites so as to further the public good. And conscience is the source of and authority for moral responsibilities, prompting humans to perform their duties.

Butler argued that self-love is not synonymous with uncontrolled satisfaction of desires. Self-love is general. It is the desire for a lifetime of happiness. Its object is inner happiness, not external objects. Thus, true self-love is superior to the impulses

---

40. Affirmation of each of these sources is found (to varying degrees) in the writings of both Luther and Calvin.

41. Wogaman, *Christian Ethics*, 151–52. Also see White, *Christian Ethics*, 241–49, 266–68.

of passion or appetite, for the objects of these are always particular and external. Hunger longs for food. Revenge seeks to inflict pain. But self-love seeks a happy existence. In short, self-love seeks the best interests of the human self. Further, Butler believed that humans have a natural benevolence or love for others. Examples and evidence of this are found in human dispositions toward friendship, paternal and filial affections, and compassion. Butler insisted that conscience is the ability to reflectively approve, disapprove, or be indifferent toward our own actions. Conscience leads us toward doing good and avoiding mischief. That humans have a conscience is evident from common experience. Butler believed that moral conscience is given by God, citing Rom 2:14–15 as evidence for the reality and authority of conscience. For Butler, then, knowledge of right and wrong is grounded in God-given moral intuitions consonant with reason.[42]

Conclusion

Christian ethical theories and practices continued to take shape after the first century CE. Anchored in the Hebrew biblical tradition and in the insights of Jesus and the first Christian communities, Christians of later periods attempted to apply and expand these ideals in their own historical and cultural contexts. Naturally, such attempts often involved Christian thinkers interacting with the varied cultural, political, and intellectual environments of their given times—often intertwining Christian ideals with thought patterns and concerns dominant in those periods. In this ninth chapter, we have examined several of the major ethical teachings of prominent Christian thinkers and movements of the classical, medieval, and Reformation eras. In Chapter 10, we will explore the ethical perspectives of Christians in the modern and contemporary periods.

---

42. See Denise et al., eds., *Great Traditions in Ethics*, 117–28; and Wogaman, *Christian Ethics*, 158–61.

10

Christian Ethics in the Modern
and Contemporary Eras

IN CHAPTER NINE, WE explored some of the central Christian ethical perspectives that emerged in the classical, medieval, and Reformation eras. In Chapter 10, we turn to consider key Christian ethical models of the modern and contemporary periods.[1]

Modern Philosophical Ethics

Close on the heels of the Protestant Reformation was the modern era, a period running roughly through the seventeenth, eighteenth, and nineteenth centuries. During this age multiple trends in Western culture blended to form states of affairs never before fully manifested in human history. The details of these changes are well beyond our concerns here. Suffice it to say the following features contributed to the modern era:

1. The rise of humanism—the celebration of human creativity, art, and reason

2. Western global expansion, exploration, and exploitation

3. The development of modern nation-states

4. The emergence of capitalism and modern financing

5. The ascendancy of empirical science, technology, and industry

6. The growth in individualism—the appreciation of the autonomy, rights, and value of individual humans

7. Secularism—a refocusing from religious to secular concerns

8. Modern philosophy—adaptation of philosophical epistemology and metaphysics to interpret modern science and modern values

---

1. By the term "modern period," I mean (roughly) the era beginning in the seventeenth century and running through the nineteenth century. By the phrase "contemporary period," I largely mean the twentieth and twenty-first centuries.

Out of this cultural and intellectual milieu several influential models of philosophical ethics arose, including theories offered by Thomas Hobbes, John Locke, David Hume, Immanuel Kant, John Stuart Mill, and Karl Marx.

Thomas Hobbes

From foundations grounded in reason, numerous modernist approaches to ethics arose in the seventeenth, eighteenth, and nineteenth centuries. Thomas Hobbes (1588–1679) offered his own essentially materialistic vision of political and ethical theory. Hobbes proposed that in a presocial material world, humans would find themselves in competition with one another for various resources. In such a state, everyone would have a "right" to whatever he or she wanted. But under such conditions, persons also would find themselves insecure; they would be ever threatened by other people seeking the same resources. Hobbes claimed that at this point reason would arise and dictate that the wisest course for self-interested humans is to enter into *social contracts* with one another. In these contracts, each person willingly gives up those rights that others are willing to relinquish too. Or another way to say this is that people demand only those rights that they are willing to grant to others.[2] Hobbes summarized the basic insight and moral maxim of such social contracts to be, "Do not do to others what you do not want done to you."[3] Hobbes insisted that people would and should enter into these agreements because it is in their long-term best interest to do so. Otherwise, humanity would be in a constant state of war. In other words, for Hobbes, the ultimate grounding of ethics and of social contracts is a kind of egoism. Ethical egoism essentially claims that an action is right if it benefits me, the individual. Hobbes called himself an *enlightened egoist* because he believed that usually it is in the best interest of someone to respect the rights of others—thus, avoiding conflict.

John Locke

Following some of the insights of Hobbes, John Locke (1632–1704) also advocated for a social-contract understanding of human government. Ultimately, Hobbes's pessimism about human nature led him to affirm the need for a sovereign monarch who—in the face of selfish, irrational, and often fickle humans—would guarantee the rule of law over anarchy. But Locke—who was more optimistic about human capacities to live in harmony—supported diverse forms of government so long as they recognized the ultimate sovereignty of the people as a whole—including their collective right to change governments should such institutions fail to attend to the demands and rights of the populace.[4] Locke also advocated freedom of religious *beliefs* as long as such beliefs did

2. Hobbes, *Leviathan*, chapters 13 and 14.

3. Hobbes, *Leviathan*, chapter 15.

4. Locke, *Concerning Civil Government*.

not generate *practices* that brought harm to others or to their rightful property.[5] Locke likewise believed ethical norms are ultimately grounded in God. But he thought (and Aquinas had thought similarly) that these core norms are knowable by a kind of natural reason. Specifically, Locke argued that right actions are those that in the long run bring about a balance of pleasure over pain in a person's or a society's life. Locke, however, also believed that the divine law is ultimately designed to help bring about precisely such a circumstance for individuals and humanity as whole.

David Hume

The philosophy of David Hume (1711–1776) shared much in common with John Locke's. Each man endorsed an empiricist approach to knowledge. This tradition insists that the primary source of knowledge is experience. Hence, the mind has no innate ideas, only ideas accrued through experience. In turn, there are two types of *experience*: (1) sense experiences (sight, hearing, taste, and so forth) and (2) the immediate experiences of the mind (such as awareness of one's own thoughts or passions).[6] According to Hume (and Locke) only through these kinds of experiences does the mind have ideas. Thus, for example, through sensation one gains the *idea* of red (redness); through the immediate experience of being angry, one obtains the general notion of anger. Unlike Locke, however, Hume recognized interesting implications of such an empiricist approach for ethics. Hume queried: if all ideas are grounded in some prior experience, what is the experiential grounding of the concepts of right and wrong? Hume denied (as a good empiricist) that such concepts are known innately. At the same time, however, Hume recognized that ethical concepts do not derive from sense experience. A person never sees, tastes, or smells wrongness or rightness when observing (or imagining) some event (such as someone being stabbed or someone being aided in time of need). Hence, Hume concluded that the concepts of wrong and right must be grounded in some inner, mental experience. Specifically, he contended that the idea of right must be grounded in the feeling of "approval," and wrong must be grounded in the feeling of "disapproval."[7] Hume's perspective on ethics is typically understood to be a form of subjectivism. An action is right if an individual approves of it; it is wrong if someone disapproves of it. Hume attempted to avoid sheer relativism of ethical norms by proposing that overall humans tend to share similar ethical feelings toward various actions (or potential actions) in the world. Hume believed that, in general, humans tend to favor those actions that are understood to benefit humanity.[8]

5. Locke, *A Letter Concerning Toleration.*

6. Examples of thoughts are believing that a claim is true, denying a claim, hoping for something to occur. Examples of passions are awareness of being angry or being afraid.

7. Hume, *An Enquiry Concerning Human Understanding*, section 2. Also see, Hume, *An Enquiry Concerning the Principles of Morals.*

8. Hume writes: "It is sufficient for our present purpose, if it be allowed, what surely, without the

Immanuel Kant

Immanuel Kant (1724–1804) was another important modern thinker. Kant insisted that ethics is grounded in reason. An action is right if it conforms with the dictates of reason. It is wrong if it does not conform with reason. The goodness of an act is not determined by the empirical consequences that it brings about. It is good solely based on whether or not the act conforms to a rule of action established by reason.

Kant agreed with Hume (and other empiricists) that knowledge begins with sense experience. But Kant insisted (contrary to Hume and Locke) that sense data is not simply passively received by the mind. Rather the human mind imposes structure upon the data that it receives from the senses. Kant agreed with Hume that rightness and wrongness cannot be sensed in external events. Thus, Kant rejected what he called "hypothetical imperatives." These are commands or recommendations to act so as to attain some nonmoral purpose, some nonmoral consequence—like attaining wealth or achieving happiness. For Kant, such external events are neither right nor wrong. They are morally neutral, capable of being used for good or evil. Kant also insisted (contrary to Hume) that rightness and wrongness cannot be inwardly felt. Rightness and wrongness are not a matter of sentiment, a matter of *feeling* approval or disapproval of a given external event. Kant argued that while certain instinctual feelings may motivate a person to act in accordance with what is right, this is not the same as acting for the sake of what is right.

In light of these denials, Kant suggested that moral knowledge is grounded in *pure moral reasoning*. The content of pure moral reasoning is any concept based solely on the formal structures of moral reasoning. It is a concept that contains no reference to sensory experiences or sensory objects. In short, it is an a priori concept. But what concepts are derived from pure moral reasoning? For Kant there is one central idea derived from pure moral reasoning, and that is the notion of *oughtness* or *duty*. For Kant, the abstract idea of duty grounds all moral reasoning. Thus, according to Kant, an action is right if and only if it is done for the sake of duty.

Kant affirmed what he called the *categorical imperative*. This is a command that demands that an action be performed solely for the sake of the action itself, and not for some further consequence. In turn, a genuinely moral categorical imperative must be one that commands an action solely for the sake of duty itself. Thus, Kant says that the moral imperative or categorical imperative commands "universal

---

greatest absurdity cannot be disputed, that there is some benevolence, however small, infused into our bosom; some spark of friendship for humankind; some particle of the dove kneaded into our frame, along with the elements of the wolf and serpent. Let these generous sentiments be supposed ever so weak; let them be insufficient to move even a hand or finger of our body, they must still direct the determinations of our mind, and where everything else is equal, produce a cool preference of what is useful and serviceable to mankind, above what is pernicious and dangerous" (Hume, *An Enquiry Concerning the Principles of Morals*, 109–13 (quoted in Denise et al., eds., *Great Traditions in Ethics*, 138–39).

conformity of its actions to law in general."[9] Kant offered several versions of this basic categorical imperative:

> "I am never to act otherwise than so that I could also will that my maxim should become a universal law."[10]

> "Act only on that maxim whereby thou canst at the same time will that it should become a universal law."[11]

> "Act as if the maxim of thy action were to become by thy will a Universal Law of Nature."[12]

For Kant, then, morality is grounded in reason, in the a priori structures of moral reasoning. To violate the categorical imperative is to act irrationally. It is to ask the will to contradict itself, to will different actions under essentially the same set of circumstances. Further, Kant believed that the rational grounding of morality implies that rational creatures are the ultimate source of morality. When humans exercise reason, they effectively impose the categorical imperative (morality) upon themselves. As rational beings, we impose morality upon ourselves simply by affirming our own a priori concepts of moral reasoning. Further still, Kant insisted that since only rational beings understand, impose, and perform moral maxims, rational creatures alone are inherently good; that is, rational beings alone are ends unto themselves. Thus, Kant offers yet another version of the categorical imperative, one that recognizes the unique value of rational beings—including humans:

> So act as to treat humanity, whether in thine own person or in that of any other, in every case as an end withal, never as means only.[13]

John Stuart Mill

Another important ethicist of the modern era was John Stuart Mill (1806–1873).

Mill agreed with David Hume that knowledge (including ethical concepts) is founded upon experience. But while Hume attempted to establish ethics in the passions of approval or disapproval, Mill sought to ground ethics in the experiences of pleasure or pain. According to Mill, an action is good if it brings pleasure or avoids

9. Kant, *Fundamental Principles of the Metaphysics of Morals* (quoted in Denise et al., eds., *Great Traditions in Ethics*, 149).

10. Kant, *Fundamental Principles of the Metaphysics of Morals* (quoted in Denise et al., eds., *Great Traditions in Ethics*, 149).

11. Kant, *Fundamental Principles of the Metaphysics of Morals* (quoted in Denise et al., eds., *Great Traditions in Ethics*, 151).

12. Kant, *Fundamental Principles of the Metaphysics of Morals* (quoted in Denise et al., eds., *Great Traditions in Ethics*, 151).

13. Kant, *Fundamental Principles of the Metaphysics of Morals* (quoted in Denise et al., eds., *Great Traditions in Ethics*, 153).

pain. Further, unlike Hume, who tended to stress the inner experiences of individuals, Mill emphasized the experiences of the majority of persons. Thus, for Mill, that action is best which brings about the greatest balance of pleasure over pain *for the greatest number of persons*. Mill called his perspective *utilitarianism*. Some in Mill's day (and today) complained that his doctrine was "swinish." That is, they protested that to root good in pleasure ultimately makes human moral actions no higher than the acts of base animals (pigs). Mill denied this. Rather, he insisted that humans are able to appreciate higher pleasures than can pigs. For example, humans can enjoy scientific inquiry, problem solving, art, and philosophical speculation. In turn, argued Mill, typically, humans prefer a life that includes higher pleasures and not just one that grants sensual indulgences. Thus, Mills writes: "It is better to be a human being dissatisfied than a pig satisfied";[14] Mill saw his theory of utilitarianism as an enlightened revision of the ancient hedonistic theory of Epicurus.

Karl Marx

Another important contributor to nineteenth-century (especially political) ethics was Karl Marx (1818–1883). Marx offered a materialistic interpretation of human history. He saw history as a series of essentially economic conflicts among social classes as they attempted to satisfy various physical and emotion needs in this material world. According to Marx, such conflicts move toward a kind of natural resolution. Marx believed that the emergence of industrial technology and capitalism had generated an economic crisis that was creating human conflict that ultimately would resolve itself when workers were no longer alienated from what they produce. Marx contended that these clashes would be resolved when property was deprivatized— that is, taken from capitalistic owners and given to the working classes as a whole. For Marx, the ideal political system was communism wherein workers generate products based on their own innate interests and abilities, and those products are then distributed within the broad society as each person needs. Marx tended to dismiss religion as nothing more than an ideology that arises to appease the anxieties of persons whose economic needs are not being sufficiently met.[15]

Spiritual Awakenings, Revival, and Evangelicalism

As the voices of modernism and rationality resounded throughout the seventeenth, eighteenth, and nineteenth centuries, other phenomena ignited and flamed across Great Britain, the United States, and parts of Continental Europe. Numerous Christians sought for and experienced what aptly has been called spiritual awakening. In

---

14. Mill, *Utilitarianism*, chapter 2 (quoted in Denise et al., eds., *Great Traditions in Ethics*, 162).

15. Jones, *Kant and the Nineteenth Century*, 178–92.

the late seventeenth century, a movement known as Pietism arose. This program was led by men such as Philipp Jakob Spener (1635–1705), August Hermann Francke (1633–1727), and Nikolaus von Zinzendorf (1700–1760). These leaders stressed the importance of personal commitment to Christ, individual and group Bible study and prayer, and pious living. A movement similar to Pietism was Methodism, which arose in England under the leadership of John Wesley (1703–1791), Charles Wesley (1707–1788), and George Whitefield (1714–1770). These writers stressed personal conversion to Christ, Bible study, private prayer, Christian fellowship, and passion for Christ. These movements (including those they inspired) are sometimes referred to as Evangelicalism since among other ideals they emphasized the need to respond to the gospel (*evangelion*; good news) of Christ.

John Wesley and George Whitefield played significant roles in the Great Awakening—a decades-long series of religious revivals that broke out in Great Britain and in the American British colonies in the eighteenth century. Other leaders of the Great Awakening were Theodorus Frelinghuyson (1692–1747), Gilbert Tennent (1703–1764), and Jonathan Edwards (1703–1758). Another series of revivals exploded during the early decades of the nineteenth century. Sometimes called the Second Great Awakening, these religious rallies splashed across the western frontiers of Kentucky, Tennessee, Pennsylvania, and Ohio. Many of these revivals were conducted in great camp meetings that drew hundreds, even thousands, to hear evangelists from various Protestant denominations deliver emotion-packed messages of repentance, faith, and spiritual renewal. Thousands converted to Christ or renewed their faith. Echoes of these revivals continued through much of the nineteenth century in urban areas through the preaching of men such as Charles Finney (1792–1875) and Dwight L. Moody (1837–1899).

Tied to these diverse spiritual awakenings was an earnest desire for an emotionally and existentially impactful faith—one that gave both meaning to existence in the present and hope for the future. Many who participated in the great revivals, while obviously yearning for communion with God, also sought relief from sometimes crushing social challenges. The early revivals in Great Britain often drew persons who "had lost the protections of the medieval feudal order without gaining the freedoms and affluence of the new industrial age."[16] In a similar manner, the hardships of the American frontier and the poverty of the working classes in Britain's and America's industrialized cities (especially in the late nineteenth century) led many to turn in faith to a transcendent gospel-message. To such audiences, the revivalists of the period stressed salvation and justification by grace through faith as well as promises of fellowship with and empowerment by the Spirit of God. Revivalists also celebrated deep emotional responses to the gospel—including remorse for sin and elation for God's gifts of forgiveness and spiritual enabling. For many people, such displays of emotion were welcome in an era when some intellectuals disparaged

16. Wogaman, *Christian Ethics*, 161.

emotional enthusiasm and admired the calm (if sometimes sterile) detachment of reason. As we will see below, these Evangelical movements often also challenged key social evils of the eighteenth and nineteenth centuries.

The Liberal-Conservative Divide

Another important feature of the modern era involved two broad and distinctive Christian reactions to the tenets of modernism. While all Christians, to some degree, imbibed aspects of the modern ethos, some were more accommodating to it than others. Several Christians—often called *liberals* (or *classic liberals*)—endorsed the modernist notion that the universe is a closed physical system. From this view, liberals often denied divine miraculous intervention in history. Consequently, many such Christians thought of divine revelation not so much as God miraculously breaking into history to reveal truths, but more as divine revelation immanent in the broad processes of human and natural history. In a similar manner, some—although certainly not all—liberals doubted the incarnation of God in Christ or Jesus' physical resurrection from the dead or belief in a general resurrection. Rather many liberals emphasized the role of Jesus as a moral teacher and downplayed the importance of his death as an atoning sacrifice for sin. Writers associated with nineteenth-century liberalism included Frederick Schleiermacher (1768–1834), Albrecht Ritschl (1822–1889), and Adolf Harnack (1851–1930).

Opposing the views of classic liberals, several Christians—often called *conservatives*—emphasized the supernatural status of Jesus and his work, accentuating Christ's deity and his atoning sacrifice on the cross as the primary means by which humans may be reconciled to God. Conservatives often believed that the modern philosophical case against knowledge of supernatural truths was grossly overstated, and that in fact a strong rational case can be made for believing in God's supernatural inbreaking into history and for the deity's miraculously conveying truths through special revelation. Further, conservatives stressed the need for personal confession of and conversion to Christ as the means by which one might be saved. Many conservatives agreed (in principle) with liberals that all people—including Christians—should live moral lives, loving God and loving their fellow humans; but conservatives also often believed that essential to such morality was the more fundamental need to get right with God by exercising faith in Christ and his saving atonement on the cross. Key nineteenth-century exponents of conservative Christianity included Charles Hodge (1797–1878) and Benjamin Warfield (1851–1921).[17]

Something of an ethical divide emerged between Christian liberals and conservatives. Liberals tended to stress the need for social morality, calling for proactive changes to evil social structures in order to produce a more Christian society. Conservatives

17. For further details on the liberal and conservative theological divide see Robinson, *Christianity: A Brief History*, 352–58.

often emphasized individualistic morality, calling for personal conversion to Christ and for personal commitment to living as a righteous individual.

Abolitionism, Feminism, and Social-Economic Ethics

Three socioethical concerns especially caught the attention of many Christians and non-Christians alike in the nineteenth century. These were concerns over slavery, women's rights, and the plight of the working-class poor. Many Christians of various stripes challenged the moral blight of American slavery. In the eighteenth century, writers such as Congregationalist Samuel Sewell (1653–1730), Quaker John Woolman (1756–1772), and Methodist John Wesley spoke out vehemently against slavery. In 1833, through the efforts of several English Christians, including especially the work of William Wilberforce (1759–1833), slavery was abolished in British territories worldwide. Around the same time, abolitionists in the United States gained ground, calling for the cessation of slavery on American soil. The American Anti-Slavery Society was founded in 1833. Sadly, not all Christians were abolitionists. Controversies about slavery (and other matters) drew the United States into civil war in the 1860s, ultimately leading to the defeat of rebel southern states and to the eradication of slavery in America. But the long-standing existence of slavery in the USA, including the racist rationales and social structures used (often by white Christians) to support it, was and still is a lingering blemish on the American Christian psyche.

Another critical ethical issue of the modern era was concern over women's rights. Historians sometimes refer to this period of feminist activity as the *first wave* of modern feminism. Fueled by political liberalism—especially as expressed by John Locke and American constitutionalism—a number of feminists arose in the eighteenth and nineteenth centuries, advocating for core rights for women. Emphasizing the pragmatic tensions that arise between fundamentally self-interested persons, as well as stressing the intrinsic value of individuals, classic political liberals often insisted that a central function of government is to grant and protect core civil liberties of citizens, including protection of property, the right to vote, the right to free speech, the right to religious freedom, and liberty to assemble. As these norms for male citizens became common in Britain and especially the United States, several advocates for similar rights for women likewise arose. One of the earliest first-wave feminists was Mary Wollstonecraft (1759–1799), who noted the negative effects of the capitalist, industrial economy on middle-class women, whose roles became restricted to economically unproductive domestic lives of leisure. According to Wollstonecraft, such circumstances truncated women's opportunities for personal autonomy, rational development, productive enterprise, and self-development. Wollstonecraft advocated for equal opportunities in education for women.[18]

18. See Wollstonecraft, *Vindication of the Rights of Woman*.

John Stuart Mill and Harriet Taylor Mill (1807–1858) also advocated for women's rights in the nineteenth century.[19] Each author argued not only for equal educational opportunities for women but also for granting women core civil rights and employment options. Harriet Taylor Mill insisted that "sexual inequality is the result not of nature's decrees but of society's customs and traditions."[20] Consequently, she proposed women be given equal education, equal partnership in business (including gains and risks), and "a coequal share in the formation and administration of laws."[21] John Stuart Mill challenged the misconception that women are intellectually inferior to men, insisting that given the opportunity generally women too will excel in rational inquiry. Further, among other arguments, Mill offered a utilitarian case for granting core civil rights (including suffrage) and economic opportunities to women; he argued that making such concessions would benefit society as a whole.

In the nineteenth century, in America, many supporters of abolition likewise championed the feminist cause. Among the ranks of feminists were both women (such as Angelina and Sarah Grimké, Elizabeth Cady Stanton, and Susan B. Anthony) and men (such as William Lloyd Garrison and Frederick Douglass). In 1848, several women's rights advocates met at the Seneca Falls Convention, issuing a declaration that decried the long-standing tyranny[22] of men over women. Among the injuries protested were denying women the right to vote, forcing women to live by laws in whose formation they had no say (including marriage laws that unjustly undermined women's rights to property and to political and economic autonomy), and limiting women to subordinate positions in churches.[23]

Through the advocacy of these early women's rights activists, several laws were enacted in America, Britain, and English-speaking territories, seeking to change various legal inequalities. In 1839, Mississippi became the first state in the USA to grant women the right to own property in their own names (rather than in the names of their fathers or husbands). In 1845, New York allowed women the right to obtain patents for their inventions and to gain and keep earnings for themselves "as if they were unmarried." In 1848, the New York legislature passed the Married Woman's Property Act, which allowed wives on their own (independent of their husbands) to own property, enter into contracts, collect rent, and file lawsuits. By 1900, all other states in the USA had similar laws. Comparable laws arose in Britain. From 1870 through 1893, a number of Married Women's Property Acts were enacted by British Parliament, each granting greater economic rights to women within the context of marriage. Often previous laws had disadvantaged married women by subsuming their ownership and control of

19. John and Harriet were longtime friends who eventually married. Each wrote separately regarding women's issues, as well as collaboratively.

20. Tong, *Feminist Thought*, 18.

21. Mary Taylor Mill, "Enfranchisement of Women" (quoted in Tong, *Feminist Thought*, 95).

22. The Seneca Falls Declaration specifically uses the word "tyranny" in this context.

23. Wogaman, *Christian Ethics*, 198.

property under the authority of their husbands. The British Married Women's Property Acts ceded various property rights to wives, including ownership and control over assets earned or inherited. Alongside demands for fair economic policies, first-wave feminists advocated for women's right to vote. Such pleas (and political activism) helped embolden lawmakers and populaces to grant suffrage to women throughout the Western world. In 1869, Wyoming became the first US state to grant voting rights to female citizens. New Zealand granted such rights in 1893, Australia in 1902, Britain in 1918, and the United States in 1920.[24]

Several Christian feminist writers of the era challenged traditional interpretations of the Bible that denied ministerial authority and offices to women—insisting instead that the Bible affirms women's leadership. Others Christian writers acknowledged scriptural restrictions upon the role of women in the church, but they attributed these prohibitions to the ancient historical context in which such passages were written. Using strategies often employed by abolitionists to undermine the Bible's implicit acceptance of slavery, several feminist authors insisted that while Scripture writers often unconsciously assumed and promoted subservient social roles for women, the higher ideals implicit in the Bible's teachings ultimately undermine such social oppression.[25]

A third paramount ethical issue of the eighteenth and nineteenth centuries was the plight of the economically underprivileged. Various Christian leaders of the period sought to address the suffering and inequalities faced by the urban and rural poor. The Industrial Revolution created a need for unskilled workers, greatly increasing the populations of British and American cities as millions migrated from farms and small towns seeking jobs. Industry brought great wealth to owners of large businesses but often squashed small businesses and trapped workers in a life-time of hard work, debt, and subsistence. In response, many Christians sought to relieve the hardships of the urban poor by sponsoring various rescue missions such as the McAuley Water Street Mission in New York City (now called New York City Rescue Mission), Goodwill Industries, the Salvation Army, the Young Men's Christian Association (YMCA) and the Young Women's Christian Association (YWCA). Many local churches—Protestant and Catholic alike—also began neighborhood food pantries, clothing distribution-centers, homeless shelters, and various health services. Many Evangelical Protestants also fought against the ills of alcohol abuse, linking poverty and alcohol consumption as interdependent phenomena. In 1866, the Women's Christian Temperance Union was formed as was the Anti-Saloon League in 1895.

24. National Women's History Alliance, "Timeline of Legal History of Women in the United States."

25. The emergence of scientific biblical, literary, and historical interpretation (sometimes called higher criticism) helped make possible such nuanced Christian feminist critiques of the biblical literature. The same may be said of abolitionist interpretations of the Bible. Wogaman suggests that biblical scholarship and these social-ethical concerns were mutually supporting phenomena—each spurring the other toward further insights. Wogaman, *Christian Ethics*, 192.

Early Twentieth-Century Christian Ethics

The twentieth and twenty-first centuries brought new wonders to the world, many of which were echoes of the previous era. Science and technology continued to expand at breakneck speeds. Automobiles, airplanes, telephones, radios, televisions, computers, the internet, and cell phones, all emerged over the course of these centuries, as well as breakthroughs in medicine and industrial productivity. Alongside these marvels of human invention were fearful weapons of war. Early in the twentieth century, many (especially liberal) Christians expressed belief and hope that the coming century would be a new era of peace and progress for humanity—a period inspired and facilitated by the ideological and technological splendors of Western, Christian civilization. Such grandiose hopes were soon dashed by the horrors of the First and Second World Wars, as well as by the Cold War and its harrowing threat of planetary nuclear annihilation.

Not surprisingly, a variety of Christian responses to the realities of the contemporary era emerged. In this section, we highlight some of the most notable of these approaches. First, we discuss the Social Gospel movement.

The Social Gospel and Walter Rauschenbusch

While admiring the varied politically conservative Christian efforts to aid the plight of the working-poor, a number of Christian writers of the late nineteenth and early twentieth centuries began calling for more drastic responses to the human dilemma fostered by the industrial age. Informed by the secular political-economic ideas of individuals such as Henry George (1839–1897) and Karl Marx, these writers argued that socialist policies best suit the Christian call to charity and justice toward humanity. Two exponents of Christian socialism were W. D. P. Bliss (1856–1926) and George D. Herron (1862–1925): each man was active in the Society of Christian Socialists (founded in 1889).[26]

Likely the most renowned proponent of what became known as the Social Gospel movement was Walter Rauschenbusch (1861–1918). Rauschenbusch was a second-generation German immigrant to the United States. His family had strong roots in Lutheranism, but early in life his father, Augustus Rauschenbusch (1816–1899), converted to the Baptist faith. Walter too was Baptist but felt strong ties to his German-Lutheran heritage. In 1886, Walter Rauschenbusch was called to the Second Baptist Church in New York City, near Hell's Kitchen. There his sensitivities to urban poverty especially were awakened, and he began seriously contemplating how Christianity could best respond. During this time, Rauschenbusch found inspiration in various Christian

26. Two other voices worthy of mention were F. D. Maurice (1805–1872) and Washington Gladden (1836–1918). These writers were transitional figures whose proposals were less radical than those of other Christian advocates of social change, but their efforts inspired and helped spur on the Christian socialist movements.

social-activists, including some socialists. In 1891, Rauschenbusch visited Germany, spending part of his time under the tutelage of Albrecht Ritschl, whose teachings about the kingdom of God greatly influenced him. In 1897, Rauschenbusch took a faculty position at Rochester Seminary in New York, teaching church history. During his tenure at Rochester, Rauschenbusch penned several influential Social Gospel works, including especially *Christianity and the Social Crisis* (1907), *Christianizing the Social Order* (1912), and *A Theology for the Social Gospel* (1917).

At the center of Rauschenbusch's approach to the Social Gospel was the concept of the kingdom of God. In *Christianizing the Social Order*, Rauschenbusch writes:

> Christ's conceptualization of the kingdom of God came to me as a new revelation. Here was the idea and purpose that had dominated the mind of the Master Himself. All His teachings centre about it. His death was suffered for it . . . The saving of the lost, the teaching of the young, the pastoral care of the poor and frail, the quickening of starved intellects, the study of the Bible, church union, political reform, the reorganization of the industrial system, international peace—it was all covered by the one aim of the Reign of God on earth . . . the divine transformation of all human life.[27]

It is not surprising, then, that in his groundbreaking major work—*Christianity and the Social Crisis*—Rauschenbusch attempted to show first that "the essential purpose of Christianity was to transform human society into the kingdom of God by regenerating all human relations and reconstituting them in accordance with the will of God."[28] Rauschenbusch sought to demonstrate this by examining the core content of the prophetic tradition of Israel, the central teachings of Christ, and the dominant themes of pre-Constantinian Christianity. Next, in the same work, Rauschenbusch catalogued a host of problems in his day, most of which he attributed to the rise of the industrial age. Among those challenges listed were the undermining of previous economic systems that more directly rewarded workers for their products, the increasing of land prices beyond the reach of workers, low wages for workers, economic insecurity, the demoralization of workers, ill health, economic and political inequality, threats faced by democratic processes, moral decline, strain upon family units, and direct challenges to the existence of Christianity as envisioned by Christ.[29]

For Rauschenbusch, the primary solution to these woes induced by the Industrial Revolution was the emergence of a socialist economic system politically supported by the working class and inspired, advocated, and reinforced by Christianity. According to Rauschenbusch, capitalism "necessarily divides industrial society into two classes—those who own the instruments and materials of production, and those who furnish the labor for it." Such a division has produced the tensions and ills of

---

27. Rauschenbusch, *Christianizing the Social Order* (quoted in White, *Christian Ethics*, 293).

28. Rauschenbusch, *Christianity and the Social Crisis*, xxiii.

29. Rauschenbusch, *Christianity and the Social Crisis*, 211–86.

modern society. Socialism, however, would "abolish the division of industrial society into two classes and . . . close the fatal chasm which has separated the employing class from the working class." In turn, it would "restore the independence of the workingman by making him once more the owner of his tools and . . . give him the full proceeds of his production instead of a wage determined by his poverty."[30] Christianity, in turn, could provide the moral support needed for such an endeavor, entering a "working alliance" with the working class, effectively providing the "soul" for the political "body" of the workers' "economic class movement," providing the "elation and faith that comes through religion."[31]

Rauschenbusch's analysis of social ills, combined with his understanding of the kingdom of God, led him to bemoan the individualistic understanding of the gospel often expressed by various conservative Christians of his era. While agreeing that personal conversion was an essential element of the gospel message, Rauschenbusch insisted that conversion of society from the systemic evil of unjust economic and political structures to just social systems also was a central concern of the Christian faith. Sin is selfishness, and while this involves personal rebellion against God, it also entails disdain for and abuse of one's fellow humans. In turn, salvation involves not only being made right with God or personal morality. It also includes fighting for and establishing righteous or just economic, political, social systems.[32] Rauschenbusch notes that evil social systems make good people do bad things, while good social systems help curtail the evils of evil individuals.[33] Rauschenbusch was aware that conservatives sometimes criticized advocates of the Social Gospel (and socialism) for failing to appreciate the gravity of sin—for naively thinking that humankind can generate political-economic systems wherein justice prevails and sinful humans willingly share economic resources. Rauschenbusch retorted, however, that conservatives likewise can be criticized for failing to recognize the systemic nature of sin whereby unjust social systems perpetuate injustice and benefit some social classes over others.

Neoliberalism: Reinhold Niebuhr

Another significant Christian ethicist of the twentieth century was Reinhold Niebuhr (1892–1971). Niebuhr had much in common with Rauschenbusch and other advocates of the Social Gospel. Like them, Niebuhr was discontent with conservative Christian tendencies to ignore the social-economic forces at play in capitalistic systems, which generate the plight of the working-class poor as well as the perennial political clout of the wealthy. Niebuhr, however, also saw early advocates of the Social Gospel as politically naive and theologically misguided. Social Gospel writers tended to believe that

---

30. Rauschenbusch, *Christianity and the Social Crisis*, 406–7.

31. Rauschenbusch, *Christianity and the Social Crisis*, 409.

32. Rauschenbusch, *A Theology for the Social Gospel*, 45–56, 95–103.

33. Rauschenbusch, *Christianizing the Social Order*, 125. See also Wogaman, *Christian Ethics*, 213.

rational enlightenment or appeal to the Christian principle of love would suffice to inspire social-economic changes. Such tactics would educate the elite toward granting greater economic power to the working class and would motivate the working class to strive for, establish, and maintain economic systems wherein each individual worked according to his or her abilities, and each member of society was supplied according to his or her needs. According to Niebuhr, however, such beliefs fail sufficiently to grasp the deep-rooted bias of humans toward self-interest, thus failing to take seriously the truth of the Christian doctrine of sin.[34] Niebuhr comments, "What is lacking among all these moralists, whether religious or rational, is an understanding of the brutal character of the behavior of all human collectives, and the power of self-interest and collective egoism in all inter-group relations."[35] In a similar manner, Niebuhr writes regarding Marxism: "The weakness of the Marxian apocalypse is that its naturalism betrays it to utopian fantasies."[36] Marxism tends to see the ills of society as grounded in capitalistic systems, failing to realize that a dictatorship of the proletariat equally is subject to the collective egoism that generates exploitation of some humans by others.

For Niebuhr, the solution to the systemic nature of sin is *justice*, not merely love. Niebuhr admits that love is the highest Christian ethical principle. This precept calls for selfless regard for others. Through love, one is inwardly motivated to consider and care for the needs of others. Love can indeed inspire a person to take into consideration the needs of others before one's own, even leading an individual to refuse to match evil with evil, violence with violence. In turn, love leads to personal forgiveness. But such selfless regard for others often is not helpful in the context of social systems where egoism and self-interest inevitably emerge. While principles of nonviolence and nonretaliation can sometimes lead an enemy-group to repent and change selfish behavior, such is not necessarily or even normally the case. Often nonretaliation leads to even deeper abuses and injustices. For Niebuhr, in the context of human collectives (which nearly always are self-serving), the primary Christian moral principle to be employed is justice. Justice involves a balance of powers and interests so that fundamental rights are protected, and the needs of all classes are addressed and met, and no group is taken advantage of. Further, establishing justice often leads to conflict and requires perennial vigilance to maintain. Ultimately, for Niebuhr, love is the highest moral principle. Indeed, justice flows from love. But also, ultimately tolerance of injustice is inconsistent with love. For this reason, Niebuhr does not think that pacifism in the face of belligerence is typically a viable option; at times, aggression must be met with violence for the sake of the higher good.

34. For a brief description of Niebuhr's view of the doctrine of sin, see Chapter 4, above (pages [x-ref]).

35. Niebuhr, *Moral Man and Immoral Society*, xx.

36. Niebuhr, *An Interpretation of Christian Ethics*, 26.

Karl Barth

Another key contributor to Christian ethics in the twentieth century was Karl Barth (1886–1968). Although trained in the classic liberal tradition, Barth became convinced that the primary function of Scripture is not to give human interpretations of God, but to offer God's address to humanity. In turn, God is transcendent, infinite, absolute. God is wholly other than humanity; hence, only by the divine will and action can humans in any way know God. Barth rejected the liberal tradition's claims that God may be known through natural human abilities—through culture, or reason, or historical progression. God may be known only by an autonomous divine act of revelation wherein the deity confronts and encounters human beings. Thus, natural theology is not possible.[37] In turn, Barth rejected the notion that *ethics* can be established by human insights or efforts. Natural law ethics, like natural theology, is impossible because God's moral will transcends the human mind and heart. Further, since humans are sinful, they are utterly helpless in their attempts to know what is right or to be righteous in God's eyes. Indeed, at times, Barth suggests that ethical theories developed by human reason alone, including alleged natural law ethics, are sinful and the products on human pride.

Barth believed that ethics flows from theology. And at the center of theology is the claim that through Christ God was reconciling the world. By God's act of grace (not by human effort or cunning) humans are made right with God. The focal point of Christian ethics, then, is to recognize this utter human dependence upon God and live accordingly. According to Barth, God has freely elected to save humans through Christ, not through human moral acts. And this gracious act of election in Christ, itself is a divine command. "It is the command to be what, by divine grace, God has chosen us to be."[38] But to be this, one does not act per se; one *receives* through faith (through passive acceptance) what God has ordained is so (through Christ). Christian ethics, then, is primarily about *being something*, not about doing something. It is being what God has elected and commanded us to be—namely, redeemed, righteous, in Christ. One implication of this ethic is that Christians are freed from any cultural, economic, or social restrictions that are not consistent with their fundamental *being* in Christ. Another implication is that the gospel (good news of salvation in Christ) is primary, and obedience to law is secondary; obedience to divine law is essentially a response to the reception of righteous-being granted in Christ. It is doing that which one has become in Christ.

37. For Barth, divine revelation is a paradox. It occurs in history, especially in and through the Word of God—that is, Jesus Christ—but its truth cannot be discerned through human efforts (reason, intuitions, historical investigations, or the like). Rather, revelation only occurs when, through the Holy Spirit, God chooses to be known. Thus, every finite means by which the deity might be known (including Scriptures and the preaching of the church) both reveals and conceals God. Ultimately only when God chooses to be revealed does revelation occur.

38. Wogaman, *Christian Ethics*, 235.

Although Barth disavowed natural law, he insisted that certain moral precepts are noticeable in the created order. Knowledge of these patterns, however, is only discernible through divine revelation as manifested in Christ, the Word of God. This knowledge arises within the context of God's electing covenant of salvation in Christ.[39] God's sheer act of will is the reason for the existence of the saving covenant, and God's rationale for creating the world was so that the divinely ordained covenant could unfold (could be actualized). The created order, thus, exists for the sake of God's redemptive covenant with humankind, but that covenant itself could not transpire unless created beings (humans) existed in an environment created for them; only in such a context could the drama of redemption or covenant play out. According to Barth, among the moral principles arising from the doctrine of divine creation are precepts regarding "the Sabbath, prayer, confession, marriage, family and communal life, capital punishment, war, and vocation."[40]

Christian Ethics since the Mid-Twentieth Century

In the mid-twentieth century, Western culture experienced immense changes, as various movements questioned traditional practices and values. The civil rights movement challenged the de facto and de jure racial, gender, and sexual inequalities at play in America. Numerous voices likewise contested traditional (often religious) sexual prohibitions regarding sex outside of marriage, divorce, contraceptives, pornography, and same-sex relationships. In turn, many advocated for legalized abortion, arguing that denying such medical measures infringed upon women's rights of autonomy over their own bodies. During the mid-twentieth century, United States legislators enacted laws and courts rendered verdicts favoring pleas for such social changes. No doubt, these cultural shifts were due to numerous causes, but almost certainly a partial root of these alterations were ideals set in motion by the modern era—including affirmations of individual rights, freedom of conscience, freedom of religion, and calls to pursue one's own happiness and fulfillment. Not surprisingly, Christians offered different responses to these cultural swings. Many moderate and liberal Christians endorsed the various calls for racial and gender equality, seeing these movements as natural allies of earlier nineteenth- and twentieth-century Christian advocacy for workers' rights and socioeconomic equality. Many likewise advocated for social policies allowing same-sex relations and disallowing discrimination against gays and lesbians. Some moderate and liberal Christians (perhaps more reluctantly) accepted calls for legalizing abortion for the sake of women's rights.

39. In Christ's incarnation, God has entered into a covenant relation with humankind.
40. Brown, "Karl Barth's Doctrine of the Creation."

Joseph Fletcher

In the midst of these cultural modifications, a number of Christian voices arose advancing differing nuances to Christian ethics. Joseph Fletcher (1905–1991) endorsed *situation ethics*. This perspective affirmed love as the singular moral norm of Christian ethics.[41] All moral quandaries and decisions are resolved by contemplating what the most loving action would be in a given situation, and then doing it. Although Fletcher was not abundantly clear, for him, love appears to be more or less synonymous with benevolence and goodwill toward fellow humans.[42] According to Fletcher, love and justice are the same; justice simply is distributed love: justice involves enacting the implications of love calculated for groups.[43] Further, Christian love is impartial, inclusive, indiscriminate (universal), and not based on feeling. It is an attitude, an act of will.[44] Fletcher saw his approach as falling between legalism (in which preestablished moral rules determine what one should do such that rules tend to proliferate over time) and antinomianism (in which there are no preexisting moral precepts for discerning right actions such that one simply capriciously chooses "there and then" what to do). For Fletcher, like antinomianism, situationism addresses each moral decision in its immediate context, but unlike antinomianism (and like legalism), situationism does not come to the decision-making process empty-handed, without moral principles to aid in the process. Like legalism, situationism comes "fully armed with the ethical maxims of his community and its heritage," but unlike legalism, situationism "is prepared in any situation to compromise . . . [moral rules] or set them aside *in the situation* if love seems better served in doing so."[45]

Paul Ramsey

Fletcher's proposals received both accolades and critiques from Christian writers. One of the more substantive critiques (of which we say more below) came from Paul Ramsey (1913–1988), whose earlier writings inspired Fletcher's love-based situation ethics. In 1950, Ramsey published his notable text, *Basic Christian Ethics*.[46] Therein, Ramsey proclaimed "obedient love" to be the central moral norm of Christian ethics.[47]

---

41. Fletcher states: "There is only one thing that is always good and right, intrinsically good regardless of the context, and that one thing is love" (Fletcher, *Situation Ethics*, 60). See especially Fletcher's chapter called "Love Is the Only Norm," in *Situation Ethics*, 69–86.

42. Fletcher speaks of Christian love as "neighbor love" and notes: "Apart from the helping or hurting of people, ethical judgments or evaluations are meaningless" (Fletcher, *Situation Ethics*, 69–86). See also Grenz, *The Moral Quest*, 178.

43. Fletcher, *Situation Ethics*, 87–102.

44. Fletcher, *Situation Ethics*, 103–19.

45. Fletcher, *Situation Ethics*, 18–26 (brackets and italics added).

46. Ramsey, *Basic Christian Ethics*.

47. Ramsey, *Basic Christian Ethics*, xxxi.

In loving fellow humans (neighbors), the follower of Christ obeys God's covenant and fulfills the law.[48] This obedient love is only understood in the light of the nature of God, specifically the God of Jesus Christ, especially as manifested by divine incarnation in Christ. The nature of this God is disclosed in the Old Testament tradition's emphasis upon the *righteousness* of God (which often is virtually synonymous with God's *justice* and *steadfast mercy*). According to Ramsey, examination of this tradition reveals that God's righteousness is closely tied to salvation so that Israel's God is not righteous *yet also* savior; rather, *because* God is righteous, God is savior. God's righteousness is not one that stands aloof simply condemning humanity and sin. Rather, it is redemptive; in it, God perceives the poverty of humanity and seeks to save.[49]

In turn, claims Ramsey, Jesus highlighted and expanded this notion of divine righteousness. Jesus came proclaiming the kingdom or reign of God, including the ethical expectations of this rule. In his proclamation, a fundamental ethic of neighbor love emerges—one in which care for the needs of the other is prioritized. Neighborly love is uninterested in personal gain and instead focuses on the needs of the other for his or her own sake.[50] It is an "enlightened unselfishness."[51] Distinct from a legalist who attempts to follow law as closely as possible while making concessions for human need, Jesus prioritized lovingly meeting human hardships and "quite spontaneously left the rules behind to take maximum care of those in need."[52] Thus, considerable flexibility arises in the ethic of Jesus so that in a sense it is "an ethic without rules," because the principle of love directs one toward right acts without reference to external moral regulations. Ramsey sees the apostle Paul accurately capturing the ethic of Jesus when Paul teaches essentially that "all things are lawful for me, all things are now permitted, *which Christian love permits*."[53] According to Ramsey, the correlate of this principle is, "everything is demanded which Christian love requires," so that there is both freedom in Christ and servitude to Christ.[54]

Ramsey saw the command to love as a deontological ethic, one concerned primarily with the right (what one should do), not with the good (a state of affairs to be obtained). Christian neighbor love defines what is right or obligatory.[55] Thus, while Ramsey's ethic is grounded in the biblical tradition, he believed it had affinities with philosophical idealism.[56] For Ramsey, Christian love also seeks to create and preserve community, not for self-serving purposes (as Jeremy Bentham [1748–1832]

48. Ramsey, *Basic Christian Ethics*, 367, 388.

49. Ramsey, *Basic Christian Ethics*, 1–14

50. Ramsey, *Basic Christian Ethics*, 95–96.

51. Ramsey, *Basic Christian Ethics*, 160.

52. Ramsey, *Basic Christian Ethics*, 56.

53. Ramsey, *Basic Christian Ethics*, 78 (italics original).

54. Ramsey, *Basic Christian Ethics*, 79.

55. Ramsey, *Basic Christian Ethics*, 115–16.

56. Ramsey, *Basic Christian Ethics*, xiii.

proposed) or for the sake of shared values (as John Stuart Mill suggested). Rather, community is sought and preserved for the sake of the neighbor.[57] In turn, like the Reformers before him, Ramsey insisted that true love for neighbors sometimes requires making efforts to protect those who are threatened by others, including through state-sponsored police actions and war.[58]

In light of the discussion above, it is easy to see how Joseph Fletcher was inspired by Ramsey's ethical theory—in particular by Ramsey's assertion that Christian love is an "ethic without rules."[59] Ramsey, however, soon took exception to Fletcher's situation ethics, finding in it both a lack of clarity and a tendency to create dire consequences for Christian morality. A central critique offered by Ramsey was that situation ethics (as well as Ramsey's own earlier views) often failed to distinguish between justifying moral *acts* and justifying moral social *practices*. Ramsey agreed with Fletcher (and with the implications of his own earlier views) that when judging which *act* to perform in a given situation, one should determine which one is the most loving, even if this means breaking moral rules.[60] But Ramsey insisted that another Christian moral concern must be attempting to establish loving social policies or *practices*. Here one seeks to discern which overarching social practice most fully embodies love; in turn, one seeks to establish that practice as a rule of behavior for society.[61] In this case, "the *practice* itself is to be justified by direct application of Christian love. But then one justifies an action falling under it by appeal to the practice."[62] That is, love establishes the rule of *practice*, but the rule of practice establishes which *acts* to perform. Such "rules of practice necessarily involve the abdication of full liberty to guide one's action case by case by making immediate appeals to what love . . . requires in each particular case. The point of a practice is to annul anyone's title to act, on his individual judgment . . . [even] from considerations of Christian love in that one instance alone."[63] The purpose of establishing such policies is to help ensure that Christian love is embodied in social practices. And since such policies overall help establish loving acts, allowing numerous exceptions to such rules could undermine not only the policies themselves but the love (typically) embodied in them. An example of such a social practice is the institution of marriage which, based on love, attempts to establish a social policy that is best for both marriage partners as well as for the progeny of the couple.

57. Ramsey, *Basic Christian Ethics*, 234–46.

58. Ramsey, *Basic Christian Ethics*, 166–71. See also, Ramsey, *War and the Christian Conscience*.

59. Ramsey, *Basic Christian Ethics*, 46.

60. Rules that often, *but not always*, produce the most loving consequences.

61. Or at least the church.

62. Ramsey, *Deeds and Rules in Christian Ethics*, 133.

63. Ramsey, *Deeds and Rules in Christian Ethics*, 135.

Liberation Theologies

Alongside the proposals of writers like Fletcher and Ramsey, a number of other Christian voices arose in the mid-twentieth century advancing calls for social justice. Several of these perspectives fall under the rubric of *liberation theologies* or *liberation theological ethics*. At the center of these movements was the belief that God's kingdom, reign, and salvation are not just about individual salvation from personal sins or ultimate removal from this world into some heavenly state. Rather, God's reign and salvation also (and, according to some theologians, exclusively) concern overcoming the evils of this world, including especially the systemic evils that impoverish and oppress whole classes of people (typically for the benefit of other groups). Three broad forms of liberation theology frequently are noted—although often different titles are given to each of these. We will refer to them respectively as *Black liberation theology*, *Latin American liberation theology*, and *feminist liberation theology*.

Black Liberation Theology

Black liberation theology emerged largely in reaction to the exploitation of persons of African descent in the West—exploitation manifested first in the long-history of African slavery (especially in the United States) as well as in the continuation of unfair (de jure and de facto) social practices after the abolition of slavery. Not long after the American Civil War, most US southern states established discriminatory policies designed to curtail African-American voting and to effectively separate Whites and Blacks. Numerous so-called Jim Crow laws were passed, requiring Blacks and Whites to use separate (and allegedly equal) public services and facilities, such as schools, hotels, restaurants, and restrooms. Unsurprisingly, the facilities for Blacks seldom were of equal quality to those for Whites. Vigilante lynching was a too-common mechanism for suppressing the Black population. Periodically, Black resistance arose against such dire circumstances, including the famous case of Rosa Parks, who in 1955 refused to yield her bus seat (as mandated by law) to a White male passenger in Montgomery, Alabama. Her act helped inspire a bus boycott in the city, forcing (minimal but real) changes in public transportation policies. Other acts of peaceful protest and civil disobedience likewise sprung-up in the ensuing years, often leading to violent White retributions.

Out of this context arose a leading figure in the American civil rights movement and a catalyst for black liberation theology—namely, Martin Luther King, Jr (1929–1968). King's stirring preaching and his courage under oppression inspired and convicted many (although certainly not all) Americans that social change was needed. His advocacy helped inspire American legislators to pass the Civil Rights Act (1964), which prohibited discrimination based on race, color, religion, sex, or national origin, and the Voting Rights Act (1965), which made it illegal to make or enforce voting laws that discriminated based on race.

King did not construct an overarching theological-ethical theory; but he did invoke theological concepts in his advocacy for social justice. King was influenced by the writings of Walter Rauschenbusch and earlier Social Gospel proponents. With them, he believed that God was concerned not only about personal sins but also about social, systemic evils. These evils were clearly manifested in the long-standing racially discriminatory practices in America. For King, a central goal of Christian righteousness is to produce a "beloved community" in which each person is valued, granted dignity, and offered equal opportunities. King disagreed with some advocates of Black power, who saw Whites and White society as irreconcilable enemies to themselves, and who sought to create an isolated Black community. Rather, King believed that the gospel of Christ offered a vision of true unity, mutual respect, and thorough equality.

King, however, also chastised various (especially White) church leaders for their tacit or explicit support of discriminatory laws and social policies, and for complaining against King's advocacy for nonviolent civil disobedience in an effort to change such unjust practices. While incarcerated in Birmingham, Alabama, for his involvement in protests against discriminatory practices in that city, King wrote a letter replying to some of his Christian critics. He noted that a

> just law is a man-made code that squares with the moral law or the law of God. An unjust law is a code that is out of harmony with the moral law. To put it in the terms of Saint Thomas Aquinas, an unjust law is a human law that is not rooted in eternal and natural law. Any law that uplifts human personality is just. Any law that degrades human personality is unjust. All [racial] segregation statutes are unjust because segregation distorts the soul and damages the personality. It gives the segregator a false sense of superiority, and the segregated a false sense of inferiority.[64]

King concluded that he must protest against unjust laws, for they are not from God or from natural law. Further, to support such laws, or to restrain from seeking to dismantle them, is to participate in such injustice. To critics who condemned his peaceful but disruptive protests for unnecessarily agitating White ire and violence, King pointed out that the laws imposing inequity upon citizens were already being enforced by violence and were also evoking hostilities.

King's primary means for seeking social change was nonviolent resistance—nonviolent protests and civil disobedience. King criticized advocates of violent resistance, contending that such efforts where neither productive nor right. King explained that "the problem with hatred and violence is that they intensify the fears of the white majority, and leave them less ashamed of their prejudices toward Negroes. In the guilt and confusion confronting our society, violence only adds to the chaos.

---

64. King, "Letter from Birmingham City Jail," 295 (brackets added).

Violence is the antithesis of creativity and wholeness. It destroys community and makes brotherhood impossible."[65] Again, King's Christian vision pulled him toward seeking a reconciled community of Whites and Blacks, not a situation of isolation and mutual suspicion. As Philip Wogaman notes, however, King was not opposed to the use of force to guarantee *just* laws; he sought "the replacement of laws upholding racial segregation with laws enforcing civil rights" and, thus, his movement pursued aid from federal courts and law-enforcement.[66]

A more strident voice for Black liberation was theologian James Cone (1938–2018). In his second major work, *A Black Theology of Liberation*, Cone wrote: "It is my contention that Christianity is essentially a religion of liberation. The function of theology is that of analyzing the meaning of that liberation for the oppressed so that they can know that their struggle for political, social, and economic justice is consistent with the gospel of Jesus Christ."[67] In a later work, Cone commented: "Theology is always a word about the liberation of the oppressed and the humiliated. It is a word of judgment for the oppressors and the rulers. Whenever theologians fail to make this point unmistakably clear, they are not doing Christian theology but the theology of the Antichrist."[68] Cone notes further that often ideological systems—including theology—express and reinforce the biases of their writers. Not surprisingly, then, many theologies constructed by White Enlightenment theologians have ignored the plight of the oppressed and have expressed ideologies that (tacitly or explicitly) buttress the will of the privileged. Cone, instead, sought to render a theology that reflects the insights, values, and experiences of the Black—oppressed—community. In *A Black Theology of Liberation,* Cone distances himself from King's calls for nonviolent resistance, insisting that violence often is the only means by which social justice can be obtained, because of the recalcitrance and hostility of the oppressors. Cone ultimately hoped for a reconciled community in which liberty (which includes equality) is granted to all. But Cone believed such reconciliation had to start within the Black community.[69]

In a still later work, *For My People*, Cone criticized White theology for often failing to see the strong connection of the Christian message with the liberation of the oppressed. In this vein, he called for several needed measures to help ensure an authentic Christian, worldwide liberation of the oppressed. Among these were the following:

1. The need to establish Black unity through celebrating Black history and culture.

---

65. King, *Where Do We Go from Here?*, 48.

66. Wogaman, *Christian Ethics*, 287.

67. Cone, *A Black Theology of Liberation*, v. This was a reprint of an earlier edition (from 1970), which included commentary from other theologians.

68. Cone, *God of the Oppressed*, 83.

69. Cone, *God of the Oppressed*, 254.

2. Embrace choice elements of Martin Luther King Jr.'s calls for integration within a blessed community.

3. Overcome sexist tendencies.

4. Follow key socialist principles within a democratic society.

5. Recognize and work for the economic liberation of the poor worldwide.

6. Recognize and celebrate the religious insights and values of the poor, including those of the Black community.[70]

Latin American Liberation Theology

The social disquiet of midcentury North America (and Europe) was similar to the so-cial-political turbulence occurring in Latin America at the same time. These upheavals were grounded in a long history of exploitation in the Southern Hemisphere. Through the 1800s, partly inspired by the revolution that formed the United States of America, many Latin American countries rebelled against their European overlords, ostensibly forming democratic republics. But many of these liberal governments were not stable and soon deteriorated into indigenous oligarchies and military dictatorships. Further, Latin American economic growth was often stymied by the protectionist economic policies of the United States and Europe, which sought to ensure that the Southern Hemisphere served its economic purposes. These policies essentially continued into the twentieth century and were exacerbated by US anticommunist policies that often turned a blind eye toward the exploitation to which right-wing South American gov-ernments subjected their citizens. By the mid-twentieth century, numerous unchecked civil rights violations were transpiring in Latin America.

Latin American liberation theology ascended out of this long history of ex-ploitation that had unfolded in the western Southern Hemisphere from the days of European colonization into the contemporary era. The catalyst for change in the 1960s and 1970s was the expanding disparity between rich and poor in most South American countries—this in spite of considerable economic growth overall in these nations. Social-economic analysis suggested that disparities arose due to capitalistic tendencies to protect the interests of owners (to the detriment of workers) and to guard the interests of developed countries over the interests and needs of develop-ing and undeveloped nations. The result was that within the economies of South American countries, "workers [were] . . . not paid a just wage, the price of raw mate-rial [was] . . . held down, [and] the interest charged on loans needed by cooperatives [was] . . . exorbitant,"[71] In short, rich individuals and nations got richer, and poor

---

70. Cone, *For My People*, 202–4. See also Crook, *An Introduction to Christian Ethics*, 48.

71. Boff and Boff, *Introducing Liberation Theology*, 47

individuals and nations got poorer. The plight of the unemployed or underemployed was even more dire.[72]

In light of these circumstances, several Latin American Christian laypersons, clergy, and theologians began calling for liberation for the poor. Among these co-workers were the theologians Gustavo Gutiérrez (b. 1928), Leonardo Boff (b. 1938), José Porfirio Miranda (1924–2001), and Juan Luis Segundo (1925–1996). Gutiérrez seems to have coined the phrase "liberation theology," offering one of the first expositions of these ideas in his work *A Theology of Liberation*.[73] At the core of Latin America liberation theology was affirmation of God's "preferential option for the poor." A two-fold meaning is derived from this principle. First, God is especially concerned for the plight of the poor; thus, the church is called to challenge and undo the political and economic systems that bring about poverty. Such arrangements essentially exploit the disadvantaged, often driving them into deeper poverty. Persons trapped in such systems are "deprived of the necessary means of subsistence—food, clothing, shelter, basic health care, elementary education, and work."[74] They often also are deprived of dignity and are evaluated essentially as nonpersons (by oppressors). Liberation theologians insist, however, that the Bible clearly shows a bias toward the poor—not because they are loved more by God, but because they are the most needy; thus, they need the most care. Typically, liberation theologians believe the only truly effective way to amend the plight of the poor is to alter the economic systems that repress them—specifically capitalism. Economic aid from the wealthy or middle classes only serves as a Band-Aid for deeper, systemic problems. Further, typically capitalistic attempts to *reform* or *develop* undeveloped economies only marginally help the poor, while increasing the wealth of rich owners significantly. In short, such reforms generally are still exploitive. In light of all this, usually liberation theologians have called for some form of Marxist socialism, obviously absent its atheistic philosophy. But liberation theologians often also note that this endorsement of Marxist ideas is *only a tool* for theology and for God's concern for the poor; Marxism is not the goal, nor is it a first-order ideology shaping or *controlling* Christianity.[75]

A second meaning of liberation theology's commitment to the "preferential option for the poor" is that the outlook of the poor is critical both for understanding their plight and for solving their dilemmas. The poor—with their insights, experiences, interpretations—play a primary role in comprehending their own dire circumstances, perceiving the theological and social ramifications of biblical and ecclesial

---

72. Boff and Boff, *Introducing Liberation Theology*, 26. Boff and Boff supplement these conclusions with several harrowing stories and stats from the two-thirds world. See Boff and Boff, *Introducing Liberation Theology*, 1–3.

73. Gutiérrez, *A Theology of Liberation*.

74. Boff and Boff, *Introducing Liberation Theology*, 46.

75. Boff and Boff, *Introducing Liberation Theology*, 27–28. See also, Gutiérrez, *A Theology of Liberation*, 86–88.

teachings, and using these insights to envision realistic, systemic solutions to their problems. With this in mind, an important term and concept for liberation theology is *conscientization* (making-conscious). Through a process of sustained conversation and study, the oppressed (in community) "become aware of the fact and causes of their victimization,"[76] move from naïve awareness to critical awareness, and reject "the oppressive consciousness" within them, thus finding their own liberated perspectives.[77] With these new insights in mind, the poor themselves become a key to solving the economic and political injustices they face.

Related to all these ideas is the notion of *comunidades de base*—often translated "base communities." In South America, these were small groups of poor, oppressed Christians gathered for Bible study and reflection—local communities that seek to envision the practical import of Christian teachings for their lives, thus offering deeper insights into biblical and church teachings. As various liberation theologians have noted, in many ways, liberation theology was first a grassroots movement. It surfaced among laypeople and local ministers attempting to discern how to live out the Christian faith and life under the dire circumstances of (frequently acute) repression and poverty. As time passed, many of these groups advocated political solutions to the problems of their oppressive circumstances. In turn, various pastors and ultimately theologians likewise saw the righteousness of these believers' cause and became advocates of social change. A central insight of liberation theology is that praxis (effective action, including ethics) is more rudimentary than beliefs (ideologies or dogmas). Thus, for liberation theologians, Christian theology is a secondary activity dependent on and reflecting Christian (moral and political) practices. Thus, Gutiérrez asserts that theology is "a critical reflection on Christian praxis in light of the word of God."[78] In turn, Leonard and Clodovis Boff note:

> In the biblical tradition it is not enough for faith to be true in the terms in which it is expressed (orthodoxy); it is verified, made true, when it is informed by love, solidarity, hunger and thirst for justices. St James teaches that 'faith without good deeds is useless' and that believing in the one God is not enough, for 'the demons have the same belief' (2:21, 20). Therefore, ortho-doxy has to be accompanied by ortho-praxis.[79]

According to Leonard and Clodovis Boff, the key themes of liberation theology include

1. Living and true faith include the practice of liberation.

2. The living God sides with the oppressed against the pharaohs of this world.

76. Wogaman, *Christian Ethics*, 284.

77. Gutiérrez, *A Theology of Liberation*, 91. Conscientization was a pedagogical technique developed by Brazilian educator Paulo Freire, adopted and adapted by several liberation-theology practitioners. See Freire, *The Pedagogy of the Oppressed*.

78. Gutiérrez, *A Theology of Liberation*, xxix.

79. Boff and Boff, *Introducing Liberation Theology*, 49–50.

3. The kingdom of God is God's project in history and eternity.

4. Jesus, the Son of God, took on oppression in order to set us free.

5. The Holy Spirit, "Father of the poor," is present in the struggles of the oppressed.

6. Mary is the prophetic and liberating woman of the people.

7. The church is sign and instrument of liberation.

8. The rights of the poor are God's rights.

9. Liberated human potential becomes liberative.[80]

Liberation theology gained considerable credence in South America when its basic tenets were endorsed in 1968 by the Latin American Episcopal Conference (CELAM) in Medellín, Colombia, and, again in 1979 at the CELAM conference in Puebla, Mexico.

Feminist Liberation Theology

A third form of liberation theology is feminist liberation theology. Feminism in general is a movement that seeks to overturn the injustices done to women in human culture. It aims to elevate women to their rightful status as fully human, granting to them the rights, privileges, and dignity due all humanity.[81] With these goals in mind, feminism often offers critical analysis of the varied inequalities and oppressions imposed upon women throughout history. These impositions occur within family, educational, economic, and political structures. Examples of such inequalities include denying to women the right to suffrage, the right to hold political offices, the right to own property, the right to enter business contracts, and the right to obtain higher education. Other concerns of feminism include protecting women from various forms of personal and systemic abuse or exploitation—including unfair labor practices, unequal legal standing within marriages or domestic partnerships, sexual harassment, domestic violence, rape, and marital rape. Also of concern for feminism is a woman's right to control her own body, including particularly reproductive rights—the right to use contraceptives or to have an abortion.

Often the history of modern feminism is divided into three or even four waves. We will focus our attention especially on *second-wave* feminism.[82] The *first wave* of feminism we discussed above: it arose in the mid- to late nineteenth century as various women (and men) advocated for changes to legal, political, and financial systems that disadvantaged women. The *second wave* of feminism arose in the 1960s and carried on at least into the 1990s. This movement was given voice by a large

---

80. Boff and Boff, *Introducing Liberation Theology*, 49–63.

81. For this definition of feminist goals, I have followed the insights of several feminist writers including Ruether, *Sexism and God-Talk*, 18–19; and Haney, "What Is Feminist Ethics?," 5–6.

82. For more detail on various approaches to feminism, see Appendix A at the back of this book. For a brief comment about third wave feminism, see footnote 101.

number of writers and activists, including Betty Friedan (1921–2006) and Gloria Steinem (b. 1934). Second-wave feminism was sympathetic toward and encouraged by the broader civil rights movement of the mid-twentieth century. Second-wave feminism focused on overcoming a host of inequalities faced by women beyond property ownership or suffrage. Broadly these inequities involved social or cultural prejudices and discriminatory practices against women, which limited their social, economic, and educational opportunities.

Among these prejudices were culturally imposed gender roles and sexist language that (unconsciously or otherwise) reinforce cultural perspectives that limited women's access to broader opportunities. Also included were unjustified stereotypes about women's rational abilities, or acumen for chores in business, science, politics, medicine, and so forth. Coupled with these largely attitudinal perspectives were a host of social-economic facts that seemed to demonstrate biased practices against women in the workplace. There were considerable wage gaps between men and women working the same jobs; there also were ongoing tendencies to hire a greater percentage of men over women in the workforce, especially for higher-paying and leadership positions (the glass ceiling). Equally (and indeed perhaps more) disturbing, there was evidence of long-standing misogynous practices in Western culture. The objectification of women (treating women as mere objects for personal gain or pleasure rather that as persons) was a continuing and common practice; such objectification found expression in advertising, media, pornography, and humor. Even worse, there were signs of long-standing, intrinsic violence toward women in some cultural practices—especially in domestic violence and rape. These and other concerns fueled the activism of second-wave feminism.

Through the activism of second-wave feminists and growing sympathies for their concerns, a number of laws were enacted in the US (and in western Europe) to curtail diverse social and economic inequalities. In 1963, the US Congress enacted the Equal Pay Act, requiring that persons (men and women) should be paid the same amount for the same job. In 1964, the Civil Rights Act passed, outlawing discrimination based on race, color, religion, sex, or national origin. It also forbade distinctive voter-registration requirements for citizens of different social groups. Title IX of the Education Amendments of 1972 required that "No person in the United States shall, on the basis of sex, be excluded from participation in, or be denied the benefits of, or be subjected to discrimination under any education program or activity receiving federal financial assistance."[83] In 1978, the Pregnancy Discrimination Act prohibited discrimination (including in the workforce) based on pregnancy, childbirth, or medical conditions.

An especially contentious concern of the second-wave feminist movement was over women's rights to choose what happens to their own bodies, including especially the right to use contraceptives and to choose abortion in the face of an unwanted

83. US Department of Justice, Title IX of the Education Amendment of 1973.

pregnancy. In 1960, the contraceptive drug Enovid was approved by the US Food and Drug Administration, thus making it possible for a woman to avoid pregnancy with relative ease. In 1965, the United States Supreme Court ruled—based on the right to privacy—that a person could use contraceptives to avoid pregnancies. The production of "the pill" and its legalization in US courts was particularly problematic for many Catholics. In 1968, Pope Paul VI issued an encyclical, titled *Humanae Vitae*, which forbade the use of contraceptives.

Even greater consternation unfolded for many Catholics and Protestants alike in 1973 when in the case of *Roe v. Wade*, the US Supreme Court legalized abortions up to the point of fetal viability. In a 7–2 decision, the court found that the right to privacy is implicit in the due process clause of the Fourteenth Amendment, and that included in the right to privacy is a woman's right to choose an abortion. The court also recognized the state's interest in protecting the health of both a pregnant woman and a fetus. With this caveat in mind, the court ruled that during the first trimester of pregnancy, the state could not regulate decisions regarding abortion; in the second trimester the state could impose some restrictions in the interest of the mother's health; in the third trimester, once the fetus attains viability, the state could impose considerable restrictions including forbidding abortions. The court's decision set off a firestorm in American politics as pro-choice and pro-life advocates faced off in various legal (and sometimes illegal) battles. For many feminists, the *Roe v Wade* ruling was a clear victory for women's rights.

It was primarily within the context of the second-wave feminist movement that feminist liberation theology emerged. Inspired both by accomplishments of first- and second-wave feminism and by other mid-twentieth-century Western cultural changes, Christian feminist theologians began pondering the nature of their faith and its ramifications for feminist concerns, including worries over the social and economic inequalities faced by women. Making matters especially difficult was a realization that (both past and present) Christianity (often deeply) contributed to the disparities and oppression faced by women. Numerous feminist theologians arose from midcentury and through the late twentieth century. Among them were Mary Daly (1928–2010),[84] Dorothee Söelle (1929–2003),[85] and Rosemary Radford Ruether (b. 1936). We spotlight Ruther's writings.

In her book *Sexism and God-Talk: Toward a Feminist Theology*, Ruether writes:

> The critical principle of feminist theology is the promotion of the full humanity of women. Whatever denies, diminishes, or distorts the full humanity of women is, therefore, appraised as not redemptive . . . This negative principle also implies the positive principle: what does promote the full humanity of women is of the Holy, it does reflect true relation to the divine, it is the true

84. See Daly, *The*; and Daly, *Beyond God the Father*.
85. Sölle, *Thinking about God*.

nature of things, the authentic message of redemption and the mission of the redemptive community.[86]

Ruether notes that affirmation of the full humanity of women is not a new Christian ideal. It is implied in the biblical tradition's affirmation that all humans (including women) are created in the image of God, and that through the redemption brought in Christ all humans (including women) are being made into the image of Christ. Sadly, claims Reuther, acknowledgment of the full humanity of women has nevertheless been distorted throughout Christian history. It has been warped by "the naming of males as norms of authentic humanity," which has resulted in women taking the blame for the emergence of sin[87] and effectively being denied their full humanity whether in their original created nature or in their redeemed state or in both.[88]

Ruether finds these patterns of women being blamed for sin and being denied their full humanity in various (male) Christian writers throughout Christian history.[89] Augustine, for instance, saw the image of God primarily in men and only secondarily in women. Aquinas, following Aristotle, envisioned women as "misbegotten" males who even before the fall were inferior to men in body, mind, and morality. This inferiority only increased after the fall. Further, due to women's natural inferiority, men are to rule over women. Martin Luther taught that before the fall, men and women were equal, but after the fall women fell under divine punishment, divinely condemned to be subjugated to men. Thus, in the unredeemed world, wives are now "compelled to obey" their husbands. John Calvin taught that women are equal to men both before and after the fall. Nevertheless, the subordination of women to men still holds, for God has ordained this for the social order. Thus, in marriage "the man rules not because he is superior but because God has commanded him to do so."[90]

Ruether finds these misogynous tendencies rooted first in the affirmation of God's maleness, which appears in both ancient Israelite and so also in Christian tradition. According to Ruether, the tradition's picture of God as exclusively male arose in part due to the ancient semi-nomadic Israelites' rejection of the gods and goddesses of their (urbanized and agrarian) neighbors, who understood deity as both male and female.[91] Reuther believes that the commitment to God's maleness can be overcome in Christianity by using sources within the faith tradition itself. In particular, the biblical condemnation of idolatry and its understanding of Yahweh as the God of the oppressed allows Christian theology to construct more inclusive

---

86. Ruether, *Sexism and God-Talk*, 18–19.

87. See especially Ruether, *Sexism and God-Talk*, 165–72

88. Ruether, *Sexism and God-Talk*, 19,

89. Ruether, *Sexism and God-Talk*, 94–99.

90. Ruether, *Sexism and God-Talk*, 98.

91. Ruether, *Sexism and God-Talk*, 47–54.

understandings of the deity.[92] Using the term "God/ess" to avoid male-biased depictions of the divine, Ruether writes:

> If all language for God/ess is analogy, if taking a particular human image literally is idolatry, then male language for the divine must lose its privileged place. If God/ess is not the creator and validator of the existing hierarchical social order, but rather the one who liberates us from it, who opens up a new community of equals, then language about God/ess drawn from kingship and hierarchical power must lose its privileged place. Images of God/ess must include female roles and experience.[93]

According to Ruether, a second source of the Christian tradition's inclination toward misogyny is its "tendency to correlate femaleness with the lower part of human nature in a hierarchical scheme of mind over body, reason over passions. Since this lower part of the self is seen as the source of sin—the falling away of the body from its original unity with the mind and hence into sin and death—femaleness also becomes linked with the sin-prone part of the self."[94] Again, various sources in Christian history have endorsed this interpretation of women, resulting in tendencies to blame women (more than men) for sin and to see men as superior to women. For Ruether, however, valid Christianity entails throwing off the oppressive tendencies of some of its history and affirming those aspects of the faith that acknowledge the full humanity of women.

In Ruether's view, sin involves the distortion of human community, including the warping of the basic "I-Thou relation" between men and women. This deformation emerges from the elevation of the individual or collective self above others, seeing oneself or one's group as superior to them; in turn, through this bent of mind, groups or individuals selfishly justify oppressing those different from themselves. Such denigration and exploitation of others is the "fundamental distortion and corruption of human relationality."[95] Redemption from such sin involves *metanoia*—a change of mind, especially regarding belief about one's own superiority over others. Ruether sees the (true) church as a liberated and liberating community. One of the church's goals is to overcome sexism, thus helping lead persons and society toward true *metanoia* or conversion. "Conversion from sexism means both freeing oneself from the ideologies and roles of patriarchy and also struggling to liberate social structure from these patterns."[96] Thus, both personal and socioeconomic liberation are important aspects of redemption and of the church's mission.[97] Ultimately, for Ruether, a central goal of

92. Ruether, *Sexism and God-Talk*, 61–68.

93. Ruether, *Sexism and God-Talk*, 68–69.

94. Ruether, *Sexism and God-Talk*, 93.

95. Ruether, *Sexism and God-Talk*, 163.

96. Ruether, *Sexism and God-Talk*, 201.

97. Ruether, *Sexism and God-Talk*, 214–15.

the church is to "affirm the equality of woman in the image of God and the restoration of her full personhood in Christ."[98]

Liberation Theologies Conjoined

To some degree, these various forms of liberation theology—Black, Latin American, and feminist—arose independently of one another, each flowing from distinguishable (but similar) historical and social contexts. Still, as the twentieth century rolled on, these various forms of liberation ethics soon found common ground—each sympathizing with the others and seeing strong continuity with them. Ruether captures this recognition well when she writes:

> Women cannot affirm themselves as *imago dei* and subjects of full human potential in a way that diminishes male humanity. Women, as the denigrated half of the human species, must reach for a continually expanding definition of inclusive humanity—inclusive of both genders, inclusive of all social groups and races . . . In rejecting androcentrism (males as norms of humanity), women must also criticize all other forms of chauvinism: making white Westerners the norm of humanity, making Christians the norm of humanity, making privileged classes the norm of humanity.[99]

Again, Ruether notes:

> Images of God/ess must be drawn from the activities of peasants and working people, people at the bottom of society. Most of all, images of God/ess must be transformative, pointing us back to our authentic potential and forward to new redeemed possibilities.[100]

Similar views are voiced by advocates of Black liberation theology and of Latin American liberation theology.[101]

Stanley Hauerwas

The last quarter of the twentieth century witnessed the emergence of yet another model of Christian ethics, one returning to the ancient concern for moral *virtues*

98. Ruether, *Sexism and God-Talk*, 214.

99. Ruether, *Sexism and God-Talk*, 20.

100. Ruether, *Sexism and God-Talk*, 69.

101. See Cone, *For My People*, 88–98, 204; and Boff and Boff, *Introducing Liberation Theology*, 4–48. One of the criticisms of second-wave feminism was that it tended to represent the concerns (and assumptions) of middle-class white women and tended to overlook the voices of women from other racial, ethnic, and economic groups. Indeed, part of the impetus of third-wave feminism was a desire to offer broader representation of feminism. See Williams, "The Color of Feminism," 42–58. Also see, Akasha et al., eds., *All the Women Are White*. For an introduction to third-wave feminism, see Baumgardner and Richards, *Manifesta*.

(ethics of being) and stressing the fundamental importance of community, tradition, and narrative both for establishing moral principles and for developing personal and social identity. While numerous Christian ethicists have endorsed such themes in the late twentieth and early twenty-first centuries, few have been as influential as Stanley Hauerwas (b. 1940).

In his book *The Peaceable Kingdom*, Hauerwas lays out the key elements of his ethics. Hauerwas rejects emotivism, existentialism, and situationism, which emphasize the role of an individual's emotions or will in freely choosing moral values and character traits. Allegedly, such approaches lead to the fragmentation of moral norms and principles. Against such views, Hauerwas insists that "moral authenticity . . . require[s] that morality be not a matter of one's own shaping, but something that shapes one. We do not create moral values, principles, virtues; rather they constitute a life for us to appropriate."[102] Hauerwas also dismisses attempts to anchor ethics in human nature or rationality. Immanuel Kant attempted to ground ethics is universal reason; various Christian natural-law theorists have attempted to secure ethics in human nature. Such moves attempt to establish ethics in alleged commonalities shared by all human beings.[103] According to Hauerwas, however, these views fail to recognize that "all ethical reflections occur relative to a particular time and place"; thus ethics cannot be grounded in some universal human trait.[104] Further, these systems attempt to root ethics *in humanity rather than in God*. But for the Christian, ethics is not founded in humans but in God and in God's historical interrelation with humanity.

According to Hauerwas, "Christian ethics is determined by the fact that Christian convictions take the form of a story . . . or stories."[105] Through such narratives, Christians learn of the nature of God, the world, the individual self, and the Christian community. Knowledge of such realities arises from stories because the world, humans, and human communities are historical entities whose transpiring nature is not discernible in isolated moments but through transitions and interrelationships that unfold through time. Narratives allow humans to rationally integrate sets of temporal events that otherwise seem (or are) disjointed, treating them as cohesive wholes. In turn, the broad *Christian narrative* allows Christians to understand reality—the universe, humanity as a whole, human communities, and individuals. It does this by placing them all "within God's story."[106] Thus, the Christian narrative is *reality-making*; it helps Christians construct a truthful understanding of reality.[107]

---

102. Hauerwas, *The Peaceable Kingdom*, 3 (brackets added). Also, Hauerwas writes: "Character determines circumstances . . . by our very ability to interpret our actions in a story that accounts for moral activity" (Hauerwas, *The Peaceable Kingdom*), 8.

103. Hauerwas, *The Peaceable Kingdom*, 11, 55–66.

104. Hauerwas, *The Peaceable Kingdom*, 1.

105. Hauerwas, *The Peaceable Kingdom*, 24.

106. Hauerwas, *The Peaceable Kingdom*, 27.

107. Hauerwas, *The Peaceable Kingdom*, 25, 29.

Through the divine historical narrative, first one perceives that humanity and all of the created order is *contingent*. Second, one perceives that individual Christians and the Christian community are *historical*—that they endure through time and find unity through the common Christian story (tradition). Further, Christians employ their narratives—their traditions—"to help individuals identify and navigate the path to the good." Indeed, the individual ultimately discovers himself or herself in and through the tradition. For this reason, says Hauerwas, Christian ethics does not begin with the musings or rational intuitions of the individual, but it arises from the Christian tradition and from the community formed around that tradition. Hence, individual Christians begin in the middle; that is, they begin within the Christian narrative and tradition. And from that vantage point, Christian ethics is explored and moral training transpires.[108]

A third implication of the divine historical narrative is that God's revelation comes through the accounts of "the history of Israel and the life of Jesus." At the root of this narrative is the story of God's redeeming efforts "through the covenant with Israel, the life, death, and resurrection of Jesus, and the ongoing history of the church as the recapitulation of that [Jesus'] life."[109]

An important aspect of the Christian narrative is its understanding that humans are sinners and thus "in fundamental rebellion" against God. Christians are expected to do something about this sin. They are called to be disciples. This is not simply a general admonition to be good, but "a concrete and definite call to take up the way of life made possible by God's redemptive action for us on the cross. To be redeemed . . . is nothing less than to learn to place ourselves in God's history, to be part of God's people . . . Redemption . . . is a change in which we accept the invitation to become part of God's kingdom, a kingdom through which we acquire a character befitting one who has heard God's call."[110] This redemption involves serving and being formed by the Christian community, "a community of peaceable people," "whose interest lies in the formation of character and whose perduring history provides the continuity we need to act in conformity with that character."[111] Indeed, in a certain sense, says Hauerwas, the goal of Christian ethics is not to become "moral" where morality is defined by an alleged universal or innate human notion of right and wrong. Rather, "put simply, we Christians are not called on to be 'moral' but faithful to the true story, the story that we are creatures under the lordship of a God who wants nothing more than our faithful service. By such service we become not 'moral,' it seems, but like God, holy."[112] Furthermore, notes Hauerwas, Christian ethics is more concerned with "who we are than what we do." What we do is important, but the Christian community (the

---

108. Hauerwas, *The Peaceable Kingdom*, 28, 62

109. Hauerwas, *The Peaceable Kingdom*, 29 (brackets added).

110. Hauerwas, *The Peaceable Kingdom*, 33.

111. Hauerwas, *The Peaceable Kingdom*, 33.

112. Hauerwas, *The Peaceable Kingdom*, 68.

church) "has a stake in holding together our being and behaving in such a manner that our doing only can be a reflection of our character."[113]

Not surprisingly, Hauerwas insists that Jesus' life provides an optimal example of how Christians are to live. "By learning to be followers of Jesus we learn to locate our lives within God's life, within the journey that comprises his kingdom." Following Jesus "involves nothing less than learning to be like God."[114] Christian ethics, then, is not primarily about "principles, laws, or values." Rather, it is an ethic "that demands we attend to the life of a particular individual—Jesus of Nazareth."[115] Being followers of Jesus means living in the manner he lived, which includes living a peaceful, nonviolent life of love and of service to others.[116] Jesus' "life reveals the effective power of God to create a transformed people capable of living peaceably in a violent world."[117] The cross of Christ indicates that God's kingdom has come. It tells us that only by God's grace are we able to receive and accept the invitation to participate in God's kingdom. "Because we have confidence that God has raised the crucified man, we believe that forgiveness and love are alternatives to the coercion the world thinks necessary for existence."[118] In turn, because of Jesus' resurrection, and the vindication of his life and practice that it affords, Christians have confidence to live as a forgiven and forgiving community, and to "take the risk to love."[119] Faith in Christ is not simply a matter of belief and trust, but an issue of fidelity to Jesus. And salvation—especially the notion of sanctification—reminds Christians that taking on the story of Jesus as our own requires faithfulness along the way.[120]

Finally, Hauerwas insists that the primary task of the Christian community—the church—is not to "attempt to make the world more peaceable or just." Rather, "the first social ethical task of the church is to be the church—the servant community." That is, the Christian community is to be the "faithful manifestation of the peaceable kingdom in the world," so that the church does not "have a social ethic; the church is a social ethic."[121] The church offers to the world a vision of what should be in the face of what is.[122] To accomplish this task, the church must be "a people of virtue,"[123] faithful "to the mode of life of the peaceable kingdom."[124]

---

113. Hauerwas, *The Peaceable Kingdom*, 33–34.

114. Hauerwas, *The Peaceable Kingdom*, 75.

115. Hauerwas, *The Peaceable Kingdom*, 75–76.

116. Hauerwas, *The Peaceable Kingdom*, 76, 80–81.

117. Hauerwas, *The Peaceable Kingdom*, 83.

118. Hauerwas, *The Peaceable Kingdom*, 87.

119. Hauerwas, *The Peaceable Kingdom*, 90.

120. Hauerwas, *The Peaceable Kingdom*, 93–94.

121. Hauerwas, *The Peaceable Kingdom*, 99.

122. Hauerwas, *The Peaceable Kingdom*, 100.

123. Hauerwas, *The Peaceable Kingdom*, 103.

124. Hauerwas, *The Peaceable Kingdom*, 106.

Hauerwas has contributed to contemporary Christian ethics in numerous ways, including especially with the following points. First, his emphasis on becoming a certain kind of person or community (over just obeying laws or preforming deeds) has helped reestablish appreciation for the ancient stress on virtue ethics (the ethics of being). Second, Hauerwas's avowal that self-identity, community identity, and moral character are *established* by narrative adds new insights into Christian ethics about the value of Christian (biblical and church-historical) narratives. While Christian ethicists long have recognized that traditional Christian sources *convey* theology and ethics through stories, many Christian ethicists today have a greater appreciation for why this is the case. If Hauerwas is correct, this is so because narratives are essential not only for *communicating* identity and character but for *establishing* them.[125]

Conclusion

As noted throughout this book, Christianity is multifaceted. Among its critical components are the key foundations of the Bible (sacred text), the story of Israel (sacred story), Jesus Christ (sacred person), and the church (sacred community). In the first two chapters of this work, we discussed these four foundations of the faith. Another important element of Christianity is a set of beliefs designed to describe the nature of God and of God's relationship to the rest of reality. These beliefs often are called the *theology* of Christianity or the *doctrines* of the church. In Chapters 3 through 7, we examined many of these core teachings. A further facet of Christianity is its ethics—its core moral beliefs and practices. In Chapters 8, 9, and 10, we examined the main features of Christian ethics, including the chief moral norms of the biblical tradition and diverse Christian perspectives on ethics across time. In the next two chapters—Chapters 11 and 12—we turn to consider some core worship practices of Christians over the centuries.

125. In these matters, Hauerwas is not alone. He was deeply influenced by the similar views in MacIntyre, *After Virtue* and McClendon, *Systematic Theology*, vol. 1 (*Ethics*).

Part Four: **Christian Worship**

11

Christian Worship

Biblical Foundations and
Early Centuries

IN CHAPTERS 1 AND 2, we discussed the foundations of Christianity which include the Bible, the story of Israel, the person and work of Jesus, and the Christian community. In Chapters 3 through 7, we investigated the core doctrines of the Christian faith. In Chapters 8 through 10 we explored Christian ethics. In these next two chapters, 11 and 12, we turn to examine the worship practices of Christianity. Because of limited space, we focus primarily on the rituals of baptism, Eucharist, prayer, preaching, penance, the Christian year, and church music; we leave for others discussions of art, architecture, and diverse spiritual disciplines such as fasting, meditation, and so forth.

A common feature of religions throughout history and across the globe is the performance of rituals. Underlying these exercises often is the belief that humans can interact with the spiritual world. Through a ritual, one can affect and be affected by the supernatural. Sometimes these interchanges are perceived to be impersonal, as if one were manipulating an unconscious object. But often rituals are understood as interpersonal—exchanges between persons. For example, prayer typically is conceptualized as humans communicating with (petitioning, praising, thanking) a supernatural person or persons. Often, one's interpretation of rituals depends upon how one perceives the supernatural world, including ultimate reality. Religions that interpret ultimate reality to be essentially personal typically understand rituals as interchanges between persons. This usually is the case with Christianity, which understands ultimate reality (the triune God) as personal.

Not surprisingly, then, many Christian rituals assume an interpersonal interchange between God and humans. God and humans commune with one another. Sometimes this exchange is verbal; sometimes nonverbal; sometimes it involves sensory stimuli (art, music, symbols), sometimes only silence; and occasionally (perhaps even frequently) it entails inner testimony—a feeling-filled awe, joy, love, peace, or awareness of the divine presence. This model of interpersonal communion between God and humanity is implicit in numerous passages of the Bible and in many of the rituals of the Christian faith.

Divine Encounters in the Bible

A central claim of the Christian faith is that God has been and still can be encountered by human beings. Sometimes this encounter involves rituals—sometimes not, and nearly always these encounters are understood to be due to divine initiative, not to human manipulation. The Hebrew Bible offers several examples of such experiences with God. In Gen 12, God comes to Abram (later called Abraham) and promises to bless him, give him many descendants, and bless all nations through them. In Gen 15, the Lord appears to Abram and reaffirms the promise to bless him, his descendants, and all nations through them, and to be his protector (shield). And God makes a covenant with Abram. In Gen 28, Abraham's grandson Jacob experiences God in a dream, observing a ladder with angels ascending and descending, and in that dream God reaffirms to Jacob promises made to Abraham. In Exod 3, God appears to Moses in the form of a burning bush (that never is consumed) and calls Moses to lead the Israelites out of slavery in Egypt. In 1 Sam 3, the young boy Samuel is awakened in the night, three times hearing a voice calling his name—the voice of Yahweh. In Isa 6, the prophet Isaiah describes a vision of Yahweh seated on the throne in the Jerusalem temple, and of six-winged creatures hovering near the throne, exclaiming "Holy, holy, holy, is the LORD of hosts!" Isaiah then experiences a calling from God to speak to the obstinate people of his generation. In Ezek 1–2, the priest and prophet Ezekiel describes a profound vision involving a great storm, bizarre images of angelic beings, and a brilliant, flashing throne upon which sits Yahweh.[1] From this experience, Ezekiel receives a call from God to speak to the people of Israel.

The New Testament likewise describes many such encounters with the divine. In both Matthew and Luke, angels appear (to Joseph and Mary respectively) to announce the conception and birth of Jesus. Likewise, in all four Gospels, accounts of varied wonders, healings, and exorcisms of Jesus are given—descriptions certainly designed to depict human encounters with the divine in Christ. The greatest of these, of course, is Jesus' own resurrection from the dead. But also recorded in the New Testament are diverse, often more subtle, encounters with God. Among these are the following:

1. Jesus' postresurrection appearance to two disciples on the road to Emmaus (Luke 24:13–35)

2. Jesus' postresurrection appearance to Mary Magdalene (John 20:11–18)

3. Jesus' postresurrection appearance to the disciples (Matt 28:1–20; Luke 24:26–52; John 20:19–29)

---

1. Ezekiel is careful not to say that he saw Yahweh proper; rather, he saw something like the likeness of God's glory (1:26–28).

4. The outpouring of the Spirit of God on Pentecost (Acts 2:1–13)

5. The several receptions of (or baptism in) the Holy Spirit in Acts[2]

6. Paul's encounter with Jesus on the road to Damascus (Acts 9:1–9; compare Gal 1:11–12)

7. Peter's divine vision permitting the consumption of unkosher foods (Acts 10:9–16)

8. The reception and influences of the Holy Spirit mentioned in Paul's Epistles[3]

9. The testimony of the Spirit assuring believers of their salvation in Christ (Rom 8:15–17)

10. The reception of varied gifts of the Spirit in Pauline churches (Rom 12:1–13; 1 Cor 12:1–11; Eph 4:11–13)

The precise nature and authenticity of these divine encounters are subject to dispute among scholars. We will not pursue these puzzles here.[4] Suffice it to say that the biblical tradition long endorsed the belief that humans can experience and have experienced God in varying ways in diverse contexts.

Religious Rituals in the Hebrew Bible

In addition to these varied encounters with God, the Bible also points to numerous ritual practices. Some of these rites memorialize divine encounters from the past, especially celebrating God's prior saving acts. Some invoke the continuing presence and salvation of God in the now. And still others are designed simply to worship God.

The Hebrew biblical tradition exhibits all these tendencies and more. After his encounter with the Lord, and during his journey through the promised land, Abraham built altars for making sacrifices to God (Gen 12:6–8). Later, the Lord gave to Abraham and to his descendants circumcision as a sign of the covenant between God and Abraham's people (Gen 17:1–14). Having encountered God in a dream, Abraham's grandson Jacob sets up a place of worship at Bethel (Gen 28). After his experience of the Lord at the burning bush, Moses goes to Pharaoh with God's demands to let the Israelites leave Egypt so that they might worship the Lord in the wilderness (Exod 3–12). After the exodus, God's people go to Sinai to worship Yahweh and to receive the Lord's stipulations. At Sinai, the people enter a covenant with the Lord, receiving life-giving instructions (torah). At the center of this covenant are the Ten Commandments. The first four of these focus on worship, directing the people how to rightly respect and honor God. Specifically, the Israelites are to worship only Yahweh, and no other gods;

2. Acts 1:4–5; 2:1–4, 37–39; 8:14–17; 10:44–48; 11:16–18.

3. Rom 8:1–8; Gal 3:1–5; 5:16–26.

4. For philosophical discussions of the nature and validity of religious experience, see Peterson et al., *Reason and Religious Belief*, 27–51. Also see Alston, *Perceiving God*; and Otto, *The Idea of the Holy*.

they are not to make molded statues depicting the Lord or any other deity; they are to treat the divine name with reverent honor; and they were to worship and rest (Sabbath) on the seventh day, making it holy (separate) from other days of the week (Exod 20:2–11). Thereafter, through much of the Torah, God lays down demands for Israel to follow. Among these instructions are a host of worship rituals.

Sacrifices to the Lord are central rites in the Hebrew Bible. There were sacrifices made by individuals and families, sacrifices made on behalf of the people of Israel as a whole, and various sacrifices for special occasions and offices. Among the individual and family sacrifices were

1. burnt offerings (Lev 1:1–17; 6:8–13)

2. grain offerings (Lev 2:2:1–16; 6:14–18)

3. well-being offerings (Lev 3:1–17; 7:11–38)

4. sin or purification offerings (Lev 4:1—5:13; 6:24–30)

5. guilt or reparation offerings (Lev 5:14–6:7; 7:1–10)

The purposes of these sacrifices is not clearly stated in the biblical text. The first three seem to function as voluntary acts of worship for individual Israelites, while the last two seem to involve mandatory actions for the atonement of unintended sins and for cleansing the temple or tabernacle sanctuary (so God might abide with the people of Israel). Even so, the precise rationale for these offerings and for sacrifices in general is not precisely clarified.

Several explanations of sacrifices have been proposed. Traditionally, Christian commentators have understood many of these sacrifices as mechanisms for making atonement for sins—for covering or forgiving moral or cultic trespasses against God. This interpretation is sometimes supported by noting that especially in the case of animal sacrifices, the religious practitioner is instructed to place his hand upon the head of the sacrificial animal, presumably as a sign that the animal somehow represents the one making the sacrifice[5] (and his family; see Lev 13:1–4; 3:2; 4:4). In this interpretation, the animal stands in the place of the person giving the offering to God and, in some sense, receives a punishment or penalty due the participant. Not all commentators agree with this interpretation of the sacrifices. Some see these offerings as means of communing with God, almost as a kind of shared meal with the Lord.[6] Others see these sacrifices as gifts to God. Whatever the precise rationale for sacrifices, such rites were common elements of Israelite worship and came to be especially connected with the temple in Jerusalem.

---

5. Usually it is a male who performs the sacrifice, or a priest (who also is male) performs it in behalf of a man and his family.

6. The idea of the sacrifice as a kind of fellowship meal with the Lord is suggested in Lev 21:6, which speaks of the offerings as "the food of their God." See also Num 28:1–8 (especially v. 2) and Num 15:2–16.

In addition to individual sacrifices, there were sacrifices made on behalf of the whole nation of Israel. Among these sacrifices were

1. those made on a daily basis (Num 28:1–8)

2. those made each Sabbath (Num 28:9–10)

3. those made each new moon (Num 28:11–15)

4. those made for the five annual conventions of all Israel, including

   a. the Passover (including the Feast of Unleavened Bread and Firstfruits) (Lev 23:4–14; Num 28:18–25)

   b. the Feast of Weeks (Pentecost) (Lev 23:15–22; Num 28:26–31)

   c. the Feast of Trumpets (Lev 23:23–25; Num 29:1–6)

   d. the Day of Atonement (Lev 23:26–32; Num 29:7–11)

   e. the Feast of Tabernacles (Lev 23:32–43; Num 29:12–38)

Just as the meanings of the sacrifices offered by individuals are not specified, so the precise meanings of these national sacrificial activities are not fully clarified in the biblical text. But similar interpretations as those given above for individual sacrifices have been proposed for these.

Whatever might be the import of sacrifices per se, one cannot miss the broader significance of the various national celebrations just mentioned. Clearly, these practices arouse a sense of God's perennial presence and interplay with the people of Israel. Through daily, weekly, monthly, and annual ceremonies, the rhythm of the nation's corporate life with Yahweh is deliberately set and applauded. Each of these moments is both a *commemoration* of God's past blessings and a request for continuing divine favor into the future. Further, in light of the sacrifices offered, each of these efforts serves as an acknowledgment of Israel's covenantal failures and need for forgiveness.

Most of these feasts serve as celebratory reminders of God's blessings to the people. The Sabbath recalls God's grace and power manifest in the creation of the world (in six days) and the divine (and human) rest thereafter, on the seventh day (Exod 20:8–11). The Sabbath also recollects God's deliverance from the hard labor of Egyptian enslavement and the need to take time (each week) to rest from labor and to honor God (Deut 5:12–15). The Passover and Feast of Unleavened Bread commemorate the Lord's mighty deliverance of Israel from Egyptian enslavement and the divine provisions in the wilderness. The Feast of Weeks (Pentecost) recognizes God's life-giving blessing exhibited in the early summer harvest. The meaning of the Feast of Trumpets, which was celebrated on the first day of the month of Tishri, is somewhat obscure in the Scriptures, but through the fanfare of trumpet blasts the event seems to have inaugurated a month of religious ceremonies; it also seems to have celebrated God's call of Israel to assembly. Later in Jewish history, this first day of Tishri became known as Rosh Hashanah, the first day of the year.

Close behind the Feast of Trumpets, celebrated on the tenth day of Tishri, was the Day of Atonement. This was a most solemn holy day, one upon which the nation of Israel gathered to repent of its sins and seek forgiveness and purification. On that day, the high priest entered the Holy of Holies, sacrificed a young bull for his sins and a goat for the sins of Israel. Through these actions, the high priest was said to have made "atonement for the sanctuary, because of the uncleanness of the people of Israel, and because of their transgressions"(Lev 16:16). The high priest also symbolically placed his hands upon the head of a second goat, confessed the sins of all of Israel, and sent the goat away into the wilderness so that it might "bear on itself all" the iniquities of Israel.

Some Christian commentators note two important principles of divine forgiveness implicit in the symbolism of the two goats. The sacrificed goat symbolized *atonement* or *purification* for sins, while the goat that was sent away symbolized the *removal* of sins. Arguably, both these symbols are aspects of divine forgiveness.[7] Other commentators see in the Day of Atonement rites, especially in the sacrifice of the bull for the high priest and the goat for Israel, mechanisms by which Israel was attempting to *purify the sanctuary* of the tabernacle or temple so that the Lord might continue to abide with the people of Israel. Thus, some commentators suggest that the Day of Atonement would better be named the day of *purification*.[8] There seems to be truth in each of these perspectives: forgiveness of sin, removal of sin, and purification of "sin-stained" persons (and places) all seem to be intimated in these verses. At any rate, the Day of Atonement (Purification) was yet another significant annual religious festival of ancient Israel (and remains important for many practitioners of modern Judaism).

A final national convocation of ancient Israel was the Feast of Booths or Ingathering, which rounded out the religious ceremonies of the month of Tishri. This six-day festival celebrated the second major harvest of the year and commemorated Israel's journey through the wilderness from Egypt to Canaan. During the Feast of Booths, the Israelites resided in small tents and so were reminded of God's provisions in the wilderness when the people lived in such shelters.[9]

In addition to these sacrifices and festivals, strong hints appear throughout the Hebrew Bible of other elements of Israel's worship. Clearly, many of the psalms in the book of Psalms played an important role in corporate (and likely in personal) worship. And many of these works suggest verbal interplay between congregations and worship leaders or cantors. The same may be true of other poetic writings in the Hebrew canon, such as the Song of Moses and Miriam (Exod 15:1–19), the Song of Deborah and Barak (Judg 5:2–31), and David's lament for Jonathan (2 Sam 1:17–27).[10] Scholars have noted a wide variety of psalms. Among them are these:

7. See Freeman, "Festivals," 604–5.

8. See notes by Jeffrey Stackert for Lev 16 in Coogan et al., eds., *The New Oxford Annotated Bible*.

9. Later Jewish tradition added lesser, but significant, annual celebrations, including Purim and the Feast of Dedication (Hanukkah).

10. See Dowley, *Christian Music*, 21–22.

1. hymns—praises to God, including using hallelujah ("praise Yah[weh]") (Pss 8, 19, 29, 33, 47, 65, 93, 95–100, 105–6, 136, 145–50)

2. laments—including personal and communal laments (personal: Pss 3, 5, 7, 13, 22, 42–43, 51, 54–56, 141–142; communal: Pss 44, 74, 79, 80, 137)

3. songs of thanksgiving—expressing gratitude for divine personal and corporate deliverance (Pss 18, 23, 30, 32, 34, 41, 67, 75, 107, 118, 124)

4. royal psalms—likely presented at royal celebrations, such as coronations; often emphasizing the virtues of Israel's kings as the agents of Yahweh (Pss 2, 18, 20, 21, 45, 72, 89, 101, 110, 132, 144)

5. wisdom psalms—commending the merits of divine wisdom (Pss 1, 37, 49, 73, 112, 127, 128)

6. liturgical psalms—involving the interplay of multiple voices (antiphonal) when read or sung (Pss 14, 15, 24, 50, 75, 82, 126)

Almost certainly, many of these psalms were used in temple- and personal-worship.

In addition to psalms and other poetic songs, it is clear that various musical instruments and choirs were employed during Israel's religious ceremonies (1 Chr 16:4, 6, 42–43; 2 Chr 5:13; Ps 150). It also is likely that oral instructions, explanations, exhortations, and historical remembrances (narratives) were expressed during corporate worship, as is suggested by the many instances of such verbal forms in Hebrew scriptures (Deut 6:4–21; 26:1—27:10; 2 Chr 6:4–11; Ps 106). Private and public prayers most certainly also were mouthed. Further, as the Hebrew scriptural tradition developed, there arose public reading and exposition of these writings (Deut 17:19; 31:9–11; Josh 8:34; 2 Kgs 22:8; Ezra 8; Neh 8:8, 18; 9:3–38; Ps 119). With little doubt, many of the activities mentioned above were used during corporate worship, although precisely how often and at what places in the various celebrations such accoutrements of devotion were used is less certain. The Hebrew biblical tradition also testifies of the importance of the rite of circumcision for the Jewish faith as well as various holiness restrictions for many Israelites, especially priests and Levites. We will not pursue these emphases here.

Worship Practices of Second Temple Judaism

Obviously, the fall of Judah to the Babylonians in 586/7 BCE was traumatic for the Jewish people. For many Jews, it meant exile to a foreign country. For others it entailed an impoverished existence scratching out a living in desolated Judah. Equally obvious, however, was that many Jews continued to worship Yahweh (both inside and outside Judah) in spite of the destruction of their beloved temple and the end of sacrifices. Further, even after the Persians allowed many Jews to return to their former homeland from 538 BCE onward, significant populations of Jews remained scattered throughout the Near

East and beyond, and many of these members of the diaspora continued to worship God even without regular access to the restored temple (which was rebuilt by 515 BCE). Over time, the practice of gathering in local venues for prayer and religious instruction became more and more common among Jews throughout the Mediterranean and Near East. These religious gatherings were called *synagogues* in the Greek language, essentially meaning "assemblies." The precise nature and timing of the emergence of synagogues are uncertain; what is clear is that by the first century CE, there were Jewish synagogues throughout the Mediterranean world, including several in major cities like Rome. The New Testament regularly mentions such gatherings.

Among the worship practices of Jews during the era of the Second Temple were the following. First, for most Jews (in Judea and beyond) the restored temple in Jerusalem remained the *ideal* center of piety. Thousands of Jews both within Judea and beyond traveled to Jerusalem annually to participate in one or more of the major religious festivals—especially Passover, the Feast of Weeks (Pentecost), and the Feast of Tabernacles. At the center of these celebrations was the Jerusalem temple. In turn, Jewish adult males throughout the Mediterranean and beyond paid an annual tax to support the temple.

Nevertheless, for most Jews (especially those outside Judea), the primary *practical* place of worship was the local synagogue. While the precise details are not certain, among the worship practices of these diaspora communities were the following. First was prayer. Indeed, a common Greek name for synagogues was *proseuchē* ("house of prayer"). Although the precise content and order of such prayers are uncertain, it is likely that some standardizations of them occurred by the first century CE while further structures were added over the ensuing centuries.[11] The types of prayers used may have been something like the stylized pleas found in Dan 9:4–19, Tob 3:1–6, 11–15, and Jdt 9:2–14.[12]

A second worship ritual in Second Temple Judaism was the confession of the Shema. This confession (still used in many Jewish houses of worship) includes the proclamation of Deut 6:4–9:

> Hear, O Israel: The LORD is our God, the LORD alone. You shall love the LORD your God with all your heart, and with all your soul, and with all your might. Keep these words that I am commanding you today in your heart. Recite them to your children and talk about them when you are at home and when you are away, when you lie down and when you rise. Bind them as a sign on your hand, fix them as an emblem on your forehead, and write them on the doorposts of your house and on your gates.

11. Later synagogue worship came to prescribe a more precise regimen of liturgical prayers, among them were the Eighteen Benedictions.

12. So proposes Hurtado in *At the Origins of Christian Worship*, 32.

Also often included in the Shema were lines from Deut 11:13–21 and Num 15:37–41. These recitations point to Israel's commitment to Yahweh as the only God and to the divine call to Israel to be faithful to the Lord's ethical and cultic instructions.

In addition to prayers and recitation of the Shema, numerous other rites were performed in the synagogues as part of Second Temple Judaism. Although the precise order of worship is debated, evidence suggests the following as a typical pattern in many synagogue services:

1. An opening invitation or call to worship

2. Recitation of the Shema

3. Recitation and/or singing various psalms

4. Reading of scriptures both from the Torah and the Prophets

5. Sermons giving commentary on and exhortations from Scripture

6. Closing formalized benedictions

There also is evidence of congregational singing, especially in the form of antiphonal responses to cantors singing various psalms.[13] Weekly Sabbath meals and annual feasts were also important features of synagogue traditions, and some aspects of these meals suggest the idea of communion with one's fellows and with God.[14] Missing in these synagogue activities were the sacrifices to Yahweh—a practice strictly limited to the temple in Jerusalem, and yet one that (until the fall of Jerusalem in 70) was a central element of Jewish religious practices.

Christian Religious Rituals in the New Testament Era

Christianity itself was initially a sect within Second Temple Judaism. Many of the followers of Christ continued to worship the God of Israel through rituals practiced by their fellow Jews. But changes also arose due to various factors, including the expanding early Christian understanding of Jesus Christ. The New Testament does not offer exact descriptions of Christian worship services in the first century, but it does (sometimes obscurely) point to several components of such activities.

Clearly, the early Christians routinely met together. A central name for these gatherings—similar to the meaning of *synagogue*—was *ecclesia* ("assembly"). In depicting the activities of the first followers of Jesus, the book of Acts names several practices that became common in early churches. According to the book of Acts, the earliest Christians

1. Devoted themselves to the apostles' teachings (2:42)

13. Dowley, *Christian Music*, 22–23. Also, such practices seem to have been performed in the Jerusalem temple.

14. Dowley, *Christian Music*, 35.

2. Experienced a sense of awe in the face of God's handiwork (2:43)

3. Engaged in fellowship (2:42)

4. Broke bread together (2:42, 46)

5. Prayed together (2:42)

6. Perennially offered praise to God (2:46–47)

7. Shared their possessions (2:42–47)

8. Engaged in evangelicalism and witness-bearing (2:32; 3:15; 5:32; 10:39)

9. Were baptized and baptized other (2:38, 41; 8:13; 9:18; 16:33)

10. Sang hymns together (16:25)

11. Cared for the needy (6:1)

12. Deliberated together over controversial issues (15:1–29)

These and other practices became common features of Christian worship and ministry, as is evidenced by their routine mention in the New Testament.

A central ritual of the early church was baptism. Precursors to baptism are found in the Hebrew biblical tradition of ablution—that is, ritual washing. Such observances often were tied to notions of ritual purification (Exod 19:10, 14; 30:19; 40:12–15; Lev 14:8–9). Also, at times, washing—including pouring—was associated with *moral* purification (Ps 51:7; Isa 1:16; Ezek 36:25; Zech 13:1). Further, occasionally, images of washing or being washed, and of pouring water were linked to promises of Israel's national renewal (Isa 4:2–6). In light of this, some sectarian Jews of the Second Temple period, such as the Essenes, performed baptisms for persons designed to symbolize both ceremonial and moral purity. Further, the Essenes (also known as the Qumran community) associated baptisms with purification by the Holy Spirit.[15]

Other Jews of the first century CE saw baptism as a sign for Gentile conversions to the Jewish faith. Proselytized Gentiles confessed faithfulness to the Torah, received circumcision, and were publicly baptized as a sign of their rebirth into the Jewish faith. Obviously, John the Baptizer's baptisms were a precursor to early Christian ritual practices. Key distinctions between his and their washings were that unlike followers of John, followers of Jesus (1) baptized *in the name of Jesus* (Acts 2:38; 10:48) and (2) affirmed that baptism in Jesus' name entailed baptism with the Holy Spirit (Acts 2:38; 10:44–48). Indeed, the Synoptic Gospels depict John the Baptist as announcing that Jesus himself had come to baptize with/in the Holy Spirit (Matt 3:11; Mark 1:8; Luke 3:16). Apparently sometime in the first century, the formula of baptizing in Jesus' name was changed to baptizing in the name of the Father, Son, and Holy Spirit (Matt 28:19).[16]

---

15. See Martin, *Worship in the Early Church*, 89.

16. See also Riddle, trans., *Didache*, chapter 7.

Ralph P. Martin (1925–2013) notes that in the book of Acts, a common sequence of actions often unfolded around the rite of baptism—namely, (1) people heard the message about Jesus, (2) came to believe in him, and (3) confessed that faith by submission to baptism.[17] James White notes a similar pattern in the account of Philip's baptism of the Ethiopian eunuch.[18] The exact means of baptism is not known. Obviously it entailed the use of water, but whether baptism happened by sprinkling, immersion, or pouring is a matter of dispute. Each of these ways of ritual washing was used in Second Temple Judaism, and differing contexts in the New Testament hint at possible distinct modes of delivery. The *Didache*, a first-century noncanonical Christian work, seems to assume baptism by immersion in running water (as in a stream or river) but quickly allows for pouring water on the candidate's head when running water is not readily available.[19]

The precise significance of baptism for first-century Christians is somewhat obscure. Various meanings seem to have been given to baptism by the New Testament writers. Broadly, one might note that many of the states associated with salvation are often closely linked to Christian baptism. Hence, baptism was correlated with forgiveness of sins (Acts 2:28), purification from unrighteousness (Acts 22:16; 1 Cor 6:11), justification and sanctification (1 Cor 6:11), and union with Christ (Gal 3:27): experiencing union with Christ entailed taking part in Jesus' death and resurrection (Rom 6:3–11; Col 2:11), partaking in Jesus' sonship (Gal 2:26), participating in the church or the body of Christ (1 Cor 12:13; Gal 3:27–29), and receiving the Holy Spirit (Acts 2:38; 1 Cor 12:13). No wonder 1 Pet 3:21 proclaims that baptism "saves you." Not surprisingly, the close association of baptism and other aspects of divine salvific blessing in the New Testament has led many Christians throughout the centuries to presume that baptism is an instrument that conveys salvation upon individuals. For details about Christian interpretations of the relationship between baptism and salvation, see Chapters 5 and 6, above.

It should be noted that in the New Testament, baptism is interpreted as a kind of initiation into the Christian faith; alongside profession of faith in Christ, baptism served as an entrance point into the church and into the salvation offered by God through Christ. In this regard, Christian baptism resembled baptism in Second Temple Judaism. (Baptism was part of the induction of Gentiles into Jewish life.) Whether they accepted Judaism or became followers of Jesus, through baptism adult converts consciously announced their allegiance to a new way of life. But as we will see below, over time, Christian writers began to liken baptism to another Jewish rite of initiation into the community—namely, circumcision. And this induction was less a matter of a

---

17. Martin, *Worship in the Early Church*, 100. See also Acts 2:37–38; 2:41; 8:12–13; 35–36; 18:8.

18. White, *A Brief History of Christian Worship*. See also Acts 8:26–40.

19. Riddle, trans., *Didache*, chapter 7.

candidate's conscious choice and more a matter of the community itself grafting into itself the newly initiated individual.[20]

A second major ritual of the early church was the Lord's Supper. All three of the Synoptic Gospels describe the origin of this meal as occurring on the night that Jesus was betrayed as he gathered to celebrate the Passover with his disciples (Matt 26:26–29; Mark 14:22–25; Luke 22:14–23). According to Mark, a centerpiece of the meal happened when Jesus gave his disciples bread and said, "Take; this is my body" (14:22); then Jesus gave them a cup of wine and said, "This is my blood of the covenant, which is poured out for many" (14:24). Luke records the latter of these phrases as "This cup that is poured out for you is the new covenant in my blood" (22:20). The apostle Paul gives the earliest known written depiction of this ceremony, although he admits that the tradition had been handed down to him by others. Paul notes that the

> Lord Jesus on the night he was betrayed took a loaf of bread, and when he had given thanks, he broke it and said, "This is my body that is for you. Do this in remembrance of me." In the same way he took the cup also, after supper, saying, "This cup is the new covenant in my blood. Do this, as often as you drink it, in remembrance of me." For as often as you eat this bread and drink this cup, you proclaim the Lord's death until he comes (1 Cor 11:23–26).

It is uncertain precisely when the earliest Christians began routinely practicing this ritual. Acts 2:46 says that the first Christians in Jerusalem "broke bread" in one another's homes. This may allude to the Lord's Supper but could mean only that Christians shared common meals. Elsewhere in the New Testament there is evidence that churches celebrated the Lord's Supper within the context of a broader shared meal often referred to as the *agapē* feast. For example, what suggests this is Paul's remarking that sometimes when the Lord's Supper was celebrated in Corinth, poorer members of the congregation went home hungry while others were full and even got drunk (1 Cor 11:20–22, 33–34). Extrabiblical evidence shows that for more than a century, this broader *agapē* meal was shared in churches alongside the commemoration of the Lord's Supper.

Perhaps the most dramatic shift from the worship practices of Second Temple Judaism was the Christian cessation of sacrifices. The book of Acts records that members of the first Christian community in Jerusalem often went to the temple grounds but typically says nothing of them offering sacrifices there.[21] It is possible that some early

---

20. For further consideration of these differences, see Chapter 6, above.

21. Acts 2:46; 3:1; 5:20, 42. One exception to this generalization is Acts 21:22–26, which describes the apostle Paul—per the request of the leaders of the Jerusalem church—accompanying four Christian men to the temple to restore their status as Nazirites. They were to undergo a purification ritual, and Paul was to pay the fees for the process. Apparently, part of this ceremony involved a sacrifice being made on their (and perhaps also on Paul's) behalf (v. 26). Some commentators wonder whether being present at such a sacrifice (and so perhaps condoning it) ran counter to Paul's dismissal of such practices in some of his writings. Other scholars contend that Paul never flatly rejected such practices as making animal sacrifices for Jewish Christians (including himself) but only denied that Gentile

Christians did offer sacrifices, but if they did, such practices quickly disappeared from Christian activities. One explanation for this, of course, is that (virtually) all Jewish sacrifices ceased after the fall of the temple in 70 CE. But the tone of the New Testament suggests that followers of Jesus discontinued or flatly rejected such activities earlier than Jerusalem's fall. For one, the apostle Paul claimed that through Jesus Christ God's definitive sacrifice had been made (Rom 3:21–26), and the book of Hebrews adamantly declares that this sacrifice was once for all (9:1–21).

In turn, the Gospels as well as Paul interpret Jesus' last supper with his disciples as anticipating and depicting Christ's sacrificial death on the cross. Thus, Paul records that Jesus "took the cup also, after supper, saying, 'This cup is the new covenant in my blood. Do this, as often as you drink it, in remembrance of me'" (1 Cor 11:25). Paul here seems to allude to Christ's blood being like that of the blood of animals shed when the covenant between God and Israel was confirmed (Exod 24:5–8). In like manner, the Gospel of Matthew portrays Jesus as saying, "This is my blood of the covenant, which is poured out for many for the remission of sins" (26:28; see also Mark 14:22–24; Luke 22:20). These writers see the Lord's Supper as representing and proclaiming Jesus' death as a sacrifice that confirms a new covenant with God, and that remits sins. Not surprisingly, then, Christians seem to have quickly discontinued offering sacrifices.[22]

A greater controversy is whether early Christians saw the Lord's Supper as a form of sacrifice per se—that is, as repeating Jesus' atoning death in some way. Certainly the death of Jesus on the cross was interpreted as the central sacrificial act, and the Lord's supper was understood as a commemoration of it. But was the Supper also a real reenactment of that sacrifice? Was the sacrificed Jesus—his body and blood—really present in the elements of the meal? It perhaps would not be surprising if several early Christians—having come out of Jewish worship practices that routinely involved sacrifices—would have seen the meal commemorating Jesus' sacrificial death as somehow taking the place of those sacrifices (as if the meal filled a void vacated by sacrifices); and it would not be a great shift in thought even to see the commemorative meal as (symbolically or really) repeating that sacrifice. Such an interpretation is suggested in the *Didache* (from the first century):

> But every Lord's day gather yourselves together, and break bread, and give thanksgiving after having confessed your transgressions, that your *sacrifice* may be pure. But let no one that is at variance with his fellow come together with you, until they be reconciled, that your *sacrifice* may not be profaned. For

---

believers had to participate in such actions. See Bruce, *Commentary on the Book of the Acts*, 430–32, especially footnote 39.

22. Paul speaks of the lifestyle of believers serving as a living sacrifice but says nothing of offering animal sacrifices (Rom 12:1); see a similar idea in 1 Pet 2:5.

this is that which was spoken by the Lord: In every place and time offer to me
a pure sacrifice.[23]

Obviously, understanding the Eucharist as a literal sacrifice is controversial. As noted
in Chapter 6, above, diverse interpretations of the Lord's Supper arose in church history and are still held today.

In addition to baptism and the Lord's Supper, the New Testament indicates
that first-century Christians participated in several other worship activities. Among
these were reading Scripture (1 Tim 4:13); preaching and teaching (Acts 11:26;
15:35; 18:25; 20:7); praying (Acts 24:2; 1 Cor 14:14–16); prophesying; speaking in
tongues; and singing psalms, hymns, and spiritual songs (1 Cor 14:26–32; Eph 5:18–
20). Alongside the celebration of the Lord's Supper, many of these practices occurred
during weekly gatherings. According to the book of Acts, the earliest followers of
Christ continued to worship at the Jerusalem temple, but they also regularly met in
one another's homes. Furthermore, there is evidence that many first-century Jewish
Christians attended local synagogues throughout Palestine and the Mediterranean
basin. Many of these gatherings almost certainly occurred on Saturdays—the traditional Sabbath. But as time progressed, Christians of the first century soon splintered
away from such congregations, meeting separately and routinely on Sundays—the
Lord's Day, the day Jesus rose from the grave.[24] On these Sundays, Christians corporately worshiped God and participated in many of the rituals mentioned above.
The precise order of such services, including when the Lord's Supper was celebrated,
is uncertain. The frequency of baptism also is unclear. The New Testament pictures
baptisms occurring at diverse times during the week—often spontaneously upon an
individual's confession of faith. But almost certainly fairly early on, baptisms were
incorporated into weekly and even annual worship services. Early Christians also
routinely engaged in outreach to the poor (Rom 15:26; 1 Cor 16:3; Gal 2:10) as well
as in private and corporate prayers throughout the day.[25]

23. Riddle, trans., *Didache*, chapter 14 (italics added). See White's further comments, in White, *A
Brief History of Christian Worship*, 29.

24. Acts 20:7 notes that on the first day of the week, an early Christian community gathered and
broke bread and heard Paul deliver a message/discussion. In 1 Cor 16:2, Paul encourages his audience
to take up an offering for the Jerusalem church on the first day of every week. The *Didache* instructs
churches to come together and break bread and give thanks "on every Lord's Day—his special day"
(Riddle, trans., *Didache*, chapter 14). Ignatius explains that early Christians "ceased to keep the Sabbath and lived by the Lord's day, on which our life as well as theirs shone forth, thanks to Him and his
death" (Ignatius, *Magnesians*, quoted in White, *A Brief History of Christian Worship*, 31).

25. There is some evidence of routine daily prayers among the ancient Israelites. Ps 55:17 mentions
daily evening, morning, and noon prayers. Dan 16:10 echoes this idea. The New Testament, likewise,
hints at early believers praying daily at more or less regular times. Acts 10:9 depicts Peter praying at
the noon hour. Acts 3:1 mentions Peter and John going to the temple at the hour of prayer at three
o'clock in the afternoon. In Acts 16:25, we find Paul and Silas praying (and singing) at midnight. Echoing these clues about daily prayer, Riddle, trans., *Didache* chapter 8 recommends praying the Lord's
Prayer three times daily, but it does not name the recommended hours. All of these depictions of daily
prayer must be tempered by the broader recommendation of Paul in 1 Thess 5:17 to pray perpetually.

Worship in the Early Christian Centuries[26]

As the first wave of first-century Christians passed away, they were replaced with new generations of believers and new church leaders, and for the next several centuries the worship practices of Christians continued to evolve. In this section, we survey some of the major developments in worship from the second century through the seventh century. Often these forms of veneration were heavily inspired by earlier practices, but innovations likewise emerged.

During the early centuries of postbiblical Christianity, baptism continued as the rite of initiation into the Christian community and increasingly as an instrument through which the saving benefits of Christ's work are received.[27] Most germane to our discussion is the development of the *procedures* of the baptismal ritual, although we will note some key theological interpretations of the rite as well. During the second century, Justin Martyr (100–165) described the following components of Christian baptism: Baptismal candidates who professed the Christian faith and were seeking to live according to it, after a period of prayer and fasting, were brought to a body of water. Having expressly repented of their sins, they were then baptized with water in the name of the Father, and of the Savior Jesus, and of the Holy Spirit. According to Justin, through these actions, the newly baptized Christian received remission of sins and illumination.[28]

Also in the second century, the *Shepard of Hermas* taught that baptism remits sins, and that thereafter a person could be forgiven only one grievous sin and still be saved. Irenaeus of Lyons (around 190) taught that baptism brings immortality and the presence of the Holy Spirit. Additional benefits ascribed to baptism by second-century Christian writers were empowerment for spiritual warfare, a supernatural seal symbolizing divine ownership and allegiance, and spiritual circumcision—a sign of being among God's chosen people.[29]

These descriptions, from the second century, of baptism are meager, but considerably more light is given by third-century writers. Tertullian (155–240) offers a somewhat cryptic description of baptism, noting that in it a person "is dipped in water, and amid the utterance of some few words, is sprinkled, and then rises again."[30] The day before baptism, says Tertullian, candidates pray and fast through the night, often on bended knees, confessing past sins. After baptism, the candidates ascend from the water, are anointed with oil and receive the Holy Spirit through the bishop's laying on of hands.[31] In another text, Tertullian also mentions the signing of the cross in the

26. I borrow this heading from the title of James White's chapter on the same topic. The heading is intended to capture the era from the second century CE through approximately the seventh century.

27. For a discussion of these matters see Chapter 6, above (pages 179–188).

28. Justin Martyr, *First Apology*.

29. Davies, *The Early Christian Church*, 104.

30. Tertullian, *On Baptism*.

31. Tertullian, *On Baptism*, chapter 20.

moments following baptism.[32] Tertullian comments that while baptisms are normally performed by ministers (that is, by bishops, presbyters or elders, or deacons), previously baptized laypersons can do the job. Further, typically baptisms are to be performed on Easter or during the Easter season.[33]

The *Apostolic Tradition* (often ascribed to Hippolytus, 170–235) offers considerably greater detail about the practices surrounding baptism. Prior to baptism, those seeking it typically went through three years of instruction as catechumens. During this period, they faced much scrutiny by the church and spent significant time in prayer, routinely receiving exorcisms. Sometimes this process was shortened for those especially gifted. Upon the completion of such training, some catechumens were selected for baptism. On the Thursday before Easter, the candidates bathed and then fasted and prayed through Friday and Saturday. At an appointed time on Saturday, the candidates were brought before the bishop. There they knelt, prayed, and received another exorcism; the bishop also breathed into their faces and made the sign of the cross upon them. Upon standing up, the candidates continued their vigil until Easter morning. At the crowing of the rooster on Sunday, participants removed their clothes, renounced Satan, and were anointed with the oil of exorcism by the bishop. They then descended into the water to be baptized by a presbyter or elder, who accompanied them. Laying hands upon the candidate, the elder interrogated the individual about the central claims of the faith, and baptized the candidate with water three times— once for each member of the Trinity. The mode of baptism is not specified in the *Apostolic Tradition*, but it likely involved immersing or possibly pouring water over each candidate. Having been baptized, the new Christian came out of the water and received from the presbyter or elder an anointing with the oil of thanksgiving. After drying off, the newly baptized believer dressed and joined others in the church building. The bishop again laid hands on the baptized individuals, thus symbolizing and ushering in the filling of the Holy Spirit. The bishop then poured oil over each new believer and made the sign of the cross upon the person's forehead. A holy kiss was given, and then the newly baptized individuals collectively partook of their first Eucharist with the rest of the congregation.[34]

Tertullian likely represents baptismal practices common in North Africa during the third century, while the *Apostolic Tradition* speaks for procedures in Rome around the same time. Slightly different rites were practiced elsewhere in the Roman Empire. Both Tertullian and the *Apostolic Tradition* make clear that baptizing young children was common by the third century. Tertullian opposed this practice, whereas the *Apostolic Tradition* described how such rites were to be performed. Further, by this period, special accommodations were being made for those too ill to endure the baptismal procedures, as well as for those unbaptized persons who had been martyred for their

32. Tertullian, *On the Resurrection of the Flesh*, chapter 8.

33. White, *A Brief History of Christian Worship*, 45–46.

34. Hippolytus, *Apostolic Tradition*, chapters 18–21.

faith. Martyrs were said to have been baptized in their own blood, and thus their sins remitted. The *Didascalia Apostolorum* (c. 230), likely from Syrian Christians, added another feature to baptism, recommending that female candidates be baptized by women deacons since candidates typically were baptized in the nude.[35]

From these sources we also see that, ideally, the baptismal ritual involved *both* bishops and presbyters overseeing key components of the rite. But exceptions soon emerged due to practical complications. First, allowances were made for persons too ill to come to or endure the rigors of the full baptismal service. Such individuals often received baptism by water from a presbyter (often by pouring or sprinkling) while postponing for healthier days those parts of the rite performed by the regional bishop (such as anointing with oil and laying on of hands to receive the Holy Spirit). Further, in times of persecution, sometimes parents (fearing the rite might not otherwise occur) asked presbyters to baptize their children even when a bishop was not available. Again, often the hope was that the rest of the ritual might occur in happier times. Likewise, as the practice of infant baptism became more prevalent (requiring numerous baptisms throughout sometimes vast territories served by only one bishop), the practice arose of presbyters baptizing babies and postponing the services rendered by a bishop for a later time. The effect of these diverse procedures was to sever the rite of baptism per se from the later actions of bishops. Over time, these disunifying ways led to a formal division between the *baptism* of infants (often conducted by presbyters or priests) and the *confirmation* of the same individuals by a bishop when the baptized infants had reached moral maturity. In turn, the formal teaching arose that while baptism brought the presence of the Holy Spirit to the baptized, the *gifts* of that presence did not arise until the later age of confirmation.[36]

Many of the patterns manifested in the third century carried over into the fourth century and beyond. If anything, with the legalization of Christianity under Emperor Constantine, the rituals of the church, including baptism, became more complex. The central procedures, however, stayed much the same as those of the third century; yet regional diversities were manifested throughout the classical period. We cannot explore these variances here. Perhaps the most significant difference between Eastern and Western Churches in the classical period was that in the Eastern Church baptismal practices tended to remain essentially unified, with baptism, anointing with oil, and conferring the Holy Spirit occurring in a single session administered by a presbyter. However, as noted above, in the West a candidate's baptism *by a presbyter* often was temporally separate from his or her anointing with oil and the reception of the Spirit through *a bishop*. Part of this procedural severance in the West was due to the doctrine of original sin defended especially by Augustine. This doctrine generated

---

35. Davies, *The Early Christian Church*, 148–49; White, *A Brief History of Christian Worship*, 46–47.

36. Davies, *The Early Christian Church*, 149.

parental anxieties about the need to baptize infants early in life so as not to consign them to an eternity outside heavenly bliss.[37]

A second major component of Christian worship in the early centuries of the church was the Lord's Supper. Earlier on, this rite also was called the Eucharist (thanksgiving). Unlike baptism, which was more sporadic, the Eucharist typically was received weekly, on Sundays and in the context of the broader weekly worship of the church. Indeed, the Eucharist soon became the center of Christian worship. From Justin Martyr and other second-century sources, we learn that weekly worship services of the period (especially around Rome) typically involved meeting in fellow believers' homes on Sunday mornings. Often the president or presider of the service (likely a bishop or presbyter) offered an opening prayer for the service and read from "the memoirs of the apostles" (the Gospels). Readings from the Hebrew prophets also were given. Often an oral exposition of these writings followed; intercessory prayers also were offered; a holy kiss of greeting was given, and soon thereafter the Eucharist meal itself was celebrated. Here, the president took hold of the bread and wine (mixed with water), displayed them to the congregation, and offered praise and thanksgiving to God for the elements. In response, the congregation replied amen, which, Justin explains, means "So be it." The deacons of the church, then, distributed the meal to those gathered, and they in turn ingested the food. Thereafter, the deacons gathered the remaining portions of the meal and took them to individuals of the community unable to attend the service.[38] Already by the second century, the Christian writer Ignatius of Antioch (d. 108/140) was teaching that the elements of the Eucharist were somehow the flesh and blood of Jesus and somehow provided salvific benefits to partakers, declaring the meal to be "the medicine of immortality."[39] Justin Martyr and Irenaeus of Lyon (130–202) shared similar views.[40]

Eucharist celebrations of the third century demonstrate essentially the same patterns as those of the second century, although the rite was becoming more elaborate and more prescriptive. Tertullian writes of readings from the Law (Torah), Prophets, Epistles, and Gospels, and singing of psalms—all occurring as precursors to the Eucharist celebration. He also speaks of prayers offered for the Roman emperor and other governmental officials. Cyprian of Carthage (210–258) adds to these services the preaching of a sermon, the use of the phrase "lift up your hearts" (*sursum corda*), and remembrances of Christ's suffering, death, and resurrection.[41]

The *Apostolic Tradition* (of the third century) focuses on the Eucharist per se, in the context of annual baptisms, saying little of the opening reading of scriptures or preaching. The author notes the giving of the kiss of peace, congregational offerings

---

37. White, *A Brief History of Christian Worship*, 50–51.

38. Davies, *The Early Christian Church*, 104. See especially Justin Martyr, *First Apology*, 65–66.

39. Ignatius, *The Epistle to the Ephesians*, chapter 20.

40. Justin Martyr, *First Apology*, chapter 66; Irenaeus, *Against Heresies*, 4.18.5.

41. Davies, *The Early Christian Church*, 150–51.

and greetings, the use of the phrase "lift up the heart," and the presentation of the bread and wine (again mixed with water) to the congregation. The bishop offered a prayer of praise and thanksgiving for the elements. Additionally, milk and honey were presented to the congregants as signs of the promised land now made available through Christ. Upon explaining the meaning of the elements, the bishop broke the bread and distributed portions to each congregant, saying, "The Bread of Heaven in Jesus Christ." The recipients replied amen. In turn, the presbyters and deacons administered the mixed wine, and the milk and honey, to each congregant three times, once for each member of the Trinity. Upon reception, the partakers replied amen. The elements having been ingested, the congregation (and the newly baptized especially) were encouraged to live according to their faith.[42] The worship and eucharistic procedures for nonbaptismal services appear to have been similar but perhaps less elaborate.[43]

Many third-century writers seem also to have believed that somehow the elements of the Eucharist, while remaining bread and wine, also became the body and blood of Jesus.[44] In turn, the elements often were understood to be a kind of repetition of Christ's sacrifice; this is especially true for Cyprian.[45] As the celebration of baptism did, so the celebration of the Eucharist also continued to expand through the first several centuries of Christianity. While the basic structure of the weekly Sunday service remained relatively consistent, regional diversities emerged regarding differing components of these observances; and along with these disparities sometimes came contrasting emphases and even dissimilar interpretations of parts of the eucharistic ceremony. We cannot explore these differences here.[46]

A third significant element of Christian worship in the early centuries was preaching. Since the first century, preaching had been a key component of Christian expression and worship. From the second century onward, preaching, along with the Eucharist, was a fundamental element of Christian weekly worship services. By the fourth century, lectionaries were in use providing lists of scriptural texts and themes for worship leaders to follow throughout the year. Many great preachers of the church arose in the earliest centuries of the faith; of particular note were Ambrose (d. 397), Augustine (354–430), and John Chrysostom (d. 407).

A fourth important worship practice among Christians in the early centuries was daily prayers. As noted above, there are hints of routine times of prayer in the biblical literature. Not surprisingly, then, some writers of the early centuries of Christianity recommended regular times of prayer throughout the day. Tertullian advised five

---

42. Hippolytus, *Apostolic Tradition*, chapter 21.

43. Hippolytus, *Apostolic Tradition*, 22.

44. According to J. G. Davies, the elements were understood somehow to be symbols that participate in the reality they symbolize. See Davies, *The Early Christian Church*, 151.

45. Davies, *The Early Christian Church*, 151–52.

46. For further detail see White, *A Brief History of Christian Worship*, 55–61; and Davies, *The Early Christian Church*, 266–69.

daily prayers—namely, at the third, sixth, and ninth hours, plus at daybreak and at nightfall. The *Apostolic Tradition* proposed seven daily prayers. In the fourth century, the rise of Emperor Constantine brought an explosion of Christian public piety. The new emperor reopened many long-standing Christian houses of worship[47] and commissioned (often with his own funds) the building of new ones. To train the broader pagan culture and to encourage participation among individuals long faithful to Christianity, daily times of prayer were established (often with considerable formality) in churches throughout the empire. Typically, daily hymns and prayers were offered in the morning and psalms and prayers in the evening.[48]

In addition to formalized prayer times for laypersons, Christian monastics developed elaborate routines for daily prayers. In the fourth century, Basil of Caesarea (330–379), who had immense influence upon Eastern Christian monasticism, established eight daily times of prayer: early morning, the third hour (midmorning), the sixth hour (noon), the ninth hour (midafternoon), workday's end, nightfall, midnight, and before dawn. Nearly two hundred years later, Benedict of Nursia (480–547) established for monks a routine of seven daily prayer times—a routine that greatly influenced Western monasticism. These prayer times were vespers (at work's end), compline (just before bedtime), nocturns or vigil (at midnight), lauds (at daybreak), prime (shortly after lauds), terce (at the third hour, midmorning), sext (at the sixth hour, noon), and none (at midafternoon). Over time, Christian clergy also adopted many of these prayer habits. Such procedures often proved to be unrealistic for laypersons and gradually the practice of formal hours of prayer for laity dropped away nearly entirely.[49]

A fifth growing practice of piety in the early Christian centuries was that of penance. Early on, several Christian writers expressed the opinion that after baptism, only one grievous sin could be reprieved. But such a policy soon proved to be too stringent in the eyes of many Christian leaders. Such sentiments led to the development of a formal mechanism for recompensing sins. While there was some variance among Christian leaders, typically a three-step process was employed. First, the fallen believer needed to confess the sin, often to the congregation. Second, some form of (often public) contrition and penitential exercises needed to be performed. Third, a formal absolution was pronounced. For ordinary sins, prayers and almsgiving might typically be required for penance. For more egregious sins (including adultery, murder, idolatry, and recanting of faith in times of persecution), more stringent and lengthy periods of contrition were required. Indeed, some early Christian writers taught that these more shocking sins were beyond forgiving.[50]

---

47. Many churches had been closed under the persecution of Emperor Diocletian (244–311).

48. White, *A Brief History of Christian Worship*, 53.

49. White, *A Brief History of Christian Worship*, 53–54.

50. Davies, *The Early Christian Church*, 154.

A sixth feature of the early centuries of Christian worship was the development of weekly and annual routines. We might refer to such routines as *sacred times*. The development of the Christian week seems to have formed first. As noted above, even first-century Christians gradually gravitated toward worshiping on the first day of the week, contrary to the Jewish Sabbath, which occurred on Saturdays. By the second century, the trend of worshiping on Sundays was second nature for Christians. In 321, Emperor Constantine declared Sunday to be a legal holiday, forbidding trade and other labor except for crucial agricultural work. Later Roman emperors banned theater and circus events on Sundays. In turn, early patterns of weekly fasting also arose. The *Didache* proposed Christian fasting on Wednesdays and Fridays in contradistinction from Jewish fasting which occurred on Mondays and Thursdays. By the fourth century, Wednesday and Friday fast days apparently were still operative, with the *Apostolic Constitution* offering the rationales that Christian fast on Wednesday to mourn Judas's betrayal of Christ and on Fridays to remember Jesus's crucifixion and death.

The Christian annual circuit emerged gradually. From the Jewish tradition, early Christians borrowed the Passover (Paschal) and Pentecost celebrations, obviously levying new meaning upon them. Jesus' death occurred during the week of Passover, and first-century Jewish Christians soon interpreted Jesus to be the Messiah whose advent at Passover had long been anticipated by many (but not all) practitioners of Second Temple Judaism. In turn, these Christians saw sacrificial significance in Jesus' execution. Jesus's was the atoning sacrifice for sin (Rom 3:22–25) and the lamb of God slaughtered to take away the sins of the world (John 1:29). First-century Christian writers also soon associated Pentecost with the long-promised outpouring of the Holy Spirit (Acts 2). In subsequent centuries, Christians continued to recognize these great events of salvation history, celebrating them not only on a weekly basis, but also through festivals each year. A third religious holiday also arose early among Christians: Epiphany. The origins of this celebration, set on January 6, are unclear. Several events became associated with this festival, including Jesus' birth, baptism, and first miracle (John 2:1–11). All in all, each of these associations connects Epiphany with the beginnings of Jesus' life and ministry. Early on, Epiphany also was correlated with the second coming of Christ.

As time progressed, these three annual celebrations (Paschal/Easter, Pentecost, and Epiphany) expanded. Much of this development occurred in the fourth century, again as Constantine's measures sought to inculcate the Roman populace to the Christian faith. The single-day celebration of Easter soon expanded to include the events of the whole holy week. This was accomplished largely through the efforts of Cyril, bishop of Jerusalem (315–386). Through his and others' labors, an elaborate series of commemorations arose in Jerusalem celebrating the events of Jesus' last week—including remembrances of Palm Sunday, Judas' betrayal (on Wednesday), Jesus' agony at Gethsemane (on Thursday), Jesus' atoning death on Friday, Holy Saturday (Easter Eve), and Resurrection or Easter Sunday. These observances, seemingly originating in Jerusalem, soon became common commemorations throughout the Christian empire. Also tied to Easter was Lent, a month-long period of self-reflection and self-denial preceding Easter week. The origins of Lent are uncertain, but this period likely grew out of the long-standing practice of requiring baptismal candidates to participate in an extended phase of contrition prior to their immersion into the Christian faith. In the West, the practice of pre-Lent also arose, likely sometime in the sixth century. These exercises were not initially widespread but involved over the three weeks prior to Lent, believers seeking divine aid against the evils (and evil spirits) of the world.

The celebrations of Pentecost also expanded over time. Most notably, two events that once were commemorated in a single holiday were spliced into separate commemorative-festivals—Ascension Day (celebrating Christ's victorious return to heaven) and Pentecost (hailing the outpouring of the Holy Spirit upon the church). Expansions likewise occurred to celebrations of Christ's advent. In the fourth century, under uncertain circumstances, the festival of Christmas (celebrated on December 25th) burst forth in Rome. Early confusion and conflict arose among some believers regarding the relationship between Christmas and Epiphany, but eventually, especially in the West, Christmas was recognized as the date of Jesus' birth and Epiphany came to commemorate the visit of the Magi to the holy family (Matt 2:1–12). Epiphany also, however, often continued to be associated with Christ's baptism (Mark 1:9–11) and his first miracle at Cana (John 2:1–11). In the late fifth century, Bishop Perpetuus of Tours (ruled 461–490) set aside a period of fasting before Christmas, commencing perhaps the earliest instantiation of the Advent celebration. The practice soon spread through Spain, eventually landing in Milan and Rome. In the sixth century, Pope Gregory the Great set the commencement of Advent as the four weeks prior to Christmas.[51] Once the date of Jesus' birth had been established, the timing for many of the other annual festivals fell into place. Commemoration of Jesus' circumcision was fixed at January 1 (eight days after his birth; Luke 2:21). And remembrance of Jesus' presentation at the temple (called Candlemas) was established on February 2 (forty days after his birth; Luke 2:22–40). In the end, then, two great seasons of celebration arose among Christians—a season commemorating Christ's advent and early ministry, and a season recalling Christ's atonement and glorious victory.

Another set of annual festivals emerged in the early centuries of the Christian faith. This was the celebrations of saints. In New Testament times, the word "saint" referenced anyone who believed in Jesus as Christ. All sincere believers were holy ones, persons set apart for God. But as time passed, Christians began to recognize truly exceptional persons of the faith as saints. This name especially was given to those whose commitment to Christ led to their execution (martyrs) or torture (confessors) by government authorities. Through the early centuries of Christianity, accounts and legends about these saints arose and many were written down. Local Christian communities began recognizing and celebrating these faithful believers through various services, including

51. Shepherd, "Church Year."

annual remembrances of their deeds and lives. Often these commemorative events were called the birthdays of the saints—that is, the days they died and entered into heavenly rest and glory. Soon, Christians began making annual visits to the burial sites of these saints, often claiming that healings and other miracles occurred while there.

When the era of persecution ended under Constantine and thereafter, the number of persons being martyred declined (although never completely ceased); and a new group of individuals arose many of whom were recognized as persons of extraordinary faith; these were various pious monks and nuns. Through lives of dying to self and living for Christ, these faithful disciples gained recognition as especially committed followers of Christ—that is, saints. The same is true of especially important Christian clergy or even secular leaders. Over time, annual commemorations of these various saintly persons transpired as well as pilgrimages to their graves. In turn, as time passed, many of these varied acts of remembrance and veneration were incorporated into the annual Christian cycle of festivals—often only in local communities but sometimes among broader swaths of the Christian empire.

A final word is needed regarding Christian worship music in the classical period. As noted above, there is evidence that music played a viable role in first-century Christian worship. We are told that New Testament churches sang psalms, hymns, and spiritual songs. We read of Paul and Silas singing and praying while in prison. And we observe songs of praise playing a central role in the book of Revelation's depiction of heavenly worship. Further, we noted the use of music and song in ancient Jewish worship as portrayed in the Hebrew Bible and in the literature of Second Temple Judaism. It is no surprise, then, that similar activities continued in the early centuries of Christianity.

The precise nature of the church's music in this era is not clear. Evidence suggests that congregational songs were sung in unison often with the deliberate intension of symbolizing congregational unity. There also were responsive songs (antiphons), where a minister, cantor, soloist, or choir would sing a refrain; the congregation would respond with a vocal refrain. Such antiphons apparently were common in the church led by St. Ambrose, whose chants often called for such interplays. Monks, in turn, practiced what was known as *plainsong*—monophonic (nonharmonious) singing of phrases, prayers, and psalms. While there is some evidence of Christians using instruments in worship, the majority of (or at least the most influential) Christian leaders rejected the use of such instruments. Thus, typically congregational singing was unaccompanied; this pattern held sway for nearly a thousand years of Christian history.[52]

The lyrical mainstay of Christian music in the early Christian centuries was the psalms of the Hebrew Bible. Psalms were recited (and often sung) during Sunday worship services as well as in the daily offices of lay and monastic prayers. Various components of Christian worship services also were sung by cantors or other

---

52. Among those condemning the use of instruments were Clement of Alexandria (c. 150—c. 215) and John Chrysostom (c. 347–407). See Dowley, *Christian Music*, 37–38.

officiants, typically borrowing words or themes from Jewish and early Christian scriptures. Among such canticles were *Gloria in excelsis* (Glory to God on high), *Gloria Patri* (Glory to the Father), and the *Ter Sanctus* (Holy, Holy, Holy). Hymns often also were composed and sung; hymns were typically inspired by biblical narratives and precepts, and often relayed specific theological perspectives honored (or in dispute) during the era. From the fourth century onward, especially in larger churches, professional choirs were employed to sing various components of worship services. Indeed, the pageantry of worship (including vocal music) greatly increased from the reign of Constantine onward, as the tastes of Roman aristocracy called for the fineries and pomp of worship long experienced in pagan and imperial worship. Such pageantry continued in the centuries following Constantine, into the Middle Ages, especially in the larger and ecclesiastically powerful churches.

Conclusion

Rooted in ancient Jewish religious experiences and traditions, Christians have long participated in varied worship practices. Inspired by diverse encounters with God through Jesus, first-century Christians engaged in a host of ritual practices, many of which echoed their Jewish heritage, but some of which were unique. Among the core rituals of the first Christians were baptizing in Jesus' name, gathering weekly, sharing the Lord's Supper, praying, reading and expositing of the Scripture, preaching and teaching, singing psalms and hymns, and (perhaps) celebrating annual festivals. As the first century passed into the second, Christian worship-routines continued to develop, often following the patterns of the earliest Christians but also expanding and augmenting into diverse forms. The same core practices listed above were still engaged, but their forms were enhanced, expanded, and sometimes rigidified. From the growing routines of daily prayers to the complexities of baptismal and eucharistic celebrations to the expanding patterns of the Christian year, Christian worship practices grew. As we shall observe in the next chapter, such growth and augmentation continued for Christian worship in the ensuing centuries.

12

Christian Worship

From the Middle Ages to
the Contemporary Era

IN THE PREVIOUS CHAPTER, we examined the worship practices of the ancient Jewish tradition and of Second Temple Judaism, as well as the worship routines of the Christians of the New Testament era. We also described the worship activities of Christians from the second to roughly the seventh century CE, observing a myriad of expansions upon earlier rituals passed down from the first-century church. In this twelfth chapter, we direct our attention to the worship practices of Christians from the Middle Ages through the contemporary era. We begin by looking at Christian worship in medieval times.

Worship in the Middle Ages

Christianity continued to expand after the sixth century. Eastern, North African, and Spanish Christianity suffered considerable turmoil from the seventh century onward as Muslims conquered vast territories, often imposing the faith of Islam upon non-Christians and restricting (sometimes severely) the religious practices of Christians throughout their lands; Muslim rulers typically also strictly forbade Christians proselytizing to Muslims, thus essentially ending any expansion of the Christian population beyond those families already faithful to Christ. Over time, Christianity virtually disappeared in North Africa, but lingered in the East and in Spain, often in diminishing pockets.

In turn, German-tribal encroachment into western Europe initially dampened Christian activities north of the Alps, and even in Italy and Spain after Germanic conquests there. Eventually, Christianity prevailed among German tribes, in no small measure due to the formal affirmation of Christianity by Charles the Great—Charlemagne (748–814)—in 800 CE. Over time, Christian missionaries converted many tribal groups in Britain and across the Rhine. In turn, with the fall of much of the Levant to Islam,

Eastern Orthodox Christianity (the Christianity of the Eastern Church, also Byzantine Christianity) managed to spread northward into the Balkans and into what became known as Russia. Further, Christians within and even east and south of Muslim territories also expanded. Two major groups of Christians often are recognized beyond the bounds of the old Roman Empire—the Nestorians and the Miaphysites. Both of these branches of the faith saw themselves as noncompliant with pronouncements made at the Council of Chalcedon of 451, and thus often were branded heretical by Roman Catholic and Eastern Orthodox Christianity. Our focus here will be on the worship practices of orthodox (that is, Chalcedonian) Christianity, although occasional attention will be given to the churches of the East.

Christian worship practices continued to develop through the Middle Ages, augmenting to greater or lesser degrees the practices of earlier generations. Baptism continued to be the primary rite of entrance into the church and into the Christian faith. More and more, infant baptism became the norm, due in no small measure to its association with the reception of divine salvation. In the West, tendencies to separate the acts of baptism and confirmation (which included the reception of the Holy Spirit) only increased. Several factors facilitated this trajectory. First was commitment to the division of labor between presbyters (priests) and bishops: presbyters typically performed the baptism while bishops blessed with the oil of confirmation (and the empowering of the Holy Spirit). Unfortunately, as the size of episcopal territories (dioceses) expanded, the availability of bishops for administering confirmations decreased, thus practically guaranteeing a bifurcation of the practices of baptism and confirmation (which once were unified). Of course, in principle candidates could wait to be baptized until both a priest and bishop were available. But such a policy was hardly appealing due to the West's further commitment to the doctrine of original sin. Since baptism was seen as the instrument through which original sin was remitted, few adults were willing to postpone baptism out of fear that eternal damnation might overtake them if they died before receiving the sacrament. And typically parents were unwilling to take the chance of consigning their infants to an eternity outside God's kingdom should the child die prior to baptism. Not surprisingly, then, in the West baptism and confirmation eventually were divided into two rites, baptism occurring in infancy and confirmation reserved until what was sometimes called the age of reason (of rational and moral autonomy) often set at seven or later. Eastern Orthodox Christian churches managed to retain the unity of baptism and confirmation by the more practical solution of allowing priests (under episcopal authority) to administer both rituals in a single ceremony.[1]

---

1. As noted in the previous chapter, Western theologians at times struggled to explain the need for confirmation since it was believed that through baptism original sin was remitted and the Holy Spirit was received. Thus arose the notion that at confirmation the use of the divine gifts was made possible through the Holy Spirit, even though earlier through baptism the Holy Spirit per se was received.

Another interesting feature of medieval baptismal-practices was the following. As early as the second century, the ritual of adult baptism typically was followed immediately by a believer's reception of his or her first communion. Yet as infant baptism became more prevalent in the late classical period into the Middle Ages, this tradition led churches to administer the Lord's Supper *to infants at baptism*. This feat often was accomplished by a priest dipping his finger into the chalice and touching it to the child's lips. By the twelfth century, however, this practice had largely dissipated in the West as greater emphasis was placed on the real presence of Christ's body and blood in the elements and as fears of spilling Christ's blood increased. Indeed, eventually in the West the routine arose of partaking of only the bread of communion out of concern that parishioners might dribble the blood of Christ. In contrast, medieval Eastern churches continued to administer the Eucharist to infants at baptism.

The celebration of the Eucharist continued to be the center of Christian worship in the Middle Ages. The core patterns of this rite remained much the same as they had been in earlier centuries. These patterns included an opening service (Synaxis) of prayers, Scripture, and homilies followed by the celebration of the Lord's Supper proper. Over time in the West, the term *mass* (*massa* in Latin) was applied to these formalized worship rituals centered on the Eucharist. A myriad of diverse sanctioned prayers grew around these services, many of which were written down in what became known as *sacramentaries*. Among the most venerated of these collections were the Gelasian and Gregorian sacramentaries. In the late eighth century, Charlemagne attempted to bring religious unity to his territories by ordering the use of a sacramentary developed by pope Hadrian I (772–795); this sacramentary was an augmented form of the Gregorian text. Supplements reflecting a broader swath of traditions from lands north of the Alps were later added to Hadrian's work. In addition to the sanctioned prayers for the Eucharist, catalogues of directions for performing the Eucharist services (called *orde*) were produced.[2]

Beyond these trends toward formalization and uniformity, another inclination of medieval piety was the growing distance between laity and participation in the eucharistic rites. Over time, the table of the elements was moved away from the nave (where laypersons stood) toward the far eastern wall of church sanctuaries; eventually, a screen was erected to separate the congregation from the priest as he prepared and blessed the elements. Further alienating laity, most of the words of the worship service, including those having to do with the Eucharist, were spoken in Latin—a language that the majority of laypersons of the Middle Ages did not know. Additionally, often such words were spoken in hushed tones, all but ensuring that members of the congregation were unable to grasp the significance of the various procedures being performed.

Just as the distance grew between laypeople on the one hand and clergy on the other, so separation also increased between parishioners and the act of sharing the

2. White, *A Brief History of Christian Worship*, 86–88.

Lord's Supper. Congregants themselves tended to avoid participating in the Lord's Supper except on especially significant celebrations, such as Easter, Christmas, Pentecost, and festivals celebrating particularly important saints. This partly came about due to the formal teaching that one must fully confess his or her sins and receive forgiveness prior to celebrating the Eucharist. As time passed, laypersons came to be denied the privilege of partaking of the cup of the Lord, and believers were given the bread only when a morsel was directly placed in each believer's mouth by the presiding priest or bishop. These practices came about largely because of the growing belief that the elements of the Eucharist mysteriously become the very body and blood of Christ. With this affirmation came the fear that average believers might partake in an unworthy manner, thus bringing judgment upon themselves; or persons might somehow defile the elements by mishandling them. To help justify these practices theologically, the teaching arose that the whole of Christ was present in each element of the sacrament. Thus, to take one element was effectively to receive both. Another doctrine also emerged: that the whole congregation was represented by the priest when he partook of both elements of the Lord's Supper. In 1415, the Council of Constance banned the practice of offering the cup to laity.[3]

A third important element of Christian worship in the Middle Ages was preaching. The use of lectionaries continued throughout the period, with similar though varied listings of passages used from region to region. In the service to preaching and theology, biblical commentaries and exegetical techniques were developed from the early centuries of Christianity forward. Because scriptural texts were typically used within the context of worship, interpretations of these passages often developed to suit theological perspectives already established by church tradition, sometimes with limited historical-critical or even expository insights in view. Among the varied methods of interpretation were the literal, moral, allegorical, and analogical modes.

Public prayers also continued to play important roles in medieval Christianity. In the East, the cathedral offices of lay-prayers (which involved morning and evening public prayers) still was practiced in several contexts. Further, in the East, the patterns of lay prayer often were blended with elements of the more extensive monistic routines of public prayer. In the West, the cathedral office of lay prayer virtually disappeared. Public prayer essentially fell under the purview of monks and clergy, and the patterns of prayer largely reflected the monistic traditions. Like other components of worship, public prayers were said in Latin, further obscuring their meanings from the laity. Over time, public prayers to the Virgin Mary and to the saints also became prevalent, and the number of ceremonies set aside for venerating saints grew, often crowding out other elements of Christian worship.

Not surprisingly, the routines of public prayer grew quite complicated in the Middle Ages. Prayers were formalized and written down, with a host of sources enveloped into the process. Since the earliest days of monasticism, the scriptural book

3. White, *A Brief History of Christian Worship*, 88–92.

of Psalms was incorporated into daily prayer times, so that over the course of each week, all 150 biblical psalms were prayed. Added to this hefty chore were numerous antiphons, responsories, hymns, formal readings, and lessons. Typically, these prayers were communal—spoken or sung by groups. As time progressed, efforts were made to unify (if not always to simplify) the wide diversity of prayer practices into books called *breviaries*. Pope Gregory VII (ruled 1073–1085) commissioned the development of such breviaries in Rome. The use of breviaries became especially prevalent in the thirteenth century with the rise of mendicant monastic orders such as the Franciscans and Dominicans; rather than remaining stationary in monasteries, these monks traveled alone or in small groups. Such friars offered daily prayers alone rather than in groups. Small book-sized breviaries made it possible for mendicant friars to continue the practice of daily prayer and worship even while traveling.

The practice of *penance* also became prevalent in the Middle Ages. Originating as a means for dealing with the most egregious sins committed after baptism, penance came to serve as a mechanism of contrition and forgiveness for a host of sins great and small. This development was inspired in part by Celtic monasticism, in which a routine had emerged of confessing sins to holy persons; these persons in turn offered advice for showing contrition and for holier living. As time passed, guidebooks for penance (called *penitentials*) were written. These works recommended various forms of contrition to match specific kinds of sins. Over time, they became complex and prescriptive. As Irish monastic missionaries spread into northern Europe, they brought with them these precepts and practices. Eventually, hearing confessions, once a role for holy people such as monastics, was taken up exclusively by clergy (priests and bishops), who in turn recommended diverse penitent actions to match the severity of particular sins.

The Christian annual calendar of the Middle Ages essentially followed those patterns established in the early centuries of Christianity. However, the number of holy days and saints' days proliferated as did the complexity of the varied celebrations. Liturgical directions for conducting these services often became more prescriptive both from a desire for consistency and for orthodox compliance. In 431 CE, the Council of Ephesus ruled affirmatively on applying the title *theotokos* ("God-bearer") to Mary; thereafter, several feasts celebrating Mary arose finding their places on the Christian calendar. The feasts of the Annunciation (celebrating the angel's announcement that Mary would bear the Christ) and of the Presentation (commemorating Jesus' being presented at the Jerusalem temple) had long been celebrated and associated with Mary. But new feasts also emerged. Among these tributes were the festival of the Nativity of the Blessed Virgin Mary on September 8, and Assumption Day on August 15 (commemorating the end of Mary's earthly life: her assumption into heaven). Other holy days set aside by Western Christians in the Middle Ages were the Feast of the Holy Trinity, institutionalized by Bishop Stephen of Liege (ruled 902–920) and celebrated on the Sunday after Pentecost. Over time, the festival was celebrated throughout northern Europe. In 1334, Pope John XXII sanctioned this celebration for churches under his watch and care. In 1264, Pope Urban IV instituted the Feast of Corpus Christi, commemorating the real presence of Christ's body in the elements of the Eucharist. This holy feast came to be observed on the Thursday following Trinity Sunday. Also, during the medieval period, a host of additional days were set aside to celebrate various saints.

Church music in the Middle Ages also largely followed the patterns established in late antiquity. Plainsong remained the core form of ecclesial singing. Such chants were monophonic and instrumentally unaccompanied, with rhythms essentially established by the words being sung. Between the fifth and eighth centuries, worship liturgies (with their sung texts) varied regionally, with distinct Celtic, Hispanic or Visigothic, Gallican, Beneventan, Old Roman, and Milanese liturgies (and chants) flourishing. But from the ninth century onward, beginning with the consolidations imposed by Charlemagne and later by Roman papal authorities, a more or less uniform liturgy and liturgical musical style became dominant in Western medieval Christendom. This mode was called the *Gregorian chant*—associated with but almost certainly not invented by Pope Gregory I (the Great), who ruled between 590 and 604.[4] Through much of the Middle Ages, typically, both the ritual prayers of the daily offices and the varied components of the Sunday and festival masses were sung using Gregorian chant melodies.

In the later centuries of the Middle Ages, ecclesial composers began experimenting with polyphonic music, including in liturgical pieces. The first extant written evidence of polyphony music theory is a ninth-century anonymous texts titled *Musica enchiridis*. Some of the earliest polyphonic liturgical music arose from the schools of Saint Martial at Limoges in France and Santiago de Compostela in northwestern Spain. At first, relatively simple harmonies were employed, called organum, but eventually richer and more complex harmonies were composed. Among some of the most significant early composers were Magister Leoninus (c 1159–1201) and Magister Perotinus Magnus (1170–1236), both tied to Notre Dame of Paris. With complex voiced-harmonies also came more and more intricate instrumental accompaniments, solos, and ensembles. As noted earlier, for centuries the church avoided instrumental music of any kind, but with the emergence of polyphonic harmonies a new place arose for the ecclesial use of diverse instruments. This was especially true for the organ, which had existed for several centuries but had not been much used by the church until the late Middle Ages.[5]

---

4. Dowley, *Christian Music*, 55–57.
5. Dowley, *Christian Music*, 64–85.

The Era of Reformation

Christian worship continued to develop after the Middle Ages, during the era of the Reformation (in roughly the sixteenth and seventeenth centuries). With the fall of Constantinople to the Ottomans in the mid-fifteenth century, Western powers soon sought new trade routes to India and China. Portuguese explorers quickly were traversing the waters of the South Atlantic, along the west coast of Africa, past the Cape of Good Hope, into the Indian Ocean to the shores of East Africa and West India. The Spanish ventured westward, first seeking a route to India, only to discover a new world. With these explorations, new trade routes both east and west were mapped out. And with trade (and exploitation) came shifts of economic power away from the Mediterranean basin to those countries with access to the Atlantic.

This era also saw the rising power of nation-states, the development of science, and the growth of early industry and capitalism. And with these changes came new insights into literary and textual studies, renewed interest in and celebration of human creativity and reason, and new technologies. The invention of the printing press played an immense role in propagating new ideas to vast numbers of people throughout Europe; disseminated was news of exciting discoveries from the great explorers, along with new scientific findings and the perspectives of dissenters challenging the status quo of Christian beliefs and practices.

Into this mix burst the calls of Martin Luther (1483–1546) for theological and ecclesiastical changes. At first, Luther set out especially to change what he saw to be the abuses of the medieval church's selling of indulgences. But soon his writings were challenging important elements of the medieval Western faith. At the center of his contestations was the rejection of the traditional Catholic understanding of salvation by the infusion of saving grace through the Church's sacraments—especially through baptism and the Eucharist. As we have noted elsewhere,[6] for Luther salvation comes only through divine grace made effective through human faith, which itself is only possible through divine aid. From these basic insights emerged a revolution in Christian thought and practices. In Chapter 6, above, we explored many of the core perspectives that arose among Protestant Reformers about the nature and use of the sacraments. We will not rehearse these views here; rather we focus on the ramifications of these ideas for concrete acts of worship. We begin, as we have in previous sections, with rituals surrounding baptism.

Baptism persisted as the primary initiation rite into the Christian faith, both in Catholic and Protestant churches. Further, for all but Anabaptists, Quakers, and later Puritan-Baptists, infant baptism continued to be practiced. Of course, European exploration and the subsequent emergence of new global mission fields greatly increased the demand for adult baptisms. But infant baptism remained a stalwart practice of most churches. One change to the rite of baptism was a move away from

6. See Chapter 6, above (pages 179–188); and Robinson, *Christianity: A Brief History*, chapter 9.

immersion. The baptismal fonts of the Middle Ages suggest, as does the literature of those times, that while infant baptism was prevalent, the mode of such baptism was immersion (dunking). This changed for many churches through the early centuries of the Protestant Reformation. But the changes occurred less for theological reasons and more because of parishioner sensitivities about the safety of infants. Martin Luther insisted on immersion as the proper mode of the rite, although over time the churches bearing his name moved away from it. Similar circumstances unfolded in the Anglican tradition, where formally immersion was the sanctioned method, but where parental concerns soon turned the tide toward sprinkling or pouring. John Calvin (1509–1564) did not think the mode of baptism was all that significant, whether immersion or pouring. But most Reformed churches, as time passed, moved toward pouring—especially when infants were involved. Practical evidence for this is found in the fact that most baptismal fonts of the Reformed and Puritan traditions were too small for immersion. Even Anabaptists, who insisted on believer's baptism, were unconcerned with the mode of the ritual, often practicing pouring. Quakers, on the other hand, simply abandoned the practice of water baptism completely, favoring in its stead the invisible baptism of the Holy Spirit. Only English Baptists, who rose up out of the Puritan tradition in the seventeenth century, insisted on believer's baptism and also on baptism by immersion.

The practice of confirmation fell on hard times during the Reformation era. Martin Luther rejected the view that it is a sacrament, contending that its sacramental status lacked scriptural support; further, for Luther, because it fails to symbolically convey the gospel's promise of salvation, it is not a sacrament proper. Nevertheless, Luther recognized the importance of solidifying faith in young Christians as they came of age, so he allowed pastors, through the symbolic laying on of hands, to confirm the faith of the young after a period of education. Huldrych Zwingli (1484–1531) dismissed the practice of confirmation deeming it nonbiblical. Like Luther, Calvin denied that confirmation is a sacrament, but he did support the notion that as young Christians come of age, they should profess their faith publicly before the church. Since Anabaptists practiced only believer's baptism, in a sense baptism and confirmation were reunited (as in ancient times). At baptism, the believer confessed his or her faith before the congregation, thus confirming that faith. Often in Anabaptist churches the bishop would lay hands upon the newly baptized believers as a sign of that person's reception of the Holy Spirit and of salvation. English Baptists followed comparable practices.[7]

Like confirmation, the sacrament of penance also faced challenges. All the Protestant Reformers dismissed the view that penance is a sacrament; nevertheless, most saw value in personal and corporate contrition and repentance. Most Protestants perceived confession of transgressions and subsequent forgiveness of sins to be an exchange between God and the individual sinner-believer. Christ was the

7. White, *A Brief History of Christian Worship*, 109–16.

true priestly mediator between God and sinners, and to him one must go for confession, repentance, and forgiveness. Nevertheless, many Reformers made room for acts of confession and contrition by individuals or groups to other persons within the church. Luther allowed confessions to ministers but also taught that in principle any believing Christian could pronounce another's sins forgiven. Often in Reformed churches, a kind of implicit demand for penance was found in the practice of restricting participation in the Eucharist to those Christians who demonstrated a morally upright life. Anabaptists often employed even harsher restrictions upon morally or doctrinally suspect brothers and sisters by banning them from worship services and publicly shunning them. Still, in every case, the formal sacrament of penance largely disappeared among Protestants but mostly was kept by the Roman Catholic faith, as evidenced in writings of the Council of Trent.[8]

The Lord's Supper continued to be a centerpiece of worship in the Catholic churches of the Reformation era. However, the Roman Church also persisted in stanchly denying to parishioners access to the cup of the Eucharist. Virtually all Protestant Reformers rejected this suppression of the chalice, contending that both bread and wine are central components of the ritual. Most Protestants saw the denial of the cup to believers as another example of church tradition superseding clear scriptural mandates. In turn, virtually all Protestants insisted that there should be no Eucharist without communion. That is, the Eucharist should not be performed only by and for the sake of clergy. Rather, it is designed for the communion of the church community as a whole—laity and supervising ministers alike. Another important change enacted in Protestant churches was conducting the Eucharist celebration (as well as other key elements of the worship service) in the vernaculars of the people. Following the lead of fellow German pastors, Luther published the Lutheran mass in German in 1526. Over the next three decades, similar vernacular masses were published in French, Swedish, Danish, Norwegian, English, and Finnish.

Luther advocated celebrating the Eucharist each Sunday, thus countering the trends of the late medieval church. But Zwingli called for masses four times a year—on Christmas, Easter, Pentecost, and in the autumn—essentially retaining the sequence established by late medieval Catholicism. Like Luther, Calvin hoped to see the Lord's Supper celebrated weekly, but he met stalwart opposition from magistrates in Geneva, who favored the practicality of Zwingli's reforms in these matters. Many Anabaptists and Presbyterians (members of the Reformed Church in Scotland) likewise retained Zwingli's sparser number of Lord's Supper celebrations. On the other hand, for many years, the German Reformed church, under the influence of Martin Bucer, followed Luther's practice of weekly communions. Later Puritan and Baptist worshipers settled for infrequent celebrations of the Lord's Supper.

For its part, the Roman Catholic Church of the Reformation era dug in its heels and refused to make most of the concessions demanded by Protestant Reformers.

8. White, *A Brief History of Christian Worship*, 128–29.

Thus, at the Council of Trent (held between 1545 and 1563), the Catholic Church retained its commitment to denying the cup to laypersons, continued saying the mass in Latin alone, allowed private masses (rather than observing the Eucharist only in congregational settings), taught that the mass was (in some way) a real enactment of Christ's sacrifice, and insisted on the doctrine of transubstantiation as an accurate understanding of the nature of the eucharistic elements.[9]

For Protestant Reformers, preaching became the central rite of Christian worship. Luther's affirmation of *sola scriptura*—which nearly all Protestants endorsed—virtually insured a place in worship for hearing Scripture read and expounded. Preaching (based on Scripture) became a primary means for educating congregations in correct doctrine (especially over against the perceived errors of Roman Catholic tradition). More profoundly, however, because of Luther's doctrine of justification through faith alone, preaching also became for Protestants the primary mechanism through which God is encountered and divine grace is received. Through preaching (proclamation), a person hears the gospel of Christ and is called to respond in faith, thus receiving the gift of salvation. Hence, no longer do the sacraments—including especially the Eucharist—serve as the core means for encountering God and receiving salvation, and no longer was preaching perceived as a preface to the more profound encounter with God experienced in the Eucharist. Now preaching took center stage in Christian worship.

Indeed, for Protestants, the sacraments (which included only the Eucharist and baptism) became the servants of preaching. Their primary role (according to Luther) is to present the promises of God (the gospel) in pictorial form, thus drawing persons to faith in Christ. Their effectiveness is the gospel message itself, which God uses to elicit faith in sinful humans. And for many Reformers, the sacraments do not even play this role in the salvation process. As noted in Chapter 6, many Protestants followed Zwingli's interpretation that the sacraments express *human* faith rather than God's saving promises. Nevertheless, most Protestants agreed that salvation comes primarily by hearing the gospel and receiving its promises in faith (through divine gracious aid).

Daily prayers continued to be common in the Reformation era. The Roman Catholic tradition retained its commitment to monasticism so that in many ways the routines of daily prayer (often called the divine office or liturgy of hours) were maintained. During this period, however, a number of monastic orders arose whose constitutions did not require congregational prayer times, allowing instead the keeping of private daily offices. The Jesuits (Society of Jesus) are a prime example of such a movement. During the Reformation, Catholic hierarchy attempted to bring greater regularity to its daily worship routines. In 1536, Cardinal Francisco de Quiñones developed an abridged version of the Roman breviary. Later, in 1568, under

---

9. White, *A Brief History of Christian Worship*, 120–27. See also Senn, "Communion, Frequency of Reception of."

the auspices of the Council of Trent and Pope Pius V, a formal *Roman Breviary* was produced and mandated for all Roman Catholic churches. Latin remained the language of liturgy and prayer.

Protestants largely dismissed monasticism with its distinction between common Christians and sects of especially saintly practitioners of the faith. For Luther and other Reformers, all Christians are called to a saintly life; further, all morally righteous forms of work (not just distinctive religious orders) are vocations (callings) from God. In turn, each Christian is called upon to live a life of communion with God, including to engage in a life of worship and prayer. Luther advocated routine daily prayers, accompanied by psalms, lessons, and extensive readings from Scripture. Zwingli likewise called for daily times of public worship—including daily hours of prayer in local churches at 5:00 a.m. and 8:00 p.m. The Reformed traditions, including later Puritans, contributed to regular piety by advancing the notion that each Christian family is essentially a church and is expected (by Christ) to engage in routine devotional activities, including family prayers, Scripture reading, and worship. With this in mind, in 1647, the Church of Scotland published a *Directory for Family Worship* to aid parishioners in familial piety. In 1549, under the leadership of Thomas Cranmer (1489–1556), the Church of England established the *Book of Common Prayer* as a tool for both private and public worship. In it were included guides and readings for the Daily Offices of Prayer.

During the Reformation era, the Roman Catholic Church essentially retained its many religious festivals of the church year, except that the number and complexities of many of the saints' days were trimmed back. Lutherans and Anglicans largely rejected the various feasts dedicated to saints but kept the essential cycle of the church year and most of the main festivals of that cycle. They especially preserved those festivals clearly tied to biblical accounts and to the life and work of Christ. Thus, Lutherans and Anglicans continued to celebrate the various festivals and liturgies of Advent, Christmas, Epiphany, Lent, and Easter. Reformed churches in Europe rejected many of the traditional annual festivals and their rote liturgies but kept celebrations clearly suggested in the biblical testimony—that is, Sunday worship, celebrations of the events of Holy Week, Easter, Pentecost, and Christmas. Scottish Reformed (Presbyterians), Anabaptists, and (later) Puritans tended to question all traditional annual festivals, favoring only Sunday worship services. However, Scottish Presbyterians and English Puritans at times would sanction days of praise and thanksgiving for contemporary events. Such practices are echoed in the United States federal holiday of Thanksgiving.[10]

The Reformation era brought changes to church music as well, and these changes varied between Christian groups. Catholic worship music essentially continued along the tracks that had arisen in the late Middle Ages and that flourished in the Renaissance era. Often composers created complex vocal and instrumental music for professional musicians to perform, clergy to oversee, and congregational audiences to hear.

10. White, *A Brief History of Christian Worship*, 116–20.

Included in these compositions were pieces for the various parts of Sunday masses, daily offices, and annual festivals. Such concerts were especially prevalent in the most prestigious cathedrals and churches of the land. Among the great composers of the era were Andrea Gabrieli (c. 1510–1586), Giovanni Pierluigi da Palestrina (1526–1594), and Orlando Lassus (c. 1532–1594).

Martin Luther celebrated music and sought to incorporate it in congregational worship. Luther commissioned the writing of German hymns, composing as many of thirty-seven of his own. Among these was his "Ein' feste Burg ist unser Gott" ("A Mighty Fortress Is Our God"). In 1524, aided by Paul Speratus, Luther published the first German Lutheran hymnal titled *Etlich Cristlich lider* (Some Christian Songs)—a set of eight hymns (chorales) of praise. Other hymnals soon followed. In 1526, Luther published the *Deutsche Messe* (German Mass), shaping it so that much of it could be sung in German paraphrases of the Latin. Even the lessons and the creed of the Mass were often sung or chanted as an interchange between the pastor or presider and the congregation. Zwingli took a reverse tactic to that of Luther. Although he was a well-trained musician, motivated by a desire to follow what he perceived as the biblical model of worship, Zwingli forbade singing in his congregations beginning in 1523. In 1527, he had the pipe organ in his church dismantled.

Calvin followed a middle path between Luther and Zwingli, allowing congregational singing in worship so long as the words were clearly grounded in scriptures. Under his watch, many of the biblical psalms were given French paraphrases and set to music. In 1542, aided by Claude Goudimel, Louis Bourgeois, and Clement Marot, Calvin published the *Genevan Psalter*, which contained thirty biblical psalms set to music. Several revisions of that *Psalter* were produced over the ensuing decades, each adding more psalms, sometimes with new melodies. In 1562, an edition containing all 150 Psalms was published. Anabaptists generated a variety of hymns. Some Anabaptists sought only to use biblically based lyrics, but most were open to greater variety, including songs of self-reflection, doctrine, and devotion, as well as hymns commemorating contemporary martyrs of their movement. The first printed hymnal of Anabaptists was the *Ausbund*, published in 1664 and containing several songs written by various congregants while imprisoned in Passau Castle, Bavaria, in the 1530s.

The Church of England largely followed Calvin's lead, initially restricting hymns to English-language paraphrases of the Psalms. Thomas Cranmer's *Book of Common Prayer*, first published in 1549, set forth a simplified Mass and daily prayers, with various components translated into English, including many psalms set in metrical paraphrases. Soon demands for congregational hymns encouraged the production of an English Psalter, collected and published by Thomas Sternhold and John Hopkins in 1562. In 1650, the Church of Scotland had likewise published the vernacular *Scottish Psalter*. An important composer in the transition between the Reformation- and modern eras was the English dissenting pastor Isaac Watts (1674–1748). Watts wrote numerous songs of worship, including paraphrased biblical psalms and English hymns. Among his many hymns were "When I Survey the Wondrous Cross," "Joy to the World," and "I'll Praise My Maker While I've Breath." While initially dismissive of nonbiblical hymns and instrumental music, toward the end of the Reformation era, many congregations of Puritan linage came to accept both.[11]

Worship in the Modern and Contemporary Eras

Christian worship continued to evolve in the modern and contemporary eras (from the eighteenth century to the present). The worldwide expansion of European influence that began in the sixteenth century continued, and escalated, in the eighteenth, nineteenth, and twentieth centuries. The Age of Reason began, emphasizing human rationality as the primary means by which the questions and problems of humanity were to be resolved. Knowledge of the natural world and of human nature increased, as did technology, largely through the efforts of empirical inquiry and invention. Secularism gained a foothold in the Western psyche, as many Europeans and North Americans did not so much reject religious faith as find it irrelevant to their basic concerns about food, health, prosperity, and pursuits of happiness; for many humans of the modern era, science and technology offered answers to these rudimentary worries.

With the Age of Reason also came modern philosophical interpretations of reality and of value, which (often) questioned traditional Christian understandings of the universe, humans, and morality. Starting from the empiricist assumption that all knowledge is grounded in experiences (either in sense experiences or in mental experiences), philosopher David Hume proposed that ethical claims are founded upon human feelings of approval or disapproval toward various actions (or possible actions). In turn, Hume mused that human ideas of God are based on human experiences, so that whatever notions humans have of God are produced by and limited by their own finite sensory or mental experiences. In similar words, modern writer Ludwig Feuerbach (1804–1872) asserted that humans are not made in God's image but rather that God is made in the image of humans. Adding to the modern challenge to traditional religion, late eighteenth-century philosopher Immanuel Kant (1724–1804) proposed that since human experiences are made possible by the structures of the human mind, and since humans cannot know reality without or beyond such structures, humans cannot rationally know that God exists or know the divine nature. Clearly, Hume's, Feuerbach's, and Kant's conclusions ran counter to the traditional claims of Christianity and forced many Christians to more closely scrutinize their faith and worship practices.

Even as the Age of Reason was coming into bloom in the eighteenth and nineteenth centuries, other events were transpiring in Western culture. A series of spiritual awakenings burst upon Western Christian experience, generating episodes of emotion-laden spiritual experiences, often accompanied by calls for personal commitment

11. Dowley, *Christian Music*, 113–17.

to Christ, Bible study, prayer, and pious living. Pietism, Methodism, and revivalism all made their marks on the worldviews of many Christians, especially in Great Britain and the United States. The revivalist spirit particularly caught fire in the growing territories of the North American frontier, as settlers moved into the wilds of Kentucky, Tennessee, Ohio, and Indiana. Great camp meetings arose where persons from varied (typically Protestant) church traditions gathered for spiritual admonishment, and where unbelievers were encouraged to repent, believe, and find salvation. From these events sprang new styles of worship that at first influenced American church culture but eventually affected Christianity across the globe.

Out of this strange mixture of strident rationality and experiential piety, several interesting trends sprang forth from the modern/contemporary Christian mindset. First were two broad responses to the Age of Reason—namely, liberalism and conservativism. As noted in Chapter 10, liberalism accepted many of the tenets of the Enlightenment era. Albrecht Ritschl (1822–1899) and Adolf Harnack (1851–1930) essentially agreed with Kant that Christian teachings cannot be established by reason; in turn, with Kant, they proposed that Christianity is primarily about morality. Friedrich Schleiermacher (1768–1834) agreed that Christianity cannot be established by reason, but he rejected the view that the faith primarily is about morality. Rather, Christianity essentially is about feelings and is founded particularly upon the human awareness of absolute dependence. Conservativism, on the other hand, largely rejected Hume's, Kant's, and liberalism's denial of intellectual knowledge of God, insisting that strong rational arguments can be made for God's existence and nature; further, a rational case can be made for the authority of Scripture—a case often appealing to the miraculous nature of the Scriptures. Further, for conservatives, the Christian faith is not merely or primarily about morality or inner experiences; it essentially is about doctrine—cognitive truths taught in the authoritative and inerrant Bible.

A second trend of modern/contemporary Christianity was *conversionism*, the emphasis upon the need for personal conversion to Christ for salvation and the distrust of teachings that salvation may be gained in ways other than through deliberate decisions for Christ. Perhaps this accent upon conscious conversion was implicit in Luther's declaration that salvation is by faith, not by works, and not by receiving infused righteousness via the sacraments.[12] Even more than in Luther's thought, conversionism was embedded in Anabaptists' commitments to believer's baptism and to the need for explicit, conscious faith in Christ for salvation. The same conversionism was also implicit in the doctrines of the seventeenth-century Baptist movement, whose members taught and practiced believer's baptism. While implicit in these earlier movements, conversionism came into full bloom in the revivalist moments that sent shock waves through the American religious consciousness in the eighteenth and

---

12. However, Luther did not fully develop the theme of conversionism and indeed implicitly seems to have rejected it in his continuing support of infant baptism and his teaching that through the sacraments faith is evoked and (thus) salvation is gained.

nineteenth centuries. Many revivalists presumed the need for heartfelt and rationally assented to conversion commitments. The revivalist movement deeply affected nineteenth-century American religion—first on the frontier but eventually throughout the nation. In turn, partly due to the growing economic and military power of Great Britain and the United States in the modern and contemporary eras, what had been largely actualized in the backwoods of North America eventually became common practice for many Christians across the globe.

Not far removed from the conversionist and revivalist ethos was a third trend of modern/contemporary Christianity—namely, Pentecostalism. The enthusiasm and emphasis on spiritual encounter underlying the spiritual awakenings of the modern period found new expression in the Pentecostal movement of the twentieth century. Pentecostalism was anticipated by the teachings of John Fletcher (1729–1785) and Phoebe Palmer (1807–1874), who helped create what became known as the Holiness tradition. Fletcher taught that through the baptism of the Holy Spirit, Christians could be sanctified (enabled to live holy lives). Palmer proposed that such sanctification could be attained instantaneously through the working of the Holy Spirit. Pentecostals likewise propounded that through the Spirit's baptism believers could be thoroughly sanctified, adding that the clearest sign of this spiritual baptism is *glossolalia*—speaking in tongues.

A catalyst of the Pentecostal movement was a Holiness preacher named Charles Parham (1873–1929). Another critical advocate of Pentecostalism was African American Holiness preacher William Seymour (1870–1922), whose worship services in the early 1900s at the Azusa Street Apostolic Faith Mission in Los Angeles, California, caught national attention for the exuberance of their celebrations and for the amazing manifestations of divine power. Among these manifestations were healings and speaking in tongues. Several pastors from across the United States visited the Apostolic Faith Mission and came away convinced that the teaching and practices of Seymour's congregation were divinely sanctioned. Among the visiting pastors were William Durham (1873–1912) and Charles Mason (1866–1961), who took their new perspectives back to their own churches and spread the Pentecostal way.

Pentecostalism spread rapidly throughout the twentieth century, first in the United States and to a lesser degree in Europe; but it soon traversed northwestern borders, moving southward into South America and Africa in the late twentieth century and becoming a major (and quite diverse) force in worldwide Christianity. Another movement, similar to Pentecostalism, was the Charismatic renewal movement, which sprang forth especially from the 1960s and after in many traditional Christian denominations. Several persons within this movement remained faithful to the core teachings of their respective denominations but believed in the empowering of Christians through baptism in the Holy Spirit and through the receiving of spiritual gifts (*charisma*) such as speaking in tongues, healing, and prophecy.

Out of the mix of these social and religious ideological currents, Christian worship practices marched on—sometimes barely changing from previous eras, sometimes altering dramatically. Baptism continued to be acknowledged by virtually every branch of Christianity as the central rite of initiation into the church. Likewise, for the most part, the distinctive interpretations of and modes of baptism that were forged by diverse groups during the Reformation persisted in the modern era. Roman Catholics continued to teach the infusion of actual righteousness via the sacraments, while most Protestants insisted that righteousness is only imputed upon believers due to their (God-given) faith.

Protestant groups continued to disagree, however, about the meaning of baptism. Lutherans still understood baptism as a depiction of the gospel that aids, even evokes, faith in believers. In turn, Lutherans tended to downplay the role of baptism as an *expression* of the faith of the believer. On the other hand, many in the Reformed tradition, including many Presbyterians, endorsed Calvin's insights that baptism is both a human pledge of allegiance to God *and* God's pledge to humanity. In turn, the Spirit uses baptism as a tool to arouse faith and thus to bring salvation to persons. Christians from the Anabaptist and Baptist traditions still endorsed Zwingli's understanding of baptism as a believer's pledge to God; yet going further than Zwingli, they insisted on believer's baptism only. Several newer Christian denominations likewise emerged and endorsed believer's baptism only. Among these were the Christian Church or Disciples of Christ (founded by Barton W. Stone, Thomas Campbell, and Alexander Campbell),[13] assorted Holiness churches, and virtually all Pentecostal churches. Each of these traditions commonly refers to baptism (and the Lord's Supper) as an ordinance (a practice commanded by God) rather than a sacrament—finding the term *sacrament* too suggestive of an infusion of grace upon the participant through the ritual.

One of the most significant trends in the celebration of baptism in the modern and contemporary eras has been an increase in the number of churches, and in the number of participants in these churches, endorsing believer's baptism only. Anabaptists and especially Baptists proliferated on American soil in the eighteenth and nineteenth centuries, as did the Disciples of Christ and Holiness churches in the nineteenth century. Pentecostals exploded numerically in the twentieth and twenty-first centuries. The membership of these churches, especially in Pentecostal churches likewise increased significantly in the Southern Hemisphere beginning in the late twentieth century onward. Each of these denominations practice believer's baptism.

The numerical increase in churches endorsing believer's baptism was partly due to the revivalist movement on the American frontier. These camp meetings emphasized the need for individual repentance and conversion to Christ. And typically baptism followed such moments. Even John Wesley (1703–1791), who affirmed the

13. This movement eventually split into the more liberal Disciples of Christ and the more conservative Churches of Christ.

regenerative power of baptism (including infant baptism), also stressed the need for personal conversion. A consequence of this mindset has been that the significance of baptism itself as the rite of initiation into the faith has diminished, and in many churches personal conversion has instead become the primary ritual of Christian induction. For example, many Baptist churches performed a long-standing practice of asking—even expecting—new believers to "walk down the aisle" of the church sanctuary on Sunday mornings to publicly announce their conversion to Christ. Walking down the aisle or making a public profession of faith has become the true initiatory rite of the Christian faith. In a nod to the spirit of conversionism, even the Roman Catholic Church of America has formalized a process for adult conversion, calling it the Rite of Christian Initiation of Adults (RCIA).[14]

Beyond the conversionism espoused in RCIA, a further irony is this: As James White notes, many assemblies that practice believer's baptism only also engage (with increasing frequency) in baptizing very young children.[15] This practice partly stems from parental concerns for their children's spiritual welfare. But it must be added that the motive for such a practice is not quite identical with the rationale that often pressed earlier Christians to baptize infants—namely fear of the damnation of the unbaptized. This is the case because most of the churches endorsing believer's baptism only do not think unbaptized children are unsaved. Instead, most endorse some notion of the *age of accountability*. This is the idea that children are not held responsible by God for their (original or actual) sins until they reach a time of moral maturity.

Here is one final note regarding baptism: Many churches of the modern and contemporary eras have continued to practice some form of confirmation. Roman Catholic tradition retains the formal process of confirmation, maintaining that the rite is one of the seven cardinal sacraments. Those Protestant churches that recognize the need for *believer's* baptism, in some sense, have essentially reinvigorated the ancient practice of combining the rituals of baptism and confirmation in single process. Ideally, in such churches, candidates for baptism are sufficiently mature to be exposed to the basic precepts of the faith, and subsequently they acknowledge those beliefs before receiving baptism. Also, ideally, such believers continue to progress in their understanding and practice of the faith long after their initial training. Of course, for those baptized at a young age in such churches, the degree of their understanding is curbed until cognitive maturity is achieved. For those Protestant churches that practiced infant baptism, processes similar to Catholic confirmations were engaged—with the caveat that such training is not a sacrament.

Like baptism, participation in the Lord's Supper or the Eucharist also has remained a central rite of Christians in the modern and contemporary eras. Many of the distinctive interpretations of this rite, established in the Reformation period, have continued to be held. Thus, Roman Catholics continue to understand

14. See White, *A Brief History of Christian Worship*, 151 and 187.
15. White, *A Brief History of Christian Worship*, 148.

the Eucharist as a ritual that infuses grace and righteousness into participants, and in this sense the Mass is necessary for salvation. Most Protestants of the modern and contemporary era, on the other hand, understood salvation as God's graciously declaring believers righteous even though they are not (yet) literally righteous—and this is due to their (God-given, divinely aided) faith. Lutherans likewise have continued to endorse Luther's doctrine of consubstantiation and his rejection of transubstantiation. Also, with him, Lutherans denied that the Eucharist is a sacrifice of Christ. Reformed churches largely followed Calvin's view that the Eucharist is both God's pledge to humans and a human testimony to the saving actions of God. Reformed churches also maintained Calvin's (admittedly somewhat obscure) teaching that while the elements of the Eucharist are not literally Christ's body and blood (and thus are not transubstantiated), Christ's *real* presence is there through his Spirit even while his resurrected body is in heaven.

Anglicans have also rejected the doctrine of transubstantiation but have endorsed the real presence of Christ in the meal. Anglican views, however, have varied about whether Christ's presence is bodily or only spiritual. Methodists hold similar views, endorsing the real presence of Christ in the meal but denying transubstantiation. Numerous churches of the modern or contemporary period accepted the Anabaptist and Baptist perspectives—that the Lord's Supper (often called Communion) is an ordinance, not a sacrament. For these churches, Communion is performed in obedience to Christ's command, not because it generates salvific changes in Christians. Its primary function is to memorialize Christ's sacrificial death and the salvation made possible through it. It also calls Christians to anticipate Christ's return in glory. Among the denominations endorsing these essentially Anabaptist and Baptist, ideals are Mennonites, Brethren, Disciples of Christ, Churches of Christ, Nazarenes (and other Holiness denominations), and most Pentecostals.

In the modern and contemporary periods, the frequency of the Eucharist celebration has continued to vary from one church tradition to the other, and often within a single tradition. Since the Second Vatican Council (1962–1965), the Catholic Church has recommended that parishioners partake of the Eucharist each time they attend Mass, which typically is offered weekly. Anglicans likewise celebrate the Eucharist weekly. Methodists, Baptists, Mennonites, Brethren, Pentecostals, and a host of other Protestant groups celebrate Communion less regularly, with each congregation establishing its own frequency. Typically, the timing of these rites ranges from monthly to quarterly. Presbyterian and other Reformed churches typically observe Communion-sometime between four and six times a year. A striking exception to these practices among Protestant is the routine of Disciples of Christ and Churches of Christ who usually participate in the Lord's Supper weekly.

One of the most significant shifts in the celebration of the Eucharist in the contemporary era has been the Roman Catholic attempt to make worship—including weekly services and celebrations of the Eucharist—more assessable to laypersons.

Thus, Vatican II called for and implemented several changes, including reciting the eucharistic liturgies (and other components of weekly services) in vernacular languages, believers' partaking of the cup as well as the bread, priests' facing the people rather than turning away from parishioners during the service, and the congregation taking part in singing, prayers, and readings.

Preaching also came to prominence in the modern and contemporary eras. This trend partly is explained by the Protestant Reformation's elevation of faith in the gospel to the center of the Christian reception of salvation. Proclamation of the Scriptures became the heart of Reformed and Puritan churches in the Reformation period and its aftermath, even as the salvific significance of participation in the Eucharist diminished. The importance of gospel proclamation became all the more pronounced in the eras of spiritual awakening and frontier revivalism in America. In the camp meetings in the American wilderness, non-Christians and wayward believers alike were challenged to repent, believe, and live by the gospel message. The basic format of these events was three-pronged: they began with (1) a time of prayer, hymns, and praise, followed by (2) a period of intense, often emotional, preaching, which warned of God's judgment and promised salvation in Christ, and then (3) a culminating call for a deliberate response to Christ—to convert or recommit to him.[16] Almost always preaching was based (sometimes quite loosely) on scriptures. Soon these practices became the hallmark of Christian worship in America—first in the Midwest, but eventually in the more settled east as well. Charles Finney (1792–1875) helped popularize this approach to worship in America in the nineteenth century, as did Billy Graham (1918–2018) in the twentieth century. Over time, this American style was transported to Great Britain and eventually to much of the world.

The Pentecostal and Charismatic movements brought new practices with ancient roots, into the twentieth and twenty-first centuries. A hallmark of these movements—especially of Pentecostalism—was *glossolalia*, speaking in tongues. But perhaps more important were various other evidences of and experiences associated with the Baptism of the Holy Spirit and with spiritual gifts (*charisma*). Among these experiences were healing, interpretations of tongues, prophetic messages, and jubilant expressions of faith.

Obviously, Christians continued to practice private and corporate prayer in the modern and contemporary periods. In large measure, the Roman Catholic tradition retained an essentially monastic form of the daily offices of prayer. And this occurred in spite of the Second Vatican Council's attempts to invigorate lay worship practices. Formal hours of lay-prayers generally dissipated in the Lutheran tradition and never truly caught on in many Reformed and Free churches. Churches in the Anglican Communion maintained some of the offices of prayer, and especially reinvigorated such practices during its so-called Catholic resurgence, starting with the nineteenth-century Oxford movement and continuing. Formal prayers and times of prayer typically were

16. White, *A Brief History of Christian Worship,*.160–61.

dismissed by members of Free Church traditions such as Anabaptists, Baptists, Disciples of Christ, Holiness, and Pentecostal groups. In these groups emphasis fell upon private prayers and upon individual or family devotions.

Nevertheless, a relatively formalized style of lay corporate and individual prayer routines did emerge in the modern and contemporary periods for Free Church traditions, as well as other Protestant groups. These routines included especially the midweek prayer service, eventually the phenomenon of Sunday school programs, and later small-group sessions. Similar activities were observed in the *base communities* of mid-twentieth-century Latin America, where often impoverished Christians gathered to pray, expound the Scriptures, and redress the economic and political woes they faced. The Pietist and Methodist traditions provided an important impetus for such gatherings in the seventeenth and eighteenth centuries—as various groups met (often in private homes) for (typically) lay-led services in order to read and discuss the Scriptures, and to offer up prayers and praise to God.

The ritual of penance continued to be practiced in Catholic churches and to be rejected in Protestant traditions. For much of the modern era, many Catholic churches provided the confessional for individuals who wish to privately confess their sins to a priest on the other side of a screen. But even this practice swiftly waned under the sway of the Second Vatican Council. After the council, more and more Catholic parishioners met with their priests face-to-face in larger counseling rooms. Some Anglican churches restored confessionals during the period of the Oxford movement, but many also reversed these patterns in the twentieth century. Anabaptists, to greater or lesser degrees depending on the tradition, continued to use the ban and shunning as tools for evoking contrition from noncompliant members. Most other Protestant churches relied on general congregational confessions during times of worship, especially while participating in the Lord's Supper and during altar calls at the ends of worship or preaching services. Conceding to the growing field of psychology, both Protestant and Catholic traditions of the contemporary era offered various forms of pastoral counseling for congregants.

Many of the practices established during the Reformation era having to do with the Christian year continued in the modern and contemporary eras—albeit with adaptations. Roman Catholics continued to celebrate the Christian year, in large measure following the cadence set from ancient and medieval days. Three new major feasts were added in modern times—namely, the Feast of the Immaculate Conception (1708), the Feast of the Sacred Heart (1856), and Christ the King (1925). Vatican II augmented the liturgical calendar in the 1960s, reaffirming the preeminence of Sundays as the chief holy days of the Christian year. Pre-Lent was eliminated from the official liturgical calendar (including Shrove Tuesday or Mardi Gras). And the ancient Roman Feast of Saint Mary, celebrated on January 1, was restored to the liturgical year. In turn, many of the formal saint's days were simplified and broken down into three categories—solemnities, feasts, and memorials. The

Catholic liturgical calendar remained highly complicated, a description of which would consume several pages of this work. For expedience, it is best simply to name some of the central celebrations of that cycle:

Advent (the four Sunday prior to Christmas)

Christmas Day (December 25)

Solemnity of Mary (January 1)

Epiphany (January 6)

Lent (the season beginning forty days before Easter, on Ash Wednesday)

Easter

Ascension

Pentecost

Holy Trinity Sunday

Feast of Corpus Christi (Thursday after Holy Trinity Sunday)

Christ the King Sunday (in autumn)

Through much of the modern era, up until the mid-twentieth century, many Protestant churches maintained the core outlooks on the liturgical year that had been established during the Reformation. Like the Catholic Church, all these churches recognized weekly Sunday services as central times of worship. Lutheran and Anglican traditions held onto many liturgical festivals of the year but vacillated on the precise number of holy days to be celebrated. Typically they kept the key seasons of Advent, Christmas, Epiphany, Lent, Passion Week, Easter, and Pentecost. Lutherans also came to celebrate October 31 as Reformation Day, commemorating Martin Luther's posting of his ninety-five theses on the door of the Wittenberg castle church. The Methodist tradition, largely following John Wesley, did not acknowledge many of the traditional holy days, preserving only Christmas Day, Good Friday, Easter Day, Ascension Day, and Trinity Sunday. Reformed and Puritan churches, as well as many congregations in the Free Church tradition (Baptist, Disciples of Christ, Pentecostals, and others) have traditionally recognized only Sundays as obligatory times of worship. However, many of these churches also came to place special emphasis on celebrations such as Christmas Sunday, Easter Week (Palm Sunday, Maundy Thursday, and Good Friday), Easter Sunday, and Pentecost Sunday.

In addition to recognizing significant days on the traditional Christian calendar, many modern and contemporary (especially American Protestant) churches developed new annual worship routines not in traditional liturgical cycles—thus recognizing days (usually Sundays) set aside for special emphases such as Mother's Day, Father's Day, revivals, homecoming, Sunday school rallies, race relations, harvest and Thanksgiving celebrations. While not formally mandated by either congregational covenants or ecclesiastical authorities, many of these celebrations became fixtures in the annual rhythm of congregational life. In the mid-twentieth century, several Protestant denominations returned to more traditional annual liturgical celebrations. In 1983, a Common Lectionary was published, which is now shared by many Protestant groups. These changes were inspired by the twentieth-century ecumenical movement as well as by the ecumenical concessions made by Vatican II. In the late 1990s, a movement dubbed the Emergent Church, made up primarily of traditional Protestant Christians, began blending elements of contemporary worship (including rock music) with traditional features of church liturgies. Several megachurches likewise have endorsed aspects of the traditional liturgy and the liturgical year.[17]

In the modern and contemporary eras, Christian worship music continued to progress, often echoing trends from the Renaissance and Reformation periods but likewise developing new and creative styles. Emerging from the polyphonic techniques of classical Renaissance chorales and orchestras, several Catholic and Protestant composers began developing church music in what became known as *baroque* style—music focusing on major and minor scales distinct from traditional Dorian, Lydian, and Ionian modes. Important Catholic composers of the period where Claudio Monteverdi (1567–1643), Antonio Vivaldi (1678–1741), Antonio Drghi (c. 1634–1700), and Marc-Antoine Charpentier (1643–1704). These composers produced various masses, laudes (vernacular hymns for congregational singing) and oratorios (nonliturgical sacred music for choruses, orchestras, and soloists). A key baroque Protestant composer was Johann Sebastian Bach (1685–1750), who created numerous motets, cantatas, and passions (oratorios on the suffering and death of Jesus), as well as his renowned Mass in B Minor. Another important Protestant baroque composer was George Frideric Handel (1685–1759), whose most celebrated oratorio was *Messiah*.[18]

Hymns also flourished in the modern and contemporary eras. In no small measure influenced by Isaac Watts, English dissenting groups (including Puritans, Baptists, and Congregationalists) began composing and celebrating with hymns, many of which went beyond direct scriptural images to expressions of personal piety. Also greatly shaping modern Protestant worship was the hymnody of John and Charles Wesley, the latter of whom wrote thousands of theologically informed and spiritually inspiring hymns. Among Charles's works are "O, for a Thousand Tongues to Sing," "Hark! The Herald Angels Sing," and "Christ the Lord Is Risen Today." The brothers Wesley published more than fifty hymn collections in their lifetimes. Many of Watts's and Wesley's hymns (along with songs of other English authors) were transported to and became popular in America. Often such works helped shape and were affected by the First Great Awakening, in the 1730s and '40s.[19]

---

17. See Veith, "Megachurches Discovering Liturgy & Traditional Christianity?"

18. Dowley, *Christian Music*, 126–42.

19. Dowley, *Christian Music*, 115–22.

The Second Great Awakening, in the early nineteenth century, which transpired in the Midwestern frontier of the United States, also contributed to the production and popularity of hymns. From these camp meetings emerged forms of music and of lyric spun from remorseful repentance, heartfelt conversions, and deep gratitude for God's grace in Christ. In styles distinct from medieval chants of divine mystery or Reformation and Wesleyan corporate celebrations of Christian doctrine and divine grandeur, the hymns of the frontier often were personal. They featured expressions of individual inner struggle, pleas for mercy, and thanksgiving for personal salvation in Christ. Typically, such songs were more enthusiastic than contemplative. Contributing to the tenor of these frontier revival-tunes were the voices of African American Christians (many of whom were still slaves), who—among various contributions— added a poignant mix of exuberance and painful hope to their songs of worship. Out of the nineteenth-century revivalist movements came hymns like Robert Lowry's "Shall We Gather at the River?", Philip Bliss's "Wonderful Words of Life," and W. H. Doane's and Arabella Hankey's "Tell Me the Old, Old Story." Similar, but distinctive, worship songs arose out of the African American heritage—songs often referred to as *spirituals*. Among these songs were "Swing Low, Sweat Chariot" by Wallace Willis, and "Were You There When They Crucified My Lord?"[20]

Revivalist Charles Finney (1792–1875) especially helped popularize the camp-meeting style of worship throughout the eastern and northern parts of the United States, including the enthusiastic hymns of that tradition. Also playing a significant role in this endeavor were revival preacher Dwight L. Moody (1837–1899) and his longtime song leader Ira Sankey (1840–1908). By the later part of the nineteenth century, most Protestant denominations were publishing their own worship hymnals, even while borrowing profusely from one another. These trends continued through much of the early twentieth century, especially in England and the United States. Technology—especially phonographs and radio—helped spread what previously had been only regional trends to wider audiences, making worship music both more diverse and more uniform across regions. The twentieth century produced numerous hymns, some of the most memorable being "The Old Rugged Cross" (by George Bennard [1873–1958]) and "He Lives" (by Alfred Ackley [1887–1960]). Newer styles of choral music also arose in the mid-twentieth century, including varied works by Bill (b. 1936) and Gloria (b. 1942) Gaither and Ralph Carmichael (b. 1927).[21]

The mid-twentieth century also brought new technology to music, including especially electric guitars and keyboards, which soon inspired American and British youth in the 1950s and 1960s. Rock and roll emerged, deeply influenced by earlier jazz and blues styles, which themselves were rooted in innovations by various African American musicians and songwriters of earlier years. A key feature of the latter half of the twentieth century and of the twenty-first century has been the introduction of and expanding

20. Dowley, *Christian Music*, 179–85, 190–94.
21. Dowley, *Christian Music*, 211–14.

use of rock-based music in Christian worship services. During the 1960s and 1970s, a movement known as the Jesus People swept across America, with ties both to the Charismatic movement and to the counterculture of the time. While controversial to many traditionalists (then and now), rock-based worship became more and more prominent especially in Evangelical churches through the latter part of the twentieth century into the twenty-first century. Not far behind the arrival of rock-based worship music was the growth of megachurches. These were churches with memberships of two thousand or more. Such churches often were neo-evangelical in disposition—typically endorsing some form of Protestant theology and practicing congregational or presbyterian church governance. While offering a variety of musical styles in worship, many of these churches especially excelled in rock-based worship music.

One final note is needed regarding worship in the modern era and especially in the contemporary era. As Christianity expanded into the developing countries of the global south and east, especially from the mid-twentieth century onward, pressures mounted to provide rituals suitable for non-Western, cultural contexts. Often Westerners had to perform a balancing act in order to help communicate the Christian message and life in forms compatible with indigenous cultures. Following principles proposed during the Second Vatican Council, African Catholic priest Nwaka Chris Egbulem advocated what he called "liturgical inculturation," which seeks to facilitate "the incarnation of Christian liturgical experience" into local African Christian worshiping communities. Such inculturation "respects the pillars of a culture" and "brings the Church and the culture into mutual dialogue and sharing" so that a blending of "authentic Christianity and authentic Africanness" occurs. According to Egbulem, while some African traditions may need to be expunged because they are contrary to the gospel, others are "connatural" with the gospel and may reinforce truths already inherent in Western Christian ritual practices. And some African cultural traditions might even convey the gospel message in ways not fully expressed or expressible by Christian rituals of the West.[22]

Obviously, many of the rituals practiced by African churches are similar, even identical, to the rituals practiced by traditional Western churches—including baptism, the Eucharist, preaching, prayer, and the like. But not infrequently subtle, even pronounced, differences appear. Many African churches—of a variety of denominational heritages—practice exuberant worship, including boisterous dancing and singing. They often incorporate into their services room for healings, visions, dreams, prophecies, and other charismatic phenomena. And many African churches express deep familial attitudes toward fellow Christians, recognizing, celebrating, and leaning upon their Christian community for practical as well as spiritual aid. Some churches even set aside time to honor and consult ancestors in ways distinct, but not far removed, from some Western practices of honoring saints.[23] And some African Chris-

22. Egbulem, "Mission and Inculturation: Africa" is quoted throughout this paragraph.
23. Egbulem, "Mission and Inculturation: Africa."

tian leaders have advocated polygamy as biblically permissible, especially in contexts where such customs have long been practiced and where women's economic welfare is dependent upon such arrangements.

The sheer number and diversity of African churches make it difficult to identify core worship distinctives. Africa is filled with churches from a variety of sources. Many come from heritages of the ancient world, such as the Ethiopian Tewahedo and Egyptian Coptic traditions. Others are tied to traditional Western denominations—Catholics, Anglicans, Lutherans, Reformed, Anabaptists, Methodists, Baptists, and so forth. And many African churches have Pentecostal and Charismatic origins. Finally, there are a number of African Initiated or African Independent churches (often designated AICs) with diverse origin stories. All of these traditions engage in Christian worship in distinctive ways, attempting to make such worship meaningful to their congregants. Diversity of worship also emerges among churches of the global east, where the core elements of Christian faith and ritual blend with local cultural distinctives to help communicate and practice the Christian ethos in those contexts.[24]

Conclusion

A centerpiece of Christian practice is worship. Throughout the ages, Christians have gathered to worship God or have engaged in varied forms of private worship. Underlying these practices is the belief that God and God's activities are worthy of praise. Also often supporting worship activities is belief that God can be, has been, and will continue to be encountered in human life, including—perhaps especially—in the life of worship. In the previous chapter, we examined the roots of Christian worship in the biblical tradition, as well as such activities in the earliest centuries of Christianity. In this twelfth chapter, we observed the continuing development of Christian worship from the Middle Ages into our current era. Rooted in earlier practices, Christian worship activities have taken varied forms, sometimes sprouting, growing, and blossoming into new and splendid forms; sometimes, entangling, knotting, and eventually dying away. Through it all, the central convictions have prevailed that God is worthy of worship and can be encountered in and through Christian worship rituals.

24. See Chupungco, "Mission and Inculturation: East Asia and the Pacific."

Part Five: **Christian Issues**

13

Christian Issues

Christianity, the Problem of Evil,
and Other Religions

THUS FAR IN THIS book, in its first two chapters, we have addressed four core foundations of Christianity: the Bible, the story of Israel, the person and work of Jesus, and the earliest community of Christian believers. We also have explored (in Chapters 3 through 7) some of the central teachings of the Christian faith—that is, its theology—as well as (in Chapters 8 through 10) the main ethical insights of the Bible and several approaches to Christian ethics manifested throughout history. In the previous two chapters (Chapters 11 and 12), we described many of Christianity's worship practices through the ages.

In these final three chapters, we examine several pivotal issues facing Christianity. Specifically, in Chapter 13, we explore (1) the problem of evil and (2) the relationship between the Christian faith and other religions. In Chapter 14, we consider (3) the relationship between science and the Christian faith. And in Chapter 15, we inspect (4) the issue of Christianity and women in ministry. We turn first to the problem of evil.

Christianity and the Problem of Evil

The existence of evil generates a considerable conundrum for Christian theism,[1] especially because theism affirms the existence of an all-powerful and perfectly good

---

1. *Theism* basically means "belief in God." Over time, this concept has come to entail relatively specific beliefs about the nature of God. Among those beliefs are affirmations of only one God (monotheism) who is creator of, sustainer of, and sovereign over all that exists. This God is omnipotent (all-powerful), omniscient (all-knowing), and omnipresent (present everywhere not in the sense of being spatially located or spread out but rather as being aware of every spatially located event and able to causally affect all events in every spatial locale). Typically, the God of theism is understood to be utterly self-sufficient (that is, not dependent on any other) as well as fully good, nonphysical, and personal (either as a singular person or as transpersonal—as in the Christian doctrine of the Trinity). Christianity is typically understood to be a form of theism, and Christian theism is the focus of our concern in this discussion.

God. In essence, the problem of evil states that the existence of evil is incompatible with the existence of a perfectly good and all-powerful God.

Preliminary Comments

Before looking at the contours of the argument, a few preliminary comments will be helpful. First, the problem of evil is an *atheological argument*. That is, it is an argument against the existence of God rather than an argument for God's existence. Second, the responses made by believers to refute the argument from evil are often called *theodicies*. The term *theodicy* comes from two Greek words: *theos*, meaning "God," and *dika*, meaning "justice." Thus, theodicy basically means justifying God—justifying God in the face of evil. Gottfried Wilhelm Leibniz (1646–1716) coined the term.[2]

A third comment concerns the notion of evil. Philosophy often recognizes two types of evil: natural evil and moral evil. *Natural evil* is defined in various ways. One way to define it is to equate it with the suffering that befalls humans as a result of natural causes. Examples of such causes might be diseases, tornados, or forest fires. Natural evil also includes animal suffering. Thus, natural evil is the suffering that befalls humans and other animals as a result of natural causes. *Moral evil*, on the other hand, is evil that result from free choices of humans or other morally conscious beings (such as demons). Both forms of evil potentially generate problems for Christian theism.

A fourth comment concerns a *paradox* that persists for believers and nonbelievers concerning the problem of evil. The believer's faith in God causes her to take evil seriously—seriously enough to question God's existence. Further, for the believer evil requires a response on behalf of God, a theodicy. On the other hand, since the unbeliever does not believe in God, evil requires no theodicy. Nevertheless, the unbeliever finds it difficult to protest the existence of evil, especially natural evil, but to some degree moral evil also. Who does one blame for the existence of evil? Indeed, what is evil outside the context of some ultimate principle, like God?

A fifth comment concerns two basic ways the argument from evil may be interpreted. On the one hand, the problem of evil can be seen as primarily a *logical problem*. In this interpretation, the existence of evil is argued to be logically inconsistent with the existence of an all-powerful, perfectly good God. Thus, the existence of evil makes the existence of God logically impossible. On the other hand, the problem of evil can be interpreted primarily as an *evidential problem*. While the existence of God may be logically possible in the face of evil, God's existence does not seem likely. In other words, the existence of evil makes it likely that God does not exist.

A sixth point is that a distinction often is made between theistic *defenses* and *theodicies*. Alvin Plantinga has made fashionable the attempt simply to *defend* theism against the logical problem of evil, contending that against such arguments the theist need not

---

2. Leibniz, *Theodicy* (trans. Huggard).

try to give a likely explanation for God's allowing evil, but only needs to show how the existence of evil and a perfectly good and omnipotent God are logically possible. In light of Plantinga's defense of theism against the logical argument from the problem of evil, the term *theodicy* now often denotes a fuller, more plausible explanation of why in fact God has allowed the existence of evil. (Part of Plantinga's point is that the theist is under no obligation to prove that there is a God, but the theist does have some obligation to show that belief in God is coherent with other known facts.)

A seventh comment is this: Responses to the problem of evil may come from an abstract, *generic theism* or from a theism that is manifested in some *specific religion* (for example, Christianity or Judaism). These religious responses attempt to address the problem of evil as it interfaces with the broader doctrinal claims of a specific religion, not just with a theistic view of God.[3] With these qualifications in mind, we turn first to consider the logical problem of evil

The Logical Problem of Evil

The logical problem of evil can be stated in a variety of ways. Here is one such statement:

1. An all-powerful (omnipotent) God can get rid of all evil in the world.

2. A perfectly good God would want to get rid of all evil in the world.

3. God does what God can do and wants to do.

4. At least some evil exists in the world.

5. Therefore, either (a) God is unable to get rid of all evil in the world and is therefore not all-powerful, or (b) God does not want to get rid of all evil in the world and therefore is not completely good, or (c) there is no evil in the world, or (d) an all-powerful, perfectly good God does not exist.

Some versions of the argument add propositions such as "An omniscient God would know how to get rid of any evil in the world."[4] This argument challenges the coherence of claiming that God is omnipotent and perfectly good, and that evil exists. In other words, it claims that such a God's existence is impossible in the face of evil.

Various Replies to the Logical Problem of Evil

Various theistic replies have been offered to this logical problem of evil, with some being theologically more acceptable from the perspective of Christian orthodoxy than others.

3. For conversations about these diverse aspects of the problem of evil see Peterson, et al., *Reason and Religious Belief*, 178–206. Also see Hick, *Philosophy of Religion*, 39–55.

4. Peterson, *Evil and the Christian God*, 47–53.

1. Denial of the Existence of Evil

Some writers simply deny that evil exists in the world. This denies premise 4 above. One of the most well-known examples of such a position is Mary Baker Eddy's Christian Science.[5] Eddy insisted that matter and evil are each unreal. Evil is an illusion of our five senses. Eddy's position is typically rejected by mainstream Christian thought because the biblical tradition clearly affirms that evil, including human sin, occurs.

2. Acceptance of Evil as a Necessary Aspect of Finite or Created Being

Another reply to the logical problem of evil is to insist that evil is a necessary aspect of finite, created beings. Omnipotence is typically understood to mean that God can do anything that is logically possible (and consistent with God's essential nature). But in light of this, some writers have suggested that it is logically impossible to create sub-God, finite beings without also creating or bringing about evil. This perspective is at least hinted at (if not directly endorsed) by Augustine of Hippo (354–430) and Thomas Aquinas (1225–1274) when they claim that evil is the lack of being. Entailed in this claim *may be* the implication that every finite being is evil (in some sense). That is, evil is an ontological aspect or element of all finite beings.[6]

Such a view suffers from various problems. First, it makes one wonder whether God is blameworthy for creating any subdivine finite things, since to do so produces evil as well. A possible reply to this objection might be to say that God's decision to create such finite beings might still be worth the evils that are produced because it also is the only way for God to create the good that also is found in that finite reality. A second counter to this objection is this: If evil is a necessary aspect of finite being, then it seems to make no sense to condemn finite beings for doing or being evil. But Christianity—at least in its more expanded traditional versions—typically does condemn finite beings for their evil. A possible explanation for this condemnation might be to propose that God only condemns finite beings for failing to live up to their finite potential, not for being finite per se. But such a counterreply seems to run aground on the claim that it is allegedly logically impossible for God to create finite creatures without evil. Presumably, it would be logically possible to create finite creatures that do not fail to live up to their full potential. That is, while finite creatures cannot not be finite, they logically can live up to or fulfill the fullness of their finite potential. And presumably an omnipotent being could ensure that created beings do this.

5. Eddy, *Science and Health with Key to the Scriptures.*

6. See Matson, *The Existence of God*, 142–43. For a rebuttal of the notion that evil is a necessary aspect of finite reality in the thinking of Augustine and Aquinas, see Kane, "Evil and Privation."

3. Denial of God's Omnipotence

A third attempt to counter the logical problem of evil is to deny God's omnipotence. This concedes the force of the atheistic argument from evil, concluding that there is a God but not an omnipotent one. Certain forms of dualism implicitly deny God's omnipotence, for they teach that there are two ultimate realities, each equally eternal, each equally supreme. According to these forms of dualism, God is engaged in an eternal battle with the other fundamental reality. Manichaeism affirmed that God (the principle of good) and matter (the principle of evil) are the two basic realities, each ensnared in an eternal struggle with the other.[7]

Process theology also denies God's omnipotence, affirming the coeternal existence of primordial processes. According to process theology, "God is subject to the limitations imposed by the basic laws of the universe, for God has not created the universe *ex nihilo*, thereby establishing its structure, but rather the universe is an uncreated process which includes the deity."[8] All reality is thus free, and thus has some power. Reality is a perpetually changing emergence that results from the creative exercise of "choice" throughout the whole of reality. In turn, according to process theology, God's power is essentially persuasive. God lures the uncreated universe towards goals that God sees as best. But the universe is ever able to deny God's persuasion, choosing lesser goals. Thus, evil is divinely unavoidable, because nondivine reality always has the power to act contrary to God's good intentions. Process theologians admit that some theodicy is still needed in their system. For one still needs to justify God's decision to lure the primal chaos toward greater complexities—since such luring also brings about evil. Allegedly, however, the ultimate justification is that the good that derives from the process outweighs (makes permissible) the evil that also emerges.[9]

A chief problem with these denials of divine omnipotence is that they cannot guarantee that good will win over evil. The universe or reality may be forever a balance and battle between good and evil, or evil may eventually win. Millard Erickson argues that such positions solve the problem of theodicy, explaining why God allows evil; but they do not give hope that evil will be conquered. Evil remains an eternal, unconquerable threat.[10] Another problem, which seems to apply especially to process theology's theodicy, is that it seems to be inappropriately elitist. Typically, process theology denies postdeath existence for individuals, affirming instead the goodness of the overall cosmic process, including the goodness that emerges in some especially outstanding individuals. But this suggests that the good of the few justifies the suffering of many.[11]

7. Erickson, *Christian Theology* (1983 [5th printing, 1988]), 414.

8. Hick, *Philosophy of Religion*, 49.

9. Hick, *Philosophy of Religion*, 50–51.

10. Erickson, *Christian Theology* (1983 [5th printing, 1988]), 416.

11. Hick, *Philosophy of Religion*, 52–55.

4. Denial of the Goodness of God

A fourth counter to the problem of evil is this. Some authors deny the goodness of God, thus rejecting the traditional claim that God is perfectly good. Two examples of such an approach are the following.

a. God is partly evil.

Some philosophical theologians argue that God is partly evil. John K. Roth affirms what he calls a "theodicy of protest."[12] He believes that God is all-powerful, powerful enough to stop evil, but God simply does not do so. According to Roth, this implies that God is evil. Roth insists that human history is an indictment against God.[13] Roth writes:

> No body is OK. Otherwise the slaughter-bench would not be drenched. And when one says "nobody," God is included as well as humanity . . . It is irresponsible to assign responsibility inequitably. God must bear his share, and it is not small unless he could never be described as one for whom all things are possible . . . The irretrievable waste of the past robs God of a perfect alibi.[14]

Roth insists that in light of God's evil, humans must call the deity to repentance, hoping that God will change. We base this hope on the fact that we see good and not just evil in God. For many Christians, the problem with Roth's view is clear: If God is evil, how can anyone hope for good to win over evil? How can humans trust God in the future if God has not been trustworthy? And even if God should repent of God's evil now, what is to keep the deity from returning to evil in the future?

b. God is not subject to human standards of good

In an attempt to justify God's tolerance of evil, some theologians redefine the terms *good* and *goodness* as they apply to God. Millard Erickson accuses staunch theological determinist Gordon Clark of doing this. Clark asserts that God causes all events, even sin. But Clark insists that the deity is vindicated for causing sin because God is above the divine law. God sets the standard of right and wrong. And so by definition God cannot do wrong. Thus, although God causes sin and evil, God cannot be judged as doing wrong.[15] Erickson rejects Clark's approach on two grounds. First, Erickson insists that in "Clark's scheme, the statements 'God does good' and 'man does good' are

---

12. Roth, "A Theodicy of Protest," 22.

13. Roth, "A Theodicy of Protest," 11.

14. Roth, "A Theodicy of Protest," 11–15.

15. Erickson, *Christian Theology* (1983 [5th printing, 1988]), 417–19. See also Clark, *Religion, Reason, and Revelation.*

so dissimilar that we virtually cannot know what it means to say, 'God is good.'"[16] This makes the notions of the good and of goodness—especially God's goodness—ambiguous. Further, it suggests that God's decision to call something good is wholly arbitrary, rather than based on God's essentially good nature. In the end, for Erickson (and others) if one were to grant Clark's reasoning, humans, including Christians, would not know what goodness is or what we mean when we say, "God is good."

5. Assertion That God May Tolerate Evil for the Sake of Freedom and Its Higher Goods

One of the classic Christian theistic replies to the logical problem of evil is to assert that although God is all-powerful and perfectly good, there may be good reasons why God would not want to get rid of all the evil in the world. This perspective denies premise 2 above, not by denying that God is perfectly good, but by asserting that God may tolerate evil for some higher purpose.

Specifically, many Christian theists have proposed that perhaps God desires to create morally free creatures—creatures with the capacity to love. God desires this because the kind and degree of good produced (or potentially produced) by free beings is greater (more significant) than the kind and degree of good produced by determined creatures. In turn, in order to create morally free beings, God could not directly cause them to do good. Rather, God had to make it possible for them to do either good or evil. In short, a perfectly good God may permit or tolerate evil because such evil (or at least its possibility) is necessary in order for God to achieve (or possibly achieve) an even higher good. This response to the problem of evil often is called *the free-will defense* or *free-will theodicy*. C. S. Lewis explains this response as follows:

> God created things which had free will. That means creatures which can go either wrong or right . . . If a thing is free to be good, it is also free to be bad. And free will is what has made evil possible. Why, then, did God give them free will? Because free will, though it makes evil possible, is also the only thing that makes possible any love or goodness or joy worth having. A world of automata—of creatures that worked like machines—would hardly be worth creating. The happiness which God designs for His high creatures is the happiness of being freely, voluntarily united to Him and to each other in ecstasy of love . . . And for that they must be free.[17]

Philosopher Alvin Plantinga makes a similar (and more thorough) argument. He notes that when an agent is free with regard to some act, that individual is able to perform the action or refrain from performing it, and no prior conditions determine which choice the agent makes. In light of this, perhaps God knows that "a world

16. Erickson, *Christian Theology* (1983 [5th printing, 1988]), 419.
17. Lewis, *Mere Christianity*, 52.

containing creatures who are sometimes significantly free (and freely perform more good than evil actions) is more valuable, all else being equal, than a world containing no free creatures at all."[18] And if this is the case, it is reasonable to suppose that a perfectly good God would want to actualize a world with significantly free moral beings, even though these beings enact some evil actions. But if God wills a world of morally free creatures, then the deity (even though omnipotent) cannot actualize just any possible world. For

> if I am free with respect to an action A, then God does not bring it about or cause it to be the case either that I take or that I refrain from this action . . . For if he brings it about or causes it to be the case that I take A, then I am not free to refrain from A, in which case I am not free with respect to A.[19]

Accordingly, if the deity desires to create free moral beings, there are possible worlds that God cannot *directly* actualize. In turn, this makes it "possible that God could not have created a universe containing moral good (or as much moral good as this one contains) without creating one containing moral evil."[20]

Plantinga insists that the atheistic argument (against the compatibility of the existence of God and evil) fails because it assumes that an omnipotent God can directly generate just any possible world. But this is false, at least in those cases where the deity wishes to actualize morally free beings. Plantinga refers to this false assumption as Leibniz's Lapse.[21] Many other theists have followed this basic line of reasoning, including Stephen Davis,[22] Millard Erickson,[23] and Michael Peterson.[24] This line of reasoning has its roots in Augustine.

Challenging and Defending the Free-Will Defense (Free-Will Theodicy)

At least three objections arise against the free-will defense or free-will theodicy. In the face of these objections, various counterreplies are employed to defend the appeal to free will.

18. Plantinga, *The Nature of Necessity*, 166.

19. Plantinga, *The Nature of Necessity*, 171–72.

20. Plantinga, *The Nature of Necessity*, 167

21. Plantinga, *The Nature of Necessity*, 184. Gottfried Leibniz seems to have assumed this when he argued that our world must be the best possible world.

22. Davis, "Free Will and Evil."

23. Erickson, *Christian Theology* (1983 [5th printing, 1988]), 423–25

24. Peterson, *Evil and the Christian God*.

Compatibilist Freedom

First, contemporary atheistic philosopher J. L. Mackie asks why God did not create beings that always (freely) choose good. Defining *freedom* as the ability to do what you desire, Mackie wonders why God did not make creatures that always desired to do good.[25] Champions of the free-will defense offer two replies: Some argue that even though God could have made humans that way, they really would not have been free.[26] Others contend that if God had made humans that way, they would have been free, but it would not have been the best kind of freedom.[27] In both cases, proponents of the free-will defense insist that the kind of freedom God has given is not only the ability to do what you desire, but also the ability to choose between conflicting desires—or perhaps even the ability to change what you desire over time. An interesting side note is worth making here: Richard Swinburne has argued that the most significant moral choices may well be those when persons have strong desires not to do what is right but choose to do what is right anyway. Thus, temptation may play a significant role in generating the most significant moral choices.[28]

Possible Worlds with Only Freely Chosen Good

A second objection to the free-will defense or free-will theodicy is this: Some atheistic or nontheistic writers have noted that there seem to be possible worlds where *every free creature freely chooses to do good*. (That is, it seems logically possible that there be a universe where all free creatures always freely choose to do good.) But if God is omnipotent and thus can do all that is logically possible, then God should be able to create just such a world. So why does God not create one of these possible worlds?

Plantinga wrestles with this objection. The atheist may contend that even if (because of freedom) God cannot *directly* actualize just any possible world, it does not follow that it was not within God's power to *indirectly* actualize a world in which creatures freely choose only good. First, there are possible worlds in which every significantly free moral agent freely chooses to do only good. More importantly, there may be some worlds where if God were to directly actualize elements of them, every moral being in those worlds would freely choose good and never choose evil. In this argumentation, Plantinga assumes that God has middle knowledge: knowledge of counterfactuals of freedom—that is, knowledge of what any possible moral creature freely *would do* in any given circumstance. Armed with such information, it seems that an omnipotent deity could directly actualize worlds wherein only those antecedent circumstances obtain that God knows creatures of those worlds freely would react

25. Mackie, *The Miracle of Theism*, 162–72.

26. Lewis, *Mere Christianity*, 52; Davies, "Free Will and Evil," 73–74.

27. Hick, "An Irenaean Theodicy," 43–44.

28. Swinburne, *Providence and the Problem of Evil*, 134–37.

to by performing good and not evil. But if this is the case, the atheist may ask why God did not actualize such a world.

At least two replies have been offered to this objection. First, Plantinga promotes the notion of transworld depravity. Perhaps in fact there are no feasible worlds where if God were to directly actualize elements of them, every moral being in those worlds would freely choose good. Perhaps every significantly free moral being that God could create would freely perform at least one evil act in every world in which that being exists. That is, perhaps every possible significantly free moral being suffers from transworld depravity. If this is so, then God cannot create a world with significantly free moral beings where only good and no evil occurs.[29]

The plausibility of Plantinga's transworld depravity defense has been questioned by a number of thinkers. For many it seems unlikely that in every possible world with morally free creatures, all of those free creatures would *in fact* perform at least some evil. Surely there are some possible worlds where all the free creatures of those worlds *in fact* would freely only perform good acts. Even if such worlds contain, say, only one creature that lives only for a few moments, it seems possible that this being might do only good and no evil. Surely there are many such worlds. A couple counterreplies might be made in Plantinga's defense. One, Plantinga himself contends that the appeal to transworld depravity need not be plausible; it only needs to be *possible* in order to defeat the atheist's claim that the coexistence of God and evil are *logically impossible*. Transworld depravity at least appears to be possible.[30] A further counterreply in defense of Plantinga's appeal to transworld depravity is this: Even if there were feasible worlds where all free creatures in those worlds in fact only perform good, it could be that in every feasible world *worth creating*, every free creature would choose at least one evil act. By "worth creating," one means a world with sufficiently significant good in it and with free creatures.

A second reply to those who claim that there are possible worlds where every free creature freely chooses good is the following. Richard Swinburne has suggested that God cannot know ahead of time which worlds in fact are worlds where every free creature freely will choose good. In other words, Swinburne does not hold Plantinga's assumption that God has middle knowledge. For Swinburne, God does not know the truth value of counterfactuals of freedom. (Indeed, Swinburne contends that to know such information would undermine the freedom of the creatures who would be making the choices. It is impossible for anyone, including God, to know ahead of time what a free creature would freely do in a given circumstance.)[31]

---

29. Plantinga, *God, Freedom, and Evil*, 45–55.

30. Plantinga, *God, Freedom, and Evil*, 54–55.

31. Swinburne, *Providence and the Problem of Evil*, 127–34, esp. 133.

The Problem of Natural Evil

A third objection to the free-will defense or free-will theodicy is that although the appeal to freedom may explain why God might allow moral evil in our world (evil done by free moral creatures), it does not clearly explain why God allows *natural evil* in our world. That is, why does God allow cancer, tornadoes, earthquakes, and so forth?

Plantinga has offered an intriguing answer to such an objection. Pointing out that all that the defender of theism must do to overcome the logical problem of evil is to show that God's existence is logically possible in the face of evil, Plantinga argues that a possible explanation for the existence of natural evil is Satan, evil demons, or both. In other words, natural evil ultimately can be explained as moral evil—evil committed by spiritual beings. Since such an explanation is logically possible, it remains *possible* that God's existence is *logically* compatible with the existence of natural evil.[32]

While Plantinga's argument is perhaps technically correct, many find it too fanciful to take seriously. They argue that while such an explanation is possible, it hardly seems plausible. (This may be particularly problematic for theists who hope that their affirmation of God is grounded in plausible and not merely possible explanations.) In light of this, many champions of the free-will defense offer another explanation for the existence of natural evil. They suggest that our world is roughly the kind of world that God had to create for moral creatures to exist. John Hick writes:

> A morally wrong act is, basically, one which harms some part of the human community; whilst a morally right action is, on the contrary, one which prevents or neutralizes harm or which preserves or increases human well being. Now we can imagine a paradise in which no one can ever come to harm. It could be a world which, instead of having its own fixed structure, would be plastic to human wishes. Or it could be a world with a fixed structure, and hence the possibility of damage and pain. Thus, for example, in such a miraculously pain-free world one who falls accidentally off a high building would presumably float unharmed to the ground; bullets would become insubstantial when fired at a human body . . . and so on . . . But such an assumption overlooks the fact that the world in which there can be no pain or suffering would also be one in which there can be no moral choices and hence no possibility of moral growth and development. For in a situation in which no one can ever suffer injury or be liable to pain or suffering there would be no distinction between right and wrong action.[33]

Thus, following Hick, one may argue that only in a world with natural laws, where natural evil is possible, is it possible to make moral choices. Perhaps not

32. Plantinga, *God, Freedom, and Evil*, 58.
33. Hick, "An Irenaean Theodicy," 47.

surprisingly, not all writers are persuaded by such reasoning. But many theists affirm similar scenarios.[34]

Lingering Problems with the Appeal to Free Will:

Various problems remain for the free-will defense or free-will theodicy. Two of these problems concern freedom and the notion of heaven. Theists often assume that in heaven[35] people will no longer desire to sin and thus will not sin. God will take persons away from the very presence of sin. But based on the assumption of the free-will defense (the assumption that genuine moral freedom requires that persons be able to change what they desire or to choose between good and evil desires), does this mean that in heaven people will not be genuinely morally free? Second, theists often presume that in heaven there will be no earthquakes, tornadoes, pain, or the like. But if the possibility of these events in this world is what makes moral freedom possible, then in heaven (where such events do not occur) will people no longer be morally free?

A third dilemma is this: Many philosophers question the coherence of the concept of libertarian freedom—the idea that one can change what one desires or can choose between contrary desires. To change what you desire seems to require that you want to change what you want. Or to choose between contrary desires seems to imply that you desire one of those desires more than the other. But all of this seems to imply an infinite regression of explanations with no ultimate explanation. A fourth difficulty rises: Some have argued that even if natural evil can be explained by the need for a stable natural environment for moral agents to function, it remains true also that "God could greatly reduce and eliminate natural evils, either by miraculously intervening in the present natural system or by creating an entirely different natural system."[36] And here is a fifth problem: If, as the free-will defense contends, good that is freely chosen is better than good that necessarily flows from a being, creaturely good is better than divine good (assuming that God necessarily does good and cannot do evil). Not surprisingly, all of these objections are subject to dispute among defenders of Christian theism. Unfortunately, such discussions are beyond the scope of our study here. It is clear, then, that the logical problem of evil remains an ongoing subject of conversation and interest among Christian writers.

---

34. See Swinburne, *Providence and the Problem of Evil*, 160–71. For an atheistic reply to defenses like Hick's and Swinburne's, see Draper, "Pain and Pleasure."

35. By "heaven" I mean the final state of the righteous or the saved. The precise nature of that existence is variously described. See Chapter 7, above.

36. Peterson et al., *Reason and Religious Belief*, 160. Michael Peterson credits H. J. McCloskey with this view. See McCloskey, "God and Evil."

The Evidential Problem of Evil

The existence of evil presents not only a logical problem for believing in the existence of God, but also an evidential problem. Even if it is logically possible that God and evil coexist, the existence of evil may make it unlikely or implausible that God exists. In other words, evil may serve as evidence, perhaps strong evidence, against belief in a perfectly good, omnipotent God. In such an argument, theism is thought of as a kind of explanatory theory, designed to interpret overall human experience. Different experiences offer evidence for or against this theory. The existence of evil serves as evidence against it.

The evidential problem of evil can be interpreted in different ways. (1) One could argue that the existence of *any evil* makes God's existence unlikely or implausible. In light of the difficulties with the logical problem of evil, however, such an approach does not appear to be very promising for the atheist. A more hopeful approach might be one of the following: (2) One could argue that the sheer *amount of evil* in our world makes God's existence unlikely or implausible. Or (3) one could insist that the existence of *gratuitous or pointless evil* makes God's existence unlikely or implausible. Or (4) perhaps the strongest form of the argument combines (2) and (3), arguing that the *amount of gratuitous or pointless evil* makes God's existence unlikely or implausible.

The Argument from Gratuitous Evil

The argument from gratuitous evil runs something like this:

1. Probably if an omnipotent, perfectly good God exists, that deity would prevent the occurrence of any evil that does not lead to some greater good. (In other words, if an omnipotent, perfectly good God exists, that deity would prevent gratuitous evil.)

2. Probably evil exists that does not lead to some greater good. (In other words, gratuitous evil exists.)

3. Therefore probably an omnipotent, perfectly good God does not exist.

A few comments about the evidential argument may be helpful. First, notice that this argument is a typical example of a form of inductive argumentation known as *disconfirmation theory*. Such reasoning follows the pattern of deductive logic called *modus tollens*. That pattern is this:

If p, then q.

Not q

Therefore, not p.

However, in disconfirmation theory, the argument is not deductive but inductive. It is inductive because it recognizes that there may be other evidence for the truth of the antecedent[37] of premise 1 above,[38] and it also recognizes that that first premise as a whole may be false. In other words, "either independent evidential support or theoretical support may override the seemingly disconfirming case."[39]

A second point to ponder is this: Premise 2[40] assumes and asserts that gratuitous or pointless evil exists. This belief is grounded in a common interpretation of events around us. There certainly seem to be events that do not lead to higher goods. William Rowe expresses this well:

> It seems quite unlikely that all the instances of intense human and animal suffering occurring daily in our world lead to greater goods, and even more unlikely that if they all do, an omnipotent, omniscient being (God) could not have achieved at least some of those goods without permitting the instances of suffering that lead to them. In light of our experience and knowledge of the variety and scale of human and animal suffering in our world, the idea that none of these instances of suffering could have been prevented by an omnipotent being without the loss of a greater good seems an extraordinary, absurd idea, quite beyond our belief.[41]

Rowe makes two points: First, it does not seem likely that every instance of evil in the world directly leads to some higher good. And second, even if each instance of evil leads to a higher good, it seems that God could have found some better way of getting the good. For many, Rowe's points are persuasive. At very least, one might admit that there seems to be pointless evil in the world, whether there actually is or not.

A third comment about this argument is worth making: Premise 1 seems to be based on what Michael Peterson has called the principle of meticulous providence—the notion that God specifically chooses every event that occurs in history, making sure that each event fits into an overall divine plan, and making sure that each contributes to some greater good.[42]

Various Responses to Evidential Problem

A number of responses to the evidential problem of evil have been proposed. These include the following.

---

37. The *antecedent* is the first statement in a conditional claim. Thus, in the claim "If *p*, then *q*," *p* is the antecedent. (And *q* is called the *consequent*.)

38. Premise 1 is, Probably if an omnipotent, perfectly good God exists, that deity would prevent the occurrence of any evil that does not lead to some greater good.

39. Peterson, *Evil and the Christian God*, 65.

40. Premise 2 is, Probably evil exists that does not lead to some greater good.

41. Rowe, *Philosophy of Religion*, 89.

42. Peterson, *Evil and the Christian God*, 76.

1. Denial of the existence of gratuitous evil

Some theists argue that there are no evil events that do not lead to higher goods. In other words, there is no gratuitous or pointless evil. This denies premise 2 (of the evidential argument from gratuitous evil). G. W. Leibniz insisted that because God is a perfect being, if the deity creates a world, it will be the best possible world.[43] A perfect being would not create anything less than the best possible world. At least two criticisms may be raised against this view. First, it seems to be countermanded by the prima facie (that is, initial-examination) experiential evidence that in fact there are evil events that lead to no obvious higher good. Second, it smacks of circular reasoning. At issue in the argument is whether a perfect God exists. And so, it hardly seems appropriate to insist that there is no gratuitous evil because a perfect God would not allow it. One might wish to affirm such a belief based on faith, but it is not clearly a sound *assumption* to make while also making a reasoned case *for* God's existence.

2. Appeal to ignorance concerning gratuitous evil

Closely tied to arguments that flatly deny that gratuitous evil exists are theistic arguments that claim that no one knows that gratuitous evil happens. It could be that in spite of the prima facie evidence, all evil events do in fact lead to greater goods. Hence, the truth of premise 2 is called into question, not by denying that it is true, but by insisting that one cannot know that it is true. In light of this, the theist might claim that the burden of proof is upon the atheist to show that gratuitous evil does exist. Stephen Davis seems to take this approach.[44]

One problem with such a defense is that it seems to be a stubborn, unassailable position. The atheist might admit that there is no way *conclusively to prove* that there are gratuitous evil events; nevertheless, considerable evidence can be and has been offered to support this conclusion, and this evidence is sufficient for the unbiased, reasonable mind to conclude that gratuitous evil occurs. For the atheist, then, theists who appeal to ignorance regarding gratuitous evil stubbornly endorse a position that they will not allow to be falsified by reasonable evidence. The atheist protests, "How much evidence do you need? If the horrendous evils that happens in human and natural history are not enough, it seems no evidence will suffice. And if this is the theist's position, it essentially is saying that belief in God is not rational but simply a matter of tenacious faith."

A second problem with the appeal to ignorance is that simply the appearance that gratuitous evil occurs may be sufficient to ground a plausible argument against belief in God. Since neither the atheist nor the theist can know for certain that there

43. Leibniz, *Theodicy* (ed. Farrer).

44. Davis, "Free Will and Evil," 76. Also see Wykstra, "The Humean Obstacle to Evidential Arguments."

are gratuitous evil events, the chief rational grounds for believing that there are such events is the way events appear to the common observer. And so, the argument from gratuitous evil still has warrant.

3. Affirmation that God permits gratuitous evil for the sake of human freedom

Some theists deny premise 1 above (the evidential argument from gratuitous evil), insisting that God may have good reasons for allowing gratuitous evil. Specifically, perhaps God permits gratuitous evil for the sake of moral freedom. Michael Peterson affirms this position. He builds from insights developed by Alvin Plantinga. Peterson writes:

> Plantinga builds his argument upon the obvious principle that logically impossible states of affairs cannot be actual. From this he shows that it is not within God's power to make persons freely obey His will, for the very notion is self-contradictory. No doubt God can make people obey His will, but then they would not be doing so freely. Conversely, people can freely obey God's will, but then they are not being forced to do so by God. Thus, as long as God is to preserve the high value of free will, there are going to be some choices which are up to us, not God. There is no way, then that God can ensure that significantly free persons always choose and do what is right.
>
> Plantinga's discussion of free will is sound as far as it goes. But it can be expanded further to cover the whole issue of whether God can allow gratuitous evil. Very simply, if the conception of human free will is taken to involve the possibility of bringing about really gratuitous evil (specifically, moral evil), then God cannot completely prevent or eliminate gratuitous evil without severely diminishing free will. That would be logically impossible. At stake here is not merely the ability of humans to choose among options, but the ability to choose among significant kinds of options: between goods and evils, even the highest goods and most terrible evils. Thus, free will is most significant—and most fitting for the special sort of creature man is—if it includes the potential for utterly damnable choices and actions.[45]

In other words, claims Peterson: "it is logically impossible for God both to preclude the possibility of gratuitous moral evil and to preserve *significant* freedom."[46] We might express Peterson's view as follows:

> God's permitting of [gratuitous] evil results from a general principle that it is better for humans freely to choose good than to be forced to perform good. Since the actualization of this principle in any given instance requires that the human person also be able to do evil, then as a general policy God also leaves

---

45. Peterson, *Evil and the Christian God*, 104.
46. Peterson, *Evil and the Christian God*, 105 (italics added).

open the possibility of humans doing evil. Often the evil that God allows persons to perform serves no further providential purpose than to make possible freely chosen good acts. Such evil acts need not and often do not lead to some further specific good. In short, there often may be gratuitous evil—evil human actions that lead to no specific higher good. Such events are permitted only because the potential for their occurrence makes it possible for humans freely to choose good. And this possibility God deems valuable.[47]

Up to this point, only an explanation of moral evil has been offered. Peterson goes on to evoke the notion of a stable natural order to explain the existence of natural evil, including gratuitous natural evil. He writes:

> God is interested in soul-making. There are some highly valuable traits which God wants each soul to possess. For example, each human being should be capable of acting virtuously toward others and of exercising faith and love toward God. Now it is plausible that only certain kinds of environments (and not others) are conducive to producing such beings.[48]

In short, then, it may be that only in a world something like our own, where natural laws apply, could moral beings make significant moral choices. Perhaps the very structures of nature that allow a person to make moral choices are also the structures that allow natural evil.

One benefit of Peterson's response to the evidential problem of evil—the response that God permits gratuitous evil for the sake of human freedom—is that it allows one to admit that gratuitous evil exists and thus to avoid some of the difficulties found in those responses that deny that gratuitous evil occurs. A key criticism of Peterson's response to the evidential problem of evil, however, is this: One might question whether the (potential or actual) good that is achieved by free moral creatures is valuable enough to justify God's allowing the immense amount of gratuitous evil that occurs in the created order. Whereas one might admit that allowing the *possibility* of some gratuitous evil or the *actual* occurrence of some gratuitous evil may be necessary for God to allow genuine moral actions, it is not at all clear that *the actual amount* of and *intensity of* such evil is needed.

William Rowe expresses this concern in terms of particular instances of gratuitous evil. He bids us to imagine the lingering death of a fawn that has been burned in a forest fire (natural evil) or the tortured death of an innocent child by a child molester (moral evil).[49] Even if one grants that in general God must create a world with natural laws that will make such events possible, it is not at all clear that in these particular instances God must allow such events to happen. Rowe writes, in response to Hick's theodicy:

47. Robinson, *The Storms of Providence*, 250–51.
48. Peterson, *Evil and the Christian God*, 118.
49. Rowe, *Philosophy of Religion*, 99–100, 105

It is simply unreasonable to believe that if the adult acted freely in brutally beating and killing that innocent child, his moral and spiritual development would have been permanently frustrated had he been prevented from doing what he did. And it is also unreasonable to believe that permitting such an act is morally justified even if preventing it would somehow diminish the perpetrator's moral and spiritual odyssey. And in the case of the fawn, it is simply unreasonable to believe that preventing its being severely burned, or mercifully ending its life so that it does not suffer intensely for several days, would so shake our confidence in the orderliness of nature that we would forsake our moral and spiritual development . . . The best that Hick [and we might add Peterson] can do is to argue that a world *utterly devoid* of natural and moral evil would preclude the realization of the goods he postulates as justifying an omnipotent, omniscient being in permitting evil . . . The problem Hick's theodicy leaves us is that it is altogether reasonable to believe that some of the evils that occur *could have been prevented* without either diminishing our moral and spiritual development or undermining our confidence that the world operates according to natural laws.[50]

In short, it seems possible that many of the actual events of gratuitous evil could be avoided without severely undermining human moral freedom.

In the face of such a criticism, Peterson offers two replies: First, he argues that such a rebuttal may well fail to grasp the contribution that the possibility of gratuitous evil makes to the possibility of extraordinary good acts. It may be that "to remove or restrict the possibility of great evil is to remove or restrict proportionately the possibility of great good."[51] Second, Peterson insists that it is not at all clear how much gratuitous evil is permissible. Such a judgment may well be more a personal assessment than a position that can be demonstrated one way or another.[52]

Closing Remarks on the Problem of Evil

In this exposition we have only scratched the surface of the debates over the problem of evil, and we in no way have resolved the puzzles to the satisfaction of all. The existence of evil remains an ongoing challenge to the Christian faith, although arguably it is not an insurmountable challenge. Ironically, part of the motive of the Christian faith, and its Judaic predecessor, is the desire to explain the existence of evil and overcome it. With further irony (as mentioned above), one of the pesky problems faced by atheistic philosophy is the inability adequately to explain what evil is and especially why it ought not be. Nevertheless, the existence of evil remains one of the reasons Christians must walk by faith and not by sight.

50. Rowe, *Philosophy of Religion*, 105–6 (italics and brackets added).

51. Peterson, *Evil and the Christian God*, 107.

52. Peterson, *Evil and the Christian God*, 107.

Christianity and Other Religions

In addition to the problem of evil, another issue faced by the Christian faith concerns how Christianity is to interrelate with other religions. A quick survey of human cultures reveals that humans are religious beings. Shrines, temples, and churches pepper the global landscape, while religious rituals permeate our practices and religious beliefs interpenetrate our ideas and ideals. Generally, humans are religious.

Diversity among Religious Teachings

A cursory examination of humanity's religions demonstrates a wide variety of contrary beliefs and practices. While religions often ask the same questions, the content of their answers differs greatly. Among the central questions asked by religions are the following:

1. What is the nature of ultimate reality?
2. What is the nature, origin, destiny, and purpose of humans?
3. What is the nature, origin, destiny, and purpose of the world and the universe?
4. What essential problem do humans face?
5. How is this problem overcome?

Many and various answers are given to these questions. For example, concerning ultimate reality: in Hinduism answers vary from belief in a singular, personal, all-powerful God to belief in many gods to belief in a nonpersonal, monistic cosmic principle. In Taoism, ultimate reality is conceived as an all-pervasive, nonpersonal universal order. In Mahayana Buddhism, conceptualizations of ultimate reality range from belief in personal gods to belief in no gods to belief in an all-encompassing cosmic principle. In Theravada Buddhism emphasis falls on Nirvana—a kind of void (or cessation) that can be described neither as being nor nonbeing. In Judaism, Christianity, and Islam ultimate reality is conceived of as a singular, all-powerful, personal God distinct from all other realities and upon whom all else depends.

Concerning human nature and our dilemma, a variety of perspectives are offered: In Judaism, Christianity, and Islam humans are believed to have originated in the free creative act of a theistic God. Humans are ontologically distinct from God, though utterly dependent upon God for existence. In Judaism and Christianity, humans face the dilemma of their own moral rebellion against God; a personal, covenantal relationship with God has been broken. In Islam, emphasis falls on human failure to obey the static, eternal commands of God.

The themes of Eastern religions tend to differ considerably from the themes of their Western counterparts. In some forms of Hinduism, all reality is thought of as one with ultimate reality. Individual human souls are in fact differing aspects of the One Great Soul, called the Brahman-atman. Thus, humans and the ultimate are intrinsically the same. Theravada Buddhism denies the substantial existence of individual souls, claiming that a soul is merely a brief combination of five essential forces of nature. At death, portions of these forces move on to form the seed of a new "soul," which in turn exists only briefly as a unity of diverse forces. At Nirvana, these forces dissipate into the bliss of utter emptiness.

Both Hinduism and Buddhism affirm reincarnation and see the continuing cycle of life-death-life as the primary problem faced by humans. Humans need to escape this hapless, potentially eternal cycle. For some forms of Hinduism, the chief cause of reincarnation is ignorance. Persons mistake the material world and the individual self (which seem most real) for genuine or ultimate reality. But genuine reality is the all-encompassing Brahman. This ignorance keeps one in the cycle of reincarnation and prevents an absorption into ultimate reality. Buddhism, one the other hand, sees the primary cause of reincarnation to be desire—including desire to exist as a self. Such desire keeps one trapped in the cycle of reincarnation and suffering; and it disallows a person to move on to Nirvana.

Not surprisingly, just as religions vary in their understanding of the human dilemma, so they differ concerning the solution to these dilemmas. Christians emphasize that salvation from sin and restoration to God and to righteousness is made possible by faith in Jesus Christ. Christ is the Mediator between humans and God, and Christ has made atonement for the sins of humans. Jews tend to see salvation as resulting both from the forgiving act of a gracious God and from the faithful commitment of an individual to God's covenant. Muslims emphasize salvation through obedience to the divine commands given in the Quran and to other traditions of Islam. Theravada Buddhism emphasizes attaining Nirvana by means of following the Eightfold Path of self-effort, a path completely followed only by Buddhist monks. Hinduism affirms a variety of methods by which one might attain release from reincarnation. Among the methods are showing devotion to personal gods, observing the laws and responsibilities of social classes, and practicing forms of meditation such as yoga.

A quick survey of these various beliefs reveals that the religions of the world differ considerably in how they conceptualize ultimate reality, human nature, the human dilemma, and the solution of the human problem.

Exclusivist Claims of the World's Religions

The considerable diversity among world-religions is complicated by the fact that many such religions claim that their teachings alone tell the truth about the nature of ultimate reality and about the means for overcoming the human spiritual problem. At the risk of oversimplification, we may point out that generally Western religions tend to be exclusivist, while Eastern religions tend to be more open to other religious views. This exclusivism is seen in the teachings of Judaism. Thus, the Jewish scriptures declare:

I am the LORD your God, who brought you out of the land of Egypt, out of the house of slavery; you shall have no other gods before me. You shall not make for yourself an idol, whether in the form of anything that is in heaven above, or that is on the earth beneath, or that is in the water under the earth. (Exod 20:2–4)

This is what the LORD says— / Israel's King and Redeemer, the LORD Almighty: / I am the first and I am the last; / apart from me there is no God. / Who then is like me? Let him proclaim it. / Let him declare and lay out before me / what has happened since I established my ancient people, / and what is yet to come— / yes, let him foretell what will come / . . . / Is there any God besides me? / No, there is no other Rock; I know not one. // All who make idols are nothing and the things they treasure are worthless. (Isa 44:6–9 NIV)

In these passages we see exclusivist claims. First, there is no other God than the God of Israel; second, at least some forms of worship (namely, the worship of idols and the gods associated with those idols) are inappropriate; indeed, these actions are worthless and subject to divine judgment.

Similar exclusivist claims are found in Islam:

To Him [Allah/God] is due the primal origin of the heavens and the earth: How can He have a son when He hath no consort? He created all things, and He hath full knowledge of all things. That is Allah, your Lord! there is no god but He, the Creator of all things: then worship ye Him.[53]

Never will the Jews or the Christians be satisfied with thee unless thou follow their form of religion. Say: "The Guidance of Allah,-that is the (only) Guidance." Wert thou to follow their desires after the knowledge which hath reached thee, then wouldst thou find neither Protector nor helper against Allah.[54]

Here Allah (God) is claimed to be the only God, and the Book (Quran) is the means to God. Other ways (Judaism and Christianity) are inappropriate.

Exclusivism is also a common element of Christianity. Central to Christianity is the claim that Jesus is the fullest revelation of God and the only true source of salvation. As Richard Cunningham puts it, "If one asks the question, How and where is God best and finally revealed and where is salvation achieved? the almost universal Christian answer has been: In Jesus Christ!"[55] This exclusivism is found in the following scriptural passages:

Jesus said to him, "I am the way, and the truth, and the life. No one comes to the Father except through me. If you know me, you will know my Father also. From now on you do know him and have seen him . . . Whoever has seen me has seen the Father (John 14:5–7, 9)

53. Quran, interpreted (i.e., translated) by Abdullah Yusuf Ali, 6:101–2 (brackets added).
54. Quran, interpreted (i.e., translated) by Abdullah Yusuf Ali, 2:120.
55. Cunningham, *The Christian Faith and Its Contemporary Rivals*, 184.

> For God was pleased to have all his fullness dwell in him, and through him to reconcile to himself all things, whether things on earth or things in heaven, by making peace through his blood, shed on the cross . . . For in Christ all the fullness of the Deity lives in bodily form, and in Christ you have been brought to fullness. He is the head over every power and authority. (Col 1:19–20; 2:9–10)

> There is salvation in no one else, for there is no other name under heaven given among mortals by which we must be saved. (Acts 4:12)

In these passages, we see the dual claim that Jesus is the fullest revelation of God and the only means of salvation. Christianity makes exclusivist claims.

We may further note that even though Eastern religions are often open to the teachings of other religions concerning ultimate reality and the means for obtaining spiritual wholeness, these religions are not utterly relativistic. When a Taoist claims that the best life is one of simplicity and nonstriving, she is necessarily precluding as the best way of life one of complexity and harsh striving to achieve difficult goals. When a Buddhist declares that the middle path is the way to Nirvana, he is explicitly excluding extreme asceticism and indulgence in pleasure as means to spiritual wholeness. Thus whereas Eastern religions are more inclusivist than Western religions, exclusivism is not completely absent from Eastern spiritual paths. Such claims to exclusivity must be taken into account in any interpretation of the relationship between the various religions.

Options for Interpreting the Diversity of Religious Teachings

All of this raises the important question: How is Christian theology to understand and interrelate with the diversity and discontinuity found in the various teachings of the world's religions? Are all the teachings of non-Christian religions somehow true? Are none of them true? Are some of the teachings true and some not? Further, are all, none, or some of the mechanisms prescribed to bring salvation, liberation, wholeness with ultimate reality effective? In addressing these concerns, we will focus on two fundamental questions: First, do the teachings of non-Christian religions reveal truth about ultimate reality? Second, do the teachings of the non-Christian religions provide a means for overcoming the human spiritual dilemma? Four major approaches arise in answering these questions.

Philosophical Naturalism

One option for answering questions about religious truth is to claim that no religion teaches the truth or provides salvation. Religions neither reveal truth about ultimate reality nor provide a means for overcoming some spiritual human dilemma. This is the case because there is no supernatural ultimate reality and no genuine transcendent human problem. At best, religions offer solutions to various mundane secular problems—such as the problem of insuring stable societies and ethical norms. But religions offer no insight into ultimate truth or reality. And they provide no means to resolve some alleged spiritual dilemma. This is the view of many philosophical naturalists. In essence, naturalists hold that there is no reality beyond the natural, physical universe.

Exclusivism

Another option in dealing with the diversity of religions is *exclusivism*. Exclusivism endorses three key principles. First, only the teachings of one religion reveal the essential truth about ultimate reality. While other religions may rightly affirm important truths, for the most part their teachings fail to offer the deepest insights regarding the nature of transcendent reality. Second, only the one valid religion provides the mechanism necessary to solve the basic spiritual problem of humans. Other religions may help participants in various ways, but they fail to provide the necessary means by which a person might be saved, liberated, or made right with ultimate reality. Third, humans must affirm certain key beliefs or engage in specified practices prescribed by the true religion in order to receive the saving or spiritual benefits of that religion. No other beliefs or practices will suffice to save a person.[56]

Often exclusivism is expressed in Christianity by endorsing the following three ideas. First, God is most fully known in the teachings of the Christian faith, especially in the biblically informed doctrines of the Trinity and of the incarnation of God in Christ. Second, only through Christ's works—especially his incarnation, atoning death, and resurrection—is salvation made possible. Third, to receive the saving benefits of Christ, devotees must have faith in Jesus Christ and must affirm certain essential beliefs or participate in certain vital rituals (such as baptism).[57] Theologically, Christian exclusivism emphasizes the role of Jesus Christ both as the fullest revelation of God and as the sole redeemer of humanity, that is, as "the one individual through whom God has reconciled the world to Himself."[58] Further, "in practical terms, this view contends that salvation requires a formal identification

56. According to the authors of *Reason and Religious Belief*, exclusivism insists that "to be saved or liberated," a person needs to "learn about, acknowledge the truths of, and appropriate the unique way" of the religion in question. In turn, "the unique salvific or liberative structure" of that religion "is both *ontologically necessary* (the objective conditions for addressing the human predicament must really be in place) and *epistemically necessary* (those seeking salvation/liberation must know about the conditions) for addressing the predicament" (Peterson et al., *Reason and Religious Belief*, 322; italics original).

57. For many Protestants, faith in Christ must be explicit or conscious. But for many Catholics, and for some Protestants, faith in Christ may be explicit, or it may be only implicit—specifically through an infant's participation in the Church's sacraments. See Chapter 6, above.

58. Cunningham, *The Christian Faith and Its Contemporary Rivals*, 187.

with Christianity."[59] Exclusivism is often expressed in traditional Roman Catholicism and in many conventional forms of Protestantism. For centuries Roman Catholicism taught that there is no salvation outside the Catholic Church. From this viewpoint, there is no salvation outside the sacraments of the Roman Church. This criterion was used to deny salvation to adherents of non-Christian religions as well as to non-Catholic Christians. For many Christians in the Middle Ages, expulsion from the Church would have meant eternal damnation. In Protestantism, exclusivism often takes the form of claiming that one must formally hear the gospel of Jesus Christ and respond to it in faith. Those who have not heard the gospel or have not responded positively to it are destined to damnation.[60]

Exclusivism offers several advantages to Christians. First, it accommodates the exclusivist tendencies expressed in significant portions of Christian Scriptures. Second, it helps provide psychological certainty for earnest devotees. Such believers often feel confident they have found the (only) way to salvation. Some disadvantages of exclusivism are these. First, as with many claims about supernatural realities, it is difficult if not impossible (at least in our current state of existence) to verify the exclusivist claims in any religion, including the Christian faith.[61] Second, it is difficult if not impossible to be epistemically (rather than merely psychologically) certain about which exclusivist religious systems is correct. Third, theological tensions emerge especially for theistic systems (including Christianity) that both incline toward exclusivism and also tend to affirm that God is loving, merciful, and just. The questions arise: How can God fairly condemn those who have not heard of Christ or of salvation through him? And how can God condemn those who have heard but sincerely seek God via their own traditions?[62]

Christian exclusivists have replies to these questions. Some propose the possibility of post-death opportunities to respond in faith to Christ. Thus, even when persons in their earthly lifetimes have not heard of Jesus Christ or of his saving work and call to faith, such individuals may be presented with the opportunity to respond positively to Christ after death in a post-death existence.[63] Other Christian authors argue that in spite of appearances, God is just to condemn persons who never hear of Christ because God's general condemnation of sin is just, even for those who have not heard the gospel of Christ.[64]

---

59. Cunningham, *The Christian Faith and Its Contemporary Rivals*, 187.

60. Although, many Protestants add the caveat that young children who die prior to a certain age of moral accountability are saved even without making a conscience decision for Christ.

61. Most, perhaps all, religions must walk by faith, not by sight—that is, they must make commitments based on limited (perhaps even insufficient) evidence.

62. See John Hick's comments in Hick, *Philosophy of Religion*, 116–17.

63. See Walls, *Hell*, chapter 4. Also see Fackre, "Divine Perseverance." For an opposing Christian perspective, see Nash, *Is Jesus the Only Savior?* Also see Nash "Restrictivism."

64. Nash, "Restrictivism," especially 110–13, 118–20.

Pluralism

A third option for dealing with the diversity of religions is *pluralism*. Pluralism insists that no religion captures the *whole* truth about ultimate reality, although each faith offers glimpses of the truth. Further, no religion describes or possesses the *sole* mechanism for solving the basic spiritual problem(s) of humans, although each religion may provide ways for practitioners to be saved, liberated, or made right with ultimate reality. Finally, no religion provides or administrates the *exclusive* teachings or rituals necessary for obtaining salvation, liberation, or right standing before the divine. Rather, according to pluralism, affirmation of multiple beliefs or participation in numerous rituals among diverse religions may bring persons into these desired states.

John Hick (1922–2012) offers one version of this pluralistic perspective. Hick insists that the religions of the world are parts of a "dynamic continuum" rather than exclusive systems. Theologically, these religions are "intersections of divine grace, divine initiative, divine truth, with human faith, human response, human enlightenment."[65] According to Hick, each religion is a different human response to a common revelatory encounter with ultimate reality. Even though the divine reality encountered is the same in each religion, the human experience of, interpretation of, and response to this reality varies from religious system to religious system.[66] For Hick, the diversity of religious traditions and teachings results from the diversity of cultures (including disparate languages and differing cognitive schemes) in which divine encounter has occurred. These traditions are simply human interpretations of a singular ultimate reality that has been experienced. None of these traditions adequately conveys the truth concerning divine reality, but each points toward this reality. According to Hick, in some ways, it is inappropriate to apply the terms *true* or *false* to religions any more than it is appropriate to apply these terms to cultures. Cultures simply are; they are neither true nor false. Likewise, religions simply are; they are neither true nor false. They are simply diverse experiences of and responses to a common ultimate reality.[67]

Hick believes that pluralism is historically inevitable—the result of divine revelation coming to diverse and isolated cultural traditions. However, Hick speculates that as the cultures of the world come into more contact with one another, and as a world culture emerges, the world's religions likely will converge as well.[68] If this should occur, current world religions might one day be seen as distinct historical

---

65. Hick, *Philosophy of Religion*, 111.

66. Hick likens the distinction between the divine reality per se and diverse human experiences of that reality to Immanuel Kant's distinction between the noumenal world (reality *itself*) and the phenomenal world (reality *as humans experience* it). According to Hick, while the ultimate divine reality does not change, the way humans experience it varies from person to person, tradition to tradition, or culture to culture. And cultures play a significant role in how individuals experience or interpret the ultimate (Hick, *Philosophy of Religion*, 117–19).

67. Hick, *Philosophy of Religion*, 112.

68. Hick, *Philosophy of Religion*, 114.

traditions of a single religion. Hick admits that there are genuine differences between world religions. He discusses three basic distinctions. First there are different modes of experiencing ultimate reality. The most fundamental distinction
is between religions that see ultimate reality as personal and those that see it as
nonpersonal. Hick, however, believes that these two approaches are complementary
rather than incompatible, for every "profound" religion holds that "ultimate reality
is infinite and exceeds the scope of our finite human categories."[69] Thus, "predicates
that are incompatible when attributed to a finite reality may no longer be incompatible when referred to infinite reality."[70]

For Hick, a second difference between world religions revolves around differing philosophical and theological interpretations of ultimate reality. Among world
religions, a wide and contradictory set of claims may be found about the nature of
ultimate reality, not to mention between ethical and cultic practices. According to
Hick, however, these philosophical or theological theories must be understood as
belonging to the historical, culturally conditioned aspects of religion. Further, these
traditions are still developing and may be ultimately transcended so that a more
cohesive system of beliefs results.

A third difference between world religions for Hick has to do with different
pivotal, revelatory events in the history of these religions. Each religion has its own
founder, scripture, or both; and often these founders or scriptures make absolute
claims upon believers. Such absolute claims among religions seem to be mutually
exclusive. Hick cites as an example the Christian claim that Christ was uniquely
divine and the only mediator between God and humans. Such a claim denies the exclusive or even inclusive claims of other religions. Hick admits that this is a problem
for pluralism. He insists, however, that such claims to exclusivity must be rejected.
Although he does not specifically say so, he apparently believes that such a rejection
is the only way for God or ultimate reality to deal fairly with the human race. He argues that exclusive claims concerning Jesus run counter to the Christian belief that
God seeks the salvation of all people. If the exclusive claims of Jesus are correct, says
Hick, "this means that infinite love has ordained that human beings can be saved
only in a way that in fact excludes the large majority of them; for the greater part of
all the human beings who have been born have lived either before Christ or outside
the borders of Christendom."[71] Hick explicitly rejects the Christian tradition's claim
that Jesus was the unique incarnation of God—that Jesus was of the same substance
as God. Rather, Hick insists that through the spiritual presence of the ultimate, any
persons (including Jesus) can manifest the nature of the ultimate reality. For Hick,
the notion of God's incarnation in Christ is a myth that, although not literally true,

69. Hick, *Philosophy of Religion*, 115.

70. Hick, *Philosophy of Religion*, 115.

71. Hick, *Philosophy of Religion*, 116.

points to the very real possibility of humans gaining an appropriate disposition and openness toward the ultimate.[72]

Hick concludes that while there are major differences among the world's religions, these differences may be transcended or ignored. Each religion may be interpreted as a human response to some form of transcendent revelation. No religion's doctrine concerning the nature of ultimate reality is completely correct, but each points to the existence of an infinite and ultimate reality. Further (although this last point is less clear), apparently for Hick, each religion offers a pathway to salvation—whatever salvation means.[73]

A number of problems may be cited against Hick's views and pluralism in general. First, his stance explicitly denies the exclusivist claims of various religions. Thus, while attempting to be inclusive, Hick's view must exclude certain claims of various religions. This involves denying of specific claims of traditional Christianity, including the uniqueness of Jesus both as the highest revelation of God and as the sole means of salvation. A second problem is this: the nature of ultimate reality remains unclear. Are human interpretations of ultimate reality completely wrong or partially wrong? If completely wrong, does this not imply that humans know nothing about ultimate reality? If partially wrong (and thus partially right), which claims are true and which are not? By what criteria is one to decide? Hick seems to believe that some claims about ultimate reality are true. For example, he seems to assume that ultimate reality is good, just, and loving. But how does one know this? Is this a core teaching of all religions? (One challenge to this premise is dualism.) Is it a core teaching of the best religions? (If so, what criteria determine which religions are the best?)

A third puzzle facing Hick's pluralism it this: the meaning of and the means to salvation are not clear. What is the goal or purpose of human life? What problem, if any, needs to be resolved in human life? Are any of the religious traditions correct in their interpretation of the human problem? If so, which ones? By what criteria does one decide? Are none of the religious traditions correct in their interpretation of the human problem? If not, then what is the correct interpretation of the human problem? Is there even a human problem? More profoundly, if there is a human problem, what is the solution? In some ways, Hick seems to assume that the solution to the human problem is sincere commitment to some religious tradition, or sincere desire to be right with ultimate reality. But how does Hick know this? And is this a fair assessment of any world religion? Is this what they all teach? Is this what any of them affirm? The answers are not clear.[74]

72. See Peterson, *Reason and Religious Belief*, 327–28. Also see Hick, "Religious Pluralism." Also see Hick, *Problems of Religious Pluralism*.

73. Hick seems to define *salvation* as "the transformation of human existence from self-centredness to Reality-centredness" (Hick, "Religious Pluralism," 615).

74. Hick seems to assume that self-centeredness is a core human problem and that a life centered on the ultimate, transcendent reality is the best. (See the previous note for insight into Hick's understanding of the human religious problem.) But how does Hick know this? And do all religions imply

From a traditional Christian perspective, Hick's view seems to deny the unique role played by Jesus as the fullest revelation of God and of Jesus' death as an atonement for sin. In the minds of some Christians, Hick's perspective may be guilty of taking the concept of sin too lightly. Salvation without atonement suggests that the sin problem is not as severe, or that the need for Christ's death is not as important as Christian theology traditionally has taught. In short, some Christians may see in Hick's pluralism an assumption that Christ's death was not necessary. As some people read John Hick, Christ's death performs a revelatory function. But what does it reveal?

Christian Inclusivism

In light of the difficulties faced by both the exclusivist and pluralist views, several Christian writers have proposed a perspective that affirms key exclusive claims of Christianity while recognizing the salvific efficacy of sincere commitments to elements of other religions. Often this approach is referred to as *inclusivism* or *Christian inclusivism*. Inclusivism is endorsed by a number of authors.[75] Here we will discuss the perspectives of Karl Rahner and Richard B. Cunningham.

According to Catholic theologian Karl Rahner (1904–1984), Christianity is the one true religion that alone most fully reveals the one true God, accurately describes the human spiritual dilemma, and offers the only remedy for human estrangement from God. This revelation, and redemption, is manifested in Jesus of Nazareth—God incarnate. Jesus most fully displays God's nature and alone provides redemption from sin. However, the revelatory and redemptive events of Christ occurred in history so that Christianity itself has a prehistory when God was active in the religion of the descendants of Abraham and even in the practices of non-Israelite religions. Although these religions did not bring a revelation as full as the manifestation of God in Christ, these faiths were "lawful" in the sense that they brought some legitimate knowledge of God, and through them divine grace was offered and positively responded to. Since the coming of Christ, persons are called upon (and expected) to respond positively to the grace and salvation offered by and made possible in Christ, for it is in the Christ-event that God truly is known and redemption is made possible.

Still, according to Rahner, many persons and cultures are in circumstances similar to those of individuals who existed before the coming of Christ. For them, the revelation of the Christ-event has not yet become a historical reality. That is, it has not been made known to them in any meaningful way. So these individuals have no real opportunity to respond positively to the gospel of Christ. But in a way analogous to persons who lived prior to Christ but who sought God through their own religious

---

this?

75. See Lewis, *Mere Christianity*, 62, 173. Küng, *On Being a Christian*; Newbigin, *The Open Secret*; Neill, *Christian Faith and Other Faiths*; Sanders, "Inclusivism"; Cunningham, *The Christian Faith and Its Contemporary Rivals*, 189–92.

understandings, contemporary religious persons can receive some revelation of God through their non-Christian religions and by divine grace are redeemed by the tacit, if not-fully informed, faith implicit in their religious beliefs and practices. According to Rahner, something like Christian inclusivism is required if Christians seriously believe both that salvation comes through Christ and Christianity alone *and* that God truly longs for all humans to be saved.[76]

Another writer who holds an outlook of Christian inclusivism is Richard B. Cunningham. According to Cunningham, salvation is only through Jesus Christ and his concrete actions in history. Through him, an objective atonement or reconciliation with God was made, the benefits of which may be received by human beings. People may appropriate these benefits through a faith response to the gospel of Christ. But persons also "may appropriate the saving efficacy of God's historic redemption in Jesus through a tentative but genuine faith response to the presence of the cosmic Christ in general revelation."[77] In other words, in various world religions, some of the truth about Christ is revealed. And a genuine faith response to this (albeit limited) revelation is sufficient for salvation. Cunningham insists that this view is not universalistic because salvation is still contingent upon a faith in Christ as Christ is revealed in general revelation.[78] Further, Cunningham maintains that such salvation is still through faith by grace alone and not by human effort.

Cunningham lists several principles often associated with Christian inclusivism. First, this approach typically affirms that all humans are sinners and thus alienated from God. Therefore, each person is responsible for his or her own sin, stands under personal judgement by God, and needs salvation. Second, "all redemption occurs through God's historic act of reconciling the world to Himself in the person and work of Jesus Christ, a once-for-all-redemptive act for the whole human race."[79] Cunningham acknowledges that different Christian authors offer divergent theories about how humans are saved through the actions of Christ, yet there is consistent agreement among Christian inclusivists that there is no salvation independent of Christ and his work.[80]

How then does a person appropriate salvation? According to Cunningham, Christian inclusivists maintain that the clearest pathway to do this is by "hearing the gospel and responding in faith to Jesus Christ as Savior and Lord."[81] Such actions provide "the fullest conscious experience of God and an informed understanding of

---

76. For Rahner's views see Rahner, "Religious Inclusivism," in *Philosophy of Religion: Selected Readings*, 606–13. Also see, Rahner, "Christianity and Non-Christian Religions," in *Theological Investigations*, 5:115–34 and "Observations on the Problem of Anonymous Christians," in *Theological Investigations*, 14:280–94.

77. Cunningham, *The Christian Faith and Its Contemporary Rivals*, 189.

78. Cunningham, *The Christian Faith and Its Contemporary Rivals*, 189.

79. Cunningham, *The Christian Faith and Its Contemporary Rivals*, 189.

80. Cunningham, *The Christian Faith and Its Contemporary Rivals*, 189.

81. Cunningham, *The Christian Faith and Its Contemporary Rivals*, 190.

the Christian way of life."[82] Nevertheless, since a mindful response is not possible for a person who has never heard the gospel, "there is a possibility that people might be saved who follow in faith what limited light they have in general revelation"[83] Christian inclusivists propose that God is revealed in various ways through general revelation (John 1:9; Acts 14:16–17; 17:22–34; Rom 1:19–20), ways such as in "the beauty and regularity of nature, an awareness of the moral law, human conscience, and reason."[84] In turn, according to the Christian inclusivist, "broken and inadequate responses to these forms of revelation may be found within the world religions."[85] And in God's grace, these responses are accepted as tacit faith in Christ.

Cunningham insists that general revelation is genuine revelation *of Christ*—for Christ is the Word (Logos or rationality) of God that is present in all creation and is the light that "enlightens everyone" (John 1:9). Further, this "general Christological revelation is capable of saving people *if* they respond to it in what corresponds to faith," for such faith implicitly is a response to the Word of God who became incarnate in Jesus and whose actions in history reconciled humanity to God.[86] Like Rahner, Cunningham likens such tacit faith to the saving faith of pre-Christian Israelites whose trust in God's promises (to Abraham and to the people of Israel) was an implicit trust in God's future saving works accomplished in Jesus.[87]

Recognizing that opponents often criticize Christian inclusivism on the grounds that such a view undermines Christian Evangelical efforts, Cunningham retorts:

> There is a strong missionary imperative to share the gospel because there is a name for the light of general revelation and a historic act of redemption to be consciously appropriated into one's life. Those who hold this theological position are willing to leave the eternal destiny of devout people in other world religions to God. But this perspective is committed to helping people enter into the fullness of the abundant life here on earth as they learn of Jesus Christ.[88]

Christian inclusivism has been criticized by a variety of writers from diverse perspectives. Pluralist John Hick offers three criticisms. First, he asks, if salvation can happen "without any connection with the Christian Church or Gospel," why bother evangelizing? In this case, "the conversion of the people of the other great world faiths to Christianity hardly seems the best way of spending one's energies."[89] (Cunningham's comments in the previous paragraph are designed to answer this kind of criticism.)

---

82. Cunningham, *The Christian Faith and Its Contemporary Rivals*, 190.

83. Cunningham, *The Christian Faith and Its Contemporary Rivals*, 190.

84. Cunningham, *The Christian Faith and Its Contemporary Rivals*, 190.

85. Cunningham, *The Christian Faith and Its Contemporary Rivals*, 190.

86. Cunningham, *The Christian Faith and Its Contemporary Rivals*, 190 (italics original).

87. Cunningham, *The Christian Faith and Its Contemporary Rivals*, 190.

88. Cunningham, *The Christian Faith and Its Contemporary Rivals*, 191.

89. Hick, "Religious Pluralism," 616.

Hick's second criticism is that Christian inclusivism (especially as expressed by Vatican II)[90] seems to allow the salvation of theists among the world's religions, but not nontheists. But Hick wonders about the plight of the multitude of nontheistic religious adherents across the globe.[91] The exclusion of nontheists means exemption from salvation of millions, even billions, of otherwise religiously earnest and faithful practitioners. Hick's third criticism of inclusivism is this: Inclusivists seem to assume that direct rejection of Christ or of the Christian gospel brings divine condemnation. But Hick questions the fairness of this for the numerous non-Christians across the globe "who have heard the Christian gospel but have preferred to adhere to the faith of their fathers."[92] For a number of such persons, their concrete historical context makes it very difficult for them to respond positively to the Christian gospel.

In an interesting reversal of Hick's third criticism, Christian author Gabriel Fackre (1926–2018) offers another dilemma for Christian inclusivism. Fackre notes that some inclusivists (including Karl Rahner) insist that divine grace, with some human cooperation, creates an "implicit faith" in good people who do not know Christ, making them "anonymous Christians." But Fackre wonders whether such a scenario does not involve God "lassoing people into Christianity without their permission."[93] In other words, where Hick ponders the fairness of condemning those who deliberately reject the Christian faith for the sake of their traditional faith, Fackre challenges the fairness of forcing (enveloping) non-Christians who sincerely reject Christianity into a faith or relationship with God that they have not deliberately accepted. (For Fackre, such a problem is avoided if one assumes a post-death opportunity for persons—including persons of other faiths—to believe or not believe in Christ, thus, offering the chance to deliberately accept or reject God.)[94] A final criticism of Christian inclusivism is that it fails to recognize the legitimacy or fairness of God's condemnation of sinful humans in general. For writers such as Ronald H. Nash, a critic of Christian inclusivism from an exclusivist perspective, the scriptural witness is that humans are *justly condemned* for their sins through what limited knowledge they have of God (and of God's expectations) through general revelation, and the fairness of this condemnation undermines the alleged unfairness of not having an opportunity to respond to Christ.[95]

---

90. Influenced by writers like Rahner, the Second Vatican Council (1963–1965) declared that "Those who through no fault of their own are still ignorant of the Gospel of Christ and of his Church yet sincerely seek God and, with the help of divine grace, strive to do his will as known to them through the voice of their conscience, those men can attain to eternal salvation." *Dogmatic Constitution of the Church*: *Lumen Gentium*, art. 16 (quoted in Hick, *Philosophy of Religion*, 116).

91. Hick, *Philosophy of Religion*, 116.

92. Hick, *Philosophy of Religion*, 116–17.

93. Fackre, "Response to Sanders," 58.

94. Fackre, "Response to Sanders," 58. Also see Fackre, "Divine Perseverance."

95. Nash, "Retrictivism," 110–13, 118–20.

Conclusion

The diversity of the world's religions, including various exclusivist claims of many such religions, remains a perennial issue for Christian theology and for Christian relations with other religious traditions. The same can be said of the problem of evil. None of this is to concede that such conundrums have no solution; indeed, as we have noted in this chapter, various Christian responses have been offered. Still, these two issues remain topics of ongoing concern and conversation for Christians. The same may be said of matters discussed in the next two chapters—namely, the relationship of science to the Christian faith and the dilemma of women in ministry. To these issues we now turn.

14

Christian Issues

Christianity and Science

IN THE PREVIOUS CHAPTER, we examined two major issues faced by contemporary Christianity—the problem of evil and the relationship between Christianity and other religions. In this fourteenth chapter, we explore the relationship between science and the Christian faith.[1]

It is no secret that we live in a scientific world. Science has brought amazing advances both in human understanding of the natural world and in technology (including an ability to control our environment). Because of science, humans now have a greater grasp than ever before of the structure and workings of the physical universe. From the subatomic level to the macrophysical level to the cosmic level, from the workings of chemical compounds to the mechanics of genetics to the processes of the human brain to the development of stars and galaxies, science has shaped and continues to shape the modern perspective of reality.

It is also no secret that science and religion at times have been in tension with each other. This is true in a general way, for the emergence of science has generated a worldview that is significantly different from all previous, prescientific perspectives, both Eastern and Western. Compared to prescientific worldviews, a scientific worldview has new perspectives on the physical development and age of the universe, the size of the universe and the earth's place in it, the origin of life (including human life) on this planet, and the nature of the human physical organism. When scientific perspectives are compared to various prescientific cosmologies from across the globe, the differences are plain.

---

1. Portions of this chapter—including its overarching structure—are based on the lectures notes of Richard B. Cunningham, retired professor from Southern Baptist Theological Seminary, whose classes I took, and for whom I later graded as a graduate student in the late 1980s and early 1990s. Over the years, these lectures have been augmented by me as I too taught with them (often creating my own emphases and new content along the way). The end result is that I am not always sure which content or wording is his and which is mine. I wish to express my indebtedness to his insights in the construction of these materials. And whatever shortcomings there may be in these materials should be credited to me, not him.

The tension between science and religion is seen particularly in the relationship between Christianity and science. This is due in part to the fact that modern science largely emerged out of the Christian West, and as a result, the history of science and the history of Christianity have been significantly entwined for a number of centuries. That history of the interaction between Christianity and science has been plagued by conflict.

The Catholic Church's rejection of the astronomy of Nicolaus Copernicus (1473–1543) and Galileo Galilei (1564–1642) in the seventeenth century offers a model example of this conflict. Copernicus had argued that mathematically it makes more sense to assume that the earth and planets revolve around the sun, than to assume that the sun and planets revolve around the earth. In turn, Galileo's observations with the newly developed telescope seemed to confirm this. Galileo also observed mountains on the moon and sunspots, and both observations served as evidence against the medieval view that celestial bodies are perfect. Further, his observation of the moons of Jupiter gave more evidence that the earth is not the central focus around which the universe revolves. In 1633, Galileo was forced to recant his views. His theories were rejected by the Church because they did not mesh with the authoritative views of Aristotle or with verses in Scripture that seem to imply a geocentric cosmos.[2] Galileo's work called the *Dialogue on the Two Chief World Systems* was soon put on the official Catholic Index of Prohibited Books, from which it was not removed until 1822!

Some commentators have seen this episode as typical of the relationship between science and religion, and between science and Christianity in particular. Over and over again, so the story goes, scientific theories (like the Copernican theory—that the earth and other planets revolve around the sun) have been opposed by religionists, only to be validated eventually by overwhelming evidence and ultimately accepted by the majority of thinking people.[3] While such an interpretation may be somewhat biased, there is certainly a grain of truth to it. Hence, the question arises: Precisely how are we to conceptualize the relationship between science and religion, and more specifically the relationship between science and Christianity?

Contemporary Interpretations of the Relationship of Science and Christianity

The relationship between science and Christianity has been conceptualized in four broad ways. These are

---

2. Barbour, *Religion and Science*, 13.
3. See White, *A History of the Warfare*.

Subordination of Science to Religion

Some writers attempt to subordinate science to religion. This approach attempts to place scientific theory under the authority of a prescientific religious worldview, often affirming a literal interpretation of some prescientific sacred literature. In Christianity, several such approaches may be noted. Some Christians simply reject the authority of the scientific method and the prevailing views of science, particularly where such views clash with a literal understanding of the Bible. Advocates of such views offer no real evidence for their perspectives outside of commitments to a literal understanding of the biblical narrative. They insist that the universe is young, that God created in six literal days, and that humans were created on the sixth day, about ten thousand years ago.

Other Christians—who often call themselves *scientific creationists*—acknowledge the need to address the claims of science. They affirm a literal[4] reading of Gen 1, and so they believe that the universe is young and was created in six literal days. But they attempt to establish this on what they perceive to be scientific grounds. They try to show that the prevailing scientific view is incorrect, and that empirical data best support a literal six-day creation. Often such writers appeal to the biblical story of Noah's flood to explain the various strata of fossils found in the geological record. Creation science authors John C. Whitcomb and Henry Morris affirm this perspective.[5]

Still other writers accept the basic cosmological views of science and try to show that such perspectives can be harmonized with a literal reading of Scripture. They attempt to find openings in the biblical account that might allow one to harmonize the Genesis creation accounts in chapters 1 and 2 with the scientific view that the universe is several billion years old. One such group affirms the *day-age theory*. They propose that the six days of Gen 1 refer not to twenty-four-hour periods but to huge epochs that correspond to the great geological ages of the earth. Nineteenth-century geologist Hugh Miller affirmed this outlook.[6] Another group affirms the so-called *gap theory*. They argue that there were two periods of God's creative work. The first creation, which is recorded in Gen 1:1, occurred several billion years ago. The second creation, which is recorded in Gen 1:2 and following, occurred only a few thousand years ago. According to this theory, after the first creation (of Gen 1:1) the universe existed for several billion years, but eventually some great cosmic upheaval (such as the fall of Satan) brought chaotic ruin upon the universe. And so God had to re-create or re-construct the universe in six literal days (as described in Gen 1:1—2:3). Advocates of

---

4. As we will see in the latter sections of this chapter, the notion of the "literal" reading of the biblical text is a tricky matter. A cornerstone of valid biblical interpretation is to seek and discern authorial intent, which often requires an appreciation of not only of the author's goals but also of the general historical, cultural, and literary conventions of the writer's era.

5. See Whitcomb and Morris, *The Genesis Flood*. See also Price, *The New Geology*.

6. See Miller, *The Testimony of the Rocks*. See also Gedney, "Geology and the Bible," in *Modern Science and Christian Faith*.

this theory see a huge temporal gap between vv. 1 and 2 of Gen 1. This model was first proposed by Scottish preacher and theologian Thomas Chalmers (1780–1847); it is currently endorsed in the Scofield Annotated Bible.[7]

All the theories above assume that the biblical stories intend to describe the physical process of the universe's creation. The chief value of such approaches is that they attempt to take seriously the Christian Scriptures. However, several difficulties may be noted. First, none of these schemes is persuasive to the scientific community as a whole, largely because empirical evidence is lacking for them. Second, considerable hermeneutical gymnastics is required to make the Bible compatible with the contemporary scientific view of the universe. This is particularly problematic for the day-age and gap theories. Most biblical scholars insist that such interpretations simply do not do justice to a historical-grammatical reading of the Genesis text. The text does not propose either six epochs or a gap between Gen 1:1 and 1:2. Such interpretations are strained at best. Further, when closely considered, theories such as the day-age theory and the gap theory still do not fit well with the current scientific perspective (or with the data that support the scientific picture). For example, the day-age theory must suppose that God created the sun (on the fourth day) after plants had been on the earth for many millennia (since the third day). But this hardly fits the scientific perspective. On the other hand, those theories (mentioned above) that ignore science or that cite empirical evidence against the current scientific perspective often are doomed to intellectual obscurity or forced to bend the empirical data beyond what is reasonable. The history of attempts to subordinate science to religion does not place religion in a favorable light. Repeatedly when the Christian church has resisted new theories of science, it has found itself forced to retreat in the face of overwhelming evidence for science-based perspectives. The conflict with Galileo's theory is but one prime example of this.

Science and Religion as Independent

A second conceptualization of the relationship between science and religion is to see the two as independent of each other. This approach emphasizes distinctions between the concerns and methods of science and the concerns and methods of religion. It alleges that each arena has a relative autonomy in its own area of study and experience. Using the empirical method, science has primary authority for investigating the natural universe. On the other hand, appealing to divine revelation and personal experience, religion has primary authority when dealing with ultimate and existential questions. Christian theologian Langdon Gilkey (1919–2004) endorses this approach. He proposes the following distinctions between religion and science.

7. See Scofield et al., eds., *The New Scofield Reference Bible*, especially notes 5, 6, and 7 for Gen 1.

1. Science seeks to explain objective, public, and repeatable data, whereas religion is concerned with order and beauty in the world and with inner experiences (such as guilt, meaninglessness, forgiveness, trust, and so forth).

2. Science asks objective *how* questions, whereas religion asks personal *why* questions—questions of meaning, purpose, ultimate origins and destiny.

3. The basis of knowledge in science is logical coherence and experimental adequacy of theories. The basis of knowledge in religion is divine revelation as experienced by various persons in the past and as validated by our own experience.

4. Science makes quantitative predictions that can be tested experimentally. Religion must use symbolic and analogical language because God is transcendent.[8]

Two key examples of this approach in Christian theology are neo-orthodoxy and existential theology. Neo-orthodoxy (especially as expressed by theologian Karl Barth [1886–1968]) rejects natural theology (knowledge of God via nature) and emphasizes knowledge of God only through revelation in Christ. Neo-orthodoxy tends to ignore the impact that science might have on religious claims and simply reasserts (and reinterprets) traditional church doctrines based on special revelation. Thus, in this view "scientists are free to carry out their work without interference from theology, and *vice versa*, since their methods and their subject matter are totally dissimilar. Science is based on human observation and reason, while theology is based on divine revelation."[9] The chief difference between neo-orthodoxy and those theologies that attempt to submit science to religion is that whereas the latter usually affirm a literal interpretation of the biblical creation accounts, neo-orthodoxy does not. It sees these accounts as stories that present religious truth that has authority over spiritual matters; but these accounts need not be interpreted as models for understanding the physical development of the universe.

Existential theology, on the other hand, emphasizes a distinction between objective and subjective truth. Science is concerned with objectively and empirically verifiable claims. Religion is concerned with questions of personal meaning and ultimate commitments. New Testament scholar Rudolf Bultmann (1884–1976) affirmed such an approach. He admitted that the Bible often uses empirical language to speak of God's acts, but he insisted that "we can retain the original experiential meaning of such passages by translating them into the language of human self-understanding, the language of hopes and fears, choices and decisions, and new possibilities for our lives."[10] Hence, for Bultmann, science and religion deal with decisively different issues. Each can go about its business without affecting the other.

---

8. Barbour, *Religion and Science*, 86. See Gilkey, *Maker of Heaven and Earth*.

9. Barbour, *Religion and Science*, 85.

10. Barbour, *Religion and Science*, 86.

The value of this overall approach is that it acknowledges that science and religion are not primarily concerned with the same arenas of study. Science's principal concern is the processes of the natural universe. Religion's prime concern is the meaning and purpose of the universe and the human place in that universe. The deficiency of this approach is that it may too severely compartmentalize science and religion. It simply is not clear that the worldview constructed by science has no impact on religious beliefs, including beliefs such as the existence of the soul or life after death or divine sovereignty over the universe. Most of us experience life as a whole and not in compartments. Further, most religious traditions, including the Christian tradition, affirm the wholeness of life and reality and thus seem to require an integrative approach to truth.

Science and Religion as Complementary

A third vision of the relationship between science and religion is to see the two as complementary. This approach sees both science and religion as seeking the same goal, namely a unified view of reality. It acknowledges that each discipline has in own basic area of expertise and authority; yet, this perspective insists that insights from each are complementary and help form an integrated synthesis. Science and religion are in dialogue with one another, each mutually aiding and correcting the other. Several examples of such an approach may be noted.

Natural Theologies

First there are various attempts to construct *natural theologies*. Throughout history, several attempts have been made to ground certain aspects of religion in reason and empirical observation. Thomas Aquinas (1225–1274) insisted that core truths about God can be obtained by reflecting on the existence and nature of the universe. Thomas offered version of both the cosmological and teleological arguments to demonstrate the existence and basic nature of God. However, Thomas also insisted that certain key truths about God can be learned only through special revelation—such as the doctrines of the Trinity, of the incarnation, and of the atonement.

Contemporary British philosopher Richard Swinburne offers an extensive argument for God's existence, based on scientific confirmation theory. He argues that the existence of God is an initially plausible hypothesis because it offers a simple and personal explanation for the existence of the universe as we know it. Further, he insists that the plausibility of this hypothesis increases in light of the ordered structure of the universe, the emergence of sentient beings, and the various types of religious experiences around the world. Swinburne concludes that in the face of evidence, theism is more probable than not.[11]

Theologies of Nature

In addition to attempts to ground religion in reason, other thinkers have attempted to interpret scientific views of nature from the perspective of a given religious tradition. Such approaches do not start with science or reason but begin with a religious tradition; however, they attempts to reformulate traditional religious doctrines in the light of science. Ian Barbour refers to these approaches as *theologies of nature*.[12] A prime example of such an approach is the work of biochemist and theologian Arthur Peacocke (1924–2006). For Peacocke, theology is grounded in the historical teachings and experiences of a religious tradition. However, he believes that theological doctrine often needs to be reformulated in response to science. He advocates the notion that God's immanent activity is discernible in the dual aspects of chance and physical necessity in the universe. For Peacocke, "God creates through the whole process of law and chance, not by intervening in gaps in the process. God creates 'in and through' the processes of the natural world that science unveils."[13]

Another example of a theology of nature is found in the writings of Jesuit paleontologist Pierre Teilhard de Chardin (1881–1955). Teilhard's vision of reality and of God was shaped by Darwinian evolutionary thought. For Teilhard, physical reality is endowed with a kind of ever-present teleology that points toward the immanence of God throughout all physical processes of the universe.[14]

Metaphysical Theologies

Another type of theory that affirms science and religion as complementary are *metaphysical theologies*. By this phrase is meant theories that begin with a basic philosophical metaphysic and then interpret both science and religion within that construct.[15] A prime example of this approach is the various forms of process philosophy and *process theology* found in the works of Alfred North Whitehead (1861–1947),[16] Charles Hartshorne (1897–2000),[17] John B. Cobb Jr. (b. 1925),[18] and others.

11. Swinburne, *The Existence of God*.

12. Barbour, *Religion and Science*, 100.

13. Barbour, *Religion and Science*, 101. See also Peacocke, *Theology for a Scientific Age*.

14. Barbour, *Religion and Science*, 102. See Teilhard de Chardin, *The Phenomenon of Man*.

15. I am following Ian Barbour, here, who calls these the Systematic Synthesis. Barbour, *Religion and Science*, 103–5.

16. Whitehead, *Process and Reality*.

17. Hartshorne, *Omnipotence and Other Theological Mistakes*.

18. Cobb and Griffin, *Process Theology*.

The basic insight of process thought is that reality is becoming and dynamic, and not static. Another key notion is that all reality, physical reality included, has a certain psychic element to it, so that the traditional philosophical dichotomy between minds and physical objects can be overcome, and divine purpose can be discerned throughout the whole cosmic process.

Conclusion regarding Science and Religion as Complementary

The value of this overall approach (viewing science and religion as compatible) is that it aims at a holistic understanding of reality—one that takes seriously both science and theology. A limitation of this perspective is that often religious tradition and revelation get the short end of the stick; that is, the views of modern science, philosophy, or both tend to play the dominate role.

Submission of religion to science

A fourth and final conceptualization of the relationship between science and religion is to see religion as submissive to science. This approach concedes the superiority of science over religion as a way of knowing and largely dismisses the cognitive value of religious claims. According to this view, religion's value, at best, is its stabilizing effect upon society and individuals, and its power to express the emotional and aesthetic sensitivities of humans. Key proponents of this approach include A. J. Ayer (1910–1989)[19] and R. B. Braithwaite (1900–1990)[20] These writers deny cognitive content to religious expressions. Rather, each sees the meaning and value of religious expressions to be found in noncognitive aspects of communication. Ayer claims that religious statements are essentially emotive expressions. Braithwaite insists that religious statements are policy statements, expressions of how one intends to live his or her life. Both Ayer and Braithwaite are willing to grant some place for the religious life and its expressions, but not as a way of understanding the nature of the universe or of human life. Rather, genuine knowledge is gained only through the scientific, empirical process.

The limitations of this view, particularly for religion, are obvious. While religion certainly plays an important role in stabilizing society and in aiding human emotional and aesthetic expression, most adherents of religion—including of Christianity—see it as doing more. Most believe that religious statements express metaphysical truth and thus have genuine cognitive value. Further, it is precisely the truth of such statements that is believed to give grounding for many of our passionate commitments and aesthetic sensitivities.

19. Ayer, *Language, Truth, and Logic.*
20. Braithwaite, *An Empiricist's View of the Nature of Religious Belief.*

A Preliminary Assessment

I am in essential agreement with my teacher, Richard Cunningham, when he notes that none of the approaches above is wholly satisfactory and that the best approach probably lies between seeing science and religion as complementary and seeing them as independent. The other two approaches—one of whcih submits science to religion, and the other which submits religion to science—simply will not work for "anyone who wants to live in a scientific world and at the same time remain committed to historic Christianity."[21] Cunningham thus advocates a view that sees "science and theology as both having legitimate, distinctive, and complementary roles to play within a holistic and unified understanding of God, world, and human life."[22]

Science in a Christian Worldview

How, then, are Christians to integrate science into their basic view of the world? Three proposals are offered here. First, seek to understand the nature and limitations of science. Second, grant the established facts of science. Third, challenge the excessive claims that some make about science.

Understand the nature and limitations of science

First, Christians should attempt to understand the nature and heuristic limits of science. Science primarily is an extension of our common way of gaining information. It involves observation, developing hypotheses, discerning implications of our hypotheses (including expected occurrences under varying conditions), and confirmation or disconfirmation of those hypotheses through experimentation. Science, then, is best suited for investigating empirical reality—the physical universe. If one wants to know the structure of the atom, the elements of a star, the processes of biological life, or the physical laws of the universe, one will employ the methods and tools of science. (Most of us would hope that our surgeon's theoretical understanding of the body and of medical techniques is based on the methods of scientific and empirical investigation and not, for example, on logical implications about the body drawn from an ancient scriptural text).

With these basic insights in mind, we may note several limitations of science. First, science is confined methodologically to *natural explanations*. Any aspect of reality not subject to empirical observation is (at some level) not capable of being investigated, described, or explained by the natural sciences. Regarding this first limitation of science, some religious thinkers immediately complain that science should not be

21. Cunningham, Introduction to Christian Philosophy course.
22. Cunningham, Introduction to Christian Philosophy course.

so close-minded, that it should be open to the possibility of nonempirical, nonnatural explanations and theoretical constructs.

But such a position faces at least two difficulties: First, as a method that is grounded in empirical observation, science could in no way confirm or disconfirm a causal connection between an empirical event (or set of events) and some proposed nonempirical, nonnatural (spiritual) entity. For example, suppose someone postulates that the biological imbalances that occur in a cancer cell are caused by a demon. How would one empirically verify such a claim? How would one disconfirm it? Indeed, how would one empirically distinguish between one nonempirical causal explanation and another? Suppose someone theorizes not that a demon caused the cancer but an angel, or an impersonal mana force, or the Great Cancer Causer? Because these explanations lie outside the scope of empirical investigation, they are outside of the scope of scientific explanation and confirmation.[23][24]

A second problem with insisting that science be open to nonnatural explanations is that the history of science points toward the *utility* of searching for causal explanation *within the natural order*. In case after case, events previously thought to have no empirical, natural causal explanation have eventually had convincing natural explanations given and have been confirmed (if not proven) by further empirical testing and observation. This does not *prove* that other puzzling empirical states of affairs will also be explained by natural conditions, but it does give considerable hope that such is the case. Indeed, the search for natural causal explanations serves as a heuristic principle for most scientific efforts. If one too readily gives up the search for natural causes, science as a whole will be unable to function. (Who needs a natural explanation when we already have a spiritual explanation?)

So much, then, for the first limitation of science—namely, that it is confined methodologically to natural explanations. A second limitation of science is that

23. A puzzle arises for scientific methodology at this point: Atoms and evolution cannot be directly observed. But they are *natural* explanations—explanations of natural events through other natural events. But since these events cannot be directly observed, what makes them *better* explanations than nonnatural explanations? What makes them better *except* that they are natural explanations? If this is the only reason they are better, then does not this assumption shows a heuristic and metaphysical *bias* against nonnatural explanations? A possible response here is to assert that the search for natural explanation is a bias, but a warranted bias that is based on the relative *success* of finding natural explanations for natural phenomena. Further, the bias toward natural explanations is a justified bias because such an approach can generate *predictions* of future empirical observations that (in principle) can be *tested*. This is not clearly the case when appeals to *supernatural* explanations are given.

24. Perhaps a caveat is needed here about the notion that nonempirical explanations cannot be confirmed or disconfirmed. As philosopher of religion, John Hick, noted some religious claims in principle are verifiable in the afterlife. If there is life after death, and if certain claims of a religion are observed in that afterlife (whatever that might mean in such a context), then in principle key nonnatural explanations are verifiable. They may simply not be verifiable in this current state of existence. So, we might need to qualify the claim that only natural explanations are confirmable, and claim instead that only natural explanations are confirmable *in this current state of existence*. See Hick, *Philosophy of Religion*, 100–108.

scientific theories are probabilistic and provisional. Scientific generalizations are nearly always subject to further investigation, possible alteration, or even disconfirmation. This is the very nature of inductive reasoning and of the discovery of what David Hume (1711–1776). called matters of fact.[25] A third limitation of science is that it deals with natural, proximate efficient causal tendencies and is not equipped to investigate final (purposive) causal claims. For example, science is not equipped to deal with ultimate explanations, with questions such as Why is there a universe (or multiverse) at all? Or why is there this particular universe (or multiverse) rather than some other? Or what is the ultimate *purpose* of this universe (or multiverse)?[26] Fourth, science is not able to deal with unique, unrepeatable events. Such events might include divine miracles or the emergence of the universe "out of nothing." Science might observe the empirical elements of such events but cannot give confirmable theoretical explanation of them. Science is at its best when dealing with routine patterns or repeatable patterns in the empirical order, or both.

Grant the Established Results of Science

In addition to recognizing the nature and limits of science, Christians should accept the established results of science. While scientific theories are provisional and probabilistic, they very often are grounded on considerable empirical evidence and experimentation. As evidence mounts, as implications of a theory are experimentally confirmed, and as alternative explanations are disconfirmed, the likelihood of a theoretical explanation grows, often to the point that the theory becomes virtually undeniable, a practical fact. In such cases, to doubt the theory requires a kind of skepticism that one is unwilling to exercise in other areas of life.

Examples of virtually undeniable theories are contemporary scientific views about the size and age of the universe, the continuity in the chain of biological life, the age of *Homo sapiens*, the basic nature of the atom, and the close connection between the brain and various mental and emotional states. In principle, Christians need not be threatened by descriptions of natural events or by natural explanations of various physical states of affairs, especially when these descriptions and explanations are grounded in careful observation and experimentation. Christians can acknowledge that any truth about the physical world is a truth grounded in the God who created the physical world.

25. Hume, *An Enquiry Concerning Human Understanding*, 15–20.

26. Related to this third limitation is the further point that science is not equipped to answer questions of ultimate value or ethics. In this sense, science cannot even answer the question of whether science is a valuable endeavor or whether humans should engage in scientific research. To make a case that science is valuable, one must step outside the purview of science *per se* and enter the domain of philosophical or theological discourse or both.

Challenge the Excessive Claims of Science

Even though Christians should grant the established results of science, they also should challenge the excessive claims that sometimes are made in the name of science. When the scientist moves from discussing theories of causal connections within the physical world or from discussing observed events in nature to speculations about the implications of those theories and observations for metaphysics or religion, the Christian must insist on evaluating such speculation as philosophy (and theology) rather than as science. For example, sometimes scientists assume a naturalistic metaphysic to match their empirical epistemology. That is, they assume that since only events empirically observable are subject to scientific methodology, therefore only empirical events are real, valuable, or both. When this occurs, the scientist (or the person speaking in the name of science) has moved from science to philosophical speculation. Science can no more verify a naturalistic metaphysic than it can confirm or disconfirm a supernatural metaphysic. At best, a naturalist metaphysic can serve as a working but unverifiable assumption. But such an assumption is subject to philosophical critique.

The Christian should caution the scientist not to abuse his or her authority. Because of the prestige of science, it is tempting for scientists to attempt to transfer their authority within their own disciplines to large-scale religious and metaphysical declarations. Part of the reason that scientists might overstep their authority and move to philosophical speculation is that many scientists are never trained in the philosophy of science proper. Often science students are introduced to the mechanics of their particular scientific research without evaluating the difficulties of such a perspective. In short, scientists often tacitly and uncritically embrace philosophical naturalism, without evaluating the difficulties of such an embrace.

Religious thinkers as much as scientists can make excessive claims; religious thinkers may, for example, overstate the utility of science for religion. Some Christians claim, for instance, that science confirms some religious truths—including, say, that there must be a Creator, or that the universe must have a transcendent Designer. Because such claims deal with alleged nonempirical causes, science cannot verify or disconfirm such supernatural claims. At best, science can conclude that no scientific explanation can be given for the universe as a whole or for the particular structures of the known universe. Further, science cannot confirm that there is such an explanation or the nature of that Explanation.

Conclusion regarding Science in a Christian Worldview

In attempting to integrate science and a Christian worldview, several insights should be kept in mind. First, science need not lead believers away from Christianity or away from religion in general. Its methods cannot confirm or disconfirm central claims of the Christian faith—for example, claims about the ultimate supernatural origin, purpose, and value of the universe and of human life. However, science can give Christians (who already believe in God for diverse reasons) a fuller understanding of the workings of the natural order, which in turn may yield deeper insight into the splendor, glory, and wisdom of the God whom Christians believe has created that order. (That is, science does not verify that God exists, but it may aid the religious believer in developing a profounder discernment of religious affirmations.) Further, given science's limitations, particularly its inability to deal with ultimate explanations and purposes, religious faith may continue to aid to the human quest for meaning and ultimate explanations.

The Place of Christianity in a Scientific World

While granting the legitimacy of science as a way of understanding the physical universe, the Christian equally must insist upon the essential role of Christianity in generating a comprehensive understanding of reality and in constructing a broader worldview within which to understand scientific knowledge itself. For the sake of analysis, we may distinguish two important steps in the process of constructing a comprehensive Christian worldview. First, we should acknowledge and attempt to articulate the unique sphere of knowledge that is available in Christianity due to its reception of divine revelation. Second, we may attempt to discern and express the implication of these revelatory insights for a comprehensive worldview—a worldview that includes the truths found in science. Let us consider each of these in turn.

The Unique Sphere of Christian Knowledge

Christians need to recognize and to express the unique insights about reality made available to them within Christianity through divine revelation. First, the chief concern and unique insights of Christianity revolve around the ultimate concerns of human existence. These concerns include questions about the meaning and purpose of human life and the universe, specifically as human life and the universe relate to the purposes of God as Creator and Redeemer. (In other words, based on divine revelation, Christians maintain that the meaning and purpose of the universe and of human existence is to be found in God and the divine purposes.) While such insights may often involve a scientific understanding of physical things, they involve much more. Such insights address questions with answers inaccessible to science, such as these: What is the ultimate origin and destiny of the universe and of human life? What ought we to do? What is of genuine value? Christianity is primarily concerned not with the nature of the atom but with who made the atom, not with how long humans have lived on this planet or with the process of human development, but with who made humans beings and what we are made for.[27]

Second, Christianity holds that answers to these ultimate questions cannot come entirely from within the natural order or through an examination of natural processes. While one might catch fleeting glimpses of ultimate truth through reason or scientific investigation, such sources are not enough to unravel the fundamental mystery of life and existence. Instead, the basic clues to the mystery of existence come from a transcendent source—that is, divine revelation. Christianity gets explanatory clues to existence from revelation, which in turn becomes the interpretive key for constructing a holistic and comprehensive understanding of the purpose of everything within the universe. Only through revelation can persons get clear insight into the nature of God (as Creator and Redeemer), the purpose of the natural order and of human life, and how to know and relate to the Creator and Redeemer God.

Third, believers can assert that Christianity's insights about ultimate questions are primarily personal truths that can be known and incorporated into life only as part of a personal relationship with the living God. These insights cannot be received simply by affirming objective, factual scientific, philosophical, or even theological statements about reality. The reception of these insights about ultimate questions is essentially bound up with God's personal self-disclosure in Jesus Christ. Ultimately, to understanding the meaning and purpose of the universe, of human life in general, and of one's own life requires that one enter into a personal, trusting relationship with Jesus Christ as Lord.

A Comprehensive Christian Worldview

Based on insights gleaned from divine revelation and from a personal encounter with God through Christ, Christians attempt to rationally develop a comprehensive worldview, including a rational understanding of Christianity itself. The Protestant tradition has largely maintained that Christians must begin with faith as trust in and commitment to God through Christ, but that from this faith stance believers go on to seek understanding through reason. Christians seek to understand the Christian faith, which includes a comprehensive understanding of reality. Opening up such understanding is the task of Christian theology. Obviously, any rational comprehension of the Christian faith today will include an attempt to understand that faith as it relates to modern science.

---

27. These distinctions of explanation need not be conceived as contradictory or as excluding one another. Each focuses on aspects of *reality as a whole*. Ultimately, in the Christian perspective, God likewise ordained the nature of the atom, the processes (and length) of biological and cosmic development, and so forth. Science is well equipped to study these patterns and processes, but not well suited to address the meanings or ultimate purposes of such phenomena.

Such an endeavor calls for understanding Christian theology and natural science as dialectically related. First, theology and science should be seen as somewhat independent, each having primary authority in a different area of experience. Science is best able to investigate and understand natural processes. Christian theology is best able to deal with ultimate questions, based upon the self-disclosure of God in the history of the Hebrews and in Jesus Christ. Second, theology and science should be seen as playing complementary roles, each providing needed insights to the other. On the one hand, Christian theology cannot explicate a comprehensive worldview without taking into account the findings of science. Especially, Christianity cannot articulate an understanding of the created order without taking into consideration the findings of science. The theologian may maintain that all truths about the natural universe are truths established by (or allowed by) its Creator, God. On the other hand, while science can perform its task of explaining and describing natural processes theoretically (without reference to the Christian faith), it cannot satisfy the human quest for answers to ultimate questions. Here the Christian faith sets science within the context of ultimate meaning, purpose, and value. That is, natural processes only have ultimate meaning in the context of the broader perspective of the Christian faith.

Science and Biblical Revelation

One of the key areas in which science has impacted Christian theology is in the theology's understanding of nature and of biblical revelation. Given that science seems to contradict traditional understandings of the nature of nature, various Christian thinkers have reevaluated precisely how they understand nature, and how they understand biblical revelation.

Nature in Contemporary Science and in the Bible

It is well known that tension exists between the biblical picture of the universe and the current scientific understanding. These differences show up in a number of areas. We will discuss two of them: (1) contrasts between the biblical picture and the scientific picture of the age and physical development of the universe, and (2) contrasts between the biblical explanation and the scientific explanation of physiopsychology.

Contrast concerning the Age and Development of Universe

First, we note differences in how science and the Bible conceive of the age and development of the universe. Current scientific cosmology (the study of the universe), particularly the *big bang theory*, contends that the universe is about ten to fifteen billion years old, developing to its current state over many millennia. Further, current geology holds that the earth is about four billion years old, with the emergence of life occurring about three to three and a half billion years ago, and the development of various species upon the earth occurring over the last three billion years.

With these theories and their supporting evidence has come a general scientific understanding of the chronological ordering of cosmic events. Evidence suggests that the universe emerged from a huge cosmic explosion that spewed atomic particles out into an expanding time-space nexus. As these particles cooled, atoms formed and eventually coagulated into vast systems of swirling gases, which eventually formed stars, and eventually solar systems, and eventually various forms of life on this planet—life that developed from relatively simple biological systems to progressively more complex systems over billions of years.

When compared with the biblical accounts of creation (especially with Gen 1), the scientific interpretation is quite different. When Gen 1 is read as a straightforward historical and chronological description of creation, it leaves the impression that the universe, earth, and life upon the earth were created over a relatively short period of time (six days). Further the biblical narrative (particularly Gen 1) suggests a rather different chronological order of development than does the big bang theory. For example, according to Gen 1, the earth and vegetation upon the earth were created before the sun, moon, and stars. (Compare Gen 1:2, 3 with Gen 1:14–19.) Such a notion hardly fits contemporary scientific cosmology.

As we have seen, various Christian attempts have been made to reconcile the biblical and scientific views. Some endeavor to interpret the biblical perspective so that it more or less fits with the main teachings of science. The day-age theory and the gap theory are examples of such attempts. Other Christians strive to interpret the scientific evidence so that it somehow confirms the cosmic age and development implied in a straightforward reading of the biblical narrative. Therefore, some endorse scientific creationism, which alleges that the scientific data support a creation in six literal, twenty-four-hour days. We have already noted difficulties with these approaches. The first two tend not to do justice to an historical-grammatical reading of the biblical text. The third approach seems to play loose and fast with the scientific evidence.

Contrasts in Cosmic Topologies

In addition to differences in assumptions about the age and development of the universe, the Bible and contemporary science also differ in how each conceptualizes the cosmic topology.[28] According to contemporary science, when an earthbound observer looks into the night sky, she sees the light of stars whose distance from the earth boggles the imagination; in many cases she sees light that is millions or even billions of years old. Contrary to appearance, the earth is not flat, nor is it at rest. Rather, it is a globe, hurling through space. Further, the sun does not revolve

28. Topology, here, has to do with spatial relationships—in this case, the spatial relationship of celestial bodies to one another and to the earth.

around the earth; rather the earth revolves around the sun. The earth also rotates on its axis, completing a rotation about every twenty-four hours, thus exposing different portions of its surface to the sun throughout the day. Beneath the outer crust of the sphere of the earth are layers of matter that grow denser and hotter toward the center of the sphere. The sky above the earthly observer is an atmosphere of gases that cling to the outer surface of the earth's sphere, held there by gravity. Rain results when the sun evaporates water, causing the water to rise into the atmosphere and eventually to condense and fall back to the earth's surface. The earth and the planets orbiting the sun are simply one of an incredibly large number of similar star systems trapped in an immense orbit around the center of a galactic star system. And the galaxy itself is a member of a cluster of galaxies that orbits around a common center. The earth is not the center of the universe. It is midway out in one of the arms (so to speak) of the Milky Way galaxy and is moving constantly in its orbit around the sun, which in turn is orbiting the center of Milky Way galaxy, which is orbiting the center of a galaxy cluster—and all of these orbits are moving away from one another.

This scientific cosmic topology is considerably different from the cosmic topology implied in Scripture. Admittedly, the Bible does not express a formal cosmic geography. However, a basic topology can be inferred from various passages throughout the literature. For Old Testament writers, when an earthbound observer peers into the sky, she sees something quite different from what is theorized (and often observed) in modern science. She interprets[29] what she sees to be a huge dome (the firmament), which encloses the "atmosphere" of the earth, and which holds back a vast ocean of water above it. She believes that occasionally windows are opened in the dome to let down rain. Also, somewhere in the dome are storehouses for snow and hail. Under the dome, the sun, moon, and stars navigate their courses from horizon to horizon. Between the dome and the earth, the animals, plants, and humans live. The earth itself is stationary and more or less flat. Below the earth is yet more water, a subterranean ocean. Also, below the earth is Sheol, the land of darkness, the land of the dead. The earth is founded on pillars that sink down into the cosmic ocean below. Somewhere above the dome-sky and above the cosmic waters is the abode of God. Although not identical, the cosmic topology implied in the New Testament is quite similar.[30]

When pieced together, several biblical passages point to a view something like the one stated above. Here are a several examples from the Hebrew Bible and a few from the New Testament.

---

29. At one level, the ancient biblical writers saw the same things contemporary observers see when peering into the sky; that is, the phenomenal experience of ancient and modern observers was more or less the same. But how each interprets such phenomena is quite different. Each interprets the phenomenal data differently due to his or her own theoretical frames of reference, so in a sense what the ancient observers saw (or how they interpreted what they saw) involved what some call "theory-laden" facts. That is, the perceiver's observations were/are (often unconsciously) interpreted within the framework of a broader theory about the nature of reality.

30. Indeed, this basic cosmic topology was assumed by most cultures of the ancient Near East.

From the Old Testament

Genesis 1:6–8

God made the expanse, and separated the waters which were below the expanse from the waters which were above the expanse; and it was so. God called the expanse heaven. (NASB)

Here God makes the sky or the heavens—a firmament or expanse—that divides the cosmic waters above it from those below it.

Genesis 7:11

In the six hundredth year of Noah's life, on the seventeenth day of the second month—on that day all the springs of the great deep burst forth, and the flood gates of the heavens were opened. (NIV)

This passage suggests that the oceans of the earth's surface are fed by hidden springs from "the great deep"—that is, from the vast cosmic ocean below the earth. Also, the "floodgates" (or windows) of the heavenly dome open to let in rain.

Exodus 20:4

You shall not make for yourself an image in the form of anything in heaven above or on the earth beneath or in the waters below. (NIV)

Here we see assumed three-storied universe.

Job 37:18

"Can you, with Him, spread out the skies, strong as a molten mirror?" (NASB)

Here is the notion that the sky is a solid metal structure.

Job 38:4–23

Where were you when I laid the foundation of the earth? / Tell me if you have understanding. / . . ./ On what were its bases sunk, / or who laid its cornerstone /. . . /? // . . . // Have you entered into the springs of the sea, / or walked in the recesses of the deep? / Have the gates of death been revealed to you, / or have you seen the gates of deep darkness? . . . // . . . // Have you entered the storehouses of the snow, / or have you seen the storehouses of the hail, / which I have reserved for the time of trouble? (RSV)

Here, in admittedly poetic language, a picture is suggested of an earth on solid foundations, of a sea that is fed by springs and whose ebb and flow is controlled by "doors." We also see "gates of death" and of "deep darkness," terms used in other passages to speak of Sheol—the place of death, the place of darkness where the dead reside. We also read of storehouses for the snow and for hail.

Psalm 24:1–2

The earth is the LORD's and the fulness thereof, / the world and those who dwell therein; / for he has founded it upon the seas, / and established it upon the rivers. (RSV)

Here it suggests that the earth rests on foundations that sink down into a cosmic sea.

Psalm 75:3

When the earth totters, and all its inhabitants, / it is I who keep steady its pillars. (RSV)

Here the idea is that the earth rests on pillars.

Psalm 104:1–3, 5

"Bless the LORD, O my soul! / LORD my God, You are very great; / You are clothed with splendor and majesty, Covering Yourself with light as with a cloak, / Stretching out heaven like a tent curtain. / He lays the beams of His upper chambers in the waters / . . . / He establishes the earth upon its foundations, / So that it will not totter forever and ever. (NASB)

The heavens are like a tent: this possibly suggests that the heavens keep out something above them. God's high chambers are founded upon the waters: this suggests that God lives above the cosmic ocean, which is itself above the sky. And again, the earth rests on foundations.

Psalm 148:4

Praise Him, highest heavens, / And the waters that are above the heavens. (NASB)

This verse presents a picture of water above the earth, similar to the picture in Gen 1.

Proverbs 8:22–31

> The LORD created me [wisdom] at the beginning of his work, / the first of his
> acts of old /. . ./ When he established the heavens, I was there, / when he drew
> a circle on the face of the deep, / when he made firm the skies above, / when
> he established the fountains of the deep, / when he assigned to the sea its limit,
> / so that the waters might not transgress his command, / when he marked out
> the foundations of the earth, / then I was beside him, like a master workman, /
> and I was daily his delight, / rejoicing before him always. (RSV; brackets added)

Here we have what some call a third biblical creation account. Here wisdom is personified and said to be present with God as the deity creates. God makes the sky firm,
suggesting a solid physical structure. God establishes or makes strong the fountains of
the deep. God makes a circle on the deep—an expression used to speak of the horizon.
(An observer looks all "around" and sees the horizon—suggesting that the earth is a flat
disc). And again, God sets limits on the sea so that it will not inundate the earth.

Isaiah 24:18b

In a prophetic warning of divine judgment, the writer warns

> For the windows of heaven are opened, / and the foundations of the earth
> tremble. (NRSV)

The heavens (sky) have windows (apparently through which rain falls), and the earth
has foundations.

Isaiah 40:22

> It is he [God] who sits above the circle of the earth, / and its inhabitants are
> like grasshoppers; / who stretches out the heavens like a curtain, / and spreads
> them like a tent to dwell in. (NRSV)

Although some conservatives have seen this verse as endorsing a spherical earth, most
Bible scholars recognize that the verse also fits well with an image of the earth as a flat
disc covered by a huge tent-like covering.

Amos 9:2

In a prophetic warning, Amos credits God as saying, "Though they dig into Sheol, /
from there shall my hand take them; / though they climb up to heaven, / from there
I will bring them down." One can dig down into the ground to reach Sheol, the land
of the dead.

From the New Testament

While the New Testament cosmic topology is somewhat different than that of the Old Testament, much is similar.

Matthew 11:23

> Jesus says: "And you, Capernaum, will you be exalted to heaven? No, you shall be brought down to Hades." (NRSV)

Hades is described as being "down" or low in a way similar to heaven being up or high.

Luke 16:23

> "In Hades, where he was being tormented, he looked up and saw Abraham far away with Lazarus by his side." (NRSV)

In Hades, one looks *up* to see those in a better place.

Philippians 2:10

> so that at the name of Jesus
>
> every knee should bend,
>
> in heaven and on earth and under the earth. (NRSV)

Here a three-level universe is assumed, with beings in the heavens above, on the earth, and under the earth.

Revelation 5:13

> Then I heard every creature in heaven and on earth and under the earth and in the sea, and all that is in them, singing, "To the one seated on the throne and to the Lamb be blessing and honor and glory and might forever and ever!" (NSRV)

Again, as a description of the whole cosmos, a three-level universe is assumed.

The assumption of a three-tiered universe in these many verses is enhanced when one notes that similar cosmic topologies were expressed in other ancient Near Eastern cultures, including Babylonian, Mesopotamian, Egyptian, and Greek cosmologies. Biblical scholars point out that while the scriptural writers greatly demythologized their account of the divine creation, they still adopted the basic topology assumed in the cultures around them.

Contrasts in Physiopsychology

In addition to difference between biblical and contemporary scientific understandings of the age, development, and topologies of the universe, contemporary science and the Bible also contrast in how they understand the relationship between human physiology and psychology. As Bernard Ramm noted long ago, "The psychological terms of the Bible are terms of ancient cultures and not the terms of strict scientific psychology. The Bible uses such terms as heart, liver, bones, bowels, and kidneys in its psychology, attributing psychic functions to these organs."[31] The Bible associates belief with the heart (Rom 10:9–10), emotional distress with the liver (Lam 2:11), love with the bowels (Phil 1:8), and mental life with the kidneys (Jer 11:20, Rev 2:23) Contemporary science does not associate such psychological activities with these organs, but with the brain and the nervous system as a whole.

General Conclusion regarding Contrasts

There are considerable differences between the contemporary scientific view of nature and the biblical view of the same.

Science and the Reliability of Biblical Revelation

The tension between contemporary science's view of nature and the biblical view(s) of nature may require a careful assessment of how contemporary Christians are to conceptualize biblical revelation. Christian theology has traditionally maintained that the Bible is inspired by God. That is, the writings of Scripture, in some sense, are the result of divine influence upon the human authors. The precise nature of this influence is subject to dispute. Several theories have emerged that attempt to spell out the basic nature of this divine guidance.[32] Nevertheless, how one interprets the mechanics of biblical inspiration perhaps is less important for our discussion here than how one understands the impact of that inspiration upon the claims and teachings of Scripture.

A central puzzle that science raises about biblical inspiration and revelation has to do with how an interpreter conceptualizes the *reliability* of biblical teachings. Are the teachings of the Bible reliable? Reliability is related to *truth*. A document is reliable if it conveys truth. But reliability also has to do with *intended usage*. A phone book may be

31. Ramm, *The Christian View of Science and Scripture*, 73. Again it should be noted that the biblical writers' views on these matters were not unique. Similar understandings of physiopsychology persisted within other ancient Near Eastern cultures.

32. See Chapter 3 (above) for discussions of biblical revelation and inspiration.

a reliable guide for getting phone numbers but not at all reliable for gaining knowledge of chemistry or astronomy or religion. It is reliable within the parameters of its intended usage. By analogy, the Bible may be reliable to the degree that it conveys truth in the area of its intended usage, but it may not be reliable for conveying information in some area outside of its intended use.[33] For example, the Bible may be an excellent source for learning of God's love for humans but not at all reliable for understanding the elements of the periodic table or for constructing techniques for dentistry.

Reliability also is a *matter of degree*. A phone book is more or less reliable. It is completely reliable if it always conveys truth in the area of its intended use—that is, if it always gets the right name with the right number. It is generally reliable if it usually conveys truth in the area of its intended use—that is, if it usually gets the right name with the right number. Closely related to degree of reliability is the notion of *sufficient reliability*. Whether a document is sufficiently reliable often is a matter of social context. A phone book may be considered sufficiently reliable even if it is not completely reliable—for example, if it accurately matches 95 percent of its names and its numbers. But the same percentage of accuracy may not be sufficient in other contexts.

Full Reliability Theory

Taking these various elements of the notion of reliability into consideration, two basic theories concerning the reliability of Scripture emerge. The first theory is that *everything that the Bible teaches (and implies) is true*.[34] We might call this the *full-reliability* theory. This view holds that the Bible is completely reliable in all the matters with which it deals, including science. Presumably, at least often, adherents of this perspective believe that only complete reliability is sufficient reliability. According to this interpretation, genuine science and the Bible cannot contradict each other.

33. A similar issue arises when considering the usage of differing literary genres in the Bible. If one finds a parable (Luke 15:1–32) or a fable (Judg 9:7–21) in the Scriptures, one will err if she insists that these narratives must be understood as descriptions of historical events.

34. This discussion of the reliability of the Bible regarding its "scientific" claims or teachings is part of a broader dialogue about the general reliability of scriptural teachings. Often among Evangelical writers, this conversation is discussed under the nomenclature of the *doctrine of inerrancy*. Analysis of these matters is complex and voluminous. My intention here is not to entertain these broad issues but to focus primarily on the reliability of scripture in its teachings (or tacit assumptions) about some aspects of the universe's physical origins, development, and topology. Note that above I have parenthetically added the phrase "and implies" to the definition of the theory of full reliability. The point is that sometimes a scriptural text (and thus the scripture writer) may imply some claim without necessarily intending to teach it. This may well be the case with many biblical passages that seem to assume a cosmic topology such as a dome holding back heavenly waters, or pillars holding up the land, or Sheol below one's feet. These last three claims may well not be the primary point the writer is wanting to *teach* or *assert*. Nevertheless, these propositions are entailed in the overall claim being made (by the writing or the writer) and, thus, in some sense, they are being *taught* by the passage in question. For a bit more on the doctrine of inerrancy, see Chapter 3. Also, on the matter of authorial intention, see further comments below.

Sometimes when scientific and biblical claims clash, the scientific claims need to be reinterpreted or reevaluated to better fit the biblical perspective. At other times when scientific and biblical claims clash, traditional *interpretations* of biblical claims need to be re-interpreted or reevaluated to better fit the scientific perspective. But in either case, *when rightly interpreted*, genuine science and genuine biblical teaching cannot contradict each other. This approach to scriptural reliability also insists that diverse religious (and moral) claims within the Bible cannot genuinely contradict one another. When apparent religious (or moral) discrepancies emerge in the Bible, some process of harmonization must be utilized.

The perspective described in the paragraph above is essentially what many Evangelical scholars refer to as the doctrine of *full inerrancy*. Millard Erickson defines this perspective as teaching that "the Bible, when correctly interpreted in light of the level to which culture and the means of communication had developed at the time it was written, and in view of purpose for which it was given, is fully truthful in all that it affirms."[35] David Dockery offers a similar definition of this viewpoint, calling it the *balanced inerrancy* model; he states that this version of biblical inerrancy holds

> that when all the facts are known, the Bible (in its autographs, that is, the original documents), properly interpreted in light of the culture and means of communication that had developed by the time of its composition, is completely true in all that it affirms, to the degree of precision intended by the author's purpose, in all matters relating to God and His creation.[36]

Dockery adds that such a view of inerrancy "regards scientific matters as phenomenal; that is, they are often reported as they appear to the human writer, which perhaps may be different from the way they really are."[37] In turn, this view "regards the historical matters [addressed in the Bible] as accurate, though sometimes in a very general way."[38]

The doctrine of biblical inerrancy takes varied forms, with some versions more nuanced than others. Both Erickson and Dockery distinguish their perspectives from what they refer to as the doctrine of absolute inerrancy.[39] According to these authors, the doctrine of *absolute inerrancy* inappropriately assumes that the Bible gives relatively precise and detailed information about scientific and historical data, a

---

35. See Erickson, *Christian Theology*, 201–2.

36. Dockery, *The Doctrine of the Bible*, 80. Dockery refers to this as *balanced inerrancy* (Dockery, *The Doctrine of the Bible*, 86).

37. Dockery, *The Doctrine of the Bible*, 86.

38. Dockery, *The Doctrine of the Bible*, 86 (brackets added).

39. Indeed, Dockery makes a further distinction, differentiating between what he dubs absolute inerrancy and naive inerrancy. Dockery, *The Doctrine of the Bible*. Erickson and Dockery credit the absolutist inerrancy view to Harold Lindsell. See Lindsell, *The Battle for the Bible*.

maneuver that (in the view of Erickson and Dockery) imposes an exactness of detail not *intended* by the biblical writers.[40]

For many proponents of the doctrine of full inerrancy (or what I am calling the theory of full reliability), to correctly interpret biblical texts, it is crucial to rightly discern the *intentions* of the biblical writers. To dismiss or misunderstand those intentions typically generates faulty understandings of the authors' writings and (consequently) produces inaccurate assessments of the truthfulness of their claims. Obviously, the task of discerning a writer's intentions is challenging. It involves considering the writer's general and specific historical context. What were the common beliefs about reality and morality of the author's community and era? What were the typical standards for acquiring and assessing knowledge? What were the general conventions regarding composing and interpreting literature, including the varied uses of literary genres? Beyond these general contextual matters, what were the explicit or implicit motives, goals, and intentions of the authors themselves when writing their documents? All of these considerations (and more) enter into rightly discerning what a given author is attempting to communicate. And only when such factors are considered is an interpreter able to discern (1) what the author is asserting or teaching (or even whether the author is asserting anything at all) and (2) whether those assertions are incompatible with propositions now known (or at least believed) through contemporary scientific investigations.

Evangelical scholar and inerrantist Kevin Vanhoozer defends the need to accurately discern authorial intent and offers a rather nuanced version of the theory of *full inerrancy* (*full reliability*). Vanhoozer insists that interpreters must distinguish between the meaning of a sentence per se (one arbitrarily abstracted from its use by an author) and the meaning of the sentence (or set of sentences) *as intended by and employed by* an author. Vanhoozer writes:

> To assert something—to say what is the case—is a thing people do by using words. There is a difference between "sentence meaning" and "speaker meaning." It is therefore not enough to speak about the *semantics* of biblical literature (its propositional content, sentence meaning); we must also account for the *pragmatics* (kinds of communicative action, speech act meaning). This distinction is particularly important when we try to determine what precisely the authors are affirming (when they are affirming). Well-versed inerrancy here comes into its own by calling attention to Scripture as composed of various kinds of discourse and to the necessity of asking, *what is the author doing in his discourse, and what is the discourse about?*[41]

In light of this, Vanhoozer insists that interpreters must read the biblical text(s) with literary acumen and not with wooden literalism. According to Vanhoozer, the

---

40. Erickson, *Christian Theology*, 191; Dockery, *The Doctrine of the Bible*, 86.

41. Vanhoozer, "Augustinian Inerrancy," 218–19 (italics original).

interpreter "must take great care to distinguish the notion of literal truth from a literalism that runs roughshod over the intent of the author and the literary form of the text."[42] Defining *literalism* as "the view that equates *what is said* (that is, meaning) with *semantic content* (that is, the proposition semantically expressed by the sentence regardless of context),"[43] Vanhoozer insists that interpreters of the Bible "must specify the *author's communicative intent* in order rightly to say what he is *doing* with his words."[44] Discerning authorial intent is critical to a literate or well-versed reading of the text, which is what Vanhoozer means by the concept of "literal truth" in the quote above. All of this requires looking for clues in the text for the author's intentions; it also calls for being aware of the common literary, cultural, and intellectual conventions of the author's historical context.[45]

Many of Vanhoozer's insights—though true and well expressed by him—are not unique to him. They are expressions of common principles in biblical interpretation. Arguably, what sets apart Vanhoozer's insistence upon rightly discerning literary, authorial meaning are the ramifications he sees in this maxim for challenging allegations that the Bible is in error regarding various assertions, including some claims about the physical world.

While Vanhoozer does not directly say so, he seems to assume that appeal to authorial intent (as the source of the meaning of biblical assertions) helps defuse allegations that the biblical writers committed errors when (for example) they wrote of God creating a domed sky (firmament) or about pillars that uphold the earth or of windows that let down rain, and so forth. Apparently, for Vanhoozer (and other inerrantists), accusations of error are dismissible because in fact the biblical writers did not *intend* to affirm many of these assertions about cosmic topology. Rather, their *intention* was to affirm that God created the world. But since in their cultural context the universe was conceived of as having these topological characteristics, the biblical authors naturally but (perhaps) unintentionally used conceptual tools typically employed in their era to speak of such things. In short, the aim of the biblical writers was *not* to describe the nature of the physical world per se but only to declare that God made that world (whatever its characteristics).

Again, I must reiterate that Vanhoozer does not explicitly apply his emphasis on authorial intention to matters of cosmic beginnings or topography, but I think it is implicit in his reasoning, and I suspect it is (ironically) part of *his intention*. Vanhoozer specifically illustrates his point by appealing to Jesus' well-known analogy of a mustard seed being like God's kingdom. In Mark 4:30–32, Jesus says:

42. Vanhoozer, "Augustinian Inerrancy," 218–19.

43. Vanhoozer, "Augustinian Inerrancy," 218–19 (italics original).

44. Vanhoozer, "Augustinian Inerrancy," 219–20 (italics original).

45. Erickson and Dockery offer similar cautions about rightly interpreting the ancient texts. Each speaks of the interpreter's need for awareness of the biblical authors' cultural context, means of communication, and purpose in writing. See quotes above.

> With what can we compare the kingdom of God, or what parable will we use for it? It is like a mustard seed, which, when sown upon the ground, is the smallest of all the seeds on earth; yet when it is sown it grows up and becomes the greatest of all shrubs, and puts forth large branches, so that the birds of the air can make nests in its shade.

Here, Jesus memorably compares the kingdom of God to a mustard seed. Jesus' point seems to be that even though God's kingdom begins as a tiny movement, it can grow to be great, in a way similar to a mustard seed (which is small) that can grow to be a great shrub.

A problem sometimes noted by critics of inerrancy about Jesus' wording is that it seems to entail the (false) assertion that the mustard seed "is the smallest of all the seeds," a claim that is biologically incorrect. Vanhoozer, however, quickly denounces any notion that Jesus (or the Gospel's author) committed an error; and this is so, not because mustard seeds in fact are the smallest seeds, but because the biblical author or Jesus (or both) never *intended* to teach this. Vanhoozer writes:

> Jesus was not *affirming* as scientific fact the proposition semantically expressed by his sentence. The subject matter of Jesus' authoritative teaching was not mustard seeds but the kingdom of God, and he was communicating truth about the kingdom in terms his audience could understand. Jesus was not making a *literalistic* truth claim (about mustard seeds), but he was speaking the *literal* truth (about the kingdom). This is no game of semantic smoke and mirrors; it is the way linguistic communication works.[46]

Vanhoozer's reasoning above can be applied to the discussion of cosmic topology as follows: even though the claims of the ancient biblical authors *semantically* entail assertions about physical topology that are false, this does not mean that the biblical authors *committed errors* about such matters, because they did not *intend* to teach/affirm such entailments.[47]

Vanhoozer's perspective helps set him apart from some inerrantists who assume that the ancient biblical writers did intend to express truths about the physical cosmos

---

46. Vanhoozer, "Augustinian Inerrancy," 221 (italics original).

47. This interpretation of how Vanhoozer might defend the doctrine of inerrancy and appease the tensions between biblical and contemporary descriptions of the universe is reinforced by the following illustration offered by him. Vanhoozer writes: "Something counts as an 'error' only if it fails to make good on its own claim. It is wrong to say that a map (or a text) is an error for not doing something it does not set out to do. Readers should judge a text by its own standards of correctness and precision only. Error is a context-dependent notion. What might count as an error in the context of scientific historiography (or natural sciences) might not count as an error in the context of less exacting, 'ordinary' forms of discourse" (Vanhoozer, "Augustinian Inerrancy," 210, n33). For example, consider the purposes of a road map versus a topographical map. It would be odd to say the road map was in error for not depicting details about the topography of the earth's surface, since that is not what the map purports to do. In a similar manner, it would be inappropriate to expect biblical writers to accurately address issues that they did not intend to address.

and its development, including claims that run counter to contemporary science's (allegedly false) teachings about such matters. According to Vanhoozer, often such well-meaning attempts to defend biblical inerrancy fail to engage in a sufficiently literate exegesis and thus fail to discern the genuine intent of the biblical writers.[48]

Vanhoozer's argumentation above goes a long way toward resolving many puzzles about seemingly erroneous claims in Scripture and thus helps uphold the doctrine of full reliability (full inerrancy). Taking Vanhoozer's position may allow a contemporary interpreter to insist that when an ancient author tacitly assumed a three-tiered universe, that biblical writer was not consciously or intentionally *denying* core beliefs now established by contemporary science. The author was not denying that the universe is billions of years old, or that the sun is millions of miles from the earth, or that the earth rotates on its axis exposing its surface to the sun's radiation, or even that the universe was not created in six twenty-four hour periods. The biblical author was not *denying* these claims because he or she was unaware (or did not consider) that such states of affairs might be the case, or that the truth of such claims could be established on strong empirical evidence. (That is, the ancient writer did not think in the same way that a contemporary scientist steeped in modern conventions about knowledge acquisition).

Further, the biblical author was not *intentionally affirming* that belief in a three-tiered universe *is grounded in evidence* gained through scientific investigation. Instead, the author (likely) was affirming a presumed truth grounded (if at all) on common beliefs of the day or (perhaps, at some level) inferred from phenomenological observations. In short, the ancient author was not attempting to address modern concerns about *evidentially* grounded claims about the natural world.

Even after all this, it is not abundantly clear that Vanhoozer's argumentation satisfies the overarching concerns of critics (including advocates of the *partial-reliability model* of scriptural inerrancy discussed below). Even granting Vanhoozer's important insights about discerning authorial intent, opponents of the full-reliability model of scriptural inerrancy may still question whether his appeal adequately resolves the problems arising from tension between biblical claims and scientific claims. Even if one grants that the *primary* concern of the biblical writers in Genesis (and elsewhere) was to make claims about God's creative power and acts, it does not follow that such authors did not also intend (at some level) to say something about the nature of the physical world. Given their ancient context, the biblical authors were not technically attempting to do science or make scientific claims. Further,

---

48. Vanhoozer, "Augustinian Inerrancy," 222. Other advocates of full inerrancy offer similar critiques of what they deem to be naïve or simplistic inerrantists' interpretations. Erickson and Dockery criticize what they call *absolute inerrancy*, which is a view quite similar to their own view, but which (unlike their perspective) often assume the Bible gives precise and detailed information about scientific and historical data. See Erickson, *Christian Theology*, 191; and Dockery, *The Doctrine of the Bible*, 86. Erickson and Dockery credit Harold Lindsell with the absolutist inerrancy model. See Harold Lindsell, *The Battle for the Bible*.

these author's styles of thinking and of writing almost certainly were not steeped in the conventions typically assumed in the modern era. Still, it is not abundantly clear that such writers *did not intend* to say something (in their own contexts) about the nature of the physical world (as they understood it).

To determine what the authors were intending (if even it is possible) would require careful exegetical examination of the immediate literary context of the sentences in question as well as consideration of ancient literary and intellectual conventions. But even then, it is not clear that contemporary interpreters can accurately determine, with any significant degree of certainty, that the author *did not intend* to say something about the physical world in the process of making theological claims. The burden of proof lies on Vanhoozer to demonstrate that it was not the intention of the author of Gen 1 or 2 to make claims, for example, about the nature of the physical world. More to the point, critics of the full reliability for or the full inerrancy in Scripture may wonder whether Vanhoozer's (implicit) assertion that the ancient writers did not intend to say something about the nature of the physical world is grounded more upon his commitment to the full inerrancy of or full reliability of Scripture and less on careful exegesis of the texts in question or on a thorough study of how ancient literary genres were used.[49]

Partial Reliability

A second theory concerning the reliability of Scripture holds that *part of what the Bible teaches is true, but not everything.* We might call this the *partial-reliability model.* This perspective can take at least two forms. The *first* proposes that *everything that the Bible teaches (or implies) about religion (and perhaps morality) is true,*[50] *but not everything that it teaches (or implies) about science is true.* Let us call this the *qualified partial-reliability* model or the *full religious- and partial scientific-reliability* model (FRPSR model). Adherents of this understanding apparently believe that the Bible is completely reliable in matters of religion,[51] but not necessarily reliable in matters of science. Further, these authors seem to maintain that complete reliability in matters of religion is critical for the Christian life of faith, although reliability in matters of science is relatively unimportant. The FRPSR model admits that modern scientific and biblical

---

49. Peter Enns makes similar criticisms of Vanhoozer's claims about Jesus' intentions in his analogy of the mustard seed and the kingdom of God. See Enns, "Response to Kevin Vanhoozer," 246.

50. While this discussion is focused on tensions between scientific and religions claims, morality often also is a source of tension in conversations about biblical reliability. Thus, those who distinguish religious from moral claims might wish to add "moral claims" to the list of items about which the Bible is reliable. Others may wish simply to collapse religion and morality into a singular area of concern, and still others might wish to include moral claims or maxims among the type of assertions about which the Bible is not reliable. Our focus here primarily is on religious claims, whatever precisely that means.

51. And perhaps morality. See the previous footnote.

claims can contradict each other. In many cases when this happens, one must simply admit that the Bible is wrong in its claims (or assumptions) about natural states and processes.[52] Still one might maintain the Bible is always right in its basic religious (and perhaps moral) claims. Hence, when *religious* discrepancies *appear* to occur within the Bible, some sort of a harmonization can and should be made.[53]

A *second* version of the partial-reliability model of scriptural inerrancy holds that *biblical teachings are subject to error both in matters of science and religion.*[54] We might call this the *unqualified partial reliability* model or the *partial religious- and partial scientific-reliability* (PRPSR) model. Adherents of this perspective contend that the Bible is generally reliable, especially in matters of religion. Further, general reliability in matters of religion is *sufficient* for the Christian life of faith. However, general reliability in matters of science may not be needed at all. Further, the PRPSR model holds that in many cases when scientific and biblical claims about nature clash, one simply must admit that sometimes the Bible is inaccurate in its claims (or assumptions) about natural processes. Further, when *religious* (and perhaps moral)[55] discrepancies occur in the Bible, the PRPSR model admits that some religious claims (or moral claims) in the Bible are incorrect and must be dismissed in submission to more noble—that is, the more Christ-like—religious ideals within the Bible.[56]

Evaluating the Reliability Models

What are we to think of the above three models of biblical reliability (inerrancy)? First, we may note that each of these models is compatible with the notion that (at least sometimes) God reveals truths or propositions through Scripture. For some theologians, this is a boon compared to models that deny propositional content to revelation.[57] However,

52. For example, ascribing thought to the heart and kidney, or emotions to liver; or assuming the sky is a dome holding back cosmic oceans, or there are pillars holding up the earth.

53. The perspective described in this paragraph is much like what Erickson calls the doctrine of *limited inerrancy*. This theory is affirmed by Daniel Fuller and holds that all that the Bible teaches about some subjects or areas of knowledge is true—such as salvation. But teachings in other areas—such as science and history—are subject to error. See Erickson, *Christian Theology*, 191–92. Also see Fuller, "Benjamin B. Warfield's View of Faith and History."

54. And possibly also morality.

55. See footnote 50.

56. The PRPS model described above is something like the perspective Erickson attributes to Jack Rogers and names the *inerrancy of purpose* model. According to this approach, "the Bible faithfully accomplishes its purpose, which is to bring people into personal fellowship with Christ." See Erickson, *Christian Theology*, 192. Thus, some or many of the Bible's statements may be untrue. Nevertheless, the Bible accomplishes its purpose by drawing persons to an encounter with God and to salvation in Christ. See also Rogers, "The Church Doctrine of Biblical Authority." Erickson also credits James Orr with holding this view in Orr, *Revelation and Inspirations*, 217–18. Erickson, *Christian Theology*, 192 n. 8. Paul Achtemeier likewise holds a perspective similar to the PRPS model. See Achtemeier, *Inspiration and Authority*, especially 132–34.

57. We address the nonpropositions view below, as well as in Chapter 3, above.

all three models face difficulties. The full-reliability model occasionally encourages its proponents to engage in poor science, poor biblical exegesis, or both in order to reconcile science and the Bible. As noted above, this essentially is the accusation that Vanhoozer, Erickson, and Dockery level against some exponents of the full-reliability (full-inerrancy) model. For Vanhoozer, Erickson, and Dockery, some proponents of full reliability fail to adequately consider the cultural, historical, and literary conventions of the biblical writers and thus fail to sufficiently take into account authorial intent. Paul Achtemeir (1927–2013) and Peter Enns direct similar criticisms toward full inerrantists such as Vanhoozer, Erickson, and Dockery.[58]

Proponents of the partial-reliability model also face problems. Specifically, they encounter the difficulty of knowing which claims of the Bible to affirm. This is perhaps less problematic for those who hold the FRPSR perspective (which says that biblical pronouncements about religious—and perhaps moral—claims are fully reliable, but claims about scientific assertions can be erroneous). Presumably a supporter of such a model can easily identify those biblical statements that run counter to well-established contemporary scientific claims and (subsequently) declare that the Bible was (clearly or likely) wrong about such matters. But even with this advantage, the advocate of the FRPSR model must still wrestles with what to do when biblical *religious* claims *seem* to contradict one another. Presumably when this happens, proponents of the FRPSR model must somehow harmonize such alleged contradictions to insure that each is true. (This is equally a problem for supporters of the theory of full reliability).

Champions of the PRPSR model (who hold that the Bible is partly reliable and partly unreliable about both science and religion) confront a different problem. Specifically, they must wrestle with the difficulty of discerning which biblical religious claims are *accurate and which are not*. In other words, while advocates of the PRPSR model may not feel a compulsion to harmonize (seemingly incongruent) religious assertions, they still feel compelled to discern *which religious teaching is correct*. What is one to do when two religious claims contradict each other? Which claim does one choose? Not surprisingly, advocates of the PRPSR model are not without a rejoinder. As noted above, often such writers appeal to the principle that religious claims that most comport with the examples and teachings of Christ are those that are most trustworthy. But even here, knowing how to rightly and precisely discern Christ-likeness is not always clear (which is not to say impossible).

Revelation as Personal Encounter

In Chapter 3, we distinguished between the propositional and personal understandings of the *content* of special revelation. The propositional understanding emphasizes the importance of divinely revealed truths or teachings. The personal understanding

58. See Achtemeier, *Inspiration and Authority*, 36–63; and Enns, "Response to Kevin Vanhoozer," 242–48.

stresses that special revelation primarily is about a personal encounter with God—an encounter that (by God's grace) can be evoked by or precipitated by various events in the spatial-temporal world, including by reading or hearing the doctrinal claims (propositions) of Scripture.

This *personal-encounter theory* of special revelation offers another means (distinct from the models of biblical reliability discussed above) by which one might address the problem of contradictions between biblical and scientific claims. Indeed, the personal-encounter theory seems in part to have been promoted in order to avoid problems associated with tensions *within* the biblical text as well as tensions *between* the Bible and contemporary science (and historiography). Proponents of the personal-encounter theory of revelation essentially propose that the disagreements between biblical and scientific descriptions are largely unimportant, for the (divinely intended) purpose of the Bible is not to convey information or doctrine but to facilitate a personal, revelatory encounter with God.[59] Admittedly, there is much overlap between this theory and the PRPSR model of inerrancy discussed above. The key difference (if there is any difference) is that the theory of *revelation as personal encounter* explicitly denies that revelation comes in propositional form, whereas the PRPSR model appears to be open to the idea that revelation (at times) is conveyed in propositions.

Duly noting this difference, however, the critic might note that even adherents of a nonpropositional understanding of revelation must admit that presumed divine personal self-revelations require some (often much) *interpretation* (assessment and declaration of what Christians are to believe in light of such encounters) and, subsequently, proponents of this view must ponder which (if any) *interpretations* are correct. While these difficulties may be ameliorated, questions about correct interpretation remain important and (at times) puzzling.[60]

Closing Thoughts on the Reliability of Scripture

To close these discussions regarding the reliability of Scripture, we might offer the following observations. First, for some readers, much of this conversation may seem to be much ado about little. This is the case because in practice often the *full-reliability* and *partial-reliability* models render similar results. This is the case especially when one compares the writings of relatively nuanced full inerrantists (such as Vanhoozer) with the proposals of authors who endorse the partial reliability of Scripture. Regarding scientific matters, no adherents of any of these reliability theories (including most absolute inerrantists) affirm that the earth is covered by a solid domed

59. See Chapter 3, below, for more details about theories that stress personal encounter as the primary content of revelation.

60. Arguably, the notion that (propositional) *interpretation* is still important even for those theologians who endorse revelation as personal encounter is evidenced by the massive (assertion-filled) theological tomes written by many such thinkers.

firmament, or that human thought is grounded in the liver, or that pillars uphold the earth. And many (perhaps most) of the more nuanced full inerrantists (alongside their partial-reliablist counterparts) deny that the universe and the earth are only a few thousand years old or were created in six twenty-four-hour periods. Typically, as we saw in Vanhoozer's work, full inerrantists (full reliablists) simply deny that the biblical writers *intended* to teach such claims; instead, the Scripture writers sought to teach important religious (theological and perhaps moral) claims. Likewise, those partial reliablists who affirm that the biblical authors *did intend* to teach claims about the physical world (and were wrong) often *emphasize the importance of the religious claims* of the texts in question, even while rejecting the ancient biblical assertions about the nature of the cosmos. In short, sometimes the practical theological differences between the full-reliability and partial-reliability models are not that great.[61]

Perhaps the greatest divide between full- and partial-reliablists is over how each assesses and approaches the hermeneutical process. For the partial-reliability theorist, earnest biblical interpretation leads to the sincere conviction that some logical and factual incongruities exist between science and the Bible, and that this is the case in spite of the interpreter's solid commitment to the truthfulness and trustworthiness of God. For the full reliablist, commitment to the truthfulness and trustworthiness of God leads to the earnest conviction that since the Bible is inspired by God, apparent discrepancy between the biblical text and science must be only apparent, and that this is true in spite of the fact that such convictions necessitate a sometimes painstaking (and, for many, implausible) attempt to reconcile these apparent tensions. Obviously, which of these two approaches to biblical hermeneutics is correct is a matter of dispute among Christians.

A third divide between full- and partial-reliability theorists involves how each assesses what constitutes *sufficient* reliability. As noted above (and in Chapter 3, below), for some Christian writers only full reliability of scriptural claims is *sufficient* for the Christian walk of faith, while for others partial reliability is *sufficient*. Granted, for many full-reliablists, part of what motivates their commitment to inerrancy is an earnest concern to affirm the truthfulness and trustworthiness of the God who inspires Scripture. But part of their motive likewise appears to be a desire for certitude regarding Christian faith and practice. That is, for some writers, the quest for certainty fuels the advocacy for biblical inerrancy.[62] On the other hand, for other writers (presumably

61. Similar comments might be made regarding the moral teachings of the Bible. None of the adherents of any of these theories affirms that the highest moral teachings of Scripture are found in the Hebrew canonical instruction to exterminate pagan cities who refuse to submit to God (see Deut 20:10–18) or in other such moral instructions. In short, both those who deny and those who affirm religious errors in the Scripture concede that certain moral teachings of Scripture are not to be mimicked by contemporary Christians—often on the grounds that such actions have been preempted by a higher ethic as found in Christ.

62. Erickson seems to express this motive when he writes, "Our basis for holding to the truth of any theological proposition is that the Bible teaches it. If, however, we should conclude that certain propositions (historical or scientific) taught by the Bible are not true, the implications are far-reaching.

many partial-reliabilists) such psychological certitude cannot be found or grounded in the biblical text per se. Rather, such certainty is available (if at all) only through a kind of personal trust in God per se, who, in turn inspires and uses the biblical text, which nevertheless possesses the flaws of its finite human authors. Hence, for this second set of writers, general but uncertain scriptural reliability is *sufficient reliability*. As with the positions discussed in the previous paragraph, it is not obvious (to many Christians) which of these two intuitions about sufficient reliability is correct.

Finally, Vanhoozer (and other inerrentists) almost certainly is correct in high-lighting the need to properly assess the *intentions* of the Bible's human authors when judging whether or not their claims were in error. To judge their writings to be in error because they fail to address the concerns of contemporary science seems to be wrong-headed if these authors had no intention of addressing such matters. As noted above, it is not all together clear that the ancient writers *were not intending* to describe the nature of the cosmos (in some sense). And if they did intend to describe the nature of the cosmos, then their assertions and assumptions about the universe were in error. Still, it may also be accurate to suspect that ultimately biblical writers were not *focused* on giving such an account, and (even more importantly) they were not seeking to give a *scientific account* (according to the modern understanding of science or of what makes an account scientific). Rather the primary concern of the biblical writers was to proclaim that God is the source and creator of the physical world (and all else). Hence, in a strong sense, it is inappropriate for contemporary critics to fault the bibli-cal authors for failing to address (or failing to accurately address) matters that were in no way at the center of their awareness, concerns, or goals.

Conclusion

The relationship between science and Christianity is an ongoing concern of the Christian faith. Various models for understanding the relationship between the two have been proposed. While tensions persist, most Christians recognize the value of science and the need to integrate it into the broad perspectives of their faith. In this chapter, we have proposed some rudimentary ways that such an integration might happen. Especially troublesome for Christians at times is discerning how best to understand the nature of Scripture in the face of tensions between the (implicit) bib-lical understanding of the physical world and contemporary science's understanding of the same. In this chapter, we also have examined two broad models for under-standing the reliability of Scripture in the face of these tensions. Into the foreseeable future, the relationship between science and the Christian faith will almost certainly remain an ongoing issue for Christians.

We cannot then continue to hold to other propositions simply on the grounds that the Bible teaches them" (Erickson, *Christian Theology*, 196).

15

Christian Issues

Christianity and Women
in Ministry

IN THE PREVIOUS TWO chapters, we examined three major issues facing contemporary Christianity—the problem of evil, the relationship between Christianity and other religions, and the relationship between science and the Christian faith. In this fifteenth and final chapter, we explore Christianity's approach to women in ministry.

Christianity and Social Exclusivism

Closely tied to the issue of women in ministry is the matter of social exclusivism. By social exclusivism, we mean (1) excluding persons from membership in a society or group or (2) barring some members of a society or group from benefits, opportunities, or rights typically afforded other members of that society or group. We might call the first of these practices *membership exclusivism* and the second *benefits exclusivism*.[1] The practice of excluding persons in these manners is sometimes called *discrimination*. Discriminatory or exclusionist practices are not necessarily wrong, depending on the circumstances. Few pundits quibble over excluding children under a certain age from voting, serving in the military, or obtaining a driver's license. Few writers protest demanding that persons demonstrate competency in medical knowledge and procedures before being granted a license to practice medicine. Still, at other times, discrimination is deemed wrong. In general, many writers assume that exclusionist practices—here defined as denying rights, benefits, or opportunities to some but not others—must be rationally or morally justified. So, for example, while denying the right to vote to a child seems to be justified, imposing such a

---

1. Another term for the first form of exclusivism might be Complete Social Exclusivism, and a term for the second might be Partial Social Exclusivism.

restriction on mature adult citizens (including women and minorities) does not seem to be rationally (or morally) defensible.[2]

Part of what makes discriminatory practices morally suspect is not only the actions themselves but also the attitudes or beliefs that accompany them. Throughout human history, multitudes of persons and groups have distinguished themselves from others. The dichotomies of me versus you, us versus them, run deep in individual and collective psyches and in social constructs. While recognizing differences among humans, or self-identifying with one group rather than another, is not wrong per se, sometimes such conceptual perspectives are conjoined with (rationally and morally unwarranted) negative evaluations of the worth, goodness, quality of "the other" compared to oneself or one's group. And not infrequently, such negative assessments motivate (unwarranted) discriminatory practices and are employed (illegitimately) to justify such behaviors. As noted in Chapters 9, 10, and 11, Christian ethics often stresses the importance of both the *ethics of being* and the *ethics of doing*, often proposing that outward practices are motivated by inward attitudes, and that persons should not only *do* good but also *be* good. Hence, both the practice of unjustified discrimination and the attitudes that accompany or justify this practice can be questioned morally.

In light of these ideas, two critical questions arise for Christianity: First, when, if ever, is it acceptable to exclude someone from the Christian community per se?[3] That is, when is it acceptable to engage in *membership exclusionism*? Second, when, if ever, is it acceptable to exclude someone *within* the Christian community *from key benefits, opportunities, or rights* typically afforded other members of that community?[4] That is, when is it permissible to engage in *benefits exclusionism*? More positively, we may ask the question of membership exclusion as follows: Who may be *included* in the Christian way of life? Theologically, this query is asking who may participate in the salvation of Christ (soteriology), or who may become a member of God's people (ecclesiology)?

The answers to these questions regarding membership in the Christian community per se seem to be straightforward: In principle, any human—of any social, economic, ethnic, or gender category—may participate in Christ's salvation and be part of Christ's church. Christianity purports to be a universal and welcoming way of life. God has created all persons; Christ died for the salvation of all humans; and now, through Christ, God calls all to join the membership of the church (which is the saved community, the people of God, the body of Christ, the congregation of God, and so forth). Such claims of inclusion are supported by biblical texts such as these:

---

2. Of course, other factors may warrant such exclusion such as engaging in treasonous or blatant criminal behaviors.

3. That is, when, if ever, is it permissible for Christians to engage in Membership Exclusivism.

4. That is, when, if ever, is it permissible for Christians to engage in Benefits Exclusivism.

For God so loved the world that he gave his only Son, so that *everyone* who believes in him may not perish but may have eternal life. (John 3:16; italics added)

The Lord is not slow about his promise, as some think of slowness, but is patient with you, not wanting any to perish, but *all* to come to repentance. (2 Pet 3:9; italics added)

For in Christ Jesus you are *all* children of God through faith . . . There is no longer Jew or Greek, there is no longer slave or free, there is no longer male and female; for *all* of you are one in Christ Jesus. (Gal 3:26–28; italics added)

According to the first two passages above, in principle, all persons are invited to participate in God's salvation. According to the third reading, Christians come from diverse social factions but in some sense are all united into one group in Christ, each being made a child of God. In principle, then, any human—of any social, economic, ethnic, or gender category—may participate in Christ's salvation and be part of Christ's church.

But here a caveat is needed. As the verses above indicate, the invitation to participate in God's salvation comes with expectations. At some level, core affirmations and commitments are expected. Specifically, repentance of sin and faith in Christ are minimal requirements for participation in the family of God.[5] And this is so even though the exact nature of faith in Christ and of repentance from sin is subject to debate among Christians.[6] But here a puzzle arises: At first glance, the Christian universal (and equalizing) call to salvation seems to clash with the particularistic conditions for receiving this salvation. This dilemma has been addressed elsewhere in this work, including in Chapter 13 (in the section about the relationship of Christianity with other religions).[7]

With these basic concepts in hand, let us examine the second form of social exclusivism mentioned above—benefits exclusivism. When is it permissible, if ever, to exclude someone *within* the Christian community *from key benefits, opportunities, or*

5. John 3:16 identifies *belief* in Christ as the condition for salvation. Second Peter 3:9 identifies *repentance*. And Gal 3:26–28 speaks of persons being united in Christ through *faith* (and baptism). Similar perspectives are found throughout the New Testament, including in Acts 2:37–38 and Rom 3:23–30.

6. See the section immediately above and chapter 5. Even the requirements of faith and repentance may need qualification. Some theologians (although certainly not all) argue that faith and repentance are expected of those who are able to perform such acts; but these actions may not be required of those who cannot so respond.

7. See also chapter 5. For some Christian interpreters, the reality of these mandatory prerequisites of faith and repentance for salvation and for membership in the church make it impossible for some social groups (without change) to participate (or participate fully) in the Christian way of life or to be members of the Christian family. For several Christian writers, such is the case for practicing homosexuals who wish to join the church or participate (or fully participate) in its life and ministries. Space and time prevent us from exploring these matters here. For discussion of these issues, see Gushee, *Changing Our Mind* and Grenz, *Welcoming But Not Affirming*.

rights typically afforded other members of that community? As is the case with society in general, so it is in the church: Not every member of the people of God engages in every activity of the church or is granted every benefit or opportunity afforded to some members of the church. Not every Christian serves as a pastor, elder, bishop, or deacon. Not every Christian teaches Sunday school or catechism classes. Not every Christian serves as a trustee of finances and properties. Not every Christian sings in the choir or leads worship music. In turn, as is the case for society in general, often such exclusions in church are believed to be acceptable *if* they are rationally or morally justifiable. Thus, not many church members protest the requirement that a cantor or song leader or praise-team member or instrumentalist audition before being given the privilege to lead a congregation in musical worship. Few Christians reject the notion that pastors or priests must demonstrate knowledge of biblical and church doctrine, or have considerable organizational and people skills.

The apostle Paul seems to recognize the truth and permissibility of differing persons performing varying functions in the church. Indeed, Paul seems to celebrate this diversity of services within the unity of the church. Rhetorically, Paul asks:

> Are all apostles? Are all prophets? Are all teachers? Do all work miracles? Do all possess gifts of healing? Do all speak in tongues? Do all interpret? (1 Cor 12:29–30)

For Paul, the obvious answer is no. Not every Christians performs all these ministries. Instead, says Paul, the church is like a human body with divergent parts that perform different roles. Though each part performs a different work, collectively these parts form a single, living body. And each function contributes to the good of the whole (1 Cor 12:12–27).

But what qualifies a person to perform a given function, ministry, or service in the church? For Paul, the answer is God. God has chosen and empowered/gifted each member of the church to perform certain ministries of the church. And this empowerment is associated with the gracious activity of God's Spirit upon believers. Thus, the apostle states:

> Now there are varieties of gifts, but the same Spirit; and there are varieties of services, but the same Lord; and there are varieties of activities, but it is the same God who activates all of them in everyone. To each is given the manifestation of the Spirit for the common good. (1 Cor 12:4–7)

For Paul, God's Spirit is the one who empowers and qualifies a person to perform specific ministries in the church.

In practical terms, of course, discerning spiritual giftedness may be tricky; and sometimes giftedness alone is not sufficient to grant someone the opportunity to minister in a specific way in the church. Sometimes life circumstances or moral improprieties or competition among numerous gifted persons or the need for formal legal licensing or the requirement of official church sanctioning or the lack of congregational or ministerial spiritual discernment or the animus of some church members toward others can play roles in determining if and how someone ministers in the church. Nevertheless, according to the apostle Paul, spiritual giftedness plays a fundamental role in determining if and when someone is *qualified* to minister in a given way in the church. And this is the case particularly because, per Paul's argument, the Spirit of God bestows such gifts.

With these previous paragraphs in mind, we turn to consider a form of social exclusivism historically practiced by the church, and still practiced in many Christians churches today. This is the barring of women from some ministries. This practice does not appear to be a form of membership exclusionism. In light of biblical passages such as those quoted above (John 3:16; 2 Pet 3:9; Gal 3:26–28), generally Christians throughout history have welcomed women into the *membership* of the church, proclaiming that God's salvation and participation in God's family are for both sexes of the human race. Nevertheless, the *exclusion of women from some ministries* does appear to be a form of benefits exclusionism. It involves barring women (as a class) from some of the opportunities and subsequent benefits offered to men (as a class) in the church. Typically, this exclusion does not involve barring women from *all* ministries in the church. Throughout history and today, woman have engaged in a wide variety of services among the people of God, including evangelism, aid to the poor, care for the sick, teaching of children, and so forth. Rather, usually the exclusions imposed upon women have involved very specific ministries. The precise ministries from which women have been barred varies among churches or church traditions, but often these exclusions are especially from positions of ecclesiastical leadership—that is, from positions of culminating authority and decision-making.

What is the rationale for such exclusions? Almost certainly, part of the answer is that such practices have been or still are (arguably unjustly) based on long-held beliefs about women in Western (and perhaps in worldwide) culture. As noted in Chapter 10, only relatively recently in the Western world were women granted the right to vote or were married women permitted to own property independently of their husbands. In the past, such exclusions were justified based on key assumptions about the nature and abilities or inabilities of women. (We will say more about these rationales and their rationality below.) While general cultural perspectives likely play a role in the exclusion of women from some forms of ministry, for many Christians another—more immediate—set of justifications is operative. These are claims and commands, regarding women and their activities, made in several key biblical passages.

Paul and Women

Ironically, these exclusionist ideals are especially found in texts associated with the apostle Paul. This is ironic, in part, because in various other passages Paul seems to acknowledge and support a wide range of women's ministerial activities and (perhaps) offices; indeed, often he seems to offer a much more egalitarian perspective regarding women's activities than was held by many Jews and Gentiles of his day. In a moment we will examine some of these more inclusive Pauline tendencies as well as broader biblical perspectives on these matters. But first let us identify the Pauline texts that seem to bar women (as a class) from some activities or privileges available to men (as a class) in the church. These are 1 Cor 11:2–16, 1 Cor 14:33–36, and 1 Tim 2:11–15. First Corinthians 11:2–16 reads:

> 2 I commend you because you remember me in everything and maintain the traditions just as I handed them on to you. 3 But I want you to understand that *Christ is the head of every man, and the husband is the head of his wife,* and God is the head of Christ. 4 Any man who prays or prophesies with something on his head disgraces his head, 5 but *any woman who prays or prophesies with her head unveiled disgraces her head*—it is one and the same thing as having her head shaved. 6 For if a woman will not veil herself, then she should cut off her hair; but if it is disgraceful for a woman to have her hair cut off or to be shaved, *she should wear a veil.* 7 For a man ought not to have his head veiled, *since he is the image and reflection of God; but woman is the reflection of man.* 8 Indeed, *man was not made from woman, but woman from man.* 9 Neither was man created for the sake of woman, but woman for the sake of man. 10 For this reason a woman ought to have a symbol of authority on her head, because of the angels.* 11 Nevertheless, in the Lord woman is not independent of man or man independent of woman. 12 For just as woman came from man, so man comes through woman; but all things come from God. 13 Judge for yourselves: is it proper for a woman to pray to God with her head unveiled? 14 *Does not nature itself teach you that if a man wears long hair, it is degrading to him, 15 but if a woman has long hair, it is her glory? For her hair is given to her for a covering.* 16 But if anyone is disposed to be contentious—we have no such custom, nor do the churches of God.[8]

1 CORINTHIANS 14:33–36:

> As in all the churches of the saints, *women should be silent in the churches.* For they are *not permitted to speak, but should be subordinate,* as the *law* also says. 35 *If there is anything they desire to know, let them ask their husbands at home.* For it is shameful for a woman to speak in church. 36 Or did the word of God originate with you? Or are you the only ones it has reached?

---

8. Italics added. I have kept the verse numbers for the convenience of easily referencing them.

1 TIMOTHY 2:11–15

11 Let a woman learn in silence with full submission. 12 I permit no woman to teach or to have authority over a man; she is to keep silent. 13 For Adam was formed first, then Eve; 14 and Adam was not deceived, but the woman was deceived and became a transgressor. 15 Yet she will be saved through child-bearing, provided they continue in faith and love and holiness, with modesty.

In these verses—particularly those italicized above—one discovers what appear to be several restrictions upon women's behavior in the church. One limitation is that they must wear veils (or according to some interpretations long hair) when praying or prophesying (presumably in Christian worship services; 1 Cor 11:5). Another constraint is that women must be silent (1 Cor 14: 34; 1 Tim 2:11–12) and be subordinate or submissive (1 Cor 14:34; 1 Tim 2:11–12) in churches, and if they have questions (seemingly about teachings in or of the church), they should wait and ask their husbands at home (1 Cor 11:35). Further, a woman (perhaps a wife) cannot teach or have authority over a man (or perhaps over a husband; 1 Tim 2:12).

For many commentators, even more puzzling (or disturbing) than these varied restrictions upon women's activities are some of the rationales offered by Paul for these prohibitions. Perplexing justifications for women wearing veils (or having long hair) include that while men are reflections of God, women are reflections of men (1 Cor 11:7), and that women were made *for the sake of men* and not vice versa (1 Cor 11:9–10), and that *nature demonstrates* that men should have short hair and women long hair (1 Cor 11:15), and finally "because of the angels" (whatever this cryptic phrase means; 1 Cor 11:10). Another befuddling claim, seemingly connected to women wearing veils (or long hair) but not clearly explained is that a man (or a husband) has authority over a woman (or wife) in a way analogous to Christ's authority over a man (1 Cor 11:3). Since Christ's authority over creation (including human males) is seemingly absolute, does this analogy imply a man's (or men's) authority over a woman (or women) is total? Further, what law (of the Torah or of the Hebrew scriptures generally) dictates that women be silent (1 Cor 14:34)? Or how does Adam being created first, before Eve (Gen 2) and not being the one deceived by the serpent (Gen 3) relate to women keeping silent in churches (1 Tim 2:14–15)? And perhaps most perplexing of all: In what sense are women (and in what sense is Eve) somehow saved in or through childbirth (1 Tim 2:15)?

In addition to these ambiguities, there are seeming contradictions between some of the statements made in the above passages and views expressed elsewhere by Paul (and other New Testament writers). In 1 Cor 11:5, Paul seems to assume that women pray and prophesy (presumably in corporate worship venues), and Paul does not condemn such actions. But in the same letter, as we have seen, Paul commands women to be silent (1 Cor 14:34), and he makes a similar command in 1 Tim 2:11–12. But how can someone pray and prophesy in a congregation without speaking?

Further, how does Paul's insistence that women not teach or have authority over men (1 Tim 2:12) square with texts in which he acknowledges and seemingly approves of (or does not condemn) women leading (in some capacity within) congregations and possibly even teaching males? To see this dilemma, consider a comment Paul makes in 1 Cor 12:28 where he notes that "God has appointed in the church first apostles, second prophets, third teachers . . ." Such phrasing suggests that these gifted-ministries involve a kind of ranking of ministries, or that these services are (in some sense) especially significant in the church.[9] Interestingly, however, in varied places Paul seems to claim that women sometimes fill these roles of apostles, prophets, and teachers, as well as other kinds of leadership positions such as deacons[10] and coworkers (in the gospel).[11] We focus here on the first three positions (apostle, prophet, and teacher). In Rom 16:7, Paul identifies a woman named Junia as someone who had been imprisoned with him and who was "prominent among the apostles." Many translators and interpreters agree that Junia was a female name, and that the phrase "prominent among the apostles" means she was (in some sense) an apostle.[12] In turn, as noted above, Paul assumes that women prophesy (1 Cor 11:5).[13] Certainly at first glance it seems reasonable to hypothesize that persons (including women) who prophesy are prophets. Finally, in the book of Acts, the author notes that a woman named Priscilla (also called Prisca), along with her husband Aquila, *taught* an important early Christian leader named Apollos. Apollos was an enthusiastic convert to Christ who was well-informed in scripture and was teaching/evangelizing in Ephesus. Priscilla and her husband took Apollos to the side and "explained the Way of God to him more accurately" (Acts 18:16). Here is a woman more thoroughly teaching a Christian man already well versed in Scripture. Admittedly, this episode is not in Paul's writings; rather, it is in Acts. Nevertheless, it describes the actions of a wife-husband ministry team (Priscilla and Aquila), and they are often mentioned and commended by Paul (see Rom 16:3; 1 Cor 16:19; 2 Tim 4:19); further, this story from Acts depicts them (including her) as teaching a bright male convert the ways of Christ. In sum, then, Paul asserts that women sometimes are apostles and prophets

9. For a similar ordering see Eph 4:11–12: "The gifts he gave were that some would be apostles, some prophets, some evangelists, some pastors and teachers, to equip the saints for the work of ministry, for building up the body of Christ."

10. A woman named Phoebe is called a "deacon of the church at Cenchreae" in Rom 16:1. And many commentators think that 1 Tim 3:11 speaks of and to women deacons.

11. Numerous women are designated as coworkers by Paul, often in the context of praising their helpful cooperative service with him to the gospel. Among those so named are Prisca or Priscilla (Rom 16:3–5), Mary (Rom 16:6), Persis, Tryphaena and Tryphosa (Rom 16:12)

12. Paul seldom spoke of the twelve as the apostles (as the Synoptic Gospels and Acts seem to do; see Matt 10:16; Mark 316–19; Luke 6:14–16; Acts 1:13). Rather, he seems to use the term *apostle* to speak of one especially commissioned by God for the gospel and (as noted above) as one (at times) having a particularly important ministerial-function in the church. Paul refers to himself as an apostle in 1 Cor 15:9.

13. Other New Testament passages likewise do this. See, e.g., Acts 21:8–9.

(or at least they prophesy). And, in turn, Paul highly celebrates a woman (Priscilla) who, we are told in Acts, taught a man.

In light of these passages, it seems odd (especially for Paul) to say that women are not to speak in church. This is peculiar, first, because the very nature of these three functions or offices of the church (apostle, prophet, teacher) almost always involve *speaking*. How might apostles or prophets or teachers perform their roles without (sometimes) speaking in congregational gatherings? It also is strange to say women cannot hold authority over men. This is odd because at least at first glance the offices or functions of apostle, prophet, and teacher carry some degree of authority in the church, as suggested by Paul's describing them in prioritized listings. But how can offices that have a presumed authority not exercise authority? Or how can women (as a class) be denied the right (and responsibility) to teach men (as a class) based on their alleged lack of authority over men when women occasionally hold offices or perform functions (such as apostle or prophet) that seem to have greater, or at least similar, authority to that of teachers? Comparable questions arise when one notes that Paul ascribes other ministry functions or ministry positions to women such as deacons and coworkers. None of this is to say that such conundrums cannot be explained but certainly, at first glance, these questions are baffling.

In addition to the three texts mentioned above (1 Cor 11:2–16; 14:33–36; 1 Tim 2:11–15), each of which seems to restrict the role of women in the church, there are a number of other passages that apparently relegate women to a subordinate position in families—specifically asserting wives are to be subject to their husbands. While these texts do not explicitly mandate the curtailment of women's roles *in the church*, they are of a similar ilk to those that do, and they are often cited by proponents of limited female ministerial roles as texts that reinforce such restrictions. Two passages stand out: Eph 5:22–24 and Col 3:18. The former says:

> 22 Wives, be subject to your husbands as you are to the Lord. 23 For the husband is the head of the wife just as Christ is the head of the church, the body of which he is the Savior. 24 Just as the church is subject to Christ, so also wives ought to be, in everything, to their husbands.

Col 3:18 proclaims, "Wives, be subject to your husbands, as is fitting in the Lord." Each passage above admonishes or encourages wives to be "subject" to their husbands. The first reading offers the rationale that as Christ is head over the church, husbands are heads over their wives. The second passage simply states that such submission of wives to husbands is "fitting in the Lord."

The Broader Biblical Literature

The tensions in the Pauline literature surrounding the role of women in the Christian life are apparent. These frictions are echoed in the broader biblical literature. Most parties in the debate over women in ministry agree that the general biblical perspective was patriarchal, as were most premodern cultural mindsets. The fundamental social unit in the Hebrew biblical tradition was the family. In nuclear and extended families, male dominance was presumed. Nuclear families consisted of a man[14] and his wife (or wives) and their children. The husband and father was the leader of the family. Wives were subordinate to husbands, and children were subordinate to both fathers and mothers, but the father was head of all. This familial unit, in turn, served as a crucial model for society in general, including for the dynamics of clans and tribes. Nearly always, a patriarch exercised great authority over these larger social units—often leading in battle, commerce, and decision-making. Moreover, nearly always, tribal lineage was traced to a founding patriarch, with tribes deriving their names from such men.

Not surprisingly, in the context of these patriarchal systems, laws and social mores typically granted greater opportunities and benefits to men than to women. In general, a woman was under the authority of her husband or nearest male relative, so she had less autonomy than her male counterparts. Even vows to God could be annulled by a woman's male guardian (Num 20:3–16). And only husbands, not wives, could actualize a divorce (Deut 24:1–4).[15] In turn, men could have multiple wives, but women could not have multiple husbands (Exod 21:10; Deut 21:15–17). Inheritance of family property typically went to only male heirs, unless a woman had no brothers, in which case she could inherent such possessions. But even then, she could marry a husband only from within her clan so that property stayed within the family group, and those material goods would then pass over to her husband (Num 27:1–11).

Typically a woman's social roles were more restricted than a man's. Normally, in the Hebrew biblical literature, men are depicted as engaging in activities of the public domain—commerce, politics, warcraft, policymaking, and so forth. And not uncommonly, when women do act in these areas there are innuendos that this is unusual, or that it is shameful for a man to be bested by a woman.[16] In turn, women often are pictured as caring for children, hearth, and home.[17] Indeed, the primary social role of women appears to have been that of bearing and rearing children. In many ways, a women's wealth and value was described in terms of her birthing children, especially boys, for the family. To not be able to bear children brought sorrow, even shame, to a woman (Exod 23:25–26; 1 Sam 1:1—2:10; Job 24:21). Obviously, there is nothing demeaning in bearing, birthing, and caring for children or in overseeing domestic affairs. Problems arise for many contemporary social critics when women are barred from other social activities (and the rewards and responsibilities

14. A subtle presumption of male dominance and perspective is found in Gen 2 in its description of the husband-wife relationship in terms of "the man and his wife." (Gen 2:23–25).

15. Wives could sue for divorce in the Israelite tradition; however, it was up to the husband whether or not to grant the request.

16. For examples, see Judg 5:4–9; 9:50–54.

17. This image of a women's work is well depicted in Prov 31.

of those activities) simply because of their sex, and with little consideration of their task-related abilities or potentials.

Perhaps more troubling than these varied forms of social inequality are some cultic (ritual) restrictions imposed upon women in the Hebrew biblical tradition, including especially the tacit rationales underlying these mandates. For example, a woman was considered ritually unclean for seven days while menstruating, and thus she was not permitted to worship at the tabernacle during this time. But a man was considered unclean for only one day for a nocturnal emission (Lev 15). More significantly, a woman was ritually unclean for seven days after giving birth to a boy, but for fourteen days after given birth to a girl (Lev 12:2, 5). Implicit in these practices (especially the latter one) is the notion that females per se are more defiling than are males. Finally, a particularly disconcerting (seemingly misogynous and inequitable) practice of the law was the following: If a husband suspected his wife of marital infidelity, he could legally force her (under the auspices of a priest) to drink a bitter concoction that apparently induced miscarriage and possibly distention of the uterus. If she lost the baby, she was presumed guilty of infidelity. If not, she was presumed innocent. Such a procedure was justified on the grounds that "the spirit of jealousy" had fallen upon her husband (Num 5:11–31)! No similar ordeal was faced by a husband suspected by his wife of infidelity.[18]

Perhaps the most glaring repudiation of women's *ministry* in the Old Testament was their banning (or at least absence) from the priesthood. Most of ancient Israel's neighbors had both male and female priests. But there is no evidence of such in ancient Israel. The reasons for this are unclear, and the biblical texts offer no explanation. Some scholars speculate that this exclusion had something to do with the fertility cults that prevailed among Israel's pagan neighbors; thus, to distinguish worship of Yahweh (whose creative power was by divine command alone) from pagan deities (whose creative activities involved sexual unions of male and female gods), ancient Israelites recognized only male priests. Not all scholars find this explanation convincing. Other writers think the ban on female priests in Israel flowed from Israel's cultic concerns over impurity, which required officiants of God's tabernacle and temple to be ceremonially clean and holy. Since menstruation made a woman religiously unclean for seven days, perhaps women were banned from the priesthood because it would have been impractical for them to serve as priests since they effectively could perform their duties only three-quarters of the time. Whatever the original rationale, women de facto were banned from the priesthood.[19]

Clearly, the Hebrew biblical tradition manifests patriarchal tendencies. While acknowledging these male-dominant overtones, however, many scholars—especially egalitarians (see below)—note several instances in the Hebrew scriptures where

18. For more details about views of women in the Hebrew scriptures, see Grenz and Kjesbo, *Women in the Church*, 64–71; and Stagg and Stagg, *Women in the World of Jesus*, 15–54.

19. Stagg and Stagg, *Women in the World of Jesus*, 29–32.

women engaged in spiritual and social leadership, and where they participated in a host of worship activities. First Samuel 25 depicts a woman named Abigail as far more socially and politically savvy than her crass husband, so that her wise actions saves her people from retribution and wins the favor of the future king, David. Second Kings 4 celebrates the spiritual insightfulness of a non-Israelite woman who recognizes God's hand in the prophet Elisha, and who subsequently receives multiple divine blessings. According to the Hebrew scriptures, like men, women heard and entered into the Lord's covenant with Israel (Deut 29:1–11, 31:9–13). On occasion, women offered sacrifices to Yahweh (Lev 12:1–8; 1 Sam 2:19) and served (in some capacity) at the tabernacle of God (Exod 38:8; 1 Sam 2:22).

Perhaps more notably in the Hebrew Bible, at times women are depicted as holding positions of significant religions and political power. Miriam, the sister of Aaron and Moses, is described as a *prophet* and leader of Israel (Exod 15). She apparently aided her brothers in leading Israel after the exodus from Egypt. Deborah served as a *prophet* and *judge* of Israel. Ministering as a prophetic spokesperson for God and as an adjudicator of legal disputes (Judg 4:4–5), Deborah rallied the tribes of Israel to fight against the Canaanite king Jabin and his warlord Sisera. Per the request of an Israelite general named Barak, Deborah even accompanied the Israelites into battle (Judg 4:6–10). Huldah was a woman *prophet* whom an all-male leadership team, representing King Josiah, consulted. She predicted a time of peace for Josiah even while warning of the ultimate decimation of Judah because of its sinful past (2 Kgs 22:14–20). Certainly such examples of women's leadership are sparse in the Old Testament, but they are present.[20]

Patriarchal tendencies persisted in the era of the Jewish Second Temple; and in some ways these propensities became more pronounced. The continuation of these inclinations may be due partly to inherent trajectories of earlier Israelite mindsets but also to Roman-Hellenistic influences in the period. Typically in Greek society, women could not vote, own property, or hold public offices. For much of ancient Greek history, female philosophers were frowned upon, and education for women was limited. If a woman was single when her parents died, her inheritance was overseen by a male guardian, and she often was forced to marry a male relative in order to keep the family's property. Often marriages of eligible women were arranged by fathers or other male custodians, and husbands held legal authority over their wives.[21] Aristotle (384–322 BCE) taught that women are intellectually inferior

---

20. One might wonder whether these instances are few because of *God's* resistance to female leadership or because of an ancient patriarchal society's hesitancy to grant leadership to women. Advocates of women in ministry often presume the latter of these, finding it more plausible that a patriarchal society might, upon occasion and perhaps begrudgingly, concede the concrete, historical, fact that sometimes females exuded extraordinary gifts and, in spite of cultural mores to the contrary, led men with spiritual and political insight. That God would make such occasional or begrudging concessions seems less credible.

21. Cartwright, "Women in Ancient Greece."

to men, and that men or husbands should rule over women or wives.[22] Aristotle likewise offered several comments regarding differences between males and females that have a hint of condescension. He asserts that "the female is softer in disposition . . . more mischievous, . . . more impulsive" than males. In turn, women are more prone to jealousy, and more deceptive, than men.[23]

Women fared almost no better in Roman society than in Greece. Families were ruled by a *paterfamilias* (a chief male leader), whose authority was often unquestioned. Women could own property; but as in Greece, women were legally required to have male guardians to oversee their interests. Women also could sue for divorce. In divorce, a woman could keep her properties (except for the dowry. which went to the husband), but legal guardianship of children went to the husband. Women could not vote in various assemblies. And often, with the exception of the venerated Vestal Virgins, women played little to no role in state religious ceremonies.[24]

Some Jewish literature of this period also reflects strong patriarchal—and at times even misogynous—tendencies. For example, in the quasi-gnostic books of *Adam* and *Eve*, Eve admits that she is to blame for human sin and its consequences; and she is depicted as being less capable of repentance than Adam. In turn, Adam is reprimanded by an angel of God for obeying his wife when she offered him the forbidden fruit. According to the text, Adam had been created by God to command his wife and not to obey her.[25] In a similar vein, the *Apocalypse of Moses* has Eve admitting to Adam that the fall into sin and its consequences were primarily her fault: She says, "My lord Adam, rise up and give me half of your pain and I will endure it; for it is on my account that this has happened to you, on my account you have these troubles."[26] The first-century Hellenistic Jewish philosopher Philo of Alexandria (c. 25 BCE—c. 50 CE), blended many Greek philosophical- and Jewish religious-themes. Like Aristotle, Philo declared women to be intellectually inferior to men, asserting that the male mind focuses on reason while the female relies primarily on sensation. Further,

---

22. Aristotle writes, "The male is by nature superior, and the female inferior; and the one rules, and the other is ruled; this principle, of necessity, extends to all mankind" (Aristotle, *Politics*, 1254b, 13–14). Aristotle often is accused of declaring that women are *inferior beings* compared to men, virtually deformed males. Aristotle writes, "The woman is as it were an impotent [often translated "deformed"] male, for it is through a certain incapacity that the female is female." See *Generation of Animals*, 728a, 16–17. However, understanding Aristotle to be asserting that women are lesser *beings* than men may be a misinterpretation, for his quote arises in the context of describing the differing contributions of men and women to the procreative process. It seems more likely that—in this particular context—Aristotle only meant that women contribute to the process of sexual reproduction in a way different than do men. For discussion of these matters see Nolan, "Passive and Deformed?" None of this denies that Aristotle demonstrated misogynous tendencies (elsewhere), or that his writings were not often interpreted by others in strikingly misogynous ways.

23. Aristotle, *History of Animals*, 608b, 1–14.

24. Cartwright, "The Role of Women in the Roman World."

25. Stagg and Stagg, *Women in the World of Jesus* 34–35.

26. *The Apocalypse of Moses*, 9.2.

since men are dominated by rationality (which is the active component of the mind), men are active by nature; but women are naturally passive since they are primarily of a sensual nature, which is likewise passive. Finally, because males are intellectually superior to women, husbands should teach their wives. Thus, according to Philo, the Hebrew scriptures instruct high priests to marry virgins, not widows, so that they might properly "mold" their wives.[27]

By the days of Jesus, the mixture of both Greco-Roman and Jewish cultural perspectives about women came together to form sometimes belittling attitudes toward women that in turn helped stifle female opportunities for social and religious advancement. Stanley Grenz and Denise Muir Kjesbo catalogue several negative dispositions or practices found among many of Jesus' contemporaries.

1. Some Jewish teachers considered women to be the source of sin and death.

2. Some Jewish teachers taught that women were more sensual and less rational than men.

3. It was common for many religious teachers to cite the mannerisms of women primarily as examples of undesirable traits.

4. Fear of being seduced by women led some religious teachers to avoid public social interaction with them.

5. Women received minimal religious instruction.

6. In Herod's temple (that is, the Jerusalem temple or the second temple), women could not enter the more sacred inner courts, which were reserved for Jewish men only.

7. Typically, in synagogues women were passive observers.

8. In a traditional synagogue prayer, likely dating to the Second Temple period, pious Jewish males prayed "Blessed art thou . . . who hast not made me a woman."[28]

When observed in the contexts of the broad Hebrew scriptural tradition and the general Hellenistic, Roman, and Jewish perspectives of the first century, the New Testament (in many places) shows a remarkable, even liberating, attitude toward women. This is observed in the writings of Paul. As noted above, Paul honored various women in the church, acknowledging their spiritual giftedness, diverse ministries, and aid to him and to the gospel. Paul also permitted and presumed feminine participation in worship services, including praying and prophesying. And Paul could even boldly claim that in Christ "there is no longer Jew or Greek, there is no longer slave or free, there is no longer male and female; for all of you are one in Christ Jesus" (Gal 3:27–28). Similar attitudes and activities are noted throughout Acts and various non-Pauline

27. Stagg and Stagg, *Women in the World of Jesus*, 41–45

28. Grenz and Kjesbo, *Women in the Church*, 72–73. For similar commentary on first-century Jewish religious attitudes toward women, see Jewett, *Man as Male and Female*, 91–94.

epistles in the New Testament. Much of this ran counter to common restriction imposed on women in the first-century Mediterranean world.

Jesus and Women

The contrast with predominant first-century attitudes toward women is especially manifested in the New Testament's depictions of Jesus. As we have noted elsewhere,[29] Jesus came preaching the dawning of the kingdom of God—a vision of God's reign that involved a shift of emphasis from outer signs of righteousness to inner rightness of attitudes, motives, and thoughts. Love for God and for neighbor was to motivate one's actions. For this reason, Jesus demonstrated deep concern for persons who often were not granted the benefits that naturally flow from love. He reached out to those deemed socially, politically, and religiously unworthy—"sinners": the diseased, the crippled, eunuchs, and, yes, women.[30]

Jesus seemed to focus on individuals as *persons* rather than as entities defined by their social classes or life circumstances. He especially emphasized who a person was before God.[31] This interpretation of Jesus comes to light in several biblical passages depicting his encounters with women. One particularly memorable exchange occurs in the Gospel of Luke (7:36–49), when Jesus is dining at the home of a local Pharisee. During the meal, a woman from the town approaches Jesus, kneels behind him, and begins anointing his feet with her own tears and with ointment, and drying them with her loosened hair. She kisses his feet repeatedly. Awkward for modern ears but also for ancient ones! The text informs us that the woman was known to be a sinner. Although her sin is not named, it is likely she was a prostitute. Adding to the tension is the fact that rabbis and prophets (such as Jesus) were expected not to associate with such women, and would certainly not allow such women to touch them or kiss their feet or loose their hair before them (which itself was provocative for many Jews of the first century). Perhaps exasperated, Jesus' host thinks to himself: "If this man were a prophet, he would have known who and what kind of woman this is who is touching him—that she is a sinner!" (v. 29). But Jesus uses these circumstances to do three things. First, he commends the woman for her love, which (the text says) was motivated by her having been forgiven; second, he assures her that she has been forgiven of her sins. And third, Jesus informs his host and the rest of the guests of the great importance of gratitude to God for divine forgiveness. This passage shows Jesus aware of the moral, social, and

29. See especially Chapter 2 (above).

30. Foster, "Jesus and Women."

31. James Hurley notes, "The foundation-stone of Jesus' attitude toward women was his vision of them as *persons* to whom and for whom he had come. He did not perceive them primarily in terms of their sex, age or marital status; he seems to have considered them in terms of their relation (or lack of one) to God" (Hurley, *Man and Woman in Biblical Perspective*, 83 (quoted by Grenz and Kjesbo, *Women in the Church*, 74). For similar remarks, see Grenz and Kjesbo, *Women in the Church*, 73–74 ; and Stagg and Stagg, 104–5.

religious awkwardness of the moment, but he is also cognizant of the deep pathos that leads this woman to express her gratitude and love so shockingly. And in that moment, Jesus affirms her intrinsic value.

Numerous other New Testament passages demonstrate Jesus' acknowledgement of the value of women as persons over against the social roles often prescribed to them. In the Gospel of John (4:1–41), we read of Jesus' encounter with a Samaritan woman. Strict Jewish piety forbade fraternizing with Samaritans, seeing them as religious heretics and political rivals. Piled onto these biases were the further restrictions against public interchanges between men and women, and especially against religious teachers speaking with women of questionable moral repute. But Jesus breached many of these expectations. In the heat of the day, as he sat at a well outside a Samaritan town, Jesus observed a lone woman approaching. He struck up a conversation, asking her to draw water for him to drink. Seemingly caught off-guard and perhaps cynically, the woman replied, "How is it that you, a Jew, ask a drink of me, a woman of Samaria?" (v. 9) In the exchange that follows, Jesus talks with her about God, true worship, the coming of the Messiah, and about living water—water that would spring up from within and bring eternal life and an end to thirst. Indeed, Jesus identifies himself as the promised Messiah and as the one who offers "living water."

In this conversation, Jesus breaks several religious restrictions. As a Jewish man and rabbi, he (1) discusses theology with a woman, (2) does so specifically with a Samaritan woman (3) interacts with a woman of questionable moral reputation.[32] And (4) he drinks from a ceremonially unclean vessel. When his disciples return from town with food, they are shocked by Jesus' behavior but say nothing to him. The end result is not only a free exchange of ideas between two persons—a man and a woman—but burgeoning gratitude and wonder within the woman because of her encounter with this caring and insightful man. When she returns to her village, she bears witness to her life-changing exchange with Jesus, and many from the town also came to faith in him.

Stanely J. Grenz and Denise Muir Kjesbo as well as Evelyn and Frank Stagg identify several other examples of Jesus's welcoming of women, as well as his positive teaching about them:

1. Countering prevailing social mores, Jesus freely associated with women, touching them and allowing them to touch him; he interacted with women who were ritually unclean (Matt 9:18–26) or of questionable morality (Luke 7:36–50).

2. Contrary to some rabbinic traditions, in his teachings, Jesus incorporated women's behavior as positive illustrations of religious principles (Matt 25:1–13; Mark 12:41–43; Luke 18:1–13) and even of the nature of God (Luke 15:3–10).

---

32. The text informs us that the woman had had five husbands and currently was living with a man—scandalous in the Jewish world.

3. Contrary to most rabbinic traditions, Jesus taught women and included them among his disciples (Luke 8:1–3). (This seems to be the central thrust of the story of Mary of Bethany "sitting at the feet" of Jesus and "listening" to him, in spite of protests from her sister Martha. The phrases "sitting at the feet" and "listening" were common synonyms for receiving religious training from a rabbi. See Luke 10:38–42).

4. In turn, especially in the Gospel John, both Mary and Martha are depicted as having deeper or quicker insight into the nature of Jesus and his mission than many of Jesus' male disciples. Martha confesses Jesus as the Messiah and as Son of God (11:27); and in anointing Jesus, Mary is pictured as understanding the nature of Jesus as a Messiah who would suffer and die (12:18).[33]

5. According to Luke 13:10–17, Jesus touched and healed a severely crippled woman in the face of criticism that he was breaching the prohibition against working on the Sabbath. In touching and healing the woman, he "gave her priority over the Sabbath, and over his own security."[34]

6. In the Sermon on the Mount (Matt 5–7), Jesus condemns the action of "looking upon a woman for the purpose of lusting after her" (5:27–28). He thus made adultery an act that could be committed against women and not just against a man's right of virtual ownership over his wife. Jesus also made adultery a matter of inner thoughts, not just of outward behaviors.

7. In turn, Jesus championed the right of a faithful wife to not be arbitrarily divorced by her husband—something that traditional interpretations of the Torah seemed to allow (Matt 5:31–32).[35]

8. A final significant feature of the gospels' vision of Jesus is this: In all of the Gospels, the first to witness Jesus' resurrection and to bear testimony to others of this event were women, especially Mary Magdalene (Matt 28:1–10; Mark 16:1–8; Luke 24:1–12; John 20:1–10).

As Evelyn and Frank Stagg note, the fact that all four Gospels share similar stories about Jesus' treatment of and teaching about women suggests two important truths. First, there were likely early Christian sources that recognized and highlighted these features of Jesus' manner and ministry, suggesting that indeed such activities went back to Jesus himself. Second, such affirmations of women were common among several important Christian communities well into the late first century.

From this summary of biblical history and ideals, it is apparent there are (at least apparent) tensions in the scriptural understanding of women and of their

33. Grenz and Kjesbo, *Women in the Church*, 73–76

34. Stagg and Stagg, *Women in the World of Jesus*, 106.

35. Stagg and Stagg, *Women in the World of Jesus*, 128–32.

place in the Christian church. How might these diverse biblical traditions regarding women be reconciled?

Contemporary Approaches to Women in Ministry

Since the 1960s, a sizable number of Christian writers has emerged addressing various interpretive riddles regarding the Bible's, and especially Paul's, understanding of women and of women in ministry. Linked to these exegetical tasks are wider issues of social inclusivism and social justice. At the risk of over-simplification, we may distinguish five general Christian approaches to the issue of women in ministry—that is, to the issue of including or excluding women from certain kinds of ministry.[36] These approaches are

1. the traditionalist approach

2. the Evangelical complementarian approach

3. The Evangelical egalitarian approach

4. The moderate egalitarian approach[37]

---

36. These approaches vary not only in terms of the limitations they place on women in ministry but also in terms of the sources they rely upon for doctrinal authority and how they use those sources. Traditionalists affirm the authority of both Scripture and the formal teachings of the church, relying heavily upon the decisions of church councils and ecclesial leaders to establish right beliefs. By Traditionalists, then, we primarily mean Roman Catholics, Eastern Orthodox, and (to greater or lesser degrees) Anglicans—although, as noted below, several key sixteenth-century Protestant Reformers and the movements that sprang from them also are included in the Traditionalist category. Evangelicals (whether complementarian or egalitarian) are Protestants and, as such, rely primarily upon Scriptures as the source of their doctrine. But how they approach scripture varies sometimes with other Protestant thinkers. Many Evangelicals (both Complementarian and Egalitarian) hold an inerrantist understanding of the Bible and, fueled by this belief, often deem it necessary to reconcile or harmonize seemingly contradictory scriptural teachings. Moderates also are Protestants who hold the scriptures in high-esteem, but they are often less comfortable using the term *inerrancy* to describe the Bible. Many prefer phrases like "general reliability" to describe how Scriptures function. (Although, many moderates feel it incumbent to endorse "inerrancy of scripture" and, thus, define inerrancy in terms of general reliability or inerrancy of purpose). An irony is that Moderates as well as "Evangelicals" (as defined above) often consider themselves to be Evangelicals, so that the nomenclature in this chapter is slippery at best and often depends on who is doing the defining. In my own estimation, all three of these groups (Evangelical complementarians, Evangelical egalitarians, and Moderate egalitarians) have a place at the Evangelical table. But obviously, not all would agree with this assessment. As Protestants, Liberals likewise endorse the authority of Scripture; but often, for Liberals, reason plays a more significant role in establishing religious teachings or truths than is the case for the other models mentioned here. While all these approaches affirm the value of reason for grasping and even (at times) establishing religious truth, Liberals often take this a step further by proposing that upon occasion reason can trump or augment principles or propositions clearly taught in Scriptures (and in church history). For a helpful commentary on the varied uses of Scripture among Christian scholars regarding feminist issues, see Japinga, *Feminism and Christianity*, especially 35–54.

37. As commented in the previous note, many writers would see those I am naming Moderates to be Evangelicals as well.

5. The liberal egalitarian approach

By *the traditionalist approach*, I mean an approach taken by those who endorse the historically held view of many Christians throughout the ages that women are not to serve as bishops, priests, or pastors of the church. Such a view was supported by various luminaries of the Orthodox and Catholic tradition, including Clement of Rome, Tertullian, John Chrysostom, and Augustine of Hippo.[38] Several early Protestant Reformers, including Martin Luther[39] and John Calvin,[40] likewise restricted the role of women as pastors and presbyters, even while endorsing the doctrine of the priesthood of believers.

Not infrequently throughout history, such denials of ordained ministry to women were accompanied by demeaning attitudes toward the character and capabilities of women. Thus, Origen writes: "Men should not sit and listen to a woman . . . even if she says admirable things, or even saintly things, that is of little consequence, *since it came from the mouth of a woman*."[41] John Chrysostom declares: "God maintained the order of each sex by dividing the business of life into two parts, and assigned the more necessary and beneficial aspects to the man and the *less important, inferior matter to the woman*."[42] Tertullian says to women:

> And do you not know that you are (each) an Eve? The sentence of God on this sex of yours lives in this age: the guilt must of necessity live too. You are the devil's gateway: you are the unsealer of that (forbidden) tree: you are the first deserter of the divine law: you are she who persuaded him whom the devil was not valiant enough to attack. You destroyed so easily God's image, man. On account of your desert—that is, death—even the Son of God had to die.[43]

The demeaning nature of Origen's, Chrysostom's, and Tertullian's words hardly needs commentary, including especially Tertullian's less than subtle proclivity to blame women for humanity's fall into sin and for the need for Christ to die!

In similar language, Augustine notes, "Woman was given to man, woman *who was of small intelligence* and who perhaps still lives more in accordance with the

38. See *StayCatholic.com*, "The Early Church Fathers on Women's Ordination."

39. In his *Lectures on Genesis* volume 1, Luther comments that currently women are ruled by men and wives ruled by their husbands by divine command as punishment for Eve's sin. So now "the rule remains with the husband, and the wife is compelled to obey him by God's command." The husband rules at home and in the state, while the wife stays at home "as one who has been deprived of the ability of administering those affairs that are outside and concern the state" (Luther, *Lectures on Genesis*, quoted in Ruether, *Sexism and God-Talk*, 97).

40. See Calvin, *Commentaries on the First Book of Moses*, 1:129–130, 172.

41. Origen, *Fragments on 1 Corinthians* (italics added). The quotes in this section from Origen, John Chrysostom, Tertullian, and Augustine all come from this internet source: https://margmowczko.com/misogynist-quotes-from-church-fathers; however, in the footnotes that follow, I also have identified the literary sources from which these quotes originated.

42. John Chrysostom, "The Kind of Women Who Ought to Be Taken as Wives" (italics added).

43. Tertullian, *On the Apparel of Women*.

promptings of the inferior flesh than by superior reason."[44] And again, Augustine writes:

> The woman together with her own husband is the image of God, so that that whole substance may be one image; but when she is referred separately to her quality of help-meet, which regards the woman herself alone, then *she is not the image of God*; but as regards the man alone, he is the image of God as fully and completely as when the woman too is joined with him in one."[45]

Thomas Aquinas likewise offers some disparaging comments about women. Attempting to defend the dignity of women, Thomas asserts that their servitude to men is not demeaning, for there are two kinds of subjugation:

> One is servile, by virtue of which a superior makes use of a subject *for his own benefit*; and this kind of subjection began *after sin*. There is another kind of subjection which is called economic or civil, whereby the superior makes use of his subjects *for their own benefit and good*; and this kind of subjection *existed even before sin*. For good order would have been wanting in the human family if some were not governed by others *wiser than themselves*. So by such a kind of subjection woman is *naturally subject to man, because in man the discretion of reason predominates*.[46]

Here Thomas declares that women are to be subject to the benevolent authority of men because reason "predominates" in men and men are wiser than women. Further, this condition of servitude exists by nature, as part of God's original design for creation, and it is not due (simply) to the fall into sin.

In addition, Thomas explains why it is fitting that woman was created from man, specifically from his rib. One reason for this was "for the purpose of domestic life, in which each has his or her *particular duty*, and in which the man is the *head of the woman*. Wherefore it was suitable for the woman to be made out of man, as out of her principle."[47] Additionally, woman was made from the man's rib "to signify the social union of man and woman, for the woman should neither 'use authority over man,' and so she was not made from his head; nor was it right for her to be subject to man's contempt as his slave, and so she was not made from his feet."[48] In the first rationale above, Thomas affirms the headship (interpreted as authority) of husbands over wives. In the second rationale, Thomas endorses the near-equal social relationship between husbands and wives. But he stops short of asserting precisely male-female social equality, and he explicitly denies that women are to rule over men. Clearly, at times, demeaning attitudes toward and beliefs about women (including tendencies to

---

44. Augustine, *The Literal Meaning of Genesis*, 11.42 (italics added).

45. Augustine, *On the Trinity*, 12.7.10 (italics added).

46. Thomas Aquinas, *Summa Theologica*, part 1, q. 92, art. 1 (italics added).

47. Thomas Aquinas, *Summa Theologica*, part 1, q. 92, art. 2 (italics added).

48. Thomas Aquinas, *Summa Theologica*, part 1, q. 92, art. 3.

question their intellectual and leadership capacities and even to blame them for the fall of humankind) are part of the Western Christian tradition.

Today while much of the more demeaning language of the past has been toned down (although not always rejected), traditionalist attitudes still often deny to women opportunities to minister, particularly in offices of leadership in the church. Roman Catholic policymakers are still opposed to ordaining women to the ecclesial offices of deacon, priest, or bishop. And until recently, the Anglican tradition had refused to ordain women—a view defended by E. L. Mascall and C. S. Lewis.[49] The traditional approach was expressed by Pope Paul VI, when who wrote in 1975:

> It is not admissible to ordain women to the priesthood, for very fundamental reasons. These reasons include: the example recorded in the Sacred Scriptures of Christ choosing his Apostles only from among men; the constant practice of the Church, which has imitated Christ in choosing only men; and her living teaching authority which has consistently held that the exclusion of women from the priesthood is in accordance with God's plan for his Church.[50]

By *the Evangelical complementarian approach*, I mean a view taken by those Protestants who typically hold a high view of scriptural authority, often even endorsing (and seeing as fundamental) the doctrine of biblical inerrancy. These conservative Protestants insist that the scriptural testimony clearly limits the ministerial roles of women and affirms the ecclesial and familial subordination of women to men. Typically, these authors also perceive the subordination of and ministerial limits of women as grounded in a deep-seated schema within creation that has been ordained by God. These conservative Protestant writers often refer to their perspective as complementarian, holding that men and women play distinct but complimentary roles in the church and in the created order.

By the Evangelical egalitarian approach, I mean a perspective held by Protestant writers who, like their complementarian counterparts, hold a high view of scriptural authority; many of these in fact endorse scriptural inerrancy. Nevertheless, unlike their complementarian colleagues, these conservative authors do not think the Scriptures (including Paul's letters) generally mandate upon women (as a class) ministerial limitations or subordination to men. Rather, these writers often interpret the restrictions found in some of Paul's letters as contextually limited (as dealing with specific problems within particular Christian congregations or within the broader context of the first-century Mediterranean culture) and not as required in all congregations at all times. These theologically conservative authors see themselves as egalitarians, insisting that men and women (as classes) can be equally equipped and called by God to bare the burdens and reap the benefits of leadership within the church and family.

49. Mascall, "Women and the Priesthood of the Church"; and Lewis, "Priestesses in the Church?"

50. Pope Paul VI, "Response to the Letter of His Grace the Most Reverend Dr. F. D. Coggan, Archbishop of Canterbury," quoted in Pope John Paul II, *Ordinatio Sacerdotalis* (1994).

Both Evangelical complementarians and Evangelical egalitarians work toward reconciling seemingly contradictory biblical teachings. Complementarians, however, tend to see those biblical passages that limit women's roles in the church and that require submission from females to male-authority as interpretively primary. Thus, these complementarian authors attempt to construe seemingly egalitarian scriptural passages so as to be compliant with the more restrictive demands of other New Testament writings. Egalitarians reverse this order. They tend to see the more egalitarian-sounding scriptural passages as foundational, and thus they interpret the more restrictive passages as situationally limited—that is, as dealing with peculiar contexts and not as universal applications. Examples of Evangelical complementarians are John Piper, Wayne Grudem,[51] and Thomas Schreiner.[52] Among Evangelical egalitarians are Stanley J. Grenz, Denise Muir Kjesbo,[53] Craig S. Keener,[54] and Alvera Mickelsen.[55]

Like the Evangelical egalitarian approach, *the moderate egalitarian approach* emphasizes those passages of Scripture that depict or explicitly affirm women as essentially equal with men.[56] In turn, moderates often attempt to soften the sharper edges of some Pauline passages and to seek to understand and reconstruct the historical contexts that may have brought about the apostle's (or the Pauline authors') more restrictive demands upon women in the church and home. If there is a difference between moderate versus Evangelical writers, it is that moderates are more open to admitting irreconcilable tensions in the biblical text rather than feeling obligated to harmonize scriptures that (in the moderate's estimation) genuinely conflict with one another. Prime examples of those I have dubbed moderate egalitarians are Evelyn and Frank Stagg,[57] Paul K. Jewett,[58] and Lynn Japinga.[59]

Those Christian writers who subscribe to what I call *the liberal egalitarian approach* are more prone to see irreconcilable claims within the biblical literature and to recommend those scriptural teachings most compliant with egalitarian ideals while dismissing scriptural teachings that are not so compliant. Such writers wish to honor, even celebrate, the grand humanizing ideals expressed in the Bible and in the Christian tradition. But they do not feel obligated to defend biblical or traditional views that (in the liberal's estimation) fall short of or even contradict these venerable principles. And they see no rationally persuasive reason to attempt to reconcile scriptural passages that are plainly ideologically at odds with one another. Some liberal egalitarians see genuine

51. Piper and Grudem, *Recovering Biblical Manhood & Womanhood.*

52. Schreiner, "Women in Ministry."

53. Grenz and Kjesbo, *Women in the Church.*

54. Keener, *Paul, Women & Wives.*

55. Mickelsen, "An Egalitarian View."

56. Equal in terms of salvation, discipleship, and leadership in the church.

57. See Stagg and Stagg, *Women in the World of Jesus.*

58. See Jewett, *Man as Male and Female,* especially 50–61, 112–13, 147–49.

59. Japinga, *Feminism and Christianity.*

if tenuous progress in human history toward more egalitarian ideals and practices, and they find this progress more compliant with the dictates of morality and reason than the more socially restrictive rationales and customs of the past. In this sense, reason at times plays the role of judge over some aspects of the biblical tradition. Rosemary Radford Ruether exemplifies the liberal egalitarian perspective.[60]

Complementarians and Egalitarians

To close out this discussion of women in ministry, we consider two broad interpretive matrixes for understanding the biblical view (or views) of the social standing of women and of women in ministry. We especially focus on perspectives offered by Evangelical egalitarians and Evangelical complementarians, although a heathy dose of moderate egalitarian ideas likewise will be noted. We highlight these writings in part because of the wealth of literature that has arisen among these groups over the last several decades, including relatively extensive discussions of the biblical literature per se. Because these discussions are voluminous, our exposition can only be cursory at best.

For convenience, I will write in terms of two camps—complementarians and egalitarians—only sporadically distinguishing Evangelical egalitarians from moderate ones. And I will not discuss the views of what I have dubbed liberal egalitarians. Both Evangelical complementarians and (Evangelical and moderate) egalitarians acknowledge that upon occasion the Old Testament literature recognizes females serving in key ministerial roles as prophets and judges. Both groups also acknowledge the countercultural, respectful, uplifting, and encouraging regard that Jesus showed toward women. Both factions likewise agree that in many ways distinct from the first-century (Second Temple) Jewish and Hellenistic tendencies, the early church allowed greater freedom to women to participate and serve in worship. Further, both camps agree that women in the early church engaged in diverse ministries, including teaching and speaking in worship services. Thus in some sense complementarians and egalitarians agree that Paul's admonition for women to be silent must be qualified in some way. Paul's comment cannot be understood to mean that women are not to say anything ever, or that women are to say nothing in worship services, or that women are to say nothing to men or not to teach men, given that the New Testament often recognizes and even celebrates many such activities practiced by women.

Complementarians as well as egalitarians often agree that women could and did perform a host of ministries in the early church, and that typically such ministries were (and still are) founded upon a person's giftedness for the task—a giftedness bequeathed by the Spirit of God and sanctioned by divine calling. Like egalitarians, complementarians often acknowledge that a few women were prophets in the Old Testament era, and that some women prophesied and thus were prophets (in some

60. See Chapter 10, above (pages 329–334).

sense) in New Testament times. Further, the prophesies of such women in the New Testament era were often spoken in public church gatherings. Many complementarians (although not all) recognize that women sometimes were deacons in the early church. And some (although not all) complementarians hold that Junia was a woman and was in some sense an apostle.[61] Finally, many complementarians acknowledge that women can and did teach in the early church, and that such teaching is still sanctioned today; first, women taught other women and children. And often, at least informally, they taught men (as Priscilla did Apollos). Often complementarians qualify the nature of all these female ministries so as to ensure that women did not somehow usurp the primary authority of men.

The principal difference between complementarians and egalitarians is that while egalitarians think women can hold any ministerial position, including the offices of elder or presbyter or priest or bishop, complementarians do not. Specifically, complementarians bar women from senior pastoral positions (that is, from what I called above positions of culminating ecclesial authority), seeing such contemporary positions as analogates of the ancient church's offices of elder, presbyter, and bishop. John Piper and Wayne Grudem make their perspective plain:

> We are persuaded that the Bible teaches that only men should be pastors and elders. That is, men should bear *primary* responsibility for Christlike leadership and teaching in the church. So it is unbiblical, we believe, and therefore detrimental for women to assume this role.[62]

Complementarians see these restrictions upon women to be the primary point Paul was making in his admonition to woman to be silent in church and to submit to men (1 Tim 2:11–15).

Whereas both complementarians and egalitarians agree that the husband-wife relationship is one of mutual love and mutual submission (Eph 5:21), complementarians tend to highlight the wife's responsibility to submit to the husband's authority (Eph 5:22–24, 33) and for the husband to love, protect, and care for the wife (Eph 5:25–33).[63] Egalitarians, on the other hand, often stress the need for mutual submission and mutual love, seeing each partner as carrying equal degrees of personal

---

61. Often complementarians qualify the sense of Junia's apostolicity to mean she was one who was sent on mission and not one who held authority (especially over men). See Piper and Grudem, *Recovering Biblical Manhood & Womanhood*, 79–81.

62. Piper and Grudem, *Recovering Biblical Manhood & Womanhood* 60–61.

63. Piper and Grudem assert: "We believe the Bible teaches that God means the relationship between husband and wife to portray the relationship between Christ and His church. The husband is to model the loving, sacrificial leadership of Christ, and the wife is to model the glad submission offered freely by the church . . . Submission refers to a wife's divine calling to honor and affirm her husband's leadership and help carry it through according to her gifts. It is not an absolute surrender of her will. Rather, we speak of her disposition to yield to her husband's guidance and her inclination to follow his leadership" (Piper and Grudem, *Recovering Biblical Manhood & Womanhood*, 61).

authority and responsibility for caring for the other's needs, concerns, aspirations, and so forth.[64]

The Evangelical Complementarian Case

For complementarians, a primary interpretive clue for understanding Paul's case for the submission of females to male authority at home and in the church is found in the apostle's appeal to the created order. In 1 Cor 11, part of Paul's rationale for men not wearing head coverings and for women wearing head coverings is that man "is the image and reflection of God; but woman is the reflection of man" (v. 7). Further, "man was not made from woman, but woman from man." Additionally, man was not "created for the sake of woman, but woman for the sake of man" (vv. 8–9). In a similar manner, for Paul a crucial rationale for women being silent and submissive in the church is that "Adam was formed first, then Eve; and Adam was not deceived, but the woman was deceived and became a transgressor" (1 Tim 2:13–14).

Clearly, Paul draws these *reasons* for various restrictions upon women from the creation narratives of Gen 1–3. The claims that Adam was created *before* Eve, and that the woman was made *from the man* seem to flow from explicit assertions of the Gen 2 narrative. The notion that the woman was made *for the sake of* the man seems to be a reasonable—but not explicit—extrapolation from the same narrative's announcement that God made the woman so that the man might not be alone and might have a helper. And the proposition that Adam was not deceived but the woman was deceived also seems to be a plausible, if not necessary, inference from the Gen 3, where the woman (and not the man) was directly addressed and subsequently deceived by the serpent. More puzzling, and seemingly questionable, is Paul's notion that man is in the image of God, but the woman is in the image of man (1 Cor 11:7). This idea is more problematic because a straightforward reading of Gen 1 says that God created humankind, both male and female, in the divine image. (In the interest of time and space, we will not explore this last interpretive caveat from Paul.) In sum, then, Paul grounds his *reasons* for certain restrictions on women on his reading of Genesis 1–3.

Less clear in Paul's exposition is how or why his reasons necessitate or explain the occurrence of divinely sanctioned restrictions upon women. Paul does not precisely articulate how these claims about creation lead to the conclusion that God wills that women be silent (in some circumstances) or be submissive to male authority or cover their heads in worship.[65] At this point, however, complementarians offer a pivotal

---

64. A subtle, but significant, difference that often arises between complementarian- and egalitarian- interpretations of Eph 5 arises over how Eph 5:21 fits within the context of the materials around it. The verse states: "Be subject to one another out of reverence for Christ." Complementarians often see this sentence summing up the ideas expressed in Eph 4:17—5:20 regarding general behaviors of Christians toward one another. Egalitarians, on the other hand, often see this verse as qualifying the ideas expressed in 5:22–32, which deal with husband-and-wife relationships.

65. In the field of logic, one would say that Paul supplies the reader with conclusions, and offers

interpretive proposal to explain how Paul connects these elements of the creation narrative to the conclusion that certain restrictions are to be imposed upon women. That crucial principle is the *headship* (interpreted as *authority*) of men over women.

Clearly, in his writings on these matters Paul links various restriction on women to the headship of men. This is most explicitly stated in Eph 5:22–24, when Paul says:

> Wives, be subject to your husbands as you are to the Lord. For the husband is the *head* of the wife just as Christ is the *head* of the church, the body of which he is the Savior. Just as the church is subject to Christ, so also wives ought to be, in everything, to their husbands. (Italics added)

Here, a wife's submission to her husband is justified (somehow) on the grounds that the husband is head (interpreted as authority by complementarians) of his wife.

Paul offers a similar rationale for women wearing head coverings in worship in 1 Cor 11, although his reasoning is less transparent. He opens his address with this comment: "I want you to understand that Christ is the *head* of every man, and the husband is the *head* of his wife" (v. 3). With this principle in mind, Paul declares that women dishonor their "heads" (likely meaning men) by not covering their physical heads in worship (v. 5).[66] While the logical link is not abundantly obvious, there seems to be some connection between the headship of men over women and the restriction that women cover their physical heads in worship.

But how does the notion of male headship relate to the creation accounts of Gen 2 and 3? The linchpin for complementarians is Paul's assertion, in 1 Tim 2:11–15, that women should "learn in silence with full submission" and should not "teach or have authority over a man" *because "Adam was formed first, then Eve."* For complementarians, because of the similarity between Paul's reasoning in 1 Tim 2 and his reasoning in 1 Cor 11, the meaning of the claim that "Adam was formed first, then Eve" is virtually synonymous (at least in terms of its implications) with Paul's assertion that men have headship (authority) over women. In 1 Timothy, Paul reasons that certain restrictions apply to women *because* Adam was formed first. In like manner, Paul reasons in 1 Cor 11 that key boundaries apply to women *because* men hold headship (authority) over them. In short, according to complementarians, the essential meaning or import of Paul's assertion that "Adam was formed first" is that men have headship (authority) over women. *Further, for complementarians, these ideas together (Adam's priority and male headship) serve as the reason that women are to submit to male authority and the reason that some ministries are forbidden to women.*

---

a few premises for such conclusions, but leaves unwritten those premises required to make the arguments complete (and thus plausible or valid). Further, it is not abundantly clear what these premises might be. This criticism especially is true about the rationales for the silence of women and for their submission to males. Paul's reasoning is a bit clearer (or explicitly stated) about women wearing head-coverings but even this argument has considerable obscurities.

66. Paul writes, "Any man who prays or prophesies with something on his head disgraces his head, but any woman who prays or prophesies with her head unveiled disgraces her head" (1 Cor 11:4–5).

All of this leads to an intriguing interpretation of the creation narratives of Gen 2 and 3. According to Thomas R. Schreiner and other complementarians, these narratives (implicitly if not explicitly) point to male leadership in several ways. First, Gen 2 suggests that because Adam was created first, he "had a particular responsibility to lead in his relationship with Eve." And "correspondingly, Eve had a responsibility to follow Adam's leadership."[67] Schreiner admits that the text does not directly state this, but he believes that such an interpretation fits well with answering the question: "Why does the narrator bother to tell us that the man was created first and then the woman?"[68] More importantly, notes Schreiner, such an interpretation is canonically warranted: Paul surmises that *because Adam was created first*, women are forbidden to "teach and exercise authority over a man."[69] In short, the Gen 2 narrative insinuates men's authority over women when it declares that Adam was created first, and Paul presumes this interpretation of that text when he calls upon women to submit to men's authority on the grounds that "Adam was first, and not Eve."

Schreiner, like other complementarians, finds several other hints in Gen 2 and 3 that allegedly point toward male authority, including that

1. Eve was created for the purpose of helping Adam, not the reverse of this (Gen 2:18, 20)

2. Adam named the woman as he did the other animals—an act often associated with having dominance (Gen 2:18–20).

3. After their sin, God questioned Adam first rather than Eve, even though the woman was the first to sin (Gen 3:8–12).

Finally, a common proposal among complementarians—including for Schreiner—is that a critical component of the serpent's enticement of Eve was not only the temptation to disobey God but also the lure for Eve of usurping the God-given leadership of Adam in religious and familial affairs. Along with other complementarians, Schreiner admits that this last interpretation is questionable—based on limited evidence and considerable conjecture. Nevertheless, Schreiner thinks this interpretation is at least hinted at by Paul in 1 Tim 1:14 when the apostle says, "And Adam was not deceived, but the woman was deceived and became a transgressor."[70]

From this long list of reasons, complementarians conclude that while women can and do perform multiple ministries in the church, and while (at times) such ministries involve some degree of authority, women cannot hold positions of primary authority in the church or in the home. Such responsibilities fall exclusively to

67. Schreiner, "Women in Ministry," 202.

68. Schreiner, "Women in Ministry," 202.

69. Schreiner, "Women in Ministry," 203.

70. Schreiner, "Women in Ministry," 203–10. For similar interpretations of Gen 1–3, as well as various other biblical texts cited above, see Piper and Grudem, *Recovering Biblical Manhood & Womanhood*.

men. In short, the mandates upon women to submit to men's authority in the church and in the home, and prohibitions against women holding culminating positions of authority in the church, are grounded in a divinely authorized social structure that is cut into the very fabric of the created order.

The Evangelical Egalitarian Case

Egalitarians offer their own interpretations of the various Pauline passages, mentioned above. Craig S. Keener, as do other egalitarians, proposes that the primary issue Paul is addressing in 1 Cor 14:34–35 is how women *learn*, rather than whether or not women should speak per se. In verse 35, Paul encourages women to ask their husbands while at home if they desire to understand something being taught (presumably during church gatherings). Hence, Paul's admonitions in v. 34 (for women to be silent, not to speak, and to be subordinate) may apply only to those specific contexts when some women were disrupting corporate meetings where teaching or preaching was occurring. According to this view, Paul's admonitions were not intended to curtail all speech from women during worship services. This is especially obvious given the fact that earlier in the letter, Paul assumed that women pray and prophesy in church (1 Cor 11:5). Keener notes that it was common in the ancient world for hearers (especially advanced students) to ask questions of and offer responses to speakers in public venues. Such interchanges, however, often were frowned upon when initiated by novices. Further, since many women in the first century were relatively uneducated, this restriction may have been designed to curtail disruptive outbursts from uninformed parishioners. This may especially have been the case for Gentile women participating in a relatively new religion of Jewish origins. Keener proposes that Paul's call for female silence was a temporary fix for a short-term problem.[71]

Regarding 1 Tim 2:11, Keener observes that Paul's "instructions are firm. The women must remain silent." Keener argues, however, that "if pressed to mean all it could mean, this would prohibit" a whole host of practices otherwise sanctioned by Paul in other texts as well as in the New Testament as a whole. Keener notes, however, that the context of these verses (1 Tim 2:11–14) suggests Paul's prohibition primarily has to do with teaching (not with speaking per se) since Paul explicitly says, "I permit no woman to teach or to have authority over a man" (v. 12). So, the restriction on women for complete silence is avoided. Nevertheless, argues Keener, even granting this emphasis in Paul, if pressed to its fullest meaning, the passage would mean that women cannot teach men at all—contrary to Priscilla's teaching Apollos (Acts 18:26) and perhaps contrary to women prophesying in worship services (1 Cor 11: 5 and 14:3). It also would de facto undermine numerous practices in contemporary churches, including many complementarian congregations.[72] In

71. Keener, "Women in Ministry," 50–52.

72. Keener, "Women in Ministry," 52–53. Incidentally, it might be noted that it is because of these

light of these tensions especially tensions with some of Paul's own writings, Keener suggests that Paul's mandates here are not meant to be applied universally but only in very specific contexts. Keener believes the historical setting of Paul's writing 1 Timothy suggests that the specific issue confronting Timothy's church was the threat of false teachers, who were exploiting the ignorance of unlearned women to spread their false beliefs—women who were promoting these same errant doctrines. Thus, according to Keener, Paul's prohibition against women teaching men (1 Tim 2:12) and his encouraging them to "learn in silence with full submission" (v. 11) may have been directed at women who were poorly informed and who were teaching (perhaps just parroting) the doctrinal nonsense of false teachers.[73]

Some complementarians criticize interpretations like Keener's above on the grounds that such readings fail to take seriously the fact that Paul grounds his commands to women (in 1 Timothy 2) in universal principles—namely, in the principles that (1) "Adam was formed first, then Eve" (1 Tim 2:13) and that (2) the woman (Eve) was deceived but not the man (1 Tim 2:14). According to such reasoning, since Paul bans females from teaching or exercising authority over males based on universal principles drawn from the created order, such bans must be universal as well. Hence, the commands that women not teach men or hold authority over them is universal.

To this criticism Keener replies that in point of fact Paul often uses scriptural passages with universal import to support principles that have only limited application. Hence, it is perfectly acceptable to suppose that Paul here is barring only women who had been deceived by false teachers in this specific congregation, not all women for all time.[74] Indeed, argues Keener, if the principle about Eve's deception were applied universally to women, it would imply that women *by nature* are more gullible, more easily deceived, than men. While some theologians across church history have endorsed this view, the majority of complementarians today wish to avoid such a conclusion. Further supporting his case, Keener notes that in 2 Cor 11:3, Paul uses the story of Eve's deception as an analogy to the kind of deception that befalls both men and women—including men and women in the Corinthian church. Nevertheless, no reader typically presumes that because men also are deceived as was Eve, men too should be banned from teaching. Rather, Keener points out that complementarians soon find themselves in trouble if they insist that principles grounded in the creation stories must be applied universally. For instance, in 1 Cor 11 Paul appeals to an "order of creation" analogy to support his claim that women should wear head coverings in

---

kinds of puzzles over universal application of sanctions on female actions that many complementarians have barred women only from senior pastoral and preaching positions and not from church-educational roles or even assistant pastoral positions.

73. Keener, "Women in Ministry," 53–54.

74. Keener, "Women in Ministry," 58–59.

church, but this too is a mandate that most complementarians do not wish to impose universally, even in their own congregations.[75]

Egalitarian Linda Belleville offers interpretations of various Pauline texts that are similar to those of Keener. Noting that much of Paul's concern in 1 Corinthians has to do with discord in worship, Belleville believes that, in 1 Cor 13:34–35, Paul is especially speaking to married women who want to *learn*, and who are thus asking questions. Their specific fault, however, was "not in the asking *per se*, but in the corporate disorder that their asking was producing."[76] According to Belleville, married women especially would have been asking such questions because of "the educational limits of married Greco-Roman women."[77] In this context, proposes Belleville, Paul calls upon certain married women to cease their disruptive behaviors and be silent and submissive (1 Cor 14:34). That Paul offers a similar admonition in 1 Cor 14:29–33 to prophets in the church reinforces this interpretation. Remarking that the spirits of the prophets are subject to (*submissive to*) the prophets, Paul encourages prophets to be *silent* when other prophets receive new revelations so that the prophets with new revelations can speak. This allows mutual learning and encouraging to occur in an orderly and respectful process. In short, Paul's concern in 1 Cor 14:34–35, as it is in much of the epistle, is to encourage orderly and considerate behavior during worship services; his intent is not to curtail women's speech universally in church.[78]

Regarding 1 Tim 2:11–15, Belleville contends that vv. 11 and 12 should be translated as "Let a woman learn in a quiet and submissive fashion. I do not, however, permit her to teach with the intent to dominate a man. She must be gentle in demeanor." Such a translation is quite different from the one rendered by the New Revised Standard Version, which reads, "Let a woman learn in silence with full submission. I permit no woman to teach or to have authority over a man; she is to keep silent." In the NRSV translation, the Greek word *hēsychia* is interpreted to mean literal silence. So, according to the NRSV, Paul is telling women to say nothing, not to speak. But, contends Belleville, Paul typically uses this word *hēsychia* in reference to calm and quiet behavior—that is, quietude or peacefulness (1 Thess 4:11; 2 Thess 3:12; 1 Tim 2:2). Indeed, this is how Paul uses the adjectival form of the word in the immediate context of 1 Tim 2 when he urges the Ephesian congregation to pray for government officials so that Christians can "lead a quiet and peaceful life" (2:2). Further, claims Belleville, interpreting *hēsychia* as "quietude" fits well with the overarching concerns of 1 Timothy—namely, concern over strife in the congregation due especially to false teachers (1:3–7, 18–20; 4:1–8; 5:20–22; 6:3–10, 20–21). Thus, according to Belleville,

75. Keener, "Women in Ministry," 62–63.

76. Belleville, "Women in Ministry," 115–16.

77. Belleville, "Women in Ministry," 116.

78. Belleville, "Women in Ministry," 119–20.

in 1 Tim 2:11–12, Paul is urging women to learn in noncontentious ways; he is not ordering them not to speak.[79]

In a similar manner, in Tim 2:12, Paul is not dictating that women can never teach or have authority over men. Rather, he is criticizing an inappropriate way of teaching men (or anyone else), namely, one that seeks to dominate or control someone. Belleville justifies this interpretation based on the fact that prior to the second century CE the Greek word *authenenein* typically denoted for "acts of violence" or domineering behavior, and not "having authority" (as the NRSV translates it). Further, the Greek grammar of *ouk . . . oude*, which links "to teach" and "to dominate" in verse 12, allows (or perhaps even supports) the interpretation that the latter word ("dominate") qualifies the former word ("teach"). Thus, as we have seen, Belleville translates verse 12 as, I do not permit a woman to "teach with the intent to dominate a man."

Linda Belleville believes that other considerations also support her interpretation of 1 Tim 2:11–12. First, such a translation fits well with Paul's overarching interest in 1 Timothy to squash congregation strife fueled by factional dissonance and arrogance. Second, such an interpretation matches well the historical context of the Ephesian church. The cult of Artemis was prevalent in ancient Ephesus, and according to the Artemis mythology "the female was exalted and considered superior to the male."[80] Hence, ideas from this cult easily could have been influencing some women of the Ephesian church to believe they were superior to men. Indeed, the evidence suggests that, in 1 Tim 2:14–15, Paul was intentionally countering aspects of the Artemis tradition. According to that tradition, women are superior to men in a way analogous to Artemis's superiority to her own spouse. And according to the Artemis myth, Artemis's superiority was founded on the fact that she was born first while her consort was born after her. In light of all this, it is not unreasonable to suppose that Paul sought to undermine the teaching of the pagan cult by pointing out that in the Jewish Christian tradition "Adam was formed first, then Eve" (v. 14). Although one might falsely interpret the temporal priority of Adam's formation to mean that men are superior to women, Paul's true point is simply that women are not superior to men (as the Artemis cult taught). Further, for Paul neither men nor women are to dominate each other.[81]

A final note is necessary here about Belleville's, and other egalitarian writers', case against the complementarian position. As we have noted above, a linchpin for

79. Belleville, "Women in Ministry," 120–23.

80. Belleville, "Women in Ministry," 128.

81. Belleville, "Women in Ministry," 123–30. There is further evidence that Paul was challenging elements of the cult of Artemis in his notoriously cryptic saying, in v. 15, that women "will be saved through childbearing, provided they continue in faith and love and holiness, with modesty." Adherents of the Artemis sect often credited the goddess with protecting women through childbirth. Paul's strange assertion may simply have been a deliberate contrast to this view, an assertion that a woman will be kept safe during the process of birthing children *through her faith in God and through holy living* (Belleville, "Women in Ministry," 128–29).

complementarian interpretations is the notion that male headship (interpreted as authority) implies female submission. However, Belleville, along with other egalitarians, argues that Paul's use of the concept of male headship may only be intended to indicate that Adam is the *source* of Eve, not the authority over her. This analogy (between the concept of head and the concept of source) seems closer to the intention of the Genesis narrative when the man declares that the woman is "bone of my bones and flesh of my flesh," and that for this reason the two are uniquely made for each other (2:23–24). The connection between the concept of head and the concept of source makes better sense of the teaching that Christ is the head of the church, argues Belleville. While Christ obviously is Lord over the church, Christ also is depicted as the head of his body, the church. In each case, claims Belleville, the notion of the head speaks of a mysterious and intimate relationship between two realities—the first a close personal unity of a husband and wife, and the second the mysterious spiritual unity of the church with Christ.

> The real bone of contention between traditionalists and egalitarians is over the meaning of the Greek word *kephalē* [head] . . . Traditionalists would argue that Paul is speaking of the church's submission to Christ as chief executive officer . . . An egalitarian view, by contrast, is *organic* ("constituting a whole whose parts are mutually dependent or intrinsically related"). It sees the male as the "source" (*kephalē*) of the female, whom God created "from him" to be his "partner." The divinely ordained relationship of male and female is, therefore, a mutually submissive one . . . Neither the male nor the female is to lead in a "domineering" (*authentein*) fashion (as the women at Ephesus were trying to do).[82]

The Moderate Egalitarian Case

Much more could be said about both Evangelical complementarian and Evangelical egalitarian views of women in ministry. The exposition above gives readers some idea of the intricacies of the debates, and it will have to suffice for now. Before closing these discussions, however, a word about moderate egalitarians is called for. As noted above, if there is a difference between Evangelical and moderate egalitarians, it is something like this: Evangelical egalitarians (as defined above) find it incumbent to harmonize the various teachings of the Bible, especially of the New Testament, as much as reasonably possible. This is done primarily in an effort to honor and maintain the authority of the Bible as a whole. The same can be said of Evangelical complementarians. Within each camp an earnest attempt is made to interpret the biblical texts so as to insure that essential agreement is found within the Scriptures as a whole. As many have pointed out, for many Evangelicals, the harmony of the biblical canon as a whole serves as a fundamental principle for interpreting particular texts. A great

---

82. Belleville, "Women in Ministry," 137–39 (brackets added).

benefit of this approach is that it often helps produce coherent systems of beliefs about what the Bible teaches. Yet a potential problem with this approach is that it sometimes generates strained interpretations of biblical passages that (at least at face value) seem to disagree with one another. This partly explains why both Evangelical complementarians and Evangelical egalitarians are reticent to apply universally Paul's mandates about women being silent or not teaching since other passages of Scripture seem to directly affirm females speaking and ministering in various ways in churches. Thus, complementarians narrow the restrictions upon women to a slender set of *ministerial offices* (the offices of elder or presbyter and the office of bishop), and egalitarians narrow the restrictions to specific *historical contexts* while affirming that (in principle) women can fill any ministerial office. In their own ways, each of these Evangelical camps tries to harmonize Paul's restrictions with broader Pauline and New Testament affirmations of women's activities in the early church.

Many moderate egalitarians feel less obligation than Evangelicals do to harmonize biblical texts (although even for them the degree of allowable dissonance between texts has its limits). Freedom for recognizing incongruities in the biblical literature is observed in writers such as Paul Jewett and Evelyn and Frank Stagg. In the following excerpt, Jewett demonstrates his willingness to recognize disharmony in the biblical text (and in Paul's writings):

> The character of redemptive history itself throws light on this antinomy. Because the society of ancient Israel was patriarchal, the man used the opportunity which such a societal pattern afforded him to dominate the woman, reducing her to the inferior status of a second-class citizen in the covenant community. Jesus, by contrast, though he was a man, never dominated women nor treated them as inferior . . . The apostle Paul was the heir of this contrast between the old and the new . . . He was a rabbi of impeccable erudition who had become an ardent disciple of Jesus Christ. And his thinking about women—their place in life generally and in the church specifically—reflects both his Jewish and his Christian experience . . . So far as he thought in terms of his Jewish background, he thought of the woman as subordinate to the man for whose sake she was created (1 Cor. 11:9). But so far as he thought in terms of the new insights he had gained through the revelation of God in Christ, he thought of the woman as equal to the man in all things, the two having been made one in Christ, in whom there is neither male nor female (Gal. 3:28).[83]

Just as Jewett acknowledges dissonance in the biblical literature, so the Staggs write:

> Compared with 1 Corinthians and the five letters containing the Domestic Code (Colossians, Ephesians, 1 Peter, Titus and 1 Timothy) woman's status as reflected in the Synoptics and Acts is amazingly free. There is no discernible disposition to place limits upon women . . . There are no references to the rib

---

83. Jewett, *Man as Male and Female*, 112.

> narrative of creation. There is no suggestion that woman is to be subordinate to man . . . There is no exclusion of women from teaching or preaching; there is rather an affirmation of woman's right to the study of the word and the ministry of the word . . . There is no hint that she is to be silent in church, and there are no directives as to her cosmetics or wardrobe.[84]

Clearly, both Jewett and the Staggs are content with the notion that there are theological and practical tensions in the biblical literature, including (at least minor) discord between the Pauline writings and the literature of the Synoptics and of Acts.

If an Evangelical should ask, How is an interpreter to choose which perspective to endorse when there is genuine dissonance in the New Testament literature? moderates seem to reply that the primary authority from which to draw Christian theological, interpersonal, and moral principles is Jesus Christ—his manners, directives, and teachings. Old Testament and even New Testament viewpoints that run counter to those of Jesus are subject to qualification if not dismissal. Such a view of tensions in the biblical literature is suggested in Jewett's comparison between insights drawn from Paul's rabbinic background and perspectives flowing from the apostle's encounter with Jesus.

The Staggs also seem to presume that Jesus' teachings, attitudes, and behaviors are the culminating guide for right theology and practice. They argue that with the passing of time, rigidity grew in the early church about women's relationships with men and with the church. In the earlier strata of the New Testament literature, Christian congregations—including women—seem to have had greater freedom to engage in diverse ministries as each congregant served the church as directed by and empowered by the Holy Spirit. The Staggs see this freer approach as more congruent with Jesus' own views than with later, more rigid perspectives. This is especially true regarding Jesus' dismissal of some traditional religious and cultural expectations of his day, in favor of stressing the value of individuals (including women) as they interrelate with God and with other humans. According to the Staggs, these more egalitarian interpretations of Jesus are especially preserved in the Synoptic Gospels, Acts, and the Johannine literature. And these traditions were still being honored by the communities by whom and to whom this literature was written late into the first century.

In the meantime, argue the Staggs, as other church-communities developed through the first century, the freer spirit of earlier days was being (somewhat) curtailed by more restrictive policies and perspectives on women and their ministry; these more rigid viewpoints were better attuned to the broader Jewish and Gentile cultures of their day. And it was these more rigid views that set the tone for some of the harsher restrictions found in later Pauline literature. The end result was dissonance between diverse factions within the late first-century church. Some of these Christian communities held onto the freer, more equalizing ethos of Jesus, while other

---

84. Stagg and Stagg, *Women in the World of Jesus*, 232–33.

communities adopted more rigid interpretations of how Christians were to interact with one another and with the broader culture.[85] With all this in mind, the Staggs close their book with the following comments:

> Hardened structures, fixed orders, and rules belong more to the developing church than to the movement [Christianity] at its rise. The church today may opt for hardened structures, thus favoring its later stages, or it may opt for more openness to the moving of God's Spirit and its own earliest flexibility. It seems to us that the greater our openness to the manner and teaching of Jesus, the greater the freedom and responsibility of woman (and all others) in the gifts and the demands of him who is the head of his body, the church.[86]

For many Christians predisposed to affirm egalitarianism and also wishing to honor the authority of Scripture, it is not obvious which approach—Evangelical egalitarianism or moderate Egalitarianism—best suits them, if either does. New Testament scholar Adam Winn offers something of a halfway house between what I have dubbed the Evangelical egalitarian approach and the Moderate egalitarian approach. Unlike Evangelical Egalitarians, and more like moderates, Winn acknowledges real tensions in Paul's pronouncements. In some passages Paul sincerely endorses egalitarian ideals, and in others he earnestly commends nonegalitarian restrictions upon women. And Paul does this fully (or sufficiently) cognizant of the tensions between his declarations. Thus, contrary to Jewett's interpretation above, Paul did not *unwittingly* contradict himself. Rather, he was well aware of the seismic implications of genuine equality in Christ—a view that Paul himself fully endorsed. That is, Paul understood and endorsed the substantial changes that such equality would require of his society. Nevertheless, Paul issued restrictive commands upon wives and women anyway; and Paul did this, knowing that such restrictions ultimately were not cohesive with the true equality implicit in Christ and in Christ's community.

But why did Paul call for such restrictions? Winn proposes that perhaps Paul did this for the sake of the Christian mission. Paul believed that an attempt to impose the implications of equality in Christ in the Greco-Roman world would have undermined the gospel's appeal to Paul's ancient audiences (Jews and Gentiles alike), who were steeped in male-authoritarian assumptions. Thus, to demand the full implications of equality in Christ would have preempted the spread of the gospel. In turn, while Paul fully understood the implications of equality in Christ, *for the sake of the Christian mission*, he did not attempt to impose all of those ramifications upon congregations steeped in an unreceptive culture. Rather, Paul sought first to establish a foothold for the gospel in the Greco-Roman world.

According to Winn, such an interpretation of Paul is supported by the apostle's approach to missions to his fellow Jews. At times, Paul employed a strategy of conforming

---

85. Stagg and Stagg, *Women in the World of Jesus*, 205–58, especially 232–33, 251–52, and 258.

86. Stagg and Stagg, *Women in the World of Jesus*, 258 (brackets added).

to some expectations of first-century Jewish culture in order to enhance the effectiveness of the Christian mission. Thus, while Paul fully recognized that following the law was not "a necessary and guiding reality for the new covenant people of God," he nevertheless "often followed the law or lived like one under the law" for the sake of missional strategy (see 1 Cor 9:19–23). Paul even circumcised a Gentile convert, Timothy, for the sake of the Christian mission to Jews (Acts 16).

Hence, when Paul mandated that wives be subject to their husbands (Eph 5:22) and that women be silent before male authority in the church (1 Tim 2:12), the apostle was not seeking to establish *universal* familial or ecclesiological principles. Rather, Paul was proposing a compromising strategy. He was recommending behaviors that would help insure that the message of Christ would be not only heard but also received by the broader culture of his day.

With a touch of irony, Winn further notes that since egalitarianism is now the favored perspective of Western culture, contemporary complementarian attempts to undermine the equality of women (by prohibiting them from engaging in key ministries and family roles) in fact generate "a major roadblock to [contemporary] missional efforts."[87] In short, the missional strategy fueling Paul's restrictions on women in the ancient world now compels the contemporary church to affirm an egalitarian approach toward women in ministry (as well as in familial and broader social roles). This is the case in part because such an approach better fits the ethos of the contemporary culture. Furthermore, and perhaps more importantly, such egalitarianism better fits the equality implicit in the Christian's and the Christian community's oneness in Christ.

Conclusion

The debates over the role of women in the life and ministry of the church will almost certainly continue into the near future, as will debates over the issues discussed in Chapters 13 and 14 of this book—namely, the problem of evil, the interplay between Christianity and other religions, and the relationship of science and the faith. In each case, our discussion here has only scratched the surface of these complex matters. For some believers and nonbelievers alike, such debates are seen as challenges to the very fabric of Christianity. But for others, these disputes are signs of the ongoing vitality of the Christian faith as it dialogues with the concrete realities of human life in this universe.

87. Winn, "Ephesians 5:21–33"; and Winn, "1 Timothy 2:11–15," unpublished lectures given in 2020 at the University of Mary Hardin-Baylor.

Epilogue

CHRISTIANITY IS A RELIGIOUS way of life centered on the person, life, teaching, death, and resurrection of Jesus the Christ. Like other religions, Christianity is multifaceted, involving numerous beliefs and practices. Throughout these pages, we have examined many of the key features of the Christian faith. Among these features are the following: Christianity is grounded on four core foundations—namely (1) the sacred story of Israel, (2) the life and person of Jesus, (3) the earliest community or communities of believers that gathered around Jesus, and (4) the scriptural heritage that arose out of these various components. From these foundations, and mixed with the ongoing experiences and insights of generations of Christians that followed, there arose a complex system (or systems) of doctrinal beliefs, moral affirmations and practices, and ways of worship.

Christian theology often focuses on nine core doctrinal areas:

1. Revelation and Authority (How are God and religious truths known?)

2. God (What is God's nature?)

3. Creation and providence (How does God relate to reality as a whole?)

4. Humans (What is the nature of humans?)

5. Sin (What is the core human dilemma?)

6. Christ (What is Christ's nature and work?)

7. Salvation (How is God resolving the human dilemma?)

8. The Church (What is the nature and function of the church?)

9. Last Things (What is the destiny of created reality, especially humans?)

Under these broad topics, numerous—sometimes disparate—theological perspectives emerged over the centuries. Still, arguably, an overarching unity threads through much of Christian doctrine.

Christian ethics is founded upon the perennial moral insights of the Hebrew Bible and of the New Testament. Flowing from these moral precepts (and the biblical narratives that undergird them), Christian ethics developed through the ages, sometimes echoing old themes in new contexts and sometimes nurturing new insights inspired by but not fully taught in the biblical literature. Likewise, stirred by ancient biblical practices, Christian worship through the centuries exploded into a myriad of vibrant (and sometimes dull) expressions, often seeking and sometimes facilitating divine-human encounters. Not surprisingly, through the ages Christianity has faced (and still faces) numerous challenges. Among them are four issues addressed in this book—namely, (1) the problem of evil, (2) the challenge of religious diversity, (3) the sometimes awkward relationship between contemporary science and Christian tradition, and (4) matters regarding the social inclusivism of women.

Christianity is indeed, multifaceted. In this work, I have attempted to address some core elements of the Christian faith. Some readers may find it ironic (even laughable) to call a book of this length *Christianity: A Brief Survey*! Nevertheless, in many ways, such a title is quite accurate; for in these pages, I have only managed to touch in cursory ways the colossal phenomenon that Christianity is. Indeed, whole libraries have been dedicated to this topic without exhausting its many features. It is my hope that this book helps equip readers with a fuller knowledge of the Christian life and faith; and I hope that, in some small measure, Christ is glorified in the process.

Appendix

Approaches to Feminism

A VARIETY OF IDEOLOGICAL approaches to feminism have been noted. These systems of thought vary in their analysis of both the causes of and the solutions to the inequities faced by women. Writing in the heyday of second-wave feminism, Rosemarie Tong distinguished seven "varieties of feminist thinking." These are

1. Liberal feminism

2. Marxist feminism

3. Radical feminism

4. Psychoanalytic feminism

5. Socialist feminism

6. Existentialist feminism

7. Postmodern feminism[1]

Liberal feminism proposes that

> female subordination is rooted in a set of customary and legal constraints that blocks women's entrance and/or success in the so-called public world. Because society has the false belief that women are, by nature, less intellectually and/or physically capable than men, it excludes women from the academy, the forum, and the marketplace.[2]

For liberal feminism, the solution to this dilemma is to grant women equal opportunities to succeed, including especially the same fundamental civil rights and educational opportunities afforded men. *Marxist feminism* insists that a primary source of women's oppression is not simply political or civil inequality; rather, it is the economic disparity generated by capitalistic systems. In such structures, owners

1. Tong, *Feminist Thought*, 2–9.
2. Tong, *Feminist Thought*, 2.

of capital inevitably exploit workers. Marxist feminists propose that "the capitalist system must be replaced by a socialist system in which the means of production belongs to one and all." In such conditions "women would be economically freed from men and therefore equal to them."[3]

Whereas liberal and Marxist feminism see the oppression of women caused especially by legal, political, and economic structures, *radical feminism* perceives oppression as grounded in broader, patriarchal social structures—such as families, churches, and educational systems. In these broader systems male hierarchical authority is often assumed and enforced so that opportunities for women are suppressed and women's activities are often controlled. For many radical feminists, women's liberation can come only by challenging these male values and by establishing values and gender roles more congenial to female liberation. For some radical feminists, this means encouraging women to adopt androgynous (both masculine and feminine) qualities. For others, it means nurturing traditional and (perhaps) biologically driven feminine qualities—such as "nurturance, emotion, [and] gentleness."[4] For still others, proper values and gender roles for women must be "gynocentric," such that femininity is no longer "understood as those traits that deviate from masculinity," but rather as those traits that stand independently of male perspectives or values and represent "true, or authentic, *female* nature."[5]

As the name suggests, *psychoanalytic feminist* theory draws insights from Freudian psychology, finding "women's oppression embedded deep in her psyche"[6] and dawning in infantile sexual socialization. To overcome these tendencies, psychoanalytic feminists have proposed differing strategies. One of these is to engage in dual-parenting, in which young children are more fully exposed to both their male and female parents.[7] *Existential feminism* discovers women's liberation in moving away from the definitions of womanhood prescribed by male perspectives, which include seeing women as "the Other" and men as the fundamental "Self." Transcending these "definitions, labels, and essences"[8] imposed by the male viewpoint, women can construct their own identities. A woman can choose to be a subject in her own right since "there is no essence of eternal femininity that prescribes a readymade identity for her."[9]

According to Tong, *socialist feminism* attempts to draw from insights of Marxist, radical, and psychoanalytic feminism while avoiding some of their pitfalls. Some socialist feminists "maintain that patriarchy and capitalism are distinct forms of social relation and distinct sets of interest, which, when they intersect, oppress women in particularly

3. Tong, *Feminist Thought*, 2.

4. Tong, *Feminist Thought*, 4.

5. Tong, *Feminist Thought*, 4 (italics original).

6. Tong, *Feminist Thought*, 5.

7. Tong, *Feminist Thought*, 6, 153, 156.

8. Tong, *Feminist Thought*, 6.

9. Tong, *Feminist Thought*, 210.

egregious ways."[10] Each of these forms of social interaction must be overcome for women's liberation to unfold. Other socialist feminists see patriarchy and capitalism as emerging from a shared source—such as gender division of labor or alienation; thus, the solution to women's oppression is to identify this source and undermine it.[11]

Finally, *postmodern feminism* is heavily dependent upon the insights of deconstructivism—a philosophical approach often associated with Jacques Derrida (1930–2004). Deconstructionism criticizes the notion that there is a singular, true vision of all reality. Rather, there are multiple visions of reality, all grasping for truth but never fully obtaining it. Truth is always perspectival. Further, deconstructionists recognize the existence of dominating visions of reality that claim to be the Truth. Typically, such visions are imposed upon others by controlling groups within a society. Often, sanctions are exacted upon those who disagree with or engage in practices outside the normative vision. Nevertheless, deconstructionists insist that such totalizing understandings of reality are never complete and often involve internal contradictions (deeply rooted in langue itself). In light of this, deconstructionists insist that persons must live with the ambiguity of multiple, myopic visions of reality.

Picking up on such insights, postmodern feminists "attempt to criticize the dominant order, particularly its patriarchal aspects, and to valorize the feminine, woman, the Other."[12] In the process, postmodern feminists acknowledge there is no singular vision of feminism. Rather, there are multiple overlapping but distinctive feminist perspectives among different individual women and different socioeconomic groups of women. Because of this, postmodern feminists often challenge attempts by various other feminists to describe precisely what feminism is, to analyze the alleged causes of women's oppression, or to prescribe the correct paths out of the dilemmas faced by women. Tong acknowledges that "some feminist theorists worry that the overemphasis on difference [by postmodern feminists] may lead to intellectual and political disintegration"[13] of the feminist cause. But Tong also notes that such writings may "offer to women the most fundamental liberation of all—freedom from oppressive thought."[14]

10. Tong, *Feminist Thought*, 175.

11. Tong, *Feminist Thought*, 175–89.

12. Tong, *Feminist Thought*, 223.

13. Tong, *Feminist Thought*, 7 (brackets added).

14. Tong, *Feminist Thought*, 223.

Bibliography

Achtemeier, Elizabeth. "Righteousness in the OT." In *Interpreter's Dictionary of the Bible*, edited by George A. Buttrick et al., 80–85. Nashville: Abingdon, 1962.

Achtemeier, Paul J. *Inspiration and Authority: Nature and Function of Christian Scripture*. Peabody, MA: Hendrickson, 1999.

Akasha, Gloria, et al., eds. *All the Women Are White, All the Blacks Are Men, but Some of Us Are Brave: Black Women's Studies*. Old Westbury, NY: Feminist Press, 1982.

Althaus, Paul. *The Theology of Martin Luther*. Translated by Robert C. Schultz. Philadelphia: Fortress, 1966.

Alston, William P. *Perceiving God: The Epistemology of Religious Experience*. Ithaca: Cornell University Press, 1991.

Ambrose. *On the Mysteries*. Translated by H. de Romestin et al. Nicene and Post-Nicene Fathers, 2nd ser., 10. Edited by Philip Schaff and Henry Wace. Reprint, Grand Rapids: Eerdmans, 1997.

Anselm. *Cur Deus Homo*. In *Saint Anselm: Basic Writings*, 191–302. Translated by S. N. Deane. 2nd ed. La Salle, IL: Open Court, 1962.

The Apocalypse of Moses. http://www2.iath.virginia.edu/anderson/vita/english/vita.gre.html/.

The Apocalypse of Peter. In "The Apocryphal New Testament." Translated by M. R. James. http://www.earlychristianwritings.com/text/apocalypsepeter-mrjames.html/.

Aristotle. *Generation of Animals*. In *The Complete Works of Aristotle: The Revised Oxford Translation*, edited by Jonathan Barnes, 1:111–218. 2 vols. Bollingen Series 71:2. Princeton: Princeton University Press, 1984.

———. *Politics*. In *The Complete Works of Aristotle: The Revised Oxford Translation*, edited by Jonathan Barnes, 2:1986–2029. 2 vols. Bollingen Series 71:2. Princeton: Princeton University Press, 1984.

Arminius, James. "A Declaration of the Sentiments of Arminius." In *The Works of James Arminius*, 1:580–722. Translated by James Nichols. 3 vols. Grand Rapids: Baker, 1999.

Athenagoras. *On the Resurrection of the Dead*. Translated by B. P. Pratten. Ante-Nicene Fathers 2. Edited by Alexander Roberts et al. Reprint, Grand Rapids: Eerdmans, 2001.

Augustine. *Against Two Letters of the Pelagian*. Translated by Peter Holmes and Robert Ernest Wallis, and revised by Benjamin B. Warfield. Nicene and Post-Nicene Fathers 1st ser., 5. Edited by Philip Schaff. Reprint, Grand Rapids: Eerdmans, 1997.

———. *City of God*. Translated by Marcus Dods. Nicene and Post-Nicene Fathers, 1st ser., 2. Edited by Philip Schaff. Reprint, Grand Rapids: Eerdmans, 1997.

———. *Concerning the Nature of Good, Against the Manichaeans, Nicene and Post-Nicene Fathers*, 1st ser., 4. Edited by Philip Schaff. Reprint, Grand Rapids: Eerdmans, 1996.

———. *The Literal Meaning of Genesis*. Translated by John Hammond Taylor. New York: Newman, 1982.

———. *On Christian Doctrine*. Translated by James Shaw. Nicene and Post-Nicene Fathers, 1st ser., 2. Edited by Philip Schaff. Reprint, Grand Rapids: Eerdmans, 1997.

———. *On Free Choice of the Will*. Translated by Anna Benjamin and G. Hackstaff. Library of Liberal Arts 150. New York: Macmillan, 1964.

———. *Of Morals of the Catholic Church*. Translated by Richard Stothert. Nicene and Post-Nicene Fathers, 1st ser., 4. Edited by Philip Schaff. Reprint, Grand Rapids: Eerdmans 1996.

———. *On the Trinity*. Nicene and Post-Nicene Fathers, 1st ser. 3. 14 vols. Edited by Philip Schaff. Reprint, Grand Rapids: Eerdmans, 1998.

———. *Tractates (Lectures) on the Gospel of John* 29.6. Translated by John Gibb. Nicene and Post-Nicene Fathers, 1st ser., 7. 14 vols. Edited by Philip Schaff. Grand Rapids: Eerdmans 1956.

Austin, William. "Religion." In *The Encyclopedia of Philosophy*, edited by Paul Edwards, 7:140–45. New York: Macmillan, 1967.

Ayer, A. J. *Language, Truth, and Logic*. New York: Dover, 1950.

Barbour, Ian G. *Religion and Science: Historical and Contemporary Issues*. San Francisco: HarperCollins, 1997.

Barnette, Henlee H. *Introducing Christian Ethics*. Nashville: Broadman, 1961.

Barth, Karl. *Church Dogmatics*, III/1, *The Doctrine of Creation, Part 1*. Edited by G. W. Bromiley and T. F. Torrance. Translated by J. W. Edwards et al. Edinburgh: T. & T. Clark, 1958.

Baumgardner, Jennifer, and Amy Richards. *Manifesta: Young Women, Feminism, and the Future*. New York: Farrar, Straus and Giroux, 2000.

Behe, Michael. *Darwin's Black Box: The Biochemical Challenge to Evolution*. New York: Free Press, 1996.

Belleville, Linda. "Women in Ministry." In *Two Views on Women in Ministry*, edited by James R. Beck and Craig L. Blomberg, 77–172. Counterpoints. Grand Rapids: Zondervan, 2001.

Benedict XVI, Pope. *Eschatology: Death and Eternal Life*. Translated by Michael Waldstein. Translation edited by Aidan Nichols. Washington, DC: The Catholic University of America Press, 1988.

Berkhof, Hendrikus. *Christian Faith: An Introduction to the Study of the Faith*. Translated by Sierd Woudstra. Grand Rapids: Eerdmans, 1979.

Berkhof, Louis. *Systematic Theology*. Grand Rapids: Eerdmans, 1941.

Berkouwer, G. C. *The Providence of God*. Studies in Dogmatics. Grand Rapids: Eerdmans, 1952.

Bloesch, Donald. *Essentials of Evangelical Theology*, Vol. 2, *Life, Ministry, and Hope*. New York: Harper & Row, 1979.

———. *The Last Things: Resurrection, Judgment, Glory*. Christian Foundations. Downers Grove, IL: IVP Academic, 2004.

Boadt, Lawrence. *Reading the Old Testament: An Introduction*. New York: Paulist, 1984.

Boff, Leonardo, and Clodovis Boff. *Introducing Liberation Theology*. Translated by Paul Burns. Maryknoll, NY: Orbis, 1987.

Braithwaite, Richard B. *An Empiricist's View of the Nature of Religious Belief*. Arthur Stanley Eddington Memorial Lecture 9. Cambridge: Cambridge University Press, 1955.

Bright, John. *A History of Israel*. Westminster Aids to the Study of the Scriptures. Philadelphia: Westminster, 1981.

Brown, Colin. "Karl Barth's Doctrine of the Creation." http://archive.churchsociety.org/churchman/documents/Cman_076_2_Brown.pdf/.

Brown, Raymond E. *An Introduction to New Testament Christology*. New York: Paulist, 1994.

Bruce, F. F. *Commentary on the Book of the Acts*. New international Commentary on the New Testament. Grand Rapids: Eerdmans, 1973.

Brunner, Emil. *Dogmatics*. Vol. 2, *The Christian Doctrine of Creation and Redemption*. Translated by Olive Wyon. 1952. Reprint, Eugene, OR: Wipf & Stock, 2014.

———. *Dogmatics*. Vol. 3, *The Christian Doctrine of the Church, Faith, and Consummation*. Translated by Olive Wyon. 1962. Reprint, Eugene, OR: Wipf & Stock, 2014.

———. *Revelation and Reason: The Christian Doctrine of Faith and Knowledge*. Translated by Olive Wyon. Philadelphia: Westminster, 1946.

Bushnell, Horace. *The Vicarious Sacrifice Grounded in Principles of Universal Obligation*. New York: Scribner 1866.

Butler, Joseph. *Sermons*. New York: Carter, 1873.

Cairns, David. *The Image of God in Man*. London: SCM, 1953.

Calvin, John. *Commentaries on the First Book of Moses Called Genesis*. Translated by John King. 2 vols. Grand Rapids: Baker, 1979.

———. *Institutes of the Christian Religion*. Edited by John T. McNeill. Translated by Ford Lewis Battles. 2 vols. Philadelphia: Westminster, 1960.

Carson, Donald A., et al., eds. *Justification and Variegated Nomism*, Vol. 1, *The Complexities of Second Temple Judaism*. 2 vols. Wissenschaftliche Untersuchungen zum Neuen Testament 2/140, 181. Tübingen: Mohr/Siebeck, 2001.

Cartwright, Mark. "The Role of Women in the Roman World." https://www.worldhistory.org/article/659/the-role-of-women-in-the-roman-world/.

———. "Women in Ancient Greece." *World History Encyclopedia* (website). www.ancient.eu/article/927/women-in-ancient-greece/.

Chupungco, Anscar J. "Mission and Inculturation: East Asia and the Pacific." In *The Oxford History of Christian Worship*, edited by Geoffrey Wainwright and Karen Westerfield Tucker, 661–77. Oxford: Oxford University Press, 2006.

Clark, Gordon H. *Religion, Reason, and Revelation*. International Library of Philosophy and Theology. Philosophical and Historical Studies Series. Philadelphia: Presbyterian & Reformed, 1961.

Cobb, John B., Jr. *God and the World*. 1969. Reprint, Eugene, OR: Wipf & Stock, 2000.

Cobb, John B., Jr., and David Ray Griffin. *Process Theology: An Introductory Exposition*. New York: Westminster, 1976.

Cone, James H. *A Black Theology of Liberation*. 2nd ed. Maryknoll, NY: Orbis, 1986.

———. *For My People: Black Theology and the Black Church*. Bishop Henry McNeal Turner Studies in North American Black Religion 1. Maryknoll, NY: Orbis, 1984.

———. *God of the Oppressed*. New York: Seabury, 1975.

Copleston, Frederick. *A History of Philosophy*, Vol. 2, *Mediaeval Philosophy, Part 1*. 9 vols. Garden City, NY: Image, 1962.

Cranfield, C. E. B. *A Critical and Exegetical Commentary on The Epistle to the Romans.* Vol. 1. International Critical Commentary. 1975.

Crook, Roger H. *An Introduction to Christian Ethics.* Upper Saddle River, NJ: Pearson Education, 2007.

Cullmann, Oscar. *Immortality of the Soul or Resurrection of the Dead? The Witness of the New Testament.* Ingersoll Lectures 1955. New York: Macmillan, 1958.

Cunningham, Richard B. *The Christian Faith and Its Contemporary Rivals.* Nashville: Broadman, 1988.

———. Introduction to Christian Philosophy. Unpublished lecture notes from course at Southern Baptist Theological Seminary, 1986.

Cyprian. *Epistle* 51. Translated by Robert Ernest Wallis. Ante-Nicene Fathers 5. Edited by Alexander Roberts et al. Reprint, Grand Rapids: Eerdmans, 1995.

———. *On the Lapsed.* Translated by Robert Ernest Wallis. Ante-Nicene Fathers 5. Edited by Alexander Roberts et al. Reprint, Grand Rapids: Eerdmans, 1995.

Daly, Mary. *Beyond God the Father: Toward a Philosophy of Women's Liberation.* Boston: Beacon, 1973.

———. *The Church and the Second Sex.* New York: Harper & Row, 1968.

Davies, J. G. *The Early Christian Church: A History of Its First Five Centuries.* Grand Rapids: Baker, 1965.

Davies, W. D. *Paul and Rabbinic Judaism: Some Rabbinic Elements in Pauline Theology.* 2nd ed. London: SPCK, 1955.

Davis, Stephen T., ed. *Encountering Evil: Live Options in Theodicy.* Atlanta: John Knox, 1981.

———. "Eschatology and Resurrection." In *The Oxford Handbook of Eschatology*, edited by Jerry L. Walls, 384–98. Oxford Handbooks. Oxford: Oxford University Press, 2008.

———. "Free Will and Evil." In *Encountering Evil: Live Options in Theodicy*, 69–99. Atlanta: John Knox, 1981.

———. *Risen Indeed: Making Sense of the Resurrection.* Grand Rapids: Eerdmans, 1993.

Dembski, William A. *No Free Lunch: Why Specified Complexity Cannot Be Purchased without Intelligence.* Lanham, MD: Rowman & Littlefield, 2002.

Denise, Theodore Cullum, et al., eds. *Great Traditions in Ethics.* 12th ed. Belmont, CA: Thomson Wadsworth, 2008.

Dockery, David S. *The Doctrine of the Bible.* Nashville: Convention, 1991.

Dowley, Tim. *Christian Music: A Global History.* Minneapolis: Fortress, 2011.

Draper, Paul. "Pain and Pleasure: An Evidential Problem for Theists." In *The Evidential Argument from Evil*, edited by Daniel Howard-Snyder, 12–29. Bloomington: Indiana University Press, 1996.

Dulles, Avery, SJ. *Models of the Church.* New York: Doubleday, 1974.

———. *Models of Revelation.* Maryknoll, NY: Orbis, 2008.

Dunn, James D. G. *The New Perspective on Paul.* Rev. ed. Grand Rapids: Eerdmans, 2005.

———. *Romans 1–8.* Word Biblical Commentary 38A. Dallas: Word, 1988.

———. *The Theology of Paul the Apostle.* Grand Rapids: Eerdmans, 1998.

Eddy, Mary Baker. *Science and Health with Key to the Scriptures.* 1875. Reprint, Boston: Christian Science, 1934.

Education Amendments Act of 1972 tit. IX, 20 U.S.C. §§1681–88 (2018).

Edwards, Jonathan. *Original Sin.* Edited by Clyde Holbrook. The Works of Jonathan Edwards 3. New Haven: Yale University Press, 1970.

Egbulem, Nwaka Chris. "Mission and Inculturation: Africa." In *The Oxford History of Christian Worship*, edited by Geoffrey Wainwright and Karen Westerfield Tucker, 678–95. Oxford: Oxford University Press, 2006.

Enns, Peter. "Response to Kevin Vanhoozer." In *Five Views on Biblical Inerrancy*, edited by J. Merrick and Stephen M. Garret, 83–116. Counterpoints. Bible & Theology. Grand Rapids: Zondervan, 2013.

Erickson, Millard J. *Christian Theology*. 3 vols in 1. Grand Rapids: Baker, 1983–1985.

———. *Christian Theology*. 3 vols. in 1. 3rd ed. Grand Rapids: Baker Academic, 2013.

Fackre, Gabriel. "Divine Perseverance." In *What about Those Who Have Never Heard?*, edited by John Sanders, 71–95. Downers Grove, IL: InterVarsity, 1995.

———. "Response to Sanders." In *What about Those Who Have Never Heard?*, edited by John Sanders, 56–61. Downers Grove, IL: InterVarsity, 1995.

Fletcher, Joseph. *Situation Ethics: The New Morality*. Philadelphia: Westminster, 1966.

Flint, Thomas P. *Divine Providence: The Molinist Account*. Cornell Studies in the Philosophy of Religion. Ithaca: Cornell University Press, 1998.

Fosdick, Harry Emerson. *The Modern Use of the Bible*. New York: Macmillan, 1961.

Foster, Ruth Ann. "Jesus and Women." In *Putting Women in Their Places: Moving Beyond Gender Stereotypes in Church and Home*, edited by Audra and Joe Trull, 81–90. Macon: Smyth & Helwys, 2003.

Freeman, Hobart. "Festivals." In *Wycliffe Bible Encyclopedia*, edited by Charles Pfeiffer et al., 599–605. Chicago: Moody, 1975.

Freire, Paulo. *The Pedagogy of the Oppressed*. Translated by Myra Bergman Ramos. New York Seabury, 1970.

Fuller, Daniel. "Benjamin B. Warfield's View of Faith and History." *Bulletin of the Evangelical Theological Society* 11 (1968) 75–83.

Garrett, James Leo. *Systematic Theology: Biblical, Historical, and Evangelical*. 2 vols. 2nd rev. ed. North Richland Hills, TX: Bibal, 2007.

Geach, P. T. *Providence and Evil*. The Stanton Lectures 1971–2. Cambridge: Cambridge University Press, 1977.

Gedney, Edwin K. "Geology and the Bible." In *Modern Science and Christian Faith*, 39–73. Chicago: Scripture Press, 1948.

Gess, Wolfgang Friedrich. *The Scripture Doctrine of the Person of Christ*. Freely translated from the German of W. F. Gess, with many additions, by J. A. Reubelt. Andover, MA: Draper, 1870.

Gilkey, Langdon. *Maker of Heaven and Earth: A Study of the Christian Doctrine of Creation*. Christian Faith Series. Garden City, NY: Doubleday, 1959.

Gilligan, Carol. *In a Different Voice: Psychological Theory and Women's Development*. Cambridge: Harvard University Press, 1982.

González, Justo. *A History of Christian Thought*. Vol. 2, *From Augustine to the Eve of the Reformation*. 3 vols. Nashville: Abingdon, 1971.

———. *A History of Christian Thought*. Vol. 3, *From the Protestant Reformation to the Twentieth Century*. 3 vols. Nashville: Abingdon, 1975.

Gregory of Nyssa. *Great Catechism*. Translated by William Moore and Henry Austin Wilson. Nicene and Post-Nicene Fathers, 2nd ser., 5. Edited by Philip Schaff and Henry Wace. Reprint. Grand Rapids: Eerdmans, 1994.

Grenz, Stanley J. *The Millennial Maze: Sorting Out Evangelical Options*. Downers Grove, IL: InterVarsity, 1992.

———. *The Moral Quest: Foundations of Christian Ethics*. Downers Grove, IL: InterVarsity, 1997.

———. *Theology for the Community of God*. Grand Rapids: Eerdmans, 1994.

———. *Welcoming but Not Affirming: An Evangelical Response to Homosexuality*. Louisville: Westminster John Knox, 1998.

Grenz, Stanley J., and Denise Muir Kjesbo. *Women in the Church: A Biblical Theology of Women in Ministry*. Downers Grove, IL: InterVarsity, 1995.

Greshake, Gisbert. *Auferstehung der Toten*. Koinonia: Beitrage zur okumenischen Spiritualität und Theologie 12. Essen: Ludgerus, 1969.

Greshake, Gisbert, and Jacob Kremer. *Resurrectio Mortuorum: Zum theologschen Verständnis der leiblichen Auferstehung*. Darmstadt: Wissenschaftliche Buchgesellschaft, 1986.

Gushee, David P. *Changing Our Mind*. Canton, MI: Read the Spirit, 2017.

Gutiérrez, Gustavo. *A Theology of Liberation*. Translated and edited by Sister Caridad Inda and John Eagleson. Maryknoll, NY: Orbis, 1973.

Haney, Eleanor Humes. "What Is Feminist Ethics? A Proposal for Continuing Discussion." In *Feminist Theological Ethics: A Reader*, edited by Lois K. Daly, 3–12. Library of Theological Ethics. Louisville: Westminster John Knox, 1994.

Harris, Stephen L. *The New Testament: A Student's Introduction*. 6th ed. Boston: McGraw-Hill, 2009.

Hart, David Bentley. *That All Shall Be Saved: Heaven, Hell, and Universal Salvation*. New Haven: Yale University Press, 2019.

Hartshorne, Charles. *The Divine Relativity*. New Haven: Yale University Press, 1948.

———. *A Natural Theology for Our Time*. Morse Lectures 1964. LaSalle, IL: Open Court, 1967.

———. *Omnipotence and Other Theological Mistakes*. International Society for Science and Religion Collection. Albany: State University of New York Press, 1984.

Hasker, William. *God, Time, and Knowledge*. Cornell Studies in the Philosophy of Religion. Ithaca: Cornell University Press, 1989.

Hauerwas, Stanley. *The Peaceable Kingdom: A Primer in Christian Ethics*. Notre Dame, IN: University of Notre Dame Press, 1983.

Hays, Richard. *The Faith of Jesus Christ: An Investigation of the Narrative Substructure of Galatians 3:1—4:11*. Society of Biblical Literature Dissertation Series 56. Chico, CA: Scholars, 1983.

Henry, Carl F. H. *God, Revelation, and Authority*. Vol 3, *God Who Speaks and Shows, Part 2*. Waco: Word, 1979.

———. *God, Revelation, and Authority*. Vol 4, *God Who Speaks and Shows; Fifteen Theses, Part 3*. Waco: Word, 1979.

Heron, Alasdair I. C. *The Holy Spirit*. Philadelphia: Westminster, 1983.

Hewitt, Harold, "Hick against Himself." In *Problems in the Philosophy of Religion: Critical Studies of the Work of John Hick*, edited by Harold Hewitt, 162–77. Library of Philosophy and Religion. London: Macmillan, 1991.

Hick, John. *Death and Eternal Life*. With a new preface by the author. Louisville: Westminster, John Knox, 1994.

———. "An Irenaean Theodicy." In *Encountering Evil: Live Options in Theodicy*, edited by Stephen T. Davis, 39–52. Atlanta: John Knox, 1981.

———. *Philosophy of Religion*. 4th ed. Prentice-Hall Foundations in Philosophy Series. Englewood Cliffs, NJ: Prentice-Hall, 1990.

————. *Problems of Religious Pluralism*. New York: St. Martin's, 1985.

————. "Religious Pluralism." In *Philosophy of Religion: Selected Readings*, edited by Michael Peterson et al., 614–22. New York: Oxford University Press, 2014.

Hippolytus. *The Apostolic Tradition of Hippolytus*. Translated by Burton Scott Eastman. Cambridge: Cambridge University Press, 1962.

Hobbes, Thomas. *Leviathan*. Great Books of the Western World 23. Chicago: Encyclopaedia Britannica, 1952.

Hovey, Alvah. *Manual of Christian Theology*. New York: Silver, Burdett, 1900.

Hume, David. *An Enquiry Concerning Human Understanding*. 1907. Reprint, Indianapolis: Hackett, 1983.

————. *An Enquiry Concerning the Principles of Morals*. Chicago: Open Court, 1907.

Hurley, James B. *Man and Woman in Biblical Perspective*. Grand Rapids: Zondervan, 1981.

Hurtado, Larry. *At the Origins of Christian Worship: The Context and Character of Earliest Christian Devotion: The Context and Character of Earliest Christian Devotion*. Grand Rapids: Eerdmans, 1999

Ignatius. *Epistle to the Ephesians*. Translated by Alexander Roberts and James Donaldson. Ante-Nicene Fathers 1. Edited by Alexander Roberts et al. Reprint, Grand Rapids: Eerdmans, 1986.

————. *Letter to the Smyrnaeans*. Translated by Alexander Roberts and James Donaldson. Ante-Nicene Fathers, 1. Edited by Alexander Roberts et al. Reprint, Grand Rapids: Eerdmans, 1986.

International Theological Commission. "The Hope of Salvation for Infants Who Die without Being Baptized." https://www.vatican.va/roman_curia/congregations/cfaith/cti_documents/rc_con_cfaith_doc_20070419_un-baptised-infants_en.html/.

Irenaeus. *Against Heresies*. Translated by Alexander Roberts and William Rambaut. Ante-Nicene Fathers 1. Edited by Alexander Roberts et al. Reprint Grand Rapids: Eerdmans, 1986.

Japinga, Lynn. *Feminism and Christianity: An Essential Guide*. Abingdon Essential Guides. Nashville: Abingdon, 1999.

Jewett, Paul K. *Man as Male and Female*. Grand Rapids: Eerdmans, 1975.

John Chrysostom. "The Kind of Women Who Ought to Be Taken as Wives." In *Women in the Early Church*, edited by Elizabeth A. Clark, 36–38. Message of the Fathers of the Church 13. Wilmington, DE: Glazier, 1983.

John Paul II, Pope. *Ordinatio Sacerdotalis*. Apostolic Letter, May 2, 1994. http://www.vatican.va/content/john-paul-ii/en/apost_letters/1994/documents/hf_jp-ii_apl_19940522_ordinatio-sacerdotalis.html/.

Jones, W. T. *The Classical Mind*. 2nd ed. A History of Western Philosophy 1. New York: Harcourt, Brace, and World, 1969.

————. *The Medieval Mind*. 2nd ed. A History of Western Philosophy 2. New York: Harcourt, Brace, and World, 1969.

————. *Kant and the Nineteenth Century*. 2nd rev. ed. A History of Western Philosophy 4 New York: Harcourt Brace Jovanovich, 1975.

Justin Martyr. *Dialogue with Trypho*. Translated by Marcus Dods and George Reith. Ante-Nicene Fathers 1. Edited by Alexander Roberts et al. Reprint, Grand Rapids: Eerdmans, 1986.

———. *First Apology*. Edited by Alexander Roberts and James Donaldson. Translated by Marcus Dods and George Reith. Ante-Nicene Fathers 1. Edited by Alexander Roberts et al. Reprint, Grand Rapids: Eerdmans, 1986.

Kaiser, Christopher. *The Doctrine of God: A Historical Survey*. Rev. ed. Eugene, OR: Wipf & Stock, 2001.

Kane, G. Stanley. "Evil and Privation." *International Journal for Philosophy of Religion* 11 (1980) 43–58.

Kee, H. C., trans. "The Testament of the Twelve Patriarchs." In *The Old Testament Pseudepigrapha*, edited by James C. Charlesworth, 1:775–828. 2 vols. Garden City, NY: Doubleday, 1983–1985.

Keener, Craig S. *Paul, Women & Wives: Marriage and Women's Ministry in the Letters of Paul*. Peabody MA: Hendrickson, 1992.

———. "Women in Ministry." In *Two Views on Women in Ministry*, edited by James R. Beck and Craig L. Blomberg, 27–73. Counterpoints. Grand Rapids: Zondervan, 2001.

Kelly, J. N. D. *Early Christian Doctrines*, Rev. ed. San Francisco: Harper & Row, 1978.

Kent, Bonnie. "Augustine's Ethics." In *The Cambridge Companion to Augustine*, edited by David Vincent Meconi and Eleonore Stump, 205–33. 2nd ed. Cambridge Companions to Philosophy. Cambridge: Cambridge University Press, 2014.

King, Martin Luther Jr. "Letter from Birmingham City Jail." In *A Testament of Hope: The Essential Writings of Martin Luther King, Jr.*, edited by James M. Washington, 289–302. San Francisco: Harper & Row, 1986.

———. *Where Do We Go from Here: Chaos or Community?* New York: Harper & Row, 1967.

Klug, Eugene. "Luther on Ministry." *Concordia Theological Quarterly* 47 (1983) 293–303.

Küng, Hans. *On Being a Christian*. Translated by Edward Quinn. Garden City, NY: Doubleday, 1976.

Kvanvig, Jonathan. "Hell." In *The Oxford Handbook of Eschatology*, edited by Jerry Walls, 413–26. Oxford: Oxford University Press, 2008.

Ladd, George Eldon. *A Theology of the New Testament*. Grand Rapids: Eerdmans, 1974.

Leibniz, G. W. *Theodicy: Essays on the Goodness of God, the Freedom of Man and the Origin of Evil*. Translated by E. M. Huggard. https://www.gutenberg.org/files/17147/17147-h/17147-h.htm/.

———. *Theodicy*. Edited by Austin Farrer and Translated by E. M. Huggard. Rare Masterpieces of Philosophy and Science. New Haven: Yale University Press, 1952.

Leith, John H., ed. *Creeds of the Churches*. 3rd. ed. Atlanta: John Knox, 1982.

Lewis, C. S. *The Great Divorce*. New York : Macmillan, 1963.

———. *Mere Christianity*. New York: Macmillan, 1960.

———. *The Problem of Pain*. New York: Macmillan, 1944.

———. "Priestesses in the Church?" In *God in the Dock: Essays in Theology and Ethics*, edited by Walter Hooper, 234–39. Grand Rapids: Eerdmans, 1970.

Lewis, Hywel D. *The Self and Immortality*. Philosophy of Religion Series. London: Palgrave Macmillan, 1973.

Lindsell, Harold. *The Battle for the Bible*. Grand Rapids: Zondervan, 1976.

Linville, Mark. "Moral Particularism." In *God & Morality: Four Views*, edited by R. Keith Loftin, 135–58. Spectrum Multiview Books. Downers Grove, IL: IVP Academic, 2012.

Locke, John. *Concerning Civil Government, Second Essay*. Great Books of the Western World 35. Chicago: Encyclopaedia Britannica, 1952.

————. *A Letter Concerning Toleration*. Great Books of the Western World 35. Chicago: Encyclopaedia Britannica, 1952.

Luther, Martin. *Large Catechism*. In *The Book of Concord: The Confessions of the Evangelical Lutheran Church*, edited and translated by Theodore G. Tappert, 357–461. Philadelphia: Fortress, 1959.

————. *Lectures on Genesis*. Edited by Jaroslav Pelikan. Translated by George V. Schick. 8 vols. Luther's Works. St. Louis: Concordia, 1958.

————. *On the Jews and Their Lies*, 1543. Translated by Martin H. Bertram. In *The Christian in Society IV*, 121–306. Luther's Works 47. Philadelphia: Fortress, 1971.

————. *Selected Psalms II*. Edited by Jaroslav Pelikan. Luther's Works 13. Saint Louis: Concordia, 1956.

————. *Luther's Small Catechism*. Edited by Jeffery S. Nelson and Elisabeth Drotning. Minneapolis: Augsburg Fortress, 2001.

————. "That Jesus Christ was Born a Jew." In *The Christian in Society II*, 195–229. Edited by Helmut T. Lehmann. Translated by Walter I. Brandt. Luther's Works 45. Philadelphia: Fortress, 1962.

MacIntyre, Alasdair. *After Virtue: A Study in Moral Theory*. Notre Dame, IN: University of Notre Dame Press, 1984.

Mackie, J. L. *The Miracle of Theism*. Oxford: Clarendon, 1982.

Marshall, I. Howard. *New Testament Theology*. Downers Grove, IL: InterVarsity, 2004.

Marshall, L. H. *The Challenge of New Testament Ethics*. New York: Macmillan, 1947.

Martin, Ralph P. *Worship in the Early Church*. Grand Rapids: Eerdmans, 1964.

Mascall, E. L. "Women and the Priesthood of the Church." In *Why Not? Priesthood & the Ministry of Women*, edited by Michael Bruce and G. E. Duffield, 99–120. Marcham Books. Appleford, England: Marcham Manor, 1972.

Matson, Wallace I. *The Existence of God*. Ithaca: Cornell University Press, 1965.

McClendon, James Wm., Jr. *Systematic Theology*. Vol 1, *Ethics*. 3 vols. Nashville: Abingdon, 1986.

McCloskey, H. J. "God and Evil." *Philosophical Quarterly* 10/39 (1960) 97–114.

McClymond, Michael. "David Bentley Hart's Lonely, Last Stand for Christian Universalism." Bible & Theology. *TGC* (website), October 2, 2019. https://www.thegospelcoalition.org/reviews/shall-saved-universal-christian-universalism-david-bentley-hart/.

McGrath, Alister E. *Reformation Thought: An Introduction*. 2nd ed. Oxford: Blackwell, 1993.

————. *Christian Theology: An Introduction*. 3rd ed. Oxford: Blackwell, 2001.

————. *The Christian Theology Reader*. 4th ed. Oxford: Wiley-Blackwell, 2011.

Melanchthon, Philip. *Melanchthon on Christian Doctrine: Loci communes 1555*. Translated by Clyde L. Manschreck. Twin Brooks Series. Grand Rapids: Baker, 1965.

Messenger, Earnest C. *Evolution and Theology: The Problem of Man's Origin*. New York: Macmillan, 1932.

Mickelsen, Alvera. "An Egalitarian View: There Is Neither Male nor Female in Christ." In *Women in Ministry: Four Views*, edited by Bonnidell Clouse & Robert G. Clouse, 173–206. Downers Grove, IL: InterVarsity, 1989.

Migliore, Daniel L. *Faith Seeking Understanding: An Introduction to Christian Theology*. Grand Rapids: Eerdmans, 1991.

Miller, Hugh. *The Testimony of The Rocks or, Geology in Its Bearings on the Two Theologies, Natural and Revealed*. Reprint, Edinburgh: Constable, 1859.

Milligan, Susan. "Stepping through History: A Timeline of Women's Rights from 1769 to the 2017 Women's March on Washington." *USNews.com* (website). https://www.usnews.com/news/the-report/articles/2017-01-20/timeline-the-womens-rights-movement-in-the-us/.

Mohler, R. Albert Jr., et al. *Five Views on Biblical Inerrancy*. Edited by J. Merrick et al. Counterpoints. Bible & Theology. Grand Rapids: Zondervan, 2013.

Molina, Luis de. *On Divine Foreknowledge (Part IV of the Concordia)*. Translated, with an introduction and notes, by Alfred Freddoso. Ithaca: Cornell University Press, 1988.

Moltmann, Jürgen. *The Church in the Power of the Spirit*. New York: Harper & Row, 1977.

Moody, Dale. *The Word of Truth*. Grand Rapids: Eerdmans, 1981.

Moore, Brooke Noel, and Robert Michael Stewart. *Moral Philosophy: A Comprehensive Introduction*. Mountain View, CA: Mayfield, 1994.

Moreland, J. P., and Scott B. Rae. *Body & Soul: Human Nature & the Crisis in Ethics*. Downers Grove, IL: InterVarsity, 2000.

Mowszko, Marg, compiler. "Misogynist Quotes from Church Fathers and Reformers." On *Marg Mowszko* (blog), January 24, 2013. https://margmowczko.com/misogynist-quotes-from-church-fathers/.

Murray, John. *Redemption, Accomplished and Applied*. Grand Rapids: Eerdmans, 1955.

Nash, Ronald H. *Is Jesus the Only Savior?* Grand Rapids: Zondervan, 1994.

———. "Restrictivism." In *What about Those Who Have Never Heard?*, edited by John Sanders, 107–39. Downers Grove, IL: InterVarsity, 1995.

National Women's History Alliance. "Timeline of Legal History of Women in the United States," *National Women's History Alliance* (website). https://nationalwomenshistoryalliance.org/resources/womens-rights-movement/detailed-timeline/.

Neill, Stephen. *Christian Faith & Other Faiths*. Downers Grove, IL: InterVarsity, 1984.

Newbigin, Leslie. *The Open Secret: Sketches for a Missionary Theology*. Grand Rapids: Eerdmans, 1978.

Niebuhr, Reinhold. *An Interpretation of Christian Ethics*. With a new preface by the author. New York: Living Age Books, 1956.

———. *Moral Man and Immoral Society*. New York: Scribner, 1932.

———. *The Nature and Destiny of Man*. Vol. 1, *Human Nature*. New York: Scribner 1941.

———. *The Nature and Destiny of Man*. Vol. 2, *Human Destiny*. New York: Scribner 1943.

Nietzsche, Friedrich. *Beyond Good and Evil*. Translated by Walter Kaufmann. New York: Vintage, 1966.

———. *Thus Spoke Zarathustra*. Translated by Walter Kaufmann. New York: Viking, 1954.

Nolan, Michael. "Passive and Deformed? Did Aristotle Really Say This?" *New Blackfriars* 76/893 (May 1995) 237–57.

Olson, Roger E. *The Mosaic of Christian Belief: Twenty Centuries of Unity and Diversity*. Downers Grove, IL: InterVarsity, 2002.

Origen. *Commentary on Matthew*. Translated by John Patrick. Ante-Nicene Fathers 9:413–512. 10 vols. Edited by Allan Menzies. Reprint, Grand Rapids: Eerdmans, 1989.

———. *Commentary on Romans, Books 1–5*. Edited by Thomas P. Scheck. Fathers of the Church 103. Washington, DC : Catholic University of America Press, 2001.

———. *De Principiis*. Translated by Frederick Crombie. Ante-Nicene Fathers 4. Edited by Alexander Roberts et al. Reprint, Grand Rapids: Eerdmans, 1994.

Orr, James. *Revelation and Inspiration*. Grand Rapids: Eerdmans, 1952.

Otto, Rudolf. *The Idea of the Holy*. 2nd ed. New York: Oxford University Press, 1958.

Paley, William. *Natural Theology: or Evidences of the Existence of and Attributes of the Deity Collected from the Appearances of Nature*. London: Faulder, 1802.

Pannenberg, Wolfhart. *Systematic Theology*. Vol. 3. Translated by Geoffrey Bromiley. Grand Rapids: Eerdmans, 1993.

Paul VI, Pope. *Humanae Vitae: On the Regulation of Birth*. July 25, 1968. https://www.vatican.va/content/paul-vi/en/encyclicals/documents/hf_p-vi_enc_25071968_humanae-vitae.html/.

———. "Response to the Letter of His Grace the Most Reverend Dr. F. D. Coggan, Archbishop of Canterbury, concerning the Ordination of Women to the Priesthood." (November 30, 1975) *Acta Apostolistica Sedis* 68 (1976) 599.

Peacocke, Arthur. *Theology for a Scientific Age: Being and Becoming—Natural, Divine, and Human*. Theology and the Sciences. Minneapolis: Fortress, 1993.

Pearce, E. K. Victor. *Who Was Adam?* Exeter, UK: Paternoster, 1970.

Pelagius. *Libellus fidei*. Patrologiae Cursus Completus: Series Graeca. Edited by J. P. Migne and Garnier Fratres. 1857–1912.

———. *The Christian Life and Other Essays*. Translated by Ford Lewis Battles. 4th printing. Pittsburgh: n.p., 1977.

Peterson, Michael. *Evil and the Christian God*. Grand Rapids: Baker, 1982.

Peterson, Michael, et al. *Reason and Religious Belief: An Introduction to the Philosophy of Religion*. New York: Oxford University Press, 2013.

Pinnock, Clark H. "Annihilationism." In *The Oxford Handbook of Eschatology*, edited by Jerry Walls, 461–75. Oxford: Oxford University Press, 2007.

———. *Flame of Love: A Theology of the Holy Spirit*. Downers Grove, IL: InterVarsity, 1996.

Pinnock, Clark, et al. *The Openness of God: A Biblical Challenge to the Traditional Understanding of God's Providence*. Downers Grove, IL: InterVarsity, 1994.

Piper, John, and Wayne Grudem. *Recovering Biblical Manhood & Womanhood*. Wheaton, IL: Crossway, 2006.

Plantinga, Alvin. *God, Freedom, and Evil*. Oxford: Clarendon, 1978.

———. *The Nature of Necessity*. Clarendon Library of Logic and Philosophy. Oxford: Clarendon, 1974.

Plato. *Euthyphro, Apology, Crito, Phaedo*. Translated by Chris Emlyn-Jones and William Preddy, Loeb Classical Library 36. Cambridge: Harvard University Press, 2017.

———. *Euthyphro*. In *The Dialogues of Plato*. Edited by. R. M. Hare and D. A. Russell. Translated by Benjamin Jowett. London: Sphere, 1970.

———. *Phaedo and Meno*. In *Ancient Philosophy*. Edited by Forrest E. Baird. Philosophic Classics 1. Upper Saddle River, NJ: Pearson Prentice Hall, 2011.

———. *Theaetetus; Sophist*. Translated by Harold North Fowler. Loeb Classical Library. Cambridge: Harvard University Press, 1921.

Price, George McCready. *The New Geology: Textbook for Colleges, Normal Schools, and Training Schools*. Mountain View, CA: Pacific, 1923.

Price, H. H. "Survival and the Idea of 'Another World.'" *Proceedings of the Society for Psychical Research* 50, Part 182 (January 1953) 1–25.

———. "What Kind of Next World?" In *Does Man Survive Death?*, edited by Eileen J. Garrett, 37–44. New York: Helix, 1957.

Quran. Translated by Abdullah Yusuf Ali. 1934 Elmhurst, NY: Tahrike Tarsile Qur'an, 2001 . http://www.wright-house.com/religions/islam/Quran/6-cattle.php/.

Rad, Gerhard von. *Old Testament Theology*. Vol 1, *The Theology of Israel's Historical Tradition*. 2 vols. New York: Harper & Row, 1962.

Rahner, Karl. "Christianity and Non-Christian Religions." In *Theological Investigations*, 5:115–34. 23 vols. New York: Seabury, 1974.

———. *Foundations of Christian Faith: An Introduction to the Idea of Christianity*. Translated by William Dych. New York: Crossroad, 1984.

———. "Observations on the Problem of Anonymous Christians." In *Theological Investigations*, 14:280–94. 23 vols. New York: Seabury, 1974.

———. "Religious Inclusivism." In *Philosophy of Religion: Selected Readings,* edited by Michael Peterson et al., 606–13 . Oxford: Oxford University Press, 2014.

Ramm, Bernard. *The Christian View of Science and Scripture*. Grand Rapids: Eerdmans, 1955.

Ramsey, Paul. *Basic Christian Ethics*. Louisville: Westminster John Knox, 1950.

———. *Deeds and Rules in Christian Ethics*. New York: Scribner, 1967.

———. *War and the Christian Conscience: How Shall Modern War Be Conducted Justly?* Published for the Lilly Endowment Research Program in Christianity and Politics. Durham, NC: Duke University Press, 1961.

Rashdall, Hastings. *The Idea of Atonement in Christian Thought*. London: Macmillan, 1920.

Rauschenbusch, Walter. *Christianity and the Social Crisis*. Edited by Robert D. Cross. American Perspectives. New York: Harper & Row, 1964.

———. *Christianizing the Social Order*. ATLA Monograph Preservation Program. New York: Macmillan, 1912.

———. *A Theology for the Social Gospel*. Apex Books. New York: Abingdon, 1917.

Rice, Richard. "Divine Foreknowledge and Free-will Theism." In *The Grace of God, the Will of Man*, edited by Clark Pinnock, 121–39. Grand Rapids: Zondervan Academic Books, 1989.

Riddle, M. B., trans. *Didache*. Ante-Nicene Fathers 7. Edited by Alexander Roberts et al. Reprint, Grand Rapids: Eerdmans, 1995.

Robinson, Michael. *Christianity: A Brief History*. Eugene, OR: Cascade Books, 2019.

———. "Divine Image, Human Dignity, and Human Potentiality." *Perspectives in Religious Studies*, 41 (2014) 65–78.

———. *Eternity and Freedom*. Lanham, MD: University Press of America, 1995.

———. "Human Potentialism and Bioethics." *Perspectives in Religious Studies* 42 (2015) 391–404.

———. *The Storms of Providence: Navigating the Waters of Calvinism, Arminianism, and Open Theism*. Dallas: University Press of America, 2003.

Rogers, Jack Bartlett. "The Church Doctrine of Biblical Authority." In *Biblical Authority*, 30–37. Waco: Word, 1977.

Roth, John K. "A Theodicy of Protest." In *Encountering Evil: Live Options in Theodicy*, edited by Stephen T. Davis, 7–22. Atlanta, John Knox, 1981.

Rowe, William L. *Philosophy of Religion: An Introduction*. 3rd ed. Belmont, CA: Thomson Wadsworth, 2001.

Ruether, Rosemary Radford. *Sexism and God-Talk: Toward a Feminist Theology*. Boston: Beacon, 1983.

Sailhamer, John H. *Genesis*. In *The Expositor's Bible Commentary*, edited by Frank Gaebelein, 1–284. 12 vols. Grand Rapids: Zondervan, 1990.

Sanders, John. *The God Who Risks: A Theology of Providence*. Downers Grove, IL: InterVarsity, 1998.

————. "Inclusivism." In *What about Those Who Have Never Heard?*, edited by John Sanders, 21–55. Downers Grove, IL: InterVarsity, 1995.

————, ed. *What about Those Who Have Never Heard?* Downers Grove, IL: InterVarsity, 1998.

Schleiermacher, Friedreich. *The Christian Faith.* Edited by H. R. Mackintosh and J. S. Stewart. Translation of the German 2nd ed. Edinburgh: T. & T. Clark, 1989.

Schreiner, Thomas. "Women in Ministry." In *Two Views on Women in Ministry*, edited by James R. Beck and Craig L. Blomberg, 175–236. Counterpoints. Grand Rapids: Zondervan, 2001.

Scofield, C. I., et al., eds. *The New Scofield Reference Bible: Holy Bible, Authorized King James Version, with Introductions, annotations, etc.* New York: Oxford University Press, 1967.

Senn, Frank C. "Communion, Frequency of Reception of." In *The New Dictionary of Sacramental Worship*, edited by Peter E. Fink, 241–45. Collegeville, MN: Liturgical, 1990.

Shepherd, Massey. "Church Year." www.britannica.com/topic/church-year/.

Simango, Daniel. "The Imago Dei (Gen 1:26–27): A History of Interpretation from Philo to the Present." https://www.researchgate.net/publication/309453039_The_Imago_Dei_Gen_126-27_a_his tory_of_interpretation_from_Philo_to_the_present/.

Snaith, Norman. *The Distinctive Ideas of the Old Testament.* Philadelphia: Westminster, 1946.

Socinus, Faustus. *The Racovian Catechism, with Notes and Illustrations.* Translated by Thomas Rees (London, 1818). N.p.: BiblioLife, 2009.

Sölle, Dorothee. *Thinking about God: An Introduction to Theology.* Translated by John Bowden. Philadelphia: Trinity, 1990.

Stackert, Jeffrey. Notes on Leviticus. In T*he New Oxford Annotated Bible with the Apocrypha* (New Revised Standard Version). Edited by Michael D. Coogan (general editor) et al. 5th ed. Oxford: Oxford University Press, 2018.

Stagg, Evelyn, and Frank Stagg. *Women in the World of Jesus.* Philadelphia: Westminster Press, 1978.

Stassen, Glen H., and David P. Gushee. *Kingdom Ethics: Following Jesus in Contemporary Context.* Downers Grove, IL: IVP Academic, 2003.

StayCatholic.com/ (website). "The Early Church Fathers on Women's Ordination." https://staycatholic.com/ecf-on-womens-ordination/.

Stiver, Dan R. *Life Together in the Way of Jesus Christ: An Introduction to Christian Theology.* Waco: Baylor University Press, 2009.

Strong, Augustus Hopkins. *Systematic Theology: A Compendium.* 1907. 28th printing, 3 vols. in 1. Valley Forge, PA: Judson, 1972.

Swinburne, Richard. *The Coherence of Theism.* Clarendon Library of Logic and Philosophy Oxford: Clarendon, 1977.

————. *The Existence of God.* 2nd ed. Oxford: Clarendon, 2004.

————. *Providence and the Problem of Evil.* Oxford: Clarendon, 1998.

Teilhard de Chardin, Pierre. *The Phenomenon of Man.* With an introduction by Julian Huxley. Translated by Bernard Wall. New York: Harper & Row, 1959.

Tennant, Frederick. *The Origin and Propagation of Sin.* Hulsean Lectures 1901–1902. Cambridge: Cambridge University Press, 1902.

Tertullian. *On the Apparel of Women.* Translated by S. Thelwall. Ante-Nicene Fathers 4. Edited by Alexander Roberts et al. Reprint, Grand Rapids: Eerdmans, 1994.

———. *On Baptism*. Translated by S. Thelwall. Ante-Nicene Fathers 3. Edited by Alexander Roberts et al. Reprint, Grand Rapids: Eerdmans, 1994.

———. *On the Resurrection of the Flesh*. Translated by Peter Holmes. Ante-Nicene Fathers 3. Edited by Alexander Roberts et al. Reprint, Grand Rapids: Eerdmans 1994.

———. *Prescription Against Heretics*. Ante-Nicene Fathers 3. Edited by Alexander Roberts et al. Reprint, Grand Rapids: Eerdmans, 1994.

Thiroux, Jacques P., and Keith W. Krasemann. *Ethics: Theory and Practice*. 11th ed. Boston: Prentice-Hall/Pearson, 2011.

Thomas Aquinas. *Summa Theologica*. Translated by Fathers of the English Dominican Province. Revised by Daniel J. Sullivan. 2 vols. Great Books of the Western World 19–20. Chicago: Encyclopaedia Britannica, 1952.

Thomasius, Gottfried. *Christi Person und Werk*. Revised. 2 vols. Charleston, SC: Nabu, 2011.

Tong, Rosemarie. *Feminist Thought: A Comprehensive Introduction*. Boulder: Westview, 1989.

Travis, Stephen H. *I Believe in the Second Coming of Jesus*. Grand Rapids: Eerdmans, 1982.

Tyndale, William. *An Answer to Sir Thomas More's Dialogue: The Supper of the Lord After the True Meaning of John VI. and 1 Cor. XI. And Wm. Tracy's Testament Expounded*. Cambridge: Cambridge University Press, 1850.

US Department of Justice. Title IX of the Education Amendments of 1972, https://www.justice.gov/crt/title-ix-education-amendments-1972/.

Vanhoozer, Kevin J. "Augustinian Inerrancy: Literary Meaning, Literal Truth, and Literate Interpretation in the Economy of Biblical Discourse." In *Five Views on Biblical Inerrancy*, edited by J. Merrick and Stephen Garrett, 199–235. Grand Rapids: Zondervan, 2013.

Vatican Council (2nd, 1962–1965).

Veith, Gene. "Megachurches Discovering Liturgy & Traditional Christianity?'" *Patheos* (Evangelical feed) (blog), May 29, 2019. https://www.patheos.com/blogs/geneveith/2019/05/megachurches-discovering-liturgy-traditional-christianity/.

Walls, Jerry L. *Hell: The Logic of Damnation*. Library of Religious Philosophy 9. Norte Dame, IN: The University of Notre Dame Press, 1992.

Warfield, Benjamin B. *The Inspiration and Authority of the Bible*. Edited by Samuel G. Craig. Philadelphia: Presbyterian & Reformed, 1948.

———. *Revelation and Inspiration*. New York: Oxford University Press, 1927.

Wassen, Gregory. "On Preexistence." *De Grondbeginselen* (blog), February 29, 2016. https://fathergregory.wordpress.com/2016/02/29/on-preexistence/.

Wesley, John. *A Plain Account of Christian Perfection*. London: Epworth, 1952.

Whitcomb, John C., and Henry Morris. *The Genesis Flood: The Biblical Record and Its Scientific Implications*. Philadelphia: Presbyterian & Reformed, 1961.

White, Andrew Dickson. *A History of the Warfare of Science with Theology in Christendom*. Great Minds Series Buffalo: Prometheus, 1993.

White, James F. *A Brief History of Christian Worship*. Nashville: Abingdon, 1993.

White, R. E. O. *Christian Ethics*. Macon, GA: Mercer University Press, 1994.

Whitehead, Alfred North. *Process and Reality*. Gifford Lectures 1927–28. New York: Free Press, 1978.

Wiley, H. Orton. *Christian Theology*. 3 vols. Kansas City, MO: Beacon Hill, 1958.

Williams, Delores S. "The Color of Feminism, or Speaking the Black Woman's Tongue." In *Feminist Theological Ethics: A Reader*, edited by Lois K. Daly, 42–58. Library of Theological Ethics. Louisville: Westminster John Knox, 1994.

Winn, Adam. "Ephesians 5:21–33" and "1 Timothy 2:11–15." Unpublished lectures, given in 2020 at the University of Mary Hardin Baylor.

Wogaman, J. Philip. *Christian Ethics: A Historical Introduction*. 2nd ed. Louisville: Westminster, John Knox, 2011.

Wollstonecraft, Mary. *Vindication of the Rights of Woman. Project Gutenberg* (website). https://www.gutenberg.org/ebooks/3420/.

Wright, G. Ernest. *God Who Acts: Biblical Theology as Recital*. Studies in Biblical Theology, Series 1, 8. London: SCM, 1966.

Wright, N. T. *Justification: God's Plan & Paul's Vision*. Downers Grove, IL: IVP Academic, 2009.

———. *Paul and the Faithfulness of God*. 2 vols. Christian Origins and the Question of God 4. Minneapolis: Fortress, 2013.

———. "New Perspectives on Paul." Lecture delivered at the Tenth Edinburgh Dogmatics Conference, hosted by the Ruterford Centre for Reformed Theology, at Rutherford House in Edinburgh in 2003. https://ntwrightpage.com/2016/07/12/new-perspectives-on-paul/.

———. *The New Testament and the People of God*. Christian Origins and the Question of God 1. Minneapolis: Fortress, 1992.

Wright, R. B., trans. "The Psalms of Solomon." In *The Old Testament Pseudepigrapha*, edited by James H. Charlesworth, 2:639–70. 2 vols. Garden City, NY: Doubleday , 1983–1985.

Wykstra, Stephen J. "The Humean Obstacle to Evidential Arguments from Suffering: On Avoiding the Evils of 'Appearance.'" *International Journal for Philosophy of Religion* 16/2 (1984) 73–93.

Yandell, Keith. "Moral Essentialism." In *God & Morality: Four Views*, edited by R. Keith Loftin, 97–116. Spectrum Multiview Books. Downers Grove, IL: IVP Academic, 2012.

Zwingli, Ulrich. *Sermon, August 20, 1530*. In *The Latin Works and the Correspondence of Huldreich Zwingli*, edited by Samuel Macauley Jackson, 2:128–1992. Translated by Henry Preble et al. 3 vols. Philadelphia: Heidelberg, 1912–1929.

Index

Abelard, Peter, 129

abolitionism, 311

Abraham (Abram), 14–15, 17, 20, 39, 46, 48, 58, 75, 144–45, 147, 149, 166, 166n26, 167–69, 195–96, 206, 248, 252–53, 255, 342–43, 420, 422, 445

Achtemeir, Elizabeth, 259n47, 501

Achtemeir, Paul J., 455

absolutism, 169n39, 241

adoptionism, 123

age-day theory, 85, 427–28, 440

age of accountability, 184, 184n67, 381, 416n60

Alexander (the Great), 21, 23, 40

Anabaptists, 163, 163n23, 183–86, 193, 220, 300, 371–73, 376, 378, 380, 382, 384, 389

annihilationism, 232–33

Anselm of Canterbury, 127

Antiochus III, 22, 25

Antiochus IV Epiphanes, 24–25, 25n15, 26, 28

Anthony, Susan B., 312

apostle, 6–7, 11, 36–38, 45, 49–50, 53, 55–56, 58–59, 71, 76, 101, 105–8, 116, 125, 134, 142–43, 146–47, 148n56, 149n58, 150n62, 151nn63–64, 160, 163–64, 166–68, 176, 188, 189n89, 190, 192, 194, 197, 204, 207, 213, 214n23, 271, 273, 293n27, 321, 349, 352, 352n21, 353, 358, 462–63, 466, 466n9, 466n12, 467, 479–80, 482–83, 485, 491–94, 504

Apostolic Tradition, 65, 190n94, 356, 356n34, 358, 359nn42–43, 360, 507

Aquinas, Thomas, 65, 68, 68n5, 70–71, 83, 83n30, 88, 89n35, 96, 101, 101n19, 105, 105n36, 106, 106n43, 180, 180n58, 219, 219n28, 242, 249, 291, 294n28, 294n30, 295n32, 296, 305, 324, 332, 396, 396n6, 430, 478, 478nn46–48, 514

Aristotle, 24, 81, 218n27, 219n28, 241, 276, 278–79, 279n4, 280,280n5, 281, 283–84, 287n9, 291–92, 292n25, 293–96, 332, 426, 470–71, 471nn22–23, 501, 510

Arminius, James

Artaxerxes I, 16, 20

Artaxerxes II, 16, 20–21

Artaxerxes III, 21

atonement
  biblical metaphors of, 47, 49, 125, 125n11, 126, 130
  Christus Victor, 126
  ransom theory, 126–27, 129
  satisfaction theory, 127–29
  penal-substitutionary theory, 128
  subjective theories, 129

Augustine, 65–66, 66n3, 70, 80–81, 83, 83nn28–29, 96, 96n6, 106, 106n41, 109, 110, 110n51, 111, 117, 117nn68–69, 120, 126, 126n17, 132, 137, 158n8, 163–64, 180, 182, 185, 215, 216n25, 219, 287, 287n11, 288, 288nn12–13, 289, 289nn14–17, 290, 290nn18–22, 294, 332, 357, 359, 396, 396n6, 400, 477, 477n41, 478, 478nn44–45, 501, 505, 508

Ausbund, 376

Augsburg Confession, 158, 162n20, 162n22

baptism, 38, 42, 44, 49, 59, 77–78, 121, 123, 131, 136–37, 141, 143, 160n15, 167n29, 179–80, 182–87, 190, 290, 296, 300, 341, 343, 350–51, 354–55, 355nn30–31, 356–62, 366, 366n1, 367, 369, 371–72, 374, 378, 378n12, 379–81, 383, 415, 461n5, 514

Baptists, 184, 186–87, 193, 372, 380, 382, 384, 389

Barth, Karl, 72, 96–97, 97n10, 318, 318n37, 319, 319n40, 429, 502–3

Basil of Caesarea, 79, 126, 360
Bible
  biblical content, 2, 6, 12, 42, 64, 67, 71–73,
    171, 173, 202, 213, 248, 306, 315, 348,
    411, 425n1, 432, 449–50, 454–55,
    456n59, 492
  biblical canon. *See* canon, biblical
  and revelation, vii, x, 5–7, 12, 63–71,
    71nn15–16, 72, 72nn18–19, 73, 75, 77,
    79, 81, 83, 85, 87, 89, 91–92, 116, 119,
    124, 133, 156, 170–71, 171n41, 177–78,
    198, 200, 200n9, 201, 204, 207, 209,
    209n19, 210, 213–15, 226, 228, 234,
    242, 248–49, 287–88, 293–96, 310, 318,
    318n37, 319, 336, 398n15, 413–15, 419–
    23, 428–30, 437–39, 445–46, 446n32,
    454, 454n56, 455–56, 456nn59–60, 488,
    491, 495, 503–4, 506, 510, 514
  sacred text, vii, x, 1–3, 5, 7, 9, 11, 13, 15, 17,
    19, 21, 23, 25, 27–29, 31–32, 55, 60, 91,
    234, 338
Bellarmine, Robert, 157
Belleville, Linda, 488, 488nn76–78, 489,
    489nn79–81, 490, 490n82, 502
Benedict of Nursia, 360
benedictions, 77, 348n11, 349
Berkhof, Henrikus, 113n63, 158n5, 170n40, 177,
    177n49, 187n82, 502
Berkouwer, G. C., 91, 91n46, 502
bishops/overseers (episcopoi), 13, 159n11,
    160–61, 163, 181, 189, 189n91, 190–92,
    192n96, 193–94, 285, 298, 356–57, 366,
    369, 477
Black Liberation Theology, 130, 132, 153,
    153n67, 154, 323, 325, 325n67, 326,
    326n71, 327, 327nn72–75, 328,
    328nn77–79, 329, 329n80, 331, 334,
    334n101, 414, 503–4, 506
Bliss, W. D. P., 314
Bloesch, Donald, 189, 189n88, 223, 223n50, 502
Boff, Leonardo, 327, 327n72, 327nn74–75, 503
Book of Common Prayer, 375–76
Bruner, Emil, 97
Bultmann, Rudolf, 429
Bushnell, Horace, 129, 129n28, 503
Butler, Joseph, 105, 105n37, 242, 242n14, 301–2,
    503

Calvin, John, 69–70, 88, 88n34, 96, 96n9, 106,
    106n45, 117, 127–28, 128nn20–24,
    132, 134–36, 136n37, 151, 157, 157n2,
    158n8, 162n22, 163, 171n41, 178,
    184–85, 185nn68–70, 185nn72–74, 186,
    186nn75–80, 187, 187n81, 188nn84–86,

219, 220, 220n31, 299, 299n39, 300,
    301n40, 332, 372–73, 376, 380, 382, 477,
    477n40, 503
canon, biblical, 2–5, 9–10, 11n6, 12–13, 23, 28,
    30, 32, 42, 45, 57n16, 159n12, 160n15,
    180n55, 229, 346, 351, 457, 485, 490
Charismatic Movement, 379, 383, 388–89
Charles the Great (Charlemagne), 365, 367, 370
Christ
  person of, 505
  return of, 42–44, 50–51, 51n10, 51n13, 52,
    55, 115, 131, 164–65, 180, 196–98, 202–4,
    206, 208–9, 212–16, 216n25, 217, 222,
    222n42, 223–24, 227, 229, 273, 362, 382
  work of, 1–2, 32, 40, 46, 49, 56–58, 119, 124,
    126, 130, 133, 136, 138, 153, 155, 163n23,
    171, 183, 185–86, 290, 310, 341, 355, 375,
    393, 415–16, 421
Christianity and other religions, vii, 157, 170,
    171n41, 393, 395, 397, 399, 401, 403, 405,
    407, 409, 411–15, 417–25, 461, 494–95
Christianity and science, vii, x, 86, 393, 396, 424–
    27, 427n6, 428–29, 431, 433, 435–37,
    439, 441, 443, 446n31, 447, 449, 451, 453,
    455, 457–59, 494, 496, 512
Christmas, 362, 368, 373, 375, 385
Christology, 76–77, 76n24, 503
Church
  doctrine of, x, 10, 57, 64, 71, 92, 136–37, 156,
    163–64, 180–82, 182n62, 184n66, 187–
    88, 190, 192–94, 211, 214, 216, 218n26,
    234, 249, 300, 338, 341, 357, 366, 368,
    374, 376, 378, 382, 415, 429, 454n56, 462,
    476n36, 477, 479, 487, 495, 503, 512
  and God's Kingdom, 33–34, 41, 43, 49, 52,
    142, 153, 156, 164–66, 169, 172–73, 197,
    197n3, 197n5, 199–200, 202, 210, 222,
    226–27, 229, 248, 268–71, 273, 285, 298,
    315–16, 321, 323, 329, 336–37, 336,
    450–51, 453n49, 473
  and Israel, 31–32, 58–59, 59nn17–18, 60, 70,
    146, 157, 164–70, 170n40, 173, 177, 204,
    209–210, 216, 336, 338, 341, 349–50, 422,
    469, 491, 495
  and other religions, 157, 170
  four marks of, 162
  governance of, 176, 193–94, 194n97, 388
  ministries of, 59–60, 139, 141, 143, 161–65,
    176–77, 181, 188–89, 193, 215, 461–63,
    466, 472, 481–82, 484–85, 492, 494
  nature of, 57, 60, 63, 92, 156–57, 162, 173,
    194, 234, 363, 467, 495

offices of, 64, 80, 161, 176, 189–91, 194, 313,
370, 375–76, 383, 464, 467, 479, 482,
490–91
purpose of, 59, 156–57, 163, 171–74, 176–77,
179, 190, 194
Civil Rights Bill, 312, 319, 323, 325–26, 330, 497
Clark, Gordon, 398, 503
Cobb, John B., Jr., 90, 431, 503
complementarianism, 476, 479–91, 494
concurrence, doctrine of, 88–89
confessors, 362
confirmation, 179, 184, 357, 366, 372, 381, 430,
434
congregational governance, 193–94, 388
Congregationalists, 157, 163, 193, 386
Cone, James, 325, 503
Conner, W. T., 97
Constantine I, 131, 191, 215, 284–85, 357, 360–
61, 363–64
conversionism, 378, 381
Council of Ephesus, 369
Council of Trent, 137, 159n12, 160n15, 180–81,
300, 373–75
creation, vii, x, 13, 49–50, 52, 63–93, 95, 97n11,
102–3, 110–11, 115, 119, 124, 131, 138,
156, 172, 175, 195, 201, 203, 212, 222,
226, 234, 251, 253, 295, 319, 345, 422,
425, 427–29, 440, 444, 446, 448, 465, 479,
483–85, 487, 492, 495, 502–3, 505
creation and science, 82, 84–85, 103, 111, 425,
427–29, 440, 446, 448, 502, 505
Cunningham, Richard B., 413, 415n58, 416n59,
420–22, 425, 433, 504
Cyprian, 157, 160, 180, 190–91, 358–59, 504
Cyril of Jerusalem, 219, 361
Cyrus the Great, 16, 20, 22n11, 39

Daly, Mary, 331, 504
Darius II, 20
Darius III, 21
Davies, W. D., 222–23, 355n29, 357nn35–36,
358n38, 358n41, 359nn44–46, 360n50,
401n26, 504
Davis, Stephen, 223, 400, 407, 504, 506, 512
Day of Atonement, 345–46
deacons (diaconoi), 189–90, 192, 285, 356–59,
466–67, 482
death, ix, 2, 6, 11, 14, 19–21, 23, 27, 30, 32, 35,
37–38, 40, 42–44, 48–52, 53n15, 55, 70,
105, 107–9, 111–12, 114, 116, 119, 121,
124–30, 133, 136, 143, 145, 152–53, 155,
178–82, 184, 188, 195–98, 200–202, 209,
211–12, 217–27, 230–32, 253, 259–60,
270–71, 273, 282, 284, 286, 288, 298, 310,

315, 333, 336, 351–54, 358, 361, 382,
386, 397, 409, 412, 415–16, 420, 423, 430,
434n24, 442–43, 472, 477, 495, 502, 506,
511
desolating sacrilege, 202–4, 212–13
dichotomism, 100
Didache, 180, 285, 350–51, 353, 354nn23–25,
361, 512
Didascalia Apostolorum, 357
Directory for Family Worship, 375
Disciples of Christ, 11, 36, 38, 40–41, 44, 50,
54–55, 58, 173–74, 193–94, 202–3, 208,
224, 247–48, 250, 271, 276, 284–285n6,
336, 353, 363, 380, 382, 385
dispensationalism/dispensationalists, 164–65,
169–70, 214, 216–17
divine encounters, 1, 64n1, 73, 318, 342–43, 456,
496
deontological (non-consequentialist) ethical
theories, 239–41, 278, 281, 321
Dockery, David, 448–50, 452, 455, 504
Dominicans, 369
Douglas, Frederick, 312
Dulles, Avery, 71n15, 72nn18–19, 156n1, 504
Dunn, James D. G., 148n56, 149, 504
Duns Scotus, 152

Easter, 287, 356, 361–62, 368, 373, 375, 385
Eastern Orthodox, 3, 5, 10, 105, 117, 160n17,
193, 366, 476n36
Edwards, Jonathan, 88, 309, 504
egalitarianism, 493–94
egoism (ethical theory), 239, 241, 282, 304, 317
elders (presbyteroi), 189
Epicurus, 24, 276, 281–82, 308
Epiphany, 361–62, 375, 385
episcopal governance, 194
episcopacy, 160, 190, 192–93
Equal Pay Act, 330
Erasmus, 133, 300
Erickson, Millard, 73n21, 97, 102, 106, 111,
114n64, 127n18, 136n37, 153n67,
159n10, 170n40, 173, 174n46, 219n29,
220, 222–23, 222n39, 224n53, 397–400,
448–449, 450n45, 452n48, 452n86,
454n53, 454n56, 455, 457n62, 458n62,
505
eschatology, 92, 135, 154, 195–96, 198, 201, 209,
211–12, 214, 223n52, 224n54, 226, 502,
504, 508, 511
Essenes, 26, 30, 350
ethics
biblical ethics, x, 115, 249, 251–52, 254,
260–61, 268, 313n25, 321, 338

ethics *(continued)*
　　general and historical Christian ethics, 246,
　　　　276–302, 515
　　general ethics, 237–40, 242–43, 248
　　ethical norms, 238, 241–42, 250, 277, 305,
　　　　415
　　ethical virtues, 237, 241–42, 248, 260, 270,
　　　　274, 278–80, 290, 294, 297, 334–35
Eucharist, 51, 179, 181–82, 186–87, 190, 290,
　　341, 354, 358–59, 364, 367–68, 370–71,
　　373–74, 381–83, 388 (*see also Lord's
　　Supper*)
eudemonism, 238–39, 245, 281
Eutyches, 122–23
Eutychianism, 122
Evangelicalism, 308–9, 350
evangelism, 173, 175, 178, 202, 212–15, 463
evil, 46, 48, 51n12, 87–88, 130, 154, 196–97,
　　324, 393–99, 401–7, 409–410, 504, 506,
　　508–9, 512
evil, the problem of , vii, x, 46, 48, 51, 120,
　　393–99, 401–402n31, 403–7, 409–411,
　　421–25, 459, 494, 496, 513
exclusivism, religious, x, 412–16, 459, 460n3–4,
　　461
existential theology, x, 110, 429

Fackre, Gabriel, 416n63, 423, 505
feminism, 311, 329–31, 334, 476, 480, 497–99,
　　502, 507, 514
feminist liberation theology, 323, 329, 331, 334,
　　506
festivals/feasts (religious), 18, 264, 345–46, 348–
　　49, 361–64, 368–69, 375–76, 384–85, 505
Feuerbach, Ludwig, 377
Finney, Charles, 309, 383, 387
Fletcher, John, 379
Fletcher, Joseph, 320, 322–23, 505
Francke, August Hermann, 309
Franciscans, 369
freedom, 21, 26, 40, 87–91, 94, 96, 98, 113–15,
　　117, 121, 125, 133–35, 201, 231–32, 234,
　　304, 309, 311, 319, 321, 399, 401–4, 408–
　　410, 481, 491–93, 499, 508, 511–12
free will, 90, 95–96, 98, 99n14, 288n13, 300, 399–
　　401, 403–4, 407n44, 408, 502, 504, 512
free will defense, 399–401, 404
free will theodicy, 399–401, 403–4, 504
Frelinghuyson, Theodorus, 309
Friedan, Betty, 330

Gabrieli, Andrea, 376
gap theory, 427–28, 440
Garrison, William Lloyd, 312

Gehenna, 200, 233
Genevan Psalter, 376
Gess, Wolfgang, 123, 505
Gilkey, Langdon, 85n31, 428, 429n8, 505
God
　　in Old Testament, 2, 7–8, 11–13, 18–19,
　　　　42, 45–49, 74–76, 82–83, 95, 97, 104–6,
　　　　111, 124–25, 139, 147, 164, 185–86, 201,
　　　　214, 252, 258, 268–70, 273–74, 321, 442,
　　　　469–70, 481
　　in New Testament, 11–12, 38, 42–45, 49, 51,
　　　　74, 76, 95, 97, 104–6, 108, 115, 124–25,
　　　　142, 165, 170, 178, 186, 208, 211, 214,
　　　　258, 268, 274, 351, 492, 515
　　Trinity, 76, 78–81, 96–97, 119, 121, 123, 172,
　　　　227, 287, 356, 359, 369–70, 385, 393n1,
　　　　415, 430
Great Awakenings, 309, 386–87
Gregory VII, 369
Grenz, Stanley, 157, 158n5, 165, 169n38, 172–
　　175n48, 214n24, 220, 237, 241, 276n2,
　　296n34, 299n39, 320n42, 461n7, 469n18,
　　472–473n31, 474, 475n33, 480, 505–6
Greshake, Gilbert, 223, 506
Griffin, David, 83n27, 90, 431n18, 503
Grimké, Angelina, 312
Grimké, Sarah, 312
Grudem, Wayne, 480, 482, 485n70, 511
Gutiérrez, Gustavo, 327–28, 506

Harnack, Adolph, 310, 378
Hart, David Bentley, 199n8, 230–31, 506, 509
Hartshorne, Charles, 90, 431, 506
Hasker, William, 90, 506
Hasmoneans, 26–27
Hauerwas, Stanley, 241, 334–38, 506
Hays, Richard B., 148n56, 506
heaven, 23, 30, 33, 37, 40–44, 49–51, 55, 82,
　　85n31, 116, 123n7, 131, 172, 180, 184,
　　188, 198–201, 209–211, 214, 216, 219–
　　20, 226–28, 257, 269–72, 359, 362, 369,
　　382, 404, 413–14, 429n8, 442–45, 505–6
Hebrew Bible, 2, 5, 10, 13, 18, 20, 23–24, 28, 41,
　　46, 59, 77, 138–41, 145, 148, 152n66,
　　169–70, 197n5, 214, 252, 254–55, 259,
　　261, 263–64, 266, 268, 271, 276, 284,
　　342–44, 346, 363, 441, 470, 495
Hedonism, 238–39, 242, 245
hell, 23, 30, 184, 199–200, 208n17, 211, 216,
　　219–20, 222n43, 229–34, 416n63, 506,
　　508, 514
Herod the Great, 27, 472
Herron, George D., 314

Hick, John, 221, 230, 403, 416n62, 417, 420, 422, 434n24, 506
Hippolytus of Rome, 167, 190n94, 356, 359, 507
history of Israel. *See* Israel, history of
Hobbes, Thomas, 304, 507
Hodge, Charles, 310
Holy Spirit, 47, 49–50, 54, 57, 64, 71, 75, 77–81, 106, 134, 138–39, 141–44, 151, 163n23, 167, 169, 171, 173, 176, 179, 185, 188–89, 248, 250–251n26, 258n45, 273, 284, 318n37, 329, 343, 350–51, 355–57, 361–62, 366, 372, 379, 383, 492, 506, 511
Humanae Vitae, 331
Humans/Humanity, vii, ix, x, 1, 13–14, 17, 19n10, 33, 41–42, 46, 49–50, 53, 55, 58, 63–64, 67–72, 74, 82–84, 86–87, 91–135, 137–38, 142, 145–46, 148–49, 151, 153–56, 163, 171–73, 175–78, 182, 184–85, 188–89, 195–96, 199, 206–7, 211, 217–18, 223, 226–27, 230–32, 234, 239, 242–43, 248, 250–53, 256, 259, 262, 266, 268, 274, 277–85, 287–88–295–305, 307–8, 310, 314, 316–21, 329, 331–36, 341–43, 374, 377, 380, 382, 394, 398–99, 401, 408–9, 411–12, 415, 417–19, 421–23, 425, 427, 432, 435n26, 437–38, 441, 447, 460, 477, 492, 495
Hume, David, 304–5, 307, 377, 435, 507
Hymns, 6, 347, 350, 354, 360, 363–64, 369, 376–77, 383, 386–87

Ignatius, 160n15, 163, 180–181n60, 190, 233, 285, 354n24, 358, 507
Image of God, 7, 51n13, 82, 95–97, 99, 101, 103, 108, 118, 195, 227, 287, 293, 332–34, 377, 464, 477–78, 483, 503
Inclusivism, Christian, 420–23, 476, 496, 512–13
Inerrancy of Scripture, 73, 447n34, 448–57, 476n36, 479, 505, 510, 514
Infusion, 137, 149, 290, 371, 380
Israel, history of, 1–2, 7–8, 15, 76, 144, 248, 336, 503

Japinga, Lynn, 476n36, 480, 507
Jesuits (Society of Jesus), 374
Jesus Christ, 1–3, 9–10, 16–19, 20, 41, 47, 48–84
    biblical narratives of, 103, 338, 364
    person and titles of, x, 1–2, 7, 31–35, 37–41, 43–46, 48–51, 53–55, 60, 76, 78, 119–20, 122–24, 155
    resurrection of, ix, 6, 35–39, 42, 51, 55, 70–71, 76, 126, 155, 178, 198, 214, 223, 250, 310, 336–37, 342, 361, 475, 495

    work of, 1–2, 12, 32, 40, 46n8, 56, 124, 130, 141, 155, 237, 310, 341, 393, 416, 421–22
Jesus People, 388
Jewett, Paul K., 472n28, 480, 491–93, 507
John Hyrcanus II, 27
Judgment (divine), 13, 18, 30, 33, 115, 142, 149, 198–99, 201, 212, 217, 252, 413, 444
Junia, 190, 466, 482
Justification, 49, 54, 125, 130, 133–35, 137–38, 144, 146–48, 150–53, 182, 296–97, 300, 309, 351, 374, 397, 463, 465, 503, 515

Kant, Immanuel, 93n1, 240, 242, 304, 306–8, 335, 377–78, 417, 507
Keener, Craig, 480, 486–88, 508
kenoticism, 123
King, Martin Luther, Jr., 323, 326, 508
Kingdom of God, 33, 43, 49, 52n14, 142, 153, 156, 164–66, 172–73, 197, 200, 202, 222, 226–27, 229, 268, 270, 273, 285, 298, 315–16, 321, 323, 329, 336–37, 366, 450–51, 453, 473
Kjesbo, Denise Muir, 469n18, 472–475n33, 480, 506
Kvanvig, Jonathan, 229, 232–34, 508

Ladd, George Eldon, 45n7, 165n25, 189n91, 205n16, 508
laments, 267, 347
Lassus, Orlando, 376
last things. *See* Eschatology
Latin American Liberation Theology, 323, 326–27, 329, 334
Leith, John, 122n6, 158n8, 159nn11–12, 160n15, 162nn20–22, 180n55, 220n32, 508
Lent, 362, 375, 384–85
Lewis, C. S., 68, 103, 231, 339, 401, 420n75, 479, 508
Lewis H. D., 225, 508
liberal–conservative divide, 310
liberation theology, 132, 153–54, 323, 325–29, 331, 334, 503, 506
limbo, 180–81, 184n66, 219–20
Locke, John, 304–6, 311, 508
Lombard, Peter, 126
Lord's Day, 353–54
Lord's Supper/Communion, 51n13, 58, 71, 80, 144, 157, 159n11, 160n15, 171, 179–182, 183n64, 186–88, 190, 226–27, 252, 298, 309, 341, 349, 352–54, 358, 364, 367–68, 373–75, 380–82, 384, 513–14
Luther, Martin, 10, 69–70, 72, 96, 106, 117, 132, 134, 146, 161, 219–20, 296, 332, 371–73, 376, 385, 477, 501, 508–9

Mackie, J. L., 401, 509

martyrs, 219, 286, 357, 362, 376

Marx, Karl, 304, 308, 314, 317, 327, 497–98

Marxism, 317, 327

Mascall, E. L., 479, 509

mass. *See* Lord's Supper

Melanchthon, Philip, 134, 162, 167, 168n32, 509

Melito of Sardis, 167

Mennonites, 184, 193, 382

Messiah, 12, 16, 30–31, 34–35, 37–40, 42, 45, 50, 55–56, 76–77, 140–42, 145, 164–70, 196, 202–3, 204n14, 208, 215, 361, 386, 474–75

Messenger, Earnest, 103, 509

Methodism, 309, 378

Miaphysites, 123, 366

Mickelsen, Alvera, 480, 509

Migliore, Daniel, 121, 129–30, 154, 156, 188, 509

Mill, Harriet Taylor, 312

Mill, John Stuart, 304, 307, 312, 322

millennial reign, 169, 202, 204, 207–8, 215–17

ministers, 144, 162, 176, 188–93, 291, 328, 356, 373, 463

ministry, vii, 34, 40, 42, 55–56, 58–60, 76, 139, 141–43, 161–162n22, 164, 174–75, 177–79, 188–92, 196, 202, 284, 361, 393, 424, 459, 461–63, 466–71, 473, 475–77, 479–81, 483, 485–94, 502, 506, 508–9, 513

Miranda, José Porfirio, 327

moderates, 476n26, 480, 492–93

monasticism, 286, 360, 368, 374–75

Molina, Luis de, 89, 510

Molinism, 89–90

Monophysites, 123

Moody, Dale, 111, 252n29, 254, 510

Moody, Dwight L., 309, 387

Morris, Henry, 427, 514

Moses, 14, 16, 28, 30, 167, 248, 253, 342–43, 346, 470–71, 477n40, 501, 503

music, 175, 341, 346n10, 347, 349nn13–14, 363–64, 370, 375–77, 386–88, 462, 504. *See also* worship, music

natural evil, 118, 175, 394, 403–4, 409

Neo-liberalism, 316

Nestorianism, 122, 366

Nestorius, 122

New Perspective on Paul, 144–48, 150n59, 150n61, 151–52, 255, 504, 515

Niebuhr, Reinhold, 106, 110, 112–14, 316–17, 510

Occasionalism, 88

Old Testament (see Hebrew Bible)

Open Theism, 512

Orde, 367

original sin, 88n33, 180, 184, 186, 219, 357, 366, 504. *See also* sin

Origen, 79–80, 100–101, 105, 121, 126, 225, 230–32, 286–87, 477, 510

Palestrina, Giovanni Pierluigi da, 376

Palm Sunday, 361, 385

Palmer, Phoebe, 379

Parham, Charles, 379

Passover, 14, 34–35, 345, 348, 352, 361

pastor (*poimenes*), 189

Paul, the Apostle, 6, 11, 36–38, 45, 49–50, 53, 56, 58–59, 76, 101, 105–8, 116, 125, 134, 143, 146–51, 166–68, 176, 188–90, 194, 197, 204, 207, 213, 271, 273, 321, 352–53, 462–63, 466–67, 479–80, 482–83, 485, 491–94, 504

Pearce, Victor, 102, 511

Pelagius, 101, 110, 113, 117, 132, 511

penance, 179–80, 182–83, 290–91, 296, 341, 360, 369, 372–73, 384

penitentials, 369

Pentecost, 70, 142, 343, 345, 348, 361–62, 369, 373, 375, 385

Pentecostalism, 193, 379, 383

Peterson, Michael, 400, 404n36, 406, 408, 507, 511–12

Pharisees, 26, 30, 33, 40, 269

Phoebe, 189, 466n10

pietism, 309, 378

Pinnock, Clark, 90, 144, 232–33, 511–12

Piper, John, 480, 482, 485, 511

plainsong, 363, 370

Plantinga, Alvin, 394–95, 399–403, 408, 511

Plato, 24, 81, 94, 100–101, 217–19, 240–41, 247nn18–19, 276–81, 283, 288–89, 511

pluralism, religious, 417–20, 422n89, 507

polyphony, 370

Pompey, 27, 40

prayer, 4–5, 35, 40, 87, 177, 189, 200, 247–48, 286, 309, 319, 341, 347–49, 354–56, 358–60, 363–64, 367–70, 374–76, 378, 383–84, 388, 472

preaching, 33, 52, 70, 72, 161, 162n22, 164–165n25, 173–74, 178, 188, 309, 318n37, 323, 341, 354, 358–59, 364, 368, 374, 383–84, 388, 473, 486–87, 492

premillennialism, 214n24, 215–17

Presbyterian, 192–94, 373, 375, 380, 382, 388, 503, 514

presbyterian governance, 193–94, 388

presbyters, 190, 193, 356–57, 359, 366, 477

Price, H. H., 225, 427n5, 511
process theology, 82n27–83n27, 397, 431, 503
providence, vii, x, 63–92, 117n70, 132, 156, 234,
    401n28–402n31, 404n34, 406, 409n47,
    495, 502, 505, 511–13
Psalms, 3–4, 6, 39, 141n41, 161n18, 177, 266–67,
    346–47, 349, 354, 358, 360, 363–64, 369,
    375–76, 509, 515
Puritans, 301, 375, 386
purgatory, 182–83, 219–20, 296

Rahner, Karl, 223, 420–23, 512
Ramsey, Paul, 320–23, 512
Rashdall, Hastings, 129, 512
Ratzinger, Joseph, 223–24
Rauschenbusch, Walter, 314–16, 324, 512
Reformation, vii, 10, 96, 135nn34–35, 151, 168,
    182n62, 188, 191, 276–303, 371–77,
    380–81, 383–87, 505, 509
relativism, 239, 305
religious diversity, x, 411, 414, 417, 496
religious experiences, ix-x, 64, 67–68, 71, 364,
    431
Religious Society of Friends (Quakers), 193, 250,
    371–72
Resurrection, ix, 6, 23, 30, 35–39, 42, 49–51, 55,
    70–71, 76, 109, 123, 126, 131, 135, 152,
    155, 178, 198, 201–2, 204–7, 209–210,
    212, 214, 217–25, 250, 310, 336–37, 342,
    356, 358, 361, 415, 475, 495, 501–2, 504,
    514
revelation
    general, 5–6, 64, 67–69, 72, 170–171n41, 248,
        421–23
    special, 64–65, 67, 69–72, 171, 248–49, 287,
        293, 310, 429–30, 455–56
revivalism, 378, 383
Rice, Richard, 91n45, 512
Ritschl, Albrecht, 71–72, 310, 315, 378
rituals, x, 18, 47n9, 179, 190, 341–44, 349, 354,
    357, 364–67, 371, 381, 388–89, 411, 415,
    417
Roe v. Wade, 331
Roman Breviary, 374–75
Roth, John, 398, 512
Rufinus, 126
Ruether, Rosemary Radford, 329n81, 331–34,
    477n39, 481, 512

sacraments and ordinances, 133, 137–38, 140,
    157, 159–64, 167–68, 176–77, 179–83,
    185–86, 188, 190–92, 290, 296–97, 299,
    371, 374, 378, 380–81, 415–16

sacred history (history of Israel), vii, x, 1–32, 55,
    60, 144 (*see also* Israel, history of)
sacred times, 361
sacrifices, 8, 15–16, 26, 28, 47, 49, 106, 124–25,
    146, 168, 183, 201, 203, 264, 343–47, 349,
    352–53, 470
Sadducees, 30, 35, 198
salvation
    biblical metaphors, 47, 130–31
    cosmic, 154–55
    doctrine of , 118–19, 124, 128, 131, 135–37,
        146, 153–54
    individual, 133–38, 200, 227, 323
    New Testament, 49, 51–53, 58, 125, 134, 136,
        142, 218, 230, 351
    social, 153–54
Sanders, John, 90, 420n75, 423nn94–95, 505,
    510, 512–13
Schleiermacher, Friedrich, 71–72, 105, 310, 378,
    513
Schreiner, Thomas, 480, 485, 513
scribes, 29–30, 33, 42, 269
science, 66, 72, 72n20, 82, 84–85, 101, 103n28,
    111, 116, 175, 278, 303, 314, 330, 371,
    377, 396n5, 426n2, 429nn8–10, 430,
    431nn12–15, 432, 434–35, 435n26, 438,
    438n27, 440, 452, 502, 504–6, 508, 511,
    514
science and the Bible, 103, 439, 440, 446–48,
    453–58
science and Christianity. *See* Christianity and
    science
science and creation. *See* creation and science
scientific creationism, 440
Second Temple Judaism, 28n21, 48, 141, 145,
    148, 153n66, 197, 206–9, 218, 347–49,
    351, 361, 363, 365, 503
Second Vatican Council, 159n11, 160, 382–84,
    388, 423n90
Segundo, Juan Luis, 327
Sewell, Samuel, 311
Seymour, William, 379
Seleucus IV, 25
Shema, 28, 348–49
Shepherd of Hermas, 180n56, 355
Sidgwick, Henry, 242
sin
    consequences of, 17, 104, 107, 110, 114–17,
        125, 133, 138, 227, 471
    nature of, 53, 104–114, 132, 154, 184, 293,
        299, 316–17
    origin of, 104, 107–110, 113n63
    original sin, 88n33, 96, 184, 186, 219, 357,
        366, 504, 513

sin *(continued)*
  sinfulness, 108–111, 113, 120, 130, 133, 154,
    170, 184, 227, 252, 297
  slavery, 7, 14, 75, 255, 262–63, 285, 311, 313, 323,
    342, 413
social-economic ethics, 311–13
social exclusivism, x, 459
Social Gospel, 314–16, 324, 512
Socinus, Faustus, 129, 513
Söelle, Dorothee, 331
sola scriptura, 179, 183, 374
soul, 28, 44, 99–101, 103, 110–11, 120, 122, 154,
    206–207, 208n17, 217–25, 232–33, 260,
    269, 277–78, 282–83, 289–90, 316, 324,
    348, 409, 411–12, 430, 443, 504, 510
Spener, Philipp Jakob, 179, 309
spiritual awakenings, 215, 308–9, 377, 379, 383,
    386–87
Stagg, Evelyn 474–75, 480, 491, 513
Stagg, Frank, 469nn18–19, 471n25, 472n27,
    473n31–475, 480, 491–93, 513
Stanton, Elizabeth Cady, 312
Steinem, Gloria, 330
Stiver, Dan, xi, 214n24, 222n39, 223–224n54,
    513
Stoics, 283–84, 287n9
Strong, Augustus, 103, 513
subjectivism (ethical theory), 239, 244–45, 305
supersessionism, 168–70
Swinburne, Richard, 90, 401–2, 404n34, 430–31,
    513
synagogue, 29, 55, 141, 203, 348–49, 354, 472

Tanak, 5, 29, 46
Tanquerey, Adolphe, 157
teleological (or consequentialist) ethical theories,
    68, 238–39, 241, 247, 278, 281, 430
Tennant, Frederick, 113–14, 513
Tennent, Gilbert, 309
Tertullian, 65, 78–79, 101, 180, 229, 355–56,
    358–59, 477, 513
theodicy, 394–95, 397–401, 403–4, 407n43,
    409–410, 504, 506, 508, 512
theotokos, 122, 369
Thomasius, Gottfried, 123, 514
transworld depravity, 402

Travis, Stephen, 223, 228, 233, 514
trichotomism, 100
Trinity. *See* God, Trinity
Turretin, Francis, 124

utilitarianism, 239, 308

Vanhoozer, Kevin, 449–53, 455–58, 505, 514
Vatican Council, First, 159nn11–12, 160, 192,
    382–84, 388, 423, 514
virtues, 143, 152, 237, 241–42, 248, 254–55, 257–
    58, 260, 267, 270–71, 273–74, 278–80,
    290, 295, 297, 334–35, 347

Warfield, Benjamin, 71, 310, 454n53, 501, 505,
    514
Wesley, Charles, 170, 179, 309, 386
Wesley, John, 132, 135n36, 136, 163n23, 179,
    309, 311, 380, 385–86, 514
Whitcomb, John C., 427, 427n5, 514
Whitefield, George, 309
Whitehead, Alfred North, 431
Wilberforce, William, 311
William of Ockham, 295, 297
Winn, Adam, xi, 493–94, 494n87, 515
women in ministry, vii, x, 55, 393, 424, 459–94,
    502, 506, 508–9, 513
Woolman, John, 311
worship, vii, x, 6, 8, 14–15, 22, 28–29, 35–36,
    55, 74–76, 120, 147, 161–62, 171–72,
    176–77, 196, 204, 207, 210, 228, 257,
    259, 261–64, 268, 274, 284–86, 338–89,
    393, 413, 462, 465, 469–70, 472, 474, 481,
    483–84, 486, 488, 495–96, 503, 505, 507,
    509, 513–14
worship music, 341, 346–47, 349, 363–64, 370,
    375–77, 386–88, 462
Wright, N. T., 141n41, 144–45, 148–52, 515

Xerxes I, 20

Zealots, 30, 40
Zinzendorf, Nikolaus von, 309
Zwingli, Ulrich, 69, 161, 171n41, 183n64, 184–
    87, 191, 372–76, 380, 515